A GLOBAL VIEW

of

CHRISTIAN MISSIONS

D0068868

J. Herbert Kane

The ring of authenticity in **A Global View of Christian Missions** may be attributed to the author's fifteen years' experience as a missionary in China, several years spent teaching missions and mission-related subjects in Barrington College and Lancaster School of the Bible, and his present position of associate professor, School of World Mission, Trinity Evangelical Divinity School, Deerfield, Illinois.

Dr. Kane has also revised and enlarged Dr. Robert H. Glover's popular missions classic, **The Progress of Worldwide Missions.** He is much in demand as a speaker at missionary conferences and seminars and is a frequent contributor to Christian periodicals.

J. Herbert Kane is a graduate of Moody Bible Institute. He received his A.B. degree from Barrington College, his A.M. degree from Brown University, and in 1971 received an L.H.D. degree from Barrington College.

A GLOBAL VIEW

of

CHRISTIAN MISSIONS

FROM PENTECOST TO THE PRESENT

By J. Herbert Kane

School of World Mission
Trinity Evangelical Divinity School
Deerfield, Illinois

Baker Book House   Grand Rapids, Michigan

ISBN: 0-8010-5308-0

Library of Congress Catalog Card Number: 77-167688

Copyright 1971 by Baker Book House Company

Printed in the United States of America

TO

MY STUDENTS

PAST AND PRESENT

at

Barrington College

Lancaster School of the Bible

Trinity Evangelical Divinity School

who are now serving the Lord

on all six continents

Preface

A well-known missiologist maintains that mission history is "rootless and remedial." If church history were properly written, so he says, there would be no need for mission history. Quite true. But the problem is that church history has seldom been "properly" written. For the most part, church history is concerned with Christian doctrine, ecclesiastical machinery, church feuds, schismatic movements, ecumenical councils, papal bulls, imperial decrees, religious wars, the exercise of discipline, the formulation of creeds, the suppression of heresy, and other episodes and movements relating to the survival and success of the church as a gigantic religious institution. Little or nothing is said about the preaching of the gospel, the translation and distribution of the Scriptures, the conversion of non-Christian peoples, or the extension of the kingdom into all parts of the world. As long as this is so, books on *mission* history will be needed.

While the book deals mostly with Christian missions, the author has been concerned to report on the development of the indigenous churches. Missions are not an end in themselves but a means to an end. The end is the emergence of strong, self-governing, self-supporting, self-propagating churches. Unfortunately, it has not always been easy to secure the necessary information regarding the indigenous churches. Some of them do not keep accurate, up-to-date records; and some that do have such records are reluctant to share them with strangers.

Except for chapter four, Roman Catholic missions are not included in this study, not because they are not important or significant, but because lack of space makes it impossible to include them.

Mission nomenclature is something of a problem in these days when many societies are changing their names. It is not always easy to be consistent in the use of new and old names. When dealing with the nineteenth century, I have usually employed the original name; when treating of the more recent past, I have used the new name. Some fifty missions have changed their names in recent years. A list of these missions will be found in the back of the book. If the reader has difficulty in recognizing either the old names or the new ones, he should consult that list.

In a work of this kind it is impossible to do justice to all the hundreds of mission boards which work in the various parts of the world. Of necessity the author must be selective. The quickest way to convert friends into enemies is to make the "wrong" selection! In the smaller countries, where only two or three missions are working, there is no problem. In other countries, such as India, Japan, or Brazil, where there are over one hundred different societies, it is quite impossible to include them all. In that case it has been necessary to be selective. In my selection I have endeavored to be both fair and objective, including in my treatment representative missions — denominational and interdenominational, American, British, and Continental.

The author wishes to express his gratitude for the fine cooperation he received from mission secretaries and executives at home and overseas, for all the questionnaires that were cheerfully filled out, for the books, pamphlets, annual and field reports, and other materials contributed so freely.

In a project of this magnitude, the author is always indebted to many friends and colleagues who responded to his call for help. The following experts read various sections of the manuscript and offered valuable critical comments, many of which have been incorporated into the final copy: Dr. Gerald H. Anderson, Dr. Everett Cattell, Dr. Allen D. Clark, Dr. Frank L. Cooley, Dr. Harry G. Dorman, Jr., Dr. Robert P. Evans, Dr. Vergil Gerber, Dr. David J. Hesselgrave, Mrs. Marion Springer, the Reverend George M. Steed, Dr. Francis R. Steele, Dr. Herman Tegenfeldt, the Reverend Warren Webster, and Dr. David F. Wells. Needless to say, these good friends are in no way responsible for any defects that still remain in the book.

A special word of appreciation is due my wife, to whom I owe an enormous debt of gratitude for her unfailing patience, wise counsel, and constructive criticism. In addition, she spent many long hours typing and proofreading large sections of the manuscript, and helping with the bibliography and the index.

Deerfield, Illinois   J. Herbert Kane
March, 1971

Contents

Maps

PART ONE

Through the Ages

I

Christianity in the Roman Empire:
A.D. 30–500

The City of God was built at the confluence of three great civilizations, the Greek, the Roman and the Hebrew. Each contributed significantly to the progress and pattern of Christianity as it developed in the first three centuries of the Christian era.

The elements of Greek civilization are not hard to trace. They include art, architecture, literature, language, science and philosophy. We are still wondering how one small race could be so prolific in ideas, so dynamic in action, and so massive in achievement. The secret is to be sought not so much in the temper of the times as in the temperament of the Greek — his inquiring mind, his restless spirit and his zest for life.

Unlike the Egyptians, whose civilization was confined to the Nile valley, the Greeks, with their penchant for trade and travel, established colonies on the shores of the Mediterranean and the Black seas between the eighth and the sixth centuries B.C. Wherever they went they carried with them the benefits of their superior civilization.

In time the Greeks replaced the Phoenicians as the mercantile masters of the Mediterranean world. Although their voyages were not as long or lucrative as those of the Phoenicians, their influence on civilization was more powerful and certainly more permanent. The earliest ideas of scientific navigation and geography came from the Greeks. The Greek travelers, Strabo and Pausanias, are our most reliable informants when we study the topography of the Acts of the Apostles.

Seldom in history have the conquests of war contributed to the advance of civilization, but such was the case with the conquests of Alexander the Great. When the unmanageable pupil of Aristotle gave up

3

the study of philosophy to mount the throne and ride the world, he embarked on a course of action destined to change the face of the Western world and prepare the way for the spread of the gospel.

> He took up the meshes of the net of Greek civilization, which were lying in disorder on the edges of the Asiatic shore, and spread them over all the countries which he traversed. The East and the West were suddenly brought together. Separated tribes were united under a common government. New cities were built as centers of political life. New lines of communication were opened as the channels of commercial activity. The new culture penetrated the mountain ranges of Pisidia and Lycaonia. The Tigris and Euphrates became Greek rivers. The language of Athens was heard among the Jewish colonies of Babylonia.[1]

Upon the untimely death of the great conqueror, Antioch and Alexandria became the capitals of the Greek kings of Syria and Egypt respectively. Both had had a large colony of Jews from the beginning. Both were residences of Roman governors. Both were centers of Christian activity and later became patriarchates of the Eastern Church.

The Greek language, regarded by some as the richest and most delicate the world has ever seen, became the language of culture and commerce from the Persian Gulf to the Gates of Hercules. It was the mother tongue not only of Plato and Aristotle in the West, but also of Ignatius and Eusebius in the East. It was used by Paul the Christian, Philo the Jew, and Cicero the Roman. Paul and his companions never had to learn a foreign language, nor had they any need for an interpreter. The Greek language was readily understood in all parts of the empire. As early as the third century B.C. the Old Testament was translated into this language, and the Septuagint was the Bible of Jesus and the apostles. Greek, the language of philosophy, became the language of theology as well.

> It was not an accident that the New Testament was written in Greek, the language which can best express the highest thoughts and worthiest feelings of the intellect and heart, and which is adapted to be the instrument of education for all nations; nor was it an accident that the composition of these books and the promulgation of the Gospel were delayed until the instruction of our Lord and the writings of His Apostles could be expressed in the dialect of Alexandria.[2]

The empire founded by Alexander and divided among his four generals did not last long. In politics integrity gave way to intrigue. Philosophy degenerated first into cynicism and later into skepticism. Social life became a round of worthless and frivolous amusements. Religion was powerless to halt the process of decay. Rome soon displaced Greece as the mistress of the Mediterranean world.

---

[1] Conybeare and Howson, *Life and Epistles of St. Paul* (London and New York: Longmans, Green and Co., 1901), p. 7.

[2] *Ibid.*, p. 9.

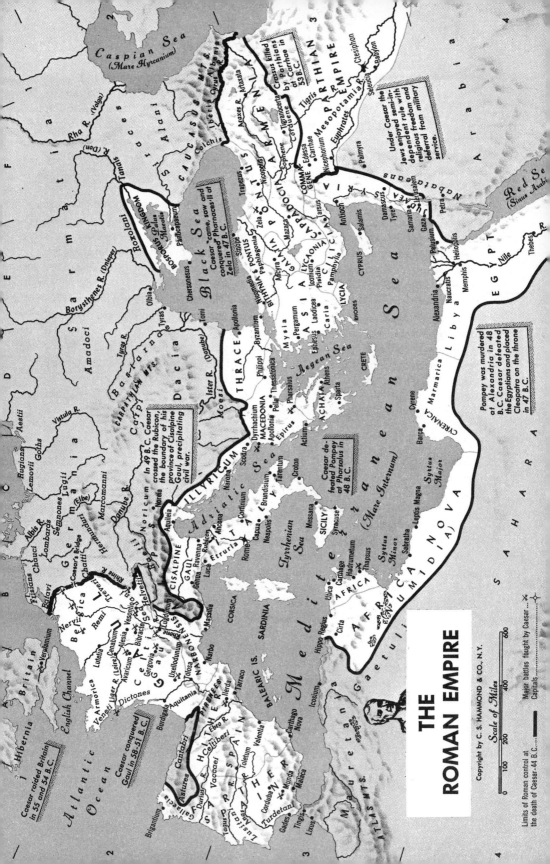

THE ROMAN EMPIRE

Copyright by C. S. HAMMOND & CO., N.Y.

Scale of Miles

0   100   200   400   600

Limits of Roman control at
the death of Caesar-44 B.C. ....
Major battles fought by Caesar ..... ⚔
Capitals .... ✦

Caspian Sea
(Mare Hyrcanium)

Red Sea
(Sinus Arabicus)

Crassus killed
by Parthians
at Carrhae in
53 B.C.

Under Caesar the
Jews enjoyed semi-in-
dependent rule with
religious freedom and
deferral from military
service.

PARTHIAN EMPIRE

Caesar came, saw and
conquered Pharnaces II of
Pontus at
Zela in 47 B.C.

Pompey was murdered
at Alexandria in 48
B.C. Caesar defeated
the Egyptians and placed
Cleopatra on the throne
in 47 B.C.

Caesar de-
feated Pompey
at Pharsalus in
48 B.C.

In 49 B.C. Caesar
crossed the Rubicon,
the boundary of his
province of Cisalpine
Gaul, precipitating
civil war.

Caesar conquered
Gaul in 58-51 B.C.

Caesar raided Britain
in 55 and 54 B.C.

Atlantic Ocean

Mediterranean Sea
(Mare Internum)

Black Sea

Aegean Sea

Adriatic Sea

Tyrrhenian Sea

English Channel

At the height of its power Rome ruled an empire comprising more than one and a quarter million square miles, that stretched from Spain to the Euphrates, from the North Sea to the Sahara Desert. It had a population of a hundred million people—Italians, Greeks, Egyptians, Germans, Celts and others. Beginning with Augustus and lasting for approximately three hundred years, this vast empire enjoyed what Pliny the Elder termed "the immense majesty of the Roman peace." With peace came prosperity.

The Romans were men of action. They swept the pirates from the seas and on land they built the most enduring roads of antiquity, along which passed, with a minimum of danger and delay, not only the merchants and the legionnaires but also the messengers of the cross. Everywhere Roman legions kept the peace and Roman magistrates administered the law. The conquests of Rome prepared for and facilitated those of Christianity.

Rome ruled her empire with an iron hand. In matters pertaining to internal security she was exceedingly strict. She collected taxes from all the provinces and punished anyone who tried to evade the universal tribute. At the same time she gave the provinces as much autonomy as she could without jeopardizing the security of the empire. She was especially tolerant in the matter of religion. Judaism was accorded preferential treatment with the designation *religio licita*; and for a time the Christians were able to capitalize on their association with Judaism. Paul was a Roman citizen, and on more than one occasion he invoked his rights as a citizen to secure for the gospel the hearing it deserved. In the Acts of the Apostles Luke takes pains to point out that Christianity, in the first generation at least, consistently enjoyed the protection of the temporal power. "The cross followed the fasces, and the Roman eagles made straight the way for Christ."[3]

More closely connected with Christianity than either the Greek or Roman civilizations was the Hebrew civilization. The dispersion of the Jewish people was the greatest single factor in preparing the world for the coming of the Messiah and the preaching of the gospel. Scattered throughout the Roman Empire, the Jews were particularly numerous in Egypt, Syria and Babylonia. In A.D. 70 Strabo reported: "It is hard to find a single place on the habitable earth that has not admitted this tribe of men, and is not possessed by it."[4]

Wherever the Jews went they carried the knowledge and the worship of the one true God, the expectation of a coming Messiah and the Holy Scriptures in the universal Greek language. Wherever possible they organized synagogues, which became the religious and cultural centers of their communities. Attracted to the synagogues were many Gentiles — proselytes and other lesser adherents known as "God-fearing men."

---

3 Will Durant, *Caesar and Christ* (New York: Simon and Schuster, 1944), p. 602.

4 Josephus, *Antiquities of the Jews*, xiv, 7.

These factors were of immense help to the Christian missionaries as they traveled throughout the Roman world preaching the gospel and planting churches. Though designated "an apostle to the Gentiles," Paul's heart was always with his own people. In every city he made his way first to the synagogue, where he found Jews and proselytes. Only when the Jews refused his message did he turn to the Gentiles. The organization of the Christian church was patterned largely after that of the Jewish synagogue.

The Geographical Expansion

Christianity is the only truly universal religion in the world. Yet its Founder was born in a stable, lived in obscurity, and died on a wooden cross in a remote province of the Roman Empire about half-way between the time of Buddha and that of Mohammed. Although His untimely death at the age of thirty-three sent His disciples into confusion, His resurrection on the third day revived their Messianic hopes, rejuvenated their flagging spirits, and sent them out to win the world.

Their task was formidable; their chances of success almost nil. They had no central organization, no financial resources, no influential friends, no political machine. Arrayed against them was the ecclesiastical power of the Sanhedrin, the political and military might of the Roman Empire, and the religious fanaticism of the Jews. Moreover, their Leader, whose life and teachings were to constitute their message, was unknown outside His small circle of friends. He had written no books, erected no monuments, endowed no institutions. The task looked hopeless.

The Book of Acts opens with 120 timid disciples meeting secretly in an upper room in Jerusalem for fear of their enemies. A generation later, when the Book of Acts closes, the gospel had been preached as far west as Rome; and there was a thriving Christian church in almost every city of significance in the eastern part of the empire. What began as a Jewish sect in A.D. 30 had grown into a world religion by A.D. 60. The details, all too few, are found in the Acts of the Apostles.

Acts 1:8 gives us a clue to the projected expansion of the Christian faith. Beginning at Jerusalem, it was to extend by way of Judea and Samaria to the ends of the earth. Prior to the ascension Christ gave the apostles two commands: to go into all the world and preach the gospel; and to tarry in Jerusalem until they were endued with power from on high.

After a ten-day waiting period, spent in prayer and fasting, the promised Holy Spirit came. This historic event marked the beginning of the Christian church and the inauguration of the missionary movement, for in those days the church *was* mission.

There was no clean break with Judaism. Regarded as a reform movement by its friends and as a heretical sect by its enemies, Christianity remained an integral part of Judaism. It took many years to develop its own theology, chart its own course, and project its own image.

Though commanded to go into all the world and disciple all nations, the disciples showed a distinct preference for Jerusalem, where they continued their association with the temple, participating in its prayers and supporting its services. Much of their teaching was done there. Later they extended their ministry to over four hundred synagogues in Jerusalem. Their message was distinctly Jewish in flavor. It centered around a suffering Messiah, called for repentance, and promised forgiveness and restoration. The church that emerged was more Jewish than Christian. A generation after Pentecost its members were still frequenting the temple, keeping the Mosaic Law, taking vows and offering sacrifices (Acts 21:20-24). The church in Jerusalem never managed to throw off the swaddling clothes of Judaism. With the destruction of the city in A.D. 70 the church there ceased to exist. This was not an unmitigated tragedy, for had Jerusalem continued to be the center of Christian worship Christianity might never have become a world religion. With the destruction of Jerusalem the church was free to become what its Founder intended it to be — spiritual and not temporal, universal and not provincial. Otherwise, Jerusalem might have become the Mecca of the Christian world, and the Jordan River might have become to Christians what the Ganges River is to Hindus.

Peter was the dominant figure among the twelve apostles. Later other leaders emerged. Two of them, Stephen and Philip, stood out from the rest. Both had a very effective ministry, Stephen in the synagogues of Jerusalem and Philip in the city of Samaria. The first contact that Saul of Tarsus had with Christianity doubtless took place in the synagogue of the Cilicians, where he encountered the irresistible wisdom of Stephen (Acts 6:9).

The martyrdom of Stephen and the ensuing persecution was a blow to the infant church; but it became a blessing for it resulted in a further extension of the Christian gospel. Those who were scattered abroad went everywhere preaching the Word. Some traveled as far as Phoenicia, Cyprus and Antioch, where they preached the gospel to the Gentiles, for the first time.

Further impetus was given to the preaching of the gospel to the Gentiles by two events of great significance: the conversion of Saul of Tarsus, who became the apostle to the Gentiles; and Peter's experience in preaching the gospel to Cornelius. That Luke attached great importance to these two events is seen from the fact that the former is recorded three times and the latter twice in the Acts of the Apostles.

Under the teaching of Barnabas and Paul the church in Antioch increased in strength and numbers until it rivalled, and later replaced, Jerusalem as the mother church of Christendom.

From its founding by Seleucus I in 300 B.C. Antioch had been a cosmopolitan city whose sophisticated inhabitants included Macedonians, Greeks and local Syrians, and a large colony of Jews. By the time of Christ it had become one of the three most important cities of the empire. Strategically located on the main highway to the east, it was a natural meeting place of East and West. Greek culture and Roman administration combined to make Antioch an ideal center for the reception of the gospel. Protected by a degree of public order not possible in a fanatical city like Jerusalem, the church in Antioch grew rapidly in size and importance. In fact, Antioch was one of the few cities in the empire in which the preaching of the gospel did not precipitate a communal riot. It was there that the disciples were first called Christians.

Paul made Antioch his headquarters during the heydey of his missionary career. His three missionary journeys, which lasted less than fifteen years, took him into four populous provinces of the empire: Galatia and Asia in Asia, and Macedonia and Achaia in Europe. Following the great Roman roads, he planted churches in all the important cities along the way. By the end of his third journey he could report " . . . that from Jerusalem, and round about unto Illyricum, I have fully preached the gospel of Christ" (Rom. 15:19). "Having no more place in these parts," he set his sights on Spain. On his way he proposed to visit Rome to make that city his base for evangelizing the western half of the empire. He reached Rome in due time, but his missionary days were over.

Paul, of course, was not the only missionary of those days. There must have been scores of others, whose names have been lost to history. We know that Christian laymen, many of them displaced persons, carried the good news of the gospel wherever they went. Casual references are made to churches in Judea, Galilee, and Samaria (Acts 9:31), Syria and Cilicia (Acts 15:23), Pontus, Cappadocia, and Bithynia (I Pet. 1:1). When and by whom were they founded? It would be interesting to know. We learn from the second chapter of Acts that Jews and proselytes from fifteen different regions of the empire were present in Jerusalem at Pentecost and heard Peter and his colleagues preach the gospel. Doubtless many of them became converts to the Christian faith and returned home to preach Christ in the synagogues and establish Christian churches in their homes.

One thing is certain; the Acts of the Apostles does not tell the whole story. There are hints in Paul's epistles that the gospel had a much wider proclamation than that described by Luke. He states that the gospel had been "preached to every creature which is under heaven" (Col. 1:23); that the faith of the Roman church was "spoken of throughout the whole world" (Rom. 1:8); that the faith of the Thessalonian believers " . . . has gone forth everywhere . . . " (I Thess. 1:8, RSV).

Coming to the second and third centuries we find that information regarding the expansion of the Christian church is even more meager. We read of large and influential churches in Alexandria, Carthage and Edessa; but we do not know when or by whom they were established. Here again there are wide gaps in our knowledge. It would seem that Christianity continued to spread along the main roads and rivers of the empire: eastward by way of Damascus and Edessa into Mesopotamia; southward through Bostra and Petra into Arabia; westward through Alexandria and Carthage into North Africa; and northward through Antioch into Armenia, Pontus, and Bithynia. Later still it reached Spain, Gaul, and Britain before crossing the borders of the empire into more remote parts such as Ireland, Ethiopia, and China.

The silence of the New Testament regarding the entrance of the gospel into Egypt in the apostolic era is as puzzling as it is tantalizing. That the gospel went north from Jerusalem to Antioch without going south to Alexandria is unthinkable, especially when communications between the two cities were constant and convenient. The fact remains, however, that we know nothing of the origin of the church in Egypt except that tradition ascribes it to the work of John Mark.

We do know that Christians were reported in Alexandria in the reign of Hadrian (c. 125) and that by the end of the century there was a strong church there. Also in Alexandria there was a famous catechetical school, founded about 180 by Pantaenus, who later took the gospel to India. Pantaenus was followed by Clement, and Clement by the brilliant Origen. "These individuals can be credited with bringing Egyptian Christianity into the mainstream of the Christian tradition."[5]

West of Egypt was Cyrene, mentioned four times in the New Testament. If Cyrenians took the gospel to Antioch (Acts 11:19), it is safe to assume that they shared the good news with their own people; but of this we have no record. From Synesius we learn that by the end of the fourth century there were half a dozen bishoprics there.

Traveling west we come to Carthage, the center of Roman civilization in North Africa at that time. Christianity may have reached Carthage across the Mediterranean from Rome or Ephesus, or it may have entered from Egypt. In and around the city were vigorous Christian churches with an extensive Latin literature, including the first Latin translation of the New Testament. By the close of the second century the Christian community had grown so large that the doughty Tertullian could threaten the Roman magistrate with rebellion unless he desisted from persecuting the Christians. Animated by the zeal of Tertullian, directed by the abilities of Cyprian, and adorned by the eloquence of Lactantius, the Christian community could hardly fail to thrive. The outstanding feature of the North African church was the large number of bishops. Every town, almost every village, had one. Most famous of all was the towering figure

---

5 Walter Oetting, *The Church of the Catacombs* (Saint Louis, Mo.: Concordia Publishing House, 1964), p. 80.

of Augustine, Bishop of Hippo (354-430), whose writings gave form to Roman Catholic theology for a thousand years.

Did Paul realize his ambition to visit Spain? The New Testament is silent on this point. Clement of Rome states that he preached the gospel in the extreme west of the empire. If this is true, Paul was the founder of the church in Spain. All we know with certainty is that by the beginning of the third century Christianity was established in the south of Spain. Spanish Christianity, then as now, was not of the highest order. Idolatry, adultery, and even homicide marred its image.

The gospel made very slow progress in the cold climate of Gaul. It is thought that Christianity entered Gaul from the east. By the second century the church was fairly well established in the southern part around Lyons and Vienne. *Irenaeus,* Bishop of Lyons (175-200), preached to both Celtic- and Latin-speaking peoples. The response was not encouraging. As late as 250 scattered churches in half a dozen communities embraced only a small number of converts. A century later when *Martin of Tours* became bishop of that diocese the surrounding countryside was still largely pagan. An ex-soldier, Martin adopted military measures to ensure immediate results. He and his monks went about the countryside demolishing temples, destroying idols, preaching the gospel and baptizing converts.

We have no sure knowledge of how Christianity entered Britain. The first authentic information relates to three bishops from Britain who were present at the Council of Arles in the south of Gaul in 314. Evidently the gospel had reached Britain some time before, perhaps as early as the middle of the second century.

Early in the second century the Christians multiplied rapidly in Asia Minor, especially in Bithynia and Pontus. So much was this the case that Pliny, Governor of Pontus, wrote to the Emperor Trajan for instructions on how to deal with a situation that threatened to get out of hand. During the third century a mass movement took place in Pontus under the leadership of *Gregory Thaumaturgus.* It was said that when he became bishop of his native city about 240 there were only seventeen Christians, but when he died thirty years later there were only seventeen non-Christians. The transition from paganism to Christianity was facilitated by the widespread use of miracles and the fact that Gregory Thaumaturgus allowed the Christians to substitute Christian festivals for pagan feasts.

Sometime during the third century Christianity spread beyond the borders of the Roman empire. In time it became established in Parthia, Ethiopia, Ireland, India, and even China.

The gospel traveled eastward from Antioch along the main trade route via Duro-Europos to Ctesiphon and Seleucia, twin cities on the Tigris River. The first Christians may have been Jews, "dwellers in Mesopotamia," who heard Peter at Pentecost (Acts 2:9). By A.D. 225, churches were found throughout the Tigris-Euphrates valley from the Caspian Sea to the Persian Gulf. Edessa became a center of strong Christian influence

and missionary outreach. By the end of the second century Christianity
had become the state religion. Syriac, the language of the church there,
was the first language into which the New Testament was translated. By
the beginning of the fourth century Edessa may have been predominantly
Christian.

The gospel entered Armenia from Cappadocia probably towards the
close of the third century. As a result of a mass movement led by the great
missionary, *Gregory the Illuminator,* and sparked by the conversion of
King Tiridates, Armenia became a Christian kingdom. The New Testament
first appeared in the Armenian language in 410. The Armenian church has
weathered many a storm and is today one of the oldest churches in
Christendom.

Tradition says that it was the apostle *Bartholomew* who first took the
gospel to Arabia. Cretes and Arabians were in Jerusalem on the day of
Pentecost (Acts 2:11) and may have taken the new faith home with them.
We know that by the end of the fourth century there was a Christian
settlement in Hirah. It seems fairly certain that by 525 Christianity was
firmly established there.

How and when did the gospel penetrate the vast subcontinent of
India? Eusebius states, and the Mar Thoma Christians firmly believe, that
their church was established in the first century by the apostle *Thomas.*
Pantaenus is reported to have left the catechetical school in Alexandria to
take the gospel to India about 180. Certainly Christianity has been in India
since the third century, making the Mar Thoma Church the oldest Christian church east of the Khyber Pass. Other Syrian churches in India are
very old.

Did the Ethiopian eunuch baptized by *Philip* (Acts 8:26-39) take the
gospel back to Ethiopia? If so, his efforts were not very successful, for we
have no evidence of a Christian church in that land until about the middle
of the fourth century. The story is a fascinating one. Two young Christians, shipwrecked in the Red Sea, were taken as slaves to Ethiopia,
where they served in the royal court at Axum. There they preached the
gospel with great effect and made many converts. When the work got
beyond their time and strength, one of them, *Frumentius,* returned to
Egypt to appeal for help. Athanasius, Patriarch of Alexandria, made
Frumentius a bishop and sent him back to Ethiopia, where he served as
head of the Ethiopian (Coptic) Church until his death.

The Goths were the first of the Teutonic peoples north of the
Danube to adopt Christianity in large numbers. Their earliest knowledge of
the gospel was received from Christian prisoners taken during their many
incursions into the empire during the third century. The systematic evangelization of the Goths, however, was the work of *Ulfilas* (c.311-c.380),
whose father was a Cappadocian and his mother a Goth. After spending
ten years in Constantinople, where he became a Christian, he returned
home to evangelize his own people. His outstanding work was the transla-

tion of the Bible into the Gothic language. To do this he had to reduce the language to writing. He was the first of a long line of illustrious missionaries who have made significant contributions to linguistics and to literature as well as to the dissemination of the Scriptures.

Latourette states that the conversion of the Franks towards the close of the fifth century "was the single most important stage in the spread of the faith among the non-Roman peoples in the northwestern part of the continent of Europe."[6] The Franks had been in touch with the Roman Empire for many years and some of them had become Christians; but the breakthrough came when their king, Clovis, with three thousand of his warriors, embraced the Christian faith and was baptized on Christmas Day, 496. His decision to become a Christian sprang from mixed motives, one of which was an obligation to keep a vow he made at the height of the battle to embrace the Christian faith if the Christian God would grant him victory. He got the victory and honored his vow to become a Christian. Though not obliged to do so, most of his subjects followed his example.

The last area to be evangelized in this period was Ireland, the most westerly part of the then known world. The apostle to Ireland was *Patrick,* who, contrary to common belief, was not an Irishman at all. Born of Christian parents in Roman Britain about 389, and with only a smattering of education, he became the greatest missionary of his time.

At the age of twelve he was carried captive to Ireland, where he was put to work herding sheep. During his exile a spiritual experience changed his whole life and made real to him the nominal faith of his childhood. After six years of lonely servitude he escaped to France, where for several years he served as a monk in the Abbey of Lerins. Finally he returned to England to receive a warm welcome from his family.

But his heart was still with the benighted people of Ireland and he could not rest. In a dream he heard voices calling him: "We beseech thee, holy youth, to come and walk again amongst us as before." This he took to be God's call to return to the land of his captivity. Ignoring the pleas of parents and friends, he returned to Ireland, where he spent the rest of his life.

A man of deep personal piety and warm evangelical fervor, Patrick gave himself without reserve for thirty-five years to the evangelization of Ireland. Exposed to many kinds of danger from Druid chieftains, Roman soldiers and robber bands, he baptized thousands of converts, planted hundreds of churches and ordained many to the clergy.

Patrick's influence continued long after his own time and extended far beyond the borders of his own country. The monasteries which became an integral part of Celtic Christianity were not only centers of Christian culture but also of missionary zeal. As such they played an important role in the evangelization of northern Europe in the following centuries.

---

6 K. S. Latourette, *The First Five Centuries* (New York: Harper and Brothers, 1937), p. 208.

By the end of the fifth century Christianity had, with varying degrees of success, become established in all parts of the empire and even beyond, from the Sahara Desert in the south to Hadrian's Wall in the north, and from India in the east to Spain in the west.

Mention should be made here of the earliest contact with the great land of China. At an early date Christianity was established in Mesopotamia and Persia. From there it spread into India, Central Asia, and China. This was the Nestorian form of Christianity, which took its name from Nestorius, Patriarch of Constantinople, who was condemned at the Council of Ephesus (A.D. 431) as a heretic and banished beyond the frontiers of the Roman Empire. In subsequent centuries the Nestorian Church became one of the greatest missionary churches of all time.

Nestorian Christianity entered China by way of Central Asia in A.D. 635, at the beginning of the T'ang dynasty, during which Chinese culture reached its zenith. Under Emperior T'ai Tsung China was probably the wealthiest and most civilized empire in the world. Changan (modern Sian), its capital, was the largest and most prosperous city on earth at that time.

Our principal and most authentic source of information regarding the Nestorian mission is the Nestorian Stone, carved at Sian in the eighth century and discovered in 1623. The inscription on this monument tells in some detail the story of the origin and spread of Christianity in China. According to this record the first Christian missionary, *Alopen,* arrived in China in A.D. 635. He was warmly welcomed by Emperor T'ai Tsung, who himself studied the religion, approved it, and gave orders for its dissemination. Alopen had taken with him a copy of the Scriptures, which he and his fellow monks translated into Chinese. In the capital he built a monastery for twenty-one monks. The new religion spread through "ten provinces" and monasteries were reported in a "hundred cities."

It would appear that Christianity was for a period of two hundred years confined largely to these monasteries, where the monks gave themselves to the study of the language and the translation of Christian books into Chinese. In spite of imperial favor Christianity met with opposition, chiefly from the Buddhists.

In A.D. 845 Emperor Wu Tsung, an ardent Taoist and opposed to all forms of monastic life, issued a decree dissolving all monasteries and ordering the monks to return to private life. The Buddhists, who had some two hundred thousand monasteries, were hardest hit. The Nestorians, with their monastic form of Christianity, likewise suffered a major setback.

They were not, however, completely wiped out. Under the Mongols in the thirteenth century they were so important that a government bureau was established to supervise their monasteries, which had been restored to them. We read of Nestorian churches in such famous eastern cities as Chinkiang, Hangchow, and Yangchow. One source gives the number of Nestorians in China as thirty-thousand.

When the Franciscans under *John of Monte Corvino* arrived in Peking in 1294 they found the Nestorian mission strongly established but bitterly opposed to the newcomers. They spread false rumors about the Franciscans and tried to bring them into disrepute with the emperor. That they were to some extent successful is suggested by a statement attributed to John of Cora. Speaking of Nestorians, he said:

> They have very handsome and devoutly ordered churches, with crosses and images in honor of God and the saints. They hold sundry offices under the said Emperor, and have great privileges from him; so that it is believed that if they would agree and be at one with the Minor Friars and the other good Christians who dwell in that country, they would convert the whole country and the Emperor likewise to the true faith.[7]

Numerical Strength

Jesus was not enamored of numbers. He was more interested in the caliber of His disciples than in the number of His converts. He chose twelve apostles and gave most of His time and thought to them. The multitudes came and went; many of them were interested only in the "loaves and fishes." Jesus did not commit Himself to them, for He knew their fickleness (John 2:25). In days of popularity He refused to be exalted to the place of kingship (John 6:15). When reverses came and the crowds dwindled He refused to be dejected (Matt. 15:12, 13). He referred to his band of followers as a "little flock" (Luke 12:32). On occasion He went out of His way to make entrance into the kingdom as difficult as possible (Luke 9:57-62). The gate He described as "straight" and the way as "narrow." He acknowledged that those who find the one or favor the other are "few" (Matt. 7:13, 14).

Nevertheless, numbers are not to be despised altogether, for quantity as well as quality is a measure of success. He did tell His apostles to "go . . . into *all* the world" (Mark 16:15) and "make disciples of *all* nations" (Matt. 28:19, RSV). How many followers did He leave behind? It is difficult to say. One hundred and twenty were found in the upper room prior to Pentecost (Acts 1:15). Paul refers to five hundred brethren who saw the Lord after the resurrection (I Cor. 15:6). Doubtless there were more.

During the early days of the Christian mission three thousand are mentioned as being baptized in one day (Acts 2:41). Later the figure increased to five thousand (Acts 4:4). As time went on the Word of God "increased" (Acts 6:7). Conversions were a daily occurrence (Acts 2:47). Believers were "the more added to the Lord" (Acts 5:14). Multitudes

---

7 Henry Yule, *Cathay and the Way Thither* (London: The Hakluyt Society, 1925), Vol. I, pp. 189-190.

were healed of various diseases (Acts 5:16). The number of disciples in Jerusalem "multiplied greatly" among them a "great company" of priests (Acts 6:7); so much so that the Sanhedrin accused Peter and John of filling Jerusalem with their doctrine (Acts 5:28).

When Philip carried the gospel to Samaria the people "with one accord gave heed," and there was "great joy in that city" (Acts 8:6-8). In Antioch the hand of the Lord was with the first messengers and a "great number" believed (Acts 11:21). Later, under the preaching of Barnabas, "much people" were added to the Lord (Acts 11:24). In Antioch of Pisidia "almost the whole city" came together to hear Paul (Acts 13:44). In Thessalonica a "great multitude" believed (Acts 17:4). "Many" of the Corinthians believed (Acts 18:8). During Paul's three-year stay in Ephesus "all they which dwelt in Asia heard the word, . . . both Jews and Greeks" (Acts 19:10). Some idea of the number of believers can be gained from the value of the magic spells and charms—"Ephesian letters" as they were called—that were burned. Fifty thousand pieces of silver would be equivalent to $10,000 if the silver *drachma* were the unit of money used.

Luke's account of Paul's labors leaves us with the impression that the churches founded by him were numerically large as well as spiritually prosperous. Athens, where only a few responded, was the exception (Acts 17:34). When we leave the Acts of the Apostles we are on less sure ground. We have very few statistics, and we cannot be sure that those we have are accurate. Figures given for primitive Christians are often exaggerated, sometimes out of piety, sometimes out of fear.

During the second century Christianity continued to make steady gains, especially in the East. Christians were especially numerous in Asia Minor. In the second decade of the second century Pliny, the governor of Bithynia, complained that the temples were almost deserted and that the new superstition had invaded not only the cities but the countryside as well. A little later Justin Martyr wrote: "There is no people, Greek or Barbarian, or any other race . . . among whom prayers and thanksgiving are not offered in the name of the crucified Jesus to the Father and creator of all things." About the year 200 Tertullian boasted: "We are only of yesterday, but already we fill the world."

Such statements, however, must not be taken too literally. They should be interpreted in the light of Origen's statement that the proportion of the faithful was "very inconsiderable when compared with the multitude of the unbelieving world."[8]

Harnack informs us that Christians were by no means numerous until after the middle of the second century. Gibbon has difficulty in accepting Justin Martyr's description, calling it a "splendid exaggeration . . . of a devout but careless writer."[9]

---

[8] Origen, *Contra Celsum*, 1, viii, p. 424.

[9] Edward Gibbon, *The Triumph of Christendom in the Roman Empire* (New York: Harper and Brothers, 1958), p. 68.

It was not until the third century, when the empire began to break up, that large numbers of people turned to Christianity. "In the chaos and terror of the third century men fled from the weakened state to the consolations of religion, and found them more abundantly in Christianity than in its rivals."[10] At the beginning of this century Christianity was already dominant in the cities of Phrygia; and throughout Asia Minor the Christians formed a large minority of the population. In North Africa conversions were so numerous as to approximate a mass movement.

A forty-year period of peace, from 260 to 300, gave the church an opportunity to extend its influence without the handicaps and hardships which accompany persecution. These four decades, just before the Diocletian persecution, were a time of unprecedented growth for the Christian church. Converts by the thousands flocked into the churches, bringing their patrimony, and in some cases their paganism, with them. The church became the richest religious organization in the empire. "In almost every city the ancient churches were found insufficient to contain the increasing multitude of proselytes; and in their place more stately and capacious edifices were erected for the public worship of the faith."[11] By the close of the third century the two greatest numerical strongholds of the faith were Asia Minor and North Africa. Edessa was well on the way to becoming the first state to make Christianity the official religion.

So far as statistics go, we have only two cities which afford anything like an accurate estimate of the strength of the church—Rome and Antioch.

We know that in A.D. 250 the church in Rome supported one hundred clergy and fifteen hundred poor persons. Assuming the population to be not less than one million, Gibbon estimates the number of Christians at fifty thousand. Harnack, working with the same figure, estimates thirty thousand. Fifty years later, according to a third opinion, the Christian community numbered one hundred thousand.

Antioch was the oldest and most illustrious church in the East. According to Chrysostom, towards the end of the fourth century Christians accounted for half of the population of five hundred thousand. Gibbon, however, considers this figure too high and suggests 20 percent rather than 50.

Exactly how many Christians were there at the close of the third century? Frankly, we do not know. We have no reliable figures for the empire, much less the church; but this has not deterred scholars from hazarding a guess. Will Durant estimates the population at one hundred million, while Stephen Neill would settle for half that figure. Estimates of the numerical strength of the church also vary. Ten per cent of the population would be a generous estimate. By far the larger portion of

---

10 Will Durant, *op. cit.,* p. 650.
11 Edward Gibbon, *op. cit.,* p. 125

these was found in the East. Durant believes that the Christians represented a fourth of the population in the East and only a twentieth in the West.

Following the conversion of Constantine Christianity entered a period of expansion. Enjoying royal patronage and supported by state funds, the church grew rapidly in the fourth century. "It seems likely that the number of Christians in the empire at least quadrupled itself in the century that followed the Edict of Milan."[12] The church in Rome reported twelve thousand men and a proportionate number of women and children baptized in one year. Barbarians, who held back when Christianity was a proscribed religion, rushed to embrace the new faith of their conquerors. In North Africa, where the native populations had remained unresponsive to the Christian message, great changes took place. In no time at all "the cities of Egypt were filled with bishops, and the deserts of Theais swarmed with hermits."[13] By the fourth century the majority of the inhabitants of Edessa had embraced Christianity.

Not content with supporting Christianity, Rome came in time to discriminate against the native religions. Gratian (367-383) withdrew state aid to the pagan cults and confiscated temple properties. Theodosius (379-395) went a step further; he closed the temples and punished those who attempted to sacrifice in secret. Emboldened by such edicts, the Christians, often led by monks, took it upon themselves to destroy pagan temples. Apostates from Christianity were deprived of civil as well as ecclesiastical rights. Anyone wanting to practice religion was virtually shut up to Christianity. Little wonder that the church quadrupled its membership in the fourth century.

The success, however, was by no means complete. In all parts of the empire pockets of resistance remained. Strangely enough, the Jews proved to be most impervious to the Christian message. They were wooed for a time, but never won. After the destruction of Jerusalem the break between the Jews and the Christians widened. Very few converts were made after the first century. The Christians grew impatient with their recalcitrant spirit and came first to hate, and then to persecute, them. "Such an injustice as that done by the Gentile church to Judaism is almost unprecedented in the annals of history . . . The daughter first robbed her mother, and then repudiated her."[14] Consequently Christianity never took root in Jewish, or even in Semitic, soil. Like Buddhism, it died out in the land of its birth and came to bloom in foreign lands.

Nor did Judaism survive in Palestine beyond 135, when the fanatical Jews under Bar Cocheba made their last desperate attempt to regain their

[12] Stephen Neill, *A History of Christian Missions* (Baltimore: Penguin Books, 1964), p. 46.

[13] Edward Gibbon, *op. cit.*, p. 64.

[14] Adolf Harnack, *The Mission and Expansion of Christianity* (New York: Harper and Brothers, 1962), p. 69.

freedom. After three flaming years and more than a million casualties the Jews were crushed, not to rise again until modern times.

> From this moment they entered their Middle Ages . . . No other people has ever known so long an exile, or so hard a fate. Scattered into every province and beyond, condemned to poverty and humiliation, unbefriended even by philosophers and saints, they retired from public affairs into private study and worship . . . Judaism hid in fear and obscurity while its offspring, Christianity, went out to conquer the world.[15]

Christianity became strongly entrenched among the Latin-speaking people in and around Carthage; but it met with considerably less success among the Punic people and left the Berbers almost untouched. In Persia, where the new faith had to compete with Zoroastrianism, it does not appear to have made much headway. In Egypt the Christian faith was for a long time confined to the city of Alexandria, which, in a sense, was a foreign colony whose culture was quite distinct from that of the surrounding areas. As late as Origen's time it was a rare thing to meet an Egyptian who was a Christian. Paganism persisted in the cities of Gaul, Italy and Spain well into the first century, and in Phoenicia and Palestine into the sixth century. Until the academies were closed by imperial decree in A.D. 529 Athens remained a stronghold of pre-Christian philosophy, while the hinterland of Greece seems hardly to have been penetrated by the gospel.

Who were the early Christians and from what classes did they come? Judged by their enemies, they were the dregs of humanity. Celsus describes them as "worthless, contemptible people, idiots, slaves, poor women and children."[16]

Paul intimates that even in the Corinthian church there were not many wise, mighty, or noble" (I Cor. 1:26). This should occasion no great surprise. Gibbon observed: "Such is the constitution of civil society that, whilst a few persons are distinguished by riches, by honor, and by knowledge, the body of the people is condemned to obscurity, ignorance and poverty. The Christian religion, which addressed itself to the whole human race, must consequently collect a far greater number of proselytes from the lower than the superior ranks of life."[17]

As time went on and the fortunes of the church improved, the upper classes were attracted in larger numbers. In the early part of the second century Pliny reported that a great number of persons of every order of men had deserted the religion of their ancestors. About A.D. 200 Tertullian claimed that "every age, condition and rank is coming over to us." Later on, when Christianity became the religion of the state, a general

---

15 Will Durant, *op. cit.*, p. 549.

16 Origen, *Contra Celsum*, iii, 49-55.

17 Edward Gibbon, *op. cit.*, pp. 69, 70

stampede brought an increasingly large number of persons of high rank into the church.

It is noteworthy that during all this time there was no organized missionary endeavor such as characterized later periods. The gospel was preached by laymen. "Nearly every convert, with the ardor of a revolutionary, made himself an office of propaganda."[18] With no weapon but truth and no banner but love, these single-minded, warm-hearted followers of Jesus traveled by land and sea to all parts of the empire, and wherever they went they gladly shared their new-found faith with friends, neighbors and strangers. As slaves, traders and, later on, soldiers, they used their secular calling to advance the cause of Christ. Even as exiles they carried the contagion of their faith to distant shores and inhospitable regions.

Cultural Penetration

Jesus was more interested in the salvation of the individual than in the reformation of society. He spoke frequently about the former, rarely about the latter. This is not to say that He was unmindful of, or indifferent to, the needs of society. He summed up the whole duty of man when He said: "Thou shalt love the Lord thy God with all thy heart, and thy neighbor as thyself." The order is important. The gospel is first personal, then social.

In the parable of the leaven (Matt. 13:33) and again in the parable of the salt and the light (Matt. 5:13-16) we are made aware of the way in which the Christian presence is to affect its environment. As salt, the Christians were to penetrate and permeate pagan society, arresting its decay, rejuvenating its institutions, and giving it new force and flavor. As light, the Christians were to illuminate the darkness of paganism by dispelling its ignorance and superstition by the truth of the gospel. Light is beneficial only if it is set on a high place where it can be seen. Salt is effective only on contact. It preserves only when it penetrates.

Jesus chose twelve men, entrusted them with His truth, imbued them with His spirit, invested them with His power, and sent them forth into the world. Everywhere and at all times they were to be as salt and light. They were to be different from other men, in character and conduct, in manners and morals, in motives and ideals; only so could they save the sinner, or reform society.

The early Christians resided for the most part in the cities, where they lived their lives, reared their children, and plied their trade side by side with their pagan neighbors. Little by little, without fuss or fanfare, these simple, wholesome, joyous Christians made their presence felt and their secret known. The light was shining. The salt was penetrating. The

---

18 Will Durant, *op. cit.,* p. 602

leaven was working its way through the fabric of society. By the year 200 Christian influence had become so pervasive that Tertullian could write:

> We are a new group but have already penetrated all areas of imperial life—cities, islands, villages, towns, market-places, even the camp, tribes, palace, senate, the law-court. There is nothing left for you but your temples.[19]

Nor did they live in isolation, for Tertullian went on to say:

> We are no Brahmins. . . . dwelling in woods and exiled from life. . . . We live with you in the world, making use of the forum. . . . the bath. . . . the workshop. . . . the weekly market, and all other places of commerce. We sail with you, till the soil with you and traffic with you.[20]

Yet all the time they were considered by themselves and others as a separate and distinct people. Peter had called them a "chosen generation, a royal priesthood, an holy nation, a peculiar people" (I Pet. 2:9). They never forgot their divine calling or their heavenly destiny. They confessed that they were "strangers and pilgrims." They were ex-patriots—a colony of heaven—and they eagerly anticipated the return of Jesus Christ to inaugurate His reign of righteousness. So different were they that they came to be called "the third race"—the Romans being the first, the Jews the second.

Their attitude toward politics was narrow and negative. They believed that the world system of which Satan was both god (II Cor. 4:4) and prince (Eph. 2:2) was alienated from (Eph. 4:18), hostile to (Rom. 8:7), and under the judgment of, God (II Thess. 1:7, 8). While they were "in" the world and could not escape from it, they were not "of" it. The insistent call was: " . . . come out from among them, and be ye separate . . . " (II Cor. 6:17).

Nevertheless they had a wholesome view of the role of government. Taking their stand with Paul (Rom. 13), they were law-abiding citizens. They believed government to be a divinely established institution and were prepared to support it loyally. They paid taxes willingly, if not joyfully, remembering the words of Christ: "Render therefore to Caesar the things that are Caesar's" (Matt. 22:21, RSV).

On the other hand, they were not wholly satisfied with the political structure, local or imperial, because it was part of the world system they believed to be essentially evil. At best, it was a necessary evil—better than anarchy. At worst it was tyrannical and demonic.

Emperor worship was universally regarded by the Christians as outright idolatry and resisted to the death. At the same time, they resolutely repudiated the charge of treason, and tried to make their point by reminding their enemies that from the earliest times they had prayed for

---

[19] Tertullian, *Apology* 37.
[20] Tertullian, *Apology* 42.

the well-being of the emperor, and had promoted the peace and prosperity of the empire.

For the first two hundred years the Christians refused to participate in any form of government service—civil or military. Gradually this attitude changed. They began by making exception of those who had been in government employ before they became Christians. By the end of the third century Christians were found in all walks of life—the court, the civil service, and the military.

By their family solidarity, their honest toil, their submission to authority, their passion for righteousness, their love of human kind, and many other virtues, Christians constituted one of the most stable elements in the social structure. Melito in his *Apology* to Marcus Aurelius was quick to point out that Christianity was helping to undergird the state, and that ever since the advent of the new religion the empire had continued to flourish.[21]

The early Christians attached little importance to worldly wisdom. Among the twelve apostles there was not one man of letters. Jesus Himself remarked that the mysteries of the gospel were hid from the wise and prudent and revealed unto babes (Matt. 11:25). Paul deplored the fact that the world "by wisdom knew not God" (I Cor. 1:21), and conceded that even in the Corinthian church there were "not many wise" (I Cor. 1:26). Though himself a man of wide learning and brilliant mind, Paul in his proclamation of the gospel purposely avoided "excellency of speech or wisdom" (I Cor. 2:1), and warned his readers of the dangers of speculative philosophy (Col. 2:8).

It is not surprising that the early Christians regarded Christianity primarily as a way of salvation, not a system of philosophy. They were content to preach "Jesus Christ and Him crucified" in terms as simple as they were direct. It was not until the second century when a more sophisticated group, among them some philosophers, entered the fold that they felt obliged to wrestle with Greek thought. "The Church now won to its support some of the finest minds in the empire. Ignatius, bishop of Antioch, began the powerful dynasty of post-apostolic fathers, who gave a philosophy to Christianity, and overwhelmed its enemies with argument."[22]

Justin Martyr considered philosophy a good thing and coupled it with piety. Clement of Alexandria declared boldly that it was a gift of God to the Greeks, conducive of piety and a schoolmaster to bring the Hellenic mind to Christ. Others went still further and found in Socrates a forerunner of the truth, and in Seneca a kindred spirit. Realizing that if Christianity were to hold its own in a sophisticated society, it must

---

[21] Eusebius, *Ecclesiastical History,* IV, 26.

[22] Will Durant, *op. cit.,* p. 611.

ultimately win the intelligentsia, these Christian apologists attempted to express Christian truth in philosophical terms.

The new venture was not without its dangers and detractors. Tatian and Tertullian denounced all philosophy, good as well as bad. Tatian went to incredible lengths and was guilty of gross injustice. Tertullian asserted that the gospel appealed to faith, not reason; and that Christianity was credible precisely because it was absurd. The two feared that the simplicity of the gospel would be corrupted by the refinements of human reason. Perhaps they were not altogether wrong, for knowledge was as often the parent of heresy as of piety.

In time Christian teachers came to regard Christianity itself as a philosophy. After all, did it not deal with the problem of being in nature, God and man? Was it not concerned with the origin of the world, the meaning of life and the destiny of man? Christians were convinced that their doctrine was really the truth, and therefore the true philosophy. Indeed, it was more, it was the wisdom of God—the highest form of philosophy. All truth, wherever found, comes from God and is therefore "Christian." Some went even further and suggested that the best in Greek philosophy had been borrowed from Christianity.

The most influential of the apologists was the brilliant Origen, who at eighteen years of age succeeded Clement as head of the Catechetical School in Alexandria. He is reputed to have written six thousand "books" and corresponded with emperors. His most famous defense of Christianity, *Contra Celsum,* which appeared in 248, "impressed pagan thinkers as no apology had done before him. With him Christianity ceased to be only a comforting faith; it became a full-fledged philosophy, buttressed with Scripture but proudly resting on reason."[23]

But the real conflict between Christian and pagan philosophy was a matter of power, not polemics. The pagan philosophers, including Socrates, had more questions than answers. The Christian philosophers did not have all the answers; but they had more and better answers. Above all, they had the answer to the greatest of all questions—How can man be *good* as well as wise? The pagan philosophers spent their time *explaining* the world. The Christian philosophers quietly went about the task of *changing* the world.

It is a mistake to suppose that any "slave question" troubled the early church. Both Jesus and the apostles accepted the institution of slavery as an integral part of the economic and political system. Slaves were admonished by Paul to "remain in the state in which" they were "called" (I Cor. 7:20, RSV). It never occurred to the early Christians to abolish slavery even among themselves. Instead they depended on Christian love to ameliorate the conditions under which the slaves lived. Masters were to be kind and considerate, and were to give to their slaves that which was just

---

23 Will Durant, *op. cit.,* p. 615.

and equal because they themselves were accountable to a Master in heaven (Eph. 6:9). Slaves, on their part, were expected to be honest, industrious, faithful, and loyal (Titus 2:9, 10), and not to take advantage of the fact that they were regarded as brethren in the Lord.

If the slave were afforded an opportunity to secure his freedom, he was to accept it; otherwise he was to be content with the spiritual freedom he enjoyed in Christ (I Cor. 7:21, 22). Masters were encouraged to set their slaves free. Congregations often allocated funds for the emancipation of slaves. In some communities, churches held special ceremonies of manumission. Instead of attacking the power structure head-on, the church was content to allow the leaven of the gospel to permeate pagan society, hoping that by precept and practice they would convince their friends and neighbors of the dignity of man and the worth of the individual.

The Character of the Early Church

The two outstanding virtues of the early church were charity and chastity. Both come to focus in James' definition of genuine religion. "Pure religion and undefiled before God and the Father is this, To visit the fatherless and widows in their affliction, and to keep himself unspotted from the world" (James 1:27).

It was said of the early Christians that they recognized one another by means of secret marks and signs, and loved one another almost before they got acquainted.

The love that became the hallmark of the Christian religion may be traced to three powerful influences: the noble example of perfect love seen in the Master (John 13:34, 35), the lofty teachings of the Savior contained in the Gospels (Matt. 5:43-48), and the dynamic afforded by the ministry of the Holy Spirit (Rom. 5:5).

Probably no parable made a greater impression on the early church than the parable of the sheep and the goats in Matthew 25. Certainly the works of charity listed there were to an amazing degree incorporated into the program of the early church.

In the early part of Acts we find the disciples practising a form of Christian communism which permitted them to have all things in common (Acts 2:44; 4:32). The church in Antioch sent relief funds to the poor saints in Jerusalem (Acts 11:27-30). Later on the Gentile churches in Macedonia and Achaia sent similar gifts to Jerusalem (II Cor. 9). Certainly Paul was concerned for the social implications of the gospel and instructed the rich to help the poor (II Cor. 8:14) and the strong to support the weak (Rom. 15:1). Converts were urged to bear one another's burdens and thus fulfill the law of Christ (Gal. 6:2). They were told to "do good to all men, and especially to those who are of the household of faith" (Gal. 6:10, RSV).

John teaches that divine love inevitably expresses itself in human compassion (I John 3:17, 18). James says the same about faith (James 2:14-16). Both love and faith express themselves in works of charity.

The early Christians began where Jesus told them to begin—by loving one another. Moreover, they followed His example and teaching, and expressed their love in deeds, not words. Harnack lists ten different areas in which early Christian philanthropy manifested itself: alms in general, support of teachers and officials, support of widows and orphans, support of the sick and infirm, the care of prisoners and convicts in the mines, the care of poor people needing burial, the care of slaves, providing disaster relief, furnishing employment and, finally, extending hospitality.[24]

All of this was, of course, in stark contrast to the pagan practices of the day. Plato suggested that allowing the poor to die shortened their misery. Cicero advised charity only for those who would use it wisely. Roman society cared nothing for orphans, allowing them to be reared for prostitution. Slaves were regarded as goods and chattels and were bought and sold as such. Christian compassion was not restricted to Christian circles. It was offered indiscriminately to all classes and conditions of men. Referring to the great plague during the reign of Maximius Daza, Eusebius reports:

> Then did they show themselves to the heathen in the clearest light. For the Christians were the only people who amid such terrible ills showed their fellow-feeling and humanity in their actions. Day by day some would busy themselves with attending to the dead and burying them; others gathered in one spot all who were afflicted by hunger throughout the whole city, and gave bread to them all.[25]

Considering the paucity of their numbers and the meagerness of their resources, the primitive Christians did more for the amelioration of human suffering than any succeeding generation of believers.

> The works of charity that Christians accomplished in the Roman Empire continue to be one of the greatest stars in the church's crown. Even the pagans noticed this. Lucian, who is known more for his satire than his appreciation, wrote: "It is incredible to see the ardor with which the people of that religion help each other in their wants. They spare nothing. Their first legislator (Jesus) has put into their heads that they are all brethren."[26]

The second great virtue of the early Christians was purity. Here again the disciples took their cue from Jesus, both His example and His teaching. The sinless character of Jesus Christ was a unique phenomenon in the world of men. Born without sin, He lived without sin. The only time He knew sin was when he "bore our sins in his body on the tree" (I Pet. 2:24, RSV). He fraternized with publicans and sinners but always with a

---

24 Adolf Harnack, *op. cit.,* p. 153.

25 Eusebius, *Ecclesiastical History,* IX, 8.

26 Walter Oetting, *op. cit.,* p. 80.

view to winning them to a life of purity. He forgave sinners but always with the proviso: "Go and sin no more." Constantly He warned men of the devastating effects of sin—sins of the spirit as well as sins of the flesh. He lived a life of holiness and tried to inculcate the same in His followers. He pronounced a special blessing on the pure in heart. The essence of His ethic was summed up in the command: "Be ye therefore perfect, even as your Father which is in heaven is perfect" (Matt. 5:48).

The early church found itself in a hostile environment every aspect of which was inimical to the pursuit of holiness. Roman life in those times was characterized by two great sins—idolatry and immorality. Her religious life was dominated by the first, her social life by the second. To live in such a world and yet keep themselves "unspotted from the world" was a perennial problem for the early Christians.

The first problem was idolatry. Apostolic preaching concerning idolatry is clearly spelled out in the New Testament. " . . . you turned to God from idols, to serve a living and true God, and to wait for his Son from heaven, . . . who delivers us from the wrath to come" (I Thess. 1:9, 10, RSV). The God and Father of our Lord Jesus Christ is the living and true God, maker of heaven and earth, and sustainer of all things (Acts 14:15). In Him we live and move and have our being (Acts 17:28). To know Him is life eternal (John 17:3). Jesus Christ came from heaven to invade Satan's kingdom (Matt. 12:29), destroy his works (I John 3:8), and deliver men from his tyranny (Heb. 2:15). Christians have been delivered from the kingdom of darkness and translated into the kingdom of light (Col. 1:13). Since this is so, there can be no communion between light and darkness, no concord between Christ and Belial, no agreement between the temple of God and idols (II Cor. 6:14-16).

> The duty of keeping oneself free from all contamination with polytheism ranked as the *supreme* duty of the Christian. It took precedence over all others. It was regarded as the negative side of *the duty of confessing one's faith,* and the "sin of idolatry" was more strictly dealt with in the Christian church than any other sin whatsoever.[27]

The war against idolatry continued during the second and third centuries when the Christian apologists intensified their polemic against the pagan gods. Their method of attack was twofold: To demonstrate the folly of pagan teaching about idols, and to rouse moral indignation against the gods by exposing their abominable vices. They were careful, however, not to encourage iconoclasm. If a Christian smashed an idol and was slain in the act, he was not reckoned among the martyrs. Idol making was declared an illegal occupation and had to be given up even if no other means of livelihood were available. Christians were not allowed to practise as astrologers or magicians.

---

[27] Adolf Harnack, *op. cit.,* p. 202.

But more subtle and dangerous than idol worship was emperor worship for it carried with it the stigma of treason. It was at this point that the Christians found themselves most sorely pressed. A pinch of incense tossed on the altar would have satisfied the demands of the imperial cultus; but this the Christians refused to do, for they regarded it as an act of worship—and therefore idolatrous. At the same time, they repudiated the charge of treason by pointing to their submission to the laws of the state and their prayers for the well-being of the emperor. They would acknowledge his authority when living and revere his memory when dead; but they adamantly refused to worship his person.

> By embracing the faith of the gospel, the Christians incurred the supposed guilt of an unnatural and unpardonable offense. . . . They dissolved the sacred ties of custom and education, violated the religious institutions of their country, and presumptuously despised whatever their fathers had believed as true or had revered as sacred. The whole body of Christians unanimously refused to hold any kind of communion with the gods of Rome, of the empire, and of mankind.[28]

Naturally this kind of conduct excited the suspicion and hostility of the Romans. Lucian regarded them as half-crazy fanatics. Tacitus called them haters of the human race. Porphyry considered them barbarians. A few gave them grudging praise; but the vast majority of writers and thinkers regarded them as an "utter abomination."

The most puzzling aspect of Christianity was its mode of worship. The philosophers could understand and even approve of monotheism; but their "secret worship" was unnatural, monstrous and repugnant. Caecilius spoke of them as a people who skulk and shun the light of day, silent in public but talkative in holes and corners, and went on to ask:

> Why have they no altars, no temples, no recognized images. . . . unless what they worship and conceal deserves punishment or is something to be ashamed of?. . . . The lonely and wretched Jews worshipped one God by themselves, but they did it openly, with temples, altars, victims and ceremonies. . . . But the Christians! What marvels, what monsters, do they feign![29]

Immorality, it was rampant in all parts of the empire, especially in the urban centers where most of the Christians lived. Such cities as Ephesus, Corinth and Rome were cesspools of iniquity, in which, according to Tacitus, "vice had charms for all orders of men." In contrast to all this was the wholesome life of the Christians whose business practices, domestic arrangements, civic responsibilities and social relationships reflected the new life in Christ.

Aristides, defending the Christians against the charge of immorality, wrote: "They do not commit adultery nor fornication, nor bear false witness, nor embezzle what is held in pledge, nor covet what is not

---

[28] Edward Gibbon, op. cit., p. 80.
[29] Caeculius, Minut. Felix, VIII, f.

theirs. . . . And their women, O Emperor, are pure as virgins, and their daughters are modest; and their men keep themselves from every unlawful union and from all uncleanness."[30]

In private life new converts were taught to live "soberly, righteously and godly in this present world" (Titus 2:12). In civic life they were exhorted to "Honour all men. Love the brotherhood. Fear God. Honour the king" (I Pet. 2:17). Not only the grosser sins of the flesh but the more refined sins of the spirit—the evil eye, the impure thought, the quick temper, the sharp tongue, and the idle word—all were to be eschewed. Anger, wrath, malice, gossip, and jealousy belonged to the old life, and were to be put away (Col. 3:8).

Once baptized, the Christian was expected to avoid all sinful practices. If he sinned, he was required to confess. If the sin were grave, he was expected to demonstrate his sorrow by becoming a public penitent. Those who persisted in sin were excommunicated.

Nowhere was the principle of separation from the world more scrupulously carried out than in the matter of entertainment. The arena, the circus, and the theater were scrupulously avoided. No church member was permitted to be an actor or a gladiator, or to teach acting. The passion for public games was almost irresistible. It required much self-discipline for the Christians to refrain from something so universally popular.

The church frowned on the theater because of the immorality of the gods and men portrayed there. The gladiatorial shows were condemned on two counts: First, they were dedicated to the gods and, therefore, smacked of idolatry. Secondly, the church took the stand that watching a person being put to death was tantamount to doing the deed oneself.

The Christians, of course, were powerless to stop the shows, but their protest paid off, because by the time Constantine came to power public opinion had developed to the point where the state was able to curtail the sadistic spectacles.

Marriage was regarded as an honorable estate, but celibacy was recommended as ideal. Christians were permitted to marry only within their own circle. Divorce, so common in Roman society, was permitted only if the unbelieving partner demanded it. The remarriage of widows and widowers was frowned upon. Homosexuality was condemned with an earnestness rare in antiquity. Children were a gift from God and were to be reared in His fear. Abortion and infanticide, which were decimating the pagan population, were equated with murder and, therefore, prohibited. Women, though emancipated by the power of the gospel, were nevertheless expected to be examples of humility and modesty especially in places of public worship. They were to adorn themselves not with cosmetics and jewels but with a "meek and quiet spirit" (I Pet. 3:4). Ornamental clothes and elaborate hair-dos were unseemly in women professing godliness.

---

[30] Aristides, *Apology* 15

With standards so high, it was easy to fall short. No church was perfect and some of them, like Corinth, were plagued with many irregularities, both ethical and theological. But on the whole it is correct to say that the Christians, for all their imperfections, represented a new breed of men whose character and conduct excited the reluctant admiration of the pagan world. Pliny the Younger reported that the Christians led peaceful and exemplary lives. Galen remarked on their self-discipline and said that in their pursuit of moral excellence they were in no way inferior to true philosophers.

Every institution, however, deteriorates with time, and the Christian church was no exception. Decline set in about the beginning of the third century and greatly accelerated during the forty years of peace from 260 to 300. Peace brought prosperity and prosperity proved more harmful than persecution. New wealth made possible the acquisition of property and the building of stately edifices. Converts flocked into the churches in large numbers.

> In the interval between the Decian and the Diocletian persecution the Church had become the richest religious organization in the empire, and had moderated its attacks upon wealth. Cyprian complained that his parishioners were mad about money, that Christian women painted their faces, that bishops held lucrative offices of state, made fortunes, lent money at usurious interest, and denied their faith at the first sign of danger. Eusebius mourned that priests quarreled violently in their competition for ecclesiastical preferment. While Christianity converted the world, the world converted Christianity.[31]

The Persecution of the Church

Jesus was extremely frank with His disciples. He told them exactly the kind of treatment they could expect from a hostile world. "In the world ye shall have tribulation. . . . Ye shall be hated of all men for My sake. . . . If they have persecuted Me, they will persecute you also." He even went so far as to warn them that "he that killeth you will think that he doeth God service."

The history of the early church verifies these words. Stephen was stoned. James was beheaded. On one occasion Peter's life was spared at the eleventh hour only by angelic interference. Paul's testimony was "I die daily." He expected his converts to live dangerously and taught that they must " . . . through much tribulation enter into the kingdom of God" (Acts 14:22). To Timothy he wrote: " . . . all who desire to live a godly life in Christ Jesus shall suffer persecution" (II Tim. 3:12, RSV). Peter warned the Christians, "Think it not strange concerning the fiery trial which is to try you" (I Pet. 4:12).

[31] Will Durant, *op. cit.,* p. 657.

During the first generation—the period covered by the Acts of the Apostles—the persecution originated with the synagogue, not the senate. Throughout the Acts of the Apostles Luke is at pains to point out that not only did Rome look with leniency on the new sect, but actually afforded protection to its chief proponents. More than once Paul and his companions owed their lives to the timely intervention of local Roman officials.

It is difficult to ascertain exactly the reason, nature, and extent of the persecution suffered by the early church at the hands of the Romans. The situation is clouded by charges and countercharges the veracity of which it is sometimes difficult to evaluate. Historical documents are tantalizingly scarce, and those we do possess leave much to be desired when it comes to objectivity. Doubtless the Christian apologists, in the heat of public debate, exaggerated the virtues of the Christians. On the other hand, their enemies patently trifled with the truth when they referred to the Christians as "imbeciles" (Lucian), "god-forsaken fools" (Celsus), and "haters of the human race" (Tacitus).

As long as Christianity was regarded as a Jewish sect, it enjoyed the privileges of *religio licita* granted to Judaism. But as time went on the rift between Christianity and Judaism widened. By A.D. 50 the followers of Jesus had acquired an image of their own and were known as Christians (Acts 11:26). Following the burning of Rome by Nero in 64 the profession of Christianity seems to have become a capital offense. In order to clear himself, Nero looked for a scapegoat and found it in the Christians, whom he subjected to the most fiendish kind of treatment. Tacitus describes the persecution in these words:

> They were put to death with exquisite cruelty, and to their sufferings Nero added mockery and derision. Some were covered with skins of wild beasts, and left to be devoured by dogs; others were nailed to crosses; numbers of them were burned to death; many, covered with inflammable matter, were set on fire to serve as torches during the night.[32]

Particularly provocative was the adamant refusal of the Christians to worship the emperor. "The rejection of the imperial cultus was a crime which came under the head of sacrilege as well as of high treason, and it was here that the repressive measures taken by the state against Christianity almost invariably started."[33]

The law regarding emperor worship was not uniformly applied. Local magistrates were often men of culture and tolerance. Many emperors enforced the ordinance with deliberate negligence. Hadrian instructed his appointees to give the Christians the benefit of the doubt. Trajan forbade Pliny, governor of the troublesome province of Bithynia, to "search" for

---

[32] Tacitus, *Annals*, XV, 44.
[33] Adolf Harnack, *op. cit.*, p. 296.

the Christians or to take action against them unless their accusers were willing to be identified by name.

The second period of persecution coincided with the reign of Domitian (81-96), during which the Apostle John was banished to the Isle of Patmos. Several years later, Ignatius, bishop of Antioch, and Polycarp, bishop of Smyrna, died martyrs. When natural calamities plagued the empire during the reign of Marcus Aurelius (161-180), the Christians were again singled out for special attention. In Vienne and Lyons the infuriated populace stoned all Christians who ventured on to the streets. Under Commodus (180-192) the situation improved but worsened again during the latter years of Septimius Severus (192-211) when baptism became a crime. In A.D. 203 many Christians suffered martyrdom in Carthage.

It is important to note that there were no empirewide, centrally directed persecutions until the third century. "No church was subjected to relentless and continuous persecution over a long period of time, and the number of martyrs was much smaller than the piety of later ages has imagined it to be."[34] In the early period, before the Church became a force in the empire, individuals who confessed Christ were simply executed. Such persons were known as "martyrs" or "witnesses." In the third century, when they could not be destroyed summarily without decimating the population, they were tortured until they recanted. Those who refused to recant were called "confessors."

During the first two centuries persecution was local and intermittent. In duration and severity it varied in time and place, depending as much on the temper of the people and the disposition of the local magistrates as on the intentions of the emperors. Government officials acted against the Christians when encouraged by an outraged populace, whose superstitious fury was sometimes provoked and sometimes assuaged by the zeal of the Christians.

The Christians were generally despised, often hated, by the people among whom they lived. They were accused of being atheists, immoral, and unpatriotic. It was also generally believed that Christians incorporated into their secret worship such hideous practices as eating human flesh and drinking human blood, and of indulging in nocturnal orgies of all kinds. That the charges were false made little difference, especially during periods when the fortunes of the empire were low and the tempers of the people were high.

Such persecutions were not wholly harmful to the Christian cause.

> These transient persecutions served only to revive the zeal and to restore the discipline, of the faithful; and the moments of extraordinary rigour were compensated by much longer intervals of peace and security. The indifference of some princes and the indulgence of others permitted the Christians to

---

[34] Stephen Neill, *op. cit.,* p. 43.

enjoy, though not perhaps a legal, yet an actual and public, toleration of their religion.[35]

The first half of the third century was marked by sporadic persecutions under Severus, Maximinius, and Decius. Then followed a forty-year period of unprecedented peace which began in 261 with the proclamation by Gallienus of the first edict of toleration. The peace was abruptly broken in 303 by the edict of persecution issued by Diocletian. Designed as a general law for the whole empire, it ushered in the last and most severe of the persecutions. The edict decreed the destruction of Christian churches, the dissolution of Christian congregations, the burning of Christian books, and the exclusion of Christians from public office. Christians who persisted in meeting in secret were marked for death.

The persecution, inaugurated with the burning of the cathedral in Nicomedia, lasted for ten years. In Italy and the East the edict was carried out with military dispatch. Martyrs were found in all parts of the empire except Gaul and Britain where only a few churches were burned. Fifteen hundred martyrs died and countless Christians lost their possessions. Thousands of believers, including the bishop of Rome, recanted.

Lasting peace came when Constantine in 313 issued the Edict of Milan, confirming religious toleration and restoring to the church the properties confiscated during the previous decade.

The patient endurance of the Christians under persecution and the triumphant faith of the martyrs facing death constitute one of the most glorious pages in church history. To a remarkable degree they followed the teachings of the Master: "Love your enemies, bless them that curse you, do good to them that hate you, and pray for them which despitefully use you, and persecute you" (Matt. 5:44).

During the first two centuries every kind of torture was used to extract the confession, "Caesar is Lord," but to little avail. Every known method of execution was employed, but few recanted. They went cheerfully to prison, to the mines, and into exile. Far from shunning death, they seemed, on occasion, to actually seek it. Condemned to be devoured in Rome by wild beasts, Justin Martyr implored both friend and foe not to intervene. Tertullian informs us that the Christians gave thanks even when condemned to die. So importunate for death were some of them that their attitude provoked the anger and disgust of the proconsul Antoninus, who exclaimed, "Unhappy men! unhappy men! if you are thus weary of your lives, is it so difficult for you to find ropes and precipices?"[36]

Far from destroying Christianity persecution only served to strengthen it. The blood of the martyrs proved to be the seed of the church. For every person who died a martyr's death, scores forsook their pagan gods and embraced the Christian faith.

---

[35] Edward Gibbon, *op. cit.,* p. 115.

[36] Edward Gibbon, *op. cit.,* p. 112.

There is no greater drama in human record than the sight of a few Christians, scorned or oppressed by a succession of emperors, bearing all trials with a fierce tenacity, multiplying quietly, building order while the enemies generated chaos, fighting the sword with the word, brutality with hope, and at last defeating the strongest state that history has known. Caesar and Christ had met in the arena, and Christ had won.[37]

The Conversion of Constantine

The Diocletian persecution, the greatest test and triumph of the church, was followed by a period of unprecedented peace. The epochal event that marked the turning point was the conversion of Emperor Constantine. About to engage in bloody battle with Maxentius for the throne, Constantine is reported by Eusebius to have seen in the sky a flaming cross and the words, "In this sign conquer!" Adopting the sign of the cross, Constantine inflicted a crushing blow on Maxentius and entered Rome as the undisputed ruler of the West.

Early in 313 Constantine issued his famous Edict of Milan, in which he granted complete freedom to all religions in the empire and ordered the restoration of church property confiscated by Diocletian. Ten years later, after defeating Licinius in the East and becoming the sole emperor, Constantine declared himself a Christian and invited his subjects to do the same.

Two events in Constantine's reign are of great significance to the Christian Church. One was the Council of Nicea, convened by the emperor in 325; the other was the completion of Eusebius's *Ecclesiastical History* in the same year.

Eusebius, the most erudite cleric of his day and a favorite of Constantine's court, placed the church forever in his debt when he produced his monumental *Ecclesiastical History,* which traced the development of Christianity from its beginnings to the Council of Nicea. The objectivity usually associated with historians is lacking in Eusebius; nevertheless, it is safe to say that he approached his sources critically and his statements are as accurate as those in any ancient work of history. It is the most comprehensive and authoritative work we have on the history of the church in the first three centuries. Without it we should be greatly impoverished.

The Council of Nicea was summoned by Constantine, whose motives were not less political than religious. The church was gravely divided; the emperor wished to unite the church as a steppingstone to uniting the empire. This first ecumenical council was attended by 318 bishops and many clergy of lower rank. It met in the imperial palace, Constantine presiding and taking part in the debate. The controversy between Athana-

---

[37] Will Durant, *op. cit.*, p. 652.

sius and Arius was most bitter. The former won the day. The council drew up a statement in which it declared that Jesus Christ was "begotten, not made, being of one essence with the Father."

Following the conversion of Constantine, Christianity suddenly became popular and people flocked in great numbers to its banner. New and finer churches were erected, sometimes with state funds, sometimes with treasures confiscated from heathen temples. The alliance between the church and the state brought a measure of prosperity and prestige, but it hardly enhanced the spiritual stature or strengthened the moral fiber of the Christian community. With thousands embracing the faith there seemed little need for missionary effort. Individual conversion and personal commitment were no longer matters of great concern. Converts entering the church brought with them their paganism as well as their patrimony. From Constantine to the present time the Christian church in the West, Protestant as well as Roman Catholic, has at different times and in varying degrees been identified with and supported by the state. Ecclesiastical power has been wedded to political power to the detriment of spiritual power.

Was the conversion of Constantine genuine? Was his espousal of the Christian religion politically motivated? Would Christianity have conquered the Roman Empire without his endorsement? There can be no final and authoritative answers to these questions. Maybe it is unfair to expect the Christian emperor of a predominantly pagan state to be absolutely genuine in the expression of his religion, or to be completely pure in his motives. Leaders in public life have always found it difficult to resist expediency. Compromise and concession form the warp and woof of political life. Even an absolute monarch cannot with impunity ignore the social, political and economic currents of his time.

Certainly there were sound reasons, some personal and some political, why Constantine should encourage the spread of the Christian religion. To begin with, Christianity was not new to him. His mother, Helena, had been a Christian and doubtless she had told him something of the new faith. His knowledge of Roman history would have impressed him with Christianity's powers of survival—ten separate periods of persecution had failed to destroy it. Under the banner of the cross his armies had achieved great victories. His support of the church was worth a dozen legions in his wars against Maxentius and Licinius. Moreover, the Christians were a stable element in society, providing a good foundation on which to build a solid empire. As a group they were hard-working and law-abiding. They made good neighbors, good citizens and good soldiers. Unlike their cousins, the Jews, they seldom revolted. Their Scriptures taught them to honor all men, to love the brotherhood, to fear God, to honor the king. What more could an emperor ask? If anybody could help him consolidate his hold on the empire, surely these strange people, members of "the third race," could.

On the other hand, it was necessary for Constantine to proceed with caution. After all, the Christians represented not more than 10 percent of the total population. While currying favor with them he could not afford to alienate the pagan element in the empire. For a time he played both sides off against the middle. Consequently there was no clean break with paganism. He built Christian churches at the same time that he restored pagan temples. At the dedication of Constantinople he employed pagan as well as Christian rites. He used magic formulas to protect crops and heal disease. To the end he continued to function as *pontifex maximus* of the traditional cult.

With the consolidation of power he took a stronger stand for the Christian faith. Pagan effigies were removed from his coins. Bishops were invested with juridical as well as ecclesiastical power. Church property was exempted from taxation. Sunday was declared to be the Christian day of worship. Large sums of money were given for church buildings and Christian philanthropy. For reasons known only to himself, however, he postponed baptism until he was on his deathbed.

Durant describes him as a "masterly general, a remarkable administrator, a superlative statesman."[38] Be that as it may, he was extravagant, capricious, ruthless, and unscrupulous. He was passionately ambitious and susceptible to flattery. As an absolute monarch he was not averse to the use of force, actually killing his own wife, his son, and his nephew.

---

[38] Will Durant, *op. cit.,* p. 664

II

Christianization of Europe:
A.D. 500–1200

During the Dark Ages Ireland stood out as a beacon in the gathering gloom. From the sixth to the eighth centuries it was the most advanced country in western Europe. Free from the disastrous invasions of the barbarians, the church there kept the lamp of learning burning when the lights all over Europe were going out. Attracting scholars from England and the Continent, she received them all with boundless hospitality, sharing with them the highest education available in that day. Had it not been for the great monastic schools of Ireland, learning would almost certainly have perished from western Europe.

Equally important, if not more so, was the missionary zeal which was the outstanding characteristic of the Irish church. From the time of Patrick the church had been thoroughly evangelical and evangelistic. During the sixth and seventh centuries it became one of the greatest missionary churches of all time. With an extensive knowledge of the Scriptures and a personal experience of the power of the Holy Spirit, its missionaries flung themselves with fiery zeal into the battle against heathenism, which threatened to engulf Christian Europe. With holy enthusiasm they gave themselves to the evangelization of foreign peoples: the fierce Picts of Scotland, the savage Angles and Saxons of England, and the Frisians of the Low Countries. In the face of hardship, persecution, and even martyrdom, they pressed on through Gaul, Holland, Germany, Switzerland, and into northern Italy. Wherever they went they founded monasteries, which became centers of Christian culture and missionary activity. From these monasteries they went out to evangelize the masses, and to them they returned for rest and renewal.

What is the debt the world owes to primitive Celtic Christianity? The answer is that it produced the greatest missionary effort the world has ever seen; that when Europe was overrun by the barbarian hordes, these wandering Irish saints pushed their settlements right into the heart of European heathendom, and that from the North Sea to the Lombardic plains, from beyond the Rhine to the borders of Brittany, Ireland kept the lamp of learning alight in those dark days, and not only made possible the Christianization of barbarian Europe, but educated and supplied the greatest teachers down to the time of Charlemagne.[1]

Britain.   The origin of Christianity in Britain is wrapped in obscurity. We do not know exactly when or by whom the gospel was first introduced into that country. That Christian churches existed there in the third century seems fairly certain. The first authentic information relates to the presence of three bishops from London, York, and Lincoln who were present at the Council of Arles in southern France in 314. When the Angles and the Saxons invaded Britain in the fifth century, much of this early form of Christianity was swept away, leaving only isolated remnants in the inaccessible regions of the west. It was not until the sixth century that Christianity took permanent root in Britain. This was effected by a twofold invasion, in the north from Ireland in 563 and in the south from Rome in 596.

It was fitting that Ireland, which earlier had been evangelized from Britain, should in turn give to Scotland her greatest apostle. He was the famous *Columba,* a man of royal birth, liberal gifts, and vast learning. A native of Donegal, he gave the first half of his life to the gospel ministry in his homeland, where he founded many churches and monasteries. The most famous were those at Derry and Darrow. Described by his biographer as "angelic in appearance, graceful in speech, holy in work, with talents of the highest order and consummate prudence," Columba in his forty-second year crossed the Irish Channel with twelve companions and established on Iona, an island off the west coast of Scotland, a monastery destined to become one of the most famous centers of missionary activity of all time. The membership of the monastery was divided into three categories: Seniors, devoted to spiritual concerns, especially the copying of the Scriptures; Working Brethren, employed in manual labor; and Juniors, who were neophytes under instruction.

> All were monks with cowl, white tunic, and leathern sandals. There was manual labor and hard service to be performed in field and kitchen, as well as study and worship in cell or chapel, and all was done to the end of bringing the gospel to those among whom Christ had not been named.[2]

Columba and his companions traveled extensively throughout Scotland and the offshore islands, evangelizing peasants and fisherfolk, teaching

---

[1] Gough Meisser, "The Mission and Expansion of Celtic Christianity" in W. A. Philips, *History of the Church of Ireland* (London: Oxford University Press, 1933), p. 49.

[2] V. Raymond Edman, *The Light in Dark Ages* (Wheaton, Ill.; Van Kampen Press, 1949), p. 149.

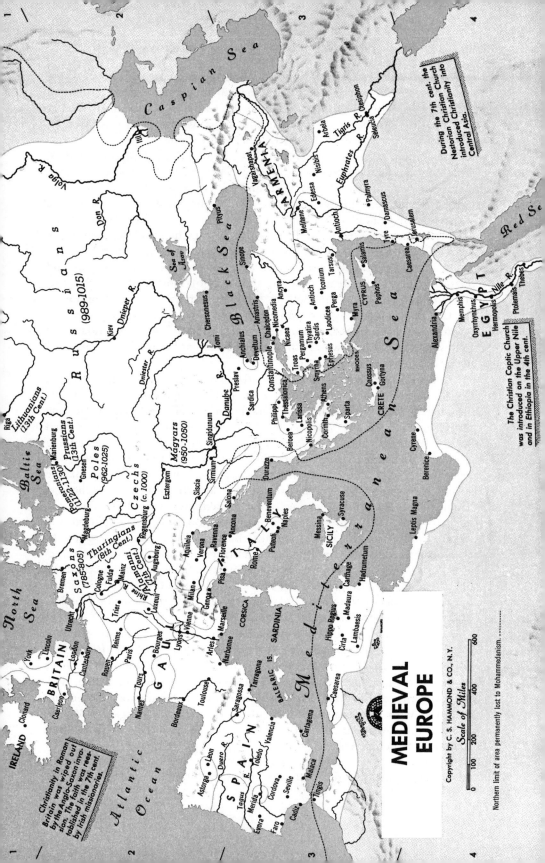

MEDIEVAL EUROPE

Copyright by C. S. HAMMOND & CO., N.Y.

Scale of Miles

0   100   200   400   600

Northern limit of area permanently lost to Mohammedanism. - - - - - - - -

During the 7th cent. the Church introduced Nestorian Christianity into Central Asia.

The Christian Coptic Church was introduced on the Upper Nile and in Ethiopia in the 4th cent.

Christianity in Roman Britain was wiped out by the Anglo-Saxon invasion. The faith was reestablished in the 7th cent. by Irish missionaries.

North Sea

Atlantic Ocean

IRELAND
Clonard

BRITAIN
York
Lincoln
London
Canterbury
Caerleon

GAUL
Rouen
Paris
Reims
Tours
Bourges
Nantes
Lyons
Vienne
Arles
Narbonne
Bordeaux
Toulouse

SPAIN
Saragossa
Tarragona
Barcelona
Valencia
Cartagena
Malaca
Cadiz
Cordova
Seville
Toledo
Merida
Leon
Astorga
Faro
Evora

Baltic Sea
Riga
Lithuanians (13th Cent.)
Prussians (13th Cent.)
Marienburg (1122-1130)
Pomeranians
Gnesen
Poles (962-1025)
Magdeburg
Bremen
Saxons (785-805)
Utrecht
Cologne
Trier
Mainz
Fulda
Luxeuil
Augsburg
Regensburg
Czechs (c. 1000)
Thuringians (8th Cent.)
Alamanni (7th Cent.)
Rhine R.

Russians (989-1015)
Volga R.
Don R.
Dnieper R.
Kiev
Dniester R.
Esztergom
Siscia
Sirmium
Magyars (950-1050)
Singidunum
Sardica
Preslav

Black Sea
Sea of Azov
Chersonesus
Tomi
Anchialus
Sinope
Pityus

Caspian Sea
Itil

ARMENIA
Vagarshapat
Melitene
Ancyra

Tigris R.
Euphrates R.
Ctesiphon
Seleucia
Arbela
Nisibis
Edessa
Antioch
Damascus
Palmyra
Tyre
Jerusalem
Caesarea

Red Sea

EGYPT
Alexandria
Memphis
Oxyrhynchus
Hermopolis
Ptolemais
Thebes
Nile R.

Mediterranean Sea

ITALY
Rome
Ravenna
Aquileia
Verona
Milan
Genoa
Pisa
Florence
Ancona
Salona
Durazzo
Benevento
Naples
Puteoli
Beroea
Nicopolis
Larissa
Thessalonica
Philippi
Sparta
Corinth
Athens
Constantinople
Nicomedia
Chalcedon
Nicaea
Pergamum
Thyatira
Sardis
Smyrna
Ephesus
Laodicea
Troas
Antioch
Iconium
Perga
Myra
Tarsus
RHODES
CYPRUS
Salamis
Paphos
CRETE
Cnossus
Gortyna

CORSICA
SARDINIA
BALEARIC IS.
SICILY
Messina
Syracuse
Catania
Carthage
Hippo Regius
Madaura
Lambaesis
Cirta
Hadrumetum
Caesarea
Tingis
Leptis Magna
Cyrene
Berenice

Marseille

converts, building churches, and establishing monasteries, all of them under the central control of Iona. A man of rare zeal and piety, Columba left his stamp not only on Iona but on the whole of Scotland. He died in 596; but the monastery at Iona continued for two hundred years to send missionaries to all parts of the British Isles and Europe.

Not content with the evangelization of Scotland, the Irish missionaries, with considerable courage and at great cost, carried the gospel to the savage Angles and Saxons of Northumbria, whose cruelties had incurred the hate and fear of the Britons. *Aidan,* the most illustrious of the successors of Columba, established a monastery at Lindisfarne, an island off the east coast of England, from which he launched his crusade into the heart of Northumbria in 635. For seventeen years Aidan, assisted by many fellow monks, preached the gospel of peace to the fierce Angles and Saxons with great effect. Oswald, the king of Northumbria, who was converted to the Christian faith in the heat of battle, actively supported the Christian mission by endowing monasteries. Churches sprang up everywhere and multitudes pressed into the Kingdom of God. Aidan was followed by *Cuthbert,* who by his godly life and arduous labors completed the evangelization of the Angles.

In the meantime a second Christian invasion of England had taken place. The year before Columba died (596), Pope Gregory the Great dispatched *Augustine* with forty Benedictine monks to England. Hearing terrifying tales of the savagery of the Anglo-Saxons, Augustine turned back in Gaul; but the pope ordered him to continue on his way. Landing in Kent, Augustine and his companions, now reduced to seven, were well received by King Ethelbert, who already had some knowledge of the gospel through his Frankish wife, Bertha, herself a Christian. Ethelbert listened attentively to Augustine, but remained unconvinced. Nevertheless, he gave him liberty to preach the new religion and provided food and lodging for him and his monks in Canterbury. Within a year, in response to the persuasion of his wife, Ethelbert embraced Christianity. Shortly thereafter, in accord with the custom of the times, his parliament adopted the new faith and in a single day ten thousand persons were baptized, Canterbury Cathedral was founded, and Augustine became the first of a long line of distinguished archbishops of Canterbury.

For a time the Celtic and Roman forms of Christianity were in conflict. Under the leadership of *Wilfrid,* Bishop of York (634-709), however, the Roman form prevailed. It remained for Theodore of Tarsus to organize England into a regular ecclesiastical province of Rome, with the authority of the Archbishop of Canterbury extending over the entire country. With the evangelization of the Saxons in Sussex by Wilfrid towards the close of the seventh century, the conversion of England is said to have been completed.

England, in receiving the gospel from the Irish church, imbibed its missionary spirit, and during the next two centuries sent a steady stream of missionaries, many of them outstanding personalities, to evangelize the pagan parts of Europe.

Gaul. Gaul had been evangelized on several previous occasions, but after each effort paganism reasserted itself; so the work had to be undertaken again in the sixth century. *Columban* led the way. He was distinguished for his unusual piety and his knowledge of the Scriptures. After training at the famous monastery of Bangor under Congall, greatest of its masters, he set out at the age of forty with twelve companions for Germany. Stopping short of his ultimate destination, he settled down in Burgundy and established a monastery at Luxeuil. After twenty years of arduous toil, like John the Baptist he incurred the wrath of the court by his outspoken denunciation of immorality in high places. Expelled from Luxeuil, he and his Celtic monks crossed the Rhine and preached the gospel to the wild ancestors of the modern Swiss. Like Martin of Tours, he waged war against paganism with fiery zeal, smashing idols and burning temples, establishing monasteries in their place. Caused to flee a second time, he repaired to northern Italy, where he established his last monastery at Bobbio. It was said of Columban that he was "always learning, always teaching, always wandering, always preaching."

Holland. The first English missionary contact with the people of the Low Countries, known as Frisians, occurred when Bishop Wilfrid stopped off in Frisia on one of his many trips to Rome. He preached with great power and baptized many of the leading men and thousands of the masses.

In 692 the Northumbrian monk, *Willibrord,* who had trained under Wilfrid in Ripon and Egbert in Ireland, and eleven companions crossed the North Sea to become the first missionaries to the Frisians. Supported by the patronage of Pepin, mayor of the palace, and suspected by the weaker Frisians and their king, Radbod, Willibrord labored through forty years of vicissitudes, setting up monasteries at Utrecht, Antwerp, Echternach, and Susteren. During those years his greatest difficulty was not persecution but politics. Not unnaturally, the missionaries were identified by the Frisians with the power-hungry Pepin and his Franks; and Willibrord found himself caught up in the political tensions existing between the two peoples. Nevertheless, on the whole the mission was successful and a strong church was established among the Frisians.

Germany. Christianity came to Germany as the gift of the Irish and English monks. Regarded by many as the greatest missionary of the Dark Ages, *Boniface* (680-754), an English noble and Benedictine monk, went to Germany in middle life. A brilliant missionary career stretching over forty years earned for him the title of the Apostle to Germany. In 722 he was consecrated by Pope Gregory II as bishop of the German frontier without a fixed see. A turning point in his ministry occurred when in a dramatic gesture he dealt a crushing blow to idolatry. Deciding that the time had come for a showdown between the pagan gods and Jehovah, he seized an axe and in the presence of thousands of enraged heathen and terrified half-Christians chopped down the sacred oak of Thor at Geismar in Hesse. When the huge tree crashed to the ground and Boniface was left unscathed, the pagans recognized the superior power of the Christian God and came in droves to be baptized.

A brilliant scholar, a great organizer, and an ardent evangelist, Boniface laid the foundation of the church in Germany. Great monasteries were established at Reichenau (724), Fulda (744), and Lorsch (763). In 741 he was called on to reform the Frankish Church, which had fallen on evil days, harboring in its hierarchy drunkards, adulterers, and even murderers. In this he was only partially successful. In 741 he was made Archbishop of Mainz. Ten years later he presided at the coronation of Pepin when he became king of the Franks.

In his old age the spirit of the pioneer reasserted itself. Leaving Germany, he repaired to a region of Holland where the Frisians were still pagan. Preaching again with great power he won many converts. As so often happens, the non-believers stirred up trouble which led to violence; and on June 5, 755, Boniface and fifty of his companions were killed.

The Saxons. The conversion of the Saxons coincided with the reign of Charlemagne (771-814). It was effected by military conquest rather than moral or religious persuasion. The unholy alliance between the church and the state, which culminated in 800 in the formation of the Holy Roman Empire, prompted the church to employ carnal means to achieve spiritual ends. Nowhere was this policy more disastrous than in the work of Christian missions, especially among the Saxons. This is one of the pages we should gladly remove from church history if we could.

Charlemagne, the first ruler of the Holy Roman Empire which was to endure for a thousand years, was one of the greatest emperors in history. Like many emperors, he was bent on conquest; but in his case he mixed religion with politics, and offered to the barbarian tribes whom he subjugated the comforts of religion as well as the benefits of civilization. "Once a German tribe had been conquered, its conversion was included in the terms of peace, as the price to be paid for enjoying the protection of the emperor and the good government that his arms ensured."[3]

Alas, the savage Saxons wanted neither Christianity nor civilization. Both had to be imposed by force of arms, and in the process atrocities were committed. On one occasion forty-five hundred Saxon men, women, and children were killed in one day by order of Charlemagne. Villages were burned, crops were destroyed, whole communities were wiped out—all in an effort to impose Christian civilization on a pagan people. Little wonder

---

3 Stephen Neill, *A History of Christian Missions* (Baltimore: Penguin Books, 1964), p. 79.

that the missionaries won few converts. The Saxons, of course, fought back, using their own brand of cruelty. Quite frequently the missionaries were made the object of attack and not a few were killed; but always there were others who came forward to fill their ranks. Gradually, by patience, pains, and prayer, the missionaries won their way, and the gospel finally prevailed. By the death of Charlemagne the "conversion" of the Saxons was complete.

Scandinavia. The Vikings of Scandinavia were the scourge of England and the Continent during the ninth century. So devastating were their raids on the monasteries and churches that for a time they threatened to terminate the missionary outreach of the English Church. The tide turned only when Alfred the Great won a decisive victory in 878 and forced some thirty leading Vikings to accept Christianity.

About this time intrepid missionaries began invading Denmark, Norway, and Sweden on preaching missions, but with little success. The Scandinavians much preferred their own way of life, including their pagan gods. Consequently the response was small. It took several hundred years for a people's movement to develop; but when it did, it occurred simultaneously in all three countries. For the most part the transition was peaceful; only in Norway was force employed.

Emperor Louis the Pious took an active interest in the spread of the Christian religion into the northern regions. In 823 he dispatched Ebo, Archbishop of Rheims, to Denmark. Without the backing of an army, Ebo achieved little by way of immediate results. Later on, following the conversion of Denmark's King Harald, the emperor sent a second mission, this time under the leadership of the greatest missionary of that period, *Anskar* (801-865), a French monk trained in the famous monastery in Corbie founded by Columba. Owing to the sullen hostility of the people, the results of this mission were limited. Later Anskar, again at the behest of Louis, made two visits to Sweden, one of them at the invitation of King Olaf. On his first journey the ship was seized by pirates and Anskar lost all his possessions. Undaunted, he finally reached Sweden, where he spent eighteen months and led many nobles into the faith. He also built the first church in that land.

On his return King Louis arranged with Pope Gregory IV to make *Anskar* the legate to all the Swedes, Danes, and Slavs of northern Europe. About 832 he was consecrated Archbishop of Hamburg. Immediately Anskar set about making his see the center of a vast network of missionary activity. He summoned monks from his old monastery at Corbie to assist in the training of missionaries to be sent into all parts of Scandinavia. With great perseverance and tact he was able to gain the confidence of King Horic of Denmark, a bitter foe of Christianity, who gave permission for the building of two churches in his realm.

It was Anskar's fate to live in an age when the political fortunes were not conducive to the rapid spread of a new faith. Consequently he did not enjoy anything like the enormous success of Boniface in Germany. Nevertheless, in spite of many handicaps and occasional reverses, including the sack of Hamburg, he managed by patience and perseverance to prepare the way for the ultimate conversion of Scandinavia, where to this day he is venerated as the Apostle of the North.

Denmark. As we have noticed, Denmark was the first of the Scandinavian countries to receive the gospel. Earliest Christian contacts were with the Hamburg See just over the German border. *Rimbert,* disciple of Anskar, carried on his work in Denmark and Sweden; but the political instability of the times and the weak state of the church rendered missionary work exceedingly difficult. Early in the tenth century King Gorm, a staunch opponent of Christianity, took steps to banish it from Denmark. Churches were destroyed and priests were killed. The tide turned when Henry the Fowler, King of Germany, in 934 subjugated the Danes and compelled one of their rulers to embrace Christianity. Archbishop Unni of Hamburg saw in this event an opportunity to renew the work laid down by Anskar seventy years before. The fortunes of the church in Denmark varied from reign to reign. Under Harald Bluetooth, successor of Gorm, Christianity flourished; under Harald's son, Sweyn, it languished. Christianity was finally established in Denmark under the world famous Canute, Christian king of Denmark and England from 1018 to 1035. Toward the end of the century twelve missionary monks from England went to Denmark at the invitation of the king and there founded monasteries. The missionary phase of Denmark's Christianization came to an end with the establishment of an archbishopric in 1104.

Norway. The gospel went to Norway not from Denmark but from England. Its introduction was attended by a good deal of violence. The leading agents were not missionaries but kings. King Haakon, who was reared in England, where he became a Christian, was the first to introduce Christianity to Norway. Meeting with rather strong opposition by people and leaders, he proceeded cautiously lest he precipitate a rebellion. He died in 961 without achieving his purpose.

Christianity took root in Norway during the reign and with the active support of Olaf Tryggvason (963-1000). Like his predecessor, Haakon, he spent some time in England and accepted Christianity there. A one-time Viking, "handsome, huge of stature, daring, and fearless," Olaf succeeded where Haakon failed. By an ingenious policy which combined force and favor, he did much to bring Norway closer to Christianity. It remained, however, for his successor, Olaf Haraldson, to administer the *coup de grâce* to paganism and make Christianity the religion of Norway shortly after the turn of the eleventh century.

Sweden. On the occasion of Anskar's second visit to Sweden in 853 the council in Gothenland declared itself in favor of the new religion; but the few missionaries who followed Anskar in Sweden failed to press forward with the vision and vigor necessary to get the new and strange religion established in a hostile environment.

As in the case of Norway, it was from England, and to a lesser degree from Denmark, that the initial thrust of the gospel reached Sweden. By the tenth century there were many English missionaries in the country. Olaf Scotkonung (993-1024) was the first monarch to profess and promote the Christian faith. Unlike the kings of Norway, Olaf eschewed the use of force to make converts. During the long reign of Olaf's son, King Anund Jacob (1024-1066), Christianity spread to all parts of Sweden. With the establishment of the first bishopric at Uppsala in 1164, Sweden became a nominally Christian country.

Eastern European Countries. As we move into this part of the world we are reminded of the fact that Christianity for many centuries had been flowing in two great streams, one emanating from Rome and the other from Constantinople. We are familiar with the former; we need to take a closer look at the latter.

> It flows mainly from Constantinople, not from Rome. Its mother language in its Bible, and in its worship services is Greek, not Latin. It is more interested in abstract theology and less in its practical application than the western arm of the church; it can claim fewer missionary conquests. The heads of the eastern church, called patriarchs, were generally controlled by the emperor in Constantinople, the emperor being the head of the eastern church, as the pope was the head of the western branch. The civilization that grew up in connection with the eastern church was called Byzantine, because Byzantium was the earlier name of the city that the emperor Constantine later named Constantinople after himself.[4]

From the time of Mohammed to the fall of Constantinople (1453) the great Byzantine Empire was a bulwark against the inroads of Islam in eastern Europe. Byzantine influence ebbed and flowed, as the influence of all empires does; but "even in its worst days, Constantinople was by far the greatest and most civilized city of the Christian world."[5]

Moravia. During the tenth century, when the Byzantine Empire underwent a renaissance, the Eastern Church began to take an interest in the non-Christians to the north. The first people to attract attention were the Slavs, and the first missionaries to go were *Constantine* and *Methodius*. These two brothers, one a philosopher and the other an artist, were sent to Moravia (now part of Czechoslovakia) at the request of Ratislav, a prince of Moravia, by the patriarch of Constantinople. The request, though

[4] Basil Mathews, *Forward Through the Ages* (New York: Friendship Press, 1960), p. 50.
[5] Stephen Neill, *op. cit.,* p. 83.

politically inspired, provided an opportunity to extend the Christian faith into virgin territory. Constantine, a teacher by training, laid the foundation of Slavic culture by reducing the language to writing and translating the Gospels and the liturgy. The use of the vernacular in worship, a practice encouraged by Constantinople but condemned by Rome, was a new departure and established a precedent which came to full bloom in the modern missionary enterprise of the nineteenth and twentieth centuries.

The pope in Rome tried to bring their work under his jurisdiction. Several visits to Rome took place; and Constantine died there in 869. Returning north by himself, Methodius completed the translation of the entire Bible into Slavic. During these years he kept in touch with the pope, who alternately condemned and condoned the use of the vernacular.

To add to his troubles the German clergy, who regarded him as an intruder into what they considered to be their ecclesiastical domain, were relentless in their opposition to the Byzantine missionary and his Slavic literature. On one occasion they imprisoned him for three years in a monastery in Swabia. After his death in 885 the Christian communities in Moravia fell on evil days. Driven out of Moravia, his disciples carried the gospel to Bulgaria, where the prevailing climate was more conducive to the development of an indigenous Christian culture.

The Bulgars. The conversion of the Bulgars was greatly accelerated by the baptism of King Boris in 865. Shortly thereafter he established a monastery, which became a radiating center of Slavic Christian culture. He sent his son Simeon to Constantinople to be educated as a monk. Later, he dispatched a famous missionary, *Clement,* to Macedonia, where he founded a missionary training college. By the time of his death (907) the Bulgars had become the Christian leaders of the Slavic world. His son, King Simeon, made history when he persuaded his bishops to declare the Bulgarian church self-governing and to elect a patriarch as its head. From Bulgaria the Christian faith spread to what is now Yugoslavia and Russia.

Though much of their work was swept away, Constantine and Methodius "can be regarded without question as the first authors of the great Slavonic Christian culture which still persists in the world today."[6] K. S. Latourette states that they "deserve to be ranked among the greatest of Christian missionaries."[7]

Russia. Two attempts were made to introduce Christianity into Russia. Both were abortive. The first occurred about the middle of the ninth century when Patriarch Photius sent an unsuccessful mission to the court of Kiev. A century later Princess Olga, after being baptized with

---

6 *Ibid.,* p. 88.

7 K. S. Latourette, *The Thousand Years of Uncertainty* (New York: Harper and Brothers, 1938), p. 166.

great pomp in Constantinople, tried to introduce Christianity into her realm; but she met with stubborn opposition from her nobles. It was under her grandson, Vladimir (980-1015), that Christianity took permanent hold in Russia. Before making up his mind Vladimir examined various religions. At one point he was deeply interested in Islam; but he finally decided in favor of Christianity. His marriage to the sister of the Greek emperor served to confirm his confession of the new faith. At the same time it provided legal grounds for Russia's claim to be the successor of the Byzantine Empire.

Poland. It is not known exactly when Christianity first reached Poland. The early agents were Slavs and Germans. The establishment of Christianity in Poland paralleled the development of the monarchy in the tenth and eleventh centuries. It began with the conversion of Duke Mieszka, whose baptism in 966 may have been prompted by the persuasion of his Christian wife, Dobrawa, sister of the king of Bohemia.

During the reign of his son, Boleslaw (992-1025), Poland became the largest kingdom in eastern Europe. Owing to Boleslaw's active support of the Christian cause, the fortunes of the church prospered along with those of the state. During his reign Christianity experienced rapid growth; but following his death both the political and the ecclesiastical power structures fell apart. A period of severe persecution ensued, during which churches and monasteries were destroyed and the clergy driven out. Under Boleslaw III (1102-1139) a measure of political stability and ecclesiastical order was restored to Poland. Missionary work was resumed and a large number of Pomeranians embraced the faith.

Space forbids any treatment of the conversion of such peoples as the Magyars, Wends, Prussians, and others. Suffice it to say that by 1200 almost the whole of Europe was nominally Christian. Bishop Stephen Neill succinctly describes the conditions under which Christianity won its way in Europe during this seven hundred-year period.

> The record in place after place tends to be much the same. The first bishop is martyred by the savage tribes; his blood then appropriately forms the seed of the Church. Initial successes are followed by pagan reactions; but the Church comes in again under the aegis of deeply converted rulers, with whom one or more outstanding bishops are able to work in harmony. The initial Christianity is inevitably very superficial; but this is in each case followed by a long period of building, in which the faith becomes part of the inheritance of the people. Political alliances, frequently cemented by marriages, form a large part of the picture; and as in the cases of Clovis and of Ethelbert of Kent, the influence of Christian queens seems to have played a notable part in the work of conversion.[8]

---

[8] Stephen Neill, *op. cit.*, p. 90.

III

Encounter with Islam:
A.D. 600–1200

"The explosion of the Arabian peninsula into the conquest and conversion of half the Mediterranean world is the most extraordinary phenomenon in medieval history."[1] So says Will Durant. Certainly, the greatest threat ever faced by the Christian church came from the sudden rise and rapid spread of Islam in the seventh century. A militant, missionary religion, Islam remains to this day Christianity's most dangerous rival.

The founder of Islam, Mohammed, was born in 570 in Mecca, an important caravan town strategically located on the main trade route between India and Egypt. He was an illiterate member of the Quraish, the ruling tribe in Mecca. At the age of forty he saw a vision that was to change the face of the world and make him the most important figure in medieval history. The angel Gabriel is said to have appeared to him and summoned him to his life's work with the words: "O Mohammed! thou art the messenger of Allah, and I am Gabriel." Thereupon Mohammed began preaching to the people of Mecca and to the pilgrims who gathered there, calling them to a new morality and a monotheistic faith. Persecution broke out and Mohammed fled from Mecca to Medina in 622. Known as the *Hejira,* this event marks the beginning of the Muslim calendar.

After his death in 632 his followers conquered and unified the warring tribes of Arabia, and in the flush of easy and rapid victory went out on their mission of conquest and conversion.

With lightning speed they conquered Damascus (635), Antioch (636), Jerusalem (638), Caesarea (640), and Alexandria (642). By 650 the Persian

---

[1] Will Durant, *The Age of Faith* (New York: Simon and Schuster, 1950), p. 155.

49

Empire had been destroyed. Across North Africa they swept, meeting little or no resistance. The Christian stronghold of Carthage fell in 697. By 715 the greater part of Spain was in Muslim hands. Crossing the Pyrenees and penetrating into France, they were stopped by Charles Martel in 732 at the Battle of Tours—one of the most decisive battles of history. About the same time the Arabs entered the Punjab in India and advanced far into Central Asia.

Following the eighth century there was a five hundred-year period of stalemate. During this time the Seljuk Turks, earlier evangelized by the Nestorians, became Muslims and occupied large areas of Asia Minor. It was against these intruders that the Crusades were launched. Certain areas in Syria and the Holy Land were regained, but on the whole the Crusades were a failure.

A second tide of Muslim conquest occurred in the thirteenth and fourteenth centuries. The Ottoman Turks and the Mongols of Central Asia became fierce and fanatical followers of the prophet and went on the rampage, pillaging and destroying everything in their path. By the fifteenth century the Ottoman Turks had invaded Greece and the Balkans. Constantinople fell in 1453. At this time the Moors were retreating in Spain, giving up Alhambra, their last stronghold, in 1492.

To consolidate their power, the Arabs established the Umayyad Caliphate in Damascus (661-750) and the Abbaside Caliphate in Baghdad (750-1058). It should be noted that while Europe was in the darkest period of the Dark Ages, Arab civilization was at its height. When the lights were going out all over "Christian" Europe, it could be said of Damascus that "if a man were to sojourn here a hundred years, and pondered each day on what he saw, he would see something new every day."[2] Baghdad boasted twenty-six public libraries and countless private ones. "Princes like Sahib ibn Abbas in the tenth century might own as many books as could then be found in all the libraries of Europe combined."[3]

It is generally believed that the Muslims in their conquests gave their victims a choice between the Koran and the sword. This is not correct. Christians and Jews were regarded by Mohammed as "the people of the book" and were accorded a special status—*dhimmis,* or "protected people." They were allowed to continue the practice of their religion, under certain restrictions, provided they rendered to the new Caesar the things that belonged to him, particularly a heavier form of taxation. Even in Baghdad, right under the nose of the Caliphate, there was a large Christian community with churches, monasteries, and schools.

In Egypt and Syria non-Catholic Christians fared better than they had under the Byzantine rulers, who were not averse to using pressure to

---

2 *Ibid.,* p. 231.
3 *Ibid.,* p. 237.

propagate the Catholic form of the faith. Likewise, the Nestorians in Persia were better off under the Arabs than they had been under the Zoroastrian rulers. The Arab conquerors, recognizing the administrative skill of the Christians, used some of them in political office. The Christians in turn shared the Greek civilization with their new rulers, translating into Arabic the classical writings of Greece.

They did, of course, suffer various forms of discrimination, which reduced them to second-class citizenship. They were required to wear a colored patch on their clothing as a mark of inferiority, much like the Jews in Nazi Germany. Intermarriage with Muslims was outlawed. In the political life of the country they could rise only so high; beyond that they could not go. They were allowed to continue the practice of their religion, but with certain well-defined restrictions. They could not build new churches; nor could they ring church bells. They could perform their worship within the quiet precincts of their own buildings, but they could not propagate their faith in the community. Conversion was a one-way street; one could convert from Judaism or Christianity to Islam, but not from Islam to Christianity. To do so was to become an apostate from the faith and a traitor to the cause. To be an Arab was to be a Muslim. To become a Christian was to cease to be both. Moreover, the Law of Apostasy, still in force in Islam, permitted the community to kill any member who defected from the faith. The Law is not always followed, but it is there and it acts as a strong deterrent. To initiate a Muslim into the Christian faith by baptism is almost certain to precipitate a communal riot in most Muslim countries. The Muslims of Iran belong to the Shi-ites and are, therefore, more tolerant than the Sunnis. Indonesia, where the government insists on a genuine form of religious freedom, is the one Muslim country in the world where Muslims in large numbers have embraced the Christian faith. In recent years a mass movement toward Christianity has taken place, involving some several million persons, many of them Muslims.

The only major faith younger than Christianity, Islam has become a world religion, second only to Christianity in its missionary zeal and worldwide outreach. Indeed, in some parts of Africa it is making converts faster than is Christianity.

It was in North Africa in the seventh century that the Christian church suffered its greatest losses. Besides being strong in numbers, the church of North Africa produced three of the greatest leaders and theologians of the early church: *Tertullian,* the brilliant defender of the faith, in the second century; *Cyprian,* the energetic builder of the church, in the third century; and *Augustine,* the greatest theologian since Paul, in the fourth century. Under this great intellectual and spiritual giant the church in North Africa, comprising some five hundred dioceses (one-fourth of all Christendom), had a better educated clergy and exercised greater ecclesiastical power than did the churches of Alexandria or Rome.

How shall we account for the demise of such a church? Doubtless there were many contributing factors of a social or political nature. Some of the Christians, not wishing to live under alien rule, emigrated to Europe. Such an exodus naturally weakened the church. Among those who remained were many who, deciding that discretion was the better part of valor, threw in their lot with the new rulers, embracing their faith and supporting their rule. Others saw in the swift and devastating military victories of the Muslims the hand of God in human affairs and decided not to fight against Him. Some undoubtedly were impressed with the claims of Islam as a later and therefore higher revelation of God. Still others preferred the protection and prestige that come from identification with the paramount power. But all of these factors combined hardly account for the disappearance of so strong a church in so short a time.

The real reason for the disappearance of the church in North Africa must be sought elsewhere. Actually, the church was not so strong as it appeared. Numerically it was large, but spiritually it was weak. To begin with, it had never become truly indigenous. It was too closely identified with Latin culture and Roman power. The congregations were composed mostly of Latin-speaking people in and around Carthage. Few of the Punic people ever embraced the Christian faith, and the Berbers were left untouched. Because of this the church never took root in the native soil. A second reason was the failure to give the Scriptures to the people in their own tongue. They were available in Latin, but no translations were ever made into the language of the Punic people or the Berbers.

Moreover, theological controversies had sapped the energies of the church. Before the time of Augustine the church had been racked by the Donatist controversy. Theologians, instead of closing their ranks and presenting a united front to the common enemy, were preoccupied with fratricidal warfare. They were more interested in defending the purity of the gospel than in demonstrating its power.

Another factor was the loss of evangelical faith and fervor among the Christians. With the passing of time the Christian gospel was gradually smothered under a growing sacramental system accompanied by sacerdotal control. Church members had long since left their first love and were Christians in name rather than fact. Consequently when the Muslim hordes swept across North Africa, the Christian church had neither the will nor the power to resist. In a few short decades it disappeared, leaving hardly a trace of its former glory.

The Crusades

The second major encounter between Christianity and Islam came with the Crusades in the twelfth and thirteenth centuries. There are two black pages in the history of the church and its relations with other peoples: one, the long-standing, almost universal, persecution of the Jews; the other, the Crusades against the Muslims.

There were seven Crusades in all, occurring at intervals between 1095 and 1272. Organized and abetted by different leaders, among them Peter the Hermit, Bernard of Clairvaux, and Richard the Lion-Hearted of England, they had the sanction and support of the Roman Catholic Church, at least in the early stages.

As usual in any great undertaking involving many diverse peoples, the motives were mixed. There were economic, political, and even personal factors. The strongest motives, however, were religious; and it is with these that we are chiefly concerned.

First there was the almost universal desire on the part of the Western church to wrest from the Seljuk Turks the sacred places in Palestine, especially the Holy City of Jerusalem. The Arabs had been in control of Palestine since the seventh century. Their continued presence there not only affronted the Christian church; it also rendered difficult, if not dangerous, Christian pilgrimages to the Holy Land.

Then there was the eagerness of the Roman Catholic Church to assist the Byzantine Empire, centered on Constantinople, to resist the inroads of the Turks. In the eleventh century the Byzantine Empire fell on evil days. The decline began in 1025 with the death of Emperor Basil II and worsened in 1056 when the Macedonian dynasty came to an end. Internal dissensions and foreign aggression threatened the existence of the state. The greatest threat came from the Seljuk Turks. Originally from Central Asia, and converts to Islam, in the eleventh century they built an empire which included Persia, Mesopotamia, Syria, Egypt, and Palestine. They fought their way into Asia Minor and in 1071 inflicted a stunning defeat on the Byzantine army at Lake Van in Armenia. Under such conditions it was only natural that the Byzantine emperors should look for help to their Christian brethren in the West; and the popes in Rome were happy to lend assistance.

In the third place, there was an admirable desire on the part of the Roman See to heal the breach between the Eastern and Western branches of the church and thus restore Christian unity. During the tenth and eleventh centuries relations between Rome and Constantinople had deteriorated. In 1054 the Patriarch of Constantinople was excommunicated by Pope Leo IX. The Crusades afforded an excellent opportunity to heal the rift.

So far as the primary objectives were concerned, the Crusades were a failure. The holy places, liberated at such cost in blood and treasure, were held for only one hundred fifty years, after which they reverted to Muslim control. Not only were the Crusaders ejected; but Islam, under the Ottoman Turks, was carried across the Balkans in the fourteenth and fifteenth centuries and to the gates of Vienna in the sixteenth century.

Instead of strengthening the Byzantine Empire against the onslaughts of Islam, the Crusades served only to weaken it. In fact, Constantinople suffered greater damage at the hands of the Crusaders than it did when it fell to the Turks in 1453.

As for healing the breach between the Eastern and Western branches of the church, the Crusades succeeded only in widening it still further.

There were, however, some lasting benefits. Through the Crusades Europe was introduced to the more advanced civilization of the East. While Europe was in the eclipse of the Dark Ages, Arab civilization, based on Baghdad, shed its light and luster over the entire Middle East. During the Crusades Arab civilization proved itself superior to Christian civilization in the arts, education, and war. Hundreds of Arab terms found their way into the languages of Europe. Printing, gunpowder, and the compass all came from the East in the wake of the Crusades. The arts, sciences, and inventions of both Greek and Saracen were introduced to Europe by the Crusaders.

The Crusades also acted as a stimulus to travel by land and sea and to the expansion of maritime trade. The knights lost the Holy Land, but the merchants gained control of the Mediterranean. European cities came to life and commerce flourished. Items which had been luxuries now became articles of common trade: spices, sugar, textiles, fruits, scents, gems, and others. "The Crusades had begun with an agricultural feudalism inspired by German barbarism crossed with religious sentiment; they ended with the rise of industry and the expansion of commerce, in an economic revolution that heralded and financed the Renaissance."[4]

The Effects of the Crusades on Christianity

The most calamitous result of the Crusades was the alienation of the entire Muslim world. The fact that the Christian church would resort to war to regain the holy places of Palestine was itself a denial of its own religion. Once the victim of Muslim aggression, it now became an aggressor. Such a course of action was a denial of the teaching of Christ and contrary to the practice of the early church.

Moreover, the atrocities committed by the Crusaders in the name of Christ left an indelible scar on the Muslim mind. When Jerusalem was liberated in 1099 the Crusaders, not content with wiping out the one thousand-man garrison, proceeded to massacre some seventy thousand Muslims. The surviving Jews were herded into a synagogue and burned alive. The Crusaders then repaired to the Church of the Holy Sepulchre, where they publicly gave thanks to Almighty God for a resounding victory.

---

[4] *Ibid.,* p. 613.

In Christendom the Crusades have largely been forgotten, but their sordid memory festers to this day in the minds of the Muslims of the Middle East. The hate engendered at that time has not been dissipated even after nine hundred years. Christianity's reputation for cruelty and revenge is a millstone around the neck of the Christian missionary in the Middle East.

IV

Roman Catholic Missions:
A.D. 1300–1700

The Roman Catholic Church is by far the oldest, largest, and most influential organization in the world. Its half billion members are to be found in practically every country of the globe. Throughout its long history it has known periods of expansion and recession. At the zenith of its power, during the Holy Roman Empire, it completely dominated the political, cultural, economic, and religious life of Europe. Its greatest losses occurred at the time of the Protestant Reformation, when large sections of Europe broke away from the Roman Catholic Church. What the Church of Rome lost in Europe, however, she regained through her missionary endeavors in Asia, Africa, and the New World during the next few centuries. While the Protestant churches of Europe were consolidating their gains in that continent, the Roman Catholic Church went out to conquer the non-Christian portions of the world.

The development of Roman Catholic missions coincided with the expansion of the overseas empires of Portugal and Spain. Franciscan missionaries accompanied the Portuguese expeditions to Madeira (1420), the Azores (1431), and the Cape Verde Islands (1450). Trinitarian missionaries sailed with Vasco da Gama to India in 1498. Franciscans arrived in Brazil with Cabral in 1500. Iberian kings, no less than the Roman popes, were zealous for the conversion of the heathen. In 1537 Pope Paul III ordered that the Indians of the New World be brought to Christ "by the preaching of the divine word, and with the example of the good life." Ferdinand and Isabella issued a royal order stating: "Nothing do we desire more than the publication and the amplification of the Evangelic Law, and the conversion of the Indians to our Holy Catholic Faith."

As early as 1454 Pope Nicholas V granted to Portugal exclusive patronage privileges in Africa and the East Indies. With Spain's incursion into the New World, Portugal's monopoly on world exploration was broken. To avoid rivalry between the two Iberian powers, Pope Alexander VI in 1493 issued a Demarcation Bull which divided the world into two spheres of influence. Portugal was to retain all the patronage privileges in Africa and the East Indies, while Spain was to enjoy similar privileges in the New World. (The following year Brazil, discovered by Cabral, was transferred to Portugal.) In return for these extensive privileges, the kings of Portugal and Spain were to be responsible for the spread of the faith and the conversion of the heathen in their overseas dominions. Ecclesiastical appointments were to be made by the civil authorities. All expenses were to be borne by the state. This system, known as the *Patronato,* meant that the missionaries had as big a stake in the explorations as the merchants.

As time went on and Catholic missions extended to all parts of the world, it became apparent that the patronage system was not altogether satisfactory. To correct its weaknesses, Pope Gregory XV in 1622 founded the Sacred Congregation for the Propagation of the Faith. Through it the Holy See was able to direct more closely the conversion of the heathen overseas and to effect the restoration of the heretics at home. In 1628 a central seminary in Rome, the College of Propaganda, was established to train native clergy from all parts of the mission world.

On the whole the civil authorities of Portugal and Spain took their Christian responsibilities seriously.

> Beginning with Columbus and Vasco da Gama, all the Spanish and Portuguese explorers regarded their expeditions as likewise crusades and missionary voyages, for the purpose of seeking Christians (as well as spices) and of opposing the unbelievers with fire and sword if they rejected the Christian law which the missionaries first preached with the spiritual sword.[1]

The Roman Catholic Church was fortunate in having at its command scores of religious orders whose dedicated members were trained and ready for any kind of service. Their vows of obedience and celibacy provided the two most desirable qualities for pioneer missionary work, servility and mobility. Their communal life, characterized by austerity, was an ideal preparation for the rigors of the missionary vocation. When, therefore, the church decided to carry its message to the heathen world, it had no need to call for volunteers. By royal decree or papal command it could, with the greatest of ease, deploy its army of servants to any part of the habitable globe.

Four orders in particular were called upon to share the burden and the glory of the missionary enterprise: the Franciscans, founded by Francis of

---

[1] Joseph Schmidlin, *Catholic Mission History* (Techny, Ill.: Divine Word Mission Press, 1933), p. 264.

Assisi (1182-1226); the Dominicans, founded by a Spanish priest, Dominic (1170-1221); the Augustinians, organized by Pope Alexander IV in 1256; and the Jesuits, founded in 1540 by a Spanish nobleman, Ignatius Loyola.

Additional missionary orders were founded during the eighteenth and nineteenth centuries, among them the Passionists (1720), the Redemptorists (1732), the Holy Ghost Fathers (1841), the White Fathers (1866), and the Divine Word Fathers (1875). The famous Maryknoll Fathers, an American mission, was established in 1911 and sent its first missionaries to South China in 1918.

Naturally, the Catholic countries of Europe supplied the greatest number of missionaries. In the early decades they came largely from Portugal and Spain, the two great colonizing powers of that period. Italy and France contributed their quota, as did Germany and Ireland. Until recent years comparatively few Catholic missionaries came from the United States.

In the long course of history Roman Catholic missions have encountered their full share of opposition and persecution. Sometimes the losses were inflicted by Protestant powers, as when the Dutch seized Ceylon (1658) and the British annexed Canada (1793). The American occupation of the Philippines in 1898 ended the Roman Catholic monopoly, but did not greatly interfere with Roman Catholic missions, in that country. At other times they were driven out by non-Christian rulers, who feared that the new religion would either undermine the local regime or destroy the indigenous culture, as was the case in China (1368), Japan (1614), and Korea (1864). In other countries Roman Catholic missions suffered at the hands of Catholic civil authorities, as in South America, where many Franciscan missions were closed during the wars of independence in 1811 and 1812.

Of all the religious orders, none has had a more turbulent history than the Society of Jesus. Wherever the Jesuits went they seemed to stir up trouble. So intolerable were their actions that they were persecuted even in Catholic countries. About the middle of the eighteenth century they were expelled from most of the countries of South America and the Philippines. So strong was the opposition that the Society was dissolved by Clement XIV in 1773. Even after its restoration forty years later, the Jesuits were expelled again from various Catholic countries of Europe.

With such a vast network of religious orders in all parts of the world, it was necessary for the Roman Catholic Church to work out some system of comity to avoid duplication, to say nothing of competition. Consequently, certain orders were assigned to certain countries. In the East the Paris Foreign Missions Society was responsible for Siam, Tibet, and Burma; the Dominicans for Formosa; and the Missioners of the Sacred Heart for Melanesia. In the larger countries, such as India, China, and Japan, most of the major and many of the minor orders were to be found. There prudence dictated that the various orders be assigned to different parts of the country. For example, in China the Dominicans worked in Fukien and the Divine Word Missioners concentrated on Shantung.

China

Roman Catholic missions outside of Europe may be said to have begun about 1294 with the arrival in China of the Franciscan friar, *John of Monte Corvino*. Friar John had labored with marked success in Persia before being sent by the pope on his historic mission to the oldest and greatest empire of the East.

Strangely enough, opposition came not from the Chinese but from the few remaining Nestorians, survivors of the Nestorian Church that flourished in China for two hundred years during the T'ang dynasty. By spreading vicious tales about the Roman Catholics, they hoped to stir up animosity against the newcomers. Nevertheless, John won the confidence of the Chinese emperor, built a church in Peking, and baptized thousands of converts. For eleven years he labored alone, devoting special care to the training of 150 Chinese seminarians. Later he was appointed first archbishop of Peking by Pope Clement V.

The Roman Catholic faith spread down the coast until it reached Fukien, some 800 miles south of Peking. When John died in 1330 there were about one hundred thousand converts in China. All this took place under the patronage and protection of the Mongol rulers of China. When in 1368 the Chinese again became masters in their own house, the Ming rulers expelled the missionaries and Christianity died out.

Two hundred years later a second attempt was made to plant Roman Catholicism in China. The leader this time was *Matteo Ricci* (1552-1610) of the Society of Jesus. Using the Portuguese colony of Macao as a jumping-off place, Ricci reached Peking after a long and arduous overland trek stretching over twenty years.

To win the favor of the Chinese, Ricci adopted their culture and appeared in the guise of a Confucian scholar. By presenting European time-pieces to local officials he gained permission to travel northward, founding mission stations in Kwangtung, Nanchang, and Nanking. Because of the Western gifts sent by Ricci to Emperor Wan Li, he was allowed to enter the capital in 1601. There Ricci and his companions acted as the emperor's official clock-winders. Intellectuals flocked to converse with the great scholar from the West. Many of them became converts. Through Ricci's influence in Peking, other Jesuits were permitted to travel and reside in various parts of the vast empire. By 1650 there were a quarter of a million converts.

Later missionaries, Franciscans and Dominicans, quarreled with the Jesuits, accusing them of compromising with heathen practices in the concessions they made to Confucianism. Particularly vexatious was the controversy regarding the term for God. The Jesuits favored *T'ien* (Heaven, or Providence), used by Confucius. The matter was referred to Rome and the pope decided on *T'ien Chu* (Heavenly Lord). The emperor took offense, and shortly after 1700 he declared that all missionaries must follow the lines laid down by Ricci and the Jesuits or leave the country. Many missionaries, including four bishops, complied. All others were expelled. In 1724, and again in 1736, edicts of persecution were issued against the Christian church. Once more Christianity suffered a major setback in China.

Japan

Regarded by many as the greatest Roman Catholic missionary of all time, *Francis Xavier* in 1540 launched the missionary work of the Society of Jesus, which was destined to become the largest and most effective missionary agency of the church. On May 6, 1542, he landed at Goa, then a Portuguese colony on the west coast of India. After three busy years in South India, during which he won thousands of converts, he made his way to the Malay Peninsula and the adjoining islands, where he spent another three years. Consumed with a holy passion "for the greater glory of God," his restless spirit would not allow him to remain long in one place. In 1549, with two other Jesuits, and a Japanese convert as interpreter, he set out for the Land of the Rising Sun, whose people, he said, were "the delight of his soul." During his two years in Japan he traveled widely, teaching, preaching, and administering the sacraments. Other Jesuits followed him and continued the work.

The chaotic political conditions prevailing at the time, together with a decadent Shintoism and a degenerate Buddhism, created a favorable climate for the Christian faith, which bore rapid and abundant fruit. By 1581 there were 200 churches and 150,000 professing Christians. They came from all classes: Buddhist monks, Shinto priests, scholars, samurai, and the common people. Two daimyos embraced Christianity and ordered their subjects to do the same or go into exile. Nobunaga, the Minister of the Mikado, gave moral support to the new religion, albeit from ulterior motives. By the turn of the century Christian converts numbered half a million.

With the assassination of Nobunaga, the Christian mission fell on evil days. The new leaders, Hideyoshi and Iyeyasu, were suspicious of the political intentions of the Jesuits and turned against the Catholic faith. Nor was the cause of Christ helped by the quarreling between the Jesuits on the one hand and the Franciscans and Dominicans on the other. Following the anti-Christian edicts of 1606 and 1614, all foreign missioners were expelled and the Japanese Christians were called upon to recant or face death. The persecutions which followed were as barbaric as any in the history of the Christian mission. Finally, in 1638, some thirty-seven thousand Christians made a last desperate stand in the old castle of Shimabara. After four months of heroic but futile resistance they surrendered, only to become the victims of wholesale slaughter. For 230 years Japan remained a hermit nation, effectively sealed off from contact with the rest of the world.

The Philippines

The Philippine Islands were discovered by Magellan on his fateful voyage around the world in 1521. Systematic missionary work began with *Father Legaspi* and the Augustinians in 1564. They were followed by the Franciscans (1577), the Dominicans (1587), and the Jesuits (1591), all of whom taught the semi-savage islanders Christianity and the arts of civilization. The women were raised from practical slavery to virtual emancipation by the introduction of the Christian concept of the family. Today almost 85 percent of the Filipinos are professing Christians. Some of the credit for this amazing achievement goes to Philip II of Spain, who made the spread of the faith the chief aim of the colonization of the distant islands named after him.

With a full complement of missionary teachers, preachers, and doctors, the Catholic mission was able to make a significant impact in the islands. Churches, hospitals, and schools soon came into being. A college for girls was established as early as 1593. In Manila the Jesuit College of San Jose, founded in 1601, was a national center of learning. The Dominican College of Santo Tomas, opened ten years later, became a pontifical university. Within a century of the discovery of the Philippine Islands the missionaries had baptized some two million persons. An indigenous clergy was gradually developed and by 1800 Filipinos had been raised to the episcopate.

To the Roman Catholic Church must go the credit for stopping the spread of Islam from Indonesia through the archipelago. The Muslims advanced from the south; the Roman Catholics from the north. They met on the island of Mindanao, where today there are 1.5 million Muslims, known as Moros.

The Roman Catholic faith achieved one of its greatest successes in the Philippines. There are several reasons for this. The Jesuits established a good educational system throughout the islands. They allowed the converts to retain many of their religious beliefs and practices. The Spanish intermarried with the local people, thus eliminating the color bar and producing a composite culture. Added to this is the fact that Spain was able to maintain political and economic control of the islands for an unbroken period of almost four centuries. During this time the church was unhindered in carrying out the progressive Christianization of the islands.

Indochina

The pioneer missionary in this part of Southeast Asia was a French Jesuit Father, *Alexander de Rhodes* (1591-1660). He mastered the Annamese language and introduced Christianity to the educated and influential classes. Among his early converts were two hundred Buddhist priests, a number of whom entered his catechetical school. Besides theology, Father Rhodes taught the catechists how to care for the sick so that they might have ready access to the homes of the people. Success attended his methods. In a comparatively short time 300,000 converts were made. On his return to France he was instrumental in establishing the Paris Foreign Missions Society in 1658. Later on, when France annexed Indochina, her colonial administrators found it advantageous to have French priests and the Catholic Church on hand to help them. Until 1911, when the Christian and Missionary Alliance was permitted to enter the country, the Roman Catholics were the only missionaries admitted to the French colony. After the Philippines, Vietnam is the most Christian country in Asia. In South Vietnam there are four million Roman Catholics, eight hundred thousand of whom are refugees from North Vietnam.

India

A new era began when Vasco da Gama rounded the Cape of Good Hope and discovered a sea route to India in 1498. The Franciscan priests who accompanied him launched the missionary program of the Catholic Church in that part of Asia.

The Muslim Moguls and the Portuguese explorers arrived in India about the same time. Several factors combined to give the Muslims the advantage over the Catholics in the winning of converts. The Portuguese, interested primarily in trade, were content with several small colonies on the west coast; whereas the Moguls, bent on political conquest, overran the greater part of the subcontinent. The profligate lives of the Portuguese merchants scandalized the Indian population and brought Christianity into disrepute. The rigid caste system of Hinduism constituted an almost insuperable obstacle to the acceptance of the new religion. Portugal's sensitive defense of her right of patronage seriously hampered the work of all non-Portuguese missionaries. Under these circumstances it is not surprising that Islam won many more converts than Christianity.

While all the great religious orders were represented in India, it was the Jesuits who made the greatest impact. As already noted, *Francis Xavier,* the first Jesuit missionary, spent three years in India in the 1540's. A generation later, Christianity excited the intellectual curiosity of Emperor Akbar, the most illustrious of the Mogul rulers of northern India. In

1579 he invited missionaries to the splendid court of the Peacock Throne. *Father Rudolf Acquaviva* (1550-1583) was chosen to head the mission band. Akbar was strongly attracted to the Jesuit leader and frequently engaged him in religious discussion. When, however, he refused to become a Christian, the Jesuits were recalled to Goa. Soon afterward Acquaviva was murdered by fanatical Hindus. When Akbar heard of the death of his friend, he wept bitterly. In the 1590's the Jesuits returned to the Mogul court and were warmly received by the emperor, who issued a decree permitting his subjects to embrace Christianity. For a time the Jesuit mission received subsidies from the court. A Christian church was erected at Lahore, but the number of converts was never very large.

The most famous of all Roman Catholic missionaries to India was *Father Robert de Nobili,* an Italian Jesuit of noble birth who reached Goa in 1605. The following year he took up residence at Madura in the south, where hitherto very few converts had been won. De Nobili discovered that the cultural barrier between East and West was a stumbling block. The Indians despised the Europeans because they ate meat and drank wine. Posing as a Roman Brahmin, he adopted the Indian way of life, including food and dress. He gave himself to the study of the Hindu Scriptures and acquired a reputation as a European holy man. Soon the Hindus were flocking to his door. For forty-two years he labored among the upper classes, making thousands of converts. After his death his colleagues carried on in the tradition set by de Nobili. By the close of the seventeenth century there were 150,000 Christians in the Madura mission.

The New World

The discovery of America had religious as well as economic and political motivation. Ferdinand and Isabella were both genuinely concerned for the Christianization of the natives. It is not surprising, therefore, that Columbus, known as "Christbearer" as well as "Colonizer," should have raised crosses wherever he went in the New World. On his second voyage he included in his company a group of priests as well as a doctor and a surgeon.

The first missionaries to the New World were Franciscans and Dominicans. The former arrived in Brazil with Cabral in 1500, in Haiti two years later, and in Mexico in 1523. The Dominicans began their missionary work in Haiti in 1510, in Cuba in 1512, in Colombia in 1531 and in Peru in 1532. They were joined by the Augustinians at an early date. In 1549 the Jesuits began to arrive in Brazil. By 1555, in the wake of the explorers and conquistadors, Roman Catholic missionaries had taken Christianity to the West Indies, Mexico, Central America, Colombia, Venezuela, Ecuador, Peru, Chile, and Brazil.

The treatment meted out to the red man by the Spaniards was so cruel that the native population in the West Indies disappeared completely and Negro slaves from Africa were brought in to take their place. The only voice raised against this form of genocide was that of the friars. Most famous of these was *Father Bartholomew de Las Casas* (1474-1566), a Dominican missioner, who made seven voyages to Spain to plead the cause of the oppressed Indians.

Strangely enough, the Spanish kings, who were so solicitous for the red man, were not disturbed by the gigantic slave trade between Africa and the New World. During the seventeenth century one thousand slaves landed each month at Cartagena for distribution among the Spanish-American colonies. For three centuries the evil traffic continued unabated, during which time, it is estimated, Brazil alone received between six and eight million slaves for the sugar plantations.

Conditions aboard the slave ships were incredibly bad. Half the human cargo died at sea. Jesuit missionaries ministered to the survivors on their arrival at Cartagena, feeding them, cleaning their sores, telling them of Christ, and baptizing those near death. The most outstanding of these was *St. Peter Claver* (1581-1654), who labored among the slaves for forty-four years. He instructed and baptized 300,000 black people. Pope Leo XIII made him the patron of all missionary work among Negroes throughout the world.

The Spanish conquest of the New World fell into three stages. During the first stage the padres with the armies checked and rebuked the excesses of the rough soldiers in their treatment of the Indians. In the second, or frontier, stage the priests founded mission settlements, known as reductions, to facilitate the Christianization of the Indians. These reductions were under the control of the religious orders. They varied in size from a few dozen to several thousand persons. In these reductions the Indians were considered wards of the crown. The Spanish kings forbade officials or settlers to interfere with the missionaries in their efforts to convert the Indians to the Christian faith and the Spanish culture. Traveling Spaniards might not remain in the reductions more than two or three days. The average reduction lasted from ten to twenty years. Then the Indians were turned over to the care of the secular clergy. In the third and final stage frontier conditions gave way to orderly, civilized municipalities. Within a century the Spaniards in Latin America filled a vast stretch of territory with churches, schools, libraries, courts of justice, aqueducts, and roads. The universities of Lima and Mexico City were nearly one hundred years old when Harvard College was founded in 1625. By 1575 books in twelve Indian languages had been printed in Mexico City.

Roman Catholic missions in colonial times were divided into eight principal regions.

Dominican and Franciscan priests arrived in 1514 in the Cumana missions of northeastern Venezuela. Cacao, coffee, and sugar plantations were established by the padres. The Indians were trained in stock raising. The decline of the Cumana missions began in the eighteenth century, when many of the reductions were prematurely handed over to the parish clergy and the civil authorities.

Between 1658 and 1758 a hundred missions were founded by the Capuchins in the llanos of Caracas, the vast Venezuelan plains, where the great cattle ranches of today are located. These reductions were ruined during the wars of independence.

Missions on the Orinoco River were established by the Jesuits in 1670. These extended over the border into the northern part of Brazil. Frequent attacks by the Carib Indians rendered settled work difficult. The Capuchins and Franciscans joined the Jesuits on the upper Orinoco in 1734 and took over the entire mission when the Jesuits were expelled some thirty years later.

The Jesuits pioneered in the eastern part of Colombia, reaching the region as early as 1629. The Indian converts risked their lives trying to persuade the more savage jungle Indians to enter the reductions. When the Jesuits were expelled in 1767 the work languished.

It was 1724 before a mission was established in Guiana through the endeavors of the Capuchins and the Franciscans. A hundred years later the mission came to a temporary end when the revolutionists attacked the missionaries. Fourteen of them died of neglect in prison and twenty others were massacred.

The pioneer in the Maynas missions of Ecuador, Peru, and western Brazil was a Jesuit who arrived in 1560. Franciscans also labored in this field. The area was quite productive; the Jesuits alone are reported to have baptized half a million Indians. Outstanding among the missionaries was Jesuit *Father Samuel Fritz* (1654-1724). Known as the apostle to the Amazon Indians, he spent forty years of his life exploring the Amazon country and persuading the jungle Indians to accept the amenities of village life. Here, as elsewhere, the missions declined upon the departure of the Jesuits.

The missions of the Chaco frontier, in the eastern part of present-day Bolivia, were founded by the Jesuits and the Franciscans. Work in this inhospitable region was difficult. The Chaco Indians were particularly intractable. Some of the early missionaries were murdered by members of their own flock.

The last, and from some points of view the most successful, mission was that of the reductions administered by the Jesuits in Paraguay. Actually, the region embraced sections of Brazil, Argentina, and Bolivia. Religion was the mainspring of life in these reductions. The day began and ended with prayer; and the great feasts of the church were celebrated with much splendor, albeit not always without residual pagan practices. Each reduction was a little town, laid out in a fixed pattern around the plaza of an impressive stone church. The Indian houses were all alike, to avoid jealousy. Various crops were successfully cultivated and cattle raising was developed on a considerable scale. Artistic work in wood, stone, silver, and gold was produced by the Indians. In the one hundred reductions founded by the Jesuits before they were expelled in 1767 almost one million Indians were baptized. Voltaire, no friend of the church, was obliged to acknowledge that the Jesuit reductions were a "triumph in humanity."

Roman Catholic missions in South America suffered two catastrophic setbacks: the expulsion of the Jesuits about the middle of the eighteenth century, and the losses incurred during the wars of independence in the second decade of the nineteenth century.

Three thousand Jesuits were expelled from various countries of South America, beginning with the Portuguese colony of Brazil in 1759. Members of the other orders did what they could to fill the gap; but they had their own missions to man and could ill afford to accept additional commitments. Nor were there any indigenous clergy to step into the void. Because of the rights of patronage granted to Spain and Portugal, the policies of the Sacred Congregation of Propaganda could not be applied in Latin America. The highest posts were given to Spanish-born clergy, who looked down on the Creole priests. As for the Indians, no adequate effort was made to train them for the priesthood. Consequently, the vacuum left by the departure of the Jesuits could not possibly be filled. When the Jesuits returned some sixty to seventy years later, it was to find their former work swept away. To this day the shortage of well-trained native-born clergy is one of the greatest weaknesses of Roman Catholicism in that part of the world.

Almost as disastrous were the wars of independence in the early years of the nineteenth century. Up to that time church and state were one. Moreover, the vast majority of the administrators, civil and ecclesiastical, were from Spain—or, in the case of Brazil, from Portugal. Under such a system the Roman Catholic Church possessed immense authority and enjoyed vast prestige. When the revolutionists went on the rampage, however, their hatred of colonialism was not confined to the civil authorities; it spilled over to the religious hierarchy. With the fall of the Spanish empire in South America, Catholic missions were deprived of the moral and economic support of the Spanish sovereigns. Moreover, the new governments were anticlerical, some of them violently so. The Roman Catholic missioners were nearly all Spanish; naturally, their allegiance was to the crown. Not a few of them returned to Spain, including some bishops; and their departure had disastrous results for their abandoned flocks. Many of the mission reductions, already declining because of the expulsion of the Jesuits in the previous century, were forcibly turned over to the jurisdiction of the secular clergy and the civil authorities before the Indians had been sufficiently Christianized. Under these conditions the patronage system broke down; and the Vatican, in an attempt to salvage what it could of its former ecclesiastical empire, was obliged to come to terms with the new regimes on an individual basis. These agreements, known as concordats, differed from country to country. Some countries called for complete freedom of religion; one, Uruguay, became a secular state; others made certain concessions to Rome. In a few instances the new governments were anticlerical to the point of interference and even persecution.

The missionary endeavors of the Roman Catholic Church were not confined to Latin America. For many years extensive missions were carried on in what is now the United States and Canada. The Franciscans entered Florida in 1526. By 1542 they had reached New Mexico. Two years later they began work in Texas. Before the end of the century they had established a mission in Lower California. By 1655 Spanish missionaries, Dominicans and Franciscans, had founded thirty-five missions in Florida and Georgia. They were later wiped out, however, by the British in 1704. Jesuit beginnings in Virginia and South Carolina were likewise shortlived. In 1612 two Jesuits founded a mission for the Abnakis in Maine. In 1626 a Franciscan, *Father Joseph de la Roche,* explored the territory of New York State, then occupied by the fierce Iroquois.

In 1632 *Father Andrew White* (1579-1656) and two other Jesuits sailed into Chesapeake Bay with Lord Baltimore in search of a land with religious liberty. Father White set about the task of converting the Indians after he learned their language. For this purpose he prepared a catechism. Ten years later, white marauders from Virginia plundered the Jesuit mission in Maryland. Father White was sent in chains to England, where he was condemned to death. The sentence, however, was never carried out.

In New France (Canada) the conversion of the Indians was a major concern of the early French explorers. Samuel de Champlain, founder of Quebec, declared, "The salvation of a single soul is worth more than the conquest of an empire." When the first explorer, Jacques Cartier, went to Canada in 1534 he took a party of priests with him; but it was not until eighty years later that organized missionary work got under way. It began with Champlain, who took the first Franciscans to Quebec in 1611. One of them began missionary work among the Hurons. Two Jesuits began work among the Micmac Indians of Nova Scotia in 1611. The Recollects arrived in 1615 and the Capuchins fifteen years later. A vicariate apostolic for Canada was established in 1658. The first diocese (Quebec) was organized in 1674. The missionaries in Canada were French and of a much higher caliber than the Spanish priests in Latin America. Missionary work in this part of the world was exceedingly difficult owing to the sparse population scattered over an immense area, the rigors of the Canadian winters, and the warlike propensities of the Indians, especially the Iroquois.

The pioneer Jesuit among the Hurons was *John de Brebeuf* (1593-1649), a Norman of noble lineage. For three years he labored alone on the banks of Lake Huron until reinforcements arrived. Several of his colleagues were murdered by the Mohawks. When the Iroquois finally destroyed the Hurons, Father Brebeuf and other Jesuits were massacred in a most barbarous fashion. The wars between the French and the British administered a further blow to Roman Catholic missions in Canada.

Judged by their passion for souls, their courage in the face of danger, their willingness to endure hardship, and their undying love for their persecutors, these missionaries must be regarded as among the greatest in the history of the church.

Africa

By virtue of the patronage system, first introduced by Pope Nicholas in 1454, Portugal was saddled with the responsibility of Christianizing Africa. In 1483 Diogo Cao, a Portuguese explorer, reached the Congo. Four years later Bartholomew Diaz discovered the Cape of Good Hope. Missions were established in Congo and Angola on the west coast and in Mozambique, Rhodesia, and Madagascar on the east coast.

Much effort was spent in an attempt to bring Christianity to the Congo. The first Christians were hostages carried away by Diogo to Portugal, where they were given Christian instruction and baptized. The first five mssionaries arrived in 1491 and received a warm welcome from the king.

The king, his wife, and one son all embraced Christianity and were baptized. The king's conversion proved to be superficial, however, for later on, under pressure, he returned to his former vices. His son, christened Alphonse, remained steadfast in the face of opposition from his brother and others. He lived a consistent Christian life and supported the mission, building churches and asking for more missionaries. Reinforcements arrived in 1509, in 1512, and again in 1521. A royal legation was sent from the Congo to Pope Julius in Rome, and a group of native princes was sent to Lisbon to be trained for the priesthood. One of the latter was Henry, the crown prince, who on his return was consecrated the first bishop of San Salvador, the national capital.

The first contingent of Jesuits, four in number, arrived in 1548 and was solemnly received by the king at the gates of San Salvador. They are reported to have baptized over five thousand converts within three months. They had grandiose plans for a special college for the nobility; but this fell through when a conflict with the king compelled them to return to Portugal.

The Congo mission received a boost when Queen Zinga of Matamba, after a serious lapse, experienced a genuine conversion in 1655 and thereafter gave moral and material support to the mission. During her reign the Capuchins arrived and threw themselves into the work of extirpating paganism. The fortunes of the Congo mission rose and fell depending on the attitudes of the various kings and queens. Some were ardent Christians and did much to strengthen Christianity among their own people. Others, after a superficial conversion, lapsed back into pagan ways and brought the Christian faith into disrepute. Still others preferred the old religion to the new and opposed, sometimes persecuted, the missionaries and their converts. By the middle of the seventeenth century Christianity in Congo gradually died out for lack of priests.

Angola was opened up to trade by the Portuguese in 1520 on condition that the king and his people become Christians. The first missionary was a priest from Congo, who succeeded in converting the king; but he later reverted to paganism. The king of Portugal sent several priests from San Thome to Angola. Their mission was unsuccessful and they returned. In 1560, after the decline of the Congo mission, four Jesuits accompanied the Portuguese ambassador to Angola to convert King Dambi; but the king would have nothing to do with the strange religion and put its emissaries in prison. Later on the tide turned with the conversion of a new king and one thousand of his subjects. By the close of the century there were twenty thousand Christians in Loando and Massagan. About the middle of the seventeenth century the Jesuits returned to Loando and four monasteries were established in connection with the bishopric of Saint Paul.

In Guinea, missions were established in Benin as early as the fourteenth century, but they were permitted to lapse. At the beginning of the seventeenth century, when the Jesuits returned to resume the work, they found several kings desirous of instruction. Some of them were baptized, along with many of their subjects. Later the mission was augmented by the arrival of the Carmelites in Upper Guinea and the Capuchins in Lower Guinea. In mid-century the mission expanded into Gambia and Sierra Leone.

Catholic missions were no more successful on the east coast of Africa. The Franciscan missioners, with Cabral in 1500 and Francis Xavier in 1541, stopped off in east Africa on their way to India to preach to the Muslims and the pagans. Neither would give them a hearing. Strangely enough, the first missionaries to Mozambique were dispatched from Goa. They proceeded up river to Tongue, where they baptized King Gamba of Inhambane and four hundred of his subjects. *Father Goncalo,* leader of the expedition, traveled up the Zambesi past Sena and Mabate, whose people he also baptized, into the kingdom of Monomotapa, whose emperor professed conversion as the result of a dream involving the Madonna which had been presented to him by the missionary. When he and his court were baptized it looked as if the Christian faith was well on its way to being firmly established in east Africa. Alas, a sudden turn of events, engineered by a Muslim conspiracy linking the missionary with the political ambitions of Portugal, resulted in the murder of Goncalo. Persecution followed and the mission was called off. A punitive expedition sent by Portugal to avenge the death of Goncalo served only to further alienate the rulers of east Africa.

In 1577 the Dominicans entered Mozambique and penetrated inland, burning Muslim mosques as they went. The Jesuit converts of another day had reverted to paganism, which did not help the cause at all. In 1607 the Jesuits made a second attempt to establish a beachhead in the hinterland of Mozambique. This time they were more successful. By 1624 they could report two dozen missionaries, twelve of them in the Mozambique college. About the same time the Dominicans had thirteen stations and twenty-five missionaries. Farther to the north, around Mombasa, the Augustinians had been at work since the turn of the century. One of their prize converts was King Jussuf, who gave great promise but relapsed into Islam and proceeded to murder all the Christians in the area. From 1630 on the Zambesi mission languished.

Madagascar proved to be one of the most difficult of all the African fields. First on the scene, in 1648, were the Vincentians, sent out by the Congregation of Propaganda. The two pioneer missionaries died within a few months of their arrival at Fort Dauphin. A second team of three missionaries met the same fate several years later. A third attempt was made, but it likewise came to nothing with the untimely death of the three members of the team. Finally, in 1674, the Madagascar mission collapsed, after only twenty-five years of abortive effort.

By the middle of the eighteenth century there was hardly a trace of Roman Catholic missions in Africa. How are we to account for failure on such a grand scale? Several factors might be mentioned: the fearfully high mortality rate among the missionaries due to the enervating climate and the lack of modern medicine; the unholy alliance between the Portuguese and the slave trade, which put the Christian religion in a very bad light since all the missionaries were from Portugal; the failure of the church to promote educational work and to train qualified leaders for the indigenous church; and the unstable political conditions in the many kingdoms of Africa, their intertribal warfare and their penchant for murder and plunder. More pertinent, and perhaps more potent, than the above were the superficial missionary methods, which resulted in hasty "conversions" and mass baptisms.

V

Origin of Protestant Missions in Europe: A.D. 1600-1800

One would naturally expect that the spiritual forces released by the Reformation would have prompted the Protestant churches of Europe to take the gospel to the ends of the earth during the period of world exploration and colonization which began about 1500. But such was not the case. The Roman Catholic Church between 1500 and 1700 won more converts in the pagan world than it lost to Protestantism in Europe. Why did the Protestant churches take so long to inaugurate their missionary program? What were some of the contributing factors?

The first, and perhaps the most potent, factor was the theology of the reformers. They taught that the Great Commission pertained only to the original apostles; that the apostles fulfilled the Great Commission by taking the gospel to the ends of the then known world; that if later generations were without the gospel, it was their own fault—a judgment of God on their unbelief; that the apostolate, with its immediate call, peculiar functions, and miraculous powers, having ceased, the church in later ages had neither the authority nor the responsibility to send missionaries to the ends of the earth.

There were, of course, exceptions to this point of view. *Hadrian Saravia* (1531-1613) and *Justinian von Weltz* (1664) wrote treatises urging the church to assume its responsibility for the evangelization of the world. But they, and others like them, were "voices crying in the wilderness." Frequently they were ignored; more often they were refuted, even ridiculed. Strangely enough, it was Erasmus who called most earnestly for the evangelization of the whole world.

That this negative view of world missions became orthodox Lutheranism is evident from the official document of the theological faculty of Wittenberg published in 1651 when it was asked by Count Truchsess for an interpretation of the Great Commission.

Moreover, there were the Predestinarians, whose preoccupation with the sovereignty of God all but precluded the responsibility of man. If God wills the conversion of the heathen, they will be saved without human instrumentality. If God does not will the salvation of the heathen, it is both foolish and futile for man to intervene. Calvin wrote: "We are taught that the kingdom of Christ is neither to be advanced nor maintained by the industry of men, but this is the work of God alone."

Added to this was the apocalypticism which anticipated, with some dismay, the rapidly approaching end of the age. Luther particularly took a dim view of the future. In his *Table Talks* he wrote: "Another hundred years and all will be over. God's Word will disappear for want of any to preach it."

A second factor is found in the sad plight of the Protestant churches of the sixteenth and seventeenth centuries. Compared with the Roman Catholic Church they were extremely small in both strength and numbers. Moreover, the Catholic Church launched the Counter Reformation and thereby regained much of the territory lost to the Reformation. The war against Rome was long and bitter and the outcome was by no means certain. The Thirty Years' War reduced Germany to economic and social chaos. The Protestant churches, preoccupied as they were with the problem of survival, may be excused for having neither the vision nor the vigor necessary for world evangelization.

Equally, if not more, enervating was the internecine warfare carried on between the Lutheran and Reformed churches themselves. If they had joined forces to present a united front to the common enemy, they might have done a better job with evangelism at home and missions overseas; but as it was they were torn asunder by ecclesiastical strife. They were united in only one thing—their hatred for the "papists." They no sooner broke with Rome than they fell to fighting one another.

In Saxony the popular saying was, "sooner papist than Calvinist." The exclusive Lutherans denied that the Calvinists were even Christians. Anathemas were hurled back and forth between the contending parties. In the middle of the sixteenth century the churches of the Augsburg Confession split in bitter controversy over the Eucharist. "Controversy over 'pure doctrine' played a larger role here perhaps than in any other period of church history, and the stage was filled with a fanatical race of scribes and pharisees abusing each other over mint, anise, and cummin."[1]

A third factor was the isolation of Protestant Europe from the mission lands of Asia, Africa, and the New World. Spain and Portugal,

---

[1] James H. Nichols, *History of Christianity, 1650-1950* (New York: Ronald Press, 1956), p. 43.

both Roman Catholic countries, were the great exploring and colonizing powers of the post-Reformation period. For more than a century they enjoyed complete mastery of the seas and a monopoly on world trade. Wherever their ships went they carried both merchants and missionaries. The kings of Portugal and Spain were deeply committed to the Christianization of their overseas colonies. Later on the Dutch and then the British got in on the act; only they were interested primarily in commerce, not colonization. The Dutch East India Company, founded in 1602, stated that one of its objectives was to plant the Reformed Faith in its territories overseas, but seldom did they work at it. The British East India Company entertained no such ambitions. While providing chaplains for its own personnel, it was adamantly opposed to missionary work among the indigenous population. Time and again it refused to transport missionaries on its ships, and forbade missionaries to reside in its territories.

A fourth factor was the absence in the Protestant churches of the religious orders which played such a prominent role in the spread of the Catholic faith throughout the world. Referring to the worldwide missionary program of the Roman Catholic Church one of its historians says:

> As papal missionary agencies, even apart from the curia, the various Religious Orders engaged ever more energetically in the missions, and vied with one another in spreading the Gospel. In the first place, the older missionary Orders renewed their activities—the Franciscans and Dominicans, and also the Augustinians and Carmelites after their internal reform. . . . The new Orders included (besides the Capuchins) one which apart from its general fitness as a regular Order, was also adapted and impelled by its deepest nature and its most intimate aims to attain the summit, to speak relatively, in missionary achievement—the Society of Jesus. The qualities which fitted it for this work were especially its cosmopolitan character, its faculty of accommodation and mobility, its military organization and centralization, its absolute obedience and the complete submerging of the individual in the common cause.[2]

When the Protestant churches, two centuries later, launched their missionary enterprise they had nothing to compare with the religious orders of the Roman Catholic Church. The largest group were the Moravians—one of the so-called sects. With few exceptions, their missionaries were unlettered men with more zeal than knowledge, artisans and farmers, married men, with ground to till, houses to build, and families to support. Fettered thus with family ties and domestic duties, the Protestant missionaries were no match for their Catholic counterparts. Certainly they had nothing comparable to the military discipline of the Society of Jesus.

Beginnings on the Continent

Several abortive attempts were made before the modern missionary enterprise got under way in Europe. The earliest attempt was made in

---

[2] Joseph Schmidlin, *Catholic Mission History* (Techny, Ill.: Divine Word Mission Press, 1933), p. 259.

Brazil, when Calvin in 1555 sent four clergymen and a group of French Huguenots to found a colony for persecuted Protestants on the Bay of Rio de Janeiro. Desultory attempts were made to Christianize the Indians, but without success. Later their leader, Villegagnon, turned traitor and abandoned the colony to the tender mercies of the Portuguese, who proceeded to destroy it. The few survivors were later killed by the Jesuits.

At the instigation of the Dutch East India Company, a seminary was established at the university of Leyden in 1622 for training chaplains and missionaries for service in the East Indies. But the venture was short-lived. It lasted only twelve years, during which time a dozen missionaries were sent forth. The majority of them returned after five years without having learned the vernacular of the people among whom they labored.

In 1661 *George Fox,* founder of the Society of Friends, sent three of his followers as missionaries to China; but they never reached their destination.

The first Lutheran to attempt missionary work was an Austrian, *Baron Justinian von Weltz,* who about 1664 issued a clarion call to the church to assume its missionary responsibilities. In three pamphlets, he set forth the missionary obligation of the church; called for the organization of a missionary society or association to get the job done; and advocated the opening of a training school for missionary candidates. But the times were not propitious. The churches, though orthodox in doctrine, were lacking in spiritual life and missionary vision. Not content with remaining indifferent, his colleagues, almost to a man, rose in indignation against him, calling him a dreamer, a fanatic, and a heretic. "The holy things of God," they said, "are not to be cast before such dogs and swine."

Undeterred by opposition and ridicule the disconcerted baron proceeded to Holland, where he abandoned his baronial title. Following ordination as an "apostle to the Gentiles," he sailed for Dutch Guiana (Surinam), where he died an early death before he could reap a harvest. Another missionary adventure had failed. Before the Protestant churches could launch a continuing missionary endeavor they must be inwardly renewed.

Pietism in Germany

The modern missionary enterprise was the direct outcome of the Pietist movement which began in Germany following the Thirty Years' War, which ended with the Peace of Westphalia in 1648. As the Protestant Reformation was a revolt against the false doctrines and corrupt morals of the Church of Rome, so the Pietist movement was a revolt against the barren orthodoxy and dead formalism of the state churches of Protestant Europe.

The father of Pietism was *Philip Spener* (1635-1705). As a Lutheran pastor, first in Strasbourg and later in Frankfort, Spener tried to raise the spiritual tone of his flock by the systematic cultivation of the spiritual life. Cottage meetings for prayer and Bible study supplemented the Sunday sermon and brought the members together in an atmosphere of fellowship hitherto unknown. Pietistic theology can be summed up in a few sentences. There can be no missionary vision without evangelistic zeal; there can be no evangelistic zeal without personal piety; there can be no personal piety without a genuine conversion experience. True religion for the Pietist is a matter of the heart, not the head; hence the emphasis on the cultivation of the spiritual life.

Like many reformers before him, Spener incurred the wrath of the hierarchy. Civil and ecclesiastical authorities denounced the man and his movement. But in spite of opposition and even persecution, Pietism proved contagious and won adherents in the Lutheran churches. When the universities of Saxony closed their doors to the new sect, the Pietists opened their own university at Halle in 1694. For ten years Spener built up the school. Following his death in 1705 the most influential leader was *August Francke* (1663-1727), who had been dismissed from Leipzig University because, following a deep religious experience which changed his whole life, he conferred with Spener and wholeheartedly embraced Pietism. Largely through his influence, Halle became the educational center of Pietism and the fountainhead of the missionary enterprise of the eighteenth century.

> The university was surrounded with other institutions; a pauper school, a boys boarding school, an orphanage, a Latin school, and some 6,000 pietist clergy were trained in the Halle theological faculty, which was the largest divinity school in Germany. Bogatzky was one of the most influential of the devotional writers of Halle, and Freylinghausen the chief hymn writer. Even the Reformed pietists in the Lower Rhine contributed regularly to Halle. Colonial Lutheranism in America was largely evangelized from Halle.[3]

The Danish-Halle Mission

Out of Halle University grew the first Protestant mission—the Danish-Halle Mission. The men, and much of the support, were furnished by Halle; the initial impetus originated in Denmark. Hence the name—Danish-Halle Mission.

In 1620 Denmark established its first trading colony at Tranquebar on the east coast of India. From the beginning chaplains were sent out to minister to the spiritual needs of the colonists; but it was almost one hundred years before missionary work was initiated among the indigenous population. In 1705 Dr. Franz Lutkens, court chaplain at Copenhagen,

---

[3] James H. Nichols, *op. cit.,* p. 84

was commissioned by Frederick IV to recruit missionaries for the East Indies. Failing to find suitable men in Denmark, Lutkens conferred with Spener and Francke in Germany, hoping that the Pietist center at Halle could furnish volunteers. Two names were suggested: *Bartholomew Ziegenbalg* and *Heinrich Plütschau,* both of whom had studied at Halle under Francke.

From its inception the mission encountered opposition both in Europe and in India. The Lutheran churches in Germany failed to support it. Instead, support, moral and material, came from Halle and interested individuals. Indeed, Warneck goes so far as to say that "but for Francke the Danish mission would soon have gone to sleep."[4] Owing to their Pietist convictions, the two missionaries had difficulty in getting the Danish hierarchy to ordain them. Belatedly and somewhat reluctantly they were ordained, and sailed for Tranquebar on November 29, 1705. Their departure raised a storm of protest in Lutheran circles in Germany. Some leaders, such as V. E. Loscher, were comparatively mild in their criticism and were content to sound a "cursory warning" against supporting the mission. Most of the critics were much more violent in their denunciation of the young mission. The faculty of theology at Wittenberg called the missionaries "false prophets" because their "orderly vocation was not ascertained."

On landing at Tranquebar on July 9, 1706, they were greeted with undisguised hostility by the Danish governor even though they carried credentials from King Frederick IV. Moreover, their Pietism did nothing to ingratiate them with the chaplains belonging to the East India Company, who regarded them as intruders and treated them accordingly. The Danish governor, uncertain as to his course of action, alternately persecuted and protected them. On one occasion he sent Ziegenbalg to prison.

Plütschau's term of service was short, lasting only five years. Ziegenbalg, never very robust, was able to give a total of fifteen years to India. On his furlough (1715) he traveled widely in Europe and aroused much interest in the Tranquebar mission. He was received by the kings of Denmark and England. He spent some time at Halle, where he met and greatly influenced young Zinzendorf, who later became the father of the Moravian missionary movement. By the time of his death in 1719 the mission had friends in Denmark, Germany, Great Britain, and even New England.

Moravian Missions

The origin of the Moravian Church goes back to 1467, when the persecuted followers of John Huss, with certain Waldensians and Mora-

---

[4] Gustav Warneck, *History of Protestant Missions* (New York: Revell, 1904), p. 44.

vians, banded together to form the *Unitas Fratrum* (United Brethren). After being almost wiped out by the Counter Reformation, the remnant, under the leadership of Christian David, migrated in 1722 to Saxony, where they were given refuge by Count Zinzendorf on one of his estates near Dresden. Known as *Herrnhut* (The Lord's Watch), this colony became the source and center of a missionary movement destined to circle the globe.

Nicolaus Ludwig Zinzendorf (1700-1760), godson to Spener and student at Francke's grammar school in Halle, decided as a young man to devote all his time and treasure to the cause of Christ. An ardent Pietist by parentage and profession, he declared: "I have one passion; it is He and He alone." He soon became the recognized leader of the colony and set about to organize its religious life. He became bishop of the Moravian Church in 1737. For thirty years he inspired and guided its worldwide missionary activities. He and Francke were, by all odds, the greatest missionary leaders of the eighteenth century.

The missionary impulse came about in a strange way. Zinzendorf, on a visit to Copenhagen in 1730, met a Negro from the West Indies and two Eskimos from Greenland, each of whom pleaded for missionaries. He was deeply moved by the appeal and decided to do something about it. On his return to *Herrnhut* he placed the challenge before the group. The response was immediate and enthusiastic.

Their first mission (1732) was to the Negro slaves on the Danish island of St. Thomas in the Virgin Islands. Greenland was next, in 1733, and St. Croix, also in the Virgin Islands, in 1734. Ten of this last group died in the first year; but it was not difficult to get recruits to fill up the depleted ranks. Other mission fields were opened: Surinam (1735), the Gold Coast and South Africa (1737), the North American Indians (1740), Jamaica (1754), and Antigua (1756). Between 1732 and 1760, 226 Moravians entered ten foreign countries.

> Within twenty years of the commencement of their missionary work the Moravian Brethren had started more missions than Anglicans and Protestants had started during the two preceding centuries. Their marvelous success was largely due to the fact that from the first they recognized that the evangelization of the world was the most pressing of all the obligations that rested upon the Christian Church, and that the carrying out of this obligation was the "common affair" of the community. Up to the present time (1930) the Moravians have sent out nearly 3,000 missionaries, the proportion of missionaries to their communicant members being 1 in 12.[5]

In almost every place their endeavors bore fruit, so that before long they had three members on the mission field for every one at home. And all of this was accomplished by men with little formal, and no theological, education. In this respect they differed radically from the Halle missionaries, all of whom were men of some erudition. Like the early apostles,

---

5 Charles H. Robinson, *History of Christian Missions* (New York: Scribners, 1915), p. 50.

they were "unlearned and ignorant men," and like them, they were despised by the cultured people of their day. The first two missionaries to Greenland were gravediggers. Of the first two missionaries to the West Indies, one was a potter and the other a carpenter. But they were men of passion and piety. What they lacked in knowledge they made up in zeal. When Sorensen was asked if he were ready to go to Labrador, he replied: "Yes, tomorrow, if I am only given a pair of shoes." When they went out they were provided with their fare. On reaching their destination they were expected to fend for themselves. They took their wives and little ones with them. They lived and died and were buried in the land of their adoption. For years they bore the stigma of their humble origin. It was only the unanswerable power of their humility, courage, industry, and endurance that gradually overcame the prejudice of the cultured classes of Europe.

After almost two hundred forty years the Moravians still maintain their missionary commitments in various parts of the world. They have four main home bases: in West Germany, England, Denmark, and the United States. Supporting agencies are found in four European countries.

These two missions, the Danish-Halle and the Moravian, occupied the center of the stage throughout the whole of the eighteenth century. Towards the close (1797) the *Netherlands Missionary Society* got under way.

During the nineteenth century some fifteen additional continental societies were organized. Germany led the way with five: *Berlin Missionary Society* (1824), *Rhenish Missionary Society* (1828), *Gossner Mission* (1836), *Leipzig Mission Society* (1836), and the *Hermannsburg Mission* (1849). Between 1821 and 1874, the four Scandinavian countries organized six societies. In France the *Paris Evangelical Missionary Society* came into being in 1822. The *Basel Evangelical Mission Society* (Switzerland), dating back to 1815, was the earliest of them all.

All these missions continue to function. The German societies took a severe beating during the first World War and again during World War II. At present German missionaries number about thirteen hundred.

The Evangelical Awakening

We have already noted that the missionary movement on the continent grew out of the Pietist movement of the seventeenth century. Now we are to trace the origin of the British missionary movement to the Evangelical Awakening under John Wesley and George Whitefield in the eighteenth century. These revivals were not two separate and distinct movements; rather they were two phases of one event—a mighty outpouring of spiritual power which eventually affected the whole of Christendom in the first decades of the eighteenth century. The leading figures in the Pietist movement were Spener, Francke, and Zinzendorf. The great preachers of the Evangelical Awakening were Wesley and Whitefield in England and Jonathan Edwards and Whitefield in America. The connecting link between the two phases was Wesley's personal contact with Zinzendorf and the Moravians and Whitefield's study of the works of Francke.

John Wesley spent several years in Georgia (1735-1737) under the auspices of the *Society for the Propagation of the Gospel.* He had hoped to do some missionary work among the Indians, but the white settlers in Savannah claimed so much of his time and strength that the Indians were neglected. Even his work among the settlers was disappointing. His legalistic approach to Christian ethics and the unbending manner in which he administered church discipline led to a virtual revolt among his parishioners. Wesley left Georgia a disillusioned man. But all was not lost. While in Georgia Wesley was introduced to Spangenberg and his Moravians, whose simple faith, personal piety, and joyous spirit were in direct contrast to his own brand of holiness. Especially was he impressed with their complete assurance of salvation—something he himself had never achieved. His sense of spiritual inadequacy was greatly accentuated when he beheld, during a storm at sea, the quiet joy and serene peace which possessed the hearts of the Moravians in the face of death.

Back in England Wesley kept up his contacts with the Moravians. On May 24, 1738, while attending an informal prayer meeting at Aldersgate Street, the light dawned and John Wesley experienced the peace of heart which he had sought so long. This simple yet profound experience, which was to change the whole course of Christendom, was described by Wesley in his journal: "I felt my heart strangely warmed. I felt that I did trust Christ, Christ alone, for salvation; and an assurance was given me that he had taken away my sins, even mine, and saved me from the law of sin and death."

Seeking to understand further the doctrines of the Moravians, Wesley visited *Herrnhut,* where he conferred for several days with Zinzendorf. Immediately upon his conversion Wesley began his evangelistic ministry—probably the greatest in the history of preaching—which lasted forty years and included an average of three or four sermons a day. His organizational genius resulted in the formation of the great Methodist Church, first in England and later in America. It is no exaggeration to say that he saved England from moral and religious disaster and laid the foundations of the modern missionary movement launched by Carey.

Early British Missions

We generally regard British missions as beginning in 1792 with the famous William Carey, the father of modern missions. Strictly speaking, this is not correct. Prior to that time there were three societies, all of them designed originally to operate within the colonial framework of North America.

The first was the *Society for the Propagation of the Gospel in New England,* founded in 1649. As its name implies, it was organized with the Indians of North America in mind. An original endowment of twelve thousand pounds was invested in land and the proceeds used to support missions in the New World. Its first missionary was *John Eliot,* who had been in Massachusetts since 1631 and who gave half a century to the evangelization of the Indians of that colony. The mission continued its work in New England until the War of Independence.

The *Society for Promoting Christian Knowledge* was organized in 1698 as an independent mission within the Anglican Church. A leading figure in its formation was *Thomas Bray,* Rector of Sheldon and Commissary in Maryland of the Bishop of London. It was not intended in the beginning to be a missionary venture. Its original purpose was to strengthen the religious life of the white colonists in the New World. This was to be done by the dissemination of Christian literature and by augmenting the meager libraries of the colonial clergy. As it branched out into many different parts of the world it became, for all intents and purposes, a missionary agency.

Through the years the SPCK has engaged in a variety of activities, mostly in the fields of education and literature. During a time of crisis in the eighteenth century it came to the rescue of the Danish-Halle Mission in South India. For over two hundred sixty years it has been a supporting mission, providing an ever increasing stream of high grade Christian literature not only for Anglicans but for others as well. Since 1835 it has been doing its own publishing. Today it has bookstores all around the world.

The *Society for the Propagation of the Gospel in Foreign Parts,* commonly known throughout the world as the SPG, is the oldest, and was for nearly a century the only, specifically missionary agency of the Church of England. The major difference between the SPG and its equally famous sister mission, the *Church Missionary Society,* is that the former is High Church and the latter, Low Church.

Here, as with the SPCK, Thomas Bray was instrumental in bringing it into being. The SPG was founded by royal charter in 1701 with a twofold purpose: to minister to the spiritual needs of the English settlers overseas, many of whom were in danger of lapsing into heathen ways for lack of religious instruction; and to evangelize the indigenous population, who were heathen to begin with.

During the entire eighteenth century the SPG maintained a rather modest program on a very restricted budget. During that time its activities were confined to the American colonies and the West Indies. Nevertheless, as will be seen in the chapter on missions in North America, the SPG filled a pressing need for chaplains and missionaries in colonial America.

VI

Origin of Protestant Missions in England and USA: A.D. 1750–1850

If Western colonialism is said to have begun with Vasco da Gama, Protestant missions may be said to have been launched by William Carey. What Luther was to the Protestant Reformation, Carey was to the Christian missionary movement. Though there were missionaries before him, it is altogether fitting that William Carey should be known as "the father of modern missions."

Many factors contributed to the inauguration of the "Great Century" of modern missions. The famous East India Companies tapped the riches of the Indies and laid the foundation of world trade. They also paved the way for European colonization which, in the providence of God, greatly facilitated the worldwide mission of the church. The invention of the steamboat made ocean travel faster and safer. Of more immediate interest to William Carey were the voyages of Captain James Cook.

Religious factors were no less potent. The Pietist Movement in Germany and the Evangelical Awakening in England and America have already been mentioned. Even before Carey's time there were stirrings of missionary interest in England. In 1719 Isaac Watts wrote his great missionary hymn, "Jesus Shall Reign Where'er the Sun." Several of Charles Wesley's compositions also bear a missionary theme. In 1723 Robert Millar of Paisley wrote *A History of the Propagation of Christianity and the Overthrow of Paganism,* in which he advocated intercession as the primary means of converting the heathen. The idea soon caught on. Twenty years later prayer groups were to be found all over the British Isles. Their chief petition was for the conversion of the heathen world.

In 1746 a memorial was sent to Boston inviting the Christians of the New World to enter into a seven-year "Concert of Prayer" for missionary work. The memorial evoked a ready response from Jonathan Edwards, who the following year issued a call to all believers to engage in intercessory prayer for the spread of the gospel throughout the world.

Almost forty years later, in 1783, Edwards' pamphlet was introduced to the churches in England by John Sutcliff in the Northamptonshire Ministerial Association. Following the reading of the pamphlet, he made a motion that all Baptist churches and ministers set aside the first Monday of each month for united intercession for the heathen world. It read:

> Let the whole interest of the Redeemer be affectionately remembered, and the spread of the Gospel to the most distant parts of the habitable globe be the object of your most fervent requests. We shall rejoice if any other Christian societies of our own or other denominations will unite with us, and we do now invite them to join most cordially heart and hand in the attempt. Who can tell what the consequences of such a united effort in prayer may be?[1]

About this time *William Carey* (1761-1834) came on the scene. At fourteen years of age he apprenticed himself to the shoemaker at Hackleton. Following his conversion at eighteen he left the Church of England to join a "nebulous body of Dissenters" and immediately began preaching in nearby churches. Later he was persuaded to join the Baptists. At twenty-six he was formally ordained by John Sutcliff, John Ryland, and Andrew Fuller. During these years he mended shoes and taught school on week days, and preached on Sundays. In his spare time he devoured every book he could lay his hands on. Doubtless it was from his father and grandfather, both schoolmasters, that he inherited his passion for learning. He taught himself Latin, Greek, Hebrew, Italian, French, and Dutch! He denied that he was a genius; he simply claimed to be a plodder.

Strangely enough, it was the reading of *The Last Voyage of Captain Cook* that first aroused in William an interest in missionary work. Thereafter he read every book that had any bearing on the outside world, including Guthrie's *Geographical Grammar*. It is certain that he read Jonathan Edwards' *Life and Diary of David Brainerd*. He was familiar with the Danish-Halle Mission, John Eliot of New England, and the Moravian missionaries. He made his own map of the world on which he inscribed every bit of pertinent information he could find. Surely there never was another cobbler's shop like Carey's. Picture the village cobbler in his leather apron, his books by his side, his map on the wall, and his beautiful flowers in the window.

In 1792 Carey published his eighty-seven-page book, *An Enquiry into the Obligations of Christians to Use Means for the Conversion of the*

---

[1] H. B. Montgomery, *Prayer and Missions* (West Medford, Mass.: The Central Committee of the United Study of Foreign Missions, 1924), p. 78.

Heathens. Believed by some to be the most convincing missionary appeal ever written, Carey's *Enquiry* was certainly a landmark in Christian history and deserves a place alongside Martin Luther's Ninety-five Theses in its influence on subsequent church history.

Carey was no armchair strategist. He was concerned with action, not theory. His immediate aim was the formation of a society that would send missionaries abroad. This was not easy, for the Baptists among whom Carey moved were staunch Calvinists. At a ministerial meeting in North-amptonshire when Carey proposed that they discuss the implications of the Great Commission, Dr. John C. Ryland retorted: "Young man, sit down. When God pleases to convert the heathen, He will do it without your aid or mine."

Undaunted, Carey used every opportunity to press home upon the church of his day the needs and claims of the non-Christian world. He was not altogether alone. There were a few who shared his vision, among them John Sutcliff, Andrew Fuller, Samuel Pearce, and others; but even they counseled caution and delay in the execution of the plan. The idea was too new, too startling; and the obstacles seemed insurmountable.

On May 30, 1792, at the Baptist Ministers' Association at Notting-ham, Carey preached his epochal sermon on Isaiah 54:2, 3, in which he coined the now familiar couplet: "Expect great things from God; attempt great things for God." The sermon had a profound effect on his hearers. The following day Carey pled for immediate action; but the brethren, while acknowledging the "criminality of their supineness in the cause of God," faltered when they faced the immensity of the task. The meeting broke up, but not before Carey persuaded them to include in the minutes a resolution that at the next meeting they would present a definite plan for the formation of a "Baptist society for propagating the gospel among the heathen." That meeting occurred on October 2 in Andrew Fuller's chapel in Kettering. The matter appears not to have been mentioned in the full public meeting of that day; but in the evening a small group of twelve ministers and one layman gathered with William Carey in the spacious home of Widow Wallis, known for its hospitality as the Gospel Inn. Again Carey pressed for action, and again the brethren wavered. After all, who were these men, ministers of poverty-stricken churches, to undertake a mission so beset with difficulty, so fraught with uncertainty? At the crucial moment, when all hope seemed gone, Carey took from his pocket a booklet entitled *Periodical Account of Moravian Missions.* With tears in his eyes and a tremor in his voice he said: "If you had only read this and knew how these men overcame all obstacles for Christ's sake, you would go forward in faith." That was it. The men agreed to act. The minutes of the meeting record their decision to form *The Particular Baptist Society for Propagating the Gospel among the Heathen.* Reynold Hogg was appointed treasurer and Andrew Fuller, secretary. The mission was to be supported by individual subscriptions. Every person subscribing ten pounds at once, or ten shillings and sixpence annually, was considered a member. Then and there the thirteen men subscribed a total of thirteen pounds, two shillings and sixpence. Carey was no longer alone in his plans for the evangelization of the world. "The ability of Ryland, the influence of Fuller, the eloquence of Sutcliff, and the enthusiasm of Pearce were now linked unreservedly with the faith and courage of Carey."[2]

It was one thing to pass a resolution to form a mission; it was another to get the mission under way. Difficulties abounded on all sides, pertaining to family, finance, and field. Carey's father considered him mad. His wife refused to accompany him. But one by one the problems were solved; and after some delay and not a little discouragement, William Carey sailed for India on June 13, 1793. He was accompanied by a reluctant wife, four children, and two companions. Five months later he arrived in India, the land to which he gave forty years of unbroken service.

Back home in Europe and America, largely through the labors and letters of Carey, missionary societies came into existence: the *London Missionary Society* (1795), the *Scottish and Glasgow Missionary Societies* (1796), the *Netherlands Missionary Society* (1797), the *Church Missionary Society* (1799), the *British and Foreign Bible Society* (1804), the *American Board of Commissioners for Foreign Missions* (1810), the *American Baptist Missionary Union* (1814), and the *American Bible Society* (1816). It is difficult to exaggerate the influence of William Carey on the missionary enterprise of the nineteenth century. Few will wish to deny him the title of "father of modern missions."

In America

About this time there was a quiet but far-reaching movement of the Spirit of God on this side of the Atlantic. The call to preach the gospel to all nations came to *Samuel J. Mills* while he was following the plow on his farm in Connecticut one day in 1802. Four years later, in obedience to the heavenly vision, he entered Williams College at Williamstown, Massachusetts, to prepare for the Christian ministry. There he kindled a fire whose sparks were destined to be carried to the ends of the earth. A group of kindred spirits—James Richards, Francis Robbins, Harvey Loomis, Gordon Hall, and Luther Rice—known as the Society of the Brethren met frequently in a grove of maples near the campus for prayer and discussion. One day on their way to prayer they were caught in a sudden thunderstorm. Taking refuge in the lee of a nearby haystack, they had their usual time of prayer for the heathen world, following which they stood to their feet and said, "We can do it if we will." They thereupon resolved to

---

[2] F. Deaville Walker, *William Carey: Missionary, Pioneer, Statesman* (Chicago: Moody Press, 1925, p. 89.

become America's first foreign missionaries and signed a pledge to that effect. Henceforth they were known as "the Haystack Group."

After graduation several of them went to Andover Seminary, founded in 1808 by the Old Calvinists and the followers of Samuel Hopkins because of dissatisfaction with the liberalism of Harvard. This young school, the inheritor and preserver of New England Puritanism and the evangelical tradition of Jonathan Edwards, became the fountainhead not only of evangelicalism in New England but also of Christian missions overseas. Here they were joined by Adoniram Judson from Brown University, Samuel Newell from Harvard University, and Samuel Nott, Jr., from Union College. Under the leadership of Judson, the brilliant valedictorian, they formed the Society of Inquiry on the Subject of Missions.

On June 28, 1810, Judson, Mills, Nott, and Newell walked six miles to Bradford to present to the General Association of the Congregational Ministers of Massachusetts a memorial in which they offered themselves for missionary service and solicited the advice, direction, and prayers of the "Reverend Fathers." The young men gave their testimonies, after which the matter was referred to a committee of three. The following day the committee approved the purpose of the young men and recommended the formation of a foreign mission board. The report was immediately and unanimously adopted. Nine men were appointed to constitute the original Board of Commissioners for Foreign Missions. The first annual meeting of the board was held at Farmington, Connecticut, on September 5, 1810, with five commissioners present. They discussed and adopted a constitution of fourteen articles and elected officers for the following year, including a Prudential Committee of three members. They also prepared an *Address to the Christian Public* to enlist support for the new enterprise. Such was the humble beginning of the American foreign missionary movement, which today provides almost 70 percent of the worldwide Protestant missionary force and about 80 percent of the finances.

From the beginning the board was concerned for home as well as foreign missions. At its second meeting (Worcester, Massachusetts) it expressed the hope that "this Board will not lose sight of the heathen tribes on this Continent." Beginning in 1817 and extending to 1883, missions were conducted among the Indians, especially the Cherokees, Chickasaws, Choctaws, and Dakotas. All told, fifteen tribes were evangelized in as many states.

Foreign missions posed more difficult problems. The Prudential Committee corresponded with the directors of the London Missionary Society, and even sent Adoniram Judson to London to inquire more specifically about fields of service and methods of work. At one point the suggestion was made that the LMS might support Judson and his colleagues until they became self-supporting. He also inquired about the feasibility of joint support by the two societies. Wisely, the LMS suggested that the American Board maintain its own identity and autonomy, and the Americans accepted the suggestion. Acting on the recommendation of the LMS, the Prudential Committee decided on Burma as its first mission field. At the third annual meeting, held in Hartford in September, 1812, the committee designated four types of field that called for missionary activity: (1) peoples of ancient civilizations; (2) peoples of primitive cultures; (3) peoples of the ancient Christian churches; and (4) peoples of the Islamic faith.

It was at the second annual meeting of the board that the four young men, Judson, Nott, Newell, and Hall, were actually appointed as missionaries of the board. As usual, finance was a problem. Only fourteen hundred dollars had been received and this was not enough to pay the cost of passage. The committee deliberated anxiously. Should they proceed with their plans or wait for additional support? At last, on January 27, 1812, they voted to send the four men but to detain the wives until sufficient funds were on hand. Perhaps the LMS would come through after all. It was a brand new venture; they oscillated between faith and fear. But their fear was shortlived. When it became known that the young missionaries had actually booked passage, gifts flowed in from all quarters. Within three weeks more than six thousand dollars was received, enough to provide for outfit, passage, and a year's salary in advance!

The first party consisted of eight missionaries: Judson, Newell, and Nott, with their wives, Gordon Hall, and Luther Rice. The five men, all graduates of Andover Theological Seminary, were ordained in the Tabernacle in Salem on February 6, 1812. It was a most impressive service. The church was crowded, and at times the entire assembly "seemed moved as the trees of the wood are moved by a mighty wind."

Two weeks later the Judsons and the Newells set sail from Salem on the *Caravan*. The other members of the party left from Philadelphia on the *Harmony* on February 24. It took them four months to reach India. The first American mission had been launched. Other fields opened in rapid succession. Ceylon (1816), the Near East (1820), China (1830), and Madura (1834) were among the earliest.

Between Salem and Calcutta Judson changed his views on baptism, and on arrival was immersed by the Reverend William Ward, one of Carey's colleagues at Serampore. With characteristic honesty, Judson resigned from the Congregational Board and offered his services to the Baptists in America. This providentially led to the formation, in May, 1814, of what is now the American Baptist Foreign Mission Society. Judson became its first and most famous missionary. In the meantime, Judson and his wife, ordered out of India by the East India Company, made their way in a "crazy old vessel" to Rangoon, where they arrived on July 13, 1813. The second American mission was under way.

Other mission boards were organized in rapid succession by the *Methodist Episcopal Church* (1819), the *Protestant Episcopal Church* (1821), the *Presbyterian Church* (1831), the *Evangelical Lutheran Church*

(1837), and others later on. Today almost every Protestant denomination of any size has its own foreign mission board. The 1970 *Directory of North American Protestant Ministries Overseas* lists 603 sending and supporting organizations engaged in overseas operations. The operating budget of these organizations totalled $350,000,000. Together they support thirty-five thousand full-time missionaries in over one hundred countries. This means that North Americans now represent 70 percent of the total number of Protestant missionaries in the world and provide an even higher percentage of the overall missionary budget.

VII

Protestant Missions in
North America: A.D. 1620-1800

We begin with New England, not because it was the earliest of all the settlements—that honor goes to Virginia; but because New England Christianity exercised an enormous influence on the religious life of the other colonies and also on the subsequent history of the Christian church in the United States. After documenting the various ways in which this was done, Latourette remarks: "In these and scores of other ways the Christianity of New England molded the entire United States and had repercussions which were felt the world around."[1]

How was Christianity nourished in the New World? It was not through state aid, but first through the private efforts of ecclesiastical bodies in the Old World, and later by the spontaneous endeavors of the more spiritually aggressive groups such as the Baptists, the Methodists, and others. Three of the ecclesiastical bodies were really missionary societies: The *Company for the Propagation of the Gospel in New England,* the *Society for Promoting Christian Knowledge,* and the *Society for the Propagation of the Gospel in Foreign Parts.* The lion's share was contributed by the last-named society, known throughout the world as the SPG—today the oldest missionary society in the English-speaking world. Up to the close of the American Revolution the SPG had maintained about three hundred missionaries in the Thirteen Colonies and had expended about a quarter of a million pounds. Only seventy-nine of the three hundred missionaries were American born; the others were sent over from England.

---

[1] K. S. Latourette, *Three Centuries of Advance* (New York: Harper & Row, 1939), p. 194.

In New England the dominant motive of the early settlers was religious. They came to these shores in search of religious liberty. The Pilgrims who landed at Plymouth in 1620 were non-Conformists who had repudiated the ecclesiastical power structure of the Church of England, had migrated to Holland to escape persecution, and had finally decided to make a new start in the New World where, hopefully, they could establish a church free of ecclesiastical tyranny.

A second group of immigrants, also from England, settled around Massachusetts Bay. These people were Puritans, not Separatists. They preferred to remain with the established church and effect, if possible, the necessary reforms from within. They gradually drifted away from the Anglican form of worship, however, and adopted a Congregational form of polity.

Strangely enough, they came in time to show the same kind of intolerance which they had found so objectionable back in the Old Country. Roger Williams, William Coddington, and Samuel Gorton, who demanded full religious freedom, were regarded as dangerous radicals and chased out of Massachusetts. Roger Williams established new communities in what is now Rhode Island.

Connecticut, with the exception of New Haven, was settled by Puritans from Massachusetts; but by this time religious fervor had begun to cool. It was not long before the Puritans and the Separatists joined hands to form a new kind of denomination—Congregationalism. It became the dominant group in New England; but the Anglicans remained a significant force. The Baptists flourished in Rhode Island. Quakers and others were tolerated.

Far more heterogeneous was the religious mosaic in New York. Under the Dutch regime, the Dutch Reformed Church was given preferential status. For a short period under Governor Stuyvesant (1647-1664) dissenters were the objects of discrimination. When the colony passed into British hands, the Church of England inherited the special status formerly enjoyed by the Dutch Reformed, though the latter continued to grow. The Anglicans, in spite of their special status, grew slowly, due to a chronic shortage of clergy. Until the turn of the eighteenth century the Church of England was confined to New York city. The *Society for the Propagation of the Gospel* sent its missionaries to fill the gap. Only then did the church make headway upcountry.

More hospitable to dissenters than the Dutch, the British attracted to New York those sects which had suffered various forms of persecution elsewhere. Huguenots were among the first settlers on Manhattan Island. Later they built up a strong colony on Staten Island. The Methodists, just branching out into the New World, came to New York in 1760. Presbyterians, Lutherans, and Catholics also established churches in New York.

New Jersey was first settled by the Dutch, though their numbers were never large. French Huguenots and Puritans from New England were also among the early settlers. After the region passed under British control in 1664, the Quakers became the dominant religious group. They were given proprietary rights to five-eighths of the land in West Jersey. *George Fox,* founder of the Quakers, visited New Jersey in 1672. *John Woolman,* an outstanding Quaker leader of the eighteenth century, was born there in 1720.

Maryland was founded by Catholics. The Jesuits were the first missionaries. Maryland thus became a center of Roman Catholic influence in colonial days. Later on, Protestants entered Maryland in large numbers and eventually became the dominant group. In 1692 the Church of England acquired special legal status. Puritans moved into Maryland to escape persecution in Virginia. Quaker missionaries were active. Methodists from England entered Maryland in the 1760's.

Granted by Charles II to *William Penn* in 1681, Pennsylvania became a haven for the persecuted sects of Europe in the closing decades of the seventeenth century. The early settlers, like those at Plymouth, were activated primarily by religious motives. Described by Penn as a "holy experiment," the new commonwealth was to be a Christian community founded on Christian principles derived from the Sermon on the Mount.

It was natural that Pennsylvania, with its advocacy of religious freedom and tolerance, should attract a large number of dissenters and independents. William Penn, himself a leading Quaker, made several tours of Europe to persuade men of like faith to join him in his experiment in the New World.

Three streams of immigration flowed into Pennsylvania. The British stream was made up largely of Quakers from England and Wales. The German stream at the beginning included the smaller sects: Mennonites, Amish, Dunkers, Moravians, and others. Later on, after 1727, when the volume of German immigration increased greatly, Lutherans and Reformed predominated. A third stream was the Scottish-Irish, who began to come in large numbers about 1728.

The outstanding Lutheran missionary in Pennsylvania was *Henry Muhlenberg,* a Pietist from Halle. Arriving in 1742, he immediately threw himself into the work, traveling extensively, preaching the gospel, organizing existing congregations, and founding new ones. He, more than any other man, laid the foundations of Lutheranism in the United States. The Moravians had as their missionary leader *Count Zinzendorf,* who spent two years in the New World. Landing in Philadelphia in 1743, he was greatly distressed by the lack of religion among the settlers. His visit greatly revived missionary interest, first among the settlers themselves and later among the Indians.

In North Carolina the progress of religion was slow. The Quakers, first on the scene, did not arrive until the latter half of the seventeenth century, and for many years they remained the dominant group. *George Fox,* their founder, visited the colony in 1672. More than any other colony, North Carolina depended for its religious life on missionaries from the outside—some from Europe and some from the northern colonies. This was especially true of the Anglicans, who never seemed to have enough clergy to go round. For many decades their clergy were missionaries of the *Society for the Propagation of the Gospel.* The Lutherans also had a shortage of clergy and had to rely on missionaries furnished by the *Society for Promoting Christian Knowledge.* The Baptists received help from missionaries sent from the Philadelphia Association. For a time the Presbyterians and the Moravians also depended for their spiritual oversight on missionaries; but later on, when the Moravians became firmly established at Salem, they sent their own missionaries into Georgia.

The first religious group in South Carolina was the French Huguenots, who came in sufficient numbers to form a significant element in the population. Their churches were later taken over by the Church of England which, here as elsewhere in colonial times, enjoyed special status in the community. Religion in South Carolina was anything but vigorous. The *Society for the Propagation of the Gospel* was the pioneer missionary organization, supplying clergy for the Anglicans and engaging in a gospel ministry. Baptists were among the early comers and thrived in the hinterland, especially after the Great Awakening in the middle of the eighteenth century.

Georgia, the last of the colonies to be settled (1733), was the scene of much missionary activity on the part of the Church of England. *John Wesley,* while still an Anglican, spent two years as a missionary in Georgia (1735-1737). It was while here that he had his first contact with the Moravians, whose Pietism so greatly influenced him and led ultimately to the "heart warming" experience in Aldersgate, the birthplace of Methodism. *George Whitefield,* the eloquent evangelist, took a keen interest in the spiritual needs of the people of Georgia, which he visited many times between 1740 and 1770. Missionaries from Halle ministered to the Moravians. Latecomers were Presbyterians from Scotland; and Baptists and Quakers formed tiny minorities.

First settled in 1607, Virginia was the oldest and most populous of the Thirteen Colonies. Religion played a minor role in its development, in spite of the fact that the Virginia Company charter called for the "spread of the gospel among the heathen." The Church of England got in on the ground floor and acquired special rights. For a time the Anglican liturgy was regarded as the legal norm. Here, as elsewhere in the seventeenth century, the Church of England suffered a severe shortage of priests. One of the outstanding clergymen was *James Blair,* who came to the colony as a missionary in 1685 and remained in a position of high leadership for almost half a century.

During the eighteenth century non-Conformist groups entered the colony: Puritans, Huguenots, and Waldensians. The first Quakers appeared in 1657, but discriminatory laws kept their numbers low until 1725, when large migrations from the north augmented them. The Baptists were latecomers, the first contingent arriving in the early part of the eighteenth century. During the second half of that century, due largely to the Great Awakening, they increased significantly in number.

The Presbyterians established a stronghold when a wave of Scottish-Irish immigrants settled in Virginia. They were helped by missionaries sent from Philadelphia and New York. Lutherans from Germany and Pennsylvania settled in the Shenandoah Valley. *Peter Muhlenberg* from Pennsylvania was their missionary pastor.

Missions to the Indians

Missionary work was not confined to the colonists. From the very beginning it was understood that the gospel would be shared with the Indians. When Charles I in 1628 granted a charter to Massachusetts it was definitely stated that "the principal end of the plantation was the conversion of the Indians." A similar clause was inserted in the Virginia charter. The *Society for the Propagation of the Gospel,* founded as a colonial missionary society in 1701, had a twofold aim: to minister to English settlers overseas and to propagate the gospel among the heathen. As early as 1710 the society went on record requesting that "immediate care be taken to send itinerant missionaries to preach the gospel among the Six Nations of the Indians according to the primary intentions of the late King William of glorious memory."

On landing at Plymouth Rock in 1620, the Pilgrim Fathers set apart one of their number to promote the conversion of the Indians. In 1636 the General Court of Massachusetts directed that the ministers appoint two of their number each year to undertake missions among the Indians. The earliest extensive mission to the Indians of New England was established on Martha's Vineyard and Nantucket, two islands south of Cape Cod. Here five generations of the famous Mayhew family worked to convert the Indians to Christianity.

Known as the Apostle to the North American Indians, *John Eliot,* a brilliant Cambridge student, came to this country in 1630 and became a Presbyterian pastor in Roxbury, near Boston. For many years Eliot combined his pastoral ministry with missionary work among the Indians, of whom there were about twenty tribes on the plantations adjoining Massachusetts Bay. His first attempt to evangelize them was made at the Falls of Grand River in 1646. His first baptisms were at Natick, where a settlement of Indians was organized in 1651. Before long there were some thirty-six hundred Christians in fourteen settlements. His translation of the Bible into the Mohican language was the first Bible ever printed in America. In addition, he published grammars and primers and translated several theological books. He died at Roxbury in 1690. It was largely through his influence that the Society for the Propagation of the Gospel in New England was organized in England in 1649.

While Eliot was busy with his "praying towns," others were working in various parts of Massachusetts and in Rhode Island and Connecticut. Roger Williams, founder of Rhode Island, preached the gospel to the Narragansetts, but without much visible success. By 1675 there were twenty-five hundred Indian Christians in Massachusetts. About twenty-five years later there were thirty Indian congregations in southern Massachusetts alone, though the Indian population had declined during the previous half-century.

Eleazer Wheelock, a founder of Dartmouth College, organized a school in Lebanon, Connecticut, to train Indian Christians to become missionaries to their own people. Young people from the Delawares of New Jersey and the Iroquois of New York came to this school and returned to teach members of their own tribes. *John Sargeant* (1710-1749) labored among the Indians at Stockbridge in the Berkshires in western Massachusetts. Using Stockbridge as a base, *David Brainerd,* most famous of all the missionaries of colonial times, made a heroic attempt to Christianize the Indians of New York and, later, New Jersey. He was supported by the *Scottish Society for Propagating Christian Knowledge.* Like Henry Martyn, he literally burned out for God, after only four years of missionary work. His *Journal,* published in 1846, and his biography, written by Jonathan Edwards, are missionary classics which have influenced many, among them William Carey and Henry Martyn, to offer for missionary service.

In New York, missions were conducted among the Iroquois and the Mohawks, being particularly successful among the Mohawks. By the middle of the eighteenth century a large number of Mohawks had been baptized, one of them being the famous chief, Joseph Brant. Outstanding among the missionaries was *Henry Barclay,* a native of Albany.

Following the teaching and the example of their founder, George Fox, the Quakers carried on extensive missionary work among the Indians in New Jersey, Pennsylvania, and the Carolinas. More than any other religious body they tried to exemplify Christian principles in their dealings with the Indians. They treated them as equals and encouraged others to do the same.

The Moravians likewise showed evangelical concern for the Indians wherever they went. During his trip to this country in 1742 *Zinzendorf* visited Indians and preached the gospel to them at every opportunity. The Moravians established in Bethlehem, Pennsylvania, a training school for missionaries to the Indians. *David Zeisberger,* who gave his life to work among the Delaware Indians and became most famous of the eighteenth century Moravian missionaries, was trained there.

Missions to the Negroes

Missionary work among the Negroes was more extensive in the southern colonies, where the plantation system created a demand for cheap labor. It was later in beginning among the Negroes than among the Indians. The latter had more glamor and therefore more appeal. Moreover, the Negroes were slaves; the Indians were not. The strongest opposition to the evangelization of the Negroes came from their white owners, who feared that Christianization might lead to emancipation, which would undermine the plantation system. It was not until some of the colonial governments passed legislation which declared that baptism did not emancipate the slaves that missionary work among them was initiated.

The earliest missionaries were the agents of the *Society for the Propagation of the Gospel.* Within a year or two of its founding (1701) the society designated missionaries to work among the Negroes of the Carolinas. In 1745 the mission opened a school at Charlestown for the purpose of training Negroes to become teachers of their own people. The school was maintained, in the face of severe opposition, for some twenty years at a time when the government made no provision whatever for the education of the fifty thousand slaves in the colony. In North Carolina the society made several attempts to evangelize the Negroes. At Chowan in 1712 upwards of forty Negroes were baptized in one year. We read of baptisms in Georgia, Pennsylvania, and New Jersey.

The Moravians also took an interest in the spiritual welfare of the Negroes, as they did in that of the Indians. The Quakers, more than any other group, took a strong stand against slavery. As early as 1717 in Newport, R.I., the most important center of the slave trade in the colonies, they went on record expressing doubt concerning the propriety of keeping slaves. Ten years later they went further and condemned the whole system. In 1775 the New England Quakers urged all their members to emancipate their slaves. Similar action was taken by the Quakers in New York and Philadelphia. *John Woolman* of New Jersey was one of their most outspoken advocates of abolition. It is to be noted that the anti-slavery movement in Great Britain and the United States was the direct outgrowth of the Great Awakening. The revivals of the eighteenth century, which had such a marked effect on the non-Conformist groups—Presbyterians, Methodists, and Baptists—made a strong appeal to the Negro.

On the Frontier

Towards the end of the eighteenth century, as the population of the new republic continued to move westward, the Congregational churches of New England became burdened for their brethren on the western frontier, many of whom were without any spiritual oversight whatever. Several isolated and abortive attempts at missions among them were made; but it was not until June, 1798, that the first society, the *Missionary Society of Connecticut,* came into being. Article four of its constitution stated: "The object of this society shall be to Christianize the heathen of North America and to support and promote Christian knowledge in the new settlements within the United States."

The good example of Connecticut was followed one year later by Massachusetts, when the *Massachusetts Missionary Society* came into being.

It should be noted that these societies were local only in name. In their genius, sympathies, and methods they were genuinely national in scope. Over a period of thirty years they sent nearly two hundred missionaries to various parts of the frontier. Into the wilds of New York and Ohio they went; among the heathen of Vermont and New Hampshire they labored; into the new settlements of Illinois and Indiana they were received. They penetrated into Kentucky and Tennessee, and made their way down the Mississippi to the Gulf of Mexico.

Following the noble example of Connecticut and Massachusetts, New Hampshire in 1801, Rhode Island in 1803, and Maine and Vermont in 1807 all formed their own home missionary societies. Thus New England became the fountainhead of the broad river of national home missions.

When the other denominations saw what was being accomplished by the Congregationalists, they took up the torch. In 1816 the *Presbyterian General Assembly* created its Board of Home Missions in succession to an earlier standing committee which had home missions as its responsibility. One of their outstanding missionaries was *Sheldon Jackson.* A native of New York State, he labored in Minnesota and the vast region of the Rocky Mountains, traveling, preaching, organizing churches, sometimes helping to put up church buildings with his own hands, recruiting and assigning missionaries, and raising funds. He served not only the whites but the Indians as well. When the Rocky Mountain area passed beyond the pioneer stage Jackson moved on to Alaska, recently purchased from Russia, where he gave himself primarily to the Eskimos.

Largely at the instigation of *John Mason Peck,* in 1832 the *American Baptist Home Missionary Society* was organized and adopted all of North America as its field. From the early 1800's Baptists had been sending missionaries to the West and had formed local and state societies for that purpose. Peck had already traveled widely in Illinois, Indiana, and Missouri, establishing Bible societies and Sunday schools.

Not content with their system of circuit riders, the *Methodists* organized their home missionary society in 1820. Indian missions were one of its objects and foreign missions were envisaged as a possibility, but it was to the advancing frontier that the new society directed its major efforts.

In that same year, 1820, the Episcopalians organized their *Domestic and Foreign Missionary Society*. In 1835 the base was so broadened that all members of the church were considered members of the society. Moreover, in that year the General Convention adopted the policy of electing missionary bishops to serve in states and territories not organized as dioceses.

Zealous as the Congregational, Presbyterian, and Episcopalian missionaries were, they did not win as many converts on the frontier as did their Methodist, Baptist, and Disciples of Christ counterparts.

A number of societies, denominational and undenominational, sought to meet the specialized needs of the frontier. Foremost among these were the Bible societies, which became the handmaidens of home and foreign missions. Between 1809 and 1815 more than one hundred Bible societies, some local and some statewide, came into being. Several of these united in 1816 to form the *American Bible Society*, which patterned itself after the famous British and Foreign Bible Society of 1804. The year 1824 saw the inauguration of two new missionary agencies: the *Baptist General Tract Society* and the *American Sunday School Union*. The following year marked the birth of the *American Tract Society*.

PART TWO

Around the World

VIII

South Asia

India

History. Indian history is divided into six periods: Indus Civilization, 3000 to 1500 B.C.; Aryan Civilization, 1500 to 500; Indian Kingdoms, 500 B.C. to A.D. 1000; Muslim Rule, 1000 to 1700; British Rule, 1700 to 1947; Independence, 1947 to the present.

India achieved independence on August 15, 1947, largely as a result of the nonviolent teaching and techniques of Gandhi. The 562 princely states, which had enjoyed special status under the British, were made part of the Indian Union soon after independence. On January 26, 1950, India adopted a new constitution and declared itself a sovereign democratic republic. Today the republic comprises twenty-nine states, including Andaman and Nicobar Islands.

The two hundred fifty-year period of British rule coincided with the heyday of Western imperialism in the Orient. It made an immense impact on the subcontinent and helped prepare India to take its place in the modern world. Today India is the largest democracy in the world and one of the very few genuine democracies in Asia. It is largely to British influence that India owes its open society with its democratic institutions: a parliamentary government, a well-trained civil service, a free press, universal education, genuine elections, and a lingua franca—English. That India and Britain have remained on such correct and cordial terms since independence is a tribute to the sagacity of British diplomacy and the civility of Indian nationalism, particularly that of Mahatma Gandhi and Jawaharlal Nehru.

It was during this period also that Protestant Christianity entered India and made such a significant contribution to the modernization of the country. Even the reform movements within Hinduism derived much of their inspiration from the dynamic of the Christian mission.

People. With a population of 530 million, India is the second largest country in the world, only China, its colossal neighbor to the northeast, being larger. Fourteen major languages and seven hundred dialects make India's population the most polyglot of all the countries in the world. Seven main physical types are commonly recognized. (1) The Dravidians, the oldest inhabitants of the subcontinent, are found mostly in the south. Included in this group are the Telugus, Tamils, Kanarese, etc. They are short in stature and of rather dark complexion. (2) The Indo-Aryans entered India through the Khyber Pass around 1500 B.C. and drove the culturally superior but militarily inferior Dravidians to the south. Today they are located in Kashmir, the Punjab, and Rajasthan. They are tall and fair, with dark eyes and fine features. (3) The Aryo-Dravidians are a mixture of the first two groups. Known also as the Hindustani type, they make their home in the Ganges valley. (4) The Scytho-Dravidians are a mixture of the Scythian invaders and the Dravidians. They are concentrated in Gugarat and the western part of Bombay. The largest group are the Marathis. (5) The Mongoloid type, originating in China and Tibet, are located in the northeastern province of Assam and the foothills of the eastern Himalayas. (6) The Mongoloid-Dravidian type are an amalgam of the Mongoloid and Dravidian elements, of which the Bengalis are representative. (7) Aboriginal hill tribes of the pre-Dravidian type include the Santals, Khonds, Bhils, Khols, Karens, etc. Found mostly in the northeast, these tribes were fierce and primitive until reached fairly recently with the gospel.

Population. With every passing year India's population crisis mounts in alarming proportions. It has only 2.4 percent of the world's land but 14 percent of its population. One out of every seven persons in the world is an Indian. The government is vigorously and openly promoting a nation-wide program of birth control; but since more than half of the population are illiterate, results are difficult to achieve. The birth rate has begun to drop slightly, but this is more than offset by a decline in the death rate from 27 per 1,000 in 1951 to 16 per 1,000 in 1966. With such communicable diseases as malaria, cholera, and smallpox brought under control, the life expectancy has risen from thirty-two years in 1950 to fifty years in 1966. The economic gains achieved by three successful Five Year Plans have been virtually wiped out by the population increase since 1955. Approximately 40 percent of the population is under fourteen years of age. And so it goes, on and on, with no relief in sight.

Language. The absence of a national language is one of the most potent divisive forces in India. The constitution recognizes fourteen lan-

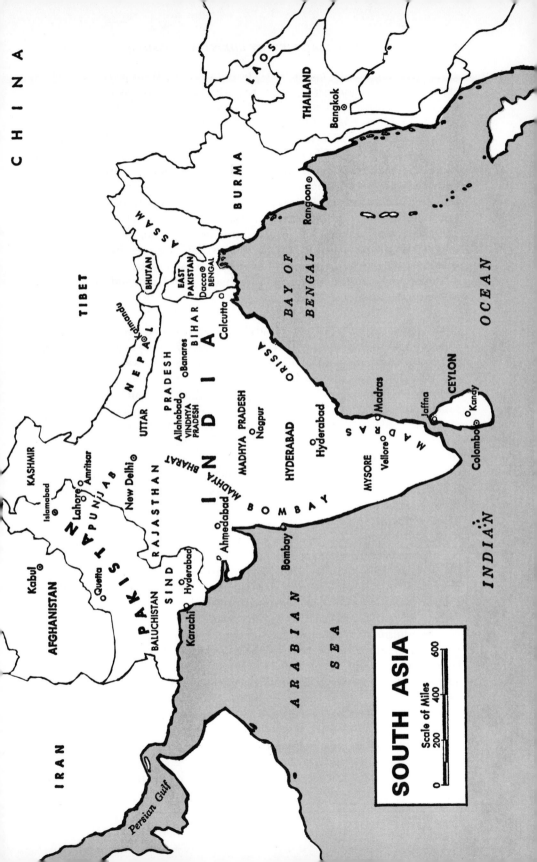

SOUTH ASIA

Scale of Miles

0 200 400 600

CHINA

IRAN

AFGHANISTAN

Kabul

TIBET

NEPAL

Kathmandu

BHUTAN

ASSAM

LAOS

THAILAND

Bangkok

BURMA

PAKISTAN

Islamabad

Lahore

Amritsar

PUNJAB

New Delhi

KASHMIR

Quetta

BALUCHISTAN

SIND

Hyderabad

Karachi

RAJASTHAN

MADHYA BHARAT

Ahmedabad

BOMBAY

Bombay

UTTAR PRADESH

Allahabad

Banares

VINDHYA PRADESH

BIHAR

Calcutta

EAST PAKISTAN

Dacca

BENGAL

Rangoon

BAY OF BENGAL

MADHYA PRADESH

Nagpur

ORISSA

HYDERABAD

Hyderabad

MYSORE

Vellore

Madras

M A D R A S

Jaffna

CEYLON

Kandy

Colombo

ARABIAN SEA

INDIAN OCEAN

Persian Gulf

INDIA

BHARAT

guages for the conduct of official business at the state level. The closest approach to a national language is English; but this, for obvious reasons, is not acceptable to the nationalists. A recent census recorded 720 languages spoken in India, most of which are mere dialects. The 1950 constitution made Hindi the official language, with English a second official language until 1965, by which time, they hoped, everyone would have learned Hindi. As might have been expected, there was widespread opposition to both measures—the adoption of Hindi and the dropping of English. In several places, notably Bombay, bloody communal riots broke out. In December, 1967, the government capitulated and passed the Official Language Amendment Bill, which provided for the continued use of English in addition to Hindi for all official purposes of the national government. In the meantime, the medium of instruction at all levels, including university, is the regional language, with Hindi and English listed as required courses.

Caste System. For thousands of years the outstanding feature of Indian social life was the caste system, by which Hindu society was divided into four broad socio-occupational groups. At the top were the *Brahmins,* the traditional priests and intellectual leaders; next, the *Kshatriyas,* the warriors and rulers; then, the *Vaisyas,* the traders and merchants; and finally, the *Sudras,* the servants and laborers, who performed all the menial tasks for the other three groups. Below this structure were the *Pariahs,* or untouchables, more recently referred to as the "scheduled classes." Constitutionally, "untouchability" has been outlawed in the new India. In the urban centers it is rapidly disappearing; in the rural areas caste remains one of the biggest obstacles to social and economic progress. So strong and pervasive is the influence of caste that even the churches in south India have been unable to eradicate it completely.

Religions. In spite of the fact that the New India has declared itself to be a secular state, in no other country does religion play such an important role. Four religions originated in India: Hinduism, Buddhism, Jainism, and Sikhism. Three others entered from the outside: Islam, Christianity, and Zoroastrianism.

Hinduism is by all odds the dominant religion; according to the latest census it claims 83.5 percent of the population. Muslims are the second largest group with 11 percent. Christians number 2.4 percent, divided almost equally between Catholics and Protestants. The others are as follows: Sikhs, 1.7 percent; Buddhists, .7 percent; Jains, .4 percent; Zoroastrians and others, .3 percent. The hill people are mostly animists.

Status of Foreign Missionaries. The constitution guarantees religious freedom, and the central government has made a sincere effort to uphold the constitution. Until October, 1966, Commonwealth missionaries were given preferential treatment and were allowed into India without visas. In recent years many missionaries, especially Americans, have been refused entrance or made to wait for their visas.

The rationale back of the government's policy is the determination to accelerate the Indianization of all foreign-sponsored organizations in India. If an Indian can fill the role, the foreigner is not needed and should not be admitted. There is nothing wrong with this expression of nationalism per se. At present the granting or withholding of visas is quite haphazard. It would be premature to regard the exclusion of all foreign missionaries as a foregone conclusion. At the same time, it is clear that the climate in the Indian government has changed. Of the applications for missionary visas made through the National Christian Council, 81 percent were successful in 1966, only 56 percent in 1968.

Obviously, the prestige of the missionary has been dropping, and his status today is rather precarious. The chief complaint is that of proselytizing. The fact that there are political as well as religious implications to this charge makes it rather serious. Several of the state governments have introduced legislation designed to curb, if not stop, all missionary activity. The State of Orissa in 1968 passed a law imposing a penalty of one year in prison or a thousand-dollar fine for missionaries convicted of converting minors, women, or untouchables. If "force, fraud, or exploitation of hunger" are used, the penalty can be doubled. In 1967 several missionary families, American, Canadian, and Dutch, were expelled from Assam on charges that they "helped rebel uprisings." Some eighty other missionaries were informed that their residence permits would not be renewed when they expired. The central government has tried to steer a middle course between the anti-missionary sentiment of the Hindu militants and the freedom of religion guaranteed by the constitution; but it can go only so far in defending missionaries in "sensitive areas."

In 1969 Mr. Shukla, Minister of State for Home Affairs, reported foreign Christian missionaries registered with the Indian government as 6,326, including those from Commonwealth countries. This was a decrease of only three hundred over four years. Of twenty applications for naturalization made by foreign missionaries during a two-year period ending April 30, 1970, nineteen were rejected. One is still pending.

Earliest Christian Contacts. According to rather well-founded tradition, the gospel was first preached in India by the *Apostle Thomas,* who arrived in A.D. 52. His twenty-year ministry was divided into two equal parts, the first in the north around Lahore and the second in the south near Madras. In the north he enjoyed the respect of King Pikuvattam and the patronage and protection of King Thanavalla. Thomas's mission in the north was suddenly terminated by the murder of the king in A.D. 63. From there he went south to Madras. Though some Western scholars doubt that Thomas ever went to India, the Mar Thoma Christians of south India insist that "the area from Madras to Cochin is studded with reminders of his work."[1] Thomas's martyrdom in A.D. 72 was occasioned by a change in succession, coupled with the conversion of the new king's wife. Thomas is reputed to have made thousands of converts during his missionary career. In later years their numbers were greatly reduced by persecution. The Christian faith, however, never died out in south India.

The second important contact with India was made by *Pantaenus* about A.D. 180. Before his conversion Pantaenus had been a Stoic philosopher. Later he became the head of the famous catechetical school in Alexandria. His pupils Clement and Origen were among the greatest Christian teachers of their time. Jerome in one of his letters says that Pantaenus was sent to India that he might preach Christ among the Brahmins. On arrival he found a group of Christians who used a Hebrew version of the Gospel of Matthew.

These St. Thomas Christians lived for centuries in isolation from Christians in the West. Now and again we catch a fleeting glimpse of this tiny Christian island in the sea of Hinduism. They appear to have clung tenaciously to their apostolic faith and to have withstood the subtle, all-pervasive influence of Hinduism. Later on they were greatly strengthened by the arrival of the Nestorian Christians, who not only settled in India following persecution in Persia, but also took the gospel to China in the seventh century.

John of Monte Corvino, on his way to China at the close of the thirteenth century, stopped off in India for a year. He found Nestorian Christians near Madras and in various other places throughout India still maintaining the integrity of their faith with the help of occasional visits from the Nestorian Patriarchs of Persia. When the Portuguese arrived in India in 1498, they discovered to their surprise over one hundred villages composed entirely of Nestorian Christians. In all India there were some fourteen hundred churches with about two hundred thousand members. In 1547 a Nestorian tablet dating back to the seventh century was unearthed near Madras. Depicted on the monument is a dove hovering over a cross. On the sides are Scripture quotations, one in Syriac and the other in Pahlavi.

Roman Catholic Missions.   Franciscan missionaries landed in India with Cabral in 1500. Three years later the Dominicans arrived. Goa, captured in 1510, became an important Portuguese colony. In 1533 it became the headquarters of an enormous diocese which extended from the Cape of Good Hope to Japan. The Roman Catholic mission in India and other parts of Asia has been covered in an earlier chapter; so there is no need to repeat the story here.

---

[1] P. Thornton-Pett, *South East Asia Journal of Theology*, Vol. 6, No. 3, January-February, 1965, pp. 43-51.

The Danish-Halle Mission. William Carey is often referred to as the father of modern missions, but Protestant missionaries were in India almost one hundred years before Carey. Mention has already been made of the origin of the *Danish-Halle Mission*—the men coming from the University of Halle and the funds supplied by the King of Denmark. Its first missionaries, *Bartholomaus Ziegenbalg* and *Heinrich Plutschau*, reached the Danish colony of Tranquebar on the east coast of India on July 9, 1706. The fact that they carried with them a letter from the king did little to ingratiate them with the local governor who, taking his cue from the Danish East India Company, did everything he could to make life miserable and work difficult for the pioneer missionaries.

Undaunted by official opposition, the two missionaries cheerfully went about the business of adjusting to life in a strange land. Starting from scratch, with no linguistic tools of any kind, they applied themselves to the study of Tamil. So remarkable was their progress that in eight months Ziegenbalg could speak it fluently, and by the end of the third year he had completed his translation of the New Testament. He thus established both a precedent and a pattern for all subsequent Protestant missionary endeavor. In addition, he produced a Tamil grammar and dictionary. Their first converts, after ten months, were five slaves belonging to Danish masters. Several months later they baptized nine Hindus and organized the first Protestant church in India. By 1719 there were 355 converts, a school, a seminary, a paper mill, a type-foundry, and a printing press.

Ill health removed Plutschau from the field in 1711. Ziegenbalg's furlough in 1715 afforded an opportunity to promote the cause of foreign missions on the Continent and in England. It also led to the recall of the hostile governor of Tranquebar. After furlough he had two more years of service in India before passing away at thirty-five years of age.

Following his death the mission continued to thrive, supported in part by grants from two Anglican societies, the Society for Promoting Christian Knowledge and the Society for the Propagation of the Gospel. Three great leaders deserve honorable mention. *Schultze* translated the Bible into Telugu and the New Testament and part of the Old Testament into Hindustani. *Philip Frabicius* spent fifty years in Tamil country, where he became an accomplished Tamil scholar. His translation of the Bible and Christian hymns made a significant contribution to the progress of the mission. The most outstanding missionary of them all, however, was *Christian Friedrich Schwartz*, who during his forty-eight years in India did more than anyone else to lay the foundations of the great Lutheran Church in that land. His first center of work was Tranquebar. Later he transferred to Trichinopoly (1761) and Tanjore (1776). His magnetic personality and administrative gifts won for him the confidence and esteem of both British officials and Indian princes. More than once he was called on to act as mediator in the many wars that plagued south India during the second half of the eighteenth century. When the Hindu rajah of

Tanjore was dying he entrusted his adopted son, Serfojee, to the protecting care of Schwartz. Later this son erected a beautiful marble monument to the memory of the great missionary.

His extraordinary linguistic gifts enabled him to master Tamil, Persian, Hindustani, English, and Hindu-Portuguese. He was a scholar of the first order and made a study of Hindu literature, religion, and mythology. He was equally at home with Indian princes, educated Brahmins, and Europeans of all classes.

The Danish-Halle Mission continued until near the end of the eighteenth century, when it succumbed to the corrosive influence of German rationalism. When men and money stopped coming from Germany, the Church Missionary Society stepped in and kept the mission going. Help was also rendered by the Dresden-Leipsic Lutheran Society. Altogether, some sixty Lutheran missionaries, all of them from Halle, had worked under its auspices. During the century fifty thousand converts had been won, most of them from the Sudras and the Pariahs. By 1800 some twenty thousand church members formed the nucleus of what is today the *Tamil Evangelical Lutheran Church.*

William Carey.   In the case of Roman Catholic countries, the Crown was genuinely interested in the conversion of the heathen; and missionaries accompanied the explorers on their early expeditions. In the case of Protestant England, it was almost two hundred years after Elizabeth I granted the first charter to the East India Company that Christian missionaries took the gospel to India.

The first British society organized especially for *foreign* missionary work was the *Baptist Missionary Society,* formed in 1792. Its first field was India. Its first and most illustrious missionary was *William Carey.* Carey reached India in 1793, after surmounting incredible obstacles. He was thirty-two years of age. He settled in the Danish colony at Serampore, fifteen miles up the Hooghley River from Calcutta. He would no doubt have preferred to work in British India; but the East India Company, which had refused him passage on its ships, regarded the presence of missionaries as a threat to the peace and safety of its possessions.

In 1799 Carey was joined by *Joshua Marshman,* a teacher, and *William Ward,* a printer. Together they were known as the "Serampore Triad," each complementing and supplementing the work of the other two. When funds from home were not forthcoming, they took up work in an indigo factory to defray expenses. Later, as a teacher of Indian languages in the new Fort William College at Calcutta, Carey managed to support the entire mission (ten adults and nine children) with his salary of $6,000 a year. The missionaries lived a communal life in frugal fashion on $500 a year. The remainder was allocated to the work. Three times a year at all stations of the mission they gathered to read their compact, which ended with these words: "Finally, let us give ourselves unreservedly to this glorious crusade. Let us never think that our time, our gifts, our strength, our families, or even the clothes we wear, are our own. Let us sanctify them all to God and His cause."

Carey's outstanding role was that of translator. Though he never claimed to be a scholar, his linguistic abilities were astounding. Before setting foot in India he had mastered half a dozen languages, ancient and modern. In India he compiled and published grammars in Sanskrit, Bengali, Marathi, Telugu, and Sikh, and dictionaries in Bengali and Marathi, besides editing numerous works in both English and the native languages. He personally supervised the translation and publication of the Scriptures in forty languages at a cost of $400,000. During their lifetime, Carey and his colleagues founded twenty-six churches, and one hundred twenty-six schools with a total enrolment of ten thousand.

Carey's influence was not confined to religious circles. For thirty years, as a professor of Indian languages at Fort William College, he helped mold the bright young men who became the backbone of the famous Indian Civil Service in Bengal. For twenty-five years he worked assiduously for the abolition of *suttee*—the Hindu practice of burning widows alive on the funeral pyres of their husbands. The evil practice was abolished on December 5, 1829.

Carey was also a trailblazer in other areas, with many firsts to his credit. He introduced the first vernacular newspaper in Bengali; the first printing press, paper mill, and steam engine ever seen in India; the first schools for Indian girls; the first seminary to train Indian ministers; the first medical mission; the first people's savings bank; the first translations into English of the Sanskrit epics, the *Ramayana* and the *Mahabharata*.

William Carey and his associates were followed by a long list of stalwart missionaries of the Baptist Missionary Society. During the early years of the nineteenth century the mission opened stations in various parts of north India. In 1903 the work was extended to Assam. Today some 112 missionaries are functioning under the auspices of the national church. In time four Baptist groups were organized into the *National Council of Baptist Churches in Northern India*. Represented in these four councils are seven hundred churches with a total membership of fifty thousand and a Christian community of over one hundred thousand. These churches are heavily dependent on overseas help to maintain their ministries, especially the medical institutions. The area of greatest growth is Orissa, where missionaries and pastors together are unable to cope with the rapid growth. Armed rebellion in the Mizo district of Assam caused the government of India to call for the evacuation of missionaries in 1968. Two hundred village churches are now left to the care of national pastors. India, nevertheless, remains the largest field of the Baptist Missionary Society.

Other British Missions. India was one of the first fields of the *London Missionary Society* when it was organized in 1795. Three years later *Nathaniel Forsyth* arrived in Calcutta, where he labored in a self-supporting role until 1816. A second LMS field was opened in Madras in 1805 and Travancore in 1818.

When first founded, the LMS was interdenominational. Its purpose as stated in the charter was not to send abroad any particular form of church polity, but the glorious gospel of the blessed God. Later on, when the other denominations formed their own missionary societies, the LMS became a Congregational board, though it has always accepted missionaries from other denominations.

Today the LMS continues its work in India. In the south its forty-six missionaries are members of the *Church of South India* and are found in all fifteen dioceses of the CSI. In north India twelve missionaries are serving under the recently established *Church of North India,* which now includes seventeen denominations.

The *Church Missionary Society* work in India goes back to the second decade of the nineteenth century, when Abdul Masih, a convert of Henry Martyn, began work in the United Province in 1813. In time, Meerut, Benares, Lucknow, and Allahabad were all occupied by CMS missionaries. The work in the northeast centered in Calcutta. Travancore and Cochin in the southwest were entered in 1816. At first the CMS attempted to cooperate with the Syrian Church of Malabar, but this did not work out. In 1837 the mission turned its attention to the non-Christians, thousands of whom entered the church as a result of a mass movement. When the Danish-Halle Mission languished for lack of support at the home end, it was the CMS that came to the rescue and took over the work. One of the outstanding national leaders of the CMS was the *Reverend V. S. Azariah* of Dornaval, who became the first Indian bishop in 1912. The ministry of this remarkable man spanned almost half a century. His address at the Edinburgh Conference in 1910 was one of the highlights of that historic occasion. Today the CMS missionaries are working with the Church of North India and the Church of South India, both of which have accepted the episcopal form of church government.

Another Anglican society in India is the *Society for the Propagation of the Gospel.* Its greatest growth in the nineteenth century took place in the Tinnevelly district. It also had work in Bengal and the Central Provinces. In 1965 the SPG merged with the Universities' Mission to Central Africa to form the United Society for the Propagation of the Gospel. Today its more than one hundred missionaries in India are divided into two groups. In the north they are cooperating with the Church of North India. In the south, a dozen missionaries are working in four dioceses of the Church of South India.

John Wesley declared that the whole world was his parish. His followers on both sides of the Atlantic have followed his lead. The

Methodist Missionary Society was organized in 1813. The first missionaries to India were Wesleyans who began to work in Madras in 1819 and later opened centers in Bangalore and Nagapatam. At first the work was mostly among Europeans. It was not until reinforcements arrived that they were able, in 1857, to establish a strong work among the Indian population. During the century the English Methodists have steadily enlarged and strengthened their work in the subcontinent, until today they have 140 missionaries in India. A large contingent is working in six of the eleven dioceses of the Church of South India. Some fifteen are serving in three northern areas: Bengal, Lucknow, and Benares.

The *Scottish Missionary Society* began work in 1823. The first missionaries settled in Bombay. *John Wilson* was the outstanding leader of the early period. During his thirty-five years in Bombay he had the joy of leading many Hindus, Muslims, and Parsees to Christ. *Alexander Duff* pioneered the work of the *Church of Scotland.* His aim was to win the upper classes of Indian society, who had proved so impervious to the gospel. To achieve this he decided to concentrate on education, using English as the medium of communication and the Bible as one of the main textbooks. Upper class Hindus flocked to his school, which became a model for Christian education in all parts of India. Duff was on friendly terms with some of the finest minds in India. Not a few of these leaders embraced Christianity; and others who never actually became Christians, such as Ram Mohun Roy, were greatly influenced by Christianity.

Other British missions of the nineteenth century included the *General Baptists,* the *Irish Presbyterians,* the *Plymouth Brethren,* and the *Salvation Army.* The Plymouth Brethren (Christian Missions in Many Lands) report 127 missionaries in India in 1970. Working alongside of them are some 110 national workers ministering in 700 assemblies. India with its teeming population and its grinding poverty continues to challenge the Salvation Army. With territorial headquarters in Calcutta, Bombay, Madras, and Kerala, the SA maintains 4,556 centers of work in India. Eighty-nine overseas officers, representing nine countries, link India with sixty-nine other countries in which the Army is still trying to cope with "sin and want and sorrow."

American Societies. Shortly after the inauguration of the *American Board of Commissioners for Foreign Missions* in 1810, its first contingent of missionaries arrived in Bombay. *Dr. John Scudder,* who sailed for Ceylon in 1819, transferred to India in 1835 and opened a mission at Madura. The following year he moved to Madras. In 1947 the Madura mission of the American Board became part of the Diocese of Madura and Ramnad of the Church of South India.

In 1961 the Congregational Church and the Evangelical and Reformed Church merged to form the United Church of Christ here in the USA. Their respective missionary boards formed the *United Church Board for World Ministries.* The UCBWM is now heavily committed in three areas of India, south, central, and west, where it contributes money or personnel or both to some ninety institutions. Among them are the two famous medical colleges, Ludhiana and Vellore. In the south the work is part of the Church of South India, in which some of their missionaries are presbyters. In the other areas the UCBWM is affiliated with the Church of North India, which has a Christian community of half a million.

India was the first mission field of the *American Presbyterian Mission,* and in 1834 Ludhiana became the first city in the world to which Presbyterian missionaries were sent. Other stations were opened in succession: Allahabad (1836), Mussoorie (1847), Lucknow (1870), Vengurla (1900). The Sepoy Mutiny in the Punjab in 1857 cost the Presbyterians the lives of fourteen missionaries, their wives, and two children, as well as the lives of several Indian Christians. In various parts of north India schools, hospitals, and churches sprang up. In 1924 the Presbyterian and Congregational Churches joined to form the United Church of Northern India.

The Presbyterian Mission, now known as the *Commission on Ecumenical Mission and Relations,* is completely integrated with the new *Church of North India.* Its one hundred fraternal workers are serving in nine of the twenty-four presbyteries (councils) of the new church. Most of them are in institutional work—medical and educational. Many of these institutions are over one hundred years old and through the decades have made a very significant contribution to the building of the church and state in India. The commission provides teachers for two famous schools for the children of missionaries: Kodaikanal and Woodstock. The most recent venture is the *North India Theological College,* founded in 1965.

Dr. Nathan Brown pioneered the work of the *American Baptists* in India in 1836. In the course of time three major fields were developed: northeast India, Bengal-Orissa-Bihar, and south India. Each of these now has its own Baptist convention. The greatest response was among the hill tribes of the northeast, where Bible translation was an important phase of the work in the early years. In the south a mass movement among the Hindu "outcastes" resulted in ten thousand converts on the Ongole field by 1880. In one day (July 3, 1878) 2,222 were baptized.

The American Baptists have not been granted a single visa in the past five years. Consequently, the number of missionaries dropped from ninety-five in 1965 to forty-four in 1970. Hardest hit is the Bengal-Orissa-Bihar region, from which all missionaries have been evacuated. The situation worsened in 1967 with the passing of the anti-conversion law. Recent communist victories further complicate the picture. Alas, the church in this area is the weakest of the three. Only nine churches out of a total of fifty-six fully support their pastors. The mission pays 90 percent of the salaries in the other churches.

The northeast area is the fastest growing field of the Baptists in India. The strongest church is in Nagaland, where half the population is Baptist and the other half is friendly to Christianity. The state government is solidly and actively Christian. The Christians tithe their meager incomes, and the churches are fully self-supporting. Because Nagaland is a "sensitive" area, no missionaries have been allowed to reside there since 1956.

American Lutherans began work in India in the 1840's. Their first field was in the Telugu country in south India, where they collaborated with the American Congregationalists. The *Reverend J. Heyer* of the *United Lutheran Church in America* opened the first station in Guntur in 1842. The *Augustana Church* sent its first missionary to the Telugu country in 1879. Out of these two missions grew the *Andhra Evangelical Lutheran Church,* organized in 1927. Education played a major role in the development of this great church. At one time it had eight hundred elementary schools (nationalized in 1960) and thirty-three secondary schools. The *Andhra Christian College* in Guntur has fifteen hundred students. Today the Evangelical Lutheran Church, with a membership of almost three hundred thousand, is larger than all the other Lutheran churches in south India combined.

The *Lutheran Church-Missouri Synod* began its mission in 1894 in the northwest corner of the Tamil country. In 1907 this was expanded to Nagercoil at the tip of India. Five years later the mission spread up the west coast to Trivandrum. Medical work got under way in 1913. A seminary was established in Nagercoil in 1922. The *India Evangelical Lutheran Church* became autonomous in 1958. Since then mission and church have been integrated. There are about 135 Indian pastors caring for forty thousand baptized members.

The *American Methodists* have been at work in India ever since 1856, when *Dr. and Mrs. William Butler* settled in Calcutta. The decision to enter India was the result of the vision of Dr. John P. Durbin, corresponding secretary of the mission, reinforced by the appeal of Alexander Duff, who visited the United States in 1854. *Miss Isabella Thoburn* and *Dr. Clara A. Swain,* the first appointees of the Women's Foreign Missionary Society, arrived in 1870. The former became an educator and founded the first Christian college for women in Lucknow. Dr. Swain pioneered in medical missions and established in 1874 the first women's hospital in Asia. Both institutions achieved outstanding fame. Two great missionary leaders were *James M. Thoburn* and *William Taylor,* both of whom became bishops. Under their leadership Methodist work in India and other parts of southern Asia greatly prospered through the years. The *Indian Methodist Church* organized its own missionary society in 1920. Its first missionaries went to Southern Rhodesia in 1938. Later on others went to Sarawak, the Andaman Islands, and Java.

Few missions in India have a bigger investment than the American Methodists. After 115 years of work their many institutions are to be found in all parts of the great country. In 1956, in celebration of the centenary of the Methodist work in India, the Central Conference set 1969 as the target date for total support of the ministry. By 1965 the church had reached approximately 60 percent of the goal. The target date has since been advanced to 1976.

The *Methodist Church in Southern Asia* is now divided into eleven annual conferences representing over six hundred thousand members. Its many hospitals, schools, and colleges are among the finest in the land. In spite of visa difficulties 165 American Methodist missionaries remain in India as fraternal workers.

The Mennonites are represented in India by the *General Conference Mennonite Church,* located in Madhya Pradesh since 1900. About thirty churches have arisen as a result of their work. An equal number of missionaries from the United States and Canada are assisting the national church. Mennonite missionaries have been seconded to Yeotmal Seminary, Vellore Medical College, and Woodstock School for missionaries' children.

During the drought in 1966-7 the *Mennonite Central Committee* organized and supervised the construction of 256 wells, twenty-one dams, three roads, and a school, in Bihar State.

In 1899 the *Mennonite Brethren Church* entered India, where it has worked for seventy years in Andhra Pradesh. The work has gone well. Today the *Andhra Mennonite Brethren Church* has twenty-five thousand members and a Christian community estimated at one hundred thousand. In 1966 it had only 121 preachers for 716 congregations. The work is still heavily subsidized from America.

Canada is represented in India by two missions of long standing: the *United Church of Canada,* whose missionaries are working with the Malwa Church Council of the *United Church of Northern India;* and the *Canadian Baptists,* working with the 110,000-member *Convention of Baptist Churches of the Northern Circars.*

Several large Pentecostal groups have made significant gains in India. Three of these are from the United States: *Assemblies of God, Church of God,* and *Church of God* (Cleveland). There are two Scandinavian groups, one from Norway and one from Sweden. In addition there are two indigenous groups, the *India Pentecostal Church* and the *Pentecostal Church of God of Andhra Pradesh.* All but one of these churches have a membership of between fifteen thousand and thirty thousand.

Continental Missions. The *Gossner Mission* (Germany) sent representatives to India in 1839. The work among the Gonds proved abortive when four of the six missionaries died of cholera. Mission stations were established in the Ganges valley in the 1840's and the 1850's. The mission's major undertaking was in Chota Nagpur, where the first baptisms took place in 1850. By 1857 there were nine hundred Christians, most of them won by fellow Kols. Steady growth characterized the latter half of the century.

The *Gossner Evangelical Lutheran Church,* established in the middle of the nineteenth century, received its autonomy in 1919. Today the church has one thousand congregations in the five states of Bihar, Orissa, Madhya Pradesh, West Bengal, and Assam. Its Christian community numbers over two hundred thousand. The mission continues to furnish fraternal workers at the invitation of the church.

The *Tamil Evangelical Lutheran Church,* the outgrowth of Ziegenbalg's mission to Tranquebar in 1706, now has a baptized membership of sixty-five thousand in 450 congregations. The well-known Indian bishop, *Rajah B. Manikam,* is the leader of this church. The *Santal Mission,* begun in 1867 and supported by missionaries from Norway, Denmark, and the United States of America, has produced the *Northern Evangelical Lutheran Church,* with over forty thousand baptized members in three hundred congregations.

Faith Missions. The American faith missions have not made the significant contribution in India that they have made in other parts of the world. Nevertheless, some of these evangelical groups have been there a long time and have done good work.

The first of the faith missions in India was the *Bible and Medical Missionary Fellowship,* which entered in 1852. Known then as the Zenana Bible and Medical Mission, it labored for the first one hundred years exclusively among the women of India, seeking to reach them through *zenanas,* hospitals, and schools. In 1952 it changed its character, began accepting men, and greatly enlarged its ministry in India, Pakistan, and, later, Nepal. In 1969 it announced plans to extend its work into Lebanon, Iran, Iraq, and probably Turkey. Today it supports over one hundred missionaries in various parts of India. BMMF in a uniquely altruistic way is not building a church or work of its own; most of its workers are seconded to institutions belonging to other missions. Non-Caucasians are welcomed as members of BMMF. An Indian council formed in 1968 is responsible for the recruitment and support of Indian colleagues.

The *Christian and Missionary Alliance* began its work in India in 1887. For a time its missionaries worked under the auspices of the North Berar Faith Mission, which merged with the C&MA in 1892. That same year seventeen missionaries were added to the group and twelve additional stations were opened. During the next five years seventy-seven missionaries went to India.

The Alliance churches in India have been self-governing and self-supporting for some years. Today fifty-four churches are organized into two synods, Gujarat and Marathi. The latter has two missionaries of its own in the Andaman Islands. Forty missionaries continue to serve with the

Alliance Church in India, principally in the fields of literature, radio, and theological education.

The Christian and Missionary Alliance, as its name implies, is a *missionary* outfit. It has one missionary overseas for every seventy-five church members at home, a record without precedent since the heyday of Moravian missions in the eighteenth century. Its nine hundred missionaries are serving in twenty-six countries and using 197 languages and dialects. Its overseas membership, now more than two hundred thousand, is twice the combined membership in the United States and Canada. Its chief emphasis is preaching the gospel and planting churches. In this it has been eminently successful. It can point to forty-five hundred fully self-supporting overseas churches and over five thousand students in thirty-three long-term Bible schools.

The *Ceylon and India General Mission* sent its first workers to south India in 1894. They settled in two districts. Working out from Bangalore, which later became its headquarters, it initiated work among the Tamils and, later on, the Telugus. In 1938 the mission transferred its Ceylon staff to north India, where they opened a second field in the United Province.

Worldwide Evangelization Crusade began work in India in 1928. Today it has some fifty missionaries scattered in various places throughout the country. They are engaged mostly in evangelistic and church planting work. WEC is one of the very few Western missions that have been able to work amicably with the three hundred indigenous assemblies headed by Bakht Singh. It draws its missionaries from the United States, Britain, Australia, New Zealand, and Canada.

The *Evangelical Alliance Mission* entered India in 1905. The *Reverend O. Dahlgren,* its first missionary, settled in Navaour in the Khandesh district of the Bombay presidency. The five years from 1945 to 1949 saw the greatest increase in the mission's staff in India. In 1952 TEAM expanded its work into the newly opened state of Gwalior. Its main work has been village evangelism among ten millions of people. The medical work includes a hospital and seven dispensaries. The Light of Life Correspondence School, which promotes Bible studies in twenty-four of the languages of India, has enrolled over a million students.

One of the more recent missions to India is the *Oriental Missionary Society,* whose first group of seven missionaries landed in 1941. Five areas of operation have been developed, three in the north and two in the south. The OMS has traditionally concentrated on Bible school work as a direct means to evangelism and church planting. Three seminaries have been established: at Allahabad (English), Madras (Tamil), and Karnataka (Karnataka). The churches brought into being by the OMS are organized under the name of the *Evangelical Christian Church of India.* Its thirty churches are divided into three regional conferences.

India was the first of twenty fields entered by the *Conservative Baptist Foreign Mission Society* since its inception in 1943. In 1945 it took over the work previously done by the Kurku and Central India Hill Mission, a British mission which had been in India since 1890. Later an adjoining mission, the Khirkian Gospel Mission, also merged with the Central Baptist India Mission, as CBFMS in India is called. By 1968 CBFMS had thirty-one missionaries in India. Evangelistic work among the Kurku and Gond peoples has not been very successful. Long-established churches, now in the second or third generation, often lack real spiritual life. In addition to medical work, CBFMS cooperates with Yeotmal Seminary and Calcutta Bible College.

Regions Beyond Missionary Union, one of the oldest faith missions, began work in India in 1890. The mission is located in north India near the border of Nepal. Through the years six main centers have been developed. The outstanding institution is the hospital at Raxaul, which is on the border of Nepal. It was established by *Dr. Cecil Duncan* of Edinburgh in 1930. Today it enjoys an honored reputation throughout north India and Nepal. It handles upwards of thirty thousand patients a year. Many Nepalese medical personnel, Christian and non-Christian, have been trained at Raxaul. The RBMU, by reason of its strategic geographical location, was a charter member of the United Mission to Nepal and spearheaded its thrust into that hermit kingdom in 1954.

Medical Missions. Wherever large numbers of poor, illiterate people live in crowded conditions, especially in a hot climate, there is bound to be a great deal of disease. Certainly this is true in India, where there is only one doctor to six thousand persons as compared with ten times that number in the United States. In this as in other areas of need, Christian missionaries rose to the challenge and combined medical skill with Christian compassion to meet the physical needs of the people.

Two outstanding medical institutions are worthy of mention: the *Christian Medical College and Hospital* in Vellore, and the *Ludhiana Christian Medical College* in north India. The former had its beginnings in 1900 when *Dr. Ida S. Scudder* started the work with an infirmary of one bed. The *Medical School for Women* came into being in 1918. In 1947 men students were admitted for the first time. When Dr. Scudder died in 1960, some sixty-two churches and missions in eight countries had combined with the churches of India to support the institution. The college and hospital currently have a staff of 315 full-time doctors, 305 graduate nurses, and 273 para-medical workers. Of this staff, forty-eight are foreign personnel from five countries. In training are 363 medical students, 354 nursing students, 90 student technicians, and 120 postgraduate students.

A similar, though smaller, institution in north India is *Ludhiana Christian Medical College,* established by *Dame Edith Brown* in 1894. It became a union institution shortly after independence in 1947. It is now supported by twenty different churches and missions. The college, now coeducational, is fully accredited and trains both doctors and nurses. To enumerate the many medical institutions maintained by Christian groups in India would be impossible; but in spite of their reputation for humanitarian service, they face an increasingly uncertain future. A survey made by the World Council of Churches in 1968 revealed that of one hundred hospitals in seven states, seventy were more than forty years old and twenty-five were more than seventy years old. All of them are obsolete and non-functional. To completely modernize these hospitals would cost well over $20 million. Moreover, the government of India, committed as it is to socialized medicine, is rapidly increasing both the number and the quality of its own medical facilities; and its hospitals are newer, better, and less expensive than mission hospitals. The *Christian Medical Association* has 450 member hospitals.

Theological Education.   India, with thirty-four high grade theological seminaries, has fared better than most countries when it comes to theological education. Nevertheless, there is still room for improvement. Too often mission boards have sacrificed quality for quantity, each mission insisting on having its own Bible school or seminary. In recent years there has been a movement toward union schools. Mergers have been taking place in various geographical areas, across denominational lines, on the basis of a common language. In 1964 three seminaries at Dornakal, Makinada, and Rajahmundry united to form the *Andhra Christian Theological College*. The following year three seminaries at Bareilly, Indore, and Saharanpur combined to form the *North India Theological College*. The academically strong schools are nearly all union institutions. The administration of these schools is largely in the hands of Indian nationals; but there is a high percentage of Western teachers, and heavy subsidies from the West are still required. There is also a paucity of theological texts in the regional languages. The four highest schools listed by the Theological Education Fund of the World Council of Churches are *Gurukul Lutheran Theological College, Leonard Theological College* at Jabalpur, *Serampore College,* and the *United Theological College* in Bangalore.

A young but growing seminary is *Union Biblical Seminary* in Yeotmal. It began as a small Free Methodist school in 1938, became a union seminary in 1953, and in 1964 was fully accredited by the Board of Theological Education of the National Council of Churches. Seventeen mission boards cooperate in its operation. It functions on two levels: a four-year post-high school course and a three-year graduate course leading to the B.D. degree. Yeotmal, with about one hundred students enrolled, is one of the largest theological schools in India.

Christian Literature.   With fourteen major languages, spoken by over 500 million people, India presents a peculiar challenge to the Christian church in the matter of Christian literature. The National Council of Churches in 1964 approved a plan to strengthen Christian literature work in all its aspects and in all the principal languages of India. Included in the plan are publishing houses, regional literature centers, and literature for tribal peoples, for non-Christians, for children, and for families. Good progress has been made in recent years in the production of theological literature in the Indian languages. Financial assistance has been provided by the Christian Literature Fund and the Theological Education Fund. At the present time some two dozen presses are operating full time turning out a steady stream of Christian literature. Scores of Christian periodicals are available in English and other languages. Much of this material is distributed through 140 distribution centers in all parts of the country. Of particular interest to India was the All-Asia Literature Conference convened in Singapore in 1970. Some one hundred Asian publishers went on record as follows: "The need of the hour is to establish publishing ministries that will outlast the missionary presence and keep on doing their work of evangelism and church growth no matter what the conditions are environmentally, politically, or militarily." Bible correspondence courses have been most helpful. The *Light of Life* course, prepared in 1949 by Dr. Donald Hillis of The Evangelical Alliance Mission, has been adopted by over a dozen other missions. It has been translated into twenty-four Indian langauges. By 1967 over a million and a half students had enrolled in the course, 85 percent of them non-Christians.

Bible Translation. With fourteen major languages and seven hundred different dialects, India poses a major problem for the Bible societies. The Calcutta Auxiliary Bible Society was the first, formed in 1811 with the help of the British and Foreign Bible Society. In 1935 the American Bible Society, which had supported the work in India since 1822, adopted a policy of collaboration with the BFBS. In 1944 the Bible Society of India, Pakistan, and Ceylon was established with the support of the American, British, and Scottish societies. Following independence, Pakistan and Ceylon established their own Bible societies. The Bible Society of India has been on its own since 1956, but it still receives large subsidies from abroad. Four Bible vans help in the work of distribution, which has increased 500 percent in the past decade to an annual figure of four million.

The entire Bible is now available in 25 languages, the New Testament in 40 languages, and Portions in an additional 65 languages, making a grand total of 130.

Wycliffe Bible Translators, known overseas as the Summer Institute of Linguistics, entered India in 1966. Already they have some forty linguists at work in eight tribes. They have singled out two hundred dialects in which they intend to work. In spite of all that has been done over the years, much still remains to be done. "For India's teeming millions the possession of even a small part of the Bible is still a dream to be realized."[2]

Mass Movements. According to Sherwood Eddy the various mass movements of the nineteenth century have accounted for 80 percent of the Christians in India. Involved in these mass movements were hundreds of thousands of Hindu "outcastes" who had been denied access to the Hindu temples and the village wells. Consequently they had nothing to lose and possibly something to gain by embracing the Christian faith. Such mass movements have both advantages and disadvantages for the Christian church. These mass defections from Hinduism are one reason for the anti-missionary spirit in India today. The missionaries have been accused of taking unfair advantage of the social conditions in which the "outcastes" found themselves. Now that "untouchability" has been outlawed, there is a feeling that these ex-Hindus should return to the fold. They also explain in part the great poverty that plagues the churches of India. Moreover, so long as the caste mentality lasts, the church in India will not be regarded as a prestigious institution. In spite of the lowly origin of most church members, however, the literacy rate among Christians is higher than it is for the country as a whole.

Interchurch Cooperation. This comes to focus in the *National Christian Council,* made up of fourteen regional councils. The greatest weakness of the council is its dependence on financial help from overseas. At the Triennial Assembly in 1967 an attempt was made to rectify the situation. The *Evangelical Fellowship of India,* founded in 1950, is a very active organization and through the years has had widespread support from evangelical missions, churches, organizations, and individuals. The general secretary is *Mr. Ben Wati.* In 1965 the EFI established the *Indian Evangelical Mission,* a purely indigenous work which now supports seven Indian missionaries. As its twentieth anniversary project the EFI sponsored an All-India Congress on Evangelism in Bombay in January, 1970. The purpose of the congress was to discover ways of implementing the findings of the Berlin and Singapore Congresses on Evangelism. Another active group is the *Union of Evangelical Students of India* which, though completely autonomous and self-supporting, works closely with the International Fellowship of Evangelical Students.

Indigenous Assemblies. *Brother Bakht Singh,* India's outstanding evangelical church planter, is the leader of a dynamic indigenous movement which is probably the fastest growing group in India. The three hundred assemblies, patterned after the Plymouth Brethren, are entirely self-supporting, self-governing, and self-propagating. A special feature of

2 British and Foreign Bible Society, *Annual Report,* 1965, p. 105.

the movement is the great Bible conferences attended by thousands of Indian Christians under tents or in the open air. Eating, sleeping, and living conditions at these conferences are purely Indian, very simple, and most economic. The ecclesiastical accoutrements, so necessary in the West, are completely missing. The preachers live by faith, supported by the freewill offerings of the Christians.

Church Union. From the very beginning of the missionary movement India has led the way in ecumenical relations. As early as 1806 William Carey suggested the convening of a worldwide missionary conference in South Africa in 1810. Missionaries looked forward to the day when God would establish one Church of Christ in India. First in their regional conferences and later in the all-India conferences, the missionaries practised intercommunion long before the idea caught on at home. In 1901 two Reformed denominations merged to form the *South India United Church*. In 1905 two Congregational denominations united to form the *Congregational General Union of South India*. Three years later these two bodies formed the *United Church of South India*. In 1947 the United Church merged with the Anglican and Methodist churches to form the *Church of South India,* which today has fifteen dioceses and a membership of 425,000. The Christian community is about 1,200,000.

The Church of South India has extended an invitation to other churches to join the union. The Baptists showed interest but later changed their minds. Ever since 1949 talks have been going on between the CSI and the Lutheran churches of south India. These churches have indicated that they do not oppose an episcopal polity in principle, but they have made it clear that they will not agree to a polity in which the office of the bishop is regarded as the essence of the church. The *Andhra Evangelical Lutheran Church,* the largest of the Lutheran churches in south India, is ready to join the union without delay. Three other Lutheran churches are in basic agreement; only minor details have to be worked out. The *India Evangelical Lutheran Church* (Missouri Synod) has shown an interest in the negotiations but remains hesitant to take definite action. In January, 1968, the CSI invited other churches to join in a wider union. Later that year the *United Basel Mission District Church Council of South Kanara and Coorg* joined the Mysore Diocese of the CSI. Other churches now engaged in union talks with the CSI are the *Methodist Church in Southern Asia,* the *Baptist Church in Northern Circars,* and the *Telugu Baptist Church*.

In the meantime the CSI has had to cope with internal strife. In 1966 a dissident group led by the Reverend V. J. Stephen withdrew and formed a new church. The move was occasioned by longstanding grievances of the low caste Pulayas, aided and abetted by the International Council of Christian Churches.

At the other end of the sub-continent is the *United Church of Northern India,* which resulted in 1924 from the union of the *Presbyterian Church in India* and the *Congregational Church in Western India.* The United Church came to include elements from four groups: Presbyterians, Congregationalists, Reformed, and Moravians, related to eleven overseas churches in six countries. Ever since 1929 efforts have been made to enlarge the union. After forty years of negotiations the fourth and final edition of the Plan of Union was adopted by six denominations, and the *Church of North India* was formally inaugurated at Nagpur on Advent Sunday, November 29, 1970. The six churches involved in the union are the *Council of Baptist Churches in North India,* the *Church of the Brethren,* the *Disciples of Christ,* the *Church of India, Pakistan, Burma and Ceylon* (Anglican), the *Methodist Church* (British and Australian Conferences), and the *United Church of Northern India.* The new church brings together more than half a million Protestant Christians.

Dialogue. India, with five or six indigenous religions and all three branches of the Christian religion, is an ideal place for dialogue. Dialogue between Protestants and Catholics dates from Vatican II. The visit of Pope Paul to Bombay in 1965 did much to advance the cause. To date dialogue has been concerned chiefly with theological matters. In April, 1967, 128 Roman Catholic, Protestant and Orthodox colleges joined to establish the *National Board of Christian Higher Education.* The Christian Union of India works closely with its counterpart, the Catholic Union of India. Together they seek to arouse and direct the political consciousness of Indian Christians, who in the past have tended to remain aloof from politics.

In February, 1969, more than forty Protestants and Roman Catholics participated in an interreligious dialogue convened in Bombay. Four workshops dealt with various aspects of dialogue. The first day a Roman Catholic priest delivered the sermon and Holy Communion was celebrated according to CSI rites. A Protestant preached during Roman Catholic mass the second day. The third day the group used a thoroughly indigenous version of the Eucharist, including a Sanskrit chant.

Dialogue in India is not confined to various branches of the Christian faith. It includes non-Christians as well. Christian-Hindu dialogue comes to focus at the *Christian Institute for the Study of Religion and Society* at Bangalore. The Christian-Muslim dialogue centers in the *Henry Martyn Institute of Islamic Studies* in Lahore.

Radio. Mass communications are extremely important in a populous country such as India, where the Protestants represent only 2.4 percent of the 540 million people. If missionaries ever have to withdraw from India, radio will become doubly important. There are no Christian radio stations in India; and it is difficult, if not impossible, to buy time on commercial stations. However, the gospel is penetrating India by means of the air waves. The principal purveyor is the *Far East Broadcasting Company,* whose powerful transmitters in Manila beam eighty programs a week in the major languages of India. Beginning in 1969 the FEBC began broadcasting into India from a powerful station erected in the Seychelles Islands. Radio Ceylon, a powerful government station in Colombo, is now used by missionaries to send the gospel into India.

Missionary Outreach of the National Churches. If India is ever to be evangelized it will be through the efforts of the national churches, not by the Western missions. There is evidence that the churches are beginning to assume more responsibility in this area. On the home front there are two indigenous groups, the *National Missionary Society* and the *Indian Missionary Society.* The former, dating back to 1905, was the brainchild of *K. T. Paul* and *Bishop Azariah.* Working in various states of India, it has become a leading factor in the Indianizing of Christianity. It has tried to make Christianity truly indigenous by rooting it in the life and soil of the East. As a result the program includes ashrams and brotherhoods as well as hospitals and schools.

The *Indian Evangelical Mission,* formed in 1965, is an interdenominational, evangelical mission operated by Indian personnel and financed by the freewill offerings of Indian Christians. Its board members are drawn from the Methodists, Anglicans, Baptists, Church of the Nazarene, and the Church of North India. Its main purpose is pioneer evangelism in India and overseas, where it seeks to place its missionaries under the auspices of other evangelical missions in those countries.

Most of the Indian churches have their own evangelistic outreach. Some of them are supporting missionaries overseas. The greatest missionary church is the *Mar Thoma Syrian Church of Malabar.* Seventy-five years ago it had one mission station. As a result of a mighty revival that swept through the whole church, it now has 145 mission stations in all parts of India. It supports 250 workers and spends annually 110,177 rupees.

Pakistan

Political History. Pakistan shares with India the long history, the rich culture, and the ancient civilization of the subcontinent of India. When Britain gave independence to the subcontinent in 1947 two nations emerged, India and Pakistan. One was predominantly Hindu and the other predominantly Muslim. The first few weeks of independence witnessed one of the greatest upheavals in history, when six million Muslims left India for Pakistan and four million Hindus fled from Pakistan to India. It was all over in about two weeks, but an estimated half-million persons were killed in the process. The death toll would have been higher had it not been for the timely intervention and protection of the Christian minority on both sides of the border.

So far Pakistan has had a turbulent history. In a five-year period six prime ministers presided over precariously balanced cabinets. Corruption became so rampant that in 1959 the military seized power and sent the politicians home. For ten years the country was ruled by General Ayub Khan, until he, too, was deposed in the spring of 1969, after five months of rioting. Pakistan's greatest problem has been its dispute with India over Kashmir. War has broken out on several occasions. Four times the United Nations ordered a plebiscite in Kashmir, but thus far India has refused to comply. This prolonged dispute has soured Pakistan's national spirit, drained its meager resources, and driven it into the arms of Red China, though it still remains a member of both CENTO and SEATO. Relations between Pakistan and India have somewhat improved since the Tashkent Agreement in 1966. Once a staunch ally of the West, Pakistan in recent years has taken a somewhat neutral stance in the Cold War.

The People. Pakistan is divided into two unequal parts with one thousand miles of Indian territory between them. West Pakistan, with the federal capital (Islamabad) and 85 percent of the territory, is the more important of the two, though it has less than half of the population. There are two official languages: Urdu, spoken in West Pakistan; and Bengali, used in East Pakistan. English is widely spoken in both parts and will remain an official language until 1972 at least.

Pakistan has only a meager supply of natural resources, insufficient rainfall, and an underdeveloped economy. Perennial drought in the west and typhoons and tidal waves in the east play havoc with Pakistan's economy. Consequently the people of Pakistan are extremely poor, even by Asian standards, in spite of the fact that three successive Five-Year Plans have been moderately successful. With only 20 percent of the population able to read, illiteracy remains a major economic and social problem. The population of Pakistan is 125 million, 45 percent in the west and 55 percent in the east.

Religion. Pakistan is an Islamic republic. Some 88 percent of the people are Muslim. Twelve million Hindus, most of them in East Pakistan, form the largest religious minority. Christians number approximately 700,000. Of these, 500,000 are found in West Pakistan, as are also more than 80 percent of the missionaries. Most of the Christians are converts from among low-caste Hindus; they came into the Christian fold as a result of mass movements many years ago. As a result the Christian church in Pakistan suffers from a poor image. Even in recent years very few converts have come from Islam. Most of them are from a nominal Christian background.

During the first fifteen years of independence Pakistan, though an Islamic state, practised a genuine form of religious liberty. The new constitution promulgated in 1962 reiterated the principle of religious freedom; but in spite of this a serious erosion took place during the sixties. Muslim extremists in and out of government called for the expulsion of Christian missionaries. Newspapers accused the missionaries of "buying" converts. Some missionaries were placed under strict surveillance and every move had to be reported to the local police. From time to time anti-Christian demonstrations broke out in various parts of the country, immobilizing the missionaries and intimidating the Christians. Some missionaries and nationals were roughed up in the course of their evangelistic work. On several occasions Scriptures were seized and burned in the streets. In East and West Pakistan missionaries were prohibited from entering certain border areas.

At one time the government was urged to nationalize all mission schools; but in spite of all the pressure it has always refused to do so. In August of 1965 Hamid Rheza Gilani, parliamentary secretary, said that his government had no intention of banning the activities of Christian missionaries. In May of the next year, accusations that Christian schools were misusing their educational activities to make converts among non-Christian students were rejected by the Commission for Education and Welfare in a report to the government. In July, 1969, the government warned that several hundred Christian schools face nationalization under a new plan designed to overhaul the entire educational structure. Time will reveal whether this means an eventual government takeover of Christian institutions or simply a more thorough "Pakistanization" of their administration, curriculum, and financing.

Early Missions. When India received its independence in 1947, the subcontinent was divided into two parts—India and Pakistan, with the latter divided into East and West. As a result, it is not easy to trace the historical development of Christian work in that part of the world, for some churches were split in two when partition took place. Only now, after more than twenty years, is the situation gradually straightening itself out. Several small missions have work in East and West Pakistan, including the Bible Society. It will be necessary then to deal with the two regions separately.

West Pakistan. The American Presbyterians have the oldest and largest work in this part of the world. Two groups shared the field: the former *Presbyterian Church in the U.S.A.* and the former *United Presbyterian Church in North America.* Most of the churches brought into existence by the first group have been on the Indian side of the border since 1947, and are now part of the Church of North India. The relatively few churches of this group which remained in Pakistan recently became, along with the Methodists and the Anglicans, part of the newly formed *United Church of Pakistan*. The churches established by the United Presbyterian Church of North America joined together in 1961 to form the *United Presbyterian Church in Pakistan*. In its seven presbyteries there are 145 self-supporting congregations, with approximately 55,000 communicant members and a Christian community of 140,000. Christians from Reformed or Presbyterian background make up about 60 percent of the Protestant Christian community in West Pakistan. Some eighty fraternal workers of the United Presbyterian Church in the U.S.A. are now serving in West Pakistan. The United Presbyterian Church in Pakistan suffered a serious rupture in April, 1968, when the moderator, K. L. Nasir, and about one-third of the synod members formed a new church, which later joined the International Council of Christian Churches.

The pioneer missionary was *Charles W. Forman,* who gave forty years of outstanding service, mostly in educational work. The first station was opened in Lahore in 1849; and to this day Lahore remains the hub of Presbyterian work in West Pakistan. Here they maintain five institutions of higher learning, three of which are over one hundred years old: *Rang Mahal High School* for boys; *Forman High School* for girls; *Forman Christian College,* affiliated with the University of Punjab; *Kinnaird College* for women; and *Kinnaird Training Center.* These are among the oldest and finest colleges in Pakistan and draw students from East Pakistan and foreign countries. Equally famous is *Gordon College* in Rawalpindi. It also is affiliated with the University of Punjab. Medical work centers in four institutions, one of which is the *United Christian Hospital,* which was founded in 1947. It is now an ecumenical institution supported by half a dozen missions. There are also some fifteen Christian high schools and dozens of primary schools throughout West Pakistan. In addition to several Bible schools for the training of evangelists and Biblewomen, the Presbyterians established the *Gujranwala Theological Seminary* in 1877. It is now an ecumenical institution training students for the Presbyterians, Methodists, and Anglicans. It has two programs, one post-high school and the other post-college.

The *Church Missionary Society* entered West Pakistan in the middle of the nineteenth century. The first station to be opened was Karachi in 1850. Peshawar, Multan, Narowal, Bannu, Lahore, and Quetta followed in rapid succession. The Diocese of Lahore was established in 1877. About 1960 a second diocese was set up in Karachi with the *Right Reverend Chandu Ray,* first Pakistani bishop, as its presiding officer. A second bishop, *Inayat Masih,* consecrated in 1968, is now bishop of the Lahore diocese. Serving with the CMS in West Pakistan are other Anglican societies: the *Church Missionary Society of Australia* and the *Church Missionary Society of New Zealand.* Much of the women's work in these parts was carried on for many years by the *Zenana Missionary Society,* which merged with the CMS in 1957. The CMS work in West Pakistan is divided into three areas. Two hospitals in Peshawar and Bannu minister to the tribesmen of the Frontier Province. Nine centers are maintained in the predominantly Hindu province of Punjab. At Quetta, the only station in Baluchistan, there is a fairly new hospital and a large church. The CMS schools are largely for the children of Christian homes.

Most of the Angelican missionaries in this part of the world appear to be theologically conservative. Howard A. Johnson, Canon of the Cathedral Church of St. John the Divine, New York, was surprised by the caliber of CMS missionary he found in West Pakistan. On a world tour in 1960, he visited Pakistan as one of eighty countries in which the Anglicans have work. This is what he said: "First in Karachi, later in Lahore, and elsewhere in Pakistan, I encountered a type of Anglicanism that was new to my experience. It was an evangelicalism marred, as it seemed to me, by Biblical Fundamentalism, Puritanism, and Pietism. In my vocabulary, these are *not* complimentary words!"[3]

The *American Methodists* have been in this part of the world for almost one hundred years. Karachi, opened in 1873, was their first station. Methodist work in Lahore was started in 1881 as an English congregation following the William Taylor revivals. In 1900 the English work was given over to the British Methodists and thereafter the Methodist Episcopal Church devoted its efforts to vernacular work, especially among the depressed classes. A mass movement began among the "outcastes" of the Central Punjab. In 1902 there were only twelve hundred Christians; by 1915 there were fifteen thousand. Until 1970 Methodist work was divided into two parts: the Indus River Annual Conference with seven districts, organized in 1924; and the Karachi Provisional Annual Conference with two districts, organized in 1959. Prior to its absorption into the United Church of Pakistan, the Methodist community numbered about fifty-six thousand and was served by 87 ordained preachers, 112 local preachers, and 10 evangelistic missionaries. Here as elsewhere the Methodists carried on a well-rounded program of educational, medical, and evangelistic work. Besides maintaining many institutions of their own, they cooperated closely with several ecumenical institutions.

The *Conservative Baptist Foreign Mission Society* entered West Pakistan in 1954 and has established several small churches and a hospital. Tribal work was begun among the Marwaris and the Odes. Bible correspondence courses have been fruitful. CBFMS now has thirty missionaries in the country engaged in village evangelism, church planting, literature, and Bible school and medical work.

Interdenominational Missions. The oldest faith mission in the world is the *Bible and Medical Missionary Fellowship,* founded in 1852 as the Zenana Bible and Medical Mission. For almost one hundred twenty years

---

[3] Howard A. Johnson, *Global Odyssey,* (New York: Harper & Row, 1963), p. 207.

its dedicated workers have served in various capacities in the subcontinent of India. It operates very few institutions of its own. Most of its missionaries are seconded to institutions maintained by others. The only BMMF institution is the *Kinnaird High School* for girls in Lahore; it has seven hundred students, both Muslim and Christian. BMMF missionaries are working in a number of cooperative projects and institutions in West Pakistan.

The *Worldwide Evangelization Crusade* has been in Pakistan since 1925 and today has three centers of work, Karachi, Quetta, and Peshawar. The *Afghan Border Crusade* is an international mission founded in 1944 by *W. Jack Ringer* and based in Great Britain. It aims to evangelize the Pathans in the northwest frontier of West Pakistan. It also has many contacts with the Afghans on both sides of the border.

With fifty-one missionaries in ten centers in the extreme north, *The Evangelical Alliance Mission* is the largest faith mission in Pakistan. Its headquarters is in Abbottabad, where the Bach Hospital is located. When workers are available and permission is granted, TEAM hopes to begin work again in nearby Kashmir. Other faith missions with work in West Pakistan are *International Missions, Incorporated; International Christian Fellowship* (formerly Ceylon and India General Mission); *Woman's Union Missionary Society,* the oldest faith mission in the United States; and *Christian Missions in Many Lands.*

East Pakistan. East Pakistan includes only 15 percent of the total land area of Pakistan, but it contains 55 percent of the population, which makes it one of the most densely populated regions in Asia. To make matters worse, only 130 of the 700 Christian missionaries in Pakistan are in the eastern region. Consequently East Pakistan is one of the most neglected parts of the non-Christian world.

Baptist Missions. The oldest and largest work in East Pakistan is that of the *Baptist Missionary Society,* under which William Carey served from 1793 to 1834. Work started at Dinajpur in 1795. Jessore was occupied in 1805, Dacca in 1816, Barisal in 1828, Khulna in 1860, Chittagong in 1881, and Rangpur in 1891. Two other centers were opened in 1901. After almost two hundred years this historic mission continues its witness to the Muslims and Hindus in this part of the world. Today its missionaries are engaged in evangelistic, medical, and educational work in connection with the *Baptist Union of Pakistan.* The largest institution is the *Chandraghona Christian Hospital,* where ten of the thirty missionaries are located. The two most important events in recent years were the addition of a new wing to the hospital and the founding of *East Pakistan College of Christian Theology.* Also working with the Baptist Union are missionaries from Australia and New Zealand.

Two Baptist missions from the United States have taken up work in East Pakistan in the postwar period. The first was the *Association of Baptists for World Evangelism,* which began in 1956. Its work now includes three main areas: Chittagong, Hill Tracts, and the Memorial Christian Hospital near Cheringa. The work has been difficult and progress has been slow. For a time the mission was plagued by illness and death, and the missionary force was reduced to four. Its missionaries now number forty-six. The ABWE is the only mission working south of the city of Chittagong. The *Southern Baptists* entered this part of the world in 1957. Their main work is in the capital of Dacca, where they have two health and welfare centers and a publication office. At present they have twenty-three career missionaries in East Pakistan. Their seven churches have been organized into the *East Pakistan Baptist Union.*

Pentecostal Missions. The *Assemblies of God* work dates back to pre-Partition days and was started by *Abdul Munshie,* son of a Muslim priest. Most of the work is located in ten centers in the Ganges Delta, with two stations in the Hill Tracts near the Burma border. Like everyone else, the Pentecostals have found Pakistan barren ground. After several decades of effort they have only fifty-five church members, most of them from low caste Hindu families. This is partially accounted for by a drop in the number of missionaries in recent years and an exodus of Christians to India. A second Pentecostal mission is the *Church of God* (Anderson, Indiana), which reports three small churches in East Pakistan.

Other Missions. These include the *International Christian Fellowship,* which has ten missionaries working in three strategic areas; and *Christian Missions in Many Lands.* These are the only two missions with work in both East and West Pakistan.

The Bible Societies. The three well-known Bible societies have worked in Pakistan for many years. The entire Bible is available in Urdu, Bengali, Sindhi, Punjabi, and Kashmiri. The New Testament is complete in seven languages. Portions are available in six other languages and dialects. The Bible House in Pakistan operates in two separate units, each with its own office, secretary, and annual report. The Bible House in the West is in Lahore; the one in the East is in Dacca.

Relief Work. During the past decade there has been a good deal of relief work done in both East and West Pakistan. In the east it was occasioned by typhoons and tidal waves, in the west by floods and the Indian-Pakistani war over Kashmir. Regular relief on a continuing basis was administered by *Church World Service* and on an emergency basis by it and the *World Council of Churches.* Most of this aid was channeled through the two National Christian Councils in Pakistan. In 1966 the CWS program was cut 40 percent by action of the government. In 1968, when the (USA) Public Law 480 program was terminated, the CWS withdrew its full-time representatives from Karachi and Dacca. In addition to these larger programs, many of the individual missions conducted their own relief programs, in this way demonstrating their concern for the welfare of the entire community, non-Christian as well as Christian.

Ecumenical Relations. Pakistan has two *National Christian Councils,* one in the east and the other in the west. Ten missionary bodies and six churches are affiliated with the East Pakistan Christian Council. The council in West Pakistan has an even wider base. In West Pakistan there is a second group, the *Evangelical Fellowship of West Pakistan.* In both East and West there is a *Christian Medical Association* which helps to coordinate the medical programs of the various groups. The three historic churches in West Pakistan—Presbyterian, Methodist, and Anglican—joined together in 1970 to form the *United Church of Pakistan.* This new church is organized around five dioceses, along the same lines as the Church of North India which came into existence about the same time.

The Christian Presence. In all Muslim countries Christians are a small minority. Pakistan is no exception. The Protestant community numbers about seven hundred thousand, most of whom are in West Pakistan. Of all the churches in West Pakistan, the United Church of Pakistan is the strongest, in terms of both membership and responsibility. All its pastors are fully supported by the congregations. Some of the most prestigious schools and colleges are church-related; but only a small percentage of the students are professing Christians. One serious handicap is the fact that many of the Pakistani Christians were converts many years ago from low caste Hindu communities; and their economic and social status has not changed much in the intervening years. Converts from Islam come one by one. Moreover, most of the churches are in the rural areas; consequently poverty and illiteracy are continuing problems. There are Bible schools, but the graduates cannot always find full-time employment in the churches. This is especially true in East Pakistan, where the church is exceedingly weak.

In recent years, however, there have appeared hopeful signs on the horizon. David Bentley-Taylor of the International Fellowship of Evangelical Students, after a visit to Pakistan in 1969 wrote: "In West Pakistan I was amazed at the progress made by the previously rather nominal evangelical student movement. With Reverend David Penman of the Church Missionary Society as its executive secretary, it has leapt into life among graduates and faces now the problems of rapid growth."[4]

In the spring of 1969 a four-man team of Indonesian Christian leaders paid a two-week visit to West Pakistan to share with the churches there

---

4 *Circular Letter,* May, 1969.

something of the revival blessing experienced in recent years in Indonesia. Wherever they went—Karachi, Sialkot, Rawalpindi, Abbottabad, Peshawar—hundreds of Christians were revived and hundreds of non-Christians were led to Christ.

> In one meeting, so many stood up indicating their desire for salvation, that the speakers had to warn them that those who did not mean business with God should sit down. Instead, even more stood up. In these meetings a large number of non-Christians were also present. In the Lahore meeting, so many came forward for salvation that the counselling team was completely overwhelmed.[5]

The Pakistani government is now in the process of revising the constitution. It is hoped that the new constitution will provide for genuine freedom of religion such as exists in Indonesia.

Afghanistan

Political History. Through the centuries Afghanistan has been invaded by the Persians, Greeks, Mongols, and Turks. Afghanistan's modern history has witnessed foreign interference but never complete conquest. King Mohammed Zahir Shah, who succeeded his assassinated father in 1933, was under the domination of his uncles until 1963; then he asserted himself and shook off their hold. On October 1, 1964, the king introduced a new constitution which provides for political parties, universal suffrage, a free press, an independent judiciary, a cabinet government responsible to parliament, and freedom of worship. In the Cold War Afghanistan has consistently maintained a neutral position. The government has accepted aid from both the United States and Russia, though the people have no love for the Russians.

The People. The population of Afghanistan is approximately sixteen million. The two major languages are Persian and Pushtu. Some 60 percent of the people are Pushtuns (Pathans) and 30 percent are Tajiks, of Iranian descent. The remaining 10 percent is divided among eighteen or twenty tribal groups each speaking its own dialect. Afghanistan must be reckoned among the more backward countries of the world. The illiteracy rate—92 percent—is one of the highest in the world. There is not a single mile of railway track in the whole country; people still travel by horse, mule, or camel, or on foot. Fewer than 10 percent of the people live in the cities.

Religion. Islam is the state religion of Afghanistan and 99 percent of the population are devotees of that religion. The constitution of 1964 guarantees freedom of worship, but this is honored mostly in the breach.

---

[5] David Bakhsh, *World News*, January-March, 1969, p. 4.

Here, as elsewhere, the power of the *mullahs* over the people is very great. They teach the principles of Islam in the village schools and are in charge of the mosques. Missionaries are not permitted to live, much less labor, in Afghanistan. Government officials deny that there is a single Christian national in the country. Yet there are signs that the winds of change are beginning to blow in Afghanistan, and it may be only a few years until a genuine form of religious liberty will be achieved. In the meantime, little by little, a Christian presence is being established in this Muslim country.

Missions on the Border.   For several decades mission groups working in countries contiguous with Afghanistan have tried to establish contact with Afghans on both sides of the border. Among these are the *Afghan Border Crusade, Bible and Medical Missionary Fellowship, Central Asian Mission, The Evangelical Alliance Mission, Church Missionary Society,* and the *American Presbyterians.* Thousands of Afghans have been treated in mission hospitals and clinics and a few have been educated in mission schools. Most of this has taken place in the Northwest Frontier Province of West Pakistan where the famous Khyber Pass provides a highway between the two countries. In recent years it has been possible for medical personnel of these various missions to visit Afghanistan to conduct temporary clinics in various parts of the country; but they have always gone in as medical practitioners.

The Christian Presence.   Leading the way and heading the list is *Dr. J. Christy Wilson,* son of Presbyterian missionaries to Iran. He first went to Afghanistan twenty years ago at the invitation of the Afghan government to teach. For a time he was principal of a boys' school of two thousand students. He also taught English to the crown prince. By his gracious manner, his quiet spirit, his evident sincerity, and his personal charm he made friends not only in the international community but also among the high Afghan officials. It was not long before Dr. Wilson became the best known, most trusted foreigner in Kabul.

Dr. Wilson started a Sunday school for the members of the American community. Out of this grew a small church which met in the Wilsons' home. When church and school grew to the point where a full-time person was needed, the American Christians in Kabul requested the government to relieve Dr. Wilson of his teaching contract to become chaplain to the American community. The request was granted and in 1956 Dr. Wilson became pastor of the Community Christian Church in Kabul. A second church was opened in Kandahar, three hundred miles southwest of Kabul. Dr. Wilson was officially pastor of this church also. His Sunday sermons were taped and sent to Kandahar, where Mr. Norman Friberg, a dedicated layman, led the services. Still later a third church was organized at Bost. These three churches are strictly for members of the international community. They are absolutely out of bounds to Afghan citizens except for Christmas services and funerals.

In connection with the church in Kabul, in 1958 Dr. Wilson opened a Christian school, Ahlman Academy, for the children of the international community. The school is self-supporting and all the teachers are dedicated Christians who go to Afghanistan for the express purpose of strengthening the Christian presence in a Muslim country still officially closed to the Christian gospel. Through the years a number of Afghan students have enrolled at the academy. Boys and girls of all nations are hearing the gospel.

Another American couple, *Rex and Jeanne Blumhagen,* both medical doctors, are very much a part of the Christian presence in Afghanistan. During their first term of duty, Dr. Rex was medical attaché for the American Embassy. Wishing to do something for the appalling needs of the Afghan people, Dr. Rex resigned from the embassy staff, returned to the United States, and joined the *Bible and Medical Missionary Fellowship.* Today he and his wife are back in Afghanistan on loan to the *Medical Assistance Program* working under contract for the Afghan government. For two terms now the Blumhagens have been traveling with a mobile clinic to the remote parts of the country, where health service is nonexistent.

Mention should be made of another couple, *Mr. and Mrs. Norman Friberg,* who taught English for eight years under the Columbia University Team. They, too, returned to the States, became members of the Bible and Medical Missionary Fellowship, and in 1966 returned to Afghanistan, where he became chaplain to the foreign community in Kandahar and Bost. He also gives time to the Afghan Literacy Project and Ahlman Academy.

Another of these Christian groups is the *National Organization for Ophthalmic Rehabilitation.* In the summer of 1969 the Minister of Health laid the cornerstone of the new Institute for the Blind, which will be used initially for an eye hospital until the proposed NOOR hospital is erected. NOOR personnel are all dedicated Christians whose professional skills and Christian compassion are quietly bearing fruit for the glory of God and the extension of His Kingdom.

The most amazing breakthrough of all was the visit to Kabul in November, 1969, of the five-member Teen Team sponsored by *Youth for Christ International.* Over seven hundred people of the international community and of the nation's intelligentsia crowded into the ballroom of the new Intercontinental Hotel to hear "Music with a Message" by five American teen-age Christians. Their youthful charm, their neat appearance, their radiant faces, and their top-flight musical artistry captivated the capacity crowd and conveyed clearly, with the use of contemporary music, their message of the love of God. The following day *The Kabul Times* carried a highly complimentary account of the performance on its front page. The president of Radio Afghanistan called the musical group a "holy delegation." A cabinet minister referred to their coming as "light from God." The following night they held a concert in the Khyber Restaurant, and over 450 world travelers, hippies, and local students crammed the private dining hall, where the manager served free tea to all in appreciation for the Teen Team's program. All this took place in a country where the Christian missionary is excluded and the Christian gospel is outlawed. There are no missionaries in Afghanistan; but there are three Christian congregations serving several hundred Christian expatriates. In addition, there are at least forty or fifty professional people, mostly medical personnel, who are in the country for the express purpose of serving the people of Afghanistan in the name and spirit of Jesus Christ.

Government permission was granted to the church in Kabul to erect its own building, the first church ever to be built in Afghanistan. On Pentecost Sunday, May, 1970, the Community Christian Church of Kabul was dedicated as "a house of prayer for all nations."

Nepal

Political History. The political unity of Nepal began in 1771, when the great Gurkha king, Prithwi Narayan Shah, conquered the kingdoms of the Valley of Kathmandu and gradually subjugated the rest of the country. The Gurkha dynasty ruled Nepal for 180 years, until its power was broken in 1950 by the National Congress Party of Nepal. Since then it has been a constitutional monarchy. King Mahendra is a popular and progressive monarch who is trying to modernize his ancient kingdom. In 1955 Nepal joined the United Nations. In 1963 King Mahendra issued a set of New Laws in which he outlawed such long-standing social evils as caste, bigamy, and child marriage.

The People. The Gurkhas descended from the Hindus who fled from Rajputana in north India during the Muslim invasions and intermarried with the tribes of the area about sixty miles west of Kathmandu. Intellect and culture gave them the advantage over their neighbors, and once they had obtained local domination the conquest of the entire country was ensured. There are ten million people in Nepal and about three million Nepalese living outside of Nepal in Sikkim and north India. The Gurkhas are among the finest soldiers in the world; at one time they formed the backbone of the British army in India.

Religion. Nepal was the birthplace of Gautama Buddha, and early in its history Buddhism spread over most of the country. Today 40 percent of the people are Buddhists; but Hinduism is the state religion, and it is unconstitutional for a Hindu to change his religion. If a Hindu becomes a

Christian he is liable to a one-year prison term; and the person who baptizes him is liable to six years in prison. In 1959 Pastor Prem Pradhan baptized nine converts, all of whom were sentenced to one year in jail. Prem Pradhan received a six-year sentence but was released after four and one-half years. Since then no further arrests have been made, even though Nepalese Christians have engaged in evangelistic work and Scripture distribution on a wide scale and Prem Pradhan has baptized more converts. Foreigners, of course, are strictly forbidden to proselytize. When the New Laws were promulgated in 1963 it was hoped that King Mahendra might relax these laws, but he did not. There are still remnants of animism among some of the hill people.

The Closed Door. For over two hundred years Nepal was sealed off from all contact with the outside world. For decades Christian missions in northern India had hoped and prayed for the door into Nepal to open. During this time they operated schools and hospitals close to the borders of Nepal on the east, west, and south. In this way thousands of Nepalese heard the gospel and not a few of them became believers. Most of these remained in north India; a few returned to their own country. *Sadhu Sundar Singh* made an evangelistic trip into Nepal in the 1920's. At his urging, the *National Missionary Society of India* sent its first missionary to Nepal; but he was able to remain only a short time. The revolution of 1950 terminated this long period of isolation. During the fifties diplomatic, economic, and other missions entered Nepal for the first time, and with them a certain number of committed Christians. Nepalese Christians began to return home.

The Open Door. The first religious group to enter Nepal was the *Roman Catholic Mission,* which had been based at nearby Patna. The four-member *Peace of Christ Brotherhood* of the Mar Thoma Church of South India established a permanent work in Nepal in 1952. The next mission to get permission to enter the country was the *Nepal Evangelistic Band,* a British faith mission which had been carrying on medical work in the border town of Nautanwa since 1936. Today the NEB has forty missionaries in three stations in central Nepal. In their hospital at Pokhra there are five doctors, four of them women—something of a record in mission hospitals. In recent years two other faith missions have entered Nepal and are working under the aegis of the NEB: the *International Christian Fellowship* in 1969 and the *Worldwide Evangelization Crusade* in 1970. In 1957 *The Leprosy Mission* (British) opened a hospital in Kathmandu. The following year the *Seventh Day Adventists* opened a hospital in Banepa. *Wycliffe Bible Translators* (Summer Institute of Linguistics) began work in Nepal in 1966. Already they have thirty-five linguists at work in ten tribes. The *National Missionary Society of India* has work in Butwal that is maintained by a Syrian Christian group.

United Mission to Nepal. Perhaps the most exciting Christian venture in this Himalayan kingdom is the *United Mission to Nepal,* which began its work in 1954. Rather than enter the country one by one, ten missionary societies decided to pool their resources and work together as a single organization with Nepal. So successful was the venture that other missions joined; today the United Mission has 130 missionaries belonging to twenty-eight missions and organizations from fifteen countries, including India and Japan. It is without doubt the largest, most inclusive of all the united missions in the world.

The UMN is unique in that it is completely separate from the emerging church in that country. It works in cooperation with, and under contract to, the government. Every new project must receive government approval and fit into the overall plans for the development of the country. The mission began in a modest way with medical work in the capital of Kathmandu. Through the years it has expanded its program to include fifteen cities and villages in all parts of the country. Its projects include three hospitals, two high schools, five clinics, one dispensary, a technical institute, and several agricultural projects. Every five years the mission must draw up a new contract with the government. If the contract is not renewed, the mission must leave Nepal. The latest contract, signed in January, 1970, restricted the mission to education and health programs, which means giving up agriculture and technology.

The mission as such is not permitted to engage in any kind of religious activity, and it has been careful to abide by the terms of the contract. Individual missionaries, however, have been able to share their faith on a man-to-man basis, and to date no one has been expelled. The missionaries with the United Mission are an unusually competent and dedicated group. They love Nepal and its people and are thrilled to be engaged in pioneer work in an exotic country. Dr. and Mrs. Robert Fleming, who have been with the mission since 1954 and who retired in 1970, have decided to stay on in Kathmandu![6]

The Emerging Church. The indigenous church in Nepal is centered around a dynamic leader, *Prem Pradhan,* a former Nepalese lieutenant in the Indian army who was converted from Hinduism to Christianity in Darjeeling. In 1959, after graduation from the Allahabad Bible Seminary in India, he returned to Nepal to evangelize his own people. After baptizing his first nine converts, in violation of the law, he spent almost five years in prison; during that time he led some twenty-five prisoners to faith in Christ. Following his release he and his converts resumed their evangelistic work throughout the country. It is estimated that there are at present about one hundred twenty-five baptized believers meeting in some twenty centers throughout the country.

---

[6] Their story has been told in *The Fabulous Flemings of Kathmandu,* by Grace N. Fletcher (New York: E. P. Dutton, 1964).

Wherever the Christians are located they have formed themselves into small groups which carry out the normal functions of a church. Where they are of sufficient size they arrange for a pastor, maintain a treasury, and administer the sacraments. In some cases they have erected church buildings, but they have developed little if any ecclesiastical structure. So far as Prem Pradhan is concerned, this is a matter of both convenience and conviction; convenience because of government restrictions and conviction because of his Plymouth Brethren background. He was converted through a member of this group and he is in touch with the Bakht Singh movement in India. The twenty congregations formed a loose Nepal Christian Fellowship in 1960. In 1966 they organized the *Evangelical Christian Church of Nepal.* It has officers and holds an annual conference for fellowship, prayer, and Bible exposition.

All this activity is illegal; but the Christians, in the glow of their first love, are determined to preach Christ. If the government wants to prosecute them they are prepared to pay the price for their faith. In fact, Prem Pradhan has the rather novel idea that religious freedom would be a bad thing for the infant church. The gospel spreads farther and the church grows faster, according to him, when Christians are a persecuted minority. Paul gloried in his infirmities; Prem exults in persecution.

Outside Assistance. The tiny church in Nepal gets indirect help from various organizations outside the country. The *Darjeeling Hills Bible School* offers a two-year course in Nepali. Over half the graduates are now working in Nepal. Christian literature in Nepali is produced by the *Nepali Christian Literature Society,* also located in Darjeeling. The *Bible Correspondence Institute,* based in India, sends Bible courses in Nepali to thousands of Nepalese inside and outside Nepal. The *Bible Society of India* supplies Scriptures. The Nepali Bible was published about the turn of the century. A revised edition of the New Testament became available in 1961. The revision of the Old Testament is under way at present. Two powerful radio stations beam the gospel into Nepal, one in Manila and the other in the Seychelles Islands in the Indian Ocean. *Missionary Aviation Fellowship* has applied for permission to fly its planes in Nepal; but to date it has not been granted.

The Christian Presence. As might be expected, the Christian presence in Nepal is rather weak. Baptized Christians, in about twenty congregations, number approximately one hundred twenty-five. It is estimated that there are another one hundred Indian Christians employed in secular jobs in Nepal. A third group of Christians, at least two hundred strong, is made up of missionaries and Christians attached to the various secular aid missions. Altogether there are between four hundred and five hundred Christians in the country. This is a tiny minority among a population of ten million; but their influence is out of all proportion to their numbers.

Ceylon

Political History. Ceylon had the dubious distinction of being under the rule of three colonial powers: Portugal, Holland, and Britain. Each remained for about one hundred fifty years; each imposed on Ceylon its own language and religion. Ceylon achieved independence in 1948. Since then it has had its share of trouble—political, economic, social, and religious. The prime minister was assassinated in 1959. Communism is fairly strong, and more than one government has remained in power only with the reluctant cooperation of leftist political parties. Injustice and discrimination against minority groups have produced a sense of frustration. Labor unrest and corruption have adversely affected the economy.

The People. The population of Ceylon stands at about twelve million. The Sinhalese, with 8,500,000, are the largest group. The second largest group is the Tamils, with 2,500,000. The Moors and the Malays account for another 750,000. A small but influential group is the Burghers who number about 60,000. Here as elsewhere in the world, the dominant group has tried to force its language on the other groups with disastrous results. Communal riots broke out in 1958, and a state of emergency was declared. Since then a precarious peace has prevailed between the Sinhalese and the Tamils. Tamil has been added as a second national language; but English continues to be widely used.

Religion. Ceylon is a pluralistic society, with each of the major groups practising its own religion. The Sinhalese have been Buddhists ever since Buddhism was introduced into the country from India in the third century B.C. The Tamils are Hindus. The Moors and the Malays are followers of the prophet Mohammed. Christians number approximately one million, with Roman Catholics outnumbering the Protestants nine to one. In 1961 the department of education made the teaching of religion compulsory in all the schools. In each case the religion taught is that of the parents, not the teachers. Christian students are taught Christianity provided there are at least fifteen Christians in the class.

A proposal that Buddhism be made the state religion was approved by the cabinet in 1964. The government is not anti-Christian. Missionaries are welcome, but on a quota basis; consequently the number of missionaries in Ceylon is at an all time low. Beginning on January 1, 1966, Sunday became a working day. It has been replaced with a Buddhist holiday, Poya Day, which coincides with the four phases of the moon. This demanded some adjustments on the part of the churches. Some churches now conduct their worship services on Poya Day; others continue to observe Sunday. Some take advantage of both. The nationalization of all the schools has been another problem for the Christian church, especially the Roman Catholics, who had quite a system of parochial schools.

Early Christianity. Ceylon has experienced three forms of Christianity. The Portuguese introduced Roman Catholicism. The Dutch came along with Reformed Christianity. The British offered the people the Anglican form of Christianity. Many of the converts made by the Dutch came from Roman Catholicism. Many of them reverted to Catholicism under the more tolerant British.

Missions. The *London Missionary Society* was the first to take up work in Ceylon; but the mission there lasted only from 1804 to 1818 when it was aborted. The first continuing work was undertaken by the *Baptist Missionary Society.* The pioneer missionary was *James Chater,* whose missionary career in Burma had been cut short by the Anglo-Burmese War in 1812. Chater remained in Ceylon and carried on an active missionary work until his death removed him in 1830. He was followed by *Ebenezer Daniel,* who became leader of the mission. The work began in Colombo but soon spread to other centers. Converts, however, were slow in coming.

Today the work is divided into five districts with missionaries in two of them. After one hundred fifty years of Christian witness, the Baptist Church has a membership of only eighteen hundred. Though fully autonomous, it still depends on financial assistance from the mission. A recent annual report bemoans the lack of growth but points out some hopeful signs.

> The churches have been disturbed out of their complacency during the past year, and a committee has been set up to look at and report on the state of the churches. It is hoped this will lead to a true spirit of repentance and a new effort. . . . All denominations are concerned about the lack of church growth, and the National Christian Council is organizing an All-island Evangelistic Campaign beginning at Pentecost, 1970.[7]

In 1814 the *English Methodists* began work in Ceylon. The leader of the first group was *Thomas Coke,* who had previously labored in the West Indies. Coke died en route to Ceylon, but his colleagues carried on and succeeded in establishing a lasting work which included schools as well as churches. The gospel was preached and converts were made among Burghers, Sinhalese, and Tamils alike. The Methodist Church became independent in 1964. With twelve thousand members, it is the second largest Protestant group in the island; but like the other churches, it is not growing very fast. In fact, the 1967 annual report showed a loss of 3 percent in membership. "On the whole evangelistic work done was inadequate. The chief reasons are the lack of interest shown by our members and their preoccupation with their own difficulties."[8] The president of the Methodist Church in Ceylon is *Dr. Daniel T. Niles,* chairman of the East

---

[7] *A Strength to the Poor,* April, 1969, p. 15.

[8] *Opportunity Now,* p. 13.

Asia Christian Conference and one of the six presidents of the World Council of Churches. Dr. Niles is one of the leading ecumenical figures in Asia today. [9]

The American Board of Commissioners (now the United Church Board of World Mission) took up work in the island in 1816. Its workers located on the Jaffna Peninsula among the Tamil people. From the beginning emphasis was on education. One of the first schools for girls in southern Asia was *Uduvil School,* founded in 1824. It is the only one of seventy UCBWM schools not nationalized by the government. It carries on, but without government subsidy; and it cannot charge fees. *Jaffna College,* founded in 1823, was the first college in Asia to offer modern higher education in English. Today it consists of two coeducational departments on separate but adjacent campuses. Its enrolment is twelve hundred. In 1947 the Ceylon mission of the UCBWM became the Ceylon Diocese of the Church of South India. When a united church of Ceylon becomes a reality, possibly in 1970, it will withdraw from the Church of South India. Present membership is five thousand.

The island of Ceylon was one of the first fields to engage the attention of the *Church Missionary Society.* It was not until 1818, however, that the mission actually got under way. Work among the Sinhalese was begun at Kandy in 1818, at Baddegama in 1819, at Kotte in 1822, and at Kurunagala in 1880. In the Tamil area, Jaffna was occupied in 1818 and Colombo in 1850. Educational institutions included four colleges for men, and two colleges and two middle schools for girls. Two teacher training schools were opened, one for Sinhalese and one for Tamils. The Anglicans have experienced more growth than any other group and today, with a membership of twenty-five thousand, are the largest non-Roman church in the island. The two dioceses into which the work is divided, Colombo and Kurunagala, are part of the Church of India, Pakistan, Burma, and Ceylon. A milestone was reached in 1965 when the Venerable Harold de Soysa became the first Ceylonese Bishop of Colombo.

The *Dutch Reformed Church,* made up mostly of Burghers, has a history dating back to the days of Dutch colonialism. Nine churches report a total membership of twenty-five hundred. The *Lutheran Church-Missouri Synod* has been in Ceylon since 1927. It has a church of five hundred members.

Ceylon Bible Society. The first Auxiliary Society was formed in Colombo in 1812. In 1905 the organization was centralized in one Ceylon Auxiliary, which in 1944 became part of the autonomous Bible Society of India and Ceylon. In 1965 the Ceylon Bible Society became independent; and by 1969 it was raising half of its budget locally. One of the main tasks at the moment is a complete revision of the Sinhala Bible. The year 1968

---

9 Dr. Niles passed away July 17, 1970.

was especially good for the Bible Society. More than three thousand persons requested a Bible correspondence course in the Gospel of Mark. Special interest in this Gospel was due to the fact that a General Certificate of Education examination uses Mark's Gospel as a textbook. Weekly advertisements in the newspapers produced over sixteen thousand inquiries for Scriptures.

Church Union. This is a live option in Ceylon. Five denominations have been negotiating for some years: Anglican, Presbyterian, Baptist, Methodist, and the Church of South India. It was hoped that union would be consummated by 1970; but the failure of the Methodists in August, 1969, to get a 75 percent affirmative vote has delayed the proceedings. When the united church comes into existence it will be called the Church of Lanka.

The Christian Presence. Approximately one million of the twelve million people in Ceylon are Christians. Of these some nine hundred thousand are Roman Catholics, most of them descendants of the converts made during the period of Portuguese colonial rule. Almost one-half of the Protestant community of one hundred thousand are Anglicans. Church growth is very slow, in some places almost at a standstill. If the Protestant churches in Ceylon are to make an impact on society they will have to be revived first.

IX

Southeast Asia

Burma

Political History. After 120 years of British rule Burma gained its independence in 1948. Unlike its neighbors, India and Ceylon, it severed all ties with the British Commonwealth. The first decade of independence was a struggle against insurrection, lawlessness, and inflation; and the end is not yet. In 1958 Dr. U Nu, premier since independence, resigned in favor of a military general with emergency powers. The government reverted to civilian rule early in 1960, but not for long. In March, 1962, General Ne Win and sixteen other officers seized power, suspended the constitution, and formed a Revolutionary Council, which has ruled Burma ever since. Doggedly dedicated to the "Burmese Way of Socialism," the government has nationalized banks, businesses, import and export enterprises, schools, and hospitals. As a result all Westerners except diplomatic personnel, and thousands of Indians, Pakistanis, and Chinese have left the country. Only authorized delegations of Burmans are permitted to travel abroad; and foreign visitors were allowed a twenty-four-hour stopover in Rangoon until May, 1970, when it was increased to seven days. Burma is today the most isolated member of the United Nations.

The People. The population of Burma stands at 26,500,000. The Burmese, who are Mongolian in race and supposed originally to have migrated from the borders of Tibet, constitute 80 percent of the population. They occupy central Burma from the Irrawaddy Delta to Mandalay. They are surrounded by mountain tribes of various ethnic origins and of primitive social organization. The largest tribe is the Karen, numbering about 2,500,000 and speaking seventeen dialects. The Karens, divided into

145

three main groups, live in both the plains and the hills of the lower and middle sections of the country. Kachin is the name commonly applied to some 500,000 tribesmen scattered across the mountains of western China, northern Burma, and eastern Assam. A third tribe, the Chin, numbers about 260,000. Other hill tribes include the Shan, Naga, Lisu, and Lahu peoples. The Christian mission has been most fruitful among these animistic tribes. They represent over 97.5 percent of all the Christians in Burma today. The overall literacy rate is quite high, 60 percent for the country as a whole and 90 percent in the towns. Before the recent exodus there were 700,000 Indians and 300,000 Chinese in Burma.

Religion. Burma has been described as the "Land of the Pagodas." The conical spires of the white and gold pagodas dominate the landscape in all parts of the country. These shrines to the memory of Gautama Buddha are a mute reminder that the Burmese people are wholly given over to Buddhism in its Theravada (orthodox) form. The lofty Shwe Dagon Pagoda in Rangoon, covered with gold leaf at a cost of a million dollars, is one of the most famous shrines in the world. In August, 1961, Buddhism was declared the state religion. The following month the government unanimously passed a constitutional amendment protecting the rights of religious minorities, much to the relief of the Christians. Until it was abolished in 1962, the Government Sasana Council aided the resurgence of Buddhism. Pagodas are being rebuilt, centers for study and meditation are being established, and Buddhist missionaries are being sent into the hill country to convert the animistic tribes. Buddhist missionaries are also going abroad, some to Western countries, with the Buddha's message of compassion and peace. The Sixth Great Buddhist Council, commemorating the 2,500th anniversary of the Enlightenment of Buddha, was held in Rangoon from 1954 to 1956 and attracted Buddhist leaders from all parts of the world. One outcome of the council was a new version of the *Tripitaka,* the Buddhist Scriptures, and a translation of the same into several modern languages. After 150 years Christianity has made almost no impact on Buddhism in Burma. Only about twelve thousand Burmese Buddhists have been won to Christ. The Christian church there is predominantly a tribal church.

The several hundred thousand Indians who remain in Burma are Hindus. There are approximately one hundred thousand Muslims; they include the Pakistanis who have stayed.

Adoniram Judson. Adoniram Judson ranks with Robert Morrison, David Livingstone, William Carey, and Hudson Taylor as one of the greatest missionaries of all time. Immediately upon his arrival in Rangoon in 1813 Judson began the study of the language. From the beginning his life was beset with difficulties and frustrations calculated to break the strongest spirit; but in spite of all the adversities he persevered until, after six long years, he won his first convert. When war broke out between

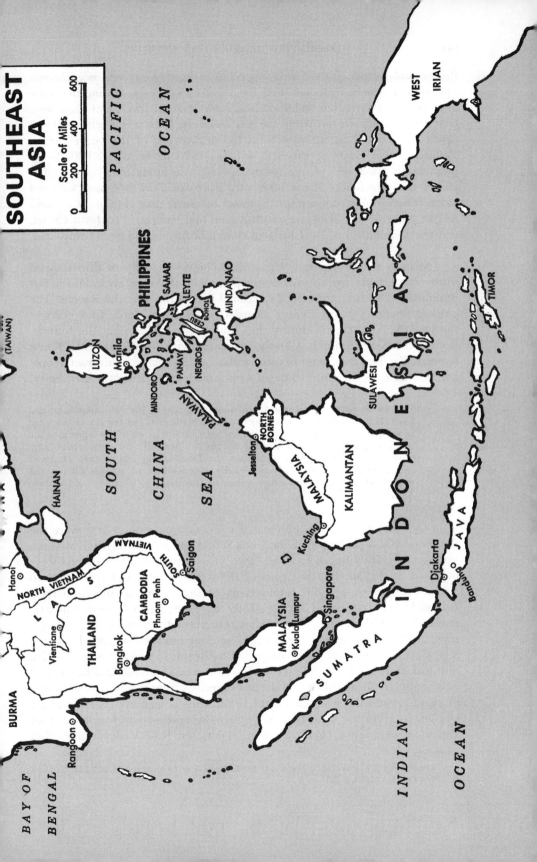

SOUTHEAST ASIA

Scale of Miles
0   200   400   600

PACIFIC

OCEAN

(TAIWAN)

PHILIPPINES

SAMAR

LEYTE

MINDANAO

BOHOL

CEBU

LUZON

Manila

MINDORO

PANAY

NEGROS

PALAWAN

SOUTH

CHINA

SEA

HAINAN

NORTH
BORNEO

Jesselton

MALAYSIA

KALIMANTAN

Kuching

SULAWESI

I   N   D   O   N   E   S   I   A

WEST

IRIAN

TIMOR

Hanoi

NORTH VIETNAM

LAOS

Vientiane

THAILAND

Bangkok

CAMBODIA

Phnom Penh

VIETNAM

SOUTH

Saigon

MALAYSIA

Kuala Lumpur

Singapore

SUMATRA

Djakarta

JAVA

Bandung

BURMA

Rangoon

BAY OF

BENGAL

INDIAN

OCEAN

Britain and Burma, Judson was suspected of being a spy and was thrown into prison, where he languished for almost two years. During this time Mrs. Judson contracted smallpox and later spotted fever, and for a long time lay at death's door. When the war was over, Judson was released from prison, and acted as interpreter in the drawing-up of the peace treaty. Following the death of his first wife in 1826 he transferred his headquarters to Moulmein. After twenty years of arduous toil, Judson completed the translation of the Bible into Burmese. Few men have suffered more or accomplished more for the cause of Christ than Adoniram Judson. At the time of his death, seven thousand had been won to Jesus Christ, and the foundation of the Christian church in Burma had been firmly laid.

Mission to the Tribes. The overwhelming majority of Christians in Burma have come from the tribespeople, most of whom are animists, not Buddhists. The first tribe to be reached for Christ was the Karens. The pioneer missionary was *George Boardman,* who spent only four years in Burma (1827-1831); but during that time he was able to lay the foundation of the Karen Church. Closely associated with Boardman was a Karen convert, Ko Tha Byu, who became a flaming evangelist to his own people and was used of the Lord to begin a mass movement towards Christianity.

> The Karen movement toward Christianity in which Judson, Boardman, and Ko Tha Byu had been pioneers continued. Wade reduced the Karen language to writing. Literature was prepared, including translations of the Bible into the tongues of various branches of the Karens. . . . Schools were organized. Clergy were trained. The Karens undertook the financial support of their churches and schools and became more nearly independent of subsidies from the outside than almost any other group of Christians in southern and eastern Asia.[1]

The first missionaries designated to work among the *Chins* were the *Reverend and Mrs. Burpe* of the Nova Scotia and New Brunswick Missionary Society. They began in 1845. Two years later the first converts were baptized at Akyab, the firstfruits of the Kemee Chins. But it was left to *Arthur Carson* to lay the foundations of the church in the Chin hills. During his short term of service, 1899 to 1908, he built two churches, reduced the Haka language to writing, established a hospital, and inaugurated a literacy program. He lived to see one hundred persons baptized. Mrs. Carson carried on until compelled by health to return home in 1920. She had translated the four Gospels and Acts and prepared a hymnal of 120 songs. In all of this work Karen evangelists were involved. The period of rapid growth did not come until 1942, when large numbers entered the church. In 1953 the *Chin* (Zomi) *Baptist Convention* was formed of four Baptist associations: Tiddim, Falam, Haka, and Kale Valley. Four other

---

[1] Kenneth Scott Latourette, *A History of the Expansion of Christianity* (New York: Harper & Brothers, 1944), Vol. VI, p. 231.

associations have since been added. All churches are required to contribute one-fifteenth of their tithes to the central organization.

Settled work among the *Kachins* began in 1876 with *Josiah N. Cushing* and two young Karen evangelists. The first baptism took place in 1882. Progress was slow. After twenty-five years there were only 150 believers, eight of whom had received sufficient private training to qualify as lay pastors. The next twenty-five years saw the development of a truly indigenous church. The Kachin Baptist Association was formed in 1910, the first of four associations which later were organized into the *Kachin Baptist Convention*. The Kachin Bible was published in 1927 and presented to the Kachin Church by its translator, *Ola Hanson*.

Another group for which the American Baptists accepted responsibility was the Shan people. Pioneer missionaries were the *Reverend and Mrs. Moses H. Bixby*. Their first charges were ten thousand Shan refugees who with the help of the British settled near Toungoo in 1861. The first Shan to be baptized was Maung Aung Myat, son of a chief, in 1862. Later Dr. and Mrs. Josiah Cushing joined the Shan mission. The Bible in Shan was completed in 1885. Dr. Gordon S. Seagrave of *Burma Surgeon* fame carried on medical missionary work among the Shan from 1922 to 1942, when the Japanese invasion terminated missionary work for the duration of the war. Other tribes reached with the gospel were the Lisu, Wa, Lahu, Akha, and the head-hunting Naga.

The tribal churches in Burma are among the largest, strongest, and most evangelistically aggressive in all Asia. They have been self-supporting, self-governing, and self-propagating for many years. They have made themselves responsible for the evangelization of their own and other tribes in Burma; and they have sent missionaries to work among the Karens in Thailand, the Kachins in China, and the Nagas in Burma. They have raised up and supported seventeen Bible schools and seminaries. Until recent action by the government nationalized all private institutions, the Baptists maintained over six hundred schools with an aggregate enrolment of forty-five thousand pupils.

Today the Burma Baptist Convention comprises seven well-organized autonomous conventions: Burma Churches Union, Sgaw Karen Convention, Pwo Karen Conference, Mon Churches Union, Asho Chin Conference, Zomi Convention, and Kachin Convention. In addition there are several other smaller or geographical groups.

Anglican Missions. Though they were the oldest and largest, the Baptists were not the only group in Burma. The *Anglican Church in Burma,* which celebrated its one hundredth anniversary in 1959, was brought into existence by two independent missionary societies within the Church of England, the *United Society for the Propagation of the Gospel* and the *Bible Churchmen's Missionary Society*. The former was launched by the educational work of *John Ebenezer Marks,* a Hebrew Christian, whose missionary career spanned forty years. Dr. Marks founded *St. John's College* in Rangoon and later established the *Royal School* in Mandalay, to which King Mindon sent his four sons to get a modern education. The USPG worked among the Burmans as well as the Karens and the Chins. The BCMS opened work in Upper Burma in 1924. Just before World War II they expanded their work among the Khumis in the Arakan Hills in western Burma. This proved to be their most rapidly growing field, the number of Christians increasing from one hundred to five hundred between 1952 and 1957. For many years the Rangoon Diocese was part of the Church of India, Pakistan, Burma, and Ceylon. The new Province of Burma was inaugurated on February 24, 1970, and the Bishop of Rangoon, Francis Ah Mya, was enthroned as the new archbishop. The new Province comprises the dioceses of Rangoon, Mandalay, Pa'an, and Akyab, which were given permission to sever themselves from the Church of India, Pakistan, Burma and Ceylon. The Anglican Church of Burma has twenty-five thousand members.

Methodist Missions. Through the years two Methodist missions have been working in Burma. The American mission is located in the south, the English mission in the north.

The American work began with a group of Methodists from Calcutta who migrated to Burma in the 1870's. The pioneer missionary was the *Reverend R. E. Carter,* who was transferred from India to work in Rangoon. The first church was composed of Europeans and Eurasians. Non-English-speaking congregations came into existence in Burma about 1900. The Methodist Church of Lower Burma received its autonomy in 1965. This led to a greatly increased interest on the part of both laymen and ministers in the organization and working of the church. "It is heartening to see how the church has been able to challenge some of its ablest young laymen to assume active leadership."[2]

The annexation of Upper Burma by the British in 1886 naturally led the British Methodists to give serious consideration to the task of taking the gospel to the northern part of the country. As a result the British Methodists established headquarters in Mandalay in 1887. Work began with the Burmese, and later spread to the Lushais. Methodist gains in this part of the world have been much smaller than those of the Baptists; nevertheless the *Methodist Church of Upper Burma* now has a baptized membership of fifteen thousand. Union negotiations between the two churches are now going on, and doubtless they will merge in the near future.

Other Missions. The *Assemblies of God's* work in Burma started with Lisu evangelists from China in the early 1930's. After World War II *Mr.*

---

[2] *1966 Report of the Board of Missions of the Methodist Church,* p. 120.

and Mrs. Clifford Morrison moved from China to Burma and laid the foundations of the work in the extreme northern part of the country. Associated with them were Lisu evangelists from China. Two Bible schools were established. In 1956 the Silver Jubilee Convention in Putao was attended by two thousand Christians. Today some three hundred churches, with a membership of twenty-five thousand, are fully self-supporting. Another thriving work among the Lisu and Rawang groups is that of the *North Burma Christian Mission* (Churches of Christ). For many years the enterprise was under the direction of the *Reverend J. Russell Morse* and his three married sons. These churches are likewise self-supporting and self-governing.

World War II. During World War II church and mission work in Burma suffered heavy losses. Missionaries were evacuated, stations abandoned, schools closed. Fearing the worst from the Japanese soldiery, many of the Christians fled to the hills. Some recanted and reverted to their former animistic worship. Others decided to remain incognito until the war was over. Of course, there were the usual casualties among the Christians. Some pastors were killed. When the missionaries returned after the war it was to find their many buildings in ruins; but they persevered, giving themselves to rehabilitation with energy and goodwill, joined by the national pastors and Christians. Soon the church was on its feet again.

The Scriptures. The first portion of the Burmese Bible was printed in 1815, the first New Testament in 1832, and the first complete Bible in 1835. This translation was the life-work of Adoniram Judson. Today the complete Bible is available in eight languages, the New Testament in eight additional languages, and portions in still another ten dialects, which makes the Word of God available in twenty-six languages and dialects of Burma. For over one hundred years the *British and Foreign Bible Society* engaged in the translation, publication, and distribution of the Scriptures in many languages. Colportage work began in 1884. An agency was established in 1889, with a full-time secretary in 1890. Burma became a joint agency of the two societies in 1962 and an independent Bible society in 1965.

A government ban on books in any language of Burma published outside the country has worked a hardship on the Christians. For several years there was a serious dearth of the Scriptures. Then in 1968 the government released $50,000 worth of Bibles held in Customs. Efforts are now being made to provide a press for the printing of the Scriptures in Burma. In spite of all the obstacles, Scripture distribution continues around two hundred thousand copies a year.

The Lisu Old Testament and a revision of the New Testament, largely the work of *Allyn Cooke* and *Allen Crane* of the Overseas Missionary

Fellowship, was published in Hong Kong in 1966. When the first copy, sent by air, was received by Pastor Lucius, he wrote:

> That which we have mourned for with tears and longing, hoping and praying, God has granted. On the evening of October 4, my own eyes saw and my own hands held His Holy Word. . . . Everyone who heard the news came running to my house. When they saw, they jumped up and clapped their hands. . . . This is the most precious thing upon this globe. Even if someone would offer me in exchange a thousand kingdoms like this whole world, I would never accept and never exchange.[3]

It was not until late 1970 that all ten thousand copies of the Lisu Bible finally reached their destination in northern Burma.

Christian Radio.   Except on special occasions such as Christmas and Easter, Christian broadcasting in Burma is not permitted; but the churches there receive immense support in their evangelistic outreach from Christian programs beamed into the country from outside. For many years station DZAS of the *Far East Broadcasting Company* has been broadcasting the gospel into Burma from Manila. The programs have been popular with the Buddhists; so much so that the Burma Christian Council decided to invite *South East Asia Radio Voice* of the National Christian Council in the Philippines to start broadcasting to Burma. A third powerful station, *Radio Voice of the Gospel,* a Lutheran station in Addis Ababa, beams the gospel to Burma. The tapes for all of these programs are made in Hong Kong and Bangkok.

The Mass Evacuation.   In March, 1966, the government, without explanation but not without warning, ordered the evacuation of all missionaries, Christian and otherwise, regardless of their length of service. The measure was part of a concerted drive to implement the "Burmese Way of Socialism," which had become the official policy of the military regime in Rangoon. All the Protestant missionaries and about half of the Catholic missionaries were out of Burma by September. Since then the churches have been on their own. It is still possible to send funds for the support of various projects; and, of course, correspondence is maintained. The churches continue to furnish annual reports to mission headquarters in the United States and Great Britain; otherwise, the isolation is well nigh complete. In 1968 church leaders were denied permission to attend the Lambeth Conference of Bishops, the World Council of Churches Assembly at Uppsala, and the Congress on Evangelism in Singapore. Churchmen from the West traveling in that part of the world are permitted a seven-day stopover in Rangoon. Until recently it was only twenty-four hours.

Nationalization.   Even before the expulsion of the missionaries the government in 1965 nationalized 129 private schools, 24 of which were

---

[3] *East Asia Millions,* January, 1969, p. 9.

Baptist. In 1966 another 720 schools and all private hospitals were included in the takeover. Christian workers were not the only ones involved; Hindu missionaries, Chinese merchants, and Indian bureaucrats were also affected. The move, of course, was highly popular with the Burmese people; but it was detrimental to both business and politics. The nationalization did not include Bible schools or seminaries; and, of course, the churches were omitted. All mission properties had to be transferred to the churches, which involved a good deal of red tape. In May, 1970, the American Baptists reported eighty pieces of property still to be transferred to the Burma Baptist Convention Property Association.

Theological Education. Now that missionaries are no longer in Burma, theological education is more important than ever. Fortunately, the theological schools were not nationalized; they continue to function under the auspices of the church. A one-week conference for church leaders and representatives of all the Bible schools and seminaries took place in April, 1969. Such subjects as coordinated curricula, exchange of teachers and students, and the unity of mission, church, and youth work were discussed. The Theological Education Fund made a grant of $750 towards the conference. The Burma Divinity School, near Rangoon, had 101 students enrolled for the second semester of 1969. Twenty-one of these students hold university degrees; the others are high school graduates. The seventeen Baptist Bible schools scattered throughout the country continue to maintain high enrolments of both men and women students. The Karen Theological Seminary and the Karen Women's Bible School in Insein graduated seventy-two young men and women in 1968.

The Future of the Church. Will the Christian Church in Burma survive the withdrawal of foreign men and money? The consensus seems to be that the Burmese Christians will weather the storm. Addison J. Eastman of the National Council of Churches in the USA observed:

> The departure of these missionaries from Burma marks the end of an era, but not the end of Christian work in the country. There is now in Burma a Christian church of approximately 600,000 members, and it is growing rapidly in some parts of the country. The church has itself become a missionary community and has developed a strong indigenous leadership.[4]

Developments in the last four years have confirmed this optimism. Not only has the church not retrenched, it has actually grown in strength and numbers and manifests an amazing degree of vision and vitality. The Assemblies of God churches have increased from 180 to 300 in three years. Enrolment in Baptist theological schools has grown from 700 to 900 in four years. Dr. Paul S. Rees spent a Sunday in Rangoon in 1969 to address an assembly of 400 pastors and 600 laymen. He wrote:

[4] *Ecumenical Press Service,* April 7, 1966, p. 101.

> Late that night I talked to a young pastor from a community of 6,000 far in the north. By jeep, by train, and by plane, he had managed to reach Rangoon for the conference. His church building, he said, is bursting at the seams. Conversions and baptisms have been on the increase. In a town of 6,000 one-third are Christians.[5]

Herman G. Tegenfeldt, the last American Baptist missionary to leave Burma in 1966, writes:

> The past few years have witnessed an increase in church attendance in almost every part of Burma. From some areas, marked growth in Sunday Schools has been reported. Conversions and baptisms have been a continuing source of real encouragement. . . . The work begun in 1966 by which Karen Baptists sent missionaries to the Nagas in northwestern Burma proceeded well for a time. During a four-month period early in 1967, a Karen evangelist baptized 102 of these Nagas, among whom there were still instances of head-hunting as late as 1953.[6]

In November, 1969, the Burmese church celebrated the sesquicentennial of the baptism of the first Burmese Christian. The main function was held in Rangoon, where church leaders from all over Burma had gathered. Only two outsiders were present on that occasion. One of them wrote: "A representative of the World Council of Churches and I were the only two non-Burmese attending this unique occasion. What struck me most was the note of triumph in the face of threatenings and difficulties, which one senses very clearly in the life and program of the Church."[7]

Malaysia

Political History. The Federation of Malaya came into existence in 1957 after 175 years of British rule. In 1963 three additional territories were added, Sarawak, Sabah, and Singapore, and the name was changed to the Federation of Malaysia. Singapore withdrew from the federation in 1965. The greatest threat to the security of the state came with the three-year Confrontation with Indonesia, which ended when President Sukarno of Indonesia was ousted. In 1967 the controversial National Language Bill made Malay the sole official language of west Malaysia. The Chinese minority dominates all aspects of society except politics; consequently they are feared and resented by the Malays. Hostility, never far from the surface, reached the boiling point in 1969 and bloody riots led to a state of emergency. Though not a member of SEATO, Malaysia is pro-Western and actively anticommunist.

---

[5] *World Vision Magazine,* September, 1969.

[6] Herman G. Tegenfeldt, *Through Deep Waters* (Valley Forge, Pa.: American Baptist Foreign Mission Society, 1968), p. 36.

[7] *World News,* January-March, 1970, p. 3.

The People. Malaysia, a multiracial country with a population of twelve million, is divided into two regions. West Malaysia includes the eleven states of the former Federation of Malaya; East Malaysia is made up of Sarawak and Sabah in northern Borneo. The two regions are separated by 400 miles of the South China Sea. In west Malaysia the Malays (4,400,000) are the indigenous and dominant race. The Chinese (4,000,000) have been in the country for several generations; they form the second largest group. The remaining 2,000,000 persons are divided almost equally between the Indians and the hill tribes. In east Malaysia the population of Sarawak is 900,000 and of Sabah, 600,000. Many of these are half-naked primitive natives who live in communal longhouses and hunt with blowguns and poisoned arrows.

Religion. As already stated, Malaysia has three main races, and each has its own religion. The Malays are Muslims, and Islam is the state religion. The Chinese are Buddhists; the Indians are Hindus. The hill tribes are animists, those in East Malaysia being very primitive indeed. The constitution provides that "subject to the requirements of public order, public health and morality, every person has the right to profess, practise and propagate his religion." Despite the progressive tone of the constitution, clause four adds: "State law may control or restrict the propagation of any religious doctrine among persons professing the Muslim religion." This means that missionary work in west Malaysia is restricted to the Chinese and Indian minorities. Christian radio broadcasts were permitted for a time and then stopped. Christian schools are not allowed to give Christian instruction. The government in recent years has begun to tighten up on visas for missionaries. Missionaries who were in the country prior to 1954 are given permanent visas; all others are issued visitors' visas; but even permanent visas are good for only ten years. In addition it is necessary to secure work permits, and these are valid for only one year. Several missionaries have been expelled for giving Christian literature to Muslims.

In east Malaysia the situation has been better, though of late Sabah has shown signs of following the lead of west Malaysia.

> Harmony between races has deteriorated since Sabah became a part of Malaysia. . . . The Church in Sabah has penetrated among most of the races, Chinese and Kadazan, Indian and Ceylonese and many others, but not at all amongst Malays whose devotion to Islam is also devotion to their family, country and racial identity. The Church, therefore, seems to stand firmly on the anti-Malay side and is therefore held in suspicion by the Malay government. Increasingly the influence of the Church is being eroded in education, medical and welfare work. The right to evangelize is being challenged and thwarted by a government that would see Islam as the state religion as soon as possible in Sabah.[8]

---

[8] United Society for the Propagation of the Gospel, *Kaleidoscope 1970*, p. 47.

Early Missions. Roman Catholicism was first introduced to Malaya in 1511 when the Portuguese conquered that part of the world. During his stay in the Orient, *Francis Xavier* spent three years in Malaya in the 1540's. Today 300,000 Catholics represent 2.5 percent of the population—twice as numerous as the Protestants. When the Dutch drove out the Portuguese in 1641 they introduced Reformed Christianity. They in turn were expelled by the British who arrived in 1786 and took possession of Malacca in 1824.

The first Protestant mission on the scene was the *London Missionary Society.* The pioneer was *Dr. William Milne* who settled in Malacca and opened the *Anglo-Chinese College.* His original intention was to go to China; but as long as that door remained closed he was content to train Chinese to become missionaries to their own country. In 1842 when China opened its door to the Christian missionaries, the LMS transferred its staff to that country. In the meantime, Milne was joined in Malacca by Mr. G. H. Thomson, who worked among the Malays. He was assisted by the Reverend S. D. Keasberry who elected to remain in Malaya after the LMS pulled out. He supported himself by teaching and operating a printing press.

Modern Missions. The Anglicans have been working in Malaya since 1848, when the *Society for the Propagation of the Gospel* sent its first missionary to work among the Chinese and Tamils. Two other Anglican societies have joined the SPG, the *Church Missionary Society* of the United Kingdom and the *Church Missionary Society* of Australia. Following the evacuation of China, the Anglican members of the *China Inland Mission* joined their colleagues in Malaya.[9] Today the membership of the Anglican Church in Malaya is approaching thirty thousand, with forty-five local clergy and fifteen missionary clergy. This includes those in Singapore.

The *American Methodists'* work in this part of the world dates back to 1885, when the *Reverend and Mrs. William F. Oldham* arrived in Singapore. He gathered an English-speaking congregation together and laid the foundations of the work in Malaya. Two years later *Miss Sophia Blackmore,* the first missionary of the Women's Foreign Missionary Society, arrived from Australia. That same year she opened a school for Tamil girls and the following year one for Chinese girls. British and German Methodists joined the work. A number of Chinese and Tamil pastors came from China, India, and Ceylon. The Malay Mission Conference was organized in 1894 and the Annual Conference in 1902. Two years later Dr. Oldham was elected missionary bishop. Through the years the Methodists have maintained a fine system of schools in which some seventy thousand students are now enrolled; but in recent years the Christian witness in these schools has been diluted.

---

[9] The difference between east Malaysia and west Malaysia is so marked that it is helpful, where possible, to keep them separate. The term *Malaya* is applied to west Malaysia.

As the government has taken over the responsibility for education, schools have become less church and Methodism oriented and have conformed more nearly to government and other private schools. They still carry the Methodist names, and, as far as possible, there is an attempt to staff them and give them training in a Christian context with Christian teachers. . . . This, with new government regulations, has become increasingly difficult.[10]

The *Methodist Church of Malaysia and Singapore* became autonomous in 1968 and elected as its first bishop Dr. Yap Kim Hao. Its baptized membership is about twenty thousand. These figures do not include their members in Sarawak and Sabah.

Christian Missions in Many Lands (Plymouth Brethren) from England has many assemblies in Malaysia, the result of several decades of work.

Other missions have been in west Malaysia for longer or shorter periods and have established churches. Some of these are ministering exclusively to ethnic groups. The *Mar Thoma Church,* the *Syrian Orthodox Church,* and the *Evangelical Lutheran Church* are ministering to the Indian "Diaspora." The *Chinese Christian Church* is working in the large Chinese community.

Postwar Missions.   The *Lutheran Church in America* has been working in Malaysia since 1953. After ten years, the *Lutheran Church in Malaysia and Singapore* was established with almost seven hundred members. The mission is confined to the two states of Perak and Selangor, and Singapore. The Lutheran Church in America is also related to two younger churches, the *Basel Christian Church of Malaysia* and the *Evangelical Lutheran Church in Malaysia.* The beginnings of the Basel Church go back to 1883 when Christian Hakka families, converts of the Basel Misson, emigrated from south China at the request of the British authorities in North Borneo. Growing by immigration, conversions, and births, Basel congregations sprang up along the eastern seacoast of Borneo, served by pastors from China and missionaries from the Basel Mission. In 1926 these congregations formed themselves into the Basel Christian Church of Malaysia. Today the church has over six thousand members in twenty congregations.

The *Evangelical Lutheran Church* is also a migrant church, its earliest members being Tamil Lutherans who came from south India in the early part of the twentieth century. They retained their connection with the church in India until 1962, when they formed the Evangelical Lutheran Church in Malaysia, a body numbering about fifteen hundred members of Indian extraction. The Church of Sweden has related itself to this church and has strengthened its witness by sending missionaries and giving financial aid.

In the postwar period a number of new missions have entered west Malaysia. Most of these have only a small contingent of missionaries and

---

[10] The United Methodist Church, *Project Handbook Overseas Mission 1969,* p. 197.

their church work is just getting under way. Among them are the *Evangelical Free Church of America* (1957), the *American Advent Mission* (1959), and the *American Baptists* (1967). Following the evacuation of China in 1950 two large missions transferred workers to Malaysia. The *Overseas Missionary Fellowship* with over one hundred workers is now one of the largest missions in the country. Many of its early workers settled in the New Villages created during the emergency from 1950 to 1953. The OMF is not establishing churches of its own; it is cooperating with other missions and independent churches, endeavoring to strengthen existing work. The Anglican members of the mission have been working with the Anglican Church of Malaysia. The other mission to transfer workers is the *Southern Baptist Convention*. Its first missionaries reached Malaysia in 1951; there are fifty-five there now, most of them in west Malaysia. More recently they have opened three stations in Sabah. Work in Sarawak began in 1970. Already thirty-four churches have been established, twenty-four of them self-supporting; and there are twenty-one national pastors.

Bible Societies. In 1814 the British and Foreign Bible Society began work in this area by printing a version of the New Testament in the Malay language. An Agency was established in 1882. In 1948 Malaya became a Joint Agency of the British and Foreign Bible Society and the National Bible Society of Scotland, under the administration of the latter. The Advisory Council, organized in 1962, coordinates the work in Malaysia, Singapore, and Brunei. The Bible Society now has nine paid colporteurs, utilizes fourteen others on a commission basis, and serves thirty-four bookstores and book stalls. A good deal of support, financial and other, comes from auxiliaries in Penang, Taiping, Ipoh, Kuala Lumpur, Malacca, and Jesselton. Translation work continues in seven dialects of East Malaysia. Contributions to the Bible Society from local sources doubled in five years. Today almost half of the budget is raised locally. Distribution in 1968 was nearly double that of the previous year. Plans are on foot to build a new and larger Bible House in Singapore.

East Malaysia. The two states of Sarawak and Sabah are quite different from the states that make up west Malaysia. Some missions, such as the Anglicans, Methodists, Plymouth Brethren, and Lutherans, have work in both areas. A few missions have concentrated on the east.

The *American Methodists* have a thriving work in Sarawak. It was begun around the turn of the century by Chinese Christian immigrants from Fukien and Methodist missionaries from Malaya. The *Reverend James Hoover* gave thirty years of strong leadership to Sarawak Methodism in the Rejang River district. The Sarawak Provisional Conference was formed in 1952 and the Annual Conference four years later. The Conference includes sixty-two churches and ten preaching places served by thirty-eight ministers. In 1962 the Sarawak Iban Provisional Annual Conference was formed. With almost ten thousand members, this is the most rapidly growing Methodist church in the world.

The *Church Missionary Society* has maintained churches and schools in these parts from the beginning of their work under *Francis McDougall* in 1848. The schools range from meagerly equipped village schools in the Sarawak jungle to the two large secondary schools in Kuching, from which graduates, mostly Chinese, have gone out to assume positions of leadership throughout Sarawak and Sabah. In Sabah the principal Anglican schools are at Jesselton and Sandakan. Recent growth of the church in Sabah has made it necessary to divide it into two dioceses, Kuching and Jesselton, the latter in charge of a Chinese bishop.

A truly remarkable work has been accomplished in little more than a generation by the *Borneo Evangelical Mission,* an interdenominational-faith mission founded in 1928 by graduates of the Melbourne Bible Institute. During the first decade a mighty movement of the Holy Spirit resulted in hundreds of primitive tribesmen turning to Christ. From the beginning the mission laid great stress on indigenous principles of mission-ary work, encouraging the tribesmen to assume responsibility for the emerging church. Founded in 1946, the *Central Bible School* is staffed almost entirely by tribesmen. It has 150 students. The missionaries have engaged widely in Bible translation, hoping to provide a complete New Testament for all the tribes represented in the church. A significant milestone was reached in 1963, when the independent *Borneo Evangelical Church* was established. It includes two hundred completely independent churches in a dozen tribes.

The *Seventh Day Adventists* have worked in east Malaysia for some time. In Sarawak they have a church of five thousand members; in Sabah there are twenty-five hundred members. The usual medical work is miss-ing.

Singapore. For two years Singapore was part of the Federation of Malaysia. It is now a sovereign city state. It is a thriving, growing metropo-lis of two million people, 76 percent of them Chinese. It is one of the most cosmopolitan cities in the world. All telephone operators must be fluent in four languages!

Singapore is important to this study for three reasons. It has a rapidly growing Christian community of its own. It is the headquarters for several large missions working in that part of the world. It is being used increas-ingly as a rendezvous for international religious conferences.

There is complete freedom of religion in Singapore; so even the Muslim Malays are not beyond the reach of the Christian missionary, though few of them ever respond. There are almost two hundred Christian churches in the city. Almost all of them are Chinese in nationality and fully self-supporting. There are three theological schools: *Trinity College, Singapore Bible College,* and the *Discipleship Training Center.* Trinity

College is the oldest. It is an ecumenical institution with staff and students drawn from the Anglican, Methodist, Presbyterian, and Lutheran churches. The student body of about one hundred is made up largely of Chinese. The Singapore Bible College is an independent school assisted by various groups, including the Overseas Missionary Fellowship. The most recent is the Discipleship Training Center, which was established in 1968. Founded by *David Adeney,* formerly with the International Fellowship of Evangelical Students, it is sponsored by the Overseas Missionary Fellowship and the Singapore Bible College. It is not just another theological school; it is pioneering in a new type of program. Already more than two dozen students are in training. A university degree is a necessary qualification. Many of them are older men who have left lucrative business and professional careers to serve the Lord in a full-time capacity.

Singapore is also the headquarters of several large missions with far-flung work in south and southeast Asia. Among these are the Anglican Church, the Methodist Church, the Overseas Missionary Fellowship, and others. The Malayan Christian Council and the Bible Society also have their headquarters in Singapore. In recent years Singapore has been the site of several international religious conferences. In 1968 it played host to the Congress on Evangelism sponsored by the Billy Graham Evangelistic Association. The All-Asia Literature Conference and the Asian Evangelical Theological Consultation were held there in 1970.

Thailand

Political History. The first kingdom was established in Thailand (Siam) in the thirteenth century. The earliest contacts with the West came with the arrival in 1511 of the Portuguese; they were followed by the Dutch and later by the British. With the Portuguese came Roman Catholic missionaries, and they have been there ever since. The modernization of Thailand began with King Mongkut (1851-1868) and his son, Chulalong-korn (1868-1910). American missionaries, especially Dr. Dan Bradley, played a major role during this era in preparing Thailand for its entrance into the family of nations. A bloodless coup in 1932 overthrew the absolute monarchy and introduced a period of political instability. In twenty-five years there were thirteen coups or attempted coups, often accompanied by assassination. The latest, in 1958, destroyed parliamentary democracy and for eleven years Thailand was ruled by a military junta. In 1969 a new constitution was promulgated by King Phomipol and representative government was restored. Today Bangkok is a thriving metropolis of two million people, served by twenty-four international airlines and visited each week by thousands of tourists. Seven agencies of the United Nations are located in Bangkok, which is also the site of SEATO headquarters.

The People. The Thai tribes emigrated from China between the seventh and the thirteenth centuries; they made their way south until they overran the whole of what is now Thailand. The population, about thirty-four million, is far from homogeneous. About 90 percent of the people belong to the Thai race, which is divided into the southern Thai, or Siamese, and the northern Thai, or Lao. The Chinese, rapidly approaching the four million mark, are the largest and most progressive minority. They are found chiefly in the Bangkok area, though large numbers are scattered throughout the country. They are well known for their business acumen; they are the leading merchants and control most of the import-export trade. They tend to keep to themselves, thus preserving their culture and their language. There are eight hundred thousand Malay Muslims, most of them in the southern peninsula. In the mountain regions of the north there are about a quarter of a million tribespeople, divided into twenty tribes, each tribe speaking a different dialect. The Thai people are very charming. They have been described as tolerant yet conservative, gracious but sensitive, proud but shy. The three main languages are Thai, Chinese, and English. One cannot graduate from high school without six years of English.

Religion. Buddhism is the state religion of Thailand, and the Thai people take their religion very seriously. "There is no Buddhist home in all Thailand that does not have its small spirit house in the garden."[11] Scattered throughout the country are 20,000 temples and monasteries housing some 170,000 mendicant monks who, in their brilliant saffron robes, go from door to door every morning to receive the food gladly given by the faithful. Every male citizen is expected to spend three months in the *Sangha* (monastic order), and men in civil service are paid during their stay. Being the state religion, Buddhism is identified with patriotism. To be a real Thai one must be a Buddhist. The people are open and friendly, and in theory there is a form of religious tolerance; but in practice it is exceedingly difficult, almost impossible, for a Buddhist to become a Christian. To do so is to cease to be a Thai. The Muslims in the south are orthodox but not fanatical. Evangelistic work among them is open and unopposed, though few of them have shown any real interest in the gospel. One mission working in that region reports one baptized convert in fifteen years!

From the beginning American missionaries have been welcome in Thailand. The nineteenth century giants made a lasting impression on both government and people; but the huge influx of American military personnel in recent years has occasioned a certain degree of resentment. American money has sparked inflation, and American morals have offended the sensibilities of a conservative populace. Some of this resentment is bound

---

11 *East Asia Millions*, April, 1963, p. 52.

to be reflected in the official treatment of the missionaries. In recent years the government has set a quota on the number of missionaries entering the country. Permanent visas are difficult to obtain, and temporary visas are good for only ten weeks. A missionary holding a temporary visa must leave the country when it expires and apply for a renewal, a process which may take several weeks; and a renewal is not always granted.

Early Missions. The first Protestant missionary to Thailand was *Dr. Karl F. A. Gutzlaff* of the *Netherlands Missionary Society.* He was there for only three years, from 1828 to 1831, but during that time he translated the Bible into Siamese and portions of it into Lao and Cambodian. In addition, he produced a dictionary and a grammar of the Siamese and Cambodian languages. Jacob Tomlin, of the *London Missionary Society,* arrived in Bangkok the same year as Gutzlaff, but remained less than a year.

In response to Gutzlaff's appeal two American missions entered Thailand: the *American Board of Commissioners for Foreign Missions* in 1831 and the *American Baptist Convention* in 1833. The leading missionary of the American Board was *Dan Beach Bradley,* whose thirty-eight-year career as physician, surgeon, publisher, diplomat, and man of God, was fabulous. Following his only furlough he returned to Thailand in 1850 under the *American Missionary Association.* As a doctor he treated thirty-five hundred patients in his first year in Bangkok. He performed the first surgical operation in Thailand in 1837. He introduced vaccination and inoculation in his fight against smallpox. He served as personal physician to three of Thailand's kings. As a publisher, he founded Thailand's first newspaper, the *Bangkok Recorder.* As a diplomat, he was entrusted by King Mongkut with the delicate task of translating state papers, foreign treaties, and other important documents. He was the best-known, most-loved foreigner in the country. To this day Mo (Doctor) Bradley is a legend in Thailand. The American Board found Thailand a barren field, and withdrew in 1849, without baptizing a single convert.

The American Baptist work got under way in 1833 when the *Reverend and Mrs. John Taylor Jones* were transferred from Burma to Thailand. Although appointed to work with the Thai, Mr. Jones was attracted to the large Chinese colony in Bangkok and found a ready response among them. In six months time he baptized three Chinese. Two years later the *Reverend William Dean* joined the Thailand mission and took over the Chinese work. The Chinese church, founded in 1837 with eleven charter members, is today the largest church in Bangkok.

The third American mission to enter Thailand was the *Presbyterian Board of Foreign Missions* whose first missionaries, *Mr. and Mrs. William P. Buell,* arrived in Bangkok in 1840. At that time there were twenty-four American missionaries in Thailand. By 1869 both the American Board and the Baptist Mission had withdrawn from Thailand, leaving the field entirely to the Presbyterians. The Baptists resumed work after World War II.

The Presbyterians did not find Thailand any more responsive than did the Congregationalists or the Baptists; but they persevered and refused to give up. They too worked for almost twenty years before winning their first convert. The early believers were fiercely persecuted and their leaders imprisoned. Just when the situation looked hopeless the hostile king suddenly died. Over night the climate changed. The new king looked with favor on the missionaries and they were able to carry on their work without further hindrance. The medical missionaries especially were held in high esteem. Some were placed in charge of government hospitals. Several lady missionaries were invited to teach the women of the royal household.

Chiengmai, the largest city in north Thailand, is the center of Presbyterian work. Besides a church, the complex includes the *Prince Royal's College* (boys), *Dara Academy* (girls), *Thailand Theological Seminary, McCormick Hospital,* and the famous *McKean Leprosy Hospital,* which cares for five hundred leprosy patients.

In 1934 the Presbyterian churches got together and organized the *Church of Christ in Thailand.* Complete integration of church and mission came in 1957. In 1970 it had twenty-five thousand members, making it by far the largest Protestant group in the country. The church is divided into twelve districts served by 135 full-time leaders. Eighty-two fraternal workers continue to assist the church, mostly in institutions located in twelve centers. The Church of Christ, though predominantly Presbyterian and belonging to the World Alliance of Reformed Churches, is really an ecumenical organization. Two other missions are part of the church: the *Disciples of Christ* and the *Marburger Mission* of Germany. Also, the Chinese churches of the *American Baptists* are affiliated with the 12th District of the Church of Christ. The church is a member of the World Council of Churches and the East Asia Christian Conference. While independent, it still receives large grants from the Presbyterian mission. Working with this church are a dozen missionaries from the Orient. In 1964 the church sent its first missionary to work among the primitive people of Sarawak.

The *Seventh Day Adventists* are the second oldest mission, having a continuing work dating back to 1918. For years they have operated a large, well-equipped hospital in Bangkok. More recently they have added two smaller hospitals, one in Bhuket and the other in Haad Yai. Most of their converts have been from the Chinese community in the Bangkok area.

The *Christian and Missionary Alliance,* occupying fifteen provinces in the northeast section of the country, began work in 1929. Over the years it has labored diligently to build up an indigenous church, but progress has been slow. There is a high incidence of leprosy in Thailand, and the C&MA

has taken a special interest in these unfortunate people. In 1968 Dr. Payton treated almost eight hundred patients in twenty-nine field clinics. In fact, this compassionate form of Christian ministry has produced more than half of the churches in the northeast. The *Central Bible School* and the *Maranatha Bible School* (for leper patients) have a combined enrolment of almost sixty students. The indigenous church, known as the *Gospel Church of Thailand,* was organized in 1950. It is still necessary for the twenty-four pastors to support themselves. In recent years violent opposition has come from the "Jesus Only" group. Several churches have defected, and others have been decimated as a result. Total church membership is close to two thousand. A new venture is the English-speaking Evangelical Church of Bangkok, which has had a full-time pastor since 1968.

Postwar Missions. Here, as in other countries of East Asia, there has been a substantial increase in the number of missions in the past twenty-five years. The first of these was the *Worldwide Evangelization Crusade,* whose first four missionaries arrived in Bangkok in 1947. For the first fourteen years an average of one new missionary each year joined their numbers, and a new station was opened every two or three years. There were very few results in the first ten years. Many professed Christ but fell away at the first hint of persecution. In 1956 work was begun among the Karen tribe. WEC work is centered in the three western provinces of Tak, Sukothai, and Kampengpet.

The second mission to enter in this period was the *Southern Baptist Convention,* whose ex-China missionaries arrived in Thailand as early as 1949. Their work began in the Bangkok area, where they now have ten centers of evangelistic outreach. More recently they have opened three centers in the extreme south not far from the border of Malaysia. During this twenty-year period they have made commendable progress. Already there is a church of thirteen hundred members served by twenty national pastors. A seminary trains pastors for the fourteen congregations. A hospital ministers to Christian and non-Christian alike. Besides working in the hospital and seminary, the missionaries, seventy in number, assist the growing church in its evangelistic outreach.

In 1952 the *Overseas Missionary Fellowship,* another ex-China mission, entered Thailand. Today its 212 missionaries are working among three distinct groups: the animistic tribespeople in the north, the Buddhist Thais in the midsection of the country, and the Muslim Malays in the south. In the mountainous regions of north Thailand live some two hundred fifty thousand primitive people belonging to twenty tribes, each with its own dialect. OMF missionaries are working with eight of these tribes; evangelism and Bible translation are important aspects of their work. Tribal work here is quite different from that in southwest China, where some of the missionaries had worked previously. The two main obstacles to the progress of the gospel have been demon worship and opium growing. In recent years communist infiltration has added a third dimension. Two OMF missionaries have been killed, Lillian Hamer in 1959 and Roy Orpin in 1960. A few converts have been made, but as yet there has been no breakthrough. In central Thailand the main work centers around the hospital at Manorom, with seven missionary doctors on the staff. An area of specialty is the rehabilitation of leprosy patients. *George K. Harris,* who gave a lifetime of service to the Muslims of north China, pioneered the OMF advance into south Thailand, where forty missionaries, working out of four centers, are seeking to reach the Muslims for Christ. In fifteen years only one convert has been baptized.

In 1951 the *United Missionary Society* of the Christian Churches (Disciples of Christ) sent its first missionaries to Thailand. They entered into partnership with the British Churches of Christ, whose work dates back to 1903. The main work through the years has been centered in Nakon Pathom, thirty-five miles west of Bangkok. Early in 1961 they joined forces with the American Baptists in a cooperative effort known as the Kwai River Christian Mission, which ministers to the Pwo Karens near the Burma border. The Disciples of Christ mission is also part of the Church of Christ in Thailand.

The *New Tribes Mission* moved into Thailand in 1952 and has developed work among three tribes, So, Lawa, and Pwo Karen. Their twenty missionaries are located in five centers and Bangkok.

The *American Baptists,* who pioneered in Thailand in 1833 and withdrew in 1869, returned to the field in 1952. Since then they have concentrated on three main areas: the Chinese in and around Bangkok, the Karen tribe in the northwest, and a joint effort with the Disciples of Christ in west Thailand close to the Burma border. Their four-thousand-member Chinese Church is now affiliated with the 12th District of the Church of Christ in Thailand. In the north the response among the Karens has been very encouraging. Some time ago there came into existence the Karen Baptist Convention. In 1968 the Lahu churches were organized into an association which was received into the Karen Baptist Convention. So rapid has been the growth that the church decided to change the name to the *Thailand Baptist Convention,* which includes five Karen associations and one Lahu association. "There is such strong emphasis on evangelism that continuing growth seems certain. Rev. James Conklin has been asked, upon his return from furlough, to give full-time leadership in evangelism."[12]

Medical Missions. Beginning with Dr. Dan Bradley in 1835 and continuing to the present time, medical work has been a very important factor in the Christian mission in Thailand. During the nineteenth century

[12] American Baptist Foreign Mission Society, *Staff Report to Board, May, 1969,* p. 45.

Thailand's most prominent killers—tuberculosis, cholera, malaria, and smallpox—claimed the lives of tens of thousands every year. Bradley and his associates did not make much headway against the first three; but they were eminently successful in their fight against smallpox, which is practically nonexistent today. At the present time there are fourteen Christian hospitals staffed by thirty missionary doctors and twenty-one national doctors. Compared with other countries, the ratio of national doctors to missionary doctors is high. The Church of Christ heads the list with six of the fourteen hospitals. Leprosy is a major health problem in Thailand. There are several leprosy hospitals and scores of leprosy clinics, most of the latter maintained by the C&MA. Before missionary medical personnel can register in Thailand they must successfully pass the government examinations.

The Bible Societies. The British and Foreign Bible Society has been involved in translation work since 1828. The American Bible Society set up an Agency in 1890. The two societies merged to form a Joint Agency in 1962 under American administration. Since 1965 the work in Laos has been under the direction of the Thailand Bible Society.

Karl Gutzlaff, with the help of his wife, performed the prodigious feat of translating the Bible into the Siamese language in three years between 1828 and 1831. With so much haste and so little help, it is doubtful if the translation was very accurate. There is no evidence that that Bible was ever published. The first portion of the Scripture in Thai appeared in 1834, the New Testament in 1843, and the Bible in 1883. In northern Thai the New Testament was completed in 1914 and the entire Bible in 1927. In addition the New Testament is now available in Tai Lu, and Portions in five other tribal dialects. The revised New Testament in Thai was published in 1967 and the Old Testament will soon be ready for publication. Production has been slightly delayed to allow for minor changes suggested by the Roman Catholic Church, which has agreed to use the new Bible in its schools. In 1967 New Testaments were printed in Thailand for the first time. Work is now proceeding on a simplified "common language" version aimed at making the Scriptures intelligible to the non-Christian Thai of limited education. Local support for the work of the Bible House is on the increase, but it is still less than 10 percent of the total budget.

Christian Radio. Some Americans may not believe in the "domino theory" for Southeast Asia; but certainly the communists are giving high priority to Thailand in their international broadcasts. Radio Peking devotes a total of 225 hours each week, in four Chinese dialects, to broadcasts to Thailand. Radio Hanoi broadcasts twenty-one hours weekly in English and eight hours in Cantonese, besides an undisclosed number of hours in tribal dialects, especially Meo. By contrast, Christian radio is hopelessly inadequate; but at least the Christian message is being heard.

For many years Christian programs have been beamed into Thailand from Manila by short wave. The effectiveness of this medium is lessened, however, by the fact that by 1967 only 5 percent of the new radios had short-wave bands, and only half of those worked! It is not surprising that a recent survey revealed that 60 percent of the Thai prefer local programs. In more recent years missions inside Thailand have begun to make use of commercial radio. The *Worldwide Evangelization Crusade* is producing "Voice of Peace" programs which they release over five local stations. Other missions borrow recorded material for broadcasting over five additional stations. The *Christian and Missionary Alliance* has the most extensive program of all. It is now producing sixty weekly programs for local broadcasts, and its mailing list increased 500 percent in one month. Time on commercial stations in Thailand is about as cheap as anywhere in the world. A fifteen-minute daily program during prime time costs only $25.00 a month.

Evangelism. Institutional work has a way of pushing evangelism to the perimeter. This has been true in all of the countries, not only in Thailand. During the postwar period, when the number of missionaries has quadrupled, much more time and attention have been devoted to evangelistic work, by which is meant winning non-Christian men and women to a personal faith in Jesus Christ as Savior and Lord. It is still too early to evaluate the results of these renewed efforts; but the Congress on Evangelism in Singapore in 1968, which attracted a dozen delegates from Thailand, set in motion a chain reaction which will have continuing repercussions in days to come. *Operation Mobilization* now has a permanent representative in Bangkok. In January, 1970, Thailand held its own Congress on Evangelism.

> As a result of the January Congress on Evangelism in Thailand spontaneous prayer cells have sprung up throughout the nation and an interdenominational committee is planning evangelistic efforts. A nationwide youth conference, planned by Thai young people present at the Congress, is another first in Thailand.[13]

The Christian Presence. Twenty-five years ago Kenneth Scott Latourette wrote: "Numerically Christianity, whether Roman Catholic or Protestant, had made somewhat slower progress in Siam than in the other major lands of south-eastern Asia."[14] The situation has not changed appreciably in the intervening period. After 140 years of church and mission work, interrupted only by the Japanese occupation during World

---

[13] *In-Depth Evangelism Around the World,* May-August, 1970, p. 1.

[14] Kenneth Scott Latourette, *A History of the Expansion of Christianity,* Vol. VI (New York: Harper & Brothers, 1944), p. 245.

War II, the Protestant community numbers little more than one tenth of 1 percent of the population. The Roman Catholics, who have been in Thailand for four centuries and outnumber the Protestants by more than two to one, have no more than one hundred thousand adherents. The largest of all Protestant groups, the Church of Christ in Thailand, is a well-organized church with a well-educated clergy; but it is not able fully to support its own pastors nor to maintain its many fine institutions without subsidies from the United States. The Christian hospitals have built up an enormous reservoir of goodwill; but the tangible results in terms of Christian commitment have not been commensurate with the huge investment of men and money. There is not a single Christian college or university in Thailand, hence it has been difficult to establish rapport with the intellectuals. Nor has there been a major breakthrough among the tribes such as took place in Burma. In spite of the presence of over six hundred missionaries, nearly all of them Americans, the Christian impact on Thailand has been negligible.

Vietnam

Political History. History in this part of the world goes back at least to 2000 B.C. For a thousand years Vietnam was under the suzerainty of China; but in A.D. 939 the Vietnamese threw off the Chinese yoke and established an absolute monarchy. As in other areas, Chinese civilization survived the collapse of Chinese rule. The literary and moral code of Confucius gave definite shape to Vietnamese thought and religion, with results distinctly seen to this day. European contacts with Vietnam began when Roman Catholic missionaries arrived in the sixteenth century, followed shortly by traders. France, which regarded itself as the guardian, if not the champion, of Christianity in Asia, gradually asserted its authority; and by 1893 Vietnam, Laos, and Cambodia were incorporated into French Indochina.

During World War II Japan overran Indochina and used it as a springboard for its attack on Malaya and Indonesia. Following the Japanese surrender, the French returned to salvage what they could of their shattered empire; but the underground forces, nationalist and communist, which had fought the Japanese continued to fight against the French. The outcome was the complete defeat of the French forces at Dienbienphu. That was followed by the Geneva Conference in July, 1954. It was there that the decision was made to divide the country at the 17th Parallel, the industrial north going to the communists and the agricultural south remaining in the hands of the nationalists. For five years all went well; then communist guerrillas, known as Viet Cong, began to harass the Saigon government. In 1964 they were joined by communist troops from North Vietnam. The United States, committed to the protection of the Saigon regime, first sent military advisors, then arms, and finally troops. The so-called civil war has dragged on now for ten years, with heavy casualties on all sides and incredible suffering inflicted on the civilian population. Needless to say, church and mission work has been disrupted; pastors, missionaries, and Christians have been among the war dead. This has been the most ruthless, most destructive, certainly the most frustrating, war in modern times.

The People. The population of Vietnam is about eighteen million, including almost a million refugees from the communist North. The Vietnamese, who constitute 85 percent of the population, are of mixed Thai and Chinese origin. They occupy the fertile plains. The remainder of the population is made up mostly of primitive tribes who live in the central highlands. There are two million Chinese in Vietnam, a sizable minority. Most of them are Vietnamese citizens, but they retain their own language and culture.

Religion. The Vietnamese, like the Chinese, are not a deeply religious people. They are more concerned with the here and now than with the life after death. Mahayana Buddhism is the dominant religion, but it is mixed with Confucianism, Taoism, and animism. Though priests and monks are found in all parts of the country, it is the scholar who is venerated. A politico-religious sect peculiar to Vietnam is Caodai, which began in 1926. It is an eclectic cult which combines the worship of Buddha, Lao Tze, Confucius, the Virgin Mary, and Jesus Christ. Its membership may run as high as four million.

Roman Catholics. After the Philippines, Vietnam is the most Catholic country in Asia. Missionary work began in the sixteenth century and by the middle of the seventeenth century there were 300,000 baptized persons. *Father Rhodes* was the outstanding missionary of that period. His transliteration of the Vietnamese (Chinese) characters is still in use today. For two centuries the mission was beset by persecution, exile, and even martyrdom. It was not until the end of the nineteenth century that settled conditions permitted peaceful, constructive work. The first Vietnamese bishop was consecrated in 1933. Three-quarters of the 800,000 refugees from North Vietnam were Catholics. This is one reason why they left. The number of Catholics in Vietnam is about 1.6 million, which is 9 percent of the population. This makes the Roman Catholic Church a religious and political force to be reckoned with. Today the church is thoroughly indigenous; in 1964 all but one of its thirteen bishops were nationals.

> All missionary work today is carried out under the direction of the Vietnamese bishops or in closest collaboration with them. An indigenous episcopate forms a normal part of the evangelization of the country; it is the sign of the maturity of the church. Today the missionary puts himself at the disposal

of the national church, which makes use of him according to his qualifications and interests. Fifteen nations are represented among the 160 Catholic foreign missionaries now resident in South Vietnam.[15]

Christian and Missionary Alliance. No other country in the world has been the sole responsibility of one mission for so long a period of time. From 1911 until after World War II the *Christian and Missionary Alliance* was the only Protestant mission in Vietnam. As early as 1895 two C&MA missionaries visited the province of Tonkin to survey the prospects for missionary work. It was not until 1911 that *Dr. R. A. Jaffray* and two south China missionaries secured property in Tourane (now Danang). The church there began with the conversion of a Confucian scholar, four members of the royal family, government officials, and other persons of high standing in the community. The church in Tourane doubled its membership each year for a number of years, until there were one thousand members. The French officials were not sympathetic and for many years the missionary work was restricted to Hanoi, Haiphong, and Tourane. With the lifting of restrictions in 1929 additional stations were opened in cities with names which have now become household words in the United States: Dalat, Nhatrang, Hue, Cam Ranh Bay, Pleiku, and many others. Work among the tribespeople, based in Banmethuot in the south central highlands, got under way in 1934. The first tribe was the Raday. Their language was reduced to writing, thus making the gospel available to 200,000 people. From the Raday the work spread to other tribes, until today it is organized into two tribal districts, central and south; and churches are emerging in dozens of tribes and dialects. In the Koho tribe there are seventy churches whose membership includes one-seventh of the 120,000 people in the tribe.

In a rapidly expanding church leadership training is very important. Hundreds of lay leaders attend short-term Bible schools each year. Two well-equipped Bible institutes, one at Dalat and one at Banmethuot, both with national principals, are training full-time leaders for the tribal churches. The Central Bible School, which for many years has trained leaders for the Vietnamese churches, has been moved to Nhatrang. Now known as the *Bible and Theological Institute,* it offered its first B.Th. degree in 1969. Present plans call for a seminary in Saigon.

With a forward-looking spirit rare in mission circles, the C&MA as early as 1927 gave autonomy to the developing church, known as the *Evangelical Church of Vietnam.* Incredible as it may seem, this church has been growing by leaps and bounds in spite of the widespread devastation of the war years. Today its baptized membership stands at fifty thousand, which makes it the largest but one of all the churches in the twenty-six fields in which the C&MA is working.

---

[15] Gerald H. Anderson, *Christ and Crisis in Southeast Asia* (New York: Friendship Press, 1968), p. 60.

Her godly president, Rev. Doan Van Mieng, has manifested unusual wisdom and courage in leading the church through the most critical experiences of her 60-year history. His earnest prayer is that the Lord will give ten million converts in Vietnam and that the church will be a source of blessing for all the people. His courage is beginning to spread throughout the church in every district with a new wave of optimism and faith and a new advance in evangelism and church planting.[16]

The War Years. Few wars in history have been more devastating, and none has been so "dirty" as the war in Vietnam. The ghastly, gory, gruesome details have been portrayed ad nauseum by the mass media of our country; but little or nothing has been said or written about the sheer heroism of church and mission personnel, who have carried on under conditions that stagger the imagination. Missionaries have been accidentally killed, kidnapped, and massacred in cold blood; yet to a man they have remained at their posts; even after the "Tet offensive" only the women and children were evacuated. Church leaders have risked their lives times without number to remain with their people. In not a few instances both pastor and people have been killed, sometimes inadvertently, at other times with malicious intent. Hundreds of churches, schools, hospitals, and even orphanages have been damaged or destroyed. One pastor rebuilt his church ten times in ten years. Christian families have been separated; parents have been killed; orphans and widows have had to beg for a living.

Death still reigns. Last night here in Dalat two men, two women and a child were killed. The night before six tribesmen and four Vietnamese were murdered. And perhaps by now you have learned of the attack the V. C. made in which they slaughtered eighteen defenseless chaplains. The morning after the senseless killing I went with Pastor Tot over to the room where their bodies were laid out on the tables for a short memorial service. I can't describe it and if I could you wouldn't want to read it. The communists write in blood what they think of religion.[17]

Yet one can read the annual reports for these war years without finding a single word of resentment or self-pity. In their place what do we find? A willingness to take joyfully the spoiling of one's goods; gratitude to God for the privilege of sharing in the fellowship of suffering; a determination to persevere in the building of a better and stronger church; and an unshakable faith in the promises of God. This kind of courage is alien to the human spirit. Only men and women fortified with a double portion of the Spirit of God could achieve such an incredible performance. This is indeed one of the brightest chapters in the history of the Christian mission.

Wartime Relief. With the American involvement in Vietnam and the daily coverage given to the war by the mass media, it was inevitable that

[16] *Annual Report for the Year 1965,* p. 65.
[17] Overseas Crusades, *Cable,* July-August, 1970.

American churches and missions should feel a special obligation to come to the aid of the longsuffering, down-trodden people of Vietnam. Some of these agencies are there on a pro tem basis, engaging in relief and rehabilitation until the emergency is over. The three largest agencies are the *Mennonite Central Committee, Church World Service,* and the *Lutheran World Federation.* To avoid duplication and competition they have been working since 1966 with the *Vietnam Christian Service.* The *World Relief Commission* of the National Association of Evangelicals, and *World Vision, Inc.,* have also sponsored relief programs. The *Christian and Missionary Alliance* has, of course, allocated large sums of money for the relief of its own large constituency and the rebuilding of churches. In addition, church bodies all over the world have contributed large sums of money for relief purposes. Some of these funds have gone to North Vietnam. The *American Friends Service Committee,* after several years of work, suspended its program in February, 1968, because, said an official, "intensified military operations have disrupted transportation, communications, supplies, and all phases of normal civilian life. Under these conditions it is impossible for us to continue."[18]

Recent Additions. *Wycliffe Bible Translators* entered Vietnam in 1957. By 1970 they had fifty-five missionaries working in twenty tribes. Language analysis and translation are proceeding. They have plans to enter ten more tribes when workers become available.

In 1958 the *Worldwide Evangelization Crusade* entered Vietnam and for nine years worked in conjunction with an independent work founded some years earlier by the *Reverend Gordon Smith,* formerly of the C&MA. The work is located in the central highlands. By 1964 the mission could report a Bible school which had already trained forty national workers, six of whom had been brutally murdered by the communists. The missionaries, then numbering twenty-four, were calling for forty more workers to help them in their church planting operations.

The *Southern Baptists* initiated work in Vietnam in 1959 and ten years later reported six churches with almost one thousand members. Their publication work centers in Danang and their seminary, opened in 1967, is located in Saigon. Each of the churches has its own pastor, but only one church is self-supporting. With seventy missionaries on hand, the Southern Baptist Convention intends to expand its program in Vietnam.

Other agencies, some of them supporting, some cooperating, entered Vietnam during the sixties. *Paul Contento* of the *Overseas Missionary Fellowship* has a fruitful work among the students in Saigon. A dynamic, hard-working man, Mr. Contento has organized local chapters of *Inter-Varsity Fellowship* and the *Scripture Union,* both of which are now under

---

[18] *Ecumenical Press Service,* February 29, 1968.

national leadership and cooperating closely with the Evangelical Church of Vietnam.

The *United World Mission* is working with the *Reverend and Mrs. Gordon Smith* among fourteen Montagnard tribes in the central highlands. Their work includes, among other projects, two orphanages and a leprosarium. In 1968 they were calling for twenty-five young couples to prepare for missionary work in Vietnam.

One or two small groups are helping out in various ways: the *Go Ye Fellowship, Navigators, Overseas Crusades.* The *Reformed Church of France* ministers mainly to French citizens and those who speak that language.

The Scriptures. The entire Bible in Vietnamese has been available since 1916. The New Testament has recently been published in Koho and Raday. Portions are available in several other tribal dialects. Several missions are engaged in translation work, but the lion's share is now being assumed by Wycliffe Bible Translators. In spite of the chaotic conditions caused by the war, Scripture distribution continues unabated. Indeed, the misery created by the war has driven many people to seek solace in the gospel.

> The strain and disruption of normal living patterns brought about by the war have, in many cases, opened new avenues of ministry for the Church and for the Word of God. Complete freedom is enjoyed to distribute Scriptures in hospitals, prisons, army camps, resettlement villages and refugee centers. The demand far exceeds the supplies of Scriptures available.[19]

In addition to the work of the Bible Societies, special agencies such as the *Pocket Testament League, Gideons International,* and *Scripture Gift Mission* were instrumental in distributing millions of Gospel Portions. Scripture distribution and evangelism go hand in hand, and both are paying high dividends in Vietnam. In its *1969 Annual Report* the C&MA reports nine thousand decisions for Christ in only one of its five main areas of work.

Christian Radio. Vietnam is the only country in Southeast Asia where the Christian church has almost unlimited opportunities for broadcasting the gospel. For the past fifteen years the government has given free time to the Evangelical Church of Vietnam on the government-operated radio network. Protestants, Catholics, and Buddhists all are allotted a half-hour weekly broadcast on government stations reaching from the Mekong Delta right up to the 17th Parallel. In 1969 the government offered the church one free television broadcast a month which will reach six million viewers. The Far East Broadcasting Company in Manila continues its twice weekly broadcasts to Vietnam.

---

[19] American Bible Society, *Annual Report for the Calendar Year 1967,* p. 84.

The Church in North Vietnam. The only two churches in the north were the Roman Catholic Church and the Evangelical Church of Vietnam (C&MA). Authentic, up-to-date information is difficult to obtain; but it is safe to assume that the pattern of church life there does not differ from that in other communist countries, where the church is allowed to exist but not to grow. "The *Catholic Annual of Vietnam,* the last issue of which appeared in 1964, reported that in North Vietnam there were 833,000 Roman Catholics with 10 bishops and 361 priests."[20]

In a letter dated February 25, 1965, the Acting Foreign Secretary of the C&MA reported that the churches in the north were permitted to hold services in the churches but not in homes. Church buildings could not be repaired or enlarged; and, of course, no new buildings could be erected. Street meetings and literature distribution were prohibited. Young people were still holding meetings, but were subjected to a heavy barrage of communist propaganda. It is doubtful if the situation has improved in the last five years. It is more likely to have deteriorated.

Laos

Political History. Once part of French Indochina, Laos received its independence in July, 1949. "Laos raised its national flag with little more than a flagpole to go on—and that only a whitewashed length of bamboo."[21] Since then the country, one of the most backward and poverty-stricken in the world, has been plagued with intrigue, nepotism, and corruption. Civil war involving the Pathet Lao, Viet Minh, and government forces has continued with varying intensity for twenty years. Cease-fires have been arranged and violated times without number. Only mammoth aid from the United States, much of which went down the drain, has kept the country afloat. Three princes heading three factions, right, left, and center, formed a coalition government in 1962. A fourteen-nation conference has guaranteed the neutrality and independence of Laos; but the eastern half of the country is under communist control. The western half remains in government hands.

The People. The population is close to three million, divided almost equally between two ethnic groups: the Lao, who live in the Mekong valley; and the mountain tribes, Meo, Man, Kwa, and Yao. In addition there are an estimated ten thousand Chinese. Other minorities include Vietnamese and Indians. The Laotian people are desperately poor, even by Asian standards. Disease and malnutrition are endemic and public sanitation is unknown. To add to their miseries, tens of thousands of refugees

---

[20] Gerald H. Anderson, *op. cit.,* p. 59.

[21] Leslie Chopard of Mission Evangelique, *East Asia Millions,* February, 1970, p. 23.

from communist areas have sought sanctuary in government controlled areas; but the government was unable to give much help.

Religion. Buddhism in Hinayana (orthodox) form was introduced into Laos before the twelfth century and is today the state religion. The king, whose royal capital is at Luang Prabang, is the civil and religious head of the state and therefore the protector of Buddhism. Vientiane, the political capital, is known as "the city of ten thousand temples." The Laotian Buddhists have been as resistant to the gospel as their coreligionists in neighboring Thailand. Only a handful of them have become Christians. The mountain tribes are animists; they live in constant fear of evil spirits who cause disease, death, and all kinds of dire calamities. These primitive peoples have been much more receptive to the gospel and the great majority of the seventy-five hundred Christians are tribespeople.

The Swiss Brethren. Protestant missionary work began in 1902 with the arrival of the *Swiss Brethren* (Mission Evangelique). They occupy the southern part of the country, where they work out from three main centers on the Mekong River: Khammouane, Savannakhet, and Pakse. Most of their work is among the Laotians and until recently the response has been anything but encouraging. The unsettled conditions in the country, however, have softened the hearts of the people, and today there is a greater willingness to listen to the gospel. Missionaries report that they enjoy excellent rapport with town officials, due in part to their medical work. A Tamil evangelist, Dr. G. D. James, founder-director of the Malaysia Evangelistic Fellowship, during an evangelistic campaign in Laos in 1968 reported an average of six hundred to one thousand present at each service. "The people listened to the message with rapt attention. . . . Many heard the gospel for the first time, and more than one hundred were counseled."[22] The Swiss Brethren in 1970 reported thirty local assemblies and one full-time national worker. Their medical work includes a leprosarium. The New Testament appeared in Lao in 1926 and the Bible in 1932, both the work of the Swiss Brethren.

Christian and Missionary Alliance. The *Christian and Missionary Alliance* work in Laos dates back to 1929, when its first missionaries arrived in Luang Prabang in the north and took over what remained of the intermittent, itinerant missionary effort of the North Siam Mission of the Presbyterian Church. Other main centers were opened in Vientiane (1931), Xieng Khouang (1939), Sayaboury (1955), and Sam Thong (1968). The national church, largely tribal, is understandably weak. Most of its leaders have not had the advantage of even an elementary education. The *Laos Bible Training Center*, opened in Vientiane in 1939, now offers a four-year

22 *East Asia Millions*, August-September, 1968, p. 130.

course with an eighteen-month in-service training program between the third and fourth years. The *Evangelical Church of Laos* comprises sixty-five organized churches with a total membership of 6,000—up from 334 in 1955. The large increase is due mostly to a mass movement in the Meo tribe during the 1950's. For a short period in the late sixties the tranquillity in church-mission relations was upset when an outside group made offers of material assistance to the national church. Two thriving churches, one Chinese and the other Vietnamese, are part of the Evangelical Church of Laos.

Overseas Missionary Fellowship. With a longstanding tradition of pioneer work, the *Overseas Missionary Fellowship* entered Laos in 1957 to take up work in the south in conjunction with the Swiss Brethren operating along the Mekong River. Working out from three Swiss Brethren bases, the OMF made itself responsible for the evangelization of some twenty tribes in the jungles along the Vietnam border. This difficult but promising work was just getting under way when that part of Laos came under communist control, and certain centers had to be abandoned. In the face of incredible difficulties and not a little physical danger, about two dozen missionaries continue to maintain a Christian witness in eleven centers.

Christian Radio. As might be expected, Christian broadcasts are not possible inside Laos. Both the C&MA and the Swiss Brethren, however, have recording studios which prepare tapes for broadcasting shortwave from Manila. The schedule includes a daily morning and evening program in Lao and three programs a week in Meo. *Gospel Recordings, Inc.* has provided gospel records in a dozen or more tribal dialects not yet reduced to writing. These are of immense help in evangelizing these primitive people.

Missionary Aviation Fellowship. In 1964 *Don Berry* flew a Wren—modified version of a Cessna 182—to Laos and inaugurated *Missionary Aviation Fellowship* service in that country. In a rugged, landlocked country without a railroad and with few all-weather roads, the air service provided by MAF is of inestimable benefit to the missions operating in Laos. Some twenty remote airstrips, carved out of the mountains and jungles by government troops, have been made available to MAF. Some of these are behind communist lines and others change hands overnight. Flying conditions in Laos are the most difficult of all the many fields in which the MAF operates. Its pilots are men of great skill and courage. Missionaries, national workers, refugees from communist areas, and all kinds of supplies are transported quickly, safely, and cheaply by the MAF plane.

In November, 1968, *World Vision International* signed an agreement with the Royal Laotian Government which prepared the way for the same sort of program—relief, educational work, and medical work—which it has pursued in Vietnam for four years.

Mention should be made of about fifteen Japanese evangelists, not affiliated with any particular mission, who are working in Laos. Several of them were captured by the Pathet Lao but later released. Christian work, whether for the missionary or the national worker, is not easy in chaotic, war-torn Laos.

Cambodia

Political History. Cambodia is heir to the famous Khmer Empire which flourished between the eleventh and fourteenth centuries, whose ancient capital of Angkor still attracts tourists from all parts of the world. During the eighteenth century Cambodia lost territory to its neighbors on the east and west. Since then mutual distrust and enmity have marred international relations in that part of Southeast Asia. Cambodia won its independence from France in 1953 and since that time has tried, not too successfully, to maintain a neutral stance between Washington and Peking. Prince Sihanouk, a very popular, playboy type of personality with great oratorical powers, abdicated the throne to become premier in 1955 and chief of state in 1960. In 1965 he severed relations with the United States. He himself was removed from power by a military coup while visiting Moscow and Peking in early 1970. The recent American-Vietnamese military incursion into Cambodia was a military success, but it may yet turn out to be a political blunder. In the meantime, United States-Cambodian relations have been restored.

The People. Cambodia is a small country with a population of about 6,600,000. Nearly 85 percent of all Cambodians are of Khmer descent. Important minorities include Chinese and Vietnamese. Tens of thousands of Vietnamese are now being repatriated to South Vietnam. Khmer (Cambodian) is the official language. French is widely used; English is taught in the schools.

Religion. Theravada Buddhism is the state religion and 90 percent of the people are Buddhists. The chief of state is also head of the Buddhist religion. Buddhist temples are found everywhere, even at the village level. They are well kept and the monks are well cared for by the populace. The state protects Buddhism and Buddhism is expected to support the government. Roman Catholic missions have been in Cambodia for four centuries. Their converts have not been numerous and have come mostly from the Vietnamese and Europeans.

Christian and Missionary Alliance. Here again the *Christian and Missionary Alliance* has the distinction of being the only Protestant mission in the country. Its work dates back to 1923, when it opened its first station in the capital of Phnom Penh. In 1933 the French government restricted missionary activity to those areas which had been worked prior to 1932. This restrictive policy was continued until 1946, when the new constitution granted religious liberty. In the meantime, the C&MA had been successful in founding three strong, self-supporting churches—Cambodian, Chinese, and Vietnamese—in the capital city. One outstanding achievement was the translation and publication of the New Testament in 1929 and the complete Bible in 1954. A Bible school was established in 1925 at Battambang. In 1949 it was moved to the outskirts of Phnom Penh. Owing to government restrictions and illness among the missionaries, only nine of Cambodia's seventeen provinces were ever occupied by full-time workers, missionary or national. The national church grew gradually to six hundred baptized members in eighteen organized churches. In 1961, at the invitation of the C&MA, the *Far Eastern Gospel Crusade* transferred a couple from the Philippines to Cambodia to work in an area south and east of the Mekong River; but the unsettled conditions forced their withdrawal in October, 1963. About the same time the *Worldwide Evangelization Crusade* announced plans to begin work in Cambodia, but subsequent events made this impossible. When Cambodia broke off diplomatic relations with the United States in 1965 all missionaries were expelled; but the national church was not left without missionary assistance. The C&MA arranged for the *French Alliance* to send a couple to Cambodia to hold the fort.

When diplomatic relations between Cambodia and the United States were renewed in the summer of 1970, missionary work was resumed immediately. The first C&MA missionary to return was the Reverend Eugene Hall, who arrived in Phnom Penh on July 6. About the same time *World Vision* representatives arrived with relief supplies. Doubtless other missions will follow suit. Everything depends on developments within the country. The present military regime might be overthrown by the communists, in which case Prince Sihanouk is almost sure to be restored to power. In that event American missionaries will probably again be expelled.

Indonesia

Political History. The Republic of Indonesia was proclaimed on August 17, 1945; but it was not until December 28, 1949, that the Dutch, after 350 years of colonial rule, reluctantly relinquished their hold on this colony so rich in natural resources. The western part of New Guinea, now known as West Irian, was ceded to Indonesia in 1963, largely through the efforts of the United Nations. The Indonesian ship of state has experienced rough sailing in the first two decades of independence. Besides the war of independence against the Dutch (1945-1949), there have been at least four major rebellions in various parts of the archipelago in addition to the Confrontation with Malaysia to say nothing of runaway inflation and economic stagnation.

The most far-reaching of all the crises was the abortive coup by the communists on October 1, 1965, which resulted in a complete reorientation in Indonesia's internal affairs and foreign policy. The Indonesian communist party was outlawed and three hundred thousand communists and suspected sympathizers were killed, as many by mob violence as by military action. President Sukarno, freedom fighter, father of the republic, author of "guided democracy," and charismatic playboy, was diplomatically and progressively removed from power. His successor, General Suharto, broke diplomatic relations with Communist China, ended the Confrontation with Malaysia, brought the country back into the United Nations, and moved Indonesia cautiously towards *rapprochement* with the United States. Inflation, vastly improved in recent years, still remains something of a problem; but it looks as if Indonesia, after twenty-five years, is beginning to set its house in order.

The People. With 120 million people, Indonesia is the fifth most populous nation in the world. Its people are Malay-Polynesian in origin. They speak over two hundred fifty dialects and twenty-five major languages. The official language is Bahasa Indonesian, which is based on Malay. English has replaced Dutch as the first foreign language. Several dialects of Chinese are spoken by the three million Chinese in the archipelago, who fall into two main groups: those born in Indonesia and those born in China. The Indonesia-born represent 70 percent of the Chinese community. Their ancestors in some cases came from South China centuries ago, even before the Dutch arrived in the islands. Approximately half of the Chinese are citizens of Indonesia. Of the other half, 250,000 are reckoned to be citizens of Red China; the remainder are stateless. Ever since 1960 the Chinese have been subjected to various forms of discrimination. In 1967 the Dayaks of Kalimantan went on the rampage, killing the Chinese and confiscating their houses and property. At one time 40,000 displaced Chinese were in refugee camps in Pontianak and Singkawang. The abortive coup in October, 1965, engineered by the communists with moral and material help from Communist China, did nothing to improve the lot of the Chinese community.

The population of Indonesia is by no means evenly distributed through the islands. Java, with only 7 percent of the land area but 65 percent of the population, is one of the most densely populated parts of the world. Kalimantan, on the other hand, though many times larger than Java, has only four and a half million people. Some of the principal groups are the Bataks and Minangkabaus (Sumatra), the Javanese and Sundanese (Java), the Menadonese and Buginese (Sulawesi), and the Dayaks (Kalimantan). In West Irian the tribespeople are just now emerging from the Stone Age—thanks to the efforts of the missionaries.

Religion. The ideological basis of the state is expressed in the five principles known as *Pantjasila:* belief in a Supreme Being, just and civilized humanity, the unity of Indonesia, guided democracy, and social justice. Although Islam is the dominant religion, the government recognizes three others: Hinduism, Buddhism, and Christianity. Indeed, Indonesia is the only Muslim country in the world where there is complete and genuine freedom of religion.

Animism, the earliest of the religions, is rapidly disappearing; but its influence still permeates the other religions. In the course of history the people of Indonesia have embraced four religions: Hinduism, Buddhism, Islam, and Christianity, in that order. Hinduism, mixed with the Balinese religion, flourishes on the small island of Bali. Buddhism has died out except among the Chinese. Islam, which first appeared in the twelfth century, today claims 85 percent of the population. Christianity, in Roman Catholic form, was introduced in the sixteenth century by the Portuguese.

Islam in Indonesia tends to be rather tolerant. There is still an underlying feeling that it, too, is an imported religion, and Indonesian Muslims are much more open and liberal than their fellow believers in the Middle East. They themselves distinguish two groups, fanatical and nominal. The Muslims in East and Central Java belong mostly to the nominal group. Those in the eastern part of Indonesia are the fanatical type and on occasion have resorted to "holy war" against the Christians. All citizens are expected to believe in God, and religion is part of the school curriculum. "Hundreds of teachers of the Christian faith are needed, because public and parochial schools are required by law to provide religious instruction to students from first grade through university. The Armed Forces have requested three hundred more Protestant chaplains to serve the military establishment—one of the most promising missionary opportunities today."[23] In the central government there is a bureau of religious affairs. Protestants and Catholics and, of course, the Muslims, all have their own political parties.

Early Protestant Missions. Roman Catholicism was first introduced into the East Indies by the Portuguese at the close of the fifteenth century. About one hundred years later, when the Portuguese were driven out by the Dutch, some eighty thousand Roman Catholics became Protestants. Here, as in Ceylon, the Dutch authorities employed coercion to

---

[23] Gerald H. Anderson, *op. cit.,* p. 131.

force the indigenous population to embrace the Christian faith, with the result that hundreds of thousands of persons "requested" baptism without undergoing a corresponding change of heart.

In order to consolidate their control and coordinate their efforts, the Dutch organized the United East India Company chartered by the Netherlands government. In keeping with the temper of the times, the company made itself responsible for the propagation of Christianity as well as the promotion of commerce. As might be expected, the company did a better job with the latter than with the former. During most of the eighteenth century it had difficulty in recruiting chaplains for the work. By 1776 there were only twenty-one Dutch ministers in the whole of the East Indies. By 1810 the number had dropped to five.

A new era began with the formation of the *Netherlands Missionary Society* in 1797. Other societies were organized in Germany in the early part of the nineteenth century, at which time missionary work in the East Indies passed into the hands of the missionary societies. However, under Dutch colonial rule, certain areas were declared off limits to the missionaries lest they stir up the animosity of the Muslims. At the same time, the colonial government divided the country into various regions, and only one mission was permitted to work in a given region. In this way there developed regional churches, each with its own language and culture. In spite of these restrictions the various missions continued to prosper, and mass movements among the animists introduced a period of rapid growth. Over one hundred thousand Muslims embraced the Christian faith.

Later Missions. Few countries in the world offer such demographic diversification and few mission fields are plagued with such religious proliferation as Indonesia. It seems best, therefore, to trace the progress of the Christian mission in each of the five main islands: Sumatra, Java, Kalimantan, Sulawesi, and West Irian.

Sumatra. The first attempt to bring the gospel to the Toba Bataks of north Sumatra proved abortive when *Henry Lyman* and *Samuel Munson* of the *American Board* were killed in 1834. The *Basel Evangelical Missionary Society* began work in western Sumatra in 1858. The largest and most successful work was that of the *Rhenish Missionary Society,* whose first converts came in 1861 from Islam. The outstanding pioneer was *Ludwig Nommensen,* who gave fifty-six years of missionary service to the cause of Christ among the Bataks. For the first twenty years progress was slow; but a people's movement in 1883 introduced two decades of spectacular growth. The *Batak Protestant Christian Church* was the first of the many Indonesian churches to receive its independence. This took place in 1930. Since 1940 it has been strictly self-supporting, self-governing, and self-propagating. Today, with a membership of one million, it is the largest church in the country.

A second large church in Sumatra, the *Nias Protestant Christian Church,* was also the work of the *Rhenish Mission.* It is located on Nias and other small islands off the west coast of Sumatra. The work began in 1865, but the first convert was not baptized until nine years later. Here, again, progress was slow, with only five thousand believers after thirty-five years. The turning point came when a remarkable revival of great spiritual power broke out in 1916 and continued for nine years. By 1940 the number of Christians had increased to 135,000. The Nias church received its autonomy in 1936 and today has a membership of 250,000.

American Methodist work in Sumatra dates back to 1905, when a Tamil teacher from Malaya opened a church and school for Chinese. By 1921 the work had spread along the east coast. In 1964 the Sumatra Annual Conference became the autonomous *Methodist Church of Indonesia.* Present membership is around fifty thousand. In the late 1960's a small group of English Methodists joined the work in Sumatra.

The *Karo Batak Protestant Church,* fruit of the work of the *Netherlands Missionary Society* begun in 1890, has experienced phenomenal growth in recent decades. From 1940 to 1946 its membership soared from five thousand to thirty thousand. During the recent revival in 1967-68 some fifty thousand additional members were received in eighteen months. Church leaders were hard pressed to provide the necessary instruction to prepare them for baptism. The church has been independent since 1940; but it has only nineteen ordained ministers for two hundred congregations.

Another church brought into existence by the *Rhenish Mission* is the *Simalungun Protestant Church.* Earliest efforts were initiated in 1903 with the arrival of the first Rhenish missionary. For several decades this work was combined with that of the Toba Batak Church and the Toba language was used in churches and schools. It was not until the Japanese occupation that the Simalungun Christians were permitted to express Christianity in terms of their own language and culture. Between 1953 and 1967 church growth reached almost 300 percent. The church has been completely on its own since 1963.

These five denominations on the island of Sumatra are all members of the National Council of Churches. Other major groups include the *Seventh Day Adventists* and the *Pentecostals.* Growth among the former has been quite modest. The Pentecostals, reported in 1961 to be divided into seven separate groups, have been working mostly among the Batak people, where they now have 300,000 members. This by no means exhausts the list of Christian groups on Sumatra. According to the Department of Religion there are no fewer than forty church organizations on the island.

Java. The Christian mission in Java has been much less successful than in Sumatra. Although Protestant missions have been there for more than one hundred fifty years and cover nine-tenths of its territory, fewer than five-tenths of 1 percent of the population is Christian. The principal reason for this is that the great majority of the people are not pagan but Muslim; and even though several hundred thousand of these have been won to Christianity, there has not been any mass movement on the scale seen in Sumatra. The outstanding mission in Java has been the *Netherlands Missionary Society.*

The oldest church now on the island of Java, is the *Western Indonesia Protestant Church,* which dates back to 1620. It was once part of the state church of colonial times, and only in 1948 did it gain its independence. It is not really indigenous to Java; it is made up largely of people from eastern Indonesia who moved to Java to find or keep employment with the colonial government or business firms. Unlike other churches, it is not an ethnic group, but embraces Dutch, Indo-Europeans, Ambonese, Timorese, Minahasans, and others. Total membership is about three hundred fifty thousand.

The *East Java Christian Church* goes back to 1815. It was the result not of missionary endeavor but of lay witness. In the early decades two outstanding men left their stamp on this church. They were C. L. Coolen, the son of a mixed marriage, who favored a Javanese form of Christianity; and a German watchmaker named Emde, who favored a Western form of Christianity. In 1849 the *Reverend J. E. Jellesma* of the *Netherlands Missionary Society* arrived on the scene and he succeeded in effecting a fusion of the two types. Jellesma and his successors preached the gospel, trained Javanese evangelists, and established Christian villages which formed the backbone of the church from 1870 to 1910. The East Java Church has been a missionary church from the beginning, which accounts in part for its large membership of eighty-five thousand today. In 1931 it became one of the earlier churches to achieve autonomy.

The *Java Christian Churches* got under way in 1858; and here, too, local Christians laid the foundations. It was not until the late 1880's that the first missionary of the *Netherlands Missionary Society* arrived. He found nine thousand believers meeting in scores of congregations. In 1891 the mission decided to branch out on its own rather than build on another man's foundation. After several decades the indigenous group dwindled, some of its members dying and others finding their way into the church established by the missionaries. Under missionary leadership the center of gravity shifted from rural to urban areas, where schools and hospitals as well as churches had a wider ministry. The Java Christian Churches became independent in 1931 and today have a total membership of eighty thousand in Central Java.

A second church on Java owes its existence to the *Netherlands Missionary Society,* whose first missionaries arrived in 1863. The Sundanese of West Java, being staunch Muslims, proved to be a most barren field. In one center after forty years of hard work the congregation numbered only seventy. The *Pasundan Christian Church* became autonomous in 1934 and now has a total membership of some sixteen thousand.

One church in Java has a Mennonite background, the *Java Evangelical Christian Church*. Beginning in 1851 the Dutch missionary, *P. Jansz,* labored for twenty years and made fewer than two converts a year. He worked among the Muslims along the north coast. During the Japanese occupation this church suffered greatly at the hands of the Muslims and the Japanese. In recent years it has been strengthened by assistance from the Mennonite Central Committee and the European Mennonite Evangelism Committee. During the past fifteen years it has grown at the rate of almost 400 percent. Present membership is about thirty thousand.

The *Southern Baptists* launched their Indonesia mission on Christmas Day, 1951, with the arrival in Djakarta of three ex-China missionaries. By the end of the first year there were ten missionaries, and the First Baptist Church of Bandung had been organized with twenty members. At the end of five years there were five churches in five cities of Java; a seminary had been opened and a publication building erected. A hospital was opened in 1957. In 1961 the work spread to Sumatra with the opening of a center in the city of Pelambang. Since then three other cities have been occupied. Work was started on the island of Madura in 1966 and plans were laid to enter Bali in 1970. In the past two decades the mission has steadily increased its staff of missionaries, which now numbers 111. Twenty-six churches, all self-supporting, have a combined membership of almost ten thousand.

Chinese Churches in Java.   It is estimated that there are three million Chinese in Indonesia, most of them in the large towns and cities, where they are very successful businessmen, merchants, and traders. The earliest Christian congregations were formed in the latter half of the nineteenth century in the homes of the first converts in various cities of Java. Through the years several missionary societies have worked among the Chinese: the *American Methodists,* the *Netherlands Missionary Society,* the *Christian Reformed Missionary Society,* and the *Mennonites.* Today there are five Chinese denominations in Java, three of which are fairly large: the *East Java Indonesian Christian Church,* the *Central Java Indonesian Christian Church,* and the *West Java Indonesian Christian Church.* The combined membership is fifty thousand. The Chinese churches are large; they are located in the cities; they all have well trained leadership and are self-supporting.

Chinese churches are not confined to Java; they are found in all parts of the archipelago. A new era began with the visit of Dr. John Sung in 1939.[24] Wherever he went revival broke out; second and third generation nominal Christians were soundly converted and non-Christians were added to the church in large numbers. Best of all he imparted to these churches a vision for the evangelization of their own communities. Since World War II

[24] See Leslie Lyall, *John Sung, Flame for God* (Chicago: Moody Press, 1954).

other well-known Chinese evangelists have conducted campaigns in Indonesia: Andrew Gih, Leland Wang, Timothy Dzao, and others. In 1952 Andrew Gih founded the Southeast Asia Bible College at Malang in East Java. It has a present enrolment of almost one hundred and is supported entirely by funds raised in Indonesia. Already its graduates are making a significant impact on the Chinese churches throughout the islands.

Another reason for the recent growth in the Chinese churches is that the Chinese have seen the handwriting on the wall and have at long last decided to abandon their policy of isolation for one of assimilation; the Christian church affords a convenient bridge between the two cultures. It is estimated that one out of every ten Chinese in Indonesia is a Christian—twice the ratio of Christians among the Indonesian people.

Kalimantan. Kalimantan occupies the southern two-thirds of the island known in the West as Borneo. Much of the island is covered with jungles, swamps, rivers, and forests. The four and a half million inhabitants occupy the southern and western areas. The Dayaks comprise the main ethnic group. Religiously the population is divided three ways, Muslims (3,000,000), animists (1,000,000), and Christians (300,000, most of them Roman Catholic). The animists are fast giving up their primitive form of religion and thousands of them are turning to Christianity. "The Dayaks are wide open to the reception of a new faith. Not many are turning to Islam; most are turning to Christianity—either Protestant or Roman Catholic. It is conceivable that within a few decades the whole of the Dayaks will have turned to Christianity."[25]

Protestant missionary work in Kalimantan started with the arrival of the *Rhenish Missionary Society* in 1836. During the early years the mission was plagued with all kinds of difficulties, including a rebellion which excluded the missionaries for seven years. After seventy years of work there were only two thousand Christians. In 1925 the work was turned over to the *Basel Evangelical Missionary Society* of Switzerland. Ten years later the Dayak Evangelical Church was organized. In 1953 its name was changed to the *Evangelical Church of Kalimantan*. With Dayaks turning to Christianity at the rate of five thousand a year, this church now has a membership of at least eighty thousand.

The *Christian and Missionary Alliance* has been at work in Indonesia since 1929. Its most famous pioneer was *Dr. Robert A. Jaffray,* who gave forty years of unremitting service, first in south China and later in Indonesia. The first party of missionaries occupied two centers in east Kalimantan with a view to reaching the Dayaks for Christ. As the number of missionaries increased three districts were developed in east Kalimantan. In 1935 the mission opened a second field in west Kalimantan, where the churches are divided into two districts. In both districts the work is

---

[25] *East Asia Millions,* July, 1963, pp. 108, 9.

among the Dayaks, in the inaccessible regions where Islam has not penetrated. Tens of thousands of Dayaks have accepted Christianity. Their
self-supporting churches are part of the *Gospel Tabernacle Church of
Indonesia,* which includes some three hundred fifty organized churches
with an aggregate membership of sixty thousand. It is, therefore, the
largest church in all of the C&MA's twenty-six fields. East and west
Kalimantan each has its own Bible school. In addition, the *Jaffray School
of Theology* in Makassar (Sulawesi) offers the most advanced training of
all eight C&MA Bible schools in Indonesia. Total enrolment in these
schools is 430. In 1969 the first *Missionary Aviation Fellowship* plane
arrived in Kalimantan and has drastically reduced the time and hazards of
missionary travel. While Kalimantan is the C&MA's first and largest field in
Indonesia, the mission has work also in Sulawesi, Java, Bali, and Timor. Its
headquarters, first established in Makassar, was moved to Bandung in 1954
and to the capital, Djakarta, in 1960.

Several faith missions have work in Kalimantan. The *Regions Beyond
Missionary Union* entered in 1947. It built on the previous endeavors of
several independent missionaries, all of them Moody graduates and supported by a Prayer Group in London. Arriving in 1933, Miss Greet van't
Eind mastered the Dayak language in six months, built her own house,
established her own medical work, and for three lonely years trekked the
jungles by herself to share the gospel with the Dayaks before she lay down
to die. In 1937 William and Sylvia Sirag, supported by the same Prayer
Group, took up the work which had been interrupted by the untimely
death of Miss van't Eind; but William died a few years later in a Japanese
concentration camp. In 1947 Mrs. Sirag returned to Kalimantan, this time
under the auspices of the Regions Beyond Missionary Union. She was
accompanied by Miss Gudrun Lima. A Bible school at Darit, with an
enrolment of sixty, is training national leaders for more than thirty
indigenous churches. In recent years the mission has also worked in
northwest Kalimantan, where it has contact with the Chinese population.

The *Worldwide Evangelization Crusade* entered Kalimantan in 1949.
This is pioneer work. It involves a rugged kind of life which includes river
travel by canoe, sleeping in Dayak longhouses, and working with primitive
people. Young women have responded to the need for workers and have
persevered in the face of overwhelming odds; but young men in larger
numbers must offer for service if these primitive people are to be adequately evangelized. In 1951 WEC extended its ministry to southern
Sumatra, where it has work among the dwindling Kubus. Two years later it
moved into East Java and in 1959 established a Bible school at Batu. In
ten years the enrolment increased from ten to one hundred. The school is
staffed by WEC missionaries, but it is incorporated as an Indonesian
organization under national leadership. Its principal, Pak Octavianus, is
one of Indonesia's outstanding evangelists; his campaigns in Indonesia and

other countries have resulted in thousands of decisions for Christ. More recently WEC has sent missionaries to the islands of Timor and Madura.

It was the presence of large numbers of Chinese in Indonesia that first attracted the *Overseas Missionary Fellowship* to that part of the world. Initial contacts were made with overseas Chinese churches, and OMF missionaries were at once invited to work in cooperation with two congregations in west Kalimantan where there is a large concentration of Chinese-speaking people. During the following twenty years more than two thousand converts were baptized and some twenty new Chinese churches established.

As the OMF became better known, invitations came from Indonesian churches in other parts of the republic, and today the OMF has a missionary task force of sixty-five working in cooperation with and under the direction and leadership of twenty different denominations or Christian institutions. With government immigration regulations, plus the deep conviction that missionary contribution could best be made in close cooperation with the already existing orthodox, Bible-believing churches of Indonesia, the OMF gladly entered wide-open doors of cooperation with local churches of many ethnic groups in Sumatra, Java, Sulawesi, and Kalimantan.

In addition, qualified personnel were sent to Christian hospitals and universities, theological colleges and Bible schools, teacher training colleges, and state universities. Missionaries are engaged in student work and Bible teaching in primary and secondary schools, and the mission has made a sizable contribution to the preparation and publication of evangelical literature, and in the training of Indonesian national writers and lay workers. OMF missionaries are also engaged in follow-up work in connection with the revival in Indonesia.

The *Conservative Baptists* have been in West Kalimantan since 1961. Their work is based on Sungai Betung, where twelve of their twenty missionaries are located. Much of it is among the Dayaks; but they also have contacts with the Chinese, especially in the city of Singkawang. The program includes evangelism, vacation Bible schools, medical work, and leadership training. As yet no Bible school has been established. Growth has been rather slow, with only two organized churches and a combined membership of 150.

Sulawesi. Several Dutch societies were responsible for the evangelization of Sulawesi. First on the scene was the *Netherlands Missionary Society,* which entered the northeastern peninsula in 1822 in an area known as Minahasa. Its pioneer missionary was Joseph Kam. So successful was the work that by 1870 the Christianization of the area was virtually complete. Today 600,000 of the total population of 700,000 are Christians. Of these, 500,000 are members of the *Minahasa Evangelical Christian Church,* which became autonomous in 1934. The remaining 100,000

Christians belong to the Roman Catholic Church and some twenty small Protestant groups.

Three other churches are also the result of the ministry of the Netherlands Missionary Society: the *Central Sulawesi Christian Church,* the *Southeast Sulawesi Protestant Church,* and the *South Sulawesi Christian Church.* The Southeast and the South Churches are comparatively small, with a combined membership of only ten thousand. There are two reasons for this. First, missionary activity was late in getting under way; and secondly, this area is the home of some of the most fanatical Muslims in all of Indonesia. The story is different with the Central Sulawesi Church, which is located in the northern region of central Sulawesi among the Toradja people. The two outstanding pioneers were *Dr. Albert C. Kruyt* and *Dr. N. Adriani,* whose indigenous policies of missionary work paid off in mass movements so great they had to call for help from the Minahasa Church. In 1947 the Central Sulawesi Church became autonomous. Since 1961 no foreign missionaries have been needed. Membership in 1968 was 125,000, divided among some 340 congregations.

The second mission was the *Dutch Reformed Missionary Society,* which sent its first missionary into Bolaang Mongondow in 1904. After more than sixty years of effort there is a sizable church, the *Evangelical Christian Church of Bolaang Mongondow.* It has thirty thousand members.

Another Sulawesi church is the *Toradja Christian Church,* which resulted from the labors of the *Dutch Christian Reformed Missionary Association.* Its first missionary, *Van Loosdrecht,* arrived in 1913. This church quadrupled its membership during twenty years of the severest persecution ever suffered by an Indonesian church. A fanatical group from the south murdered their pastors, burned churches and Bibles, and sought to force the Toradja Christians to renounce their faith at the point of the sword. Today it is one of the larger churches in Indonesia with a membership of almost two hundred thousand.

Before we move over to West Irian we should make mention of two other large churches in the eastern part of the archipelago. One of these is the *Protestant Church of the Moluccas,* the oldest Protestant church in Asia. Its present membership is over four hundred thousand. The second one is the *Timor Evangelical Christian Church,* which dates back to 1612. With some seven hundred thousand members it is the second largest church in Indonesia.[26]

West Irian. This is the last major area of the world to be occupied for Christ. Its hundreds of tribes are just now emerging from the Stone Age, helped by the missionaries and, more recently, by the Indonesian government, which gained control of West Irian in 1963. The mountainous

---

[26] In preparing this section on Indonesia the author has made extensive use of materials found in Frank L. Cooley's excellent book, *Indonesia: Church & Society* (New York: Friendship Press, 1968).

terrain and a complete absence of roads make travel impossible except by plane; and the Missionary Aviation Fellowship has done yeoman service for the half dozen missions in this part of the world. In recent years several planes have crashed, taking the lives of pilots and missionaries.

The picture in West Irian is spotty. In some areas the missionaries have been welcomed, mass movements have developed, and thousands have turned to the Lord. In other areas the opposition has not been only stubborn but satanic. In some places missionaries and evangelists have been killed. Since 1963 the Indonesian government has tried to impose its rule on the primitive tribes in the interior and this has resulted in opposition and rebellion. For a time new missionaries were not admitted, and missionaries already there were caught in the crossfire between two opposing forces. Both they and the Christians tried to remain neutral, but this is not always easy to achieve. Mr. Harold Lovestrand of The Evangelical Alliance Mission was suspected of collaborating with the tribespeople and spent some months in prison in Djakarta.

The *Utrecht Missionary Union* was the pioneer society in this part of the world. Its work in West Irian dates back to 1855. For the first forty years only the utmost perseverance kept the missionaries at their task. During the first twenty-five years, there were only some twenty converts. The first breakthrough did not occur until the turn of the century. A period of rapid growth began in 1910 and lasted until 1940. During that period the number of believers increased from five hundred to fifteen thousand. Today there is a Christian community of one hundred thousand.

It was under the leadership of Dr. R. A. Jaffray that the *Christian and Missionary Alliance* entered West Irian. The first mission station was established at Enarotali in 1939 after two missionaries and three Indonesian Christians traveled eighteen days on foot from the coast. The work was held up during the Japanese invasion but resumed in 1946. In June, 1949, the work was extended to the Kemandora Valley and to the Baliem Valley in 1954. The work is now divided into three districts with 263 organized churches and 110 unorganized groups. The national church, known as the *Gospel Tabernacle Church of West Irian,* has a total membership of twenty thousand. There are four hundred national workers. In most areas church growth has been rapid, aided by miracles of healing and instances of persons actually raised from the dead. Such phenomena are not unusual when the Holy Spirit moves in power. In a few cases the church members have already grown cold and indifferent and need a fresh touch of the Spirit.

The government requires all missions in West Irian to provide education for the tribespeople. This means that education plays a major role in the missionary program. The C&MA has eighty-five primary schools and one teacher training school. Most of the teaching is done by trained tribespeople under the supervision of the missionaries. As the literacy rate has increased the demand for literature has become overwhelming, and the mission must provide reading material on a vast scale. The New Testament in Moni and Uhmunduni should be off the press this year (1970). The mission maintains six Bible schools, five in the tribal languages and one in Indonesian.

The Evangelical Alliance Mission has been working in West Irian since 1952, when two pioneer missionaries on an exploratory trip into unknown jungle territory were brutally slain by their native carriers. Undaunted, other missionaries volunteered to take their place. The mission is working in two districts, Bird's Head in the extreme northwest and among the cannibals of the south coast. The *Erikson-Tritt Bible Institute,* named for the two martyrs, was opened in 1959. Three years later its first nine graduates took up work in various parts of West Irian. Today TEAM has forty missionaries in fourteen centers engaged in evangelism, church planting, Bible translation, literature, medical work, and primary education.

The first station of the *Unevangelized Fields Mission,* located at Lake Archbold, was established in 1954 by missionaries from Australia. Three years later the first contingent of North American workers arrived. By 1965 there were thirteen couples in half a dozen stations. Part of their field is located among the Dani tribe, where thousands have burned their fetishes and turned to Christ. Intertribal warfare has been abolished and demonism is gone. Thirty-five churches have been established with almost three thousand baptized believers. Adherents number twenty thousand. A central Bible school is in operation and already some three dozen pastors have been appointed.

The *Regions Beyond Missionary Union* with a team of four missionaries established a beachhead at Lake Sentani on the north coast in 1957. An MAF plane flew them to Lake Archbold and from there they trekked five days through jungle territory to Bokodini, where they set up their first station in the central highlands among the Dani tribe. Today they have sixty-three churches with eight thousand baptized members. Seven of their thirteen missionary couples are working with this tribe. The Vine Memorial Hospital and the Maranatha Bible Institute are also there. In 1969 the Dani Christians took up a missionary offering of twelve hundred rupiahs to support five of their own missionary couples. Through the years five other tribes have been entered; but in all of them the work has been difficult and the results disappointingly small. In all five tribes combined there are fewer than one hundred believers. Two RBMU workers, Stanley Dale and Philip Masters, were killed by hostile tribesmen on September 25, 1968, while on trek through unexplored territory.

There is close cooperation among the missions in West Irian. The UFM, C&MA, and RBMU are working together on the translation of the Dani New Testament, which is almost completed. In September, 1968, missionaries and evangelists from these three groups met in conference to lay plans for a joint advance into the Lakes Plain district. The *Maranatha Bible Institute* is sponsored jointly by the C&MA and RBMU.

Nowhere in the world are the missionaries more dependent on air travel than in West Irian, where the terrain is covered with jungles and the mountains rise to twelve thousand feet. The *Missionary Aviation Fellowship* has been the sole mode of transportation since 1954. Well over one hundred missionaries and many national pastors and evangelists depend on MAF for transportation, supplies, and emergency help. The MAF fleet of seven planes each year carries three million pounds of food, mail, equipment, fuel, school supplies, and medicines from five supply bases. From headquarters at Sentani MAF maintains daily contact with all the mission stations in West Irian.

Bible Translation. Though the *British and Foreign Bible Society* began work in 1811 and some work has been done by the *National Bible Society of Scotland,* the main burden has fallen on the *Netherlands Bible Society.* The *Bible Society of Indonesia* was established in 1951; but it still receives support from the other three societies. The complete Bible is now available in eight languages, the New Testament in twelve additional languages, and Portions in another thirty. The principal translation project is a new interconfessional version in Bahasa Indonesian, the national language. It is expected that the new Bible will be ready by 1971. Three factors have combined in the last decade to place a severe strain on the resources of the Bible societies: the rapidly increasing literacy rate, the sudden influx of hundreds of thousands of new converts into the church, and the government embargo against the importation of literature. To solve this problem the Indonesian Bible Society established its own printing plant in 1966. The demand still far outstrips the supply.

Ecumenical Relations. The great majority of the churches have long since been independent of missionary control. The Batak Protestant Christian Church led the way in 1930. Eight others received their autonomy in that decade; fourteen more followed in the 1940's. Twenty-seven churches became charter members of the *National Council of Churches* when it was inaugurated in 1950. There are now thirty-eight member churches, representing 75 percent of all Protestants. Three of the churches are Pentecostal. Fifteen are also members of the World Council of Churches.

The Christian Presence. The 1960 census placed the number of Christians at six million. According to the moderator of the Reformed Church of West Indonesia, the latest census has increased this figure to nine million. With recent mass movements into the churches, accurate, up-to-date figures are difficult to secure. The Protestants, who outnumber the Roman Catholics three to one, are found in all twenty-five provinces; but they are by no means evenly distributed. Fewer than 1 percent of the population of Java are Christians; in Minahasa 90 percent are Christians. Both the Roman Catholics and the Protestants have their own political parties. Many Christians hold high offices in the government.

Church Growth. Following the abortive coup of October 1, 1965, there was a mass movement into the Christian church. It was not confined to any one area of the country; practically every church experienced a period of rapid growth. In some instances church membership doubled in a few years. The Karo Batak Church, one of the smaller churches, baptized forty thousand persons in 1968. Several factors contributed to this phenomenal growth. (1) The government requires every citizen to belong to one of the four recognized religions. Animists, who represent about 2 percent of the population, were obliged to state their preference. Hinduism, which is virtually confined to the island of Bali, was hardly a live option. Buddhism, the smallest of the four religions, had little to offer. That left Christianity and Islam as the sole contenders, and more persons opted for Christianity than for Islam. (2) The destruction of communism and the chaotic conditions following the attempted coup created a moral as well as a political vacuum, especially among the Chinese, whose connections with Communist China rendered them suspect. In their dilemma many of them sought comfort in religion, and most of these turned to Christianity. (3) Many persons were ripe for conversion to Christianity prior to the events of 1965 but were held back by fear of reprisals from the communists. With the destruction of the communist party and the liquidation of three hundred thousand communists, these people were free to embrace Christianity. (4) These factors by themselves hardly explain the true nature and full extent of the movement. Undoubtedly it was a genuine revival of spiritual religion brought about by the mighty moving of the Spirit of God, in some places accompanied by charismatic manifestations reminiscent of the Acts of the Apostles.

The Characteristics of the Indonesian Church. Briefly they are as follows. (1) With few exceptions, the Batak Church being one, the churches are Dutch Reformed in background. All are theologically orthodox. (2) At the same time there is great diversity and proliferation. In north Sumatra alone the government lists forty Christian groups. (3) The churches are divided along tribal and ethnic lines. (4) Finance is a continuing problem, carried over from colonial days when the state subsidized the church. Many of the largest churches are tribal and therefore rural in background, and the people are poor even by Asian standards. (5) The Chinese churches are an exception to this rule. They are located in the urban areas and their members are business and professional people. Finance is no problem with them. (6) Qualified leadership is woefully inadequate. In the Batak Church, which has one million members, there are only two hundred pastors. The ratio is much the same in the other churches. (7) The churches are large numerically as compared with other Asian countries. Only India offers any comparison. Not only are the denominations large; the local congregations are also large. (8) The recent mass movements in all parts of the archipelago have placed a severe strain on the meager resources, human and material, of the churches. Without adequate preparation and instruction the new converts may possibly retain their animistic tendencies to the future detriment of the churches. (9) The churches of Indonesia have more converts from Islam than all the other churches of the world combined. (10) The churches have strong ecumenical ties, with thirty-eight of them in the National Council of Churches and fourteen in the World Council of Churches. Only Germany, the United Kingdom, and the United States have more members in the World Council.

Philippines

Political History. The Philippine Islands were discovered by Magellan in 1521 and annexed by Spain in 1565. In 1898 the islands were ceded to the United States following the Spanish-American War. After almost half a century of American political tutelage, the Republic of the Philippines became an independent sovereign nation July 4, 1946. It has often been referred to as the showcase of democracy in Asia, and on the whole the government has managed to preserve the democratic institutions inherited from America in spite of communist agitation, bureaucracy, corruption and, more recently, student unrest. The Philippines has a bilateral military agreement with the United States, and America has military bases and personnel in the islands, both of which are a source of irritation to the Filipinos. American economic policy *vis-s-vis* the Philippines is not altogether equitable, and this makes for bad feeling. In recent years anti-American sentiment has been running high. All of this does not help the cause of the Christian mission, especially when the overwhelming majority of missionaries are American.

The People. The people of the Philippines may be divided into three main families: the Negritos, the Indonesians, and the Malayans. The Negritos, about forty thousand in number, are exceedingly primitive in life and habits. The Indonesians invaded the Philippines and drove the aborigines into the forests and mountains. Later on, the Malayans came to the islands. They were of a higher order than the Indonesians and in time overran the islands, introducing rice growing, weaving, pottery, and woodwork. These people eventually came to dominate the country and today the lowland Filipinos are regarded as the descendants of these Malay invaders.

These three main groups are divided into smaller groups. They speak 130 different languages and dialects. Eight trade languages are understood by about 90 percent of the population which now stands at thirty-eight million. The growth rate of 3.3 percent is one of the highest in the world. Tagalog, Visayan, and Ilocano are the principal trade languages. Tagalog has been selected as the basis of the national language, which is called

Filipino. English continues to be widely used. Half of Manila's daily newspapers are in English. Spanish culture and American influence remain strong. The modern Filipino is a mixture of Western and Oriental, with the Oriental predominating. There are approximately three hundred thousand Chinese, most of them successful merchants, traders, and bankers, whose business acumen excites the jealousy of the Filipinos.

Roman Catholicism.   The Christianization of the Philippines started in earnest with the arrival in 1565 of Lopez de Legaspi and five Augustinian monks. Franciscans, Dominicans, and Jesuits followed, all teaching the doctrines of Christianity and the arts of Western civilization. A combination of religious passion and military conquest enabled the Roman Catholic Church to effect the conversion of the islands during the first century of occupation. Christianity has done much for Philippine society, and today 72 percent of the Filipinos are professing Roman Catholics, which makes the Philippines the only nominally Christian country in Asia. Some credit for this achievement must go to Philip II of Spain, who made the spread of the faith the chief aim of his colonial policy. Churches, hospitals, and schools were opened. An indigenous clergy was trained; but the first Filipino bishop, Jorge Barlin, was not raised to the episcopate until 1905. To the Catholic Church belongs the credit for stopping the advance of Islam as it spread north through the archipelago from Indonesia. Here, as in South America, the church suffers from a paucity of priests. While the constitution recognizes the principle of separation of church and state, Protestants have expressed concern regarding the rapid increase in the number of Roman Catholics in control of education and social welfare and within the political parties. The Vatican has a papal nuncio in Manila, and a Philippine ambassador is accredited to the Vatican. The first Philippine cardinal was consecrated in 1960. All presidents since independence in 1946 have been practising Roman Catholics.

Other Religions.   Non-Christian groups include about one million pagans, tribesmen who have through the years been driven into the mountainous regions of the main islands. In addition there are two million Muslims, known as Moros, concentrated largely in the southern island of Mindanao. The three hundred thousand Chinese in Manila and the other large cities are mostly Buddhists by religion and Confucianists by culture.

The *Philippine Independent Church,* sometimes referred to as the Aglipayan Church, was formed in 1902 when its leader, Gregorio Aglipay, broke with Rome and established a national Catholic church. To some extent the new church was a product of the chaotic conditions prevailing at the turn of the century; and there were political as well as ecclesiastical reasons for this rather unorthodox development.

> Filipino clergy by the tens and laity by the thousands, if not millions, flocked to the new church . . . For a while, the prospects for the new young church

seemed good, but the Roman Catholic Church filed suit for the return of the buildings and other property occupied by the "apostate" congregations. In a momentous Supreme Court decision handed down in 1906 the *Independientes* were ordered to surrender the disputed property to the Roman Catholic Church; and, in the process of obeying, many of the clergy and a large percentage of the laity went back to Rome, unable to give up forever the beautiful parish churches which their forefathers had built with blood, sweat and tears under the Spanish system of forced labor.[27]

Through the years the Philippine Independent Church has suffered many vicissitudes. A split in the church, due to a feud between the liberals and the conservatives, brought it to the brink of disaster. Since 1948, when three bishops of the Philippine Independent Church received consecration at the hands of the American Episcopate, the two denominations have worked in close cooperation. St. Andrew's Theological Seminary in Quezon City is now a union institution and trains priests for both churches. Since 1961 there has been full communion between them. The Philippine Independent Church, with a membership of over a million and a half, has some forty bishops in two dozen dioceses.

Protestant Missions. With the American annexation at the turn of the century came an influx of Protestant missionary societies from the United States. The first was the *Presbyterian Church in the USA,* whose pioneer missionary, *Dr. James B. Rodgers,* arrived in April, 1899. The famous Silliman University in Dumaguete City was founded by the Presbyterians in 1901. From the beginning the Presbyterians fostered an ecumenical spirit. In 1907 they joined with the Methodists to establish Union Theological Seminary in Manila. In 1929 they merged with the Congregationalists and the United Brethren to form the *United Evangelical Church.* In 1947 church and mission merged, after which the missionaries served as fraternal workers under the church. Since 1948 the Presbyterian work has been an integral part of the United Church of Christ in the Philippines. During the last decade the number of fraternal workers has decreased from sixty-seven to forty. Approximately one-third are in church work; the others are in medical, educational, and administrative work.

The second mission to enter the Philippines was the *Methodist Episcopal Church.* Bishop James M. Thoburn visited Manila in 1899 and made arrangements for Methodist work in the islands. Pending the arrival of the first missionaries, the *Reverend Nicolas Zamora,* an early convert, carried on the work. The first missionaries were five women of the Woman's Foreign Missionary Society, who reached Manila in February, 1900. The *Reverend Thomas H. Martin* arrived a month later, and the following year *Dr.* (later Bishop) *Homer C. Stuntz* arrived to take over the superintendency of the work. The first Bible school for women was

27 Gerald H. Anderson and Peter G. Gowing, "Four Centuries of Christianity in the Philippines: An Interpretation," *Encounter,* Vol. 25, No. 3, p. 358.

opened by *Miss Winifred Spaulding* in 1903. The first Mission Conference was organized in 1905 and the first Annual Conference in 1908. The Methodist Episcopal Church split three times, in 1905, 1909, and again in 1933. Its first Filipino bishop was elected in 1944. Today the Methodist Church is organized into five Annual Conferences. All top posts are held by Filipinos; American missionaries serve in supporting roles. Total membership is about seventy-five thousand with the Christian community almost three times that size, making it one of the largest Protestant churches in the Philippines. Something of a problem was posed in 1968 by the merger in the United States of the Methodist Church and the Evangelical United Brethren. The latter had been a member of the United Church in the Philippines, whereas the Methodist Church has never been part of the United Church. Until 1952 Methodist work was confined to the island of Luzon in the north; but since then church and mission work has been extended to Mindanao. Most of the two million Muslims (Moros) live on this large island. Evangelistic work has been directed to them; but to date there has been little or no response.

The *American Baptists* arrived on the field in 1900 and concentrated their efforts on the islands of Panay and Negros. *Dr. Eric Lund,* a Swedish Baptist missionary, was the first representative of the American Baptist Foreign Missionary Society. He and his companion, *Braulio Manikan,* a native of the province of Capiz, completed the translation of the Bible into Panayan Visayan by 1912. The first mission hospital in the islands was opened at Iloilo by *Dr. J. Andrew Hall.* Later Emmanuel Hospital was opened in Roxas City. In 1905 the *Reverend W. O. Valentine* established the Jaro Industrial School, which grew into the Central Philippine University. In the same year *Miss Anna V. Johnson* founded the Baptist Missionary Training School. Today it is part of the College of Theology in the university. Some schools started in the early years were later relinquished; but Filamer Christian Institute, founded as an orphanage in 1906, grew into an elementary school, then into a high school. The *Convention of the Philippine Baptist Churches*, formed in 1935, today includes some three hundred churches with a total baptized membership of thirty thousand. Six hundred full-time national workers are assisted by two dozen missionaries.

Next on the scene were the *Disciples of Christ,* who made their appearance in 1901. Avoiding Manila, they went to northern Luzon and established a station at Laoag. Between 1901 and 1954, some seventy missionaries of this board served in the islands. In 1943 the Disciples merged with the United Brethren to form the Evangelical Church, which later became a charter member of a larger union when the United Church of Christ in the Philippines was organized in 1948.

In 1902 the *American Board of Commissioners for Foreign Missions* (now the United Church Board for World Ministries) was assigned by comity agreement to the southern island of Mindanao. At that time 50 percent of its population was nominally Roman Catholic, 30 percent was Muslim (Moros), and the remainder was pagan. Pioneer missionaries were the *Reverend and Mrs. R. F. Black,* who located at Davao. They were joined in 1908 by *Dr. and Mrs. C. T. Sibley.* In 1929 the Congregation-alists joined with the Presbyterians and the United Brethren to form the United Evangelical Church. In 1948 it became part of the newly formed United Church of Christ in the Philippines. Today its two dozen missionaries are serving in various capacities with the United Church.

The *Protestant Episcopal Mission* began work in 1902. It has always maintained a significant ministry to the Anglo-American communities in Manila and elsewhere through the country. The mission also maintains a strong, self-supporting work among the Chinese in Manila. Other areas of interest are a well-established work among the Igorots of Mountain Province in Luzon and among the indigenous peoples of southern Mindanao. The medical work centers in St. Luke's Hospital and School of Nursing. *St. Andrew's Theological Seminary* and *Trinity College* are now operated jointly with the Philippine Independent Church. The Philippine Episcopal Church has a baptized membership of almost sixty thousand.

In 1902 the *Christian and Missionary Alliance* initiated work in the southern island of Mindanao. It was suspended several months later when the only missionary died of cholera. For several years after work was resumed in 1908, the mission had only two couples on the field; but beginning in 1923 reinforcements began to arrive and by 1941 there were thirty workers in the islands, all of whom survived the horrors of the Japanese occupation. In 1947 the Christian and Missionary Alliance Church in the Philippines became independent. In 1965 it sent its first missionary couple to Sumatra. Four years later a second couple followed. In 1969 the national church had 558 congregations, all of them self-supporting. Total baptized membership is in the neighborhood of twenty thousand. Church and mission jointly operate four Bible schools offering Christian training at various levels. Great importance is attached to lay leadership. Lay preachers institutes are held quarterly. As a result over two hundred self-supporting laymen have the oversight of small churches. While English is used in most city churches and in all schools, Alliance missionaries and national workers are teaching and preaching in thirty Filipino dialects. The Alliance Press in Tituan publishes more than two million pages of gospel literature annually. Radio broadcasting is a vital part of the Christian and Missionary Alliance program in Mindanao. *Good News Time,* a program begun in 1958, has now expanded to twenty-two weekly broadcasts over four commercial stations and one church-related station.

The *Seventh Day Adventists* initiated missionary work in the Philippines in 1910. Here as elsewhere they have developed strong institutions, including 174 elementary schools, twenty high schools, two colleges, and six hospitals. Church planting has not been neglected, however; in 1970 they reported no fewer than 1,165 churches with an aggregate membership of 125,000.

The *Association of Baptists for World Evangelism* has been at work in the Philippines since 1928. Its first missionaries were *Dr. and Mrs. R. C. Thomas* and *Miss Ellen W. Martien,* who resigned from the American Baptist Board in the Philippines. During the first ten years the mission rapidly extended into the islands of Luzon, Panay, Negros, Mindanao, and Palawan. A gospel ship had an effective medical-evangelistic ministry among the islands of the Sulu Sea. Since then two additional islands, Leyte and Guimaras, have been added. The missionary force now numbers seventy-two. With the Association of Baptists for World Evangelism, medical work is a means to an end; it is always correlated with evangelism and church planting. Two Bible schools are maintained, one in Manila and the other in Iloilo. The latter offers training on four levels to ensure a steady stream of pastors, evangelists, and Bible women for the more than two hundred fifty indigenous churches. The Filipino Christians have organized their own associations, locally and nationally. They have their own home and foreign mission boards.

The *Assemblies of God's* work in the islands is unique in that it was started by Filipinos who were converted in the United States and trained in American Bible schools. With a burning desire to witness to their own people they returned to the Philippines in the 1930's and established Assemblies of God churches. Today some of these men are outstanding leaders in the work. Here, as in other countries, the Assemblies of God have concentrated on evangelism and church planting. To this end they have established six Bible schools in various parts of the archipelago. The Far East Advanced School of Theology was opened in Manila in 1964 to provide advanced training for graduates of their Bible schools throughout the Far East. Baptized members numbering almost fifty thousand are found in their 425 churches and 370 outstations, which are served by almost 700 national workers and forty-four missionaries.

United Church of Christ. In 1948 three denominations merged to form the *United Church of Christ in the Philippines.* These were the *United Evangelical Church* (Presbyterian and Congregational), the *Evangelical Church* (United Brethren and Disciples), and the *Philippine Methodist Church* (Independent). Five American denominations cooperate with the United Church: Disciples, United Presbyterian, United Methodist, Reformed Church, and United Church of Christ. Besides assigning some seventy fraternal workers to the United Church, these mission boards make large annual grants to its educational, medical, and administrative work. An Interboard Office in Manila coordinates the activities of the five boards related to the United Church.

With a growth rate of from 4 to 5 percent per year, the United Church finds it impossible to support a seminary-trained ministry for all of its fourteen hundred congregations. Only four hundred of its ministers are ordained. With a total baptized membership of 160,000 the United Church of Christ is by far the largest Protestant church in the Philippines. The United Church has included in its form of government the office of bishop. It serves its people and its country through more than twenty schools—Bible schools, academies, junior colleges, nurses' training schools, two theological seminaries, and Silliman University. It also operates five hospitals and half a dozen dispensaries. Its Board of Missions has sponsored a score of missionaries in Thailand, Indonesia, Okinawa, Hawaii, Canada, Brazil, and Taiwan. The chairman of the general assembly, the highest ecclesiastical body, may be a minister or a layman, and along with the bishops who serve for four-year terms, he has oversight of the church. These bishops are ineligible for reelection after three terms. One of its bishops, *Onofre Geneta Fonceca,* described by *World Vision Magazine* (Sept., 1969) as "an evangelist by conviction, a revivalist in action and a bishop by position," served as vice-chairman of the Asia-South Pacific Congress on Evangelism sponsored by the Billy Graham Evangelistic Association in Singapore in 1968.

Protestant Universities. Not many mission fields can boast of one, much less two, Christian universities. Founded in 1901 by the Presbyterians as a boys' vocational school, Silliman University in Dumaguete City has grown to become one of the outstanding universities of the country. It has a teaching faculty of 207 and an enrolment of thirty-five hundred. In addition to the elementary and high school departments, there are six colleges, including theology, and a graduate school. Silliman University is now an ecumenical institution related to the United Church of Christ. Its faculty includes some thirty fraternal workers from the cooperating mission boards. *Central Philippine University,* an American Baptist related institution, began as a small industrial school for boys at Iloilo in 1905. It provided elementary education for older boys who otherwise would have had no schooling. Eventually a high school was added and then a junior college. In 1923 it acquired status as *Central Philippine College.* During World War II its buildings were completely destroyed. By 1947 the college was rebuilt and in full operation with a thousand students. In 1953 it was granted university status by the government. It now comprises ten colleges, one of which is theology, and a graduate school. It still retains its kindergarten, elementary school, and high school. Of the total enrolment of three thousand, more than two-thirds are in the university. Bible instruction is offered to all students from grade school through college.

Theological Education. The Philippines is fairly well supplied with training schools for the Christian ministry. Almost three dozen of them are to be found in all parts of the archipelago. Most of them are Bible schools and colleges with rather low academic requirements for entrance. Even the best seminaries usually have two programs, one for college graduates and the other for high school graduates. The oldest is *Union Theological Seminary* near Manila. Started in 1907 by the Presbyterians and the Methodists, it is today an ecumenical institution training ministers for the United Church of Christ and The United Methodist Church. *St. Andrew's Theological Seminary* in Quezon City, established in 1947 by the Episcopalians, prepares priests for both the Philippine Episcopal Church and the Philippine Independent Church. Other seminaries include the *Divinity School, Silliman University* (United Church of Christ); the *College of Theology, Central Philippine University* (American Baptist); (Missouri) *Lutheran Theological Seminary,* Baguio City; *Philippine* (Southern) *Baptist Theological Seminary,* Baguio City; and the *Baptist Bible Seminary* (Association of Baptists for World Evangelism) near Manila. The *Far Eastern Bible Institute and Seminary,* founded in Manila in 1947 by the Fear Eastern Gospel Crusade, established in July, 1969, a sister school known as the *Asian Theological Seminary,* which operates on the graduate level and offers a Master of Divinity degree. The theological faculty of the *Philippine Union College* in Manila prepares ministers for the Seventh Day Adventist churches.

Postwar Missions. The Philippines, like many other fields in the Far East, has seen a large influx of new missions since World War II. Some of these, such as the *Far Eastern Gospel Crusade* and *Overseas Crusades,* were newly-organized missions starting work for the first time. Other fast growing missions, such as the *Southern Baptist Convention,* the *Lutheran Church-Missouri Synod, Wycliffe Bible Translators, Baptist General Conference, Conservative Baptist Foreign Mission Society, New Tribes Mission, Evangelical Free Church,* and others had existing work in other parts of the world and were simply adding the Philippines to their list of mission fields. One group, the *Overseas Missionary Fellowship* (formerly the *China Inland Mission*), took up work in the Philippines following the evacuation of the China mainland.

The *Lutheran Church-Missouri Synod* was the earliest of the new missions to enter the Philippines after the war. The work began with the arrival of *Alvaro Carino* on July 6, 1946, and the first service was held in the Lutheran Service Center in Manila. Some months later a second missionary, *Herman Mayer* and his family, arrived in Manila, followed a year or so later by others. With the addition of five missionaries who evacuated China early in 1949, the Lutheran Church in the Philippines had enough men to fan out from Manila and expand its missionary outreach to the major regions of the country—north and south Luzon, Visaya, and Mindanao. The numerical growth of the Lutheran Church in the Philippines has not been nearly so great as in Nigeria and New Guinea; nevertheless after twenty-four years of work the baptized membership stands at thirteen thousand.

The *Far Eastern Gospel Crusade* is of unusual origin. One spring day in 1945 eight Christian servicemen knelt on board an army transport as it neared the Philippines. They asked God to lead them into some evangelistic work in Manila, among both the GI's and the Filipinos. Out of this came the Christian Service Center in Manila, whose first meeting was conducted in a mortuary owned by a Roman Catholic. Through these GI's the Far Eastern Gospel Crusade was launched in 1947. Through the years it has engaged in church planting, training of national leaders, literature production and distribution, medical work, and student work. Far Eastern Gospel Crusade is confined to the island of Luzon and some of its work is among primitive tribes quite untouched by four hundred years of Spanish culture and religion. Its outstanding institution is the Far Eastern Bible Institute and Seminary founded in 1948 in Manila. With almost one hundred students it is one of the largest Bible schools in the islands. Students come from many parts of the Philippines as well as from Thailand, Malaysia, Indonesia, and the Caroline Islands. Of its more than three hundred graduates 95 percent are in full-time Christian service.

The *Southern Baptist* work was begun in 1948 by ex-China missionaries among the Chinese in Manila. Since then it has grown rapidly to include some twenty centers divided almost equally between Luzon in the north and Mindanao in the south, with one city, Cebu, in the center. Including associates and journeymen, the mission now has one hundred missionaries in the Philippines. Already 145 churches have been established, 131 of which are reported to be self-supporting. Total baptized members number thirteen thousand.

The *Overseas Missionary Fellowship* entered the Philippines in 1952 and took up work on the island of Mindoro, which up to that time had never had a resident Protestant missionary. Today about half the total force of one hundred missionaries are involved directly in church planting, equally divided between lowland towns and tribal groups. Work is proceeding in six main tribes of the Mangyan population of about thirty thousand. These people are exceedingly primitive and among them work has been hard but rewarding. Small self-governing churches have been formed in all six tribes, and a Mangyan Bible school is training church workers and evangelists for three areas. Christian literature produced in Manila is a major contribution of the Overseas Missionary Fellowship to the evangelical churches in the Philippines. Also in Manila, several couples are seconded to other organizations, such as the Bible Institute of the Philippines (Chinese), the Philippine Missionary Institute (indigenous), and the Far East Broadcasting Company.

Dr. Richard Pittman of *Wycliffe Bible Translators* led the first group of twenty-two linguist-translators into the Philippines in 1953. In 1970 there were 150 members working in forty-two tribes, each with its own language. Some portions of the Scriptures have been produced in twenty-three languages. The pagan tribes were the first to claim attention. More recently the work has been extended to Muslim groups. Although Wycliffe Bible Translators does not engage in direct evangelism, there are now believers in some thirty-six tribes. Plane and radio service span the islands and link the workers to the main bases at Nasuli in the south and Bagabag in the north, where facilities for administration, housing, rest, recreation from long stints of isolation in the tribes, and schooling for the children are provided. The Philippine branch has given on-the-field training to new in-transit members and contributed several of its own experienced field workers for advance into the tribes of New Guinea, Australia, Vietnam, India, and Nepal. To finish the job in the Philippines, Wycliffe Bible Translators is calling for thirty more translation teams and several categories of supporting personnel.

Also working among the primitive people of the Philippines is the *New Tribes Mission,* which now has fifty missionaries in six tribes. *Missionary Aviation Fellowship,* in the Philippines since 1962, provides fast, convenient, and economical transportation for missionaries and national pastors on the islands of Luzon, Palawan, and Mindanao. In 1968 the Palawan-based plane crashed, killing the pilot and one missionary.

The Republic of the Philippines became an official field of the *Conservative Baptist Foreign Mission Society* in 1955, although missionaries there had been on loan to other missions for several years. The mission is at work in three provinces on the island of Luzon: Laguna, Batangas, and Quezon. Approximately half of its nearly three dozen missionaries are located in Manila. They are engaged in radio and literature work, assisting in Faith Academy for missionaries' children, and teaching in the Baptist Bible College, which was opened in 1968. After fifteen years of pioneer work the mission reports sixteen organized churches with a baptized membership of 1,325.

No account of Christian work in the Philippines would be complete without mention of a rapidly growing, fiercely nationalistic, unorthodox group known as *Iglesia ni Cristo,* founded in 1914 by Felix Manalo. In spite of its name, the church is unitarian in doctrine, dictatorial in administration, and authoritarian in discipline. It is probably the fastest growing church in the islands, with a reputed constituency of two million, though the actual figure may be considerably lower. It is building large, impressive churches all over the country, and the faithful pay rent for their pews thus ensuring an adequate supply of church funds. Indirectly the church is active in politics with the hierarchy telling its membership how to vote; consequently its influence is strong and its patronage is sought by leading politicians running for office. Alas, its peculiar doctrines place it outside the pale of orthodox historical Christianity.

The National Council of Churches. From the beginning of Protestant missions at the turn of the century the principle of comity has been observed with happy results. Cooperation, leading in many instances to church union, has been the prevailing practice. As early as 1901 the *Evangelical Union* came into existence. It gave way in 1929 to the *National Christian Council,* which in turn became the *Philippine Federation of Evangelical Churches* in 1938. In 1949 the name was changed to the *Philippine Federation of Christian Churches,* and finally, in 1963, to the *National Council of Churches.* Eight denominations are members of the National Council of Churches, including the *United Methodist Church* and the *Convention of the Philippine Baptist Churches,* both of which have not joined the United Church of Christ. Though the Lutheran Church-Missouri Synod is not a member of the National Council of Churches here in the United States, the daughter church in the Philippines is a member of the NCC. For two or three years the NCC published the *Philippine Ecumenical Review,* but it was discontinued in 1966 for lack of financial support. The NCC in the Philippines does not appear to be as viable an organization as similar organizations in other countries of East Asia.

Christian Radio. One of the most amazing developments in postwar missions in the Far East has been the rapidly expanding ministry of the *Far East Broadcasting Company,* which was organized in 1948 by a group of American GI's who served in the Philippines during the war. Located in Radio City, a twelve-acre piece of land outside Manila, and known as the *Voice of the Orient,* Station DZAS has built twenty stations and uses eight medium frequencies and fifteen international frequencies to broadcast almost one thousand hours each week in forty major languages of the world. Most of these stations are in the Philippines; two are in Okinawa; one is in San Francisco. The latest station to go on the air (October 8, 1969) is located in the Seychelles Islands in the Indian Ocean. These stations vary in power from 1,000 watts to 250,000 watts. FEBC has its own recording studios in Tokyo, New Delhi, Bangalore, Bangkok, Djakarta, Hong Kong, and Singapore. Some thirty-five additional studios belonging to various cooperating missions throughout Asia make tapes in the languages of their respective countries and send them to Manila for broadcasting. Mail is received at an average of twelve thousand letters a month from fifty-eight countries around the world. Follow-up includes Bible correspondence courses in Oriental languages, Spanish, and English. In 1969 the course in the Philippines enrolled its 1,250,000th student. Pre-tuned radios, known as portable missionaries, have been placed in *barrios* all over the islands; and thousands of persons, literate and illiterate, in inaccessible regions hear the Christian message every day. Ever since the evacuation of missionaries from China in 1949, FEBC has been broadcasting the gospel to eight hundred million Chinese by shortwave from Manila and by medium wave from Okinawa. Following the destruction of Bibles by the Red Guards in 1966 it began broadcasting the Bible in Chinese at dictation speed, giving the Christians in China the opportunity to make their own Bibles. FEBC, with three hundred members on its staff, is a *big* operation, supported entirely by the freewill offerings of interested Christians and churches of many denominations all over the world.

In February, 1971, the Far East Broadcasting Company announced plans for the erection of two powerful radio stations, one on the island of Cheju in Korea and the other on the island of Luzon in the Philippines. Both are to be 250,000-watt medium wave facilities. The Korea station on Cheju will operate less than 250 miles from Shanghai. The entire project will cost about one million dollars and will be completed by March, 1972.

There are three other Christian radio stations in the Philippines, related both to the National Council of Churches in the Philippines and to the Radio, Visual Education and Mass Communication Committee of the Division of Overseas Ministries of the National Council of Churches of Christ in the United States. *Station DYSR* was established in 1950 by Silliman University in Dumaguete City. *Station DZCH* in Manila began in 1964 with an FM station and added an AM station the following year. In 1969 these stations began accepting commercials. They also changed the style and content of their programming to emphasize youth and music on the Manila station, and news and rural programming for the Dumaguete station.

A third radio station in the Philippines is the South East Asia Radio Voice (SEARV) which began broadcasting in May, 1968, to Burma and Thailand over its first 50,000-watt shortwave transmitter. SEARV is an independent radio station which is related to the Broadcasting and Audio-Visual Aids Committee of the East Asia Christian Conference. SEARV is now beaming its message into all parts of Southeast Asia and the mainland of China. Recording studios in these various countries (except China) provide tapes which are mailed to the Philippines and used by SEARV.

The Lutheran Church-Missouri Synod has been making use of gospel broadcasting since the beginning of its work in 1946. More recently it has branched out into television. Other missions use commercial stations in various parts of the islands for gospel broadcasting. The *Back to the Bible Hour* from Lincoln, Nebraska, is heard over some three dozen stations in the Philippines.

Bible Translation. The *British and Foreign Bible Society* opened an agency in Manila in 1899, but withdrew in 1918 in favor of the *American Bible Society*. In 1963 a Joint Agency was set up under the administration of the American Bible Society. In 1968 the United Bible Societies reported the complete Bible to be available in eight main languages, the New Testament in two other languages, and Portions (one or more books) in thirty-three languages. In 1970 Wycliffe Bible Translators reported that selected Bible passages in twenty-three additional dialects had been published on their own press in Nasuli. This means that some portion of the Word of God is now available in sixty-six languages and dialects.

Roman Catholic co-operation continues in the field of translation. Five joint translation committees of three to six members have been organized to translate the Bible into Iloko, Tagalog, Bicol, Hiligaynon, and Cebuano. The members of the five committees began their work in May 1968 at the Translators Institute for Southeast Asia, held in Baguio. Ninety-three people were in regular attendance representing thirty-four languages and ten countries.[28]

Ecumenical Relations. Eight denominations, including the Philippine Episcopal Church and the Philippine Independent Church, are members of the National Council of Churches in the Philippines. The NCC is affiliated with the East Asia Christian Conference and the Commission on World Mission and Evangelism of the World Council of Churches. Only two churches, the United Church of Christ and the Philippine Independent Church, are members of the World Council of Churches. Christian medical work in the islands is coordinated through the Inter-Church Commission on Medical Care. Over fifty church-related educational institutions are affiliated with the Association of Christian Schools and Colleges. Since Vatican II relations between the Roman Catholics and the Protestants have greatly improved. The former are now participating in Bible translation and distribution. Several of the theological seminaries are affiliated with the Association of Theological Schools in Southeast Asia.

Missionary Outreach. A new day is dawning in Southeast Asia. The churches there are beginning to assume responsibility for home and foreign missions, and the churches in the Philippines are carrying their share of the burden. The *United Church of Christ* has a dozen missionaries in eight countries on four continents. The *United Methodist Church* has eight missionaries in Okinawa and Sarawak. The *Christian and Missionary Alliance Church* has two couples in Indonesia. The *Association of Fundamental Baptist Churches* has its home and foreign mission boards. In the past twenty years the *Seventh Day Adventists* have sent 175 missionaries to various parts of the world. In 1964 the *Philippine Missionary Fellowship,* a purely indigenous group, reported twenty-nine missionaries plus twelve associates working in Tagalog-speaking areas of Luzon and Mindoro.

Christian Presence. Roman Catholics represent about 72 percent of the population. The Protestant community (including the Philippine Independent Church), numbering about 4,500,000, represents another 12 percent, for a total of 84 percent. This makes the Philippines the only Christian country in Asia. It must be remembered, however, that millions of Roman Catholics are Christians in name only and seldom attend mass. Even today there is a good deal of pagan superstition mixed with Roman Catholicism in the Philippines. Protestant growth is slightly higher than the

---

[28] British and Foreign Bible Society, *Annual Report,* 1969, p. 46.

growth rate for the country as a whole; but most of the converts have come from nominal Catholicism. With many of the postwar faith missions concentrating on the pagan population, an increasing number of converts is coming from this group. To date, very few converts have been won from Islam. There are strong Chinese churches in Manila and other cities. Protestant missionary personnel, greatly increased in the last twenty-five years, now stands at about fifteen hundred. All but a handful are Americans.

X

Far East

China

History. The history of modern China may be said to have begun with the Treaty System which followed the Opium War. The Treaty of Nanking in 1842 opened five treaty ports to foreign commerce and to Christianity.

Slowly and with considerable reluctance China adopted Western ways. From time to time political reforms were introduced; but in each case it was too little and too late, with the result that China became the victim of Western imperialism, which reduced it to colonial status without granting it colonial benefits. The internecine Taiping Rebellion (1850-1865), with quasi-Christian overtones, came close to overthrowing the central government and failed only when the Western powers refused to support it. Had it succeeded, it is just possible that China would have become a Christian country. The Boxer Rebellion of 1900, designed to drive the "barbarians" out of China, was the last great paroxysm of a dying dynasty. The Revolution of 1911 overthrew the Manchu government and brought to an end the most enduring empire in human history. This was followed by a period of instability which invited Japanese aggression and ultimately paved the way for the triumph of communism. Under the tutelage of the Kuomintang China tried valiantly to become a democratic nation; had it not been for the Sino-Japanese war, it would no doubt have succeeded. Weakened by eight years of war, wracked by inflation, and honeycombed with corruption, the Nationalists fell easy prey to the communists, who came to power in 1949 after two decades of guerrilla warfare. In twenty years the communists have completely changed the face of China. Until the Red Guards went on the rampage in

1966 it looked as if China might settle down to become a peaceful member of the family of nations. Today she is the most powerful nation in Asia, the most unpredictable and potentially the most dangerous country in the world.

People. It is difficult to believe that one-quarter of the human race is concentrated in one country; but such is the case. With over 800 million people, China is the most populous country in the world. By 1980 the population will be almost a billion.

The outstanding feature of the Chinese is their homogeneity. All 800 million of them look alike, dress alike, write alike, and, to a lesser degree, speak alike; and, thanks to Confucius, they think and act alike. They are found in large numbers outside of China—fifteen million in Taiwan and an equal number elsewhere. There is hardly a city of any size in the Western world that does not have its Chinatown. When they live abroad, wherever they go, they live together, work together, and play together. To preserve their culture they speak their own language, print their own newspapers, and establish their own schools. They prefer to marry their own people, maintain their own businesses, patronize their own shops, and in general manage their own affairs. As a people they are patient, frugal, peace-loving, hard-working, and law-abiding. Juvenile delinquency, a universal problem, is virtually unknown among them. Filial piety, the greatest of all Confucian virtues, is the cement that holds Chinese society together. Even when separated by thousands of miles, Chinese families manage to keep in close touch. They always come to the aid of their own. Those who make good overseas seldom fail to send money home to support their parents and grandparents and to educate their younger brothers and sisters. They are a remarkable people.

Religion. Unlike the people of India, the Chinese are not by nature religious. They are "of the earth, earthy." They are confirmed humanists, like their greatest sage, Confucius. The Chinese always refer to three religions in China. These are Confucianism, Taoism, and Buddhism. Buddhism, of course, is not indigenous to China. It came from India in the first century, about the time that Paul was arriving in Rome. Taoism in its original form was more a philosophy than a religion. As for Confucianism, it cannot, strictly speaking, be called a religion. It is rather a system of political and social ethics.

One must not assume that the individual Chinese follows only one of these religions. Actually, they all practice all three at once as time and circumstances dictate. They hire Taoist priests at a wedding, Buddhist priests at a funeral. Confucianism has no priests, only scholars; and they are never out of place on any occasion, private, public, or state.

Confucianism is the political and social philosophy of Confucius, the greatest and best known of all of China's sages. He lived in the sixth

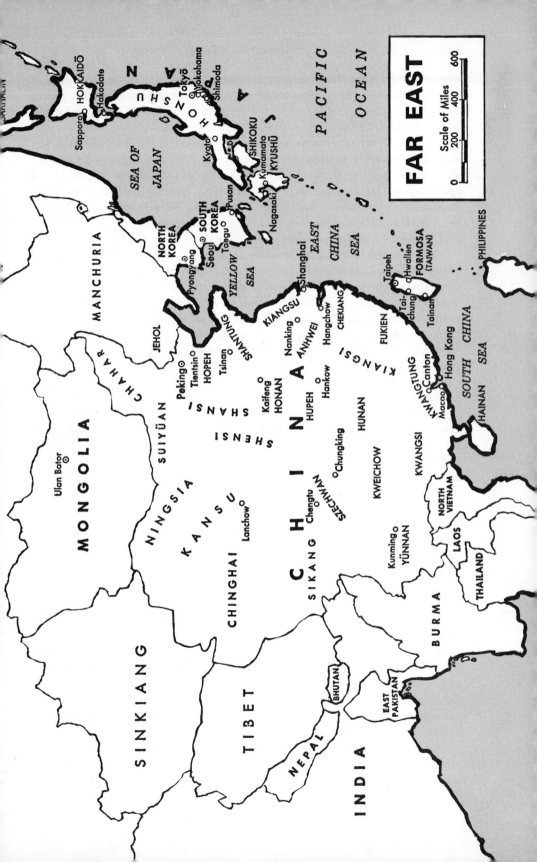

FAR EAST

Scale of Miles

0 200 400 600

century B.C. Confucius taught that man is essentially good and that human nature can be perfected by self-cultivation reinforced by the power of example. Confucius spoke of five relationships around which all human society is built, each with its privileges and responsibilities. He advocated five cardinal virtues to correspond to the five relationships. His vision was almost completely earthbound. He did refer now and again to Heaven or Providence, but he showed no real interest in religious or philosophical speculations. He was not an atheist; he was a humanist. He refused to be drawn into controversy over religious matters. His influence in China has been enormous. No other man in history has so completely molded the life and thought of so many people over so long a period of time.

Taoism takes its name from the word *tao,* which literally means way, path, or road. It is often translated truth, doctrine, word, or law. It is the central thought in the *Tao Teh Ching,* the sacred book of Taoism, which is supposed to contain the teachings of the founder, Lao-tze, who was contemporary with Confucius. There are two forms of Tao, the Tao of Heaven and the Tao of Man. The Tao of Heaven represents the Absolute, the eternal and ubiquitous impersonal Principle by which the universe was produced and by which it is supported and governed. The universe consists of two souls, or breaths, one called *Yang* and the other, *Yin.* Every physical phenomenon in the universe—the stars in their courses, the earth on its axis, the phases of the moon, the rotation of the seasons—is the result of the interaction of the *Yang* and the *Yin.* The Tao of Heaven includes the moral order as well as the physical. It is the moral law at the heart of the universe. It is essentially good, invariably right, universally true; it works inexorably and will ultimately destroy anything that opposes it.

The Tao of Man is man's imitation of the Tao of Heaven. Health, peace, and well-being depend on harmony between man and nature. Man's happiness here and his immortality hereafter depend on the extent to which he can bring his life into line with the Law of Heaven. The system of ethics built up in this way is what is known as the Tao of Man. It is therefore synonymous with virtue. The ethical teachings of Taoism are of a very high order.

Buddhism, which originated in India in the sixth century B.C., divided into two great schools, Hinayana and Mahayana. The former is found in Southeast Asia; the latter in China, Korea, and Japan. Mahayana Buddhism is rejected as heresy by the Hinayana or Theravada school. Mahayana Buddhism has many more scriptures, provides saviors in the form of Bodhisattvas, advocates faith rather than works as a means of salvation, and looks forward to the Western heaven rather than Nirvana as the place of final rest.

About A.D. 67 two Buddhist missionaries from India arrived in China at the invitation of Emperor Ming Ti. They brought with them all kinds of relics, and sacred books which they translated into Chinese. During the first two hundred years these immigrant monks held positions of leadership; but after this period administration gradually passed into the hands of the Chinese and Buddhism became indigenous.

The man responsible for this achievement was a former Taoist, Hui-yuan, who lived in the fourth century. A famous Indian monk, Kumarajiva, played an important role in the development of Buddhism in China. He reached China about A.D. 400. Supported and encouraged by Emperor Yao Hsing, he threw himself heart and soul into the work of translation. His most important translation was *The Lotus Gospel,* which has been called the most important religious book of the Far East.

With the coming to China of Bodhidharma, the great Indian monk, in 520, the center of gravity shifted from India to China; thereafter Buddhism gradually died out in the land of its origin. Bodhidharma was the twenty-eighth patriarch in the direct line from Buddha. He was India's last patriarch and became China's first patriarch. He was received with great honor by Emperor Liang Wu Ti, the Asoka of China.

Buddhism in China developed into various schools, each having its own favorite doctrines and scriptures. The three most important schools were the Pure Land School, the Meditation School, and the Tien Tai School. Additional schools were developed in Japan after the introduction of Buddhism to that land in A.D. 538.

Islam has been in China for hundreds of years. Like Christianity, it has never been regarded as truly indigenous. Although Muslims are to be found all over China, the largest concentration is in the northwest. It has always been difficult to estimate the number of Muslims in China, even though they are a distinct entity. Like all other religions, Islam has suffered under the communists. The *Voice of Islam* for December, 1965, gave the number of Muslims in China as sixty million. This may be a trifle high.

Nestorian Mission. The *Nestorian Church,* which followed the teachings of Nestorius, Patriarch of Constantinople in the fifth century, spread rapidly eastward from Antioch and Edessa to Mesopotamia where it established its own patriarchate in Baghdad. Thereafter Nestorian merchants and missionaries traveled widely throughout Central Asia. The first missionary, *Alopen,* arrived in China in 635, the same year that Aidan established his famous monastery at Landisfarne. At that time, the beginning of the T'ang Dynasty, China represented the highest form of civilization and Hsianfu, the capital, was probably the most cultured city in the world.

Our chief source of information on the Nestorian mission is derived from the famous Nestorian Stone found in Hsianfu in 1625. The inscription, in Chinese and Syriac and dated 781, records fascinating details concerning the introduction of Christianity into China.

Alopen and his Syrian monks were warmly received by Emperior T'ai Tsung, who built them a monastery and encouraged them to teach the new religion throughout the empire. Favored with imperial sanction, Alopen and his colleagues set to work to learn the Chinese language, study the indigenous culture, and translate the Scriptures and some thirty-five Christian books. The new religion is said to have spread through "ten" provinces, with monasteries in a "hundred" cities.

For two hundred years Nestorian Christianity flourished in China until Emperor Wu Tsung in 845 decided that monasticism, as practised by the Buddhists and the Christians, was alien to the Chinese way of life. He issued an edict dissolving the monasteries and ordering all monks to revert to civilian life. Hardest hit were the Buddhists, who had forty-six hundred monasteries and more than a quarter million monks and nuns. Nestorian monks numbered only three thousand.

The subsequent history of the Nestorians in China is not clear. Abou'l Faradj, writing in 987, reports that there was not a Christian then left in the country and that the church buildings had been destroyed. That some Christians survived is certain, for when the first Franciscan missionary, John of Monte Corvino, arrived in Peking in 1294 he encountered the Nestorians, whom he described as being "strongly established and bitterly opposed" to his mission. It is doubtful, however, if the Nestorian Church made much impact on the Chinese Empire.

Robert Morrison. Protestant missionary work in China began with *Robert Morrison* of the *London Missionary Society* in 1807. Denied passage on the East India Company's boats, Morrison decided to go to China via the United States. This was all to the good, for while in Washington he received from James Madison, then Secretary of State, a letter of introduction to the American consul in Canton. Armed with this letter, he set sail for China on an American ship bound for Canton. The owner of the ship evidently considered Morrison's venture a little rash. Said he one day with a cynical smile: "And so, Mr. Morrison, you really expect to make an impression on the idolatry of the great Chinese Empire?" Morrison's characteristic reply was, "No, sir, but I expect God will."

He landed in Canton in September, 1807, and immediately addressed himself to the formidable task of learning the complicated Chinese language. From the very beginning he was beset with difficulties of all kinds. Antiforeign feeling, which has been the plague of missionary work in China through the decades, made it necessary for him to keep out of sight most of the time. To render himself as inconspicuous as possible he adopted Chinese dress and wore the Chinese queue. He lived for a time in a warehouse and carried on his literary work behind closed doors. Starting from scratch, he built up his own Chinese vocabulary as he went along. Later he prepared a grammar and a dictionary. By 1819 he had completed his translation of the entire Bible. His *Chinese Dictionary,* bound in six massive volumes and requiring sixteen years to complete, was a monumental piece of literary work. "Hercules never undertook such a task," was Gladstone's appraisal of Morrison's work.

All of this was accomplished in the face of overwhelming odds. Added to the open hostility of the populace was an imperial edict forbidding the publication of Christian literature. As a result he lived daily in fear of imprisonment. More than once his life was threatened. Finally, when driven from Canton, he made his way ninety miles south to the Portuguese colony of Macao. Later he was expelled from Macao because of Roman Catholic intrigue. For a time he acted as interpreter for the East India Company. In this capacity he was permitted to return to Canton. He was paid a salary of $2,500 a year, all of which, except for his living allowance, he devoted to his work.

The enervating climate, the unsanitary condition of his lodgings, hard work, and poor food all combined to play havoc with his health. He died in 1834 at the comparatively early age of fifty-two.

Early Attempts at Missionary Work. In the meantime others had come out from England and the United States to join him in the work. *William Milne,* of Scottish birth, arrived in 1813. Unable to gain entrance to Canton, he was content to settle in Malacca, where he founded an Anglo-Chinese college and a printing press. Three years later *William Medhurst* arrived to help Milne in Malacca. Together they engaged in a vigorous and widespread ministry of teaching, preaching, and publication in Chinese settlements all the way from Singapore to Hong Kong.

The first American missionaries to China were sent out by the *American Board* and arrived in 1829. Of these, the two most famous were *E. C. Bridgman* and *Dr. S. Wells Williams,* both of whom made a name for themselves as brilliant sinologues. The former edited *The Chinese Repository,* which for twenty years was a veritable mine of information on things Chinese. Dr. Williams' best known work, *The Middle Kingdom,* remains to this day the standard authority on the Chinese Empire.

Dr. Peter Parker, also of the American Board, was the first medical missionary to China. He arrived the same year that Morrison died and set up the Ophthalmic Hospital in Canton. In no other mission field has medical skill been more effectively employed than in China. Of Dr. Parker it was said that he "opened China at the point of the lancet." He was the vanguard of a mighty army of medical missionaries who were willing to forego a lucrative practice in the homelands to devote their time and talent to the ministry of healing overseas.

Opening Doors. Missionary work in China proper did not really begin, however, until 1842. Before that time, as we have already seen, it was carried on for the most part from outside the borders of China, principally Macao. The foothold in Canton was a precarious one and the missionaries were in danger of being ousted at a moment's notice.

The Opium War, which ended with the Treaty of Nanking in 1842, marked the beginning of Protestant missions in China. One of the clauses of that historic treaty stipulated that the five ports of Canton, Amoy, Fuchow, Ningpo, and Shanghai were to be opened to foreign residence and trade. While we can never condone the dastardly attempt of the British to force opium on China at the point of the sword, we can now see how God used this event to accomplish His own purpose. Missionaries as well as merchants and traders took advantage of this concession and pressed in through the newly opened door. During the next five years nine societies began work in China. These men and women formed the spearhead of the greatest invasion in the history of modern missions.

Shanghai, which at that time was a little village on the mud flats of the Whangpoo River, became the headquarters of missionary societies from all over the world. With the help of Western enterprise and capital this little town soon mushroomed into the busiest port in the Far East.

In those early days the *London Missionary Society* was the largest and most influential society in China. Among its first missionaries were such intellectual and spiritual giants as *Lockhart, Muirhead, Griffith John, James Legge,* and others. These men helped to lay the foundation of the Christian church in China. *Alexander Williamson* was the founder of the *Christian Literature Society.*

On the American side, the Baptists sent missionaries to all five treaty ports; at the same time the Presbyterians established themselves in Canton, Ningpo, and Shanghai. Among the Presbyterians were the famous *W. A. P. Martin,* whose book on Christian evidences had such an enormous circulation in China and Japan; and *John L. Nevius,* whose indigenous methods were attended with spectacular success, first in the province of Shantung and later in Korea.

It was during this period that the continental societies entered the field, the *Basel Missionary Society* in 1846 and the *Rhenish Mission* the following year. *Karl Gutzlaff* of the *Netherlands Missionary Society* was the outstanding man in this group. His prodigious labors and wide travels up and down the coast of China from Hong Kong to Chefoo make fascinating reading. In 1850 he organized a group of Chinese Christian workers and sent them inland to preach the gospel and distribute Christian literature. These men betrayed his trust and the whole enterprise came to an ignominious end. But the man himself made a lasting contribution to the Christian cause in China.

Another milestone coincided with the signing of the Treaty of Tientsin in 1860, following the Arrow War. Again the foreign powers forced concessions from a prostrate China. Ten additional cities were opened to foreign trade. Protestant missionaries were given the right to travel anywhere throughout the country, and Christian converts were protected by law from persecution.

The ten new treaty ports were occupied immediately, while exploratory journeys involving many months of arduous travel were undertaken in many parts of the vast empire never before visited by the white man.

China Inland Mission. It was in 1865 that the *China Inland Mission,* which was destined to become the largest mission in China, came into being. The rapid development of this mission marked the beginning of the great faith missions movement whose missionaries, now numbering over ten thousand, are found in all parts of the world. For almost forty years *Hudson Taylor* directed the work and shaped the character of the CIM, and in so doing he set the pattern for the whole of the faith missions movement. Hudson Taylor has become a household name in evangelical circles; and his two-volume biography is not only a missionary classic but for decades it has been a perennial source of inspiration to pastors and missionaries all over the world.

The CIM, as its name suggests, purposely avoided the large cities on the main lines of communication and concentrated on the smaller cities and towns of inland China. To disarm prejudice and facilitate missionary work, CIM missionaries adopted Chinese dress, ate Chinese food, lived in Chinese houses. The male missionaries even wore the despised Chinese queue. They incurred the ridicule of other Westerners in China, including some missionaries; but they went quietly about their business, preaching the gospel and planting churches in fifteen of the eighteen provinces of China. The mission grew to be the largest in China, with nine hundred members and four hundred associates. It ended up with over three hundred thirty main stations, thousands of outstations, and a self-supporting church of a hundred thousand members. Only a few missions have been larger than the CIM and none has ever had all its missionaries in one country. At one time one out of every four missionaries in China was a member of the CIM. At the height—or depth—of the depression, when other missions were retrenching, the CIM issued a call for two hundred new workers in two years and got them. The evacuation of China in the early 1950's was a severe blow to all the missions working there; but to the CIM, which had all its eggs in one basket, so to speak, it was well-nigh catastrophic. When the mission evacuated China it did not possess a vacant lot or a stick of furniture in the whole of the Far East. That the mission survived is a testimony to the faithfulness of God and the vision and vitality of its leaders. Now known as the *Overseas Missionary Fellowship,* it has some eight hundred fifty missionaries working in ten countries of East Asia.

The Taiping Rebellion. No account of Christianity in China is complete without some reference to the most bizarre revolution in China's history, the Taiping Rebellion. Its leader was a southerner, Hung Hsiu-ch'uan (1814-64), whose many unsuccessful attempts to pass the civil service examinations left him frustrated to the point of mental illness. In this frame of mind he had a vision in which he went to heaven, where he was washed clean and given a new heart and other organs. There he was introduced to an old man, and to a middle-aged man who instructed him in the art of demon slaying. Later on he came into possession of Christian tracts which he thought threw light on the meaning of his visions. The Old Man he identified with God, the Older Brother with Jesus. Hung himself was the Younger Brother. For a time he studied under a missionary in Canton, but this contact did little to straighten out his weird theology.

In 1850 Hung began preaching his strange doctrine, and disenchanted peasants flocked to his colors. At first the movement was religious and peaceful; but as it gained momentum it took on the aspect of an armed conflict. Government troops were powerless to halt the advance of the Taipings. Hung proclaimed the *T'ai P'ing T'ien Kueh* (Great Peaceful Heavenly Kingdom), with himself as the *T'ien Wang*, or Heavenly King.

To his Christian beliefs Hung added elements from Confucianism, Buddhism, and Taoism, which gave him a rather eclectic creed. He preached One True God, Father of all mankind, who had sent His Son, Jesus, into the world to redeem mankind by His suffering. The chanting of hymns, baptism, and the observance of Saturday as a day of rest were features of his religion. The great sin was idolatry; hence the desecration of temples and the smashing of idols. Adherents had to memorize the Ten Commandments and attend divine worship. Prostitution, foot-binding, slavery, adultery, gambling, opium, and wine were all prohibited. On the economic front they advocated land reform, promising to give the land to the peasants who tilled it. Peasants joined by the tens of thousands as the Taipings made their way north. By the time they reached Nanking they were a motley crowd of half a million men, women, and children. Wherever they went they pillaged and killed, leaving a swath of destruction in their wake. They established the Heavenly Kingdom in Nanking, but it did not last long. The leaders, now made "kings," fell to fighting among themselves. Victory led to prosperity and prosperity produced immorality. The central government, with the support of the Western powers, moved against the Taipings and finally crushed the rebellion, but not before twenty million persons had been killed over a fifteen-year period.

Period of Expansion. The period from 1860 to 1900 was one of rapid expansion. Wherever missionaries went, churches, schools, and hospitals were established. In addition to the three Bible Societies—the British and Foreign, the American, and the Scottish—eleven tract societies were organized and eleven mission presses turned out a steady stream of Christian literature.

The first all-China conference was held in Shanghai in 1877. A decade later the Second Decennial Conference, meeting in the same city, issued an appeal for a thousand missionaries to be sent to China within five years to speed up the "evangelization of China in this generation." By the time of the Centenary Celebration in 1907, Protestant forces comprised a total of ninety-four societies with a combined membership of 3,445 missionaries residing in 632 stations. There were 166 hospitals and 389 schools of higher learning.

Opposition and Persecution. Let no one imagine that this growth was accomplished without opposition. Antiforeign feeling has always run high in China. It seems to be in the bloodstream of this otherwise docile people. In no other major mission field has the cause of Christ suffered so many setbacks or sustained greater losses. In every province of the empire progress was made in the face of determined opposition, sometimes on the part of the officials, sometimes on the part of the people. The Yangchow riot in 1868 attracted the attention of the House of Commons in England. In 1870 similar outbreaks took place in Tientsin and Hankow, resulting in the death of a score of foreigners. In 1890 violent disturbances were reported in various cities along the Yangtze River. Five years later the Kucheng massacre wiped out the entire ten-man staff of the Church Missionary Society in that city.

Then came the Boxer uprising in 1900, when 189 Protestant missionaries and their children lost their lives. Of these seventy-nine belonged to the China Inland Mission and thirty-six to the Christian and Missionary Alliance. Scores of other missionaries barely escaped to the coast, suffering untold hardships along the way. This was, without doubt, the largest massacre of missionaries in the history of modern missions.

The missionaries were not the only ones to suffer. Their Chinese brothers and sisters, regarded as "the running dogs of foreign imperialism," were hauled before the magistrates and called upon to recant. Those who refused were first tortured and then killed. The exact number of those who thus laid down their lives for the name of Christ is unknown; but it is safe to assume that thousands from China will one day wear the martyr's crown.

Peace and Progress. The storm blew over, and with the signing of a new treaty the missionaries returned to their devastated stations in the interior to pick up the threads and begin the long and costly work of rehabilitation.

The material losses, however, were more than compensated for by the spiritual gains. Once again it was proved that "the blood of the martyrs is the seed of the church." If statistics are any criterion, more progress was made in the decade from 1900 to 1910 than in the previous half century. Missionaries enjoyed more prestige than ever before. People began to join the churches in large numbers for the sake of the standing it gave them in the eyes of their countrymen.

The missionaries, while fully alive to the dangers of such doubtful popularity, were nevertheless wise enough to take advantage of every opportunity to press forward with their work while favorable conditions lasted. By 1914 there were 543 high schools, with an enrolment of thirty-three thousand. There were also thirty-three colleges and universities, with a student body of two thousand. Of these students, more than four-fifths were men. Medical work, too, went ahead by leaps and bounds. Hospitals now numbered 265 and dispensaries 386, ministering to more than a million people a year. The foreign medical staff in these institutions consisted of 328 male doctors, 92 women doctors, and 127 nurses. In ten years the Bible societies had stepped up their output of Bibles and Portions from 2,519,758 to 6,148,546. Church members numbered approximately two hundred fifty thousand.

Aftermath of the Revolution.   Mention must be made in passing of the Revolution of 1911, which resulted in the downfall of the crumbling Manchu dynasty. The moving spirit behind this revolution was a Christian, Sun Yat-sen, the Father of the Republic. It was he who organized the Kuomintang (the Nationalist Party); and he remained at the helm until his untimely death in 1925. The period from 1911 to 1925 was one of political instability. The central government in Peking was torn by internal strife. In the provinces, local warlords with their private armies roamed to and fro, living off the land, issuing their own currency, and collecting their own taxes. Not infrequently they got in one another's way and battles ensued, working untold hardship on the patient, poverty-stricken populace. Chiang Kai-shek finally emerged as the Strong Man of China. His victorious march from Canton to Shanghai made him the undisputed leader of all China south of the Yangtze. After the capture of Nanking and the "takeover" of Shanghai, the various warlords decided that discretion was the better part of valor. One by one they made their peace with Chiang or were liquidated by him, and the whole country was unified under one command. After the capital was transferred to Nanking, the communists, who had their headquarters in Kiangsi, were the only sizable group refusing to acknowledge Chiang's leadership. For twenty years they remained a thorn in his side and ultimately brought about his downfall in 1949.

All this political upheaval was not without its effect on the missionary movement. Because of their reputed wealth, missionaries made good pickings for the bandits who roamed the country in large numbers. During the eleven years from 1924 to 1935, twenty-nine missionaries were killed and eighty were kidnapped. These figures do not include Catholic casualties, which were probably higher.

Christian Presence. It was only natural that China, with one quarter of the world's population, should claim the largest number of Christian missionaries. The year 1926 marked the peak of missionary personnel. At that time there were some one hundred sixty Protestant societies at work in all parts of China. Together they represented over eight thousand missionaries. Following the communist troubles in 1927 the number of missionaries declined, and never again exceeded sixty-five hundred. The number of Chinese won to Christ was comparatively small. Protestant church membership never surpassed the one million mark. After the communists came to power in 1949 the figure dropped to about six hundred thousand, exactly one-tenth of 1 percent of the population. However, it must be said that Christianity in China exercised an influence far greater than its numbers would suggest. In the 1930's, some 35 percent of the influential people in all walks of life had received at least a part of their education in a Christian school. Ninety percent of the nurses were Christians. At that time almost 70 percent of all the hospitals in China were mission institutions. The fact that Sun Yat-sen and Chiang Kai-shek both were Christians lent a certain degree of prestige to Christianity. It is a well-known fact that most of the reforms in China were due, directly or indirectly, to the influence of Christianity.

National Christian Council. The first great missionary conference took place in Shanghai in 1877. Others followed in 1887 and 1907. With each succeeding conference there was a larger number of Chinese participants. The conference of 1922 marked the end of the missionary era and ushered in the church era, for the most notable achievement of that conference was the creation of the National Christian Council with a Chinese general secretary and two assistant secretaries, one Chinese and the other foreign. Another achievement of the conference was the formation of a home missionary society controlled and supported by the Chinese churches. The NCC did not a little to strengthen the Christian churches of China. It continued to function effectively until it gave way to the Three Self Patriotic Movement inaugurated in 1950.

Church Union. With the emergence of Chinese leadership came a growing desire for church union. Denominational differences which have kept the Western churches apart for centuries mean little or nothing on the mission field. Church union is, therefore, a much simpler problem there than here. As early as 1912 the Anglicans in China came together to form the *Chinese Episcopal Church.* Five years later the Lutherans formed the *Chinese Lutheran Church.* In 1930 the *China Baptist Alliance* came into being. By far the most comprehensive union was the *Church of Christ in China,* which held its first assembly in Shanghai in 1927. Participating groups included the American Presbyterians, the United Church of Canada, the London Missionary Society, the American Board of Commissioners for Foreign Missions, the Swedish Evangelical Free Church, the United Brethren in Christ, and the English Baptists. Its first general secretary was A. R. Kepler. Some of the conservatives remained aloof, and in 1920 they formed the *Bible Union of China.*

Indigenous Groups. A number of purely indigenous groups sprang up in various parts of the country. Chief among these were the *Jesus Family* and the *Little Flock.* The Jesus Family began in a little village in Shantung called Machuang. Later it spread to other provinces, particularly Honan and Kansu. The Jesus Family was a Pentecostal group confined almost entirely to the poorer classes in the rural districts, though some well-educated persons, attracted by the evident sincerity of the members, joined the Family.

The Little Flock was very much like the Plymouth Brethren movement at home. Its leader was the well-known *Watchman Nee,* a well-educated, deeply spiritual man and author of several books which have been translated into English. It had its headquarters in Shanghai. It was indigenous, self-supporting, self-governing, Bible-loving, and deeply spiritual. It had no ordained ministers, but it did have full-time workers.

Sino-Japanese War. The war began in 1937 and lasted for eight years, during which church and mission work suffered staggering losses. Prior to Pearl Harbor (1941) the missionaries opened their compounds to Chinese women and girls to save them from the atrocities of the invading armies. When Nanking fell the only foreigners in the city were the missionaries, who risked their lives for the sake of their Chinese friends. One newspaperman was so impressed that some years later he wrote:

> Japan's attack on China raised hundreds, nay thousands, of Christian missionaries from the status of nice, devoted but rather humdrum workers in the vineyard of the Lord to that of true heroes and heroines. . . . It was the time of supreme test which Christian missions met superbly. They braved Japanese bombs and bayonets to save hundreds of thousands of Chinese lives. No honest person of any race or nationality could watch the Christian missionaries in China during Japan's brutal onslaught and feel anything but fervent admiration. [1]

Overnight Pearl Harbor converted Western missionaries into enemies, after which they could no longer befriend the Chinese. Those in occupied territory went into concentration camps for the duration. Those in Free China kept one jump ahead of the advancing Japanese armies.

Aftermath of the War. When Japan surrendered, the missionaries returned to China. Four hundred missionaries, the largest number ever to travel on one ship, sailed from San Francisco in 1946 on the *Marine Lynx*

---

[1] Randall Gould, *China in the Sun,* p. 285.

bound for Shanghai. Others followed until almost four thousand had returned. But they had barely settled in their stations when the Red armies from north China swept southward carrying everything before them. In the final stages of the civil war the Nationalist soldiers defected in large numbers to the enemy, taking with them thousands of tons of modern weapons furnished by the United States. Even before Chiang Kai-shek fled to Taiwan, the People's Democratic Republic of China had been established in Peking on October 1, 1949.

One or two mission boards pulled their missionaries out of China in advance of the communist victory; but the vast majority of the missionaries elected to remain, hoping that some kind of *modus operandi* could be found whereby they might be able to carry on a modified form of Christian witness. They were not very optimistic but they thought it was worth a try.

The Christian Manifesto. During the first year of "liberation" the missionaries up-country were left severely alone. The first intimation of impending trouble came suddenly with the publication in the national press on September 23, 1950, of a manifesto signed by 1,527 church leaders. It read in part as follows:

> Christianity was first introduced into China more than 140 years ago. During that time it has made considerable contribution to Chinese society. Unfortunately, however, shortly after the coming of Christianity, imperialism also commenced activities. Since the missionaries came chiefly from these imperialistic countries, wittingly or unwittingly, Christianity has been associated with imperialism. . . . Christian churches and organizations in China must, by utmost effort and effective means, enable the masses in the churches to clearly recognize the crimes committed by the imperialists in China, and also the fact that imperialism in the past has made use of the Christian church. They must wipe out all traces of imperialistic influence in the church. They must be on the alert against any conspiracy on the part of the imperialists, especially American imperialists, to use religion to foster the growth of reactionary forces.

The Manifesto was circulated among and studied by all the Protestant churches in China. By 1952 it had been signed by four hundred thousand Christians belonging to seventy-nine denominations. As such it was supposed to represent the will of the people, always an important factor in communist strategy. The Manifesto was important from two points of view. It marked the beginning of the struggle between the church and the state. It was in a very real sense a declaration of war. Moreover, it revealed the strategy which the state would use in the prosecution of that war. There is no doubt that the Chinese communists regarded the missionaries as wolves in sheep's clothing, unscrupulous, treacherous, very dangerous, and highly undesirable. They accused them of being political agents working hand-in-hand with their respective governments, all the while using religion and philanthropy as a cloak for their real intentions—intrigue and espionage.

The communists were not alone in this regard. Many nationalists felt the same way; and even Chiang Kai-shek, himself a Christian, had some harsh things to say about Christian missions in his book, *China's Destiny*. It is a matter of record that the Western powers took advantage of China's weakness in the nineteenth century to wrest from her certain political and economic concessions which reduced her to the status of a semi-colony. Almost to a man the missionaries were in favor of the unequal treaties, regarding them as an answer to their prayers and an expression of the providence of God. To make matters worse, when the treaties were drawn up the missionaries acted as interpreters. Hence the old story about "the gospel and the gunboat." The fact that many missionaries, from Peter Parker in the 1840's to Leighton Stuart in the 1940's, left missionary work to join the American diplomatic corps in China served only to confirm the belief that missionaries were all along in the secret employ of their governments. Given this basic assumption, it is no wonder that the Chinese communists determined to get rid of the missionaries.

Under such conditions it is not surprising that antimissionary sentiment began to build up. Church and state publications engaged in anti-American propaganda. Individual missionaries were denounced in public. It was not long before the presence of the missionaries became an embarrassment to their Chinese colleagues. Chou En-lai declared in April, 1951, that the government was not prepared to implement Article 88 of the constitution—the one which guaranteed religious freedom—until the church purged itself of imperialism. This meant getting rid of the missionaries and severing all ties with the West. After an agonizing reappraisal the mission leaders concluded that the time had come for the missionaries to withdraw and allow the church to free itself of the stigma of imperialism. It was recognized by both sides that so long as the missionaries remained, the church would be obliged to fight a war with the communists on two fronts—the political as well as the religious. It was believed that the church would stand a better chance if it were free from all entangling alliances with the West.

The General Evacuation.   Evacuation got under way in the early part of 1951. For the most part it proceeded smoothly, with only minor irritations and delays. Some missionaries were placed under house arrest and others spent time in jail; but on the whole the casualties were low. Not more than half a dozen died along the way. By the middle of 1953 the evacuation was complete except for a few stragglers. The mass evacuation of China was the greatest reverse ever suffered in 250 years of Protestant missions.

The Three Self Movement.   One might imagine that with the missionaries out of the way the church would have been given a clean bill of health; such was not the case. The church then had to purge itself of all "reactionary elements." Its leaders must "change their thoughts" and rid themselves and their people of all "bourgeois thinking." The agent appointed to undertake this task was the Three Self Patriotic Movement. The origin of this movement is somewhat obscure; but this much is clear. The movement, while it purported to be an interdenominational organization functioning within the sphere of the Christian church, undoubtedly was a government-inspired, government-sponsored organization, the sole purpose of which was to render the church subservient to the state.

The leader of the Three Self Movement was Y. T. Wu, who had spent most of his life in YMCA work. As early as the 1930's he was known as a leftist. Other influential members of the movement were Cora Deng, Marcus Cheng, Liu Liang-mo, and T. C. Chao. Whether Dr. Wu was put forward by the churches, or chosen by the government, or simply volunteered his services is not known. Whether he had been a communist in disguise during these years or was just a confirmed leftist also is not known. In any case, he was sufficiently to the left to be regarded as reliable by the government and entrusted with the task of bringing the churches into line. The churches for their part had no other man of such stature to represent them before the government. Doubtless they were thankful at that stage to be represented by a person who was friendly to them and at the same time on speaking terms with the communists. It looked like a happy solution to a difficult problem.

The first task of the Three Self Movement was to supervise the housecleaning process by which the church was to be purged of all imperialism, feudalism, and bourgeois thinking. The chief instrument was the denunciation meeting. Initially the denunciations were aimed at the missionaries. The government was determined to debunk the whole missionary enterprise of the past one hundred years by exposing the "crimes" of the missionaries. During 1951 no fewer than 228 denunciation meetings were held in 133 cities. Leighton Stuart, Frank Price, Ralph Mortensen, and others were singled out for special attention. Two leading church periodicals, *Tien Feng* and *Hsieh Chin*, devoted issue after issue to the denunciation meetings. Not satisfied with that, these periodicals delved into history and carried on a veritable tirade against the missionaries of the nineteenth century: Robert Morrison, Karl Gutzlaff, S. Wells Williams, Timothy Richard, and Hudson Taylor, all of whom they accused of "imperialist designs" on China.

If the denunciations had ended with the missionaries it would not have been so bad; but following that the church leaders were called on to confess their own sins. Two means were used to bring this about, study sessions and accusation meetings. All church leaders were obliged to attend study sessions once or twice a year, during which they studied the basic principles of Marxism, the communist party line, and, of course, the evils of the capitalist system in general and of American imperialism in particular. With their hands clean and their thoughts changed, the leaders returned to their churches where they were expected to conduct mutual accusation meetings in an effort to purge them of their "reactionary elements."

Every local church and every Christian organization in China was required to conduct a mutual accusation meeting. It was assumed that anyone who had had any contact with American missionaries was infected with bourgeois thinking, and this had to be eradicated root and branch. In these meetings the leaders had to make a full and frank confession of every thought, word, and deed now known to be "reactionary" and not in the best interests of the people. The greatest of all crimes was failure to understand the diabolical nature of American imperialism as reflected in the missionary movement of the nineteenth and twentieth centuries.

One of the first organizations to be examined was the Christian Literature Society. Miss Liu and Mr. Kia were singled out to make confessions. The pressures brought to bear on them by their own colleagues within the organization were almost unbearable. In desperation Miss Liu said to her bishop: "How can I say what I don't believe, and keep on doing what I don't want to do?" The Bishop replied: "Our country is going through a life-and-death struggle. We, as a people, must endure this, even at great sacrifice to ourselves. After you have made your confession, you will feel differently about it." She ended up by confessing thirty-seven "crimes" and was set free.

The Seventh Day Adventists had three accusation meetings in Shanghai, one for each of their three departments, medical, educational, and publications. The church was filled for the occasion. Three Chinese staff members were on public trial. One by one different members of the SDA staff rose and read accusations. These were punctuated by shouts from the audience: "Drive out the running dogs.... Make them pay the blood debt.... Kick them out of the church." At one point pandemonium broke loose, with the entire audience on their feet roaring approval of the "blood debts" to be exacted from the criminals. The three accused men, white and trembling, slowly raised their hands in support of the resolution demanding their death and the confiscation of their goods and property. They smiled a strange smile to show that they were in agreement with "the will of the people."

Dr. Y. T. Wu, Chairman of the Three Self Movement, made the concluding speech and thanked the audience for its "forceful demonstration." He praised the organizers for their "originality," saying that they had done a good job. The three criminals were dragged from the church and taken away on a weapons carrier. The Bureau of Religious Affairs was favorably impressed. The meeting was declared a success. The Seventh Day Adventist Church got a clean bill of health and was designated a "reformed church," the first in Red China.

Some of the finest church leaders received similar treatment in accusation meetings held all over the country. Among them were Kimber

Den, Bishop of Chekiang; Dr. Baen Li, Secretary of the China Bible House; Dr. Henry Liu, President of Shanghai University; Reverend Wang Ming-tao, Peking pastor; Watchman Nee, leader of the Little Flock; and Ching Tien-ying, founder of the Jesus Family of Shantung.

As each church and organization successfully completed its accusation meeting it was given a clean bill of health and permitted to join the Three Self Patriotic Movement. This gave it a certain measure of security. It was regarded as "reliable" and could function as a "free" institution in a "democratic" society. Those leaders who could not conscientiously go through with this ghastly piece of hypocrisy were placed on the official black list. Some were brainwashed; some were imprisoned; some were sent to labor camps; some were executed. Most tragic of all was the final end of those church leaders who did go along with the new regime and who wholeheartedly supported the party line, only to find themselves tossed aside when their services were no longer needed. Professor T. C. Chao, Marcus Cheng, Y. T. Wu, and others shared this fate.

The churches which survived the mutual accusation ordeal and gained legal status in the community were never given the religious freedom guaranteed by the constitution. The churches continued for some years to be fairly well filled on Sunday mornings, but that was the extent of their activities. There were no week-night meetings, no special services, no open-air gatherings; in short, there was no evangelistic outreach whatever. Sunday schools were permitted; but parades, demonstrations, and theatricals, all of a patriotic character, were usually held on Sunday, and all school children were expected to attend. Consequently Sunday school attendance at best was very uncertain. In 1964 it became an offense to teach religion to children under eighteen years of age, and the Sunday schools ceased to function.

The Indigenous Groups. China, like other mission fields, had indigenous groups that never had any connection with foreign mission boards. The three largest were the *True Jesus Church*, founded in Peking in 1917, and the *Little Flock* and the *Jesus Family* both dating back to 1921. By 1949 these three groups represented a total of almost two hundred fifty thousand Christians, one-fourth of all the Protestant church members. Throughout their history these groups had been self-governing, self-supporting, and certainly self-propagating. Moreover, they were fiercely independent and often antiforeign.

If any Christian group could survive in communist China, surely these groups could. They could not be accused of being "running dogs of Western imperialism," nor were they infected with "bourgeois thinking." In fact, the Jesus Family practised a form of Christian communism which was in advance of anything the Chinese communists were able to achieve. But did they survive? They did not. Indeed, they received harsher treatment than did the conventional churches, which for decades had been supplied with Western missionaries and supported with foreign funds. Watchman Nee and Ching Tien-ying were brought to public trial, accused by their own people of atrocious crimes, and sentenced to long prison terms. Following their liquidation the indigenous groups shared the fate of all the other churches in China.

A Fiery Ordeal. Some people in the West have wondered how Christian leaders in China could say and do the things they did. Some of them seem to have gone the second mile in their support of a godless, totalitarian regime. Others have been unnecessarily harsh in their denunciation of American missionaries. As a consequence they have been accused of "compromising their faith" and "selling out to the communists." No person who has not lived under a communist regime can possibly know how complicated are the issues and how enormous are the pressures involved.

In every communist country the intellectuals have a hard time; but in China the Christian leaders had several additional factors which militated against them. So long as the communists regard religion as the opiate of the people, they are not likely to look with favor on those whose business it is to propagate religion. Secondly, Christianity, unlike Buddhism, never became indigenous to China. To the end it was regarded by all as a foreign religion. Given China's traditional xenophobia, this was quite a serious charge. Thirdly, the Christian mission in China had for a hundred years been identified with Western imperialism, which gave the church in China a stigma unknown in the West. Fourthly, the church in China was a very small and feeble institution compared with its counterpart in the West. In 1949 all the Protestant groups combined numbered about nine hundred thousand church members. This number dropped to six hundred thousand after "liberation," or about one-tenth of 1 percent of the population. This was a far cry from the Russian Orthodox Church, which had fifty million members out of a population, at the time of the revolution, of 170 million people.

Ecumenical Contacts. Long before the last missionary crossed Freedom Bridge into Hong Kong the church in China had severed all official contacts with the ecumenical movement. China, which sent a very strong delegation to the Madras Conference in 1938, has not been represented at any ecumenical gathering since 1949. In July, 1950, Dr. T. C. Chao, Dean of the Yenching School of Religion, resigned as president of the World Council of Churches, denouncing it as a tool of American imperialism. Even the entrance of the Russian Orthodox Church into the WCC at New Delhi in 1961 had no influence on the church in China.

Contacts with the West, however, were not completely severed. Delegations of Western churchmen were permitted to visit China from time to time. Nearly every major Protestant country except the United

States was represented in these groups. Christian leaders from India and Japan have also visited China. Four well-known churchmen, Bishop R. B. Manikam (India), Rev. Gustav Nystrom (Sweden), Professor J. L. Hromadka (Czechoslovakia), and Bishop Janos (Hungary) were present at the All-China Christian Conference in Peking in 1956. Dr. Walter Freytag (Germany) spent three weeks in China in 1957 lecturing in the theological seminaries. A few former missionaries have been permitted to go back for brief visits, among them James Endicott and Homer Brown, both of the United Church of Canada. Dr. Hewlett Johnson, the "Red Dean" of Canterbury, made several visits to Red China. After his 1952 visit he wrote *China's New Creative Age.*

Everywhere the visitors went they received the same stock answers to their questions, until they got the impression that they were listening to a broken record. Obviously, the church leaders had been duly indoctrinated, or else they had been told what to say. To a man they appeared to be happy under the new regime. They reported that the New China was a vast improvement on the old. They were actually enthusiastic about China's progress at home and, of course, not unhappy with China's growing prestige abroad. There was no apparent desire to return to former days, nor was there any suggestion that missionaries would be welcomed back to China. Less understandable was the statement, made times without number, that under the communist regime the churches enjoyed complete freedom of religion.

Several top leaders of the Three Self Patriotic Movement have traveled abroad, principally in the interests of international peace, a topic dear to the hearts of the communists. Dr. Y. T. Wu made a dozen or so trips to Europe to attend peace conferences in Paris, Berlin, and Prague. Liu Liang-mo represented China at the Sixth Party Congress of the German Christian Democratic Union in East Germany in 1952. Newton Chiang did the honors at the Eighth Congress in 1956. That same year Bishop Ting paid a visit to England. On his way home he dropped in at a meeting of the Central Committee of the World Council of Churches in Hungary. But apart from these rather sporadic contacts, the church in China has kept pretty much to itself. The National Council of Churches in the United States has from time to time discussed the matter of reestablishing contact with the Christians of China. More than once it has gone on record favoring the admission of Red China to the United Nations. Nothing very substantive is likely to come from such ventures until Peking and Washington have at least a meeting of the minds. This will be difficult so long as the first generation, die-hard revolutionaries are in power in Peking. There are signs, however, that China's attitude may be changing.

The People's Communes. A major setback was suffered by the Christian church when the people's communes were introduced. They were first organized in the summer of 1958 and by the fall they were in full swing. In the system there were 26,500 communes with an average of five thousand each. At first regimentation was exceedingly strict; later on it was relaxed. The system made no provision for church buildings; consequently public worship was impossible. The churches in the rural districts were hardest hit. Most of them were numerically small and lacked competent leadership. They simply ceased to exist. When the communes were introduced into the urban areas, the city churches also felt the pinch. In Tientsin the churches were reduced to four, one in each section of the city. Shanghai's two hundred churches were reduced first to twenty and later on to twelve. Local congregations in other cities shared a similar fate.

The Hundred Flowers. In February, 1957, Mao Tse-tung made his famous rectification speech, in which he said, "Let a hundred flowers bloom; let a hundred schools contend." This was understood to be an open invitation for the people to criticize the communist party and the people's government. It is not clear whether Chairman Mao was sincere when he invited criticism or whether this was just another gimmick to flush out the reactionary elements among the intellectuals. In every communist country a certain amount of criticism is not only tolerated but encouraged, if for no other reason than to give a semblance of legitimacy to their claim of freedom of speech for their people. At the same time it should be understood that there are certain sacred cows which are beyond criticism. To attack them is to invite destruction. This is what happened in China in 1957-58.

Among the critics of the party and the government were Christian leaders in various parts of the country. When the axe fell six months later, it cut them down, too. Many of them were tried as rightists and found guilty of subversive activities and other "crimes" usually leveled against the "enemies of the people." As a result the churches suffered another severe blow. Not only were their leaders removed, but the more timid members fell away.

From 1958 to 1966 the churches managed to maintain their precarious existence in the hostile environment. The Three Self Movement, organized on the local, state, and national levels, kept a close watch on them and relayed to them the directives of the Religious Affairs Bureau, which also operated on three levels. More and more the Three Self Movement became the tool of the Religious Affairs Bureau. On several occasions its leaders attempted to remonstrate with the government in matters involving discrimination against religion; but little was ever accomplished. The few churches that remained open were little more than a sounding board for the Religious Affairs Bureau, whose responsibility it was to ensure that religion, like everything else, served the interests of the party.

The Red Guards. Then came the final and most devastating blow of all, the Great Proletarian Cultural Revolution launched by the Red Guards in August, 1966. The Red Guards were school children from eight to fourteen years of age. They were the chosen instruments of the cultural revolution, which was directed against the Four Olds: old ideas, old culture, old customs, and old habits. The schools were closed for more than a year, releasing one hundred million students to participate in the strangest revolution in China's long history. Chairman Mao himself was present for the initial send-off in Peking on August 15. He told them: "Revolution is not wrong; it is right to rebel." Between August and November Chairman Mao reviewed over eleven million Red Guards at eight massive parades in Heavenly Peace Square in Peking. Supported and encouraged by the highest authority in the land, the Red Guards launched their Children's Crusade. Armed with a little red book, *Quotations from Chairman Mao Tse-tung,* and provided with free transportation on the state railways, they went on the rampage, physically attacking all organizations and institutions which harbored any one of the Four Olds.

The few remaining churches which had survived the previous purges were entered and desecrated. Bibles, hymnbooks, pictures, images, and other religious symbols were removed from the churches and burned. The houses and shops of the Christians were ransacked. In the process property was destroyed and persons were molested, sometimes humiliated. The *South China Morning Post* (August 25) reported:

> The final page of the history of the Christian religion in Shanghai was written on August 24. On that day all churches, active or inactive, whether conducted by their meager congregations or preserved by the Shanghai Municipal Bureau of Religious Cults, were stripped of the crosses, statues, icons, decorations and all church paraphernalia by the revolutionary students, wearing "Red Guard" armbands, and determined to eradicate all traces of imperialist, colonial and feudal regimes.

The Red Guard attack was, at least, indiscriminate. It included not only Christian churches, but Muslim mosques and Buddhist temples. Everything that smacked of "bourgeois culture" was marked for destruction; and they did their work well. Nothing escaped their attention, not even the Greek, Roman, and Chinese art objects in Peking.

In 1967 Dr. Masao Takenaka of Doshisha University in Japan visited China. He requested permission to see former Christian friends, but he was refused. "Early one morning," he reported, "I went to examine a church in Shanghai. There was no cross. Instead a huge picture of Chairman Mao and red flags and revolutionary slogans were displayed. I thought it looked like the symbol of the suffering church of China."[2]

Baden Teague, a Christian student from Australia, spent twenty-five days visiting eight cities in China in 1968. He saw eleven churches, not one of them used for religious purposes. He asked to see Christians but was told that this was impossible.

---

[2] *Ecumenical Press Service,* No. 23, June 29, 1967.

It seems safe to say that the institutional church has ceased to exist in the People's Republic of China. Individual Christians, of course, remain. The manner and extent of their witness is not known. An underground church may develop, but this is both difficult and dangerous under a totalitarian regime. It is doubtful if the Christians can meet, even in secret. Yet refugees and letters coming out of China indicate that God is still at work and that the believers there still continue to hope and pray.

Penetrating the Bamboo Curtain. Even though the institutional church in China lies in ruins, the gospel is still getting into the country. Tapes produced by *The Evangelical Alliance Mission* in Taiwan are beamed into China from three powerful radio stations located around the perimeter of that closed land. The most powerful station is KSBU on Okinawa. It is owned and operated by the *Far East Broadcasting Company*. Its 100,000 watt medium-wave transmitter aims its China beam on Shanghai and covers central, north, and northwest China. From its main base in Manila FEBC uses four shortwave transmitters to beam the message on Sian and Canton, blanketing all of China except the northeast. From a third station, HLKX in Korea, The Evangelical Alliance Mission, using medium wave, beams the gospel into north, central, and northeast China. It is estimated that there are six million shortwave radios in China. Medium-wave sets would be much more numerous. The American Bible Society is sponsoring a Bible reading program from Manila, at a pace slow enough to enable the Bibleless Christians of China to make their own copy of the Holy Scriptures. The *Radio Voice of the Gospel* (Addis Ababa) is also beaming the gospel into China. The Far East Broadcasting Company in February, 1971, announced plans for the erection of two powerful radio stations, one on Cheju Island in Korea and the other on the island of Luzon in the Philippines. Both are to be 250,000-watt medium-wave facilities. The Korea station will be within 250 miles of Shanghai.

Taiwan

Political History. Formosa was known to the Chinese as early as the seventh century, but Chinese emigration to the island did not begin until the seventeenth century. In the meantime, the Portuguese discovered the island in 1590 and named it Formosa—"Beautiful Isle." The Dutch and the Spanish both established settlements there during the 1600's; but the Dutch drove out the Spanish. They in turn were ousted in 1662 by the famous Chinese pirate, Koxinga, who used the island as a base from which to harass the Ch'ing dynasty of China. In 1683 Formosa fell to China and became part of Fukien province. Sizable migrations of refugees from China increased the population to two hundred thousand. The Chinese ruled Formosa until it was ceded to Japan in 1895, a period of about two hundred years. It was occupied by Japan for fifty years, then reverted to China at the end of World War II, at which time its name was changed to Taiwan. When the Chinese communists overran the mainland in 1949, Generalissimo Chiang Kai-shek transferred the Nationalist government and the remnants of his defeated army to Taiwan, where they have remained ever since.

With mammoth aid from the United States the Nationalist government has been able to achieve reforms which evaded it on the mainland. Taiwan is one of the few places where the American foreign aid program has been an unqualified success, so much so that it was terminated in June, 1965. Today, with a booming economy, Taiwan's standard of living is second only to Japan in Asia.

The People. There are four distinct groups in Taiwan. (1) The *Aborigines* number about 240,000 and are divided into ten tribes, five large and five small, each speaking its own language. Their origin is obscure. Two or three tribes may be Malayan in origin; others, more fair-skinned, are probably Polynesian. They live in the mountains and along the east coast. Until recently they were headhunters and even the Japanese did not completely subdue them. (2) The *Hakkas,* one million strong, came originally from the mainland. They are located in the foothills in south and central Taiwan. They speak Hakka, which is similar to Cantonese. (3) The *Taiwanese* form the main section of the population and are the backbone of the economy. They inhabit the fertile plain along the west coast. They migrated in the seventeenth century from the Amoy district of Fukien and speak the Amoy dialect. There are approximately nine million of them. (4) The *Mainlanders* are the Chinese who fled the mainland with the Nationalist government in 1949-50. They number close to three million. This includes several hundred thousand soldiers who came with the army. These people belonged to the wealthy, educated elite who preferred exile to life under a communist regime. They speak Mandarin, the national language of China, which is now the official language of Taiwan. There is no love lost between the Taiwanese and the Mainlanders. The population of Taiwan is fourteen million.

Religion. Buddhism and Taoism are the dominant religions of Taiwan. The Chinese brought them with them when they began their migrations in the 1700's. Today they have a strong hold on the people. Well-built and beautifully decorated temples abound and new ones are being built in many places. Each family has its own idol shelf and prays to its ancestors. Religious festivals and processions, a common sight in the bigger cities, never fail to draw huge crowds. There are fifty thousand Muslims in Taiwan. They have an imposing mosque in the capital of Taipei. Animism was the dominant religion of the tribespeople until after the war, when they turned en masse to Christianity.

Early Missions. Protestant missions began with the *English Presbyterians* in 1865. *Dr. James L. Maxwell* led the way. They worked in the southern part of the island and by the end of the first decade they had twenty-two churches with about one thousand members. The *Canadian Presbyterians* began their work in the north in 1872. After ten years they could report twenty organized churches. Their pioneer was *George Leslie Mackay*. These were the only two missions in Taiwan until 1950, when many missions formerly in China began to enter the country.

In 1885, after twenty years of labor, there were twenty-nine national workers in the church in south Taiwan. In the following year this church began its own outreach by opening three stations in the Pescadores. During the first decade of Japanese occupation (1895-1905) church membership doubled. Significantly enough, the greatest gains in Taiwan coincided with periods of stress and strain during two world wars.

The first presbytery was organized in the south in 1896 and in the north in 1904. In 1912 these presbyteries united to form one synod for the whole island. The General Assembly was constituted in March, 1951, and the same year the church joined the World Alliance of Reformed Churches. The following year it became a member of the World Council of Churches. Five Presbyterian missions from the West now cooperate with the *Presbyterian Church of Formosa*. Their missionaries are known as "fraternal workers." Although dozens of missions have entered Taiwan in the past twenty years, the Presbyterian Church of Formosa remains by far the largest Protestant group, having a membership of about seventy-five thousand and a Christian community of 175,000. The rapid growth of the Presbyterian Church in recent years is due mostly to the mass movement among the tribes. Today the tribal Christians make up about one-half of the membership of the church.

People's Movement. Taiwan can boast of the only genuine people's movement in the Far East. It got under way during World War II and has been called "Pentecost in the Hills." During the war a remarkable work was begun among the tribespeople by a Taiyal woman, Chi-oang by name, who had previously received some Christian instruction at the Presbyterian Bible school in Tamsui in 1930, when she was fifty-eight years of age. During the year she went from village to village in the mountains along the east coast, preaching the gospel and leading thousands of simple tribespeople to faith in Christ. The Japanese set a price on her head; but the tribal Christians hid her in their homes and farms, and they were unable to find her.

When the war was over the missionaries returned to find a Christian community of four thousand Taiyals meeting in churches which they themselves had built. From the Taiyals the movement spread to other tribes. Today all ten tribes have embraced the Christian faith in a mass movement that is without precedent in that part of the world. Incorporated into the Presbyterian Church of Formosa, these tribal churches now have their own elders, deacons, and pastors. Other groups besides the Presbyterians have been working in the tribal churches, conducting Bible schools, operating clinics, and translating the Scriptures. Approximately one-half of the tribal Christians have joined the Roman Catholic Church. Outstanding work has been done among the tribes by *Mrs. Lillian Dickson,* a Presbyterian missionary, who single-handedly established and maintains *Mustard Seed, Incorporated.*

Postwar Missions. When mainland China was evacuated in 1950 many China missions transferred some of their workers to Taiwan, where they could continue to work among the Chinese, whom they had come to love and with whose language they were familiar. As a result there was a sudden influx of ex-China missionaries during the 1950's. Other groups also were attracted to this country in which the United States had such high stakes. The result has been a vast proliferation of foreign missions. According to the 1968 edition of the *Taiwan Christian Yearbook* there are 850 missionaries in Taiwan, representing seventy-eight religious organizations. Some of these are service agencies which have only a supporting role. Even so, some fifty church bodies now exist in Taiwan. Only ten of the seventy-eight missions have more than twenty missionaries in the country. Five boards have only five; nine boards have four; three boards have three; sixteen boards have two; and twelve boards have only one. In addition, there are twenty-three independent missionaries who operate on their own. One or two societies have run out of manpower and have pulled out of Taiwan in recent years. A large majority of these missions are from the United States. Some of the missionaries, especially those from China, are working among the Mandarin-speaking Mainlanders, who form only 20 percent of the population.

Some of these groups, such as *The Evangelical Alliance Mission, Southern Baptists, Lutheran Church-Missouri Synod, Seventh Day Adventists, Overseas Missionary Fellowship, United Methodists, Southern Presbyterians, Mennonite Mission, Conservative Baptists,* and the *Finnish Missionary Society,* have a large enough commitment in Taiwan to make a significant contribution to the Christian cause. Most of them are establishing churches of their own. Five Presbyterian missions are integrated with the Presbyterian Church of Formosa. The Overseas Missionary Fellowship is not attempting to establish another denomination but is cooperating with the Presbyterian church and some of the independent churches and Bible Schools.

Inter-Mission Cooperation. It must not be assumed that the seventy-eight missions in Taiwan are working at cross purposes or engaging in competition. While many of them are supporting their own cause, there is considerable cooperation at various levels. Much of this is found within confessional bounds. As already stated, there are five Presbyterian missions working in connection with the Presbyterian Church of Formosa. Five conservative Presbyterian missions have formed themselves into the *Reformed and Presbyterian Missions Council*. Seven Lutheran missions have formed the *Taiwan Lutheran Mission*. Four of the seven actively support the work of the *Taiwan Lutheran Church,* which was established in 1955. The *Lutheran Church-Missouri Synod* operates independently of the other seven Lutheran groups.

Cooperation across confessional lines has also been achieved. Taiwan has never had a National Christian Council. Until recently there was no need. The nearest equivalent is the *China Association of Christian Churches,* which was organized in 1966. Membership in the association is open to denominations, local churches, and individuals. The oldest and widest association is the *Taiwan Missionary Fellowship*. "Committed to the evangelical Christian faith, this Fellowship now includes a peak membership of more than 800 missionaries representing seventy-eight missionary societies and agencies."[3] Each year it sponsors a summer conference for all the missionaries in Taiwan. It has prepared and published three editions of the *Taiwan Christian Yearbook,* 1960, 1964, and 1968. Other cooperative agencies include the *China Sunday School Association,* the *Christian Literature Association,* and the *Taiwan Christian Service*. The last named coordinates the relief activities sponsored by Church World Service and Lutheran World Relief. There is also the *China Evangelical Fellowship,* which is aligned with the *World Evangelical Alliance*.

Ecumenical Relations. The *Taiwan Lutheran Church* is a member of the Lutheran World Federation. In 1967 the *Taiwan Holiness Church* (linked with the Oriental Missionary Society) joined with sister churches in Japan and Korea to form the Asian Holiness Church Federation. The *Presbyterian Church of Formosa,* the oldest and largest church on the island, holds membership in the World Alliance of Reformed Churches and the East Asia Christian Conference.

Christian Education. For its size Taiwan is fairly well supplied with Christian higher educational institutions. In 1968 there were nine middle schools, six colleges, and three universities. The three universities are: *Tunghai University* in Taichung, *Soochow University Law School* in Taipei, and *Fu Jen University* near Taipei. Tunghai is an interdenominational school established in 1955 by the United Board for Christian Higher Education in Asia. Soochow is a Methodist institution dating back to 1900 in China. It was closed by the communists in 1949 and reactivated by alumni in Taiwan in 1951. Four years later it reaffiliated with the

---

3 *Taiwan Christian Yearbook,* 1968, p. 11.

United Methodist Church. Fu Jen is the famous Catholic university which was formerly in Peking.

Medical Work. Christian medical facilities consist of eight hospitals and eight clinics. Two of the hospitals and one of the clinics belong to the Presbyterians and date back to 1912, 1896, and 1865. The other institutions are all postwar ventures of the newer missions. Medical work in the island is afforded some degree of coordination by the efforts of the *Consultative Committee for Christian Medical Work.*

Theological Education. Church growth depends to a large extent on theological education. Taiwan, with seven Bible schools and fourteen seminaries, seems to be adequately supplied with theological institutions. Each major denomination has its own school. As might be expected, the Presbyterians lead the way with four schools. The *Tainan Theological College,* with twenty-five full-time faculty members and 240 students, is one of the largest and strongest in East Asia. It was founded in 1876. Historically it has been related to the Presbyterian Church of Formosa; but recently it has become an ecumenical school with Methodists and Episcopalians participating in the program. The *Taiwan Theological College,* near Taipei, is the successor to Oxford College, which was started in Tamsui by Dr. George L. Mackay in 1882. The *Yu-shan Theological Institute,* founded in 1946 in Hualien, is preparing pastors for the hundreds of tribal churches along the east coast. A fourth school, founded in 1952, is a Bible institute for laymen. The schools belonging to the other missions have a short history and a small enrolment. The Seventh Day Adventist school trains workers for the tribal churches only. The *China Evangelical Seminary,* sponsored by twelve conservative groups, began classes in the fall of 1970.

Indigenous Movements. No account of Christian work in Taiwan is complete without mention of two indigenous groups with considerable numerical strength. The *Little Flock* began on the mainland in 1926 under the leadership of a remarkable Christian known to the Western world as Watchman Nee. The movement, known as the Christian Assemblies and patterned after the Plymouth Brethren, grew rapidly in Chekiang and Fukien. It is a purely indigenous work which has never had any connection, official or unofficial, with any organized groups in the West. Following the communist takeover in China, the Little Flock spread to Taiwan, where it grew rapidly. By the mid-fifties it was estimated that their numbers had increased to more than forty thousand. In more recent years there has been a decline in membership owing in part to their militant exclusiveness. The second group is the *True Jesus Church,* a Pentecostal group founded by Paul Wei in Peking in 1917. In 1926 it spread to Taiwan, where it had a gradual but steady growth until 1945. During the postwar period membership has quadrupled to about thirty thousand, most of the new members being tribal converts. A large building completed in Taichung in 1967 provides facilities for the Taichung church, the general assembly, and a seminary.

Bible Translation. With the people's movement among the mountain tribes, Bible translation suddenly became of prime importance. Several of the ten tribes already have portions of the Bible. The Sediq and Paiwan tribes have the complete New Testament, the work of Ralph Covell and John Whitehorn. Translation work is proceeding in the other languages. One problem is a government regulation which requires the use of Chinese phonetic as the official language. The Taiwanese Bible, dating back to 1884, is in romanized script. A revision of this is now under way, a joint project of the Roman Catholics and the Protestants. In 1967 the Bible Society distributed two million Portions to non-Christians. This was accomplished with the cooperation of fifty Christian bookstores throughout the island. One of the weaknesses of the Bible Society work in Taiwan is the fact that only 6 percent of the budget is raised locally.

Radio and Television. There is no Christian broadcasting station in Taiwan, but the various missions have made good use of government and commercial stations to blanket the island with Christian programs. During the 1960's, twenty-four missions were responsible for some two hundred hours of radio broadcasting each week. These programs were broadcast in Mandarin, Taiwanese, Hakka, English, and several tribal languages. Tapes were also prepared for use in Singapore, Manila, Okinawa, and Korea. *The Evangelical Alliance Mission* produces a thirty-minute program which is released daily over ten stations throughout the island. The *Assemblies of God,* using two 650,000-watt government stations, beams the gospel into mainland China in three languages. The well-known *Lutheran Hour* is broadcast weekly over eleven stations. Designed primarily for non-Christians, the programs serve as a preevangelism tool to condition the unchurched for the reception of the gospel through a purposeful follow-up ministry.

Television was introduced in Taiwan in 1962. Christian TV began the following year when *Overseas Radio, Inc.* initiated its weekly program, *Heavenly Melody.* For several months in 1966 it was removed from the air; but in response to popular demand it was reinstated. In 1966 the *Lutheran Church-Missouri Synod* in cooperation with the *Taiwan Lutheran Church* launched a weekly TV program called *Sunday Theater* during prime time on Sunday evenings. The program is one of the most popular on the air. The *Southern Baptists* launched their TV program in 1969.

The Christian Presence. Dr. Hollington Tong said on one occasion that Christianity is the dominant religion in Taiwan; but this is obviously a gross exaggeration, for the Christian community, including the Roman Catholics, is only about 4 percent of the population. Most of the church growth has occurred in the past twenty-five years, during which time the majority of the 240,000 tribespeople have embraced the Christian faith. Approximately one-half of these joined the Roman Catholic Church; 40 percent joined the Presbyterian Church; the remaining 10 percent were divided among the other Protestant groups. In recent years the growth of the Roman Catholic Church has been almost three times that of the Protestants. Of course, the Roman Catholics started from a much smaller base. Moreover, in this postwar period they have made a huge investment of both men and money in their Taiwan mission. Apparently it has paid off, because in ten years their constituency grew from 5,000 to 200,000. Today they number between 300,000 and 350,000. The total Protestant community stands at about 250,000, making a grand total of 600,000.

The fact that President and Madame Chiang Kai-shek are practising Christians lends a certain degree of prestige to the Christian cause in Taiwan. Through the influence of Madame Chiang regular Bible classes are conducted for the Chinese officials. Many of the wives of the military officials are Christians. Some 20 percent of the student body at Tunghai University are professing Christians, compared with 6 percent for the total population. Andrew T. Roy offers the opinion that no other faith has had more influence on the modern, educated segments of the population.[4]

The American involvement in Taiwan has doubtless had some influence on the growth of the church. American stock in Taiwan remains high, and American missionaries are accorded preferential treatment. As might be expected, missionaries and church leaders almost to a man have staunchly supported the claim of the Taiwan government to represent China in the United Nations. Statements made by the World Council of Churches regarding Red China have not been well received by the Presbyterian Church of Formosa. In fact, the General Assembly in the summer of 1970 voted to withdraw from the WCC over this issue.[5]

Here as elsewhere the fortunes of Christianity are bound up with the political situation. It is just possible that when Chiang Kai-shek passes on, Taipei will make a deal with Peking. With American public opinion hardening against involvement in Asia, it is conceivable that the United States may withdraw its support of Nationalist China. Either of these contingencies would have an adverse effect on the Christian cause in Taiwan.

---

4 Andrew T. Roy, *On Asia's Rim* (New York: Friendship Press, 1962), p. 103.

5 *Ecumenical Press Service,* August 9, 1970, p. 5.

Japan

Political History. According to Japanese history Emperor Hirohito is a direct descendant of the first emperor, Jimmu Tenno, who is reputed to have lived about 660 B.C. The origin of the Japanese people is wrapped in mystery, though they are thought to have migrated from the mainland centuries before the Christian era. Authentic Japanese history begins about A.D. 400. From the sixth to the eighth century Japan came under the strong influence of China. It was during this time that Buddhism was introduced by way of Korea. The Portuguese in 1543 were the first Westerners to establish contact with the Japanese. They remained for one hundred years until Japan decided on a policy of complete isolation which lasted for 230 years until Commodore Perry sailed into Tokyo Bay in 1853. The Meiji Restoration (1868) marked a decisive turning point in Japanese history and completely changed its domestic and foreign policies. The defeat of China in 1895 and the destruction of the Russian navy in 1905 were stepping stones in Japan's bid for world power. The Mukden Incident in 1931 provided an excuse for Japan to invade and annex Manchuria. On July 7, 1937, the Sino-Japanese War broke out. On December 7, 1941, Japan launched a devastating air attack on Pearl Harbor and the United States declared war. For the first time in history the white man suffered defeat at the hands of the yellow race. With lightning speed Japan conquered all the countries of Southeast Asia and stood on the doorstep of India. But Japan lost the war and with it all its overseas territories.

Under General MacArthur Japan made an amazing comeback, both politically and economically. The peace treaty signed by forty-eight nations was the most generous in the history of war. Japan regained full sovereignty in 1952 and four years later joined the United Nations. The 1946 constitution outlaws war and commits Japan to unarmed neutrality guaranteed by a Mutual Security Pact with the United States. The pact, though opposed by the Socialists, has been renewed twice, the last time in 1970.

The People. Although Japanese origins are obscure, we do know they belong to the Mongoloid stock and doubtless migrated from the continent by way of Korea. As they advanced north from Kyushu they drove the aborigines, the Ainu, ahead of them. Today the Ainu, about fifteen thousand strong, are concentrated in the northern island of Hokkaido. Half of Japan's one hundred million people live in a narrow corridor between Kobe and Tokyo, one of the most densely populated parts of the world. The government has halted the population explosion by promoting birth control and legalizing abortions, which now number about one million a year. The Japanese have been called the Anglo-Saxons of Asia. Certainly they are ambitious, industrious, aggressive, and dynamic. They are almost 100 percent literate. One quarter of their high school graduates go on to college. There are more students in Tokyo than in any other city in the world. They are the most Westernized of all the countries in Asia and have the highest standard of living.

Like all Orientals, the Japanese are exceedingly polite. Two outstanding characteristics are filial piety and patriotism. Soldier and statesman alike have been known to commit *hara-kiri* rather than bring disgrace on emperor or country.

Religion. Shinto is the national religion of Japan. The word means "the way of the gods," and there are some eight "million" of them in the pantheon. In 1889 Shinto was divided into two parts. One part, known as cult or Sect Shinto, was regarded as a religion. It dealt with ritual, prayers, divination, and charms. The other part was State Shinto, which was not supposed to be a religion but a national cult which every patriotic Japanese was required to accept. State Shinto was supported by the government, enforced in the schools, and later exploited by the militarists. Shrines were converted into national monuments. Priests were civil servants under the Home Office. According to Japanese mythology the first historical emperor, Jimmu Tenno, was the great-great-grandson of the Sun Goddess, hence divine. All his successors likewise were divine. Thus State Shinto culminated in emperor worship.

General MacArthur realized that if militarism was to be eliminated from Japanese life State Shinto had to go. Emperor Hirohito was not tried as a war criminal even though he had been commander-in-chief of the Japanese forces. He was not even removed from the throne; but he was required to renounce his divinity in an Imperial Rescript on January 1, 1946. In the meantime, on December 12, 1945, the occupying forces announced the disestablishment of State Shinto. However, it is one thing to outlaw religion on the books; it is another thing to eradicate it from the hearts of the people. There is no indication that State Shinto is on the wane. To the contrary there are signs that it is slowly but surely making a comeback. More than once the Japanese Diet has tried to nationalize the Yasukuni Shrine, sacred to the war dead. Several official attempts have been made to revive the observance of Kigensetsu, the anniversary of the founding of the Japanese empire by the mythological emperor, Jimmu Tenno. The Christian church has protested both these moves.

Now that Buddhism has been destroyed in China, Japan has become the stronghold of Mahayana Buddhism in Asia. It entered Japan from China by way of Korea in the sixth century of the Christian era, gaining a foothold after an initial period of opposition. Later on, supported by royal patronage, it was widely accepted. With forty million believers, Buddhism is today a powerful influence in Japan. Actually most Japanese practise both Shinto and Buddhism indiscriminately. The average home has a Shinto family shrine and a Buddhist family altar. Every morning members of the family light candles and offer flowers to the Shinto deities. They also light candles and offer a small bowl of rice, sweets, and fruit at the Buddhist altar. Birthdays and national holidays are linked with Shinto; funerals and memorial services are usually conducted according to Buddhist rites. Both Shinto and Buddhist festivals are attended. Religion in Japan is a family matter and most of the ceremonies are performed in the home. For an individual, old or young, to break with family tradition is exceedingly difficult. This is one reason for the paucity of Christian converts in Japan.

Soka Gakkai. Mention should be made of Soka Gakkai, the best known and fastest growing cult in the country. Its religious exclusiveness, militant nationalism, forced conversions, political ambitions, and worldwide missionary aims make it Christianity's most formidable foe in Japan. *Soka Gakkai* means "value-creating society." Although it began in the early 1940's, it has its roots in Nichiren Buddhism, which dates back to the thirteenth century. The movement has experienced phenomenal growth since 1960, when youthful and dynamic Daisaku Ikeda became president. In the first five years of his leadership he established 114 headquarters with 1,672 chapters, 58 of them overseas. In 1967 they reported a membership of 6,500,000 families. Ikeda predicts a membership of ten million families by 1979 and fifteen million by 1990.

Beginning in 1956 Soka Gakkai ventured into politics under the name *Komeito*—Clean Government Party. In 1962 Komeito ran 136 candidates for Tokyo ward councils and elected every one. It aims to control the Japanese Diet in fifteen years. In the December, 1969, election Komeito doubled its seats in the Diet to forty-seven, making it Japan's third largest party.

Soka Gakkai is openly critical of Christianity with its emphasis on the sinfulness of man, the salvation of the soul, and glory by and by. Soka Gakkai offers salvation here and now, not from guilt or sin but from sorrow, suffering, poverty, and pain. Its advocates practise what they preach. They are the first to help earthquake and typhoon victims, feed the hungry, fight fires, and face floods.

Each member is a fisher of men, sold on the idea of converting others to his faith. Every believer must study the *Manual of Forced Conversions,* the central concept of which is *shakubuku,* meaning "to break and subdue." At the local level the members are organized into cells, where most of the personal work is done. Cells are organized into squads, squads into companies, companies into districts, and districts into regional chapters which are responsible to Tokyo. Money is no problem. A four-day fund-raising campaign in 1965 for the purpose of building a new Hall of Worship on the slopes of Mount Fuji was expected to raise fourteen million dollars. It netted about $100 million!

Writing in the English-language *Seikyo Times*, Mr. Ikeda said: "We have a message! We are committed to the salvation of mankind. Our aim is to save the masses from misfortune and misery and to establish a happy life for every individual. We must create a peaceful world. Soka Gakkai is not only the hope of Japan, but the hope of the world."

There are signs that Soka Gakkai may be running out of steam. Its sudden surge of strength, especially in politics, has stirred labor and religious groups to join forces in combating the challenge of Soka Gakkai. More recently Mr. Ikeda has intimated that he might be willing to abandon forced conversions.

First Protestant Contacts. Even before Commodore Perry's historic visit to Tokyo in 1853 efforts were made to get the gospel into Japan. One such attempt was made in 1837 when an American ship with three missionaries on board (Karl Gutzlaff, Peter Parker, and S. Wells Williams) delivered seven shipwrecked Japanese sailors to Japan. It was hoped that by this humanitarian gesture Japan might be persuaded to open its door to commerce and Christianity. Japan was not ready for contact with the outside world; consequently the mission was a failure, and the ship had to return to Macao. Gutzlaff had already translated the Gospel of John and the First Epistle of John into Japanese in preparation for the day when missionaries would be permitted to enter that long closed land. But the Christian missionaries had to wait another twenty years before they were to gain access to Japan.

The historic role played by Commodore Perry in opening Japan to foreign commerce in 1853 is too well known to be repeated here. The treaty signed by Perry on March 31, 1854, opened two treaty ports to American trade; but it was not until Townsend Harris, the first American envoy to Japan, concluded a second and more liberal treaty in 1858 that Western missionaries were permitted to enter the country.

Pioneer Missionaries. The first missionaries on the scene were two Episcopalians transferred from China, *John Liggins* and *Channing M. Williams*. They arrived in May, 1859, almost two months before the date stipulated by the treaty. Liggins remained only a short time, health problems making it necessary for him to return to America. Williams, who later became the first bishop of the Episcopal Church, remained to give a lifetime of devoted service, during which he laid the foundations of the Episcopal Church in Japan. In October of the same year *Dr. James C. Hepburn* of the Presbyterian Board arrived. He, too, had seen service in China. In addition to his medical work, which spanned a period of thirty-three years, Hepburn was a first-rate educator and linguist. Among his many achievements were an English-Japanese, Japanese-English lexicon containing forty thousand words, and a Bible dictionary, both of which were an enormous help to all succeeding missionaries. He was also one of the chief translators of the Bible. "His versatility as physician, linguist, educator and church builder made him the most venerated of all the early missionaries."[6]

Two outstanding pioneers of the Dutch Reformed Church arrived in November, 1859. They were *Samuel R. Brown* and *Guido F. Verbeck*. Brown, like the other pioneers mentioned, had seen service in China. He was primarily an educator, having been headmaster of a school in Connecticut. He opened the first English-speaking school in Japan. His reputation as a scholar, his ability as a teacher, his deep and sincere love for the Japanese attracted the bright young samurai, who flocked to his school to imbibe the learning of the West. It was largely due to his influence that the government decided to send the first Japanese students to study in England and America.

Of even greater stature was Guido F. Verbeck. Born in Holland and educated in the United States, Verbeck was a born linguist who spoke the difficult Japanese language with a fluency and accuracy that amazed his missionary colleagues and charmed his Japanese friends. He was at once educator and evangelist, orator and translator, brilliant statesman and humble personal worker. He played a significant role not only in laying the foundations of the Christian church but also in helping to build the Japanese empire. He made his services available to the Japanese government at a crucial time when it was building a new system of education based on the learning from the West. It was largely through his influence that in 1871 an imperial embassy was sent to visit Western countries. Later he had a hand in the framing of a new constitution. A man without a country, Verbeck was issued a special passport by the Japanese government. He was awarded the highest of all decorations, that of The Rising Sun. At his death he was given a state funeral.

The *Reverend James C. Ballagh* of the Reformed Church arrived in 1861 and joined Hepburn, Simmonds, and Brown near Yokohama, then little more than a fishing village. The following year the missionaries were able to secure premises of their own. Hepburn built a dispensary and clinic, which he operated with remarkable results for sixteen years. Hepburn, Brown, and Ballagh all opened private schools and trained an unusual roster of students who later filled influential positions in all walks of life. These schools were the forerunner of the famous Meiji Gakuin University in Tokyo.

Hostile Climate. In those early years the situation was anything but favorable to the proclamation of the new faith. Christianity was a proscribed religion and public edicts to that effect were found in every town and village. The missionaries were confined to Yokohama and

---

6 Charles W. Iglehart, *A Century of Protestant Christianity in Japan* (Tokyo: Charles E. Tuttle Co., 1959), p. 32.

Nagasaki; and even there they had to find shelter in Buddhist temples, where the priests could keep an eye on the suspicious foreigners. In this way the missionaries were pretty well isolated from the people. Under these conditions conventional methods of evangelism were out of the question. For many years they were restricted to operating schools and clinics.

The decade between the Townsend Harris Treaty of 1858 and the Meiji Restoration of 1868 was a time of social and political turmoil in Japan. The nation was trying desperately to emerge from 230 years of self-imposed isolation and take its place in the family of nations. As might be expected, there were those who preferred to cling to the past, and they fought tenaciously to retain the old forms of political and social life. These were the people who supported the Shogunate. On the other side were the progressive clans in the west, whose war cry was, "Honor the Emperor; down with the Usurpers." Finally, in 1867 Keiki, the last of the Shoguns, submitted his resignation to the Throne, and the new emperor, Meiji, only fifteen years of age, became the sole ruler of Japan. Thus began the long period of the Meiji reign, which lasted until 1912.

In the meantime the fortunes of the Christian mission hung in the balance. There was no way of knowing how the impasse would be resolved. Everywhere the new faith was banned. The missionaries were viewed with suspicion by the government and with mingled hostility and fear by the people. It was an offense to preach the gospel or make converts. The first convert, Mototaka Yano, was baptized by Ballagh in 1864, but not before he had conferred with Hepburn and Brown and consulted Yano's wife and sons. Even then he acted with fear and trembling, not knowing what the consequences might be.

Initial Success. The year 1872 was important for the fledgling mission, inasmuch as it marked the beginning of a modest movement towards Christianity. In January the missionaries held a week of prayer led by James Ballagh. The Holy Spirit moved among them in a mighty way. Japanese students who attended the meetings were so impressed that, with Ballagh's permission, they planned a similar week early in February. About thirty attended, a revival broke out, and the meetings were continued for several weeks. As a result nine persons became Christians and were baptized by Ballagh on March 10. These nine joined two previously baptized persons in establishing the first Protestant church in Japan. The following year five others were baptized and became members of the church. Almost all the converts were from samurai families belonging to the Shogunate party. Out of this group came the Yokohama Band. In September of 1873 a second church was opened in Tokyo.

The first missionary conference was held in Yokohama in September, 1872. Three denominations were represented, Presbyterian, Reformed, and Congregational. The problems discussed were the organization of

Japanese churches along nondenominational lines, theological education, and Bible translation. The first theological school, really only a class, was opened by Samuel R. Brown in Yokohama. In that first class were men of outstanding ability who later became leaders of the Japanese church. In 1877 three theological schools united to form the Union Theological Seminary in Tokyo. In the matter of Bible translation they unanimously decided to cooperate with the American Bible Society. Three missionaries (Brown, Hepburn, and Greene) and two Japanese (Okuno and Matsuyama) were chosen to serve on the translation committee. The New Testament was published in 1880 and remained the authorized translation until 1917. The Old Testament translation was begun in 1876 and completed in 1887. It remained in use until a new translation appeared in 1955.

In the meantime other missions were taking up work in Japan. The *Church Missionary Society* entered in 1869. The *Woman's Union Missionary Society* opened the Doremus School for Girls in Yokohama in 1871, the first school of its kind in Japan. *Nathan Brown,* an American Baptist, in 1872 picked up the work laid down by Jonathan Goble. He established the First Baptist Church in Yokohama. A man of great linguistic ability, he undertook and completed his own translation of the New Testament.

The year 1873 was crucial for the success of the mission, for it was on February 21 that the government removed the anti-Christian edicts from all public places. With their removal came a sudden influx of new missionaries which in one year doubled their number from twenty-nine to fifty-eight. With these reinforcements the work spread to Osaka, Kobe, Kyoto, and Hakodate on the northern island of Hokkaido. Among the new boards were the *Methodist Episcopal Church,* the *Canadian Methodists,* and, from Great Britain, the high church group, the *Society for the Propagation of the Gospel.*

Literature. With so many literate persons, Japan was a natural for Christian literature. The earliest literature consisted of Christian books in Chinese printed in Shanghai. Townsend Harris ordered and distributed many copies of W. A. P. Martin's *Evidences of Christianity,* which had been so influential in China. This was possible because the Japanese written language is based on the Chinese characters. As early as 1864 Hepburn wrote a tract, *An Easy Introduction to Christian Doctrine.* Considerable impetus was given to the publication of Christian literature when the American Board established its own printing press. The first Christian periodical, *The Weekly Miscellany,* came out in 1875. So voracious was the appetite of the early converts, mostly samurai, that they were willing to go without food to purchase copies of the magazine. For many years one of the most widely read periodicals was *Cosmos Magazine,* produced by Kozaki who, in 1880, founded the Japanese YMCA.

Japanese Christianity. As the churches developed, three significant features began to appear: nondenominationalism, nationalism, and liberal theology which led to syncretism. The last two have plagued the Japanese church to the present time.

From the beginning the Japanese Christians were opposed to the denominational fragmentation imported from the West. The first church formed in Yokohama in 1873 was called simply the Church of Christ. James Ballagh was called as its temporary pastor. Though Presbyterian in government, it breathed an air of interdenominationalism and manifested a strong spirit of independence. The pattern was repeated when a second Church of Christ was established in Tokyo. Some of the missionaries gave encouragement to this spirit of independence. Its Japanese leaders rejected the more elaborate historic creeds of the church and settled for the brief statement of the World Evangelical Alliance. They stated quite clearly: "Our church does not belong to any denomination; its basis is in the name of Christ alone, in whom all are one." Most of the young men who made up the membership of the church were from militant samurai families and their strong nationalistic sentiments were quite obvious. In 1877 five churches which had been Presbyterian and four which originally carried the title of the Church of Christ united to form the United Church of Christ in Japan.

In the northern island of Hokkaido the early Christians, after meeting for some time in their private rooms, decided to build a Methodist church and to throw in their lot with the *Reverend M. C. Harris,* a Methodist missionary. They decided to build a Methodist church only to discover to their dismay that the Episcopalians were about to do the same. Their leader, Kanzo Uchimura, who was to become one of the most influential Christian thinkers and writers of Japan, expressed the sentiments of the little group when he stated: "What is the use of having two separate Christian communities, when even one is not strong enough to stand upon its own feet? We felt for the first time in our Christian experience the evils of denominationalism."

Nationalism per se is not a bad thing. Indeed, no nation can long endure without it. But like everything else, nationalism can go too far and become divisive. That is what happened in the church in Japan. The early converts came largely from the samurai class and to the end they remained loyal samurai. This perfectly natural tendency prompted them to advocate a "Japanese Christianity." Uchimura wrote: "It is Christianity received by Japanese directly from God without any foreign intermediary; no more, no less. . . . The spirit of Japan, inspired by the Almighty is Japanese Christianity. It is free, independent, original and productive, as true Christianity always is. . . . Only Japanese Christianity will save Japan."[7] On another occasion he wrote: "I love two J's and no third: one is Jesus and the other is Japan. I do not know which I love more, Jesus or

---

[7] Kanzo Uchimura, *The Works of Uchimura,* vol. 15, p. 9.

Japan."[8] This failure to differentiate between God and Caesar was a contributing factor in the Kyodan's capitulation to the Japanese militarists during World War II.

Liberal theology was introduced into Japan by two German missionaries, Wilfred Spinner and Otto Schmiedel of the Evangelical Protestant Mission. By means of a monthly magazine, *The Truth,* they introduced the Japanese Christians for the first time to the study of higher criticism. Moreover, they belittled the conservative theology of the Anglo-American missionaries. In the name of science they denied the inspiration of the Scriptures and destroyed the faith of many. About this time the Unitarians from the United States entered the picture and their watered-down version of Christianity further strengthened the cause of liberalism. The greatest impact was made on the members of the Kumamoto Band, which owed its origin to the work of Captain L. L. Janes, himself a layman who accepted the findings of higher criticism. As a result many of the fine young men who in 1876, during a time of spiritual revival, had taken an oath of Christian fealty defected from the faith. So much was this the case that Kanzo Uchimura, writing in 1920, said:

> If we should make a list of prominent Japanese who once converted and are now apostates, their number would be found to be very large. The ranks of government officials, especially diplomats, journalists, men of letters and arts, and educationalists abound in apostate Christians.[9]

From liberal Christianity to syncretism was but a small step. It was not long before liberal theologians were identifying Christianity with Shinto and Christ with Buddha. Danjo Ebina announced that Jehovah God was the same as the Shinto god, Ame-no-minaka-nushi no Kami, and that Christianity was the religious form into which the Japanese spirit was to develop. Kanzo Uchimura chided those who affirmed that there is any antagonism between Buddhism and Christianity. "The two are essentially one in magnifying love. . . . All other differences amount to nothing," he said. Writing on the subject of Buddha and Christ, he stated:

> Buddha is the Moon; Christ is the Sun. Buddha is the Mother; Christ is the Father. Buddha is Mercy; Christ is Righteousness. . . . I now love the Sun more than the Moon; and I know that the love of the Moon is included in the love of the Sun and that he who loves the Sun loves the Moon also.[10]

The Period of Rapid Growth. The removal of the anti-Christian edicts in 1873 prepared the way for a period of rapid growth in the 1880's. Three factors contributed to this growth. To begin with, the sphere of evangelism was enlarged. Up to this time the missionaries were barely tolerated and their evangelistic work had to be carried on with great

---

[8] *Ibid.,* p. 599.

[9] *Ibid.* p. 352.

[10] *Ibid.,* p. 390.

caution lest they stir up the antiforeign sentiment of the populace. The only Christian witness possible was that presented in the private schools opened by the missionaries for the sons of the samurai, who were desirous of getting a Western education. With the ban lifted it was possible to hold public meetings in the open air, rented halls, and large theaters.

Secondly, the work of evangelism passed from the hands of the missionaries into the hands of the early converts. Most of these were men of high standing and good character; and many of them had unusual gifts. A third factor was the disestablishment of all religions. Buddhism, which over a period of thirteen centuries had acquired wealth, power, and prestige, was reduced to the status of a voluntary faith. Shinto, which had from time immemorial been a national cult, was declared not to be a religion at all but simply a divinely appointed "Way of the Subject." As for Confucianism, it was ruled to be a philosophy rather than a religion—which, of course, is true. This gave Christianity at least a fighting chance in its struggle with the well-entrenched indigenous religions.

In April, 1883, the Second Missionary Conference was held in Osaka. It was truly an ecumenical gathering, attended by about one hundred missionaries representing a score of churches, missions, and Bible societies. The mood of the conference was one of optimism, looking forward to the rapid evangelization of Japan.

The following month the Third National Christian Conference took place in Tokyo. This was a gathering of Japanese Christians, laymen as well as ministers. Delegates came from all over Japan. It was a popular rather than a working conference, the chief feature of which was the great preaching services held in a rented theater. These continued for five nights and drew large crowds of people, many of whom were hearing the gospel for the first time. So great was the attendance that on the last night it was necessary to close the doors on three thousand persons milling about outside.

During the week of prayer in 1883 revival broke out in Yokohama, again under the influence of John Ballagh. The spirit of prayer continued through the month of March and the revival spread to Tokyo and other centers. As is customary at such times, there were unusual manifestations of the power of God: deep emotional experiences, confession of sin, restitution, and a consuming desire to share Christ with others. The revival spread from the Tokyo-Yokohama area to central Japan; and in 1884 it swept through Doshisha College like a hurricane. For weeks all classes were suspended and the students gave themselves to prayer and testimony. All efforts to resume academic work were futile. At the end of the period some two hundred students were baptized. In 1886 a similar revival broke out in Sendai, afterwards spreading to Nagoya and Nagasaki.

During this time there was a steady influx of missionaries, mostly from 100 to 409. It could not be described as a people's movement, but increased from 145 to 383. Happily there was a corresponding growth in the Japanese churches. Not only was the gospel widely preached, but converts were baptized in large numbers. Churches and outstations increased from 83 to 448. In a period of seven years church membership rose from four thousand to thirty thousand, the number of ordained pastors increased threefold, and evangelists multiplied even more rapidly, from 100 to 409. It could not be described as a people's government, but it was steady, solid growth that greatly cheered the hearts of the missionaries and augured well for the future of Christianity in Japan. Indeed, there were leading Japanese educators who advocated making Christianity the national religion of Japan. This was indeed the heyday of Protestant Christianity in Japan. Alas, it did not last long.

> Thus Japanese Protestantism passed through its summer harvest. It proved to be a brief Indian summer followed by early frosts, but it stands as a period to which Christians may look back with nostalgia and pride. Perhaps never again in Japan's modern century was the church so close to the intellectual, the political and the social leadership of the nation, nor did it ever again attract quite such wide attention and interest. Never again was it so near to a mass movement in growth. It probably did not again register so high a level of spiritual experience on the part of the ordinary members of the churches. An imposing roster of names, among both ministers and laymen, was posted. Its accomplishments in proportion to its size were impressive.[11]

The Period of Reaction. In any situation the pendulum sooner or later swings in the opposite direction. This is what happened in Japan in the last decade of the nineteenth century. Doubtless both the government and the people became alarmed at the growing influence of the Christian religion. Particularly disturbing was the large number of samurai who were embracing the new faith. If the trend were permitted to continue Japanese culture, to say nothing of Japanese sovereignty, might be undermined.

The first and most decisive step to bolster the spirit of nationalism was the promulgation in 1890 by the Ministry of Education of the Imperial Rescript on Education. Described by one writer as "the most damaging blow that ever struck the Christian cause in Japan,"[12] the Rescript declared in no uncertain terms that the Christian view of God and morality was strictly rejected. The basic concept underlying the Rescript was that Japan, with a divine origin and mission, was unique among the nations. At the head of the great Japanese people was the emperor, a direct descendant of Jimmu Tenno, the first god-emperor of Japan. The opening words of the Rescript reiterated the essential connection between the Japanese people and the ancestral gods of Shinto. These gods demanded "filial affection," which involved an act of obeisance before the portrait of the emperor. Copies of the Rescript were sent to every public school, with instructions that it be ceremonially read by the principal,

[11] Charles W. Iglehart, *op. cit.*, pp. 84, 85.
[12] John M. L. Young, *The Two Empires in Japan* (Tokyo: The Bible Times Press, 1958), p. 44.

wearing white gloves, on all public holidays. During the reading the entire student body was to stand at attention with bowed heads before the portrait of the emperor. The psychological effect of this simple but impressive ceremony, carried out in all the public schools of Japan over a period of fifty years, was enormous; it goes a long way towards explaining the enthusiasm with which the Japanese people supported their government in the militarism of the 1930's and the events which led up to Pearl Harbor in 1941.

The initial reaction among both the missionaries and the Japanese Christians was antagonistic. They regarded the rite as an act of idolatry and refused to comply. Kanzo Uchimura, just returned from four years in the United States, refused to worship during the reading of the Imperial Rescript and was discharged from his teaching post at the First High School in Tokyo. This episode touched off a series of heated debates running through some thirty books and more than two hundred articles. All over the country champions of nationalism took up the cudgels and lashed out at Christianity. Its cosmopolitan emphasis, they complained, was inimical to the best interests of Japan and would lead ultimately to the downfall of the empire. No patriotic Japanese could be expected to view such a prospect with complacency.

The Sino-Japanese War of 1894-95 was not without its influence on the Christian church. Nothing stirs the emotions of a patriotic people like a foreign war. Christians and non-Christians alike are swept along on a mighty wave of national sentiment in favor of the government. "My country, right or wrong," becomes the battle cry of the nation. In this vein all the churches gave their support to the war. Even Kanzo Uchimura declared that the war was just. Ten years later, during the war with Russia, the Christians again displayed their loyalty to the emperor.

> This was Christianity's opportunity. In the camps, at home, on the battlefield, Christian men were in the van. With a Christian admiral to lead her fleets, a Christian American missionary to lead in prayer to the God of battles, Christian women to care for the wounded and sorrowing, it became evident that a Christian Japan might not be less Japanese than the old dreams of the samurai."[13]

That may be so, but the preoccupation with patriotism and the growing spirit of nationalism did nothing to advance the cause of Jesus Christ in Japan. The earlier progressive character of the church was disappearing. A period of stagnation set in and church growth came almost to a standstill.

> The state of the church for two or three years before and after the war was utterly deplorable. National self-conceit bred by victory in the war . . . encouraged anti-foreignism, lessened confidence in the missionaries, and set up direct and indirect barriers to mission work. Most unfortunate of all was the trend

---

[13] E. M. Bliss, *The Missionary Enterprise* (New York: Revell, 1932), p. 311.

towards the nationalization of the inner core of the church itself, by which it gradually became defenseless against the current of nationalism without.[14]

The Three Bands. One of the unique features of Japanese Christianity was the development of three "bands." The *Sapporo Band* represented Puritanism or orthodoxy. It stressed an indigenous brand of Christianity and attempted to adapt the Western faith to the culture of Japan. Its leader was Dr. William S. Clark. The *Yokohama Band* represented reformed theology and had a deep concern for social reform. This band had a galaxy of leaders: James Hepburn, Guido Verbeck, Samuel Brown, James Ballagh, and Nathan Brown. The third band was the *Kumamoto Band* which grew out of the witness of Captain L. L. Janes at Doshisha University, which had been established by the American Board of Commissioners. This band tended to be liberal in theology, though some of its members, such as Paul Kanamori, later became leading evangelists.

Interdenominational Missions. Just before the turn of the century the so-called faith missions came into existence here in North America. Most of them were patterned after the China Inland Mission, founded by J. Hudson Taylor in 1865. One of the earliest was *The Evangelical Alliance Mission*. It was founded by Fredrik Franson in 1890. Its first fifteen missionaries arrived in Japan in 1891. Three years later there were twelve stations, thirty outstations, and sixty baptized believers. In 1888 a *Christian and Missionary Alliance* missionary destined for central China died of smallpox en route and was buried at Kobe. Soon afterwards three Alliance missionaries launched the C&MA program in western Honshu and the island of Shikoku. In 1903 *Barclay F. Buxton* and *Paget Wilkes,* both formerly in Japan under the Church Missionary Society, teamed up to form the *Japan Evangelistic Band.* Through the years the Band has concentrated on village evangelism and Bible school work. Its leaders, with a "deeper life" emphasis of the Keswick type, had a spiritual ministry far beyond their own mission. The *Oriental Missionary Society,* founded by *Charles E. Cowman,* began work in Japan in 1901. Associated with Cowman were *E. A. Kilbourne* and a Japanese evangelist, *Juji Nakada.* The OMS concentrated on church planting and Bible school work. It emphasized four truths: a new life, sanctification, divine healing, and the second coming of Christ. After two decades of work a strong indigenous church of four hundred congregations had emerged.

Denominational Development. It was only natural that the missionaries should export their denominationalism to the mission field. In Japan there was the usual fragmentation. The principle of comity, applied with good results in other countries, was not employed to any degree in Japan.

---

[14] T. Yanagita, *A Short History of Christianity in Japan* (Sendai, Japan: Bible Library Publisher, 1957), p. 50.

Nevertheless, the various missions worked together in harmony and developed along denominational lines with a minimum of rivalry and competition. From the beginning both missionaries and church leaders were in favor of church union. In 1877 three missions joined forces to bring into existence the *United Church of Christ in Japan:* the Presbyterian Church in the U.S.A., the Presbyterian Church of Scotland, and the Dutch Reformed Church. In 1890 the word "united" was dropped from the title.

In February, 1887, three Anglican missions (the Church Missionary Society, the Society for the Propagation of the Gospel, and the Protestant Episcopal Church of America) united to form the *Japan Episcopal Church.* By 1894 the denominational organization was firmly rooted. The first Japanese bishops were consecrated in 1923. Today the Episcopal church, with dioceses all over Japan, is the third largest denomination in the country.

The Methodist denomination took shape more slowly. The *Japan Methodist Church* resulted from a union in 1907 of three groups: the Methodist Episcopal Church, North; the Southern Methodist Episcopal Church; and the Methodist Church of Canada.

Here as elsewhere the Baptists, with their emphasis on the autonomy of the local church, have been slower to merge. Apart from one small merger in 1873 between the Baptist Free Mission Society and the Baptist Missionary Union, no unions were formed until the *Japan Baptist Union* came into existence in 1957. The Southern Baptists began work in 1889, but to date they have preferred to go it alone. The latest *Christian Yearbook* lists thirteen Baptist missions in Japan.

In 1892 the *United Lutheran Church of America* sent its first missionary to Saga on the island of Kyushu. The Lutheran witness through almost eighty years has extended from Kagoshima on the lowest tip of Kyushu to Sapporo in the northern island of Hokkaido. In 1953 the Japan Evangelical Lutheran Church and ten postwar Lutheran missions from four countries began negotiations to form a united Lutheran church. The plan called for the establishment of the new church on Reformation Day, 1962. When it was finally consummated in May, 1963, two churches and six missions had joined to bring into being the new *Japan Evangelical Lutheran Church.* This leaves seven other Lutheran groups still on their own. No union negotiations have taken place since 1963.

Second Period of Growth. During the fifteen-year period from 1912 to 1926, when the political climate in Japan was favorable to the spread of democratic ideas, Christianity made substantial progress. John R. Mott, Chairman of the Continuation Committee set up by the Edinburgh 1910 Conference, visited Japan in 1913 and held five important conferences. He brought some of the enthusiasm for world evangelization engendered by that conference; and out of his visit came a nationwide campaign, officially called the "Cooperative Campaign of Evangelism." It turned out to be the most comprehensive evangelistic effort up to that time. Some five thousand meetings were held in all parts of the country, with a total attendance of three-quarters of a million. Almost thirty thousand persons indicated their desire to learn more. About the same time the "Kingdom of God Movement" was inaugurated, its goal set at a million souls. Twenty tracts on various Christian themes were published and distributed in large numbers. Fifteen hundred Christians in Tokyo alone distributed millions of pieces of literature.

Those were the days of Paul Kanamori, with his famous three-hour sermons; Yamamuro Gunpei of the Salvation Army; and a host of other great evangelists, who turned many to Christ. Those were also the days of stalwart missionaries who trekked the hills and valleys of Japan, many of them giving two or three decades to one province. They gave no thought to earthly comforts as they went on foot, staying for weeks in inns and huts, and living on native food. During this exciting period church membership increased from 79,000 to 110,000; and many from the highest stations in life became Christians.

Second Period of Stagnation. This was followed by a period of stagnation during the years when militarism was rampant. Militarism was not new in Japan. It had its roots in the samurai tradition, which reaches far back into Japanese history. The resurgence of militarism can be traced back to the Sino-Japanese War of 1894-95, when Japan humiliated her giant neighbor. This was followed ten years later by her swift and devastating naval victory over the Russian fleet, which paved the way for the outright annexation of Korea in 1910. Then came Japan's "Twenty-One Demands" on China during World War I; but Japanese militarism roared into high gear with the Mukden Incident in 1931, which was really the beginning of World War II in the Pacific.

During all this time the United States of America was the only Western power which offered even token resistance to Japanese aggression in the Far East. The great majority of the missionaries in Japan were Americans, who could be expected to share the concern of the United States regarding Japanese aggression. Naturally, they were suspect with the Japanese authorities and the church became the victim of guilt by association. Christianity, always regarded as a foreign religion, fell on evil days. Missionaries who came home on furlough were not permitted to return. By 1941 their ranks had been severely depleted.

The plight of the church leaders was greatly exacerbated by the practice of shrine attendance and emperor worship, which were strictly enforced during the 1930's. The legal basis for this was the Imperial Rescript on Education which was promulgated in 1890. The government took the position that bowing to the portrait of the emperor was simply a patriotic gesture and that attendance at the Shinto shrines was devoid of religious significance. But the church took another view. As early as 1917 the Federated Churches of Japan stated: "To lead the people into a vague religious exercise under the pretext of reverence towards ancestors, and thus mix the two things, is not only irrational, but results in harm to education, and hinders in many ways the progress of the people."[15] In 1930 the National Christian Council came out with an even stronger statement:

> To treat the Shinto shrines, which from of old have been religious, as unreligious has been unreasonable. The shrines of Shrine (State) Shinto are actually engaged in religious functions. This has given rise to much confusion. Furthermore, recently the Government in its effort to foster religious faith has promoted worship at the shrines of Shrine Shinto and even made it compulsory. This is clearly contrary to the policy that Shrine Shinto is non-religious."[16]

Under extreme pressure from the government, then in control of the militarists, however, the National Council of Churches in 1936 reversed its position and declared: "We accept the definition of the government that the Shinto shrine is non-religious."[17]

The situation was further complicated by the passing in 1939 of the Religious Bodies Law, which brought all religion under state control. According to this law, all Christian churches were forced to come together in a *kyodan*—a religious party or association. In July of that year thirty Salvation Army leaders were arrested as spies. Four years later the Army was dissolved altogether. The same fate befell the Seventh Day Adventists. The Anglican Church disbanded and went underground. Some two hundred fifty pastors of the Holiness church went to jail when they insisted that Jesus Christ would return to judge the world—including Japan. Towards the end of the war the militarists organized the Japan Wartime Religious-Patriotic Association, which forced the Shintoists, the Buddhists, and the Christians (Roman Catholic and Protestant) into one body.

The Origin of the Kyodan. As Japan drew closer to a confrontation with the United States it became necessary for the government to establish absolute control over all segments of Japanese society, including the Christian church. This was effected by the formation of the Kyodan. In its original form the Kyodan was a political maneuver on the part of the government to organize one great Protestant church, which could be controlled more easily than dozens of small denominations. On October 17, 1940, the leaders of the various denominations held a huge Christian convention at Aoyama University to announce their decision to unite under the banner of the Kyodan. It was hardly by chance that October 17 coincided with the annual Festival of First Fruits, when the emperor

---

15 D. C. Holtom, *Modern Japan and Shinto Nationalism* (Chicago: University of Chicago Press, 1943), p. 96.

16 *Ibid.,* p. 97.

17 *Ibid.*

himself performed *yohai* toward the Grand Shrine of the Sun Goddess at Ise. The convention opened with an act of obeisance—*kyojo yohai*—towards the imperial palace. A hymn, composed especially for the occasion and honoring the emperor as the descendant of the Sun Goddess, was sung. At the close of the convention the delegates in a body repaired to the Meiji Shrine to announce their momentous decision to the spirits of the dead emperors.

The inaugural assembly took place in June, 1941. At first eleven blocs, composed of thirty-two affiliating groups, were organized. At the second assembly in November, 1942, the bloc system was abolished and government control was complete. Several denominations refused to cooperate and immediately became the objects of attack. Among the dissenters were the Salvation Army, the Seventh Day Adventists, the Holiness Church, and the Episcopal Church, all of which either were dissolved or went underground for the duration of the war.

The War Years. Church services continued throughout the war, but as time went on government pressures built up. Church attendance dwindled as women and children were evacuated from the cities and pastors were mobilized for work in the munitions factories. The abolition of Sunday as a day of rest further eroded church attendance. Compulsory emperor worship, formerly confined to educational institutions, was introduced into the churches. Church services were required to open with the five-minute *kyojo yohai* ceremony, when the congregation did obeisance in the direction of the imperial palace and prayed for the war dead. Hymnbooks were revised. All hymns referring to the Lordship of Christ were removed, as were such hymns as "Onward, Christian Soldiers," and "A Mighty Fortress Is Our God." In their place were substituted new hymns extolling the virtues of the emperor and identifying the military expansion of Japan with the spread of the Kingdom of God. Sunday school materials became a potent vehicle for the dissemination of government propaganda.

As might be expected under such conditions, church leaders were by no means united on the crucial issues of the day. There were those who knuckled down and went along with government policy, some doubtless with a clear conscience and others out of fear, feeling that compromise was the easiest way out of a delicate and complicated situation. One Methodist pastor wrote: "It is our mission to protect the Chinese people from having their whole body cast into Gehenna, even though their right eye must be plucked out. With love in our hearts we have resolved on the completion of the Holy War."[18]

At the other end of the spectrum were those whose convictions did not permit them to cooperate in any way with a government whose

---

[18] *Ibid.*, p. 109.

religious policy involved them in idolatrous practices. For them the issue was clear. It was a choice between God and Caesar. Individuals of this stripe emerged in all the denominations; the largest number were found in the Holiness Church. Some two hundred fifty of their pastors went to jail rather than deny the faith. The Episcopal Church was divided. At first it refused to join the Kyodan; but later on, in 1943, sixty churches joined the union on their own.

Then there was a third group who tried, but not too successfully, to bridge the gap between the church and the state. One of the leaders of this group was the Reverend Arika Ebisawa, General Secretary of the National Christian Council. In an article entitled, "Christianity and the Establishment of the New Order in East Asia," he made the following statement:

> What then is the plan for the long-term reconstruction of East Asia? Its purpose is that of realizing the vision emblazoned on the banner, "The world one family;" and that purpose, we must recognize afresh, coincides spontaneously with the fundamental faith of Christianity. . . . This is the Christian concept of the Kingdom of God. The basis of the Japanese spirit also consists in this; and thus, wonderful to relate, it is one with Christianity. Nay, this must indeed be the Great Way of Heaven and Earth.[19]

Postwar Developments. The total collapse of the Japanese Empire and the ensuing disillusionment of the Japanese people presented the Christian church with an unprecedented opportunity. The Occupation Authorities were determined to democratize Japanese society, and were glad for the help that missionaries could afford. General MacArthur personally made an appeal for one thousand missionaries, and was prepared to facilitate their return to Japan at the earliest possible moment. When they returned, the missionaries found the Japanese people amazingly receptive to the gospel, and that in spite of Hiroshima and Nagasaki. Everywhere they went they found eager crowds willing to listen to the gospel. It looked for a time as if Japan might embrace Christianity en masse.

Missions, new and old, converged on Japan and threw themselves unreservedly into the work of rehabilitation and evangelism. Seven of the old-line denominations organized the Interboard Committee to work in cooperation with the United Church of Christ (Kyodan), and to help reestablish the National Christian Council. During the first decade these organizations sent out four hundred missionaries. *The Evangelical Alliance Mission,* the *Christian and Missionary Alliance,* the *Oriental Missionary Society,* and the *Southern Baptists* were also among those that returned.

Scores of new missions crowded into Japan during the first decade of the postwar period. Ten new Lutheran groups began work, among them the *Lutheran Church-Missouri Synod.* Other denominational missions in-

---

[19] *Ibid.,* pp. 109-110.

cluded the *Advent Christian Church*, the *Evangelical Free Church*, the *Baptist General Conference*, the *Independent Board for Presbyterian Foreign Missions*, and the *Conservative Baptists*, to mention only a few. A number of so-called faith missions also took up work in Japan for the first time: *Far Eastern Gospel Crusade, Overseas Missionary Fellowship, World Vision, Association of Baptists for World Evangelism, Baptist Mid-Missions, Worldwide Evangelization Crusade*, and others. Some fifteen European societies have entered Japan since World War II, most of them coming from Norway and Sweden. There are more missionaries in Japan today than ever before. The latest figure stands at 2,620. The majority of new missionaries have come from the United States and represent the conservative wing of the Christian church.

Proliferation. According to the latest edition of the *Japan Christian Yearbook*, there are 143 missionary societies in the country. Alongside of these are 110 Protestant denominations and 46 other religious organizations. In 1966 some sixty-two denominations reported a membership of less than one thousand; and nine claimed fewer than one hundred adherents. The Big Six of Japanese Protestantism are the *United Church of Christ (Kyodan), Spirit of Jesus Organization, Japan Episcopal Church, Japan Baptist Union, Japan Evangelical Lutheran Church*, and the *Presbyterian Reformed Church of Japan*. No Christian in his right mind can condone the scandal of such proliferation. On the other hand, it should be borne in mind that Christianity, in spite of all its divisions, has no monopoly on fragmentation. The Japanese Buddhists are divided into 14 main branches and 159 sub-sects.

The United Church of Christ. Known in Japan as the *Kyodan*, it is by far the largest of all the denominations. Its membership is about two hundred thousand, which is 44 percent of the total Protestant church membership in Japan. It has over sixteen hundred churches served by almost fourteen hundred ordained pastors, which gives the Kyodan a higher ratio of pastors to congregations than any other church in the world. It supports seven seminaries, with an enrolment of approximately six hundred fifty. About three hundred fifty foreign missionaries serve as fraternal workers under the Kyodan, most of them in institutional work. The Kyodan has some thirty overseas missionaries of its own serving in seven or eight countries. It still receives financial aid from the seven missions which form the Interboard Committee; but it is trying to reduce these subsidies by 10 percent a year. In 1967 the Kyodan for the first time publicly expressed its war guilt in a "Confession of War Responsibility." It aroused both support and opposition. In 1969 the United Church in Okinawa merged with the Kyodan.

New Religions. One of the outstanding features of postwar Japan has been a resurgence of indigenous religions dating back to the nineteenth century. Between the two world wars they were suppressed by the militarists; but following the collapse of Japan in 1945 they again came to the fore. Their teachings tend to be syncretistic, embracing various elements of Shinto, Buddhism, Confucianism, and animism. As might be expected, they are highly nationalistic and stress their Japanese origin and character in contrast to Christianity which is foreign. Their leaders, some of them women, are usually charismatic personalities whose main appeal is to the middle class. They have adopted missionary methods and their meetings include testimonies, faith healings, hymn singing, and other evangelistic features. They even employ such Christian terms as faith, confession, new life, and salvation. They are very aggressive, and have won millions of converts in the past twenty-five years.

Non-Church Movement. *Kanzo Uchimura* (1861-1930) was the founder of the Non-Church Christian Movement, known as *Mukyokai*. The purpose of the movement is to get back to the primitive form of Christianity found in the New Testament. Himself a Bible scholar, Uchimura attached great importance to the study of the Scriptures. His followers meet in rented halls rather than churches. They observe none of the sacraments. They are confirmed pacifists and number about fifty thousand.

The Character of the Japanese Church. The Japanese must be numbered among the resistant peoples of the world when it comes to the reception of the gospel. After one hundred years of blood, toil, and tears the total Protestant community numbers little more than half a million souls, or five-tenths of 1 percent of the population. While the Protestant denominations in Japan are, with the exception of the Kyodan, numerically weak, it must be said that the Japanese church as a whole has its elements of strength. First, it is an urban church. Ninety percent of its thirty-six hundred organized churches and many of its preaching centers are located in the great cities of Japan. There are fewer than ten thousand Christians in rural Japan. Secondly, it is a highly literate church, which is to be expected in a country were 99 percent of the people are literate. Thirdly, it is a middle- to upper-middle class church, in contrast to India where 80 percent of the Christians came originally from the lowest class, formerly known as "outcastes." Fourthly, it is a church with a well-educated ministry. Theological schools of high caliber are found in all parts of Japan. A very high percentage of the pastors are ordained men with seminary training, in contrast to Africa where the vast majority of pastors have only a grade-school education with one or two years of Bible school.

It should be noted that there are weaknesses also. First, the local churches are without exception small even by Asian standards. There are no mass meetings, no vast crowds. The average church in Japan has fifty members. Some denominations report an average membership of only thirty-five. Secondly, the church in Japan is universally regarded as a "foreign" institution. It has not succeeded in penetrating Japanese culture. It has made little impact on Japanese society. Thirdly, it suffers from a ghetto complex, which no doubt grows out of the other two weaknesses. Fourthly, it lacks evangelistic zeal. Very few churches are doing anything like an adequate job of evangelizing their own areas. Too often the churches are willing to allow the missionaries to carry the ball at this point. Fifthly, Japanese pastors tend to be scholars rather than preachers, with the result that the sermons are over the heads of the people in the pews. "Even Dr. Toyohito Kagawa, who made a strenuous effort to generate a popular Christian movement, delivered some sermons that were so filled with learning and erudition that the common man found them difficult to understand."[20]

Evangelism. The spiritual bankruptcy of the Japanese people at the close of the war provided the Christian church with a unique opportunity for mass evangelism on an unprecedented scale. In response to General MacArthur's appeal for the Scriptures, the *Pocket Testament League* in two years distributed ten million Gospels in Japan. In the early 1950's the *Oriental Missionary Society* through its Every Creature Crusade covered most of Japan with the gospel. The *Kyodan* sponsored several evangelists-at-large, one of them *Dr. William Axling,* the veteran Baptist missionary. *Youth for Christ International* in 1953 sponsored a World Congress on Evangelism in Tokyo. Delegates from thirty-five countries met with one thousand missionaries and an equal number of Japanese colleagues. Following the congress, sixty teams toured Japan for a two-week mission and reported twenty thousand decisions. The *Lacour Special Evangelism Crusade,* a Methodist venture, visited Japan for several summers, beginning in 1954. *Dr. E. Stanley Jones,* under the sponsorship of the National Christian Council of Japan, conducted nine evangelistic campaigns, the last in 1969 when he was eighty-three years old! The *Billy Graham* ten-day Tokyo Crusade in 1967 was attended by two hundred thousand persons, almost sixteen thousand of whom registered a decision for Christ. Half of them were young people. Japan also has her own evangelists, outstanding among them being *Dr. Akira Hatori* and *Koji Honda.*

Missionary Outreach. No Asiatic power has made a greater impact on Asia than Japan. Militarily during World War II and economically since that time, Japan has greatly influenced the fortunes of its neighbors; nor has it fallen behind in the religious sphere. Japanese missionaries have gone to every major country of East Asia except Korea, and to several countries outside of Asia. Two organizations are largely responsible for this achieve-

---

[20] *The Japan Christian Yearbook,* 1968, p. 122.

ment: the *Overseas Evangelism Committee* of the Kyodan and the *Japan Overseas Medical Co-operative Service*. At the present time the former has about thirty missionaries in seven or eight countries of the world. Other groups not connected with either of the above organizations have also sent their missionaries to other countries. Chief among these is the *Japan Holiness Church*, which over the years has founded missionary churches among the Japanese people in Taiwan, Manchuria, the Pacific Islands, Hawaii, Brazil, and the United States. Another group is the *Japanese Evangelical Missionary Society*, headed by Dr. Akira Hatori.

Radio and Television.   Japan is far ahead of the rest of the East when it comes to modern communications. In fact, there are few, if any, countries in the West that can match Japan in this area. Radio broadcasting in Japan goes back to 1925. Television got under way in 1953. Color television came in 1960. In March, 1968, there were 34,500,000 radio receivers served by 345 government and 143 commercial stations, covering 99.7 percent of the population. In May, 1969, there were reported to be thirty million TV sets in use, with 97 percent of the households owning at least one set.

Christian missions and churches have not been slow to take advantage of this means of communicating the gospel. In 1966 there were thirty-eight missions using radio and TV. The *Pacific Broadcasting Association*, supported by half a dozen evangelical missions, produces tapes that are used by various missions over one hundred commercial stations. Pastor Akira Hatori is known as Japan's radio pastor. More recently PBA has ventured into the more costly field of TV, using the Moody Institute of Science films with gratifying results. The *Audio Visual Activities Commission* of the National Christian Council has three recording studios in Tokyo and supplies tapes for broadcasting in different parts of the country. The Kyodan's *Joint Broadcasting Committee* works closely with AVACO in four of the major geographical areas of Japan. The most popular program, carried over 106 stations, is the Lutheran Hour drama, *Behold the Christ*. During 1965 they received an average of 1,640 new contacts each month.

The National Christian Council.   The first National Christian Conference was held in Tokyo in 1878. At the fourth meeting, in 1884, it voted itself into the World Evangelical Alliance, in which capacity it served all the denominations until 1906, when it was dissolved. In 1911 it was succeeded by the Christian Church Federation, which became the *National Christian Council* in 1922. In 1936 the Federation of Christian Missions transferred its functions to the National Christian Council and resolved itself into an informal Fellowship of Christian Missionaries, which continues to the present. The NCC was dissolved during World War II, but it was reestablished afterwards with the help of the Interboard Committee.

Today it comprises six denominations (including the Kyodan) and twelve other agencies. The council has three divisions: mission, service, and education. At its March, 1969, meeting it voted down a resolution to change the name to the National Council of Churches. It is affiliated with the World Council of Churches and the East Asia Christian Conference.

Missionary Associations. Nowhere has evangelical fragmentation been more conspicuous than in postwar Japan. With a sudden influx of new missions the problem of cooperation became acute. At one time there were half a dozen associations, each doing its own thing; but in recent years there has been a healthy tendency to active cooperation. In January, 1968, the *Japan Council of Evangelical Missions* merged with the *Evangelical Missionary Association of Japan* to form the *Japan Evangelical Missionary Association.* Three months later JEMA linked up with two Japanese associations, the *Fukuin Renmai* and the *Japan Protestant Conference,* and formed a wider fellowship known as the *Japan Evangelical Association.* The *Japan Bible Christian Council,* an ultraconservative group, ceased to exist in 1967 for lack of support.

In addition to these conservative associations there is the *Fellowship of Christian Missionaries,* which is the oldest and most inclusive of all the associations. In 1936 it grew out of the Federation of Christian Missions, which goes back to 1902. The official organ of the FCM is the *Japan Christian Quarterly.* At the annual meeting in 1967 there was some thought that the FCM had outlived its usefulness and should be dissolved; but the majority of the missionaries present decided to continue their enthusiastic support of the fellowship.

Protestant-Catholic Cooperation. Even before the Second Vatican Council the Roman Catholic Student Organization was interested in dialogue with the leaders of the Protestant Student Christian Movement. In 1961 and again in 1962 Protestant theologians addressed the Roman Catholic National Assembly. At the first Ecumenical Roundtable, in July, 1966, the officials of the Kyodan and the Roman Catholic Church issued a joint statement calling for closer cooperation. Specific proposals included the setting up of joint Faith and Order study circles and ecumenical dialogue groups, preparation of a common version of the Japanese Bible, and increased cooperation in educational and social welfare agencies. In 1968 for the first time the *Japan Christian Yearbook* was a joint publication of the National Christian Council and the National Catholic Council of Japan. In 1969 some one hundred Protestant and Roman Catholic clergy and laity joined to form the *Japan Ecumenical Association.* Its goals include initiating contact and cooperation aimed at Christian unity and the strengthening of Christian dialogue with non-Christians. The Christian Pavilion at Expo 70 was sponsored jointly by the NCC and the National Catholic Council.

The Christian Presence. There has never been a people's movement in Japan, nor anywhere else in the Far East except among the tribes of Taiwan. Nevertheless the church in Japan has experienced moderate growth. From 1945 to 1963 Protestant church membership doubled, from 200,000 to 400,000. This gratifying growth does not tell the whole story. According to the latest census almost three million persons listed Christianity as the religion of their choice. Obviously there are more Christians in Japan than appear on the church rolls. Most recent statistics show 540,000 Protestants, 350,000 Roman Catholics, and 20,000 Eastern Orthodox, making a total of 910,000. This is slightly less than 1 percent of the population—after 110 years of Christian witness.

Can 1 percent of the population ever evangelize the other 99 percent without outside help? Perhaps there is some justification for the large number of foreign missionaries in a country so advanced as Japan. The number now stands at 2,620. The overwhelming majority of these come from North America. Several hundred come from the Commonwealth countries. An estimated forty missionaries are from Norway and Finland. There are more than two hundred Swedish missionaries in Japan, and Germany is represented by about seventy missionaries.

Korea

Political History. Tradition traces Korean history back to 2333 B.C., when the legendary first king, Tangun, is said to have established his kingdom at Pyengyang. The first authentic date is 1122 B.C., when a Chinese noble called Kija, having incurred the anger of the Chinese emperor, migrated with five thousand retainers to Korea and organized a new state. Recorded history begins with the period of the Three Kingdoms: Silla, Koguryo, and Paekche, all of which arose in the first century B.C. The three kingdoms waged war on one another for seven hundred years, until around 600 Silla gained the upper hand and absorbed the other two. Modern history dates from the beginning of the Yi dynasty in 1392. A buffer state between China and Japan, the peninsula of Korea has been a battleground for opposing forces for many centuries. Korea was able to preserve its isolation until 1876, when Japan forced a treaty on the Hermit Kingdom. By defeating China in 1895 and Russia in 1905, Japan established itself as the paramount power in Korea. Then in 1910 it formally annexed the country and held it until the close of World War II, when Korea was liberated by the Allies. It was, however, divided at the 38th Parallel; and the Republic of Korea (South) came into existence in August, 1948. A month later the North Koreans formed their own government and called the new state the People's Democratic Republic of Korea. North Korea launched an unprovoked attack on the South on June 25, 1950. A truce was signed three years later at Panmunjom. The country is still divided, with no sign of permanent peace, much less unification.

The People. The precise origin of the Korean people is wrapped in mystery. Doubtless they came originally from the mainland, via Siberia and Manchuria, about the third millennium B.C. Basically, the Koreans have the same Mongoloid background as the Chinese and the Japanese. Those in the north tend to resemble the Chinese; those in the south are more like the Japanese. The Korean people, however, have distinct features of their own. They tend to be taller than the Japanese and shorter than the Chinese. Korean culture is predominantly Confucian. The spoken language is distinctly Korean and is said to be exceedingly difficult to learn. It is universally understood in all parts of the country. The written language is a combination of Chinese characters and the Korean *hangul* alphabet of twenty-six letters invented in the fifteenth century. The population of Korea is thirty-one million, about 60 percent of whom live in the rural areas.

Religion. Government figures released in 1962 indicated that 90 percent of the people professed no religion at all. This, however, is misleading; the vast majority of the Koreans practise *Shamanism,* a form of animism which is indigenous to Korea and dates back to the dawn of Korean history. It embraces a vast number of gods, demons, and spirits, the legacy of centuries of nature worship. The good spirits are to be invoked, the evil ones appeased. As elsewhere in the animistic world, the evil spirits outnumber the good spirits, and the people live in constant fear of their malevolent influence.

Buddhism, in Mahayana form, entered Korea from China in A.D. 372. The golden age of Buddhism coincided with the Koryu period of the twelfth to the fourteenth centuries, when monasteries and temples, some of them very ornate, abounded on every hand. Buddhism never recovered from the blow it received during the Yi dynasty. Today it claims less than 5 percent of the population and Buddhist priests tend to be despised.

Confucianism, which is not, strictly speaking, a religion but a system of political and social ethics, entered Korea from China in the first century B.C. As a state religion it vied with Buddhism for dominance until its final triumph in 1392. Though fewer than 1 percent of the people list Confucianism as their religion, the teachings of Confucius have had enormous influence on Korean culture.

The Opening of Korea. Japan was an apt pupil of the West. No sooner had the "black ships" of Commodore Perry forced Japan to open its doors to Western commerce than Japan turned around and applied the same tactics to Korea. In 1876 Japan, now a modern power, sent a naval task force against Korea. In the face of superior force Korea capitulated and signed a treaty in February, 1876, by which Japan secured extraterri-toriality, the opening of several ports, and regular diplomatic relations. Six years later the United States signed a similar treaty with Korea. The other Western powers followed in quick order: England, Germany, Italy, Russia, and France.

Early Protestant Contacts. As early as 1832 the famous German missionary, *Karl Gutzlaff,* in his capacity as interpreter for the East India Company, visited the coastal areas of Korea and left behind copies of the Scriptures in Chinese which had been given to him by Robert Morrison. He succeeded in sending two copies of the Bible to the king. The next Protestant missionary to contact the Koreans was *Robert J. Thomas,* a member of the *London Missionary Society* in China. He spent some time in the fall of 1865 sailing up and down the Whanghai coast as an agent of the *National Bible Society of Scotland.* The following year he returned on the ill-fated *General Sherman,* an American ship loaded with goods for Korea. When the ship ran aground on a sandbar in the River Taidong on the way to Pyengyang, it was set afire by the Koreans. All on board perished, but not before Thomas had knelt down to pray and had offered his slayer a Bible. This man's nephew later became a Christian and worked with *Dr. W. D. Reynolds* on Bible translation. In 1867 *Alexander William-son,* the China agent of the National Bible Society of Scotland, visited the Yalu River valley and sold Christian books and Scripture portions to the Koreans there. In the 1870's *John Ross,* a Scottish Presbyterian missionary in Mukden, established contact with the Koreans in Manchuria. With their help he translated the New Testament into Korean. In the process at least three of his informants became Christians. The Scottish Bible Society provided a printing press and a typesetter and later arranged for Korean colporteurs to carry the Scriptures into Korea. When missionaries arrived on the scene some years later, they found whole communities of pro-fessing Christians waiting for further teaching. The first Korean Christians were baptized by Ross in 1884 in Manchuria. In the meantime, in 1882 the *British and Foreign Bible Society* had printed Ross's translation of Luke. Three years later they published the Four Gospels and The Acts, and in 1887 the entire New Testament. Thus Bible translation was well under way before missionaries were permitted to enter the country.

Pioneer Missionaries. Two years after the signing of the treaty be-tween the United States and Korea, in 1884, the *American Presbyterians (North)* sent the first Protestant missionary to Korea, *Horace N. Allen.* Allen was a medical missionary who had already seen service in China. Upon his arrival he was made physician to the American and other legations in Seoul. In the providence of God he was able to save the life of the queen's nephew, thus securing for himself and the other missionaries the favor of the royal family. In 1885 Dr. Allen was invited to take charge of the first government hospital in Seoul. Two years later he retired from the mission to enter diplomatic service. He was decorated three times by the king.

On Easter Sunday, 1885, two American missionaries, destined to become the giants of their day, arrived in Korea via Japan. They were *Horace G. Underwood* (*Presbyterian*) and *Henry G. Appenzeller* (*Methodist*). These two men laid the foundations of the two denominations which have carried the lion's share of the Christian witness in Korea right down to the present.

Presbyterian Advance.   Shortly after the arrival of Dr. Underwood three other Presbyterian missions began work in Korea: the *Australian Presbyterians* (1889), the *American* (*Southern*) *Presbyterians* (1892), and the *Canadian Presbyterians* (1898). From the outset these four groups agreed to work in harmony and set up a central committee to insure cooperation. In 1907 the four missions united to form the *Presbyterian Church in Korea*. Later, in 1912, the Assembly divided into seven presbyteries. From the beginning the national leaders were in the majority. The first moderator was a missionary, *Dr. Samuel A. Moffett;* but only once after 1915 did a missionary hold that high post. That was in 1919 and was brought about by fear of Japanese reprisals.

Methodist Advance.   Appenzeller of the Northern Methodists was joined in 1896 by the *Southern Methodists,* whose pioneer missionary was the *Reverend C. F. Reid.* The Southern Methodists began evangelistic work in Seoul and within ten years were firmly established in Seoul, Kaesung, and Wonsan. The two Methodist missions had much in common and worked in close cooperation from the start. They established a joint seminary and cooperated in several schools. Each mission had its own church; but the two churches came together in 1930 and formed the *Methodist Church in Korea.*

The Anglican Church.   The third confessional group to enter Korea was the Anglican Church. *Bishop C. J. Corfe* of the *Society for the Propagation of the Gospel* arrived in 1890 and work was begun in Seoul. Anglicanism has never been strong in Korea. In the 1930's they were opening six new churches a year. The peak was reached in 1939, when membership grew to ten thousand. When Korea was divided between North and South the Anglican Church lost half of its members. The church is largely rural and made up mostly of women; hence self-support is a continuing problem. In 1963 only three of the sixteen Korean priests were supported locally. The first Korean bishop was consecrated in 1965. Today there are two dioceses, Seoul and Taejon; both are directly under the jurisdiction of Canterbury.

Other Missions. Though the Presbyterians have completely dominated the picture in Korea and the Methodists have been the number two
group, some mention should be made of the smaller missions. The *Seventh
Day Adventists* began work in 1903, followed by the *Oriental Missionary
Society* in 1907, the first workers of which were Korean students trained
at the OMS seminary in Tokyo. The first resident American missionary of
OMS was the *Reverend John Thomas,* who opened a seminary in Seoul in
1912. In 1921 the OMS moved its international headquarters from Tokyo
to Seoul. That same year the *Reverend E. A. Kilbourne* organized the
work in Korea into the *Korea Holiness Church.* The Central Executive
Committee of this church was made up of missionaries and Koreans for
many years; but in the 1940's the church became fully self-governing and
self-supporting. At that time the membership had grown to forty thousand. The *Salvation Army* began work in Seoul in 1908.

Patterns of Church Growth. Korea has been the most fruitful field
in Asia for Protestant missions. Whereas in other countries the missionaries
had to wait five, ten, and even twenty years for the first converts, in Korea
the response was almost immediate. In the early years the missionaries
were cautious in their approach to evangelism until they were sure that the
anti-Christian laws on the books were a dead letter. Moreover, they
remembered the wholesale slaughter of Roman Catholics barely twenty
years before. When it became clear that the government did not intend to
enforce the laws, the missionaries gave themselves to the work of evangelism with a will. Appenzeller baptized the first convert on June 24, 1887.
In 1889 he and Underwood together made a trip into the north country.
Pyengyang soon became a major center of Christian activity. By 1892 the
Koreans were openly asking for instruction in the new faith.

The decade beginning with 1895 was marked by solid growth in all
areas of the work. In the year 1900 alone, church membership increased by
more than 30 percent. Converts were being made faster than the missionaries could instruct them, and preaching centers were opening up in rural
areas where missionaries had never been. Much of this work was the result
not of organized evangelistic campaigns but of the simple, earnest witness
of the Korean Christians as they went about their daily tasks. The
missionaries spent most of their time conducting Bible classes and preparing converts for baptism and church membership.

Bible classes played a major role in the spread of the gospel and the
growth of the church. The system of Bible training classes began in 1890
with seven men who met in Dr. Underwood's study in Seoul. In 1901 the
mission adopted a policy whereby every missionary should prepare a
course of biblical instruction for each outstation in his area. By 1904, 60
percent of the members and catechumens were attending one or more
classes. By 1909, in the Northern Presbyterian territory alone, there were
some eight hundred Bible classes with a total attendance of fifty thousand.

Following the annexation of Korea in 1910 the Japanese occupation had an adverse effect on church growth. To avoid economic exploitation many Koreans emigrated to Manchuria. In some centers, such as Pusan, the migration of Christians left the church denuded of members. The educational policies introduced by the Japanese in 1915 and the subsequent restrictions on teaching religion in mission schools precipitated a controversy which affected church and mission morale for several years.

The decade from 1930 to 1940 witnessed another significant advance in spite of the repressive measures of the Japanese. During that time the Christian community increased almost 75 percent from 200,000 to 350,000.

Throughout this time Presbyterian growth was much greater than that of the Methodists, and not without reason. The Presbyterians had more evangelistic missionaries in the field, while the Methodists had more missionaries tied up in institutions. Moreover, the educational policies of the two groups were not the same. With the Presbyterians the schools were intended to contribute directly to the building of a strong church and an educated ministry; with the Methodists the schools were an end in themselves, though hopefully they would minister indirectly to church growth.

The Nevius Method of Church Growth. In June, 1890, Presbyterian missionary *John L. Nevius* of Chefoo, China, spent two weeks in Seoul discussing with the missionaries the methods he had found so helpful in Shantung. With one accord the Korean missionaries decided to adopt his methods, which came to be known as the "Nevius Method." His four main principles, as outlined by Underwood, were:

1. To let each man abide in the calling wherein he was found, teaching that each was to be an individual worker for Christ in his own neighborhood, supporting himself by his trade.

2. To develop church methods and machinery only so far as the native church was able to take care of and manage them.

3. So far as the church itself was able to provide the men and the means, to set aside the better qualified to do evangelistic work among their neighbors.

4. To let the natives provide their own church buildings, which were to be native in architecture and of such style as the local church could afford to put up.

Presbyterian Principles. Altogether apart from Mr. Nevius, the Presbyterian missionaries in Korea decided on the following principles: (1) The acceptance of the entire Bible as the inspired Word of God and as the basis for true Christian faith and service; (2) the emphasizing of personal evangelism and witnessing as the sacred privilege and duty of every professing Christian; (3) the necessity of regeneration through the Holy Spirit and the manifestation of Himself in supernaturally transformed

Christian lives; (4) the training of the children of the church to furnish Christian leaders and to prepare for Christian life and service; (5) the use of medical work as an evangelizing agency; and (6) inculcation of the principles of self-support, self-propagation, and self-government from the beginning of the indigenous church.

The Revival of 1907. There were many contributing factors to the unique character of the Korean church. One of the most potent was the great revival that broke out in Pyengyang in January, 1907. For five months prior to that time both missionaries and Christians had been meeting daily for prayer, seeking for a deeper, more satisfying experience of the power of the Holy Spirit. On January 14 the Holy Spirit fell on the seven hundred Christians gathered in Pyengyang from the surrounding countryside for the annual Bible classes conducted by the missionaries.

All those assembled, including the missionaries, experienced the convicting, cleansing power of the Holy Spirit in a new and deeper way. The usual manifestations of a genuine revival were all present: an overwhelming sense of the holiness of God with a concomitant sense of the exceeding sinfulness of sin; public confession of wrongdoing followed by restitution; and a deep compassion for the lost, accompanied by a consuming desire to share the gospel with the unconverted. The religious excitement continued for two weeks, during which all classes were suspended and everyone gave himself to prayer.

The revival spread to Seoul and other cities in Korea and beyond the borders of Korea into Manchuria and China. Jonathan Goforth, China's greatest missionary evangelist, visited Korea and carried back with him to China the embers that later burst into revival flame in all parts of China. [21] The 1907 revival made a lasting impression on the church in Korea. The spirit of prayer and the passion for piety which have been its outstanding characteristics for more than half a century can be directly traced to this source.

Japanese Colonialism. In Africa and Asia the Christian mission has been identified with colonialism. In India it was British colonialism. In the East Indies it was Dutch colonialism. In Indo-China it was French colonialism. In the Philippines it was American colonialism. In Africa all but two countries were parceled out among half a dozen colonial powers in Europe. China had all the disadvantages and none of the advantages of colonialism. The Chinese people could never understand how the same European power could send them merchants with their opium and missionaries with their Bible. There as elsewhere Christianity suffered from an unholy alliance between the gospel and the gunboat.

---

[21] The story is told by Jonathan Goforth in his book, *By My Spirit* (Grand Rapids: Zondervan, 1942).

Not so in Korea. Here was the happy exception. In Korea colonialism was perpetrated by Japan, a non-Christian, Asiatic power. Not only were the missionaries not identified with colonialism; they took their stand against it. The vast majority of the missionaries were Americans, and the United States was the only Western power that offered even token resistance to Japanese encroachments on the continent. So the missionaries, by politics as well as by persuasion, identified not with colonialism but with nationalism.

Nor was that all. The Korean church was in the vanguard of the resistance movement. In the Conspiracy Case of 1912, 123 Koreans were arrested. Ninety-eight of them were Christians. When the Koreans defied the Japanese authorities in 1919 by issuing a Declaration of Independence, sixteen of the thirty-three signatories were Christians—at a time when only 4 percent of the population was Christian.

> In many countries the Christian, because of his association with the West, was suspect and in danger of being regarded as a second-class citizen. In Korea exactly the opposite was the case; to be a Christian was to be a patriot; the Churches were widely identified with the Korean national cause.[22]

Persecution. The Koreans have a proverb: "He that is born in the fire will not faint in the sun." Certainly this has been the experience of the church in Korea. No church in the twentieth century, not even the Russian Orthodox Church in Russia nor the Christian church in Communist China, has suffered so much oppression, persecution, and devastation as the church in Korea. First under the Japanese, then during World War II, and more recently at the hands of the communists, the Korean church has been tortured almost beyond endurance.

In 1910 an attempt was supposedly made on the life of the Japanese governor-general in north Korea. Suspicion fell on the church, and leading Christians all over the country were arrested. During the uprising in 1919 hundreds of church leaders and thousands of church members were arrested, including women and students. Scores were executed and hundreds more simply disappeared.

During the 1920's there was a brief period of respite; but the rise of Japanese militarism in the 1930's, which coincided with the Sino-Japanese War, again subjected the nation to oppression. Enforced emperor worship was particularly hard on the Christian church whose members refused to bow the knee to Baal. Many church leaders were sent to prison. Since the great majority of missionaries were Americans, it was only natural that they should come under suspicion, especially after Japan's invasion of China in 1937. In late 1940 a mass evacuation of missionaries took place. Those that remained were placed in concentration camps. Following the war, a limited number of missionaries returned, but they were confined to South Korea.

---

[22] Stephen Neill, *Colonialism and Christian Missions* (New York: McGraw-Hill, 1966), p. 219.

At the end of the war the church leaders in the north, many of them just released from prison, others emerging from the underground, gathered in Pyengyang to prepare for the rehabilitation of the church. Alas, their freedom was short-lived. As the communist regime became more and more repressive it was again the church leaders who led the opposition, though the church was not against the red regime *per se* and did its best to cooperate wherever it could. But cooperation was not possible for very long. Following the attack on South Korea in June, 1950, and the subsequent defeat of the communist armies under MacArthur, the church in North Korea was liquidated. Nothing remains above ground today. In the meantime the church in South Korea suffered staggering losses. One-third of all church buildings were damaged or destroyed. In Seoul alone more than two hundred churches were damaged. When the communists retreated over the 38th Parallel they took with them several hundred Christian pastors. None ever returned; they are presumed dead.

Rehabilitation. Although the Korean churches had long since become self-supporting, the task of rehabilitation was beyond their means; so it became necessary for the missions to give mammoth aid to the churches. The American Methodist Mission provided $840,000 to rebuild Methodist churches and $275,000 for schools and hospitals. The Presbyterian Mission paid 25 percent of all rehabilitation costs for its churches. World Vision and the Christian Children's Fund have taken a special interest in the many war orphans. The Leprosy Mission opened clinics in the rural areas. The Friends Foreign Service Unit opened a hospital at Kunsan.

Evangelistic Activities. The postwar period with its tale of human misery gave the Christian church an excellent opportunity for evangelistic endeavor. Most unusual was the work among the 164,000 prisoners of the Korean War. *W. E. Shaw* of the Methodist Mission and *Harold Voelkel* of the Presbyterian Mission, with about twenty Korean pastors, worked with the men in the POW camps for the three years until they were released. The work of *Earle Woodberry,* an ex-China missionary, and *Lee Tai Young,* for thirty-three years a Korean missionary in China, was outstanding. Altogether 100,000 men registered their names and some 60,000 professed to accept Christ.

The Bible Club Movement, founded in Pyengyang in 1930, was reactivated after the Korean War to meet the appalling needs of tens of thousands of orphans and other poverty-stricken, homeless children. These clubs meet in churches all over the country and offer general education and instruction in Bible to the many children who otherwise would not have received any education whatever. In 1969 the Presbyterians reported sixty thousand members in their Bible clubs. The Methodist Church has its Wesley Clubs; the Holiness Church also operates many children's clubs.

Evangelistic campaigns were conducted for the United Nations forces as well as for the civilian population. *Billy Graham* visited Korea twice. *Bob Pierce,* founder of World Vision, Inc., was in and out of Korea several times a year in connection with the many orphanages supported by his organization. In 1950 and again in 1955 he held campaigns in Seoul and other cities. In 1965 the churches celebrated the eightieth anniversary of Protestant work by conducting a nationwide evangelistic campaign. It was supported by seventeen denominations of extreme diversity and resulted in a harvest of twenty thousand souls. In spite of all this activity, however, there are signs that church growth in Korea may be slowing down. Peace and a measure of prosperity in the 1960's have raised the specter of materialism, and the Christian church worldwide has not yet learned how to cope with this.

Radio and Television.   Korea is the only non-Christian country with a network of Christian radio stations. Station HLKY in Seoul began broadcasting in 1954. This powerful 50,000-watt station reaches most of central Korea and beams the gospel into communist North Korea. Since its inception four other stations have been added to the network, which is a project of the evangelical churches and missions which cooperate with the Korean National Christian Council. The popularity of these Christian broadcasts was indicated by a professional audience survey conducted in three cities in 1967. Despite commercial competition, over 300,000 persons mentioned the Christian network as their favorite; 900,000 persons listened daily and more than three million listened to some programs each month. Of this number 72 percent were non-Christian.

Station HLKX, located ten miles south of Inchon and operated by *The Evangelical Alliance Mission,* went on the air in December, 1956. In 1963 its power was increased from 20,000 watts to 50,000 watts. Besides covering North and South Korea, it beams the gospel daily into China, Mongolia, and Siberia. Letters received from these countries attest the effectiveness of the programs. Today HLKX is broadcasting in five languages twenty-three hours a day.

For some ten years the *Lutheran Church-Missouri Synod* has been broadcasting the *Lutheran Hour* in Korea. During that time a quarter of a million persons have enrolled in the Christian Correspondence Course. The largest graduation in the history of the course took place when 536 inmates of the Korean army prison received certificates in September, 1968. Here as elsewhere the Lutherans have pioneered in Christian television. Since 1965 a Korean version of *This Is The Life* has been telecast from Seoul and Pusan.

Christian Higher Education.   Through the years the various missions have made a substantial contribution to Christian education at all levels. The Presbyterians are responsible for five boys' high schools and six girls' high schools. The oldest was founded in 1888, the most recent in 1967. In addition they operate three colleges: *Soong Sil* (1907), *Keimyung Christian College* (1954), and *Seoul Woman's College* (1961). The Evangelical Alliance Mission opened a Christian college on the east coast in 1961. It has two divisions, Bible and commercial. Four Korean denominations and five overseas churches cooperate in *Yonsei University,* the result of a merger in 1955 of two union schools, Chosun Christian University and Severance Union Medical College. There are five thousand students enrolled in seven colleges. All of these institutions are headed by Koreans. *Dr. Helen Kim* (she died in 1969) and *Dr. George L. Paik* are internationally famous educators. These institutions continue to exert a strong Christian influence and their graduates are found in all walks of life. *Ewha Women's University* is reputed to be the largest of its kind in the world.

Theological Education. There are forty-eight Bible schools and seminaries in Korea. Most of them are new since the war and are, therefore, still young and small. The Presbyterians maintain five seminaries and a number of Bible institutes. The seminary in Seoul is one of the largest in Asia, having an enrolment of 240. The second largest, also in Seoul, belongs to the Holiness Church. Since its inception in 1912 it has produced over fifteen hundred graduates. In 1966 the *United Graduate School of Theology* opened on the campus of Yonsei University, offering theological education on a higher level than ever before in Korea. Financed largely through the Theological Education Fund, the new school serves Presbyterians, Methodists, Anglicans, and other denominations.

Church Divisions. Since World War II the churches of Korea have been plagued by divisions. The greatest havoc occurred in the Presbyterian ranks, where there are now four major denominations in the place of one. There is some present hope that two of them will again unite. The fifty-year-old Holiness Church split into two almost equal parts in 1961. The breach was healed four years later, but about 150 churches refused the reconciliation and are still on their own. The Korean Baptist Church, related to the Southern Baptists, divided in 1959 and was not reunited until 1968. The Methodists, likewise, had their divisions. Of the larger denominations, only the Anglicans, Seventh Day Adventists, and the Salvation Army have been free of strife. In some cases the cause was theological. In others it was the matter of shrine attendance during World War II. In one or two instances the International Council of Christian Churches was responsible. One denomination divided over the issue of membership in the World Council of Churches.

Postwar Proliferation. Following World War II there was a large influx of new missions from the United States. According to the 1968 edition of the *North American Protestant Ministries Overseas Directory,* there are almost fifty mission organizations in Korea. Thirty-seven of these entered Korea since 1945. Only four of these thirty-seven new missions have more than ten workers. Some have only two or three. No other mission field, not even Taiwan, is so completely dominated by American missions. Only three missionary societies out of a total of forty-seven are completely non-American. Two other missions, being international, include non-American personnel.

Ecumenical Relations.   The churches in Korea have been among the most conservative in the world. Certainly they have been more conservative in their theology than their mother churches in the United States, especially in the postwar period. Consequently it is not surprising to read that "ecumenism is still a shocking word in some quarters."[23] Nevertheless the winds of change are blowing in Korea and ecumenism is on the way. The first ecumenical venture was the *Federal Council of Churches and Missions* organized in 1919. In 1924 the name was changed to the *National Christian Council.* In 1969 a change in name and structure took place. It is now the *National Council of Churches.* Six churches are members. In addition to the NCC there are other ecumenical organizations. The *Christian School Association* serves eighty middle schools with 150,000 students enrolled. The *Korean Christian Student Movement* is supported by six Protestant denominations and works with students in 45 colleges and 152 high schools. There is also the *Korea Council of Christian Education.*

The Roman Catholics in Korea are beginning to show an interest in ecumenical cooperation. In 1965 they participated in a Good Friday service in the Anglican Cathedral in Seoul which was sponsored by seven denominations. In 1968 for the first time the Roman Catholics and the Methodists held joint services during the Week of Prayer for Christian Unity. That same year a Roman Catholic-Protestant committee for the common translation of the Old Testament into Korean was set up in Seoul. The committee will follow the guidelines laid down by the Secretariat for Christian Unity and the United Bible Societies.

Bible Translation.   The first translation of the New Testament was the work of the *Reverend John Ross* in Manchuria. It was so Chinese in style that revision was begun almost before the ink was dry. A revised New Testament appeared in 1900 which replaced the work of Ross. The Old Testament was completed in 1910. This version was used until 1935, when a second revision was made. After Liberation in 1945, this was republished in the reformed *Hangul* spelling which is in use today. A new translation of the entire Bible was begun in 1960. The New Testament went on sale just before Christmas of 1967 and sold 100,000 copies in the first year. Work

---

[23] *International Review of Missions,* January, 1967, p. 6.

on the Old Testament began in 1968 with five Roman Catholics and five Protestants on the committee.

Through the years three Bible societies have worked in Korea: the *National Bible Society of Scotland,* the *British and Foreign Bible Society,* and the *American Bible Society.* The *Korean Bible Society* has been independent since 1945. In 1964 a concerted effort was made to render the Korean Bible Society financially independent as well as autonomous. Progress has been made but there is still a long way to go. In 1968 only 15 percent of the budget was raised in Korea. The Bible House employs twenty-two colporteurs, who give their entire time to Scripture distribution throughout the country. In 1968 almost three million pieces were distributed. In 1970 the government of Korea awarded the Bible Society a special citation for its part in helping to keep alive the Korean language during the Japanese occupation, when the Bible was the only non-Japanese book permitted to be published.

Characteristics of the Korean Church.   Several outstanding characteristics should be noted. (1) The Korean church has been a *suffering* church, first at the hands of the Japanese for thirty-five years, and after World War II from the depredations of the communists. (2) The Korean church is a *witnessing* church. From the beginning the converts were taught to share their faith with others. Indeed, up to the present time in some churches a prospective member is encouraged to lead at least one person to Christ before he can be baptized. (3) The Korean church is a *praying* church. This dates back to the Great Revival of 1907, which was born in a five-month period of prayer. Most churches in Korea still have an early morning prayer meeting every day. (4) The Korean church is a *giving* church. Most of the churches achieved self-support in the early days. The devastation brought about by the communist invasion set the church back at least ten years. They required outside help to rebuild, but they are back on their financial feet now. (5) The Korean church is a *missionary* church. As far back as the 1930's there were Korean missionaries in Manchuria and China. Today Korean Presbyterians have forty missionaries in thirteen countries. The Holiness Church and the Methodist Church have also sent missionaries overseas. (6) The Korean church is a *spiritual* church. It is definitely pietistic in its emphasis on salvation as a personal experience, the cultivation of the spiritual life, and the evangelization of the world. There are signs, however, that under the influence of postwar missionaries from the United States, the younger people are giving more thought to the social implications of the gospel. (7) The Korean church is a *conservative* church. In fact, it is so conservative that on occasion it has refused to accept some liberal missionaries sent out from the United States. The large Presbyterian Church split over the question of membership in the World Council of Churches. Today only one of the four major Presbyterian denominations is a member of the WCC.

The Christian Presence Today.   According to the 1970 *Prayer Calendar of Christian Missions in Korea,* the Protestant community now stands at 2,650,000 persons. There are about 750,000 Roman Catholics. Together they account for approximately 9 percent of the population of South Korea. The three largest groups are the *Presbyterians, Methodists,* and *Holiness Church.* Through the years the Presbyterians have dominated the scene. At present, with 5,750 churches, they represent 65 percent of the Protestant community. The Methodists report 1,425 churches and a constituency of 300,000. The two Holiness groups with 750 churches support a constituency of 225,000. Other large groups include the *Seventh Day Adventists* (95,000), *Baptists* (32,000), *Assemblies of God* (30,000), *Salvation Army* (25,000), *Church of the Nazarene* (11,000), and the *Episcopal Church* (10,000). In addition there are ten smaller groups with a total constituency of 25,000.

What about North Korea?   The churches north of the 38th Parallel have been completely wiped out by the communist regime, though many of the five million refugees who fled south were Christians. Some denominations lost half of their membership when the country was divided. There is still no contact between North and South Korea. Less is known about North Korea than about any other communist country in the world. It is almost completely sealed off from the rest of the world. We do know, however, that the visible church has been completely destroyed.

XI

Middle East

Turkey

Political History. Asiatic Turkey is one of the oldest inhabited regions in the world and for centuries served as a battleground for foreign conquerors. With the fall of Constantinople in 1453 the Ottoman Empire was born. With its collapse in 1918, modern Turkey came into existence. Mustafa Kemal became the first president of the Republic of Turkey. It was he who introduced the reforms which brought Turkey into the twentieth century. The new constitution introduced sweeping reforms in all areas of life, public and private. Islam was disestablished, polygamy was outlawed, religious garb was prohibited. With the abolition of the Caliphate came a complete separation of church and state. Overnight Turkey became a secular state.

The present constitution, adopted in 1961, provides for a parliamentary form of government with all the civil and human rights generally expected of such an establishment. Turkey is a member of NATO and CENTO and, of course, the UN. In recent years there have been anti-American demonstrations, but basically Turkey is a staunch ally of the United States. The communist party is outlawed.

The People. The dominant ethnic group are the Turkish people, who represent almost 90 percent of the population of thirty-four million. The only significant minority are the Kurds, who account for 6.5 percent. Still smaller groups include Arabs, Greeks, Armenians, and Bulgarians. The literacy rate, about 50 percent, is high for that part of the world. Seventy percent of the people live in the rural areas of the country.

Religion. Ninety-nine percent of the people are Muslims. Though Turkey by constitution is a secular state, there are indications that Islam is on the move. New mosques are being built and Islamic literature is on the increase. The Koran is now available in a Turkish edition. Since 1956 Islam has been taught in the schools. The Christian minority is small indeed: Eastern Orthodox, 175,000; Roman Catholic, 20,000; and Protestant, 10,000, composed almost entirely of Armenian and Assyrian Christians. A union church in the capital ministers to English-speaking Christians, mostly American and European. Missionary work is extremely difficult. An embargo on the import of foreign language Scriptures has caused hardship to the small Greek and Armenian Christian communities.

Early Missions. Permanent missionary work in Turkey began with the arrival of *William Goodell* of the *American Board of Commissioners* in Istanbul in 1831. His greatest achievement was the translation of the Scriptures into Armeno-Turkish. Converts came not from Islam but from the nominal Christians of the Armenian Church. When the converts were excommunicated, they had no choice but to organize their own church in Istanbul in 1846. The new Protestant sect received government approval in 1850.

In the meantime other missions entered Turkey and for a time continued to work there. These included the *Church Missionary Society,* the *Basel Evangelical Missionary Society,* and the *Society for the Propagation of the Gospel.* The famous *Karl Pfander* was the outstanding leader during this period. Efforts were made to convert the Muslims. Violent persecution broke out, and in the 1870's the work in Istanbul was discontinued. Later, other societies took up work for longer or shorter periods: the *American Baptists, Disciples of Christ, Church of the Brethren, British Quakers,* and the *London Jews' Society.* Eventually they all retired from the field, leaving the American Board to bear full responsibility for the evangelization of Turkey.

In 1970 the United Church reported eighty-four missionaries in Turkey. What do eighty-four missionaries do in a land where evangelism and church planting are virtually impossible? They minister to the physical, intellectual, and social needs of the people in the name and spirit of Jesus Christ, in the hope that this nonverbal form of Christian witness will ultimately lead some interested persons to faith in Christ as Savior and Lord. Under these conditions an analysis of the Christian presence in this Muslim country is not without interest to the student of the Christian mission. Of the eighty-four missionaries, thirty-three are located in Istanbul; eleven in mission administration, four in the *Redhouse Press;* fifteen in the *American Academy for Girls.* The Reverend and Mrs. Perry D. Avery minister in the historic Union Church. Twenty-three missionaries are attached to the *American Collegiate Institute* (for girls) in Izmir. Eighteen are on the faculty of the *American College* (for boys) in the

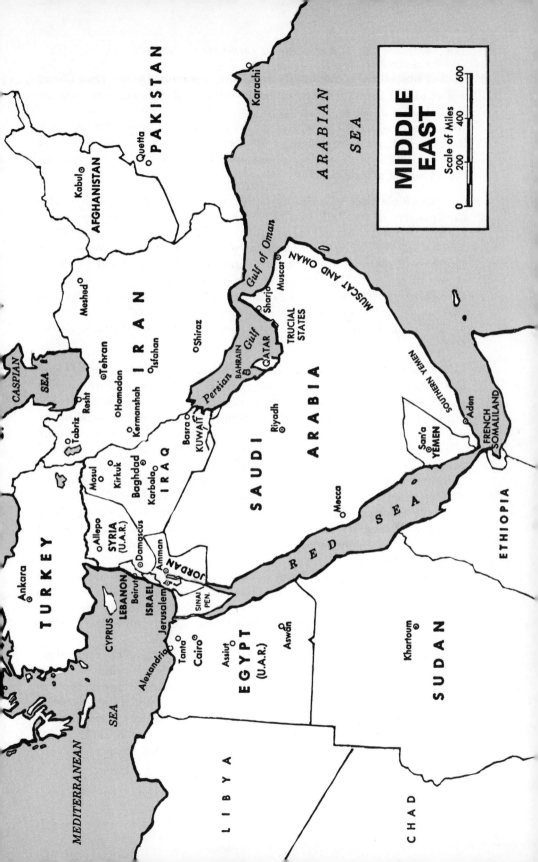

ancient hometown of Saul of Tarsus. Three are serving in the *Talas Clinic,* a government sponsored institution. The United Church also maintains the *Azariah Smith Memorial Hospital* at Gaziantep, where seven medical workers are engaged. Twenty-four of the eighty-four missionaries are single ladies, a high ratio explained by the fact that two of the schools are for girls. In 1967 lack of funds and personnel forced the closing of a seventy-eight-year-old school in Talas.

The Bible Society. The Levant Agency was established in 1820 with headquarters in Istanbul. In 1937 Turkey became a separate Joint Sub-agency. In 1962 it became a Joint Agency of the *British and Foreign Bible Society* and the *American Bible Society,* still under BFBS administration. The New Testament was first translated into Turkish in 1819 and the entire Bible in 1827. After 1929 the publication of books in Arabic characters was forbidden. In 1963 the Scriptures were circulated in forty-two languages, including thirteen diglots. The complete Bible is available in Turkish in both the modern Roman characters and the old Arabic characters.

Recent Developments. In recent years certain outside groups, *Operation Mobilization* among them, have engaged in widespread distribution of gospel literature and Bible correspondence courses. In 1966 OM was responsible for 66 percent of the Scriptures sold in Turkey. Some of the workers were arrested and spent time in prison. Most of them were released; but in 1970 a few were still imprisoned. In 1969 ten thousand tracts entitled "Permanent Revolution" were distributed by *Plymouth Brethren* missionaries on the university campuses of Istanbul. "We trust that in the very near future there will be an assembly of believers in Istanbul, Ankara and Izmir."[1] Thomas Cosmades, himself a Turk by birth and now a member of *The Evangelical Alliance Mission* stationed in Greece, makes periodic visits to Turkey for evangelistic meetings and personal follow-up.

The *Southern Baptist Foreign Mission Board* began work in Ankara in 1966. Its first services were held in the snack bar of the American Embassy. Later they were moved to an auditorium owned by the American military. In three years the church had slightly over one hundred members, most of them expatriates working in Ankara.

The *Seventh Day Adventists* have been in Turkey for some time. Their latest annual report shows one church with fifty-four members, three missionaries, and two ordained ministers. Turkey is one of the very few countries out of the 193 in which they work in which the Adventists have no medical or educational work. The *Worldwide Evangelization Crusade* worked in Turkey for several years beginning in 1962, but at present it has no representative there.

---

[1] *Voices from the Vineyard,* October, 1969, p. 5.

Christian Radio. Of course there are no Christian broadcasts originating within the country. Beginning with a fifteen-minute weekly program in 1968, *Trans World Radio* in Monaco is now broadcasting the
gospel message into Turkey seven days a week.

United Arab Republic

Political History. Better known as Egypt, the United Arab Republic
has a continuous recorded history of five thousand years, the longest in
the world. Great Britain, the last of many foreign powers to rule Egypt,
left in 1956. In 1952 a military coup engineered by Gamal Abdal Nasser
exiled playboy King Farouk, and Egypt became a republic on June 18,
1953. For a time Egypt united with Syria to form the United Arab
Republic. Syria seceded in 1961, but Egypt retains the name. Three times
Egypt has gone to war with Israel and each time has lost. Nasser, for
sixteen years president of the UAR, was the outstanding leader of pan-
Arabism; but even his charismatic personality was not sufficient to bring
unity to the Arab world. Nasser did much good for his country and
doubtless would have accomplished more but for his preoccupation with
the Arab-Israeli conflict. Officially the UAR takes a neutral position
between East and West, but America's support of Israel and Russia's aid to
Egypt have done nothing to improve American-Egyptian relations. British
missionaries evacuated Egypt during the Suez crisis in 1956; Americans
left during the Six Day War in 1967.

People. The population of the UAR is about thirty-two million.
There are two major religious groups, Muslims and Copts, though all are
Arabs in that they speak Arabic. The Copts are the true Egyptians, the
direct descendants of the men who built the pyramids. They represent
about 10 percent of the population. Only 3.5 percent of the land is arable;
the rest is desert, making a population density of almost twenty-four
hundred per square mile, one of the highest in the world. Since 1952 grade-
school attendance has risen from 40 percent to 90 percent.

Religion. Muslims comprise about 90 percent of the population.
Indeed, the UAR is the heartland of Islamic culture. The oldest university
in the world, Al Azhar, is in Cairo. At present it has thirty-six hundred
foreign students, many of whom become "missionaries" for Islam upon
their return to their own countries. The Coptic Church, which in 1968
celebrated the nineteen hundredth anniversary of the martyrdom of St.
Mark, enjoys full freedom. In 1968 President Nasser participated in the
dedication of the new St. Mark's Cathedral, which replaced the one burned
in 1963. The Egyptian government made a grant of $230,000 towards the
construction costs. For many years Islam has been taught in all public

schools. Since 1953 the government, at its own expense, has made provision for the teaching of Christianity to Christian students.

Early Missions. The earliest work was undertaken in the eighteenth
century by the *Moravians,* who maintained a mission to the Copts. They
remained for a time and then withdrew. Two other missionaries spent time
in Egypt; but they likewise did not remain for any length of time. They
were *William Jowett* of the *Church Missionary Society* and *Joseph Wolff*
of the *London Jews' Society.* Jowett was cordially received by the Coptic
patriarch, but nothing came of his visit.

Continuing work in Egypt began with the *Church Missionary Society*
in 1818, but the mission did not really get under way until reinforcements
arrived in 1825. In the early years the CMS tried to cooperate with the
Coptic Church. When this proved impractical, attention was turned to the
conversion of the Muslims; but little success was achieved. The outstanding
missionary was *W. H. Temple Gairdner,* who arrived in 1899 and served
until 1928. Medical work was begun in Old Cairo in 1899. Three other
centers were occupied by 1910. In 1920 Egypt and the Sudan were
separated from the See of Jerusalem. Sudan became a separate diocese in
1945. The Arabic-speaking Anglican Church has five parishes, four in Cairo
and one in Menouf.

Total communicant membership is about one thousand. Two Angli-
can missions, the *Church Missionary Society* and the *Jerusalem and the
East Mission,* cooperate with the Episcopal Church. Egypt, Libya, and
North Africa now form one of the five dioceses of the Archbishopric in
Jerusalem. For several years now it has been without a bishop.

Modern Missions. The arrival in Cairo in 1854 of three Associate
Reformed Presbyterian missionaries marked the beginning of what came to
be known as the *American Presbyterian Mission.* Unlike the Church
Missionary Society, which eschewed "proselytizing," the Presbyterians
sought and won thousands of nominal Copts to genuine faith in Christ. An
indigenous church, now known as the *Coptic Evangelical Church,* was
organized in 1863 as the Presbytery of Egypt of the United Presbyterian
Church of North America. Growth was sufficiently rapid that the Synod
of the Nile was formed in 1899 with four presbyteries. The Coptic
Evangelical Church became completely independent in 1957, and after
1967 the American missionaries served as fraternal workers under the
church.

The Six Day War in June, 1967, led to a mass evacuation of American
missionaries and brought about some drastic changes in church-mission
relations in the UAR. It was decided that the American Mission, which had
operated in Egypt for 113 years, was to be dissolved and that future aid to
the Coptic Evangelical Church should be channeled through ecumenical
agencies. It was further agreed that the church would assume responsibility

for all existing programs except medical work and audiovisual and music services, which are now under the Near East Council of Churches. Moreover there was to be an internationalization of the missionary staff, with a significant reduction in American personnel and a corresponding increase in non-American expatriates. The latest report (1969) indicates that only twenty-three American Presbyterian missionaries remain in the UAR, most of them in secondary education, in medical work, and in the *Evangelical Theological Seminary* in Cairo. The Coptic Evangelical Church, with almost thirty thousand communicant members in 180 organized churches served by 154 ordained ministers, is the largest and strongest Protestant church in the Middle East. It is a member of the Near East Council of Churches and the World Council of Churches.

The first girls' school in Port Said was established in 1897 by the Peniel American Mission, which later merged with the *World Gospel Mission*. Enrolment, which reached a peak of six hundred in 1946, is now down to 275. Following the crisis of June, 1967, the bookshop in Port Said was closed. The other two, in Cairo and Assuit, continue operation as a joint venture with three other missions. There are two churches under national pastors at Port Said and Port Fouad.

The *Egypt General Mission,* an independent faith work of British origin, began evangelistic work in Alexandria in 1898. The first group of missionaries was made up of seven young men who settled in the thickly-populated Delta area. After fifty years of work the mission had ten stations, the largest of which was at Shebeen-el-kanater, where the mission's only hospital was located. It ministered to some fifty thousand patients a year. Its two schools were closed in 1948, when the Free Schools Law was passed. The *Nile Mission Press,* an offshoot of the Egypt General Mission, provided Christian literature for Egypt and the Middle East for fifty years.

What is now the *Free Methodist Church of Egypt* was begun in 1899 by the *Reverend Herbert F. Randall,* a member of the Canadian Holiness Movement Church. It began in Assuit. The church in Egypt is now independent and has its own organization. Since 1959 it has been associated with the *Free Methodist Church* (USA), along with its sister church in Canada. It now has almost one hundred congregations in Upper and Lower Egypt. Its *Wesleyan Theological College* has both nationals and missionaries on the staff. The enrolment is small and only two or three men have been entering the ministry each year.

In 1905 Egypt became the first mission field of the *Evangelistic Faith Missions, Inc.* The *Reverend and Mrs. Lewis Glenn* and two others opened the first station in Alexandria. On one occasion Mr. Glenn was stoned and left for dead. The Glenns lost both their children in the first few years. Shortly thereafter smallpox took the lives of two missionaries. But they persevered, and reinforcements arrived in time to save the mission from extinction. It is committed to a church planting ministry and in 1967 had nineteen churches and a Bible school in Girga in Upper Egypt. In 1968 a new congregation was begun in Cairo. Already the building seating two hundred is overcrowded and the church is planning to erect its own building.

The *Assemblies of God* work began with prayer meetings in a private house in Assuit in 1908. The first missionary was the *Reverend G. S. Brelsford,* who died after eighteen months but not before he had established a small church. Others followed him and a station was opened in Alexandria in 1910 and in Cairo a little later. A Bible school in Port Said trains leaders for a strong indigenous church which now numbers almost ten thousand members in some one hundred fifty congregations. By far the outstanding institution is the American Orphanage founded in 1911 and for fifty years directed by *Lillian Trasher,* fondly known as the "Nile Mother." From the first the orphanage was a work of faith supported by freewill offerings from Egypt and abroad. In fifty years of loving service Miss Trasher had only three short furloughs. The orphanage, now under Egyptian leadership, is the home of fourteen hundred children.

British Assemblies of the *Plymouth Brethren* have been at work in Egypt for a long time and today they report nine thousand believers in 165 assemblies. By virtue of their New Testament pattern of work with emphasis on lay leadership, the Brethren Assemblies suffered least from recent upheavals in mission circles in Egypt. Foreign missionaries are not essential to the ongoing of that kind of indigenous work.

The *Church of God* (Cleveland) began permanent work in Egypt in 1946. The mission got off to a flying start when it received into its organization a Pentecostal leader of thirty years' standing and his twenty-three indigenous churches located along the Nile Valley. The church came to be known as the Pentecostal Church of God. Today the churches extend from Cairo for five hundred miles up the Nile. Total membership is three thousand.

Aftermath of Two Wars. The two Arab-Israeli wars of 1956 and 1967 played havoc with the Christian mission in Egypt. The first was particularly hard on the British missionaries, and the second made necessary the evacuation of all American missionaries. After both wars the missionaries were able to return; but in all such cases there is a certain degree of attrition. The Egypt General Mission transferred its workers to Lebanon and some, later, to Eritrea, where they now work under the new name of *Middle East General Mission.* The Nile Mission Press moved to Beirut, where it is now the *Arabic Literature Mission.* Anti-American sentiment continues to run high in the UAR, and churches in association with, or receiving aid from, American missions are naturally suspect. Until the Arab-Israeli confrontation is settled once and for all, American missionaries in Arab lands will continue to live and work under grave difficulties.

The Christian Presence. There has been a Christian church in Egypt since the first century. Before the onslaught of Islam in the seventh century most of Egypt was at least nominally Christian. After the Muslim scourge Christianity survived in the form of the Coptic Orthodox Church, which has continued down to the present time. Estimates of its numerical strength vary from three to five million. It has twenty-six dioceses in Egypt, thirty bishops, fifteen hundred priests, one thousand churches, and missions in South Africa, Sudan, and Kuwait. In addition there are twenty-one Protestant denominations at work, together with five Separatist churches (bodies led by national Christians who have broken with the missions), making 110,000 Protestants and 12,000 Separatists. Of the nation's nine major ethnic groups, eight, in which Christianity flourished until the fifteenth century, are now 100 percent Muslim and have no Christian witness at all.

Ecumenical Relations. Three denominations, the *Coptic Evangelical Church, Coptic Orthodox Church,* and *Greek Orthodox Church,* are members of the World Council of Churches. Only one of them, the Coptic Orthodox Church, is a member of the All Africa Conference of Churches. Seven groups belong to the *Evangelical Fellowship of Egypt,* which was formed in 1966.

Lebanon

Political History. Lebanon is the most democratic, best educated, least political, and most cosmopolitan country in the Arab world. For several centuries it was part of the Ottoman Empire. From 1920 to 1941 it was administered by France under a mandate of the League of Nations. It has none of the oil reserves that have enriched the other Arab countries; but its capital, Beirut, with over one hundred banks, forty-one of them foreign, is the financial hub of the Middle East. Though a member of the Arab League, it has never been militantly anti-Israel. It fought against Israel in 1948 and again in 1956; but it took no part in the Six Day War in June, 1967. Lebanon has been called the Switzerland of the Middle East.

The People. Lebanon has a population of 2,600,000, which makes it the second smallest country in the Middle East. Two million Lebanese live outside of the country, many of them in the United States. Arabic is the official language; French and English are widely known. Free primary education was introduced in 1960. As a result it has a literacy rate of 80 percent, the highest of all the Arab states. There are nine universities and other institutions of higher learning in Beirut, including the famous American University, which was originally a missionary institution.

Religion. Lebanon has the distinction of being the only country in the world whose population is divided almost equally between Muslims and Christians. For almost all except the Armenians, Arabic is the mother tongue. The president of the country by common agreement must be a Maronite Christian and the prime minister, his appointee, must be a Sunni Muslim. Other high officials are similarly divided equally between Christians and Muslims. Religious quotas govern the selection of judges, ambassadors, and military officers. The membership of the unicameral legislature, now ninety-nine, must always be a multiple of eleven to give the Christians a six-to-five edge over the Muslim members. Truly a unique form of religious coexistence, the arrangement seems to work well. There are only fifteen thousand Protestants in Lebanon; the other Christians, well over one million, belong to the Roman Catholic or the Eastern Orthodox churches.

The capital city of Beirut is the largest and most important Christian center in the Arab world. It has more educational institutions than any other city in the Middle East. It is the home of two vastly influential mission presses: the *American Press,* originally in Malta; and the *Arabic Literature Mission,* formerly the Nile Mission Press in Cairo. Practically every missionary organization in the Middle East has at least an office in Beirut; and it is the Middle East headquarters of the British and Foreign Bible Society. The Near East Council of Churches, founded in 1928 as the Near East Christian Council, now has its headquarters here.

Early Missions. The first Protestant mission to establish a continuing work was the *United Church Board of World Ministries.* The date was 1823 and the pioneer was *Pliny Fiske.* He died two years later, but the work was not allowed to languish. Reinforcements arrived and schools were opened. In 1824 *Mrs. Bird* and *Mrs. Goodell* took girls into their homes to educate them—when girls were not considered worth educating. Ten years later the first girls' school in the Ottoman Empire was opened in Beirut. Little by little confidence was established and converts were won, mostly from the existing Christian groups. In 1866 *Dr. Daniel Bliss,* then a Congregational missionary, founded the *Syrian Protestant College;* in 1920 it became the *American University of Beirut.* Today it has three thousand students from sixty countries. It is the largest American university overseas and has exercised an enormous influence on all aspects of professional life in the Middle East. It has been described as America's best investment in the Arab world. Certainly if there remains among the Arab peoples any residue of goodwill for Uncle Sam, it can be traced in large measure to this one outstanding institution. From the beginning it was intended to be primarily an academic institution. No direct effort was made to convert the students to Christianity. This was made clear in the words of its founder:

A man white, black or yellow; Christian, Jew, Mohammedan, or heathen, may enter and enjoy all the advantages of this institution for three, four, or eight years; and go out believing in one God, in many gods, or in no God. But it will be impossible for one to continue with us long without knowing what we believe to be the truth and our reasons for that belief.[2]

In 1969 the UCBWM had two couples in Beirut, one with the American University and the other with the Near East School of Theology.

When in 1870 the American Congregationalists decided to concentrate on Turkey, they turned their Syria-Lebanon mission over to the *American Presbyterians,* who have continued to be the major mission in Lebanon ever since. Through the years they have sent a steady stream of unusually dedicated missionaries to this part of the world. Schools, clinics, and hospitals have flourished under their supervision. The church which resulted from their efforts is now autonomous; it is known as the *National Evangelical Synod of Syria and Lebanon.* It has some four thousand communicant members and a Christian community almost five times that number. Not all, of course, are in Lebanon. Educational work includes twelve primary schools, thirteen secondary schools, a college, and a seminary. The thirty-five fraternal workers, all in Lebanon, are serving in various institutions: educational, medical, and theological. All are under the jurisdiction of the National Evangelical Synod, which has its headquarters in Beirut.

Another organization with over one hundred years of service in Lebanon is the British Syrian Mission, since 1959 known as the *Lebanon Evangelical Mission.* Founded in 1860 as an independent faith mission, its main emphasis has been educational evangelism. Its largest institution is the *Training College for Girls* in Beirut. The *Lebanon Bible Institute* in Shemlan has trained scores of evangelists, pastors, and Biblewomen for many missions besides its own.

The *Reformed Church in America* sent its first missionary to Lebanon in 1889. The work has never been large, and today two missionaries are engaged in joint programs with other churches.

Modern Missions. The *Southern Baptist Convention* as early as 1921 accepted responsibility for Baptist missions in Palestine and Syria; but it was not until 1948 that missionaries took up residence in Beirut. Since that time considerable progress has been made. Twenty-three career missionaries are busy in educational, theological, publication, and radio work. A seminary was opened in 1960. The *Lebanese Baptist Convention* comprises nine churches, six of them self-supporting, with a total membership of 450.

Although the Lutheran Hour has been heard in Lebanon since 1950, the *Missouri Synod* did not move in until 1960. Originally efforts were

---

[2] United Church Board for World Ministries, *Calendar of Prayer and Directory,* 1968-1969, p. 112.

made to establish churches; but because there were already thirty-five denominations in Lebanon it was decided to specialize in radio and thereby reach a wider audience. Bible correspondence courses are used as follow-up; in 1968 there were over twenty-three thousand active enrollees from many countries. Every effort is made to link interested listeners with local churches. Two missionaries and a local staff of eight are involved in the program.

Lebanon was the last of the three Arab countries entered by the *Christian and Missionary Alliance;* it still has the smallest work. After twenty years there are two churches in Beirut, one for Arab Christians and the other, only three years old, for the international community. The church's ministry in Monsouriye includes work among the orphans of the Near East Boys' Home.

The *Assemblies of God* have eight missionaries in Beirut. They divide their time among a small church with only fifteen members, a Bible school, and a printing press.

In the last year or two the *Bible and Medical Missionary Fellowship* has moved into western Asia and now has several workers in Beirut. Mr. and Mrs. Raymond Joyce, through the Muslim World Evangelical Literature Service, are promoting literature for Muslims in fifty countries. Dr. and Mrs. George Bush are attached to the Beirut College for Women. The *Worldwide Evangelization Crusade* is a newcomer to Lebanon, having sent its first three workers to Beirut in 1970.

Christian Radio. Repeated efforts have been made to erect a Christian broadcasting station in the Near East, but no government has been willing to give the necessary permission. The Christian message is beamed into this part of the world by powerful transmitters in Monaco, Addis Ababa, Monrovia, and, more recently, the Seychelles Islands. Half a dozen recording studios are maintained in Beirut where programs in Arabic and other Near Eastern languages are prepared.

Theological Education. The *Association for Theological Education* in the Near East was created in 1966 with financial assistance from the Theological Education Fund. It has nine member schools, one of which is the *Near East School of Theology* in Beirut. This ecumenical institution is the heir of 130 years of Protestant theological education in the Near East. Among the constituent bodies of the seminary are four local churches and two Western groups, the United Presbyterian Church in the USA and the United Church of Christ. In 1967 the school began to build on a new location not far from the American University. Enrolment in 1970 was at an all-time high, with 55 regular students and 120 special students. In addition to the basic B.D. program, there are graduate study programs leading to Th.M. and Th.D. degrees in Biblical Studies.

The Bible Societies. An Agency of the *British and Foreign Bible Society* was established in the Levant in 1820. A Joint Agency, known as Bible Lands Agency North, was formed in 1937 under the administration of the *American Bible Society.* In 1963 the Joint Agency was reorganized to cover Iraq, the Persian Gulf States, Jordan, Lebanon, and Syria; it is still under ABS administration. The Bible Society office and main shop in the heart of Beirut receives a steady stream of visitors. All church bookstores (Orthodox, Roman Catholic, and Protestant) and even some secular bookstores now stock Bible Society publications. Evangelical, Orthodox, and Roman Catholic leaders are planning to produce a common translation of the Arabic Bible to replace the Van Dyck translation of 1864.

Near East Council of Churches. Beirut is the headquarters of the *Near East Council of Churches,* which dates back to 1928. As presently constituted it comprises two regional councils: the *Egypt Inter-Mission Council* and the *United Christian Council of Southwest Asia* (Syria, Lebanon, and Jordan). Geographically its member churches extend from Morocco to Iran and from Turkey to Ethiopia. It embraces within its fellowship churches belonging to different confessional groups: Anglican, Armenian, Syrian Orthodox, and Protestant. For many years the executive secretary was the Reverend Harry G. Dorman, Jr. In 1965 the Reverend Albert Isteero became the first Arab national to hold this important post. Programs include radio broadcasting, literature, audio-visual and fine arts, Christian education, and a study program in Islam. The Western missions cooperating with the NECC do so through the Commission on Outreach and Witness. Since 1948 the NECC has been heavily engaged in relief work among the Palestinian refugees. Much of the aid has come through the World Council of Churches and Church World Service.

Church Union. In 1962 four denominations agreed to begin negotiations looking forward to organic union. Meetings were held in 1963 and 1964, and by 1965 a draft constitution was prepared. The four groups are the *Evangelical Episcopal Church* (Diocese of Jordan, Lebanon, and Syria), *Evangelical Synod of Syria and Lebanon* (Presbyterian), *National Evangelical Church of Beirut* (Congregational), and the *Lutheran Evangelical Church in Jordan.* A fifth church has joined the negotiations, the *National Evangelical Church of Damascus.* The new church will be known as the *United Evangelical Church in the Middle East.* The united church will adopt the Episcopal polity. Three bishops will be consecrated, one each for Jordan, Syria, and Lebanon. It was hoped that the final meeting would be held in the summer of 1970 to make concrete plans for the inauguration of the united church; but unsettled conditions have brought plans to a virtual standstill.

Syria

Political History. After four centuries of Turkish rule Syria was mandated to France in 1920 and gained its independence in 1944. Since then it has been dominated by left-wing governments and at one time it looked as if the communists might seize power. For a brief period (1958-1961) Syria and Egypt formed the United Arab Republic; but dissatisfaction on Syria's part led to the dissolution of the union. Syria is the implacable foe of Israel. Diplomatic relations with the United States were broken in 1967 and anti-American sentiment continues to run high.

The People. The population of Syria is 5,800,000, 90 percent of whom are Arabs. Kurds, Armenians, and Turks form the principal minorities. With the exception of 200,000 desert nomads, the population is clustered in the areas of heavier rainfall and river irrigation. Arabic is the official language. Illiteracy is about 65 percent.

Religion. Today Syria is a Muslim state but it was not always so. Prior to the introduction of Islam, Syria was the scene of much Christian activity. Antioch, one of the largest cities in the Roman Empire, had a large and flourishing church. Paul made it his base of operations for the eastern half of the empire. It was in Antioch that the disciples were first called Christians. After the fall of Jerusalem, Antioch became the headquarters of the church. In the seventh century the Muslim Arabs conquered Syria and from that time it has been a Muslim country. Various branches of the Christian church have managed to survive, and today the following groups are found in this region: Greek Orthodox, Jacobites, Nestorians, Armenians, and Maronites. They account for about 13 percent of the population. In recent years the government has taken an increasingly hard line against Christian missions from the West. At present there are no missionaries in Syria. Christian churches, largely because of their antiquity, continue to enjoy a measure of freedom. A difficult situation developed in 1967 when the government decreed that all private schools should be staffed with administrators appointed by the government. Roman Catholic authorities refused to agree; as a result their schools were closed. Orthodox and Protestant leaders came to terms with the government and their schools continue to function, but not without problems.

Early Missions. When reading missionary literature of the nineteenth century it is very difficult to separate the work in Syria from that in Lebanon. In those days Turkey, Armenia, Syria, Lebanon, and Palestine were all part of the Ottoman Empire. Often these areas were lumped together under the one name of Syria. It is known that Beirut, then as now, was the hub of the evangelical missionary movement from the West.

"This busy seaport, with healthful mountains close by and a friendly English consul at hand, was soon recognized as the most promising center for a permanent establishment."[3]

The *Reverend Joseph Wolff,* the much-traveled representative of the *London Jews' Society,* visited Syria in 1822 and 1823 in search of Jewish communities in need of a Christian witness. *Pliny Fiske* and *Levi Parsons* of the *American Board* (now the United Church Board for World Ministries) arrived in the Middle East in 1819 and traveled extensively in Palestine and Syria. Fiske's arrival in Beirut in 1823 marked the beginning of the American Board's work in that part of the world. Strangely enough, opposition came not from the Muslims but from the Roman Catholics and the Orthodox churches. The patriarch of the Maronite Church warned his flock against the missionaries: "They are therefore accursed, cut off from all Christian communion. . . . We permit no one to visit them, or employ them, or do them a favor, or give them a salutation, or converse with them in any form or manner; but let them be avoided as a putrid member and as hellish dragons."[4]

A good deal of exploration was done in the early years to ascertain the most advantageous centers for missionary outreach. As the number of missionaries increased, stations were opened in various places, Damascus and Aleppo in particular. One of the outstanding educational institutions in the Middle East is *Aleppo College,* now supported by four Christian groups; namely, the Armenian Evangelical Union, the Arab Protestant Synod, the United Presbyterian Church in the USA, and the United Church of Christ. No foreign representatives are allowed on the staff and funds from the West are being provided on a decreasing scale.

The American Board pulled out of Syria and Iran in 1870 and turned their mission over to the United Presbyterian Church in the USA, which has maintained a large mission in the Middle East ever since. Much of the work has been medical and educational. Most of the converts came not from the Muslim population but from the Eastern churches. The indigenous church, now autonomous, is the *National Evangelical Synod of Syria and Lebanon,* described in more detail in the section on Lebanon. All of the fraternal workers cooperating with this church are located in Lebanon. The *Reformed Presbyterian Church in North America* initiated work in the coastal city of Latakia and two schools were established. The work was integrated with the National Evangelical Synod in 1961. A hospital and several schools were maintained in Nebek and Qaryatain by the *Danish Mission in the Orient.* In 1960 this work was taken over by the National Evangelical Synod.

The *Christian and Missionary Alliance* began work in 1922. Dera'a became the center for all of south Syria, with two to five missionaries

---

[3] William E. Strong, *The Story of the American Board* (Boston: The Pilgrim Press, 1910), p. 83.
[4] *Ibid.,* p. 99.

located there at different times. Five main centers were opened, including the ancient city of Damascus. During the 1960's the missionaries were forced to leave. The *National Evangelical Church of Syria,* with six churches and a combined membership of 450, is carrying on under the leadership of nine national workers, two of whom are ordained ministers. In 1969 the church in Damascus erected a modern, commodious building with a capacity of over five hundred. The opening of the new church was celebrated by holding special evangelistic meetings led by the Reverend Maurice Gerges of Lebanon. Nightly attendance filled the church and all available space was occupied. Each night there were decisions for Christ.

The *Church of the Nazarene* has had work in Syria for a number of years. In 1970 seven organized churches with eighteen national workers were carrying on without the aid of missionaries.

The small group of *Anglicans* in Syria are part of the Diocese of Jordan, Lebanon, and Syria. Since 1958 the bishop has been an Arab.

Evangelical Baptist Missions, an American faith mission, has work in Syria. The director is Abraham Brake, a native of Syria and a graduate of the Lebanese Bible School. In recent years two stations have been opened in Damascus, where upwards of two hundred attend Sunday school. A building for permanent headquarters was acquired in 1969.

The *Lebanon Evangelical Mission,* known for one hundred years as the British Syrian Mission, withdrew its last missionaries in 1963. *St. Paul's School* in Damascus is now operated by the Damascus Evangelical Church. The *Near East Bible Center,* founded by the Reverend Peter G. Shadid, a Christian Arab, in 1959, is engaged in evangelistic work in Syria.

Jordan

Political History. The Hashemite Kingdom of Jordan was born out of the Arab-Israeli war of 1948. Its first king, Abdullah, was assassinated in 1951. The present ruler, the dynamic and apparently indestructible King Hussein, came to the throne in 1952. Jordan fought Israel in all three wars—1948, 1956, and 1967. In the last war it lost its territory west of the Jordan River and its section of Jerusalem. These losses greatly added to its economic woes and only large grants from the oil-rich countries of Kuwait, Saudi Arabia, and Libya have kept Jordan afloat. Of all the Arab states, Jordan has shown the most willingness to negotiate a permanent peace with Israel. Pressure from the other Arab states, particularly the United Arab Republic, has prevented King Hussein from making a separate peace with Israel.

The People. The population of 2,200,000 is almost 100 percent Arab. About half of them live in territory occupied by Israel. More than half a million Arab refugees were created by the war of 1948. For more than twenty years about half of these have lived in indescribable squalor in refugee camps supported by the United Nations. Many of the Arab guerrillas that have been causing chaos in the Middle East are the product of these camps. These desperate insurgents pose a threat not only to Israel but to the government of Jordan as well.

Religion. Roughly 90 percent of the Jordanians are Muslim; the remainder are Christian. These live in Jerusalem, Bethlehem, Ramallah, and other towns which, for the time being, are held by Israel. The Christians are mostly Roman Catholic or Eastern Orthodox. Protestants form a small minority of 1 percent. The Christians are all Arabs by race. Jordanian law forbids missionaries to preach to Muslims.

Dilemma. It is difficult to write about the Christian mission in Jordan while Jerusalem and everything west of the Jordan River is under Israeli control. Much of the Christian work in Jordan was in this area before the Six Day War of 1967. Who is to say whether this territory should be considered as part of Jordan, or treated in a later section under Israel? Mission publications must exercise the greatest discretion at this point lest one or other of the governments takes offense and expels the missionaries. Missionaries in Arab lands tend to support the Arab cause in the Arab-Israeli conflict, whereas missionaries in Israel can find good reason to espouse the position taken by Israel. It could hardly be otherwise. Without trying to cut the Gordian knot, the author will recognize the international boundaries prior to June, 1967, and when referring to Jordanian territory west of the Jordan River will speak of it as "occupied Jordan." Certainly it behooves us to pray not only for the peace of Jerusalem, but also for justice for the Arabs who have been displaced.

Missions. It seems only right and proper that Great Britain, which has played so important a role in the Middle East, should be represented by the *Church of England.* For over a century the Anglicans have manned mission stations in Palestine and other parts of the Middle East. In Jordan they have been represented by two missions, the *Church Missionary Society* and the *Jerusalem and the East Mission.* However, the war of 1948 reduced their staff and curtailed their work. Only one of seven hospitals in the Middle East remains—the Old Hospital at Nablus; and it is now maintained by the Arab Episcopal community. The CMS girls' school in Amman, founded in 1926, is still functioning. The mission also has relief work in Zerka and Salt. The JEM operates two excellent schools which through the years have acquired a fine reputation—*Bishop's School for Boys* in Amman and *St. George's School* in Jerusalem. About 80 percent of the students in these schools are Muslims.

The *Christian and Missionary Alliance* has been working here for more than thirty-five years. The work in Amman began in the living room of the mission house in 1949. In 1951 they moved into a spacious hall in the market place. In 1968 a fine property was purchased, and a new church building is under construction. The work continues to flourish with near capacity attendance. There is an organized church in the Old City of Jerusalem in occupied Jordan, composed almost entirely of people who settled there after the war of 1948. In addition there are three other C&MA centers, at Madaba, Mufraq, and Kerak. In 1969 the Youth for Christ Teen Team visited Amman and held meetings in churches and schools. One of the highlights of the tour was the evening when they packed the USIS auditorium with an enthusiastic audience, a large number of whom were Muslim youth. The team appeared on government television during prime time and was invited by King Hussein to sing at a dinner given in his honor. At present the situation in Jordan is hardly conducive to Christian, much less missionary, work. The C&MA is in the process of turning over all its buildings and properties to the *Evangelical Church of the Christian Alliance,* which has three organized congregations and two ordained national workers. There are no missionaries there now.

The *Southern Baptists* began work in Jordan in 1952 when they assumed responsibility for a hospital founded fifteen years earlier by a British doctor in the village of Ajloun. Following the war of 1956 a mob attacked the hospital and school, burning one building and damaging the other. During the 1967 crisis all of the missionaries evacuated except one doctor; they returned later. Today there are two schools in Ajloun. A government requirement that Islam be taught in all schools presented the mission with a serious dilemma. As a result one school was closed in 1969. The only other center of mission activity is the capital of Amman, where there is a bookstore and where some student work is done. Sixteen missionaries are cooperating with the *Jordanian Baptist Convention,* which now includes five churches, 173 members, and eight national pastors.

The *Independent Board for Presbyterian Foreign Missions* has work in occupied Jordan south of Jerusalem. A sanatorium for tuberculosis patients was founded at Baraka by *Dr. Thomas Lambie* after he had served almost a lifetime in Africa. A school of nursing was added in 1954. The Bible Presbyterian Church in Bethlehem was dedicated in 1953. Sunday morning attendance varies from 125 to 150. A kindergarten was opened in 1969. The mission has worked entirely among the Arabs, and when they fled to the East Bank in the summer of 1967 there was no further need for the Baraka Hospital. It has since closed, and the mission has decided to convert the property with its complex of buildings into a training center. The *Baraka Bible College* began its first class in September, 1970. It offers a four-year course leading to a B.Th. degree. It is the only institution of its kind in occupied Jordan.

World Presbyterian Missions has work in the extreme southern part of Jordan. It has two centers, Aqaba and Ma'an. The mission is constructing a hospital at Mafraq in the north. During the 1967 war the missionaries left the country; but Dr. Eleanor A. Soltau, Nurse Aileen Coleman, and Lester Gates, a technical specialist, are back in Mafraq. The church in Aqaba is under a national pastor who was formerly with the C&MA in Syria. The weekly services in Ma'an are held in the home of a layman.

For many years the *American Friends* have had two excellent schools, one for boys and one for girls, at Ramallah on the West Bank. Combined enrolment is about five hundred. In spite of the upheaval in the Middle East these schools have been able to function with little interruption, largely because of their long history and fine reputation. In connection with the Monthly Meeting there is a Sunday school which draws some two hundred children from all denominations. The 1969 Report stated: "Our Sunday School is our most meaningful work."[5]

Church World Service and the *Lutheran World Relief* along with the *Mennonite Central Committee* have been doing relief work in Jordan for some years. Their ministry is mostly to the Palestinian refugees, who even before the war of 1967 numbered over half a million. During the winter of 1968-69 the MCC imported two hundred tons of used clothing, blankets, Christmas bundles, and other items. Their program includes feeding centers, sewing schools, needlework, self-help projects, temporary housing, child care centers, women's activities centers, and others. They have work both in Jordan proper and on the West Bank.

Jordan became a field of the *Conservative Baptist Foreign Mission Association* in 1956 when one couple went there to work with an independent missionary. They worked among the national Christians to establish and enlarge the struggling churches. During the 1967 war the missionaries evacuated, but they were back at their work within a few months. Church and mission work are located in Amman, where there are three missionary couples and three churches with a total membership of 170.

Other missions with small commitments in Jordan include *Baptist Mid-Missions, Assemblies of God, Church of the Nazarene,* and *Church of God* (Cleveland).

Iran

Political History. Iran is a constitutional monarchy. Shah Mohammed Reza Pahlevi, one of the few remaining monarchs of the twentieth century, ascended the throne in 1941. One of the most progressive monarchs of our times, the Shah has enacted his own land reform program, but not without opposition from the feudal aristocracy. There were eighteen premiers in the first twenty-two years of the Shah's reign. Since 1953 his "White Revolution," financed by oil revenues, has sparked an economic boom, with factory workers in new industries receiving 20

---

[5] Friends United Meeting Board of Missions, *Communicating the Gospel, 1970,* p. 30.

percent of the profits. The American Point Four Program, initiated in 1951, was successfully terminated in 1967. Although Iran has a 1,200-mile border with Russia and cannot afford to incur its displeasure, it has close ties with the West. Iran does not share its neighbors' animosity towards Israel.

The People. The population of Iran is about twenty-seven million, which makes it one of the three largest countries in this part of the world. The people are Aryans and not Arabs and speak their own language —Persian. They are the descendants of the Persian people mentioned so often in the Old Testament. Through the centuries they have survived wave after wave of foreign invaders, and have managed to preserve their language and culture intact.

Religion. For over one thousand years Islam has been the dominant religion of Iran; but it was not always so. Christianity and Zoroastrianism both antedate Islam in Iran. The latter is indigenous to Iran, having been introduced by the prophet Zoroaster in the seventh century before Christ. The former was firmly planted in Iran in the third century by Syriac-speaking Christians from Mesopotamia, later known as Nestorians. After the onslaught by Islam the Christian church survived as a small remnant not far from the Turkish border. Today there are 65,000 Armenians, 25,000 Nestorians, 50,000 Jews, and 13,000 Zoroastrians.

Islam is divided into two major sects—the Sunnis and the Shiites. The schism originated with a dispute regarding the fourth successor of Mohammed as caliph (leader) of Islam. The Sunnis are orthodox and fanatical. The Shiites are less numerous and more tolerant. The Muslims in Iran belong to the Shiah sect and have their own holy city of Meshed. The government recognizes four religions: Islam, Judaism, Zoroastrianism, and Christianity. The constitution guarantees religious liberty, and evangelical churches have complete freedom to hold evangelistic services in their own buildings. In most Muslim countries the baptizing of a convert from Islam might easily precipitate a communal riot; not so in Iran. Islam is taught in all public schools; but Christian schools under national leadership may give instruction in ethics and observe Sunday as the weekly day of rest.

Early Pioneer. In the beginning of the nineteen century *Henry Martyn* became the first Protestant missionary to Iran. After spending four or five years in India as a chaplain of the East India Company, he went to Persia to regain his health and to complete his translation of the New Testament into Persian. He was there less than two years; but during that time he preached extensively to mullahs and students and cogently presented the claims of Christ to the ardent followers of the prophet Mohammed. Failing health forced him to return to England. He went overland by way of Constantinople; but death overtook him at Tacat in

Turkey on October 16, 1812. Though his entire missionary career lasted only six years he completed the monumental task of translating the New Testament into Hindustani, Persian, and Arabic.

Permanent Work. The *American Board of Commissioners* was the first mission to enter Iran. The date was 1834 and the pioneers were the *Reverend and Mrs. Justin Perkins.* The following year they established headquarters in Urmia. As reinforcements arrived, they were able to expand their work to include medical and educational projects as well as evangelistic work. In the interests of comity and economy the American Board pulled out of Iran in 1870 and turned the mission over to the American Presbyterians. At the time of the turnover there were about three thousand converts.

Through the years the *United Presbyterian Church in the USA* developed a strong missionary program along educational and medical lines. At one time it operated half a dozen hospitals; they have been reduced to two. On January 1, 1965, a three-year Agreement on Cooperation between church and mission was drawn up whereby responsibility for the life and program of the Evangelical Presbyterian Church was transferred to the Synod. The agreement ended January 1, 1968; since then the Synod has been drawing up a new constitution. "As leadership has shifted from missionaries to nationals, laymen have to carry great responsibilities due to the shortage of trained pastors."[6] The mission, however, continues to give aid, in men and money, to the church. Seventy-five fraternal workers are assisting the church, which at present sponsors eight Christian service institutions offering medical, educational, and social services to the people of Teheran and Tabriz. The thirty-three-hundred-member *Evangelical Presbyterian Church of Iran* is a member of the Church Council of Iran, the Near East Council of Churches, and the World Council of Churches.

The *Church Missionary Society* in Britain established its Persia mission in 1875 in the city of Isfahan. In 1912, a century after the death of Henry Martyn, the Episcopal diocese of Persia was inaugurated. Today, under its first Iranian bishop, the Right Reverend Hassan Dehqani-Tafti, it is a tiny minority of some two thousand persons with six Iranian and five expatriate clergy. The principal opportunities for witness are in medical and educational work. The diocese of Iran operates two hospitals, at Isfahan and Shiraz, and two church schools under Iranian principals, besides a children's hostel and a school for the blind at Isfahan. The Anglican missionaries now in Iran number thirty-four, including seven from Australia. The *Episcopal Church of Iran* is a member of the Church Council of Iran and the Near East Council of Churches.

6 *International Review of Missions,* January, 1969, p. 28.

The Pentecostal message was taken to Iran in 1909 when a group of Assyrian Pentecostal brethren returned from Chicago to their homes in Urmia (now Rezaieh) in northwest Iran. During World War I many of the Christians were martyred. Others were scattered, and the work came to a halt. When Mr. and Mrs. John Warton were appointed to Iran in 1924, they established churches in Kermanshah and Hamadan and ministered in Rezaieh, John Warton's birthplace. One of the workers who assisted Warton was Tooma Nasir, who continues to serve as superintendent of the Assyrian work. In 1955 the work spread to the Muslim population. In 1959 it was organized under the name of Filadelfia Churches. In 1965 the four churches of this group merged with the *Assemblies of God.* Until the appointment of Mr. and Mrs. Mark Bliss in 1966 there had been no American Assemblies of God missionaries in Iran for nearly thirty years. In 1970 they had eighteen churches with a total membership of 550. Their Bible school, the only one in Iran, has already produced eighteen national workers.

In 1954 *International Missions, Inc.* entered Iran from India, where its work dates back to 1932. It absorbed the Iran Interior Mission founded in 1923 by the Reverend F. M. Stead, and took charge of its only institution, Faraman Orphanage at Kermanshah. The orphanage is now being phased out in favor of more direct forms of evangelism and church planting. Today IM has twenty-one missionaries in Kermanshah and Teheran. The most exciting development in the 1960's was the burgeoning Bible correspondence courses which resulted from several summers of intensive literature distribution by Operation Mobilization. Thirty thousand persons, almost all of them Muslims, from three hundred cities and towns, have enrolled. The mission is hard pressed to keep up with the demands growing out of this avalanche of Bible students, who write papers, ask questions, want literature, and need follow-up. Most of the Christians in Iran are found in five or six cities. IM has decided to launch a program of village evangelism looking forward to church planting in the rural areas, which have been almost totally neglected. Two churches have been established, both under Iranian leadership.

Worldwide Evangelization Crusade entered Iran in 1963. The first missionaries were William and Rhoda Longenecker. Their number has since grown to seven. The work is located in the capital of Teheran, where the program includes Bible teaching, literature production and distribution, correspondence course follow-up, and medical work. A radio ministry is in the planning stage. More recently a Swiss member of the mission has taken up residence in Isfahan.

In 1968 George and Joan Braswell went to Teheran as representatives of the *Southern Baptist Convention.* They were warmly received by the Presbyterian missionaries. A good relationship has been established with the Presbyterian student center; and a most unusual opportunity has come to teach English to Muslim theological students at the University of

Teheran. The future of the Baptist program in Iran is still to be determined.

In 1969 the *Bible and Medical Missionary Fellowship* was invited to join the other missions in Iran. Specific requests were for doctors, nurses, physiotherapists, agriculturalists, teachers, hostel wardens, and pastors. Two missionaries of the *International Christian Fellowship* entered Iran in 1969. The mission plans to open a Bible school. The *Go-Ye Fellowship,* a recent newcomer to Iran, is represented by *Jean and Kaare Wilhelmsen* in Teheran.

Evangelism. The Shiah form of Islam found in Iran has always been more tolerant than the more orthodox Sunni sect found in other parts of the Middle East. Consequently evangelism has been less difficult in Iran than elsewhere in the Muslim world. Numbers of Muslims, Zoroastrians, and Jews came into the church in the early years through direct evangelism. Such evangelists as *William Miller* (Presbyterian) gave their entire lives, with wonderful effect, to direct evangelism. A tremendous impetus was given to evangelistic work in the early sixties when *Operation Mobilization* carried out the most extensive literature distribution campaign ever held in Iran. Today thousands of Muslims are studying the Word of God by correspondence. In 1965 the Episcopal Church held an evangelistic campaign in Isfahan. The evening meetings were particularly well attended and drew a large number of Muslims.

> Iran is enjoying an atmosphere of increasing religious tolerance. Opportunity for Christian mission lies everywhere, with especially great interest evinced among youth. The sale of Bibles has almost trebled in a little over a decade.... The Church in Iran's greatest need is for full-time evangelists and Christian leaders. The time is ripe for a great Christian advance, but national leadership is wanting.[7]

Even the Eastern churches, long afflicted with a ghetto complex, are becoming aware of the possibilities of evangelism. "For the first time in Iran some Assyrian and Armenian Christians have shown great zeal in the evangelization of the country, which has led to a number of conversions. Plans are now under way for a Bible school and for similar evangelistic work on a country-wide basis."[8]

The Bible Societies. The *British and Foreign Bible Society* began work on behalf of Persia in 1814 by subsidizing the publication of Henry Martyn's New Testament. In 1880 the Persian Agency was established with a depot in Baghdad. A bookstore was opened in Teheran in 1910. In 1914 a Bible House was acquired but later sold. In 1963 BFBS and ABS established a Joint Agency. The following year a new Bible House was

---

[7] *Ibid.,* January, 1967, p. 18.

[8] *Ibid.,* January, 1968, p. 27.

completed in Teheran. The entire Bible is available in Persian and Armenian. There is a growing interest in the Christian Scriptures on the part of Muslims, especially students. In three years, from 1964 to 1967, distribution doubled. This was due in large part to the almost thirty thousand persons who were taking Bible correspondence courses. The Bible societies are now placing ads and publishing Scripture portions in the newspapers and magazines with good results. The Eastern churches have not shown much interest in the work of the Bible societies, and only a small fraction of the budget is raised locally. During 1967 the Armenian Orthodox and Evangelical churches celebrated the three hundredth anniversary of the printing of the Armenian Bible. During this anniversary, and for the first time in Bible Society work in Iran, the doors of the Orthodox and Roman Catholic churches were opened for the sale of the Scriptures.

Christian Radio. For a time the gospel was beamed into Iran by Trans World Radio from Monaco, but reception was poor. The newly-opened station in the Seychelles Islands is heard clearly in Iran. The Lutheran station, RVOG, broadcasts from Addis Ababa programs prepared by the Iran Radio Committee of the Near East Council of Churches.

Iraq

Political History. Iraq was the home of the ancient Sumerian and Babylonian civilizations. One of the earliest Arab countries to do so, Iraq gained its independence and joined the League of Nations in 1932. Since that time the country has staggered from one political crisis to another, with four coups d'etat in a single decade. The leaders of recent regimes have been members of the Baath party, a hypernationalistic, left-wing, pan-Arab group whose animosity towards the United States is surpassed only by its hatred for Israel. Iraq has an expeditionary force stationed in Jordan, ostensibly to protect Jordan from Israeli aggression. In June, 1967, it broke off diplomatic relations with the United States and to date they have not been restored. American missionaries, while enjoying the confidence and friendship of the Iraqi people, have been persona non grata with the government.

The People. The population now stands at 8,700,000. About 80 percent are descendants of the Arabs who migrated from Arabia centuries ago. The largest ethnic minority are the Kurds, who account for 15 percent of the population. Some 3.5 percent are Persians. The large colony of 120,000 Jews migrated to Israel in a mass exodus in 1950-51 and have long since been absorbed into Israeli society. The Kurds, who live in the north, would much prefer to have their own Kurdistan and from time to time rebel against the central government.

Religion. Islam is the religion of Iraq. The Muslims there are very fanatical and it is virtually impossible for a person to change his religion. Christian minorities who have been there for centuries and who belong to the Eastern churches are permitted to preserve and practise their religion provided they do so unobtrusively within the confines of their own churches. The Christians number almost two hundred thousand.

Early Missions. Between 1820 and 1850 sporadic efforts were made by various societies to establish Christian work in Iraq. In the 1820's *Joseph Wolff* of the *London Jews' Society* paid a visit to contact the large Jewish colonies. Twenty years later *Henry A. Stern* of the same mission visited Baghdad several times. For about fifteen years this society carried on a Jewish work in Iraq and was able to report a number of conversions. The first continuing work was launched by the *American Board of Commissioners* from their existing base of operations in Armenia. Entering from the north they established a station at Mosul in the 1850's. Here, as in Iran, they did not remain long. The *Church Missionary Society* entered the country in 1882 and made Baghdad its headquarters. Their work lasted only until World War I.

Modern Missions. The *Reformed Church in America* launched the Arabian Mission in 1889 and the first station to be opened was Basrah, where the *Reverend James C. Cantine* arrived in 1892. Basrah, at the confluence of the Tigris and the Euphrates, became the center of their work in the southeastern part of the country. Amarah was occupied in 1901. In 1919, with additional personnel and more money, the Arabian Mission was able to expand its work in southern Iraq.

Another early mission was the *American Lutheran Orient Mission,* founded in 1911. Its principal station was at Sauj Boulak, which was evacuated by government order because of its proximity to the frontier. Other Lutherans entered Iraq in 1942 and worked among the Kurds.

Following the withdrawal of the Church Missionary Society in 1914, Anglican church work in Iraq came under the care of the *Jerusalem and the East Mission.* The schools were taken over by the *United Mission in Iraq.* The Anglican mission in Iraq has always been small. In 1965 only one missionary couple was responsible for the three small Anglican churches in Baghdad, Kirkuk, and Basrah. The Iraqi mission is part of the Jerusalem diocese.

The United Mission in Iraq. When the *United Presbyterian Church in the USA* entered Iraq in 1924 it did so as a joint operation with two other groups: the Arabian Mission of the *Reformed Church in America* and the *Evangelical and Reformed Church.* Together they organized the *United Mission in Iraq.* In 1957 the *Presbyterian Church in the U. S.* joined the United Mission. Iraq has been one of the most unresponsive of all mission fields, and the dedicated missionaries have shown an unusual degree of perseverance, tenacity, and courage. Following the Arab-Israeli confrontation in 1948 the position of the American missionaries in Iraq became precarious and they lived under almost daily threat of expulsion. In fact, they were actually expelled on more than one occasion, only to find their way back when the dust settled.

Direct evangelism was always part of the program but the United Mission concentrated on institutional work. It inherited three institutions from the Church Missionary Society. One of these was the *Mosul Girls' School,* which was taken over in 1924 and closed in 1929 for lack of qualified American supervision. Another was the *Mosul Hostel for Girls.* It lasted until 1941, when the exigencies of World War II made it impossible to continue. The third institution was the *Evangelical School for Boys* in Baghdad. In 1929 this project was also abandoned.

Through the years the United Mission maintained its own schools, two of which deserve mention: the *Baghdad School for Girls,* opened in 1925; and the *School of High Hope* for boys, founded a half century ago in Basrah by the Arabian Mission. Through good times and bad these schools remained open. They not only offered excellent education; they also created not a little goodwill. Unlike Iran, where the Presbyterians at one time had half a dozen hospitals, the United Mission in Iraq had no medical work.

All American missionaries were expelled from Iraq in June, 1969, and all mission schools were closed or taken over by the government. The six organized churches, in Mosul, Basrah, Baghdad, Kirkuk, Basheeqa, and Hillah, continue to operate under national leadership; but the churches are small and the pastors, in at least two of them, are from other parts of the Middle East.

The Christian Presence.   The expulsion of the missionaries does not mean the end of the Christian cause in Iraq. There were Eastern churches there long before the missionaries arrived, and they will be there long after their departure. These include the *Nestorian Church,* the *Syrian Orthodox Church,* two Uniate churches (*Syrian Catholic* and *Armenian Catholic*), and two Evangelical churches (*Armenian Evangelical* and *Assyrian Evangelical*). There are also a small number of Roman Catholics there. The total Christian community is somewhere in the neighborhood of two hundred thousand.

Israel

Political History.   The Balfour Declaration of 1917 paved the way for the return of the Jews, after almost two thousand years of exile, to Palestine, where they were authorized to establish a "national homeland."

The partition of Palestine by action of the United Nations in 1947 led to the establishment of the State of Israel on May 14, 1948. This touched off the first Arab-Israeli war. Two other wars followed, one in 1956 and the other in June, 1967; and in all three wars the Arab armies were badly mauled and their leaders greatly humiliated. As a result the Arab world is seething with hatred for Israel and would certainly resort to war again if the leaders thought they could win. The million and a half refugees, with no hope of compensation or repatriation, are the greatest single cause of tension in the Middle East. Forgotten in all the turmoil is the fact that little Israel has accepted and rehabilitated well over one million of its own refugees from some seventy countries of the world. Of course, it must be recognized that without mammoth financial aid from the United States and West Germany, Israel's economy would have collapsed long ago.

The People. The population of Israel is not far from the three million mark. The Jews make up 85 percent and the Arabs account for 13 percent. This does not include the half million Arabs in occupied Jordan. One of Israel's greatest problems is to control the Arabs on the West Bank and in the Gaza Strip, taken in the war in June, 1967. Under existing conditions it is only natural that the Arabs in Israel find themselves living under restrictions which at times are rather irritating. If Israel ever agrees to repatriate the Palestinian refugees, it would immediately and drastically alter the demographic balance of power inside Israel. The Jews in Israel today are divided into two groups: those who came as refugees from Europe in the thirties and forties and from the Arab countries in the fifties; and those born in Israel since 1948. The latter are more liberal religiously and more tolerant politically.

Religion. Not more than 25 percent of the Jews belong to the orthodox group; their influence, however, once greater than their numbers would suggest, seems to be waning. Most of the Arabs are Muslims. Christians make up about 2.5 percent of the population. They are Arab, not Hebrew, Christians, and belong in the main to the Roman Catholic and Eastern Orthodox Churches. Hebrew Christians probably do not number more than three or four hundred.

The constitution guarantees religious liberty; but here, as in other countries, there is often a gap between the promise and the performance. In 1965 a law was passed prohibiting the conversion of Jewish minors to Christianity, except where one parent is already a Christian and both parents give their written consent. In the same year the Israeli Cabinet fixed the Sabbath as the official day of rest; but it did make allowances for enterprises owned by non-Jews. During the Six Day War in 1967 several religious buildings were damaged, but the government promised to repair them. About that time at a meeting attended by forty religious leaders, Christian, Jewish, and Muslim, the Minister of Religion guaranteed complete freedom and protection in administering their holy places. Christians under Israeli rule increased from 56,000 to 105,000 as a result of territory gained in 1967. This represents thirty denominations and twenty-five hundred clergymen, monks, and nuns.

Orthodox Jewish leaders at a world gathering in Zurich in February, 1966, sharply attacked the activities of some thirteen hundred Christian missionaries in Israel. Rabbi Jungermann of Tel Aviv declared: "Every Jewish child baptized into the Christian faith is stolen from the Jewish people. He becomes a Christian missionary and often an enemy of the Jews."[9] From time to time missionaries have been harassed and church buildings have been attacked; but in every case the government has brought the culprits to justice.

The Protestants are the only religious group in Israel which has never been granted recognition as a legal community. It is difficult for a Protestant to get married in Israel, and impossible to get a divorce. Protestant church leaders on May 8, 1968, presented a petition requesting official recognition. The application followed six years of study and interchurch cooperation involving the Lutheran, Baptist, Church of the Nazarene, British Pentecostal, Christian and Missionary Alliance, and Mennonite groups.

Early Missions. The Anglicans were the pioneers in this part of the world. Their work there dates back to 1820 when the *London Jews' Society* started work among the Jews in Jerusalem. The historic Christ Church, built on the ruins of Herod's palace, was erected in 1833. In 1848 a hospital was opened in Jerusalem. One hundred years later, as a result of the war, the hospital was closed and never reopened. It was not until 1851 that a second Anglican mission, the *Church Missionary Society*, began work in Jerusalem. The CMS work has been confined largely to the Arabs. Hospitals were maintained at Jaffa and Lydda, as well as an orphanage at Nazareth. A third Anglican mission, the *Jerusalem and the East Mission,* has been at work in Palestine ever since 1888.

Several other missions have supported work in Israel. The *Edinburgh Medical Missionary Society* maintained a hospital at Nazareth. The *Mildmay Mission to the Jews* had a medical work in Hebron which was later given over to the *United Free Church of Scotland.*

Aftermath of the War. The Arab-Israeli war of 1948 resulted in widespread damage to the Christian mission. Some properties were destroyed; others were taken over by the military or the government. Some pieces of property were never recovered. Other properties that were given back were in need of major repairs. In a few cases the government helped to defray the cost of rehabilitation.

---

9 *Ecumenical Press Service,* February 24, 1966, p. 9.

The *Church Missionary Society* was particularly hard hit by the war. The hasty flight of hundreds of thousands of Arabs resulted in the closing of CMS institutions in Jaffa and Lydda. Because Nazareth remained an Arab enclave, the orphanage there continued to function. In 1951 these three centers were turned over to the *Jerusalem and the East Mission.* The *Bishop Gobat School* (Jerusalem) was closed. The *Southern Baptists* were invited to assume responsibility for the hospital in Gaza.

The Six Day War. The war of 1956 was fought in the Sinai Peninsula and had little effect on the internal situation in Israel; but the Six Day War in June, 1967, was a different matter. This time Israel captured and kept all territory between the Nile and the Jordan rivers, including the Old City of Jerusalem. Missions and churches on the West Bank now find themselves cut off from sister organizations in Jordan proper. Some organizations have their headquarters in Jerusalem, but their churches and institutions are in Jordan; and passage between the two countries is not always easy. Even Pope Paul on his pilgrimage to the Holy Land in 1964 had to make sure that his travel route was acceptable to both Jordan and Israel. Since 1967 Arab guerrillas have been increasingly active in these parts.

Recent Missions. The Anglican Church in the Middle East has its headquarters in Jerusalem. The Archbishopric in Jerusalem, created in 1957, comprises five dioceses: Jerusalem; Iran; Egypt and Libya; Sudan; and Jordan, Lebanon, and Syria. Total baptized membership is one hundred sixty thousand. Three of the ten independent missions of the Church of England are working today in Israel, but with greatly reduced forces: *Church Missionary Society, Jerusalem and the East Mission,* and *Church's Mission Among the Jews.* The CMS has one missionary at St. Margaret's School in Nazareth. The JEM supports the Archbishopric in Jerusalem and St. Luke's Hospital in Haifa, but the latter is without a chaplain at present. The CMAJ has a small work in Jaffa, Tel Aviv, Lydda, and Mount Carmel.

The work of the *Christian and Missionary Alliance* began in 1890 in Jerusalem, Hebron, and Jaffa. Beersheba was opened as a fourth station in 1911. Before the Israelis took over, Beersheba was a sleepy, dusty little town at the gateway to the Negev. Today it is a modern, bustling, booming city of almost half a million people, nearly all of them Jews. Here the C&MA has a Bible shop, the only one in the southern part of the country; it sells Bibles and books in twenty-five languages. The only other center of activity is Jerusalem. The Arab Christians meet in a modest upper-room chapel in the Old City. Also in Jerusalem the Alliance has an international church which ministers to the large international community. As a public service the local radio station makes available to various Protestant groups a forty-five minute program once a month; the C&MA participates in that. It no longer has work in Hebron and Jaffa.

The *Southern Baptists* accepted responsibility for Palestine in 1921 and have had missionaries there most of the time since then. It was not until after the war of 1948 that they launched out on an aggressive program which began with relief work in Nazareth. An elementary school was begun that year, and a few years later a high school was added. The church in Nazareth, one of six in Israel, is now the hub of their evangelistic work in Galilee. In time other centers were opened: Petah Tiqva, Haifa, Jerusalem, and Ashkelon. The program includes leadership training, student work, literature production and distribution, Bible conferences, youth camps, several schools, and a farm. With twenty-eight career missionaries, Israel is the largest mission field of the SBC in Europe and the Middle East. Its six churches, with a total membership of 190, are organized into the *Association of Baptist Churches in Israel.* The Southern Baptists are the only evangelical group working in occupied Gaza, where there are almost a half million Palestinian refugees. As mentioned above, in 1954 they took over the one-hundred-year-old Gaza hospital from the Church Missionary Society. Besides the hospital, literature work and a study center occupy thirteen missionaries. A small self-supporting church of twenty-five members completes the picture in Gaza.

Several smaller missions have token forces in Israel: the *Church of the Nazarene, Church of God* (Cleveland), and *Plymouth Brethren* (England). Two Mennonite groups have relief programs.

Dialogue. Jews and Muslims proved to be the most resistant of all religious groups to the gospel; yet they have more in common with Christianity than any of the other non-Christian religions. Especially is this true of the Jews. Jesus was a Jew. The apostles were Jews. The early church, at least in the first generation, was more Jewish than Christian in flavor. The New Testament was written by Jews. And yet the Jews have stubbornly resisted the gospel. This phenomenon is strange only in the context of theology, not in the light of history. Some of the darkest pages in church history are those which record the persecution of the Jewish people. Certainly Jews have no reason to love Christians.

Nevertheless, in Israel today there are indications that the Jews are beginning to show an interest in Jesus. Dwight L. Baker, missionary in Israel since 1950, has written: "Israelis are exhibiting an almost compulsive curiosity about Jesus. . . . The impression is strong that they must somehow deal with him. Criticize him or praise him, yes. But forget him, no." One article published recently in a Hebrew language magazine carried the caption, "Jesus Yes, Christianity No."[10] At least they seem to be taking Him seriously.

Dialogue has begun. Theologians meet regularly in Jerusalem for Christian-Jewish dialogue. In October, 1968, more than one hundred fifty

---

[10] *World Vision Magazine,* February, 1969, p. 13.

Arabs, Jews, and missionaries met at Southern Baptist Village in Petah Tiqva for their annual conference, which coincided with the Feast of Tabernacles. Reporting on the conference, a missionary wrote: "Can you imagine hearing a prominent Jewish psychiatrist preaching to Arabs and Americans that Jesus of Nazareth is the Messiah of Israel? Yet just such a man addressed the conference at the invitation of an Arab pastor who was in charge of the program."[11]

Ecumenical Relations. There is only one ecumenical group in Israel, the *United Christian Council in Israel.* It is located in Jerusalem and has no affiliation with any outside organizations.

Arabian Peninsula

Political History. Saudi Arabia is completely closed to resident missionaries, though the Arabian American Oil Company has its own chaplains there. Around the perimeter of the peninsula are seven small sheikhdoms and several independent states. The latter include Kuwait, Bahrain, Qater, Muscat and Oman, Yemen, and the newly created Republic of Southern Yemen. Some of the states have huge oil reserves and are very wealthy; and they are using their wealth to modernize the country and improve the livelihood of the people. Others, such as Yemen and Southern Yemen, are desperately poor and are just now slowly emerging from feudalism and slavery.

The People. Accurate census figures for this part of the world are difficult to obtain. A rough estimate places the population at about ten million, of whom five million are in Yemen. The overwhelming majority are Arab by race and Muslim by religion. In the coastal cities are small colonies of Indians, Pakistanis, and Somalis.

Introduction. In all but two small sheikhdoms there is some form of Christian witness. In some places, such as Aden and Southern Yemen, it goes back almost a century; in Bahrain and Kuwait, half that time. In other places, such as Yemen, the Christian mission is just beginning. Here, as elsewhere in the Arab world, Christian missions have of necessity restricted themselves to institutional work, most of it medical. There has been almost no educational work except in Aden, Kuwait, Bahrain, and Muscat. In recent years, in some oil-rich states such as Bahrain and Kuwait, free medical facilities in brand new, well-equipped government hospitals have greatly reduced the number of patients now coming to the mission hospitals.

---

11 *Ibid.*

Early Christianity. How did Christianity first reach Arabia? Luke indicates (Acts 2:11) that Cretes and Arabians were present in Jerusalem on the Day of Pentecost and heard Peter preach on that occasion. If Arabians were among the three thousand who believed, it is quite likely that they were the first evangelists to Arabia. According to tradition the apostle Bartholomew was the first person to take the gospel to Arabia. The apostle Paul spent three years in Arabia (Gal. 1:17, 18); but we are not at all sure that by Arabia Paul meant present-day Arabia. We do know that by the end of the fourth century there was a Christian community in Hirah. There is every reason to believe that by 525 the Christian faith was firmly established in Arabia. Certainly Mohammed was well acquainted with both Judaism and Christianity. Alas, Christianity was conquered by Islam in the seventh century.

First Pioneer. *Ion Keith-Falconer,* a Scottish nobleman and Cambridge graduate, was the first missionary in modern times to take the gospel to the Muslims of Arabia. Arriving in 1885 he established a center at Skeikh Othman, near the port of Aden. Before he could do much more than explore the surrounding territory the hot, enervating climate sapped his strength; and after two short years he succumbed to weakness and died at the age of thirty. Upon his death the work was taken over by the *Church of Scotland* and named the *Keith Falconer Mission.* For eighty years this mission maintained a hospital in Sheikh Othman. The civil war in 1965 forced the missionaries to evacuate, but not before a member of the little church had been ordained pastor of the flock—the first national to hold the position. In that same year two more Muslims were baptized into the Church of South Arabia: Aden, bringing the total of South Arabians baptized to thirty-five. In 1961 plans were made to integrate church and mission, but general unrest prevented the implementation. The *Danish Mission* pulled out of Aden about the same time, after its church and house there had been set afire by a gang of hooligans. The *Red Sea Mission Team's* property suffered the same fate. Anticipating just such an emergency, the *Sudan Interior Mission* evacuated its base in Aden in 1965. In 1968 three of these missions returned to South Yemen with the full cooperation of the government and a hearty welcome from the local populace.

When news of Keith Falconer's death reached the theological seminary of the Dutch Reformed Church in America at New Brunswick, N.J., several young men immediately offered themselves for missionary service in Arabia, among them *James Cantine* and *Samuel M. Zwemer.* Unable to secure funds from their own denomination, they decided to organize an independent mission, the *American Arabian Mission.* Cantine set out in 1889, followed a year later by Zwemer. After a period of language study in Beirut they proceeded to Arabia. In 1894 the *Reformed Church in America* decided to support the mission and expanded it later by opening hospitals in Bahrain, Kuwait, Muscat, and Basrah. Through the years these hospitals have maintained a quiet but consistent Christian witness in the heartland of Islam.

One day *Dr. Paul W. Harrison* was summoned to the royal palace in Riyadh to stem an epidemic in the capital. This proved to be a turning point in the fortunes of the mission. Thereafter the missionaries were much freer to carry on their Christian work.

The best-known missionary in Arabia was the famous *Samuel Zwemer* who gave sixty years of loving service to the cause of Christ not only in Arabia but throughout the Muslim world where he was widely known as "the Apostle to Islam." Zwemer was a rare combination of the pious and the practical, the saint and the scholar. He was a world traveler, a prolific writer, a dynamic speaker, a brilliant scholar, and a great personal worker. He knew more about Islam and the Christian approach thereto than any other man in the first half of the twentieth century. He founded and for many years edited *Muslim World,* a scholarly journal devoted to the Christian mission in the Muslim world. Towards the end of his life he occupied the chair of missions at Princeton Theological Seminary. He remained active to the end of his life and died in harness at the age of eighty-five.

For eighty years the Arabian Mission has carried the lion's share of missionary work in the Persian Gulf. Times have changed and the mission resources, both men and money, are not what they once were. The men's and women's hospitals in Kuwait were closed in 1967 because of the great advance in the government medical program. Only four hospitals remain, men's and women's units in Bahrain, Muscat and Oman. In the light of all these factors the mission in 1968 proposed a complete restructuring of the entire program. The Bahrain Hospital is to be coordinated with the Bahrain Health Department, and the medical program in Oman is to be upgraded to meet the standards of a new day. The number of missionaries has been reduced (in 1970) to thirty-three.

The *Worldwide Evangelization Crusade* has been interested in Arabia for half a century. An abortive attempt to enter was made in 1925 from a base in Palmyra. From 1931 to the outbreak of World War II three WEC missionaries were stationed in Arabia. A new beginning was made in 1964, first in the Sheikhdom of Dubai and later in the Sheikhdom of Fujaira. The gospel is presented through medical clinics and pioneer evangelism to both Arabs and South Indians. Literature and the teaching of English provide additional avenues of witness. Eight missionaries are there at present.

The *Red Sea Mission Team,* a British faith mission founded in 1951 by Dr. Lionel Gurney, has had work in the Republic of Southern Yemen for more than a decade. In the mid-1960's it had sixteen missionaries in three inland cities, only four of them men. During the upheaval prior to independence these stations were all evacuated, including Aden. Following independence (1967) the new government invited RSMT to resume its work, imposing no restrictions whatever. The mission now has four nurses in Southern Yemen and is badly in need of reinforcements, especially men.

For years the RSMT tried to gain access to Yemen; but it was not until 1970 that permission was finally granted. Known in Yemen simply as the Red Sea Team, the mission established its base in Sana, the capital. It has since opened a clinic at Uarim, two hours' drive to the south. In the summer of 1970 a government request came to open work immediately in Tihama. As early as 1967 Vivienne Pennel, now Mrs. Peter Back, assisted the Southern Baptists with their medical work in Taiz.

Dr. James Young, at the invitation of the Ministry of Health, pioneered the *Southern Baptist* mission in Yemen. The year was 1964. The work began with a clinic in Taiz. In 1968 a clinic and a hospital were opened in Jibla in the southern tip of the country. The SB missionaries remained in Yemen during the troubles of 1967, when all other Americans left the country. Today there are eight career missionaries and two associate missionaries in Jibla. Yemen is one of four countries which have opened their doors to the Christian missionary in the last twenty years. The other three are Somalia, Afghanistan, and Nepal.

The work of the *Independent Board for Presbyterian Foreign Missions* in Arabia goes back to 1941 when *Dr. Sarah L. Hosmon,* who had served in that part of the world for twenty-eight years under another mission, was appointed a missionary under the IBPFM. After several unsuccessful attempts to establish medical work in various places, a mission was established in the Sheikhdom of Sharjah, where the *Sarah Hosmon Hospital* is now located. The medical ministry is primarily among women and children. There are no restrictions on evangelistic work at the hospital. The patients—Persians, Baluchees, Indians, and Pakistanis, as well as local Arabs—hear the gospel daily in the clinic and also in their rooms. There is no doctor at the hospital at present. Three missionary nurses, assisted by Indian nurses, make up the staff.

Ras al Khaima is one of seven small independent sheikhdoms which comprise the Trucial States of the Arabian Gulf. Until 1952 this area was closed to missionaries. Since that time, prayers have been answered and doors have been opened, and today there are mission stations sponsored by four mission boards in five of the sheikhdoms. Only one of these stations includes nonmedical work. The *World Presbyterian Missions, Inc.* entered Ras al Khaima in December, 1959, at the invitation of the sheikh, who gave permission to preach the Christian faith as well as to minister to the physical needs of his people. The mission was initiated by the *Reverend Glenn A. Fearnow,* who had already seen five years of service under another mission in the Sheikhdom of Sharjah. The work began with an outpatient clinic. In 1963 a small midwifery unit was added. Both operations, especially the latter, give opportunity for a gospel witness.

In 1960 the first missionaries of *The Evangelical Alliance Mission* began work in Buaimi Oasis in the northeast corner of what is now the independent Sultanate of Muscat and Oman. The move came in response to repeated requests by the sheikh for a mission doctor. He promised complete freedom to teach and preach the Bible. "My people," he said, "are free to believe if they wish." During the past ten years the Oasis Hospital has ministered to the physical and spiritual needs of thousands of Arabs, many of them Bedouins. *Dr. Burwell Kennedy* pioneered the medical work in 1960. Today he has a staff of twenty missionaries.

All around the southern and eastern perimeter of the peninsula, from Aden to Kuwait, there are small colonies of expatriates, many of them British subjects belonging to the Anglican communion. In Basrah, Kuwait, Bahrain, and Muscat there are small Anglican churches, often with a local priest, sometimes without. The *Jerusalem and the East Mission* has the spiritual oversight of the Anglican communion in these parts. Several times a year the Archbishop of Jerusalem, who is also president of JEM, visits these outlying places for the installation of priests, the confirmation of communicants, and general spiritual counsel.

For many years the *British and Foreign Bible Society* maintained an office in Aden. In 1965 the work of the Society was transferred to the Bible Societies in the Near East with headquarters in Beirut.

XII

North Africa

Libya

Christian missionaries are not permitted in Libya, so there is little to report. The *North Africa Mission* and the *Seventh Day Adventists* were the only missions in Libya. For many years the NAM maintained a small dispensary in Tripoli as medical personnel were available to oversee the work. The last doctor to serve there was Dr. Patrick McCarthy. In 1957 he wrote hopefully: "How we wish you could be here to witness the founding of the Libyan Church. For the first time that we know of in more than a thousand years, Libyans are meeting together as Christians to worship the Lord and study His Word."[1]

The situation deteriorated, however, and the McCarthy family and two nurses had to sever their relationship with the NAM in order to remain in Libya as medical personnel, not as missionaries. They opened a second clinic in the European section of the city and used the proceeds from that to support themselves and the original clinic in the poor section of town.

A visitor to Libya in 1968 made exhaustive inquiries and compiled a detailed list of all Christian churches in the country. All are churches for expatriates who are working in Libya as oil men, military personnel, technical advisors, or diplomatic representatives. He counted ten Protestant churches, the largest being the Union Church in the capital with fifteen hundred adherents. According to this report there appear to be no national Christians, Protestant or Catholic, in this country where Christianity was once very strong.

---

1 *North Africa*, January-February, 1958, p. 5.

Tunisia

Political History. Tunisia became independent in 1956 after seventy-five years of French colonial rule. Although a member of the Arab League, Tunisia has never been rabidly anti-Israel, and it is more friendly to the West than any of the other Arab states. President Bourguiba, now in his third term in office, is immensely popular with his people and quite friendly towards the West.

The People. The population is estimated at 4.8 million, almost half of whom are under twenty-one years of age. The official language is Arabic, but French is widely used and continues to be taught in the schools. The illiteracy rate is about 65 percent. Following independence in 1956 there was an exodus of Europeans, a move that was repeated in 1964 when all foreign-owned lands were nationalized. Today they account for less than 1 percent of the population.

Religion. The constitution of 1959 recognizes Islam as the state religion. At one time there were two hundred thousand Europeans in Tunisia, most of them Roman Catholics; but under an agreement between Tunisia and the Vatican in 1964, all but 7 of the 109 Roman Catholic churches were closed. The churches, including the cathedral in Carthage, have been converted into museums, historical monuments, public libraries, or schools. In recent years the government has maintained strict surveillance over missionary activities.

Missions. The earliest missionary work was undertaken in 1829 by an Anglican mission, the *Church's Ministry Among the Jews*. The work is located in the capital, Tunis. In addition to St. George's Church and a bookstore, the mission has two fine schools for Jewish children, with an increasing number of Muslim pupils. Both schools start the day with prayer. The CMJ staff members maintain close personal contact with former pupils and are warmly welcomed into their homes.

The *North Africa Mission,* the largest in North Africa, sent its first missionaries to Tunis in 1882. At one time it occupied seven centers, but a paucity of workers in the 1940's reduced the number to two, Tunis and Sousse. Originally a British faith mission, NAM in 1948 established home offices in the United States and Canada. Today more than half its support comes from North America. In 1962 the mission initiated a Bible correspondence course in the Gospel of John, and by 1964 some twenty thousand Muslims had sent in a written request to be enrolled in the course. When the government became aware of this it closed down the bookstore, which had been the headquarters for the correspondence school work. The mission then transferred the operation to Marseilles,

EUROPE

ASIA

MEDITERRANEAN SEA

Rabat ⊙
Algiers ⊙
Tunis ⊙
TUNISIA
MOROCCO
RIO DE ORO

ALGERIA

Tripoli ⊙
Benghazi ⊙

LIBYA

Cairo ⊙

EGYPT
(U.A.R.)

RED SEA

SAUDI
ARABIA

MAURITANIA
Nouakchott ⊙

MALI

NIGER

CHAD

Bamako ⊙
Niamey ⊙
UPPER VOLTA
Ouagadougou ⊙

Khartoum ⊙

SUDAN

YEMEN
ADEN
FR. SOMALILAND

SENEGAL
GUINEA
akry ⊙
RRA LEONE
town ⊙
Monrovia ⊙
LIBERIA
IVORY
COAST
Abidjan ⊙
Accra ⊙
GHANA
TOGOLAND
DAHOMEY
Lome ⊙
Porto-Novo ⊙

NIGERIA

Lagos ⊙

Ft. Lamy ⊙

CENTRAL
AFRICAN REPUBLIC

Bangui ⊙

Addis Ababa ⊙

ETHIOPIA

SOMALIA

Mogadiscio ⊙

CAME-
ROON
Yaoundé ⊙
SPANISH
GUINEA
Libreville ⊙
GABON
CONGO
REP.

CONGO

Brazzaville ⊙
Leopoldville ⊙

RWANDA
BURUNDI

UGANDA

*L.
Victoria*

KENYA

Nairobi ⊙

*L.
Tanganyika*

TANZANIA

Dar es Salaam ⊙

ZANZIBAR ⊙

ATLANTIC

Luanda ⊙

ANGOLA

*L.
Nyasa*

INDIAN

ZAMBIA
MALAWI

MOZAMBIQUE

MALAGASY

OCEAN

SOUTHWEST

Salisbury ⊙
RHODESIA

Tananarive ⊙
REPUBLIC

Windhoek ⊙
AFRICA
BOTSWANA
Mafeking ⊙
Pretoria ⊙
Johannesburg ⊙

Lourenco
Marques ⊙
SWAZILAND

OCEAN

SOUTH
AFRICA

LESOTHO

Capetown ⊙

AFRICA

Scale of Miles

0   200 400 600 800 1000

France. The Bible correspondence courses now in France are tied in with the Radio School of the Bible. Gospel programs are beamed into North Africa from three powerful stations, and listeners are invited to write for the Bible courses, now available in French and English as well as Arabic. Each month an average of three thousand lessons are sent out and two thousand test papers are corrected. In the first four months of this ministry over thirty-five hundred students sent a written profession of faith in Christ. The NAM plans to initiate mission work among the eighty thousand Muslims in the south of France. Work is still maintained in Tunis and one other center.

The *American Methodists* began in Tunisia in 1908. Their work has never been large, and through the years it has been confined to the city of Tunis. In 1967 the staff was limited to two families. In recent years Methodist missionaries have lent a helping hand to the Swedish Women's Society in the seaport of Bizerte. In Tunis the workers maintain ecumenical relationships with French Reformed, Anglican, Orthodox, and Catholic groups. The program is limited to Sunday services, nursery groups, sewing clubs, and personal contacts.

The first *Pentecostal* missionary to Tunisia was Josephine Planter, a native of Bohemia, who arrived in 1912. She established a Bible depot and did personal work, but was never permitted to conduct public meetings. Over a period of forty years she won numerous converts to Christ. The *Church of God* (Cleveland) contributed to her support from 1946 until her death. Margaret Gaines was the first actual Church of God missionary in Tunisia. Miss Gaines remained with Miss Planter until May, 1953, when she moved to Megrine, a suburb of Tunis. By 1957, with the help of two leaders from Germany, the first Pentecostal church was formed, with twenty members and thirty-five or forty adherents.

Since 1969 the *Worldwide Evangelization Crusade* has been represented in Tunisia by two workers known as "Christians In Service Overseas."

Algeria

Political History. In July, 1962, Algeria, after eight years of guerrilla warfare, became an independent, sovereign nation; it had been part of Metropolitan France since 1848. France continues to pour $100 million annually into Algeria, in spite of the fact that the government nationalized all European-owned farmland and a number of French industrial and commercial enterprises. Algeria has also been the recipient of mammoth aid from both government and private agencies in the United States. This, however, did not prevent a break in diplomatic relations in June, 1967. There have been two military coups since independence, and the country is now governed by a revolutionary council. Algeria has been moving progressively to the left and today has close economic and military ties with the USSR.

The People. Algeria has a population of almost thirteen million. One-tenth used to be made up of Frenchmen; but with independence and nationalization came a mass exodus of seven hundred thousand foreigners, mostly French. The illiteracy rate is 85 percent, one of the highest in the world. The Arabs account for almost 90 percent of the population. The remaining 10 percent are Berbers, whose origin goes back to prehistoric times.

Religion. Islam has been the religion of Algeria ever since the seventh century, when the Muslim hordes swept across North Africa carrying everything before them. The Berbers, who had been conquered many times by various invaders, had no choice but to adopt Islam along with the Arabs. They do not, however, make staunch Muslims. The Europeans who are left are mostly Roman Catholics.

Missions. The *North Africa Mission* is the oldest and largest Protestant mission in North Africa. Its work in Algeria dates back to 1881 when *Edward H. Glenny*, founder of the mission, arrived in Algiers with two other brethren—a Swiss, Henry Mayor, and a Druse, Salim Zeytoun. The North Africa Mission has developed two distinct fields in Algeria—the Arab-speaking area of Cherchell on the coast and Kabylia, where the Berber-speaking people live. Of the two fields, Kabylia proved to be the more productive. One reason for this is the fact that the Berbers, being an independent people, were never completely subjugated by the Arabs. They are Muslims, but their acceptance of Islam has never been whole-hearted. Consequently they proved to be more receptive to the gospel. Even so, the number of converts has not been large and like the rest of the Muslim world, Algeria proved to be stony ground.

The *Algiers Mission Band*, a small British faith mission which had worked among the Muslims of North Africa since 1888, merged with NAM in 1965.

The *American Methodist* work in Algeria dates back to 1909. The first missionaries were two English women, members of an independent organization, who had been in Algeria since 1891. In 1908 they joined the Methodist Episcopal Church and transferred their work to its care. It was not until 1922 that the first single women were sent out from the United States. Through the years the United Methodist Board has expanded its work to include Algiers, Constantine, Fort National, Les Quadhias, Il Maten, and Oran. The only mission hospital in Algeria, opened in 1966, is located in Il Maten, a Berber village 150 miles east of Algiers. A major setback occurred on December 30, 1969, when ten Methodist missionaries, including five Americans, were summarily expelled from the country. All were stationed in Algiers. They were accused of being agents of the Central Intelligence Agency and engaging in subversive activities. The missionaries in Oran had withdrawn for medical reasons in 1968, which leaves missionaries now in only four centers. The *Methodist Church for Algeria and Tunisia* has a membership of 215, with 50 persons under instruction.

The British branch of the Plymouth Brethren (*Christian Missions in Many Lands*) has been in Algeria since 1910. Today they have about a dozen small assemblies. The *British and Foreign Bible Society*'s Agency for North Africa, dating back to 1881, is located in Algiers. The entry of the *American Bible Society* in 1962 resulted in a Joint Agency, still administered by the BFBS. Two Algerian colporteurs sell approximately five hundred books a month in market places, on the streets, and from door to door. More and more Algerians are visiting the Bible shop recently opened on the main street. Algerians, especially young people, are showing an increasing interest in the Christian Scriptures. Distribution increased 40 percent in 1968. The entire Bible is available in both classical and colloquial Arabic, the New Testament in Kabyle and Algerian-Tunisian Arabic.

Relief Work. The devastation wrought by the revolutionary war called for relief services on a grand scale. The *Salvation Army*, which has been in the country since 1934, continued its good work along this line. Other organizations that have engaged in widespread relief programs include the *Mennonite Central Committee*, the *Eastern Mennonite Board of Missions and Charities*, the *Friends Service Council*, the *World Council of Churches*, and the *Church World Service*. Most of the relief supplies were channeled through the *Christian Committee for Service in Algeria*, which cooperated closely with the government in an attempt to coordinate the overall relief and rehabilitation programs. This whole program is being phased out.

Ecumenical Relations. In a Muslim country where the Christian church is weak and small and understandably preoccupied with its own survival, it has little time for ecumenical ventures beyond its borders. There is within the country, however, the *Council of Evangelical Missions*, which was founded in 1940. The name was changed to the *Association of Churches and Protestants in Algeria*. Four missions joined the association during the past year and two withdrew because of its affiliation with the *World Council of Churches*. The *Christian Center for North African Studies* had its origin in Algiers in 1961. Although closely allied with the Methodist Church, the center receives support from other groups as well. Attempts have been made to form an Algerian Evangelical Church, but to date they have not been successful.

Morocco

Political History. After being a protectorate of France for forty-four years, Morocco gained its independence in 1956. It is supposed to be a constitutional monarchy, but parliament was suspended in 1965. Since then King Hassan II, as a "benevolent sovereign," has ruled the country by decree. The border dispute with Algeria, which from time to time erupted into open warfare, was amicably settled in 1969. The country is peaceful and the government stable.

The People. The population is estimated at fifteen million, including one hundred fifty thousand Europeans and forty thousand Jews. The majority of Moroccans are of Arab descent; about 30 percent are of Berber origin. The latter are divided into three tribes, each with its own unwritten dialect.

Religion. Islam is the state religion and Muslims are forbidden to defect from the faith. The Berbers as well as the Arabs are Muslims; but the Berbers, with their own primitive and nomadic culture, are more open to the gospel. Very few missionaries have worked among the Berbers, for two reasons. They live in the mountains, some of which are difficult of access; and, secondly, a missionary to the Berbers must learn three languages, French, Arabic, and Berber—enough to scare the stoutest heart. Opposition to the Christian mission began to appear in the mass media in 1962. In the last few years government surveillance has been especially strict. In 1969 some missions were expelled.

Missions. Here, as in other countries of North Africa and the Middle East, the pioneering agency was the *Church's Ministry Among the Jews;* they went in in 1875. The *North Africa Mission* arrived in 1882. The city of Tangier, with the *Tulloch Memorial Hospital* and the *Nurses Training School,* is the largest NAM center in North Africa. Tulloch is the oldest, and until recently was the only mission hospital in North Africa west of Egypt. Through the years work has been carried on in such centers as Fez, Tetuan, Alcazar, Rabat, Casablanca, and Settat. At various times certain stations were left vacant for lack of workers. Today NAM has forty missionaries in nine centers, all but two of them engaged in medical work of one kind or another. At the local level the missionaries continue to enjoy the favor of both people and officials. In 1888 the third group, the *Southern Morocco Mission,* began operations here. This Scottish society once had a thriving work in the southern part of the country and some of its veterans gave fifty years of service to Morocco. Following World War II the mission found it increasingly difficult to maintain its commitments, and in 1961 it merged with the North Africa Mission. In 1889 the

Mildmay Mission to the Jews began its work among the many Jewish people in Morocco.

The first American mission to enter the country was the *Gospel Missionary Union* in 1894. It was missionaries of GMU who translated the Scriptures into the colloquial Arabic of Morocco. It operated a Bible school for men and *Bethel Academy,* a school for missionaries' children. In 1961 it launched a correspondence course, and in seven years forty thousand Muslims, representing every town in Morocco, had requested courses. Doubtless it was the phenomenal success of this venture that prompted the government to restrict, and finally in 1969 to expel, all GMU missionaries from the country. The Bible correspondence course was transferred to Malaga in Spain, where it continues its program unabated. In addition, it is now sponsoring three radio broadcasts from Trans World Radio in Monaco. Two of them are in Arabic and one in Berber. All three programs are during prime evening time. Evidently the mission does not expect to return to Morocco in the near future, for it has decided to sell its properties there.

In 1929 the *Bible and Churchmen's Missionary Society* took up work in Morocco as a part of the Diocese of Sierra Leone. The first station, opened in 1929, was at Marrakesh in central Morocco. Two years later the mission suffered a great loss in the death of its leader, Archdeacon Cecil Hyde Hills. A new diocese was formed in 1936 which is now under the Archbishopric of Jerusalem. The first two converts were baptized in 1940. After the fall of France in 1940 British missionaries in Morocco found themselves in a very unenviable position and the work suffered accordingly. In 1945 the BCMS accepted responsibility for the *Raymond Lull School* for boys in Tangier; it had been carried on for thirty-eight years by an independent missionary. In 1968 the mission was harassed in various ways by the government. As a result three stations were closed and four missionaries expelled. In August, 1969, only five stations remained open.

The *Plymouth Brethren* have maintained a small work in Morocco for a number of years. In 1969 five missionaries shared the work in Tangier and Marrakesh. The *Berean Mission* entered in 1966. Mr. and Mrs. Ray Tallman were the first workers. Another couple have since joined them. They have a special burden for the Berbers, who have been largely neglected.

The *Southern Baptists* sent their first couple to Rabat in 1969. *Worldwide Evangelization Crusade* began work in Morocco that same year. Social and relief work have been conducted by *Church World Service* and the *Mennonite Central Committee* in recent years.

XIII

West Africa

Senegal

Political History. In 1958 Senegal became an independent republic within the newly formed French Community. In January, 1959, it joined the republic of Sudan to form the Mali Federation, which fell apart after eighteen months.

People. Senegal has an estimated population of 3.8 million, 70 percent of which is rural. Forty-five percent of the people are under fifteen years of age. The largest tribe, the Wolof, accounts for 36 percent of the population. Other important tribes are the Fulani, 17 percent, and the Serer, 16.5 percent. The official language is still French, but it is used only by the 5 percent of the people who are literate. The tribespeople speak their own languages.

Religion. Islam is the religion of 80 percent of the people. Christians, mostly Roman Catholics, represent 4.5 percent. The remainder are animists.

Missions. The *Paris Evangelical Missionary Society,* which began work in 1862, is by far the oldest Protestant mission in Senegal, which turned out to be the most discouraging of all its fields. Most of the men sent out during the first sixty years either died or were invalided home after only a few months. Conversions were disappointingly few. Financial stringency after World War I made conventional missionary work difficult. Today it is confined to one church, a dispensary, and a bookstore in Dakar. The *Worldwide Evangelization Crusade* entered Senegal in 1936. It too has found Senegal a very barren field. After twenty-five years of seed-sowing the harvest has been scant—four small groups with a total of twenty-five Christians. In 1970 the mission had twenty-nine workers in Dakar and eight other centers in the eastern part of the country.

The *New Tribes Mission* sent its first missionaries to Senegal in 1955; they established work at Casamance. This is their only station. In 1970 there were six couples on the station.

The *Assemblies of God* has been in Senegal since 1956. Three stations were established within the first few years. Temple Evangelique was opened in Dakar in 1963. A Bible institute was begun in 1964. Thirteen missionaries are currently under appointment to Senegal.

The *Conservative Baptists* entered in 1961, after the exodus from Congo, and settled in Thies, a city of eighty thousand on the coast. CBFMS missionaries have found the Senegalese quite receptive to the gospel; street meetings and gospel films shown outdoors have drawn large audiences as well as police protection. The climate, however, is not salubrious. As a result the mission has been plagued with illness, which reduced the staff to six in 1967. In 1970 only two remained in Thies. Short-term workers are teaching in *Dakar Academy* for missionaries' children. The bookstore was closed and publication work was terminated for the time being. The latest mission to serve in Senegal is the *Southern Baptist Convention*. It is still too early to report any progress. They have one couple in the capital of Dakar.

Ecumenical Relations. The French-speaking Protestant churches in various countries, including Senegal, joined the *French Protestant Federation in Paris* in 1965. In 1967 the Evangelical Federation of Senegal was dissolved when the conservative missions refused to cooperate with churches affiliated with the World Council of Churches. Instead, they formed their own *Evangelical Fellowship of Senegal,* which is affiliated with the Association of Evangelicals of Africa and Madagascar. One church, the *Protestant Church of Dakar,* is a member of the All Africa Conference of Churches.

Gambia

Political History. During the sixteenth century Gambia was the center of the Portuguese slave trade. In the seventeenth and eighteenth centuries Britain and France struggled for political and commercial control of the region. Britain won out and Gambia became a British colony in 1843. It achieved independence in 1965 as a constitutional monarchy within the British Commonwealth. Queen Elizabeth, who is chief of state, is represented by a governor general. Gambia is one of the few African countries with a multi-party system of politics.

The People. The population of Gambia is estimated at 360,000. Except for Bathurst, the capital, which has thirty thousand, no town has more than five thousand inhabitants. The principal ethnic group, the Mandingos, make up 40 percent of the population. Other tribes are Fula, Wolof, Jola, and Serahuli. The literacy rate is about 10 percent.

Religion. The principal religion is Islam, which claims about 80 percent of the people. There are fewer than ten thousand Christians. The remainder are animists.

Missions. The country is small and has never attracted much missionary interest. The *Wesleyan Methodists* (England) began work back in 1821 before Gambia became a British colony. Here, as elsewhere in West Africa, the climate is unhealthful and the work is hard. For almost one hundred fifty years the Methodists have persevered, with not too much to show for such a long investment. Today three men and a nurse constitute the total missionary staff. Three primary schools and two clinics are maintained. The church has seven congregations with a total membership of thirteen hundred.

The Anglicans have been represented in Gambia by the *United Society for the Propagation of the Gospel,* and, of course, they have been there for a long time. The diocese includes the Rio Pongas as well as Gambia. The first African bishop was consecrated in October, 1965. Schools are still operated; the enrolment is 95 percent Muslim.

The *Worldwide Evangelization Crusade* entered Gambia in 1957. Their six missionaries are primarily engaged in a medical outreach with a view to evangelizing the Mandingos and other tribes. Five clinics serve more than seventy thousand patients annually.

Ecumenical Relations. There is no Christian council in Gambia. The only church with ecumenical relations is the *Anglican Diocese of Gambia and Rio Pongas.* It is a member of the All Africa Conference of Churches.

Guinea

Political History. Of the twelve French colonies in Africa to gain their independence in 1958, Guinea was the only one that voted against joining the French Community. De Gaulle punished Guinea by withdrawing all French administrators and removing all government records from the country. The United States, for fear of offending De Gaulle, withheld diplomatic recognition of Guinea for almost six months. In the meantime, the USSR stepped into the vacuum and Guinea veered sharply to the left. It broke off diplomatic relations with France in 1965. The Peace Corps was expelled in 1966 but was invited back in 1969.

The People. The population of Guinea is close to four million, divided into sixteen tribal groups. The three principal tribes are the Fullah, the Malinke, and the Susu. The literacy rate is low—between 5 and 10 percent. French is the official language.

Religion. The Fullahs and the Malinkes are fervent Muslims. In the forest regions the tribes are under the power of fetish priests and sorcerers, and so far have proved impervious to Islamic influence. It is estimated that Muslims constitute 70 percent of the population.

Missions. The oldest and by far the largest work in Guinea is that of the *Christian and Missionary Alliance.* Baro, in the Niger Valley, was first opened in 1918. From there the work expanded to include eleven centers in all parts of the country. Kankan in the eastern part of the country is the site of their mission press, which serves all of West Africa. The *Guinea Bible School* is at Telekoro. Muslim converts have been few. Most of the fifteen hundred church members have come from pagan tribes.

On June 1, 1967, President Sékou Touré called for the complete Africanization of all churches and ordered all foreign missionaries to leave the country within thirty days. His main complaint was against the Roman Catholics, but he could hardly discriminate; so the order included Protestants as well. This set off a flurry of activity between the C&MA missionaries and the government on the one hand and the national church on the other. Finally the government allowed twenty-six missionaries to remain in three areas: the Bible school at Telekoro; *Manou Alliance Academy* (school for missionaries' children); and headquarters in Conakry. Although the scope of missionary work was greatly restricted, complete freedom is permitted within the framework of the new government policy. No restrictions were placed on travel; and in 1968 the missionaries were again preaching in the churches at the invitation of the local pastors. The government even permitted replacements to enter Guinea to fill vacancies in the three recognized areas. The partial expulsion of the missionaries has not been an unmitigated tragedy. It has jolted the church leaders out of their complacency and forced them not only to assume responsibility but also to provide leadership. Latest reports indicate that church services continue, giving has increased, Bible translation goes forward, theological training continues, and radio programs (broadcast from ELWA) are being prepared—all under national leadership, with the help of the remaining missionaries.

Three other Protestant missions were involved in the expulsion order of 1967, only in their case the evacuation was complete. These were the *Open Bible Standard Mission,* which since 1952 had worked among Muslims and pagans in both rural and urban areas; the *Paris Mission;* and the *Anglican Church.* The last two had work only in the capital of Conakry.

Sierra Leone

Political History. Sierra Leone's connection with the British Empire goes back to 1580 when Sir Francis Drake visited West Africa. The earliest settlements were planned as a haven within the empire for freed slaves. When the slave trade was abolished in 1807 thousands of slaves were liberated and settled in Freetown. During the nineteenth century Sierra Leone was the educational center of British West Africa. *Fourah Bay College,* established in 1827, became the Mecca for English-speaking Africans on the west coast. Unlike other African colonies, Sierra Leone's march to freedom was peaceful. In April, 1961, Sierra Leone achieved full independence and became a constitutional monarchy with membership in the British Commonwealth.

The People. During the nineteenth century Sierra Leone was a melting pot for freed slaves. Today about eighty thousand persons are the descendants of settlers from other parts of Africa. The indigenous population is divided into some twenty tribes, of which the Temne and the Mende are the largest, each representing about 30 percent of the population of 2.6 million. English is the official language.

Religion. The Mende tribe is wholly Muslim. Some, such as the Temnes, Fullahs, and Mandingos, are largely Muslim. Others are still pagan. Christians represent about 5 percent of the population, made up mostly of Roman Catholics, Anglicans, and Methodists.

Missions. Sierra Leone has the distinction of being the earliest Protestant mission field in West Africa. Two abortive attempts were made to plant the church there, one by the *Baptist Missionary Society* and the other by the *Glasgow and Edinburgh Societies.* The first continuing work was that of the *Church Missionary Society,* whose pioneers began work among the Susu tribe on the Rio Pongas. After twelve fruitless years the project was abandoned and in 1816 the mission moved to Sierra Leone. One of the outstanding missionaries of those days was *William A. B. Johnson,* whose brief career of seven years coincided with a remarkable people's movement.

Most of the work was done in the coastal area, where the descendants of the freed slaves—Creoles, as they are known—lived. These Creoles were a people apart. They developed their own *patois* and in time they all became Christians, at least in name. Here, as elsewhere in West Africa, missionary casualties were high. In Sierra Leone the CMS lost fifty-three missionaries in the first twenty-nine years. Doubtless this was one reason why the mission as early as possible shifted responsibility to the church; but this was a mistake.

In 1860 Sierra Leone suffered from what is now recognized as a premature attempt to create an independent Church. CMS withdrew most of its missionaries and left the newly formed Native Church Council to look after the congregations and be responsible for further outreach. The plan did not work; the Creoles were less in touch with the up-country people than the missionaries had been and promising evangelistic work was mostly given up.[1]

The CMS concentrated its forces in Freetown, where it founded two famous schools, *Fourah Bay College* in 1827 (now a university) and the *Annie Walsh School* for girls in 1845. It is quite impossible to exaggerate the influence of these two institutions on the educated classes in West Africa. There are now ten CMS missionaries serving with the Diocese of Sierra Leone, which has a Christian community of twenty-five thousand. Its first African bishop, Moses Scott, is also the Archbishop of the Province of West Africa formed in 1951.

The *English Methodists* entered Sierra Leone in 1811, and after several failures established a continuing work. Besides church work, they established the *Girls' High School* in Freetown, a hospital, a Bible school, a women's training center, and a number of elementary schools. The latter were hard hit in 1967 when the government reduced its grants and prohibited an increase in salaries.

The *Evangelical United Brethren Church* initiated work in Freetown in 1855. The first mission was established at Shenga. By 1880 the West Africa Conference was organized. Within the next three decades a hospital, a boys' school, and three new churches were established. By 1910 there were seventy-five national workers. In 1950 the first African superintendent was appointed. Today the *Sierra Leone Conference,* now part of the autonomous Methodist Church, has ten thousand communicant members. Twenty-two missionaries are serving with this church.

In 1889 Sierra Leone became the first missionary venture of the *Wesleyan Methodist Church* of America. From the beginning a well balanced program of evangelistic, medical, and educational endeavor has been conducted, with church planting as the prime objective. Since the first three converts were baptized eighty years ago, the church in Sierra Leone has grown to a membership of over thirty-six hundred in four tribal groups: Themne, Limba, Loko, and Susu. Attached to the church are thirty-five missionaries assisting in all forms of activity. The American Wesleyans cooperate in the *Sierra Leone Bible College* in Freetown and have a printing plant as well.

The first three missionaries of the *Church of the United Brethren in Christ* arrived in Freetown in 1855 and two years later established work at Shenga, about one hundred miles down coast from Freetown. In 1875 the mission was augmented by single ladies sent out by the newly organized Women's Missionary Association. By 1880 the West Africa Conference was organized. In 1883 the mission assumed responsibility for the Mende

---

[1] Ena Price, *Those Who Say Yes* (London: Highway Press, 1965), p. 29.

mission started some forty years before by the American Missionary Association of New York. Two church mergers here in the USA, in 1946 and 1968, brought this work under the aegis of the United Methodist Church. In 1950 the *Sierra Leone Conference* was given the status of an Overseas Annual Conference, with its first African superintendent. Today the Sierra Leone Conference has a communicant membership of more than twelve thousand persons. Most of the work is among the animistic tribes. Thirty-two career missionaries assist in the work.

The *Christian and Missionary Alliance* sent missionaries to Sierra Leone in 1890 as a stepping-stone to the great Sudan beyond. Having gained entrance to the Sudan, the mission in Sierra Leone was abandoned in 1918. From the early years the *Missionary Church Association* worked in close cooperation with the C&MA. When *David C. Rupp, Sr.,* arrived in Sierra Leone in 1905 illness and death had reduced the C&MA staff to five members. For a number of years after the withdrawal of the C&MA, the Sierra Leone mission was without missionaries. In 1945 a group of six Missionary Church Association workers returned to Sierra Leone to reopen the work. Today the mission has work in three tribes, Kuranko, Yalunka, and Temne. The New Testament in Kuranko has been completed. The mission maintains a Bible school among the tribes and cooperates with the *Sierra Leone Bible College* in Freetown for English-speaking Africans. Through its *Rupp Memorial School* for missionaries' children the mission is making a contribution to all the missions in Sierra Leone. It has thirty-five missionaries in the country. Twenty-four churches, served by twelve national pastors, have a combined membership of 315.

The *Assemblies of God* work in Sierra Leone dates back to 1905 when two young ladies opened a station in Freetown. The oldest work is among the Kru tribe. Three other tribes have been entered, all in the extreme eastern part of the country. The mission has two Bible schools. Growth has been much slower than in other countries. After more than half a century church membership in all four tribes is only 230. Full-time national workers outnumber the missionaries two to one.

Seventh Day Adventist work in Sierra Leone began in 1907. Like all other missions, progress was slow, especially in the first several decades. It was not until 1960 that membership began to increase appreciably. Today their church has approximately twenty-five hundred members.

Bible Societies. In July, 1966, the Sierra Leone branch of the Bible Societies of West Africa opened a center in Freetown. Bible translation in Sierra Leone has been rather slow. After 150 years of missionary work only one tribe has the complete Bible, the Mende. Three other tribes have the New Testament, but two of these were completed in the nineteenth century. Four other tribes have at least one portion of the Scriptures, but the most recent of these is already fifty years old.

Church Growth. Except among the Creoles along the coast, church growth in Sierra Leone has been disappointingly slow. Almost 70 percent of the Creoles are professing Christians; but upcountry where the tribal peoples live only 2 percent are Christians. The main reason for this is the fact that many of the tribes had already embraced Islam before the missionaries got there. The New Life For All campaign conducted in 1969 was expected to awaken the churches to their evangelistic responsibilities and mobilize their resources for a concerted effort to bring Christ to the masses. In Makeni five thousand people crowded into the Wusum Stadium each night to hear the gospel. By the end of the week, eleven hundred had registered their decision for Christ.

Ecumenical Relations. A new move was made in January, 1968, when the leaders of the *Evangelical United Brethren,* the *Methodist Church,* and the *Anglican Church* agreed to unite for training catechists, evangelists, and church leaders. In addition, there are two ecumenical organizations: the *United Christian Council,* which is a member of the Division of World Missions and Evangelism of the World Council of Churches; and the *Sierra Leone Evangelical Fellowship,* affiliated with the Association of Evangelicals of Africa and Madagascar. The *Methodist Church Sierra Leone* has recently joined the World Council of Churches. Three churches and the *United Christian Council* are affiliated with the All Africa Conference of Churches.

Church Union. The first tentative steps toward church union were taken in 1969. At its 1970 meeting the Methodist Church resolved to invite all interested parties to meet in June, 1970, to ask each Methodist circuit to approve the beginning of talks on church union.

Liberia

Political History. The Republic of Liberia is unique among all the countries of Africa. It had its origin in 1816 when the American Colonization Society was given a charter by the United States Congress to send freed slaves back to Africa. The first settlers arrived in 1822 with grants from the United States government. Twenty-five years later Liberia became the first independent republic in Africa. President William Tubman was first elected to office in 1944 and has been head of state ever since. Politics in Liberia is a one-party affair. The True Whig Party, which dates back to 1869, has been in power for the past ninety years.

The People. The population is estimated at 1.2 million. About 95 percent are indigenous Africans belonging to twenty-five or thirty tribes which fall into three main ethnological groups, Kru, Mandingo, and Gola.

The descendants of the emancipated slaves, known as Americo-Liberians, number about fifty thousand. They are highly civilized and live for the most part in the capital city, Monrovia. The government is largely under their control and they virtually run the country. Along the coast another sixty thousand Africans may be considered civilized. The tribes in the hinterland retain their primitive way of life. English is the official language, even though only a very small minority speak it.

Religion. As might be expected, the Americo-Liberians are all professing Christians. The tribespeople are animists, but in recent years Islam has been making headway among them. There is complete freedom of religion. President Tubman, a practising Methodist, looks with distinct favor on the Christian mission. The Roman Catholics are numerically weak in Liberia.

Initial Difficulties. It was said of the early apostles that they "hazarded their lives for the name of the Lord Jesus." The same may be said of the pioneers in West Africa. In Liberia the losses in the early years were staggering. Forty-four of the seventy-nine missionaries sent out by the *Church Missionary Society* before 1830 died during their first year.

Early Missions. The first missionaries to Liberia were black. Two Baptist ministers, *Lott Carey* and *Colin Teague,* were sent out by the Richmond African Missionary Convention, an auxiliary of the General Baptist Convention of America. They established the first Baptist church in Monrovia. The first white missionaries went to Liberia in 1833, the year that witnessed the beginning of *Methodist, Presbyterian,* and *Congregational* work in that country. During the first two decades the *American Baptists* sent out a few white missionaries. After 1856 they sent out only black missionaries. In 1875 they withdrew entirely from Liberia. The *Southern Baptists* transferred their missionaries to Nigeria in the 1870's. Two black missions continued in Liberia—the *Lott Carey Baptist Foreign Mission* and the *National Baptist Convention.*

The first *American Methodist* missionary, *Melville B. Cox,* arrived in 1833 but died within four months of his arrival. His last words were: "Let a thousand fall before Africa be given up." Reinforcements continued to be sent from America but they were insufficient to compensate for the many who died. Only the timely help of Bishops Taylor and Hartzell revived the flagging mission during the latter half of the nineteenth century. In more recent years the work has centered around two main stations—Ganta, opened in 1925, and Gbarnga, opened in 1948. The most important educational institution is the *College of West Africa* in Monrovia, which dates back to 1839. The Methodist mission also cooperates with the American Episcopal Mission in the *Cuttington College and Divinity School.*

The first missionary of the *American Episcopal Church* arrived in 1835. He was *John Payne*. In 1851 he was consecrated the first missionary bishop of Liberia. A fine educational system was developed under the leadership of *Bishop Samuel Ferguson* (1884-1916). Included in the system were scores of village and church schools. *Cuttington College and Divinity School* is the center of their educational work. The Episcopal Church in Liberia is not part of the Anglican Province of West Africa, but a Missionary District of the Protestant Episcopal Church here in the United States. Howard A. Johnson, Canon of the Cathedral of St. John the Divine, New York, deplores this situation and suggests that American funds are responsible for the anomaly. "There lurks at the back of my mind," he writes, "the thought that where American dollars go, American control would like to follow."[2]

The *United Lutheran Church* began work in 1860, when the *Reverend Morris Officer* established the first station twenty-five miles up the St. Paul River and called it Muhlenberg. Many missionaries came, served for a while, and left again. Some of them died in Liberia. After languishing for more than a decade owing to lack of recruits, the moribund mission took on new life with the coming of *David and Emily Day*. It was not until the end of the century, however, that recruits arrived in sufficient numbers to permit the expansion which got under way with the opening of Kpoloelle in 1908. Six other centers across Liberia were opened between 1912 and 1958. The *Evangelical Lutheran Church in Liberia* was organized in 1948. Ten years later came the election of the first Liberian president. Medical work includes six dispensaries and a leprosy clinic. *Phebe Hospital* is an ecumenical institution in which the Methodist and Episcopal churches of Liberia cooperate. In 1967 all the work, including medical and educational institutions, which had been mission oriented, was placed under the aegis of the church. Self-support, however, has not yet been fully achieved.

Recent Missions.   Since the turn of the century several missions have entered Liberia and today are making a sizable contribution to the upbuilding of the church in that land. The first of these was the *Assemblies of God,* which launched its Liberian mission in 1908. Newaka was the first of fifteen stations, all of them in the eastern part of the country southeast of the Cess River. The oldest and largest school, opened in 1931, is at Feloka. A girls' school is located at Newaka and a coeducational school has been developed in Monrovia. With five Bible schools in operation, the Assemblies of God have led the way in the training of national leaders. Its medical work centers in New Hope Town, a 350-acre leper colony established by *Florence Steidel* in 1947. Church membership has doubled in the past decade, and national workers have increased from 125 to 315.

The *Pentecostal Assemblies of Canada* have been in Liberia since 1915 and today report a church of over five thousand believers.

---

[2] Howard A. Johnson, *Global Odyssey* (New York: Harper & Row, 1963), p. 65.

In 1931 *Baptist Mid-Missions* entered Liberia and took over the work abandoned by a former Baptist group in the Central Province. The present work centers in four stations. Medical work includes rural dispensaries and a leper colony. A three-year Bible institute is located at Tappi. Mid-Missions operates its own press and plane. The 1970 Directory lists fifty-two missionaries in Liberia.

The *Worldwide Evangelization Crusade* moved into Liberia in 1938 and has engaged in medical and educational work as well as in church planting in all of its inland centers. It also has an important ministry at one of the large Firestone plantations. In 1947 WEC opened the first Christian bookstore in Monrovia. It also operates its own plane.

The *Southern Baptists* have been in Liberia for exactly ten years. In that time they have brought into being almost one hundred fifty churches with an aggregate membership of twenty-two thousand. Their main center is Monrovia.

One of three Christian radio stations in Africa is located in Monrovia. It is the radio voice of the *Sudan Interior Mission*. It has grown from a small 5,000-watt station in 1954 to a 100,000-watt station today. Known as *Radio Station ELWA*, its staff now includes fifty missionaries from eight countries and some one hundred fifty Africans from six countries. In recent years it has added television programs. It broadcasts the gospel in forty languages to all parts of Africa and the Middle East. It has enrolled over ten thousand students in its Bible correspondence courses. On the occasion of its fifteenth anniversary President Tubman sent ELWA the following message:

> I congratulate you and wish that within the next fifteen years your broadcasting power will increase in volume so that, like the BBC or the Voice of America, it can be heard throughout the world. May God bless you, prosper and preserve you and the great work of your hands. Convey to your principals in the United States and elsewhere the appreciation of the government and people, as well as my own, for the great services that you are rendering to this country and Africa.[3]

In connection with ELWA the mission also operates a hospital. Its director, Dr. Robert Schindler, was recently decorated by the government when it made him Knight Grand Commander of the Humane Order of African Redemption.

Bible Societies. Bible translation in Liberia has been greatly hampered by the fact that government decree made English the sole medium

---

[3] *ELWA Celebrates 15 Years of Broadcasting* (New York: Sudan Interior Mission, 1969).

of communication in church and school. Consequently, comparatively little Bible translation has been done. After 140 years of missionary work only eleven tribes have any portion of the Word of God. The first complete New Testament did not appear until 1967, in Kpelle. Loma readers are eagerly awaiting their New Testament translated some time ago by the Lutherans. Similarly the Bass readers are looking forward to having their own New Testament. Today's English Version of the New Testament, *Good News for Modern Man,* has been enthusiastically received and continues to be a best seller.

Ecumenical Relations.   The *Liberia Evangelical Fundamental Fellowship,* formed in 1968, has twelve members. One church, the *Presbytery of Liberia,* is an associate member of the World Council of Churches. The *Lutheran Church in Liberia* is a member of the All Africa Conference of Churches. Another organ of cooperation is the *Christian Rural Fellowship* formed in 1967.

Ivory Coast

Political History.   Ivory Coast became a colony of France in 1893. In December, 1958, it became an autonomous republic within the French Community. Compared with other African states, Ivory Coast has enjoyed relative political stability.

The People.   The population is estimated at 4.8 million; it is increasing at 2.3 percent each year. The ethnic makeup of Ivory Coast is rather heterogeneous. Non-Africans number some thirty-seven thousand, most of whom are French. Not all Africans are indigenous to the country. About one million come from contiguous countries: Upper Volta, Mali, and Guinea. Ivory Coast has more than sixty tribes usually divided into seven major groups. French is the official language. The literacy rate is about 20 percent.

Religion.   The largest group are the animists, who represent about two-thirds of the population. The Muslims account for another 25 percent. Roman Catholics number 250,000. Protestant Christianity claims 75,000. There is complete freedom of religion.

Mass Movement.   Mass movements have not been uncommon in Africa, but few movements can match the one that occurred in the Ivory Coast in the first part of the present century. The remarkable outpouring of God's Spirit centered around a colorful personality known as *Prophet Harris,* who appeared on the scene in 1913 when he was already sixty years of age. His uncle had been the pastor of a Methodist church in

Liberia, so William Harris as a young lad had been under Christian influence. At twenty years of age he underwent a profound spiritual experience; but it was not until forty years later that he entered on his great life's work in the Ivory Coast.

His physical appearance alone was sufficient to attract attention. Dressed in a long white robe and a large white turban, and carrying a well-worn Bible in one hand and a calabash of water in the other, the old man presented a striking appearance. When in the act of preaching, he held aloft a large bamboo cross for all to see, explaining that it was on the cross that God's Son died for the sins of the world. The effect on his primitive audiences was electric. A hundred thousand persons are said to have given up their idols, and the practice of fetishism all but disappeared along the coast. Wherever he preached, congregations were organized and churches erected for the worship of the one true God, Maker of heaven and earth. A preacher was installed in each congregation, while "Twelve Apostles" were appointed to rule the church as a whole. Evangelists, known as "Minor Prophets," went into the hinterland to evangelize the more primitive tribes. The French colonial government took a dim view of the movement, and after two years deported Prophet Harris to his native Liberia and ordered the burning of all his churches. Undeterred, the Christians built bigger churches on the ashes of the old ones. It was one of the most complete and astounding victories Christianity has ever scored over the forces of paganism.

Missions. In 1924 the Harris churches were taken over by the *English Wesleyans* though some elected to remain independent. The Methodist Church continues a full program of work. Its main center is at Dabou, where a secondary school and the *Women's Training Center* are located. The *Dabou Hospital* was opened in October, 1968. Financial support for church projects comes not only from Britain but also from Germany and the Netherlands. Church work varies from circuit to circuit. "In some circuits leaders are almost non-existent and one circuit report says our people seem content with the mere name of Christian, without seeing the need to 'press on and know the Lord.' In another circuit some members have relapsed into paganism and set up as clairvoyants and mediums."[4] The Methodist Church with a full membership of over seventeen thousand is by far the largest in the country.

There is one French Protestant mission in Ivory Coast. It is *Mission Biblique,* which began work in 1927 as the Paris Tabernacle Mission. Through the years it has grown and is now a large mission with a French and a Swiss Committee representing several evangelical churches and groups in these two countries. Its field of operation is in the southwest of Ivory Coast, where there are 600,000 inhabitants. Its educational work

---

4 *Opportunity Now,* Annual Report, 1969, p. 49.

includes elementary schools, primary schools, and a high school with a total of eighty-six African teachers. The *Union of Evangelical Churches of Southwest Ivory Coast* has twenty-five hundred members and a Christian community of eight thousand. There are 46 pastors and 175 lay preachers. Fifty-three missionaries are serving in various capacities.

In 1930 the *Christian and Missionary Alliance* entered Ivory Coast and opened its first center in Beuake, the largest inland city, which has a population of 150,000. Between 1930 and 1958 six additional centers were opened. In 1957 the *Evangelical Protestant Church of the Ivory Coast* became fully independent. Since then the two dozen missionaries have been able to give themselves unreservedly to evangelism, church planting, and leadership training. Since 1967 the government has permitted Bible teaching in the public schools. Missionaries are now teaching Bible in eighteen primary and eighteen secondary schools. The Yamoussoukro Bible Institute is a union school serving all the evangelical churches in the country. Each year the C&MA publishes half a million pages of Christian literature. In 1969 two weekly radio programs were begun. The *Alliance Church,* with over seventy-five hundred members, is the third largest in the country.

The *Worldwide Evangelization Crusade* sent its first missionaries to Ivory Coast in 1934. WEC ministry is established in Abidjan, the capital, and in seven inland centers. Evangelism, church planting, translation, literature, and student work are carried on by thirty missionaries among six tribes. Known in Ivory Coast as the *Evangelical Mission of West Africa,* it has a membership of over three hundred.

Conservative Baptist work in Ivory Coast began in 1947 in the northwestern part of the country. The missionary force was greatly augmented when seventeen CBFMS evacuees from Congo transferred to Ivory Coast in 1961. The work among the Senufo tribe has not been easy; but steady progress has been made and today there are thirty-seven organized churches and a combined membership of almost five hundred. The *Ivory Coast Academy* for missionaries' children had ninety youngsters enrolled in 1970.

The *Free Will Baptist* mission in Ivory Coast was launched by Mr. and Mrs. Lonnie Sparks in 1957. Two languages have been reduced to writing, and portions of the Bible have been translated. Twenty-two missionaries and seven national workers are seeking to build some five hundred twenty-five believers into a strong indigenous church.

The British branch of the *Unevangelized Fields Mission,* after amalgamating with the Alpine Mission in France, undertook to open a new field in Ivory Coast in 1963. The work is getting under way in four main centers close to the coast.

A newcomer to Ivory Coast was the *Southern Baptist Convention* in 1966. Six career missionaries, all in Abidjan, have brought into existence eighteen churches with a membership of slightly over one thousand.

Literature. The *Sudan Interior Mission* entered Ivory Coast in 1968, when the French language magazine *Champion* was transferred from Nigeria to Abidjan. There it has become part of the *Intermission Evangelical Publishing Center,* a venture which has great potential for reaching the twenty-two countries in Africa where French is the major language. *Champion* is a popular newsmagazine designed to be sold on the news-stands of Africa. Interspersed with the secular articles and features is a strong Christian message with a gospel appeal. The Publishing Center is supported by a dozen different missions and churches.

Bible Societies. Abidjan is the headquarters for the Bible societies' work in French-speaking West Africa. The entire program was greatly strengthened with the purchase in 1968 of a new Bible House in the commercial center of the capital city. Bible translation has not been given the priority it deserves. In forty-five years of missionary work only two tribes have acquired the whole New Testament, one in 1953 and the other in 1960. Eleven other tribes possess portions of the Scriptures. The complete Bible does not exist in any tribal language.

Ecumenical Relations. There is no National Christian Council or its equivalent in Ivory Coast. There is, however, the *Evangelical Federation of the Ivory Coast,* which is one of a dozen national associations in the Association of Evangelicals of Africa and Madagascar. One church, the *Methodist,* is a member of the All Africa Conference of Churches. All the evangelical missions in Ivory Coast have begun a joint Bible institute at Yamoussoukro.

Mali

Political History. Soudan (the old name for Mali) became an autonomous member of the French Community in 1958. The following January it joined Senegal to form the Mali Federation, which was discontinued after eighteen months when Senegal seceded. On September 22, 1960, Soudan proclaimed itself the Republic of Mali and withdrew from the French Community.

The People. There are five million people in Mali. These people pride themselves on being the descendants of the ancient kingdom of Malinke and Songhai, which flourished from the twelfth through the sixteenth centuries in the great cities of Timbuktu and Gao.

Religion. The dominant religion is Islam. About one-third of the people are pagans. Christianity has made little headway.

Missions. The *Gospel Missionary Union* was the pioneer Protestant mission in Mali. The first station was opened in 1919 at Bamako, the capital city. For the first twenty-five years progress was slow owing to the paucity of workers. Following World War II the flow of missionaries increased and the work began to prosper. In 1970 the mission had forty-six workers assigned to Mali, with a full program of medical, educational, evangelistic, church planting, and Bible correspondence work. There is a Bible school in Mana and a bookstore at Bamako. The Christian community, not yet organized into an independent church, numbers about twenty-five hundred. The New Testament was published in Bambara, the trade language, in 1937. The complete Bible appeared in 1962.

The *Christian and Missionary Alliance* built its first station in 1923 at Sikasso in the southeastern part of Mali. Since then ten other stations have been opened in all parts of the country. Not included in this figure are Timbuktu and Gao, opened in 1924 and 1928, which were turned over in 1950 to the Society of Christian Missions. The C&MA has two Bible schools in Mali: the *Central Bible School* at Ntorosso, which in 1969 had forty-seven men and thirty-six women enrolled; and the *Girls' Bible School* at Barama, with fifty girls in attendance. These two long-term schools are fed by nine or ten short-term Bible schools held throughout the year.

The *Evangelical Baptist Missions* opened stations in the ancient capitals of Gao (1951) and Timbuktu (1952). Bible stores were opened in 1953 and the gospel boat was launched on the Niger River in 1959. Several other stations have been opened since that time. Medical and dental work are also part of the program. The aim of the mission is to establish strong indigenous churches that will be able to carry on without the aid of the missionaries.

The *United World Mission* in 1954 made itself responsible for the evangelization of five counties in the Region of Kayes in western Mali, where almost half a million people were still without a knowledge of Christ. The hub of their work is Kenieba where, besides evangelism and church planting, there are several institutions: the *Correll Memorial Hospital,* an orphanage, a technical school, and a Bible school. In 1969 there were four African pastors and an organized church officially recognized by the government. The mission, however, continues to give financial aid to the congregations which are either too small or too poor to fully support their pastors.

The *New Life For All* campaign conducted in 1969 enjoyed the full support of all the churches and missions in Mali and brought great blessing to all concerned.

Ecumenical Relations. The only inter-mission organization in Mali is the *Evangelical Association of Churches and Missions* formed in 1963.

Upper Volta

Political History. Upper Volta was under various forms of French rule from 1896 to 1960, when the country became independent on August 5. Its membership in the French Community was allowed to lapse. Shortly after independence the National Assembly was suspended, and Upper Volta has been under military rule ever since.

The People. The population stands at 5.3 million, with the largest concentration in the south and center of the country. Nearly half of the people are Mossi, who are believed to have come from East Africa in the eleventh century. The literacy rate is estimated at 5 to 10 percent.

Religion. Unlike its neighbors, Mali and Niger, Upper Volta has been penetrated only slightly by Islam, which is confined largely to the pastoral people of the north and west. Roman Catholicism is much stronger than Protestantism.

Missions. Two branches of the *Assemblies of God* are in Upper Volta. The American mission got under way in 1921 in the capital city of Ouagadougou in the center of the country. The French missionaries joined the work in 1948, and Swiss workers came later. A Bible school, established in 1933, has moved three times. It is now located at Lake Nagabageré. In the past thirty-seven years it has graduated over three hundred students, which is one reason why the church today has 260 national workers. A genuine revival swept through the churches in the mid-sixties with the usual charismatic manifestations. As a result the total number of Protestants doubled in four years to about thirty-one thousand. The complete Bible has been translated into Moré, the language of the Mossi. The AOG in Upper Volta have a strong Sunday school and publishing work. Some twenty thousand pupils are in Sunday school each week. From the beginning the work proceeded along indigenous lines and as early as 1949 the church became autonomous and received government recognition. Today the church has seven thousand members with an equal number of adherents.

The *Christian and Missionary Alliance* has its headquarters in Bobo-Dioulasso, a city of sixty thousand which dominates the western part of the country and is second only to the capital city. The work began in 1923; since then nine other centers have been opened, the latest in 1963. The national church was given its independence in 1962. The New Testament in Red Bobo was published in 1954 and in Dogon in 1958. The complete Bible is now available in Bambara.

The *Sudan Interior Mission* was the third mission to take up work in Upper Volta. The first station was opened in 1930 at Fada N'gourma, where the Bible school is now located. The major part of its work is in the Gourma country. The national church received government recognition in 1966. That year the number of baptized Gourmas increased 30 percent. Twenty-five missionaries assist the national pastors in all phases of church life and work.

The *Worldwide Evangelization Crusade* in Upper Volta is a truly international group with fifteen missionaries from six countries. The work began in 1937. Through the years the mission has been working among two tribes, the Lobi (200,000) and the Birifor (100,000). The New Testament has been translated into Lobi. Only the Gospel of Mark is available in Birifor. One missionary is giving his full time to this and it is hoped that the Birifor New Testament will be completed shortly.

Ecumenical Relations. The only inter-mission, interchurch organization is the *Evangelical Federation of Upper Volta,* one of a dozen national associations of the Association of Evangelicals of Africa and Madagascar.

Ghana

Political History. Ghana gained its independence in March, 1957, the first British colony in Africa (after South Africa in 1910) to do so. Under President Nkrumah the government became increasingly oppressive and the country veered off to the left. All opposition parties were eliminated in 1964. In 1966 Nkrumah was overthrown by a military coup, which had widespread support among the populace. Representative government was restored in 1969. Ghana remains a member of the British Commonwealth.

The People. The population is estimated to be eight million, with the greatest concentration in the coastal areas, the Ashanti region, and the two largest cities, Accra and Kumasi. The fifty tribes break down into five main linguistic groups: Akans, Ashanti, Guans, Ga and Ewe, and the Moshi-Dagomba. English is the official language and is taught in all the schools.

Religion. During Nkrumah's regime several missionaries, including the Anglican Bishop of Accra, were expelled from the country when they objected to the government's attempt to deify Nkrumah. The new constitution recognizes the authority of God and guarantees freedom of religion. Most of the tribespeople are animists. The Hausa people are Muslims, who are said to represent about 15 percent of the population. Christians number almost 1,750,000, of whom about 60 percent are Protestant and 40 percent Roman Catholic.

Early Missions.   As far back as the eighteenth century the *Moravians* made several abortive attempts to establish a mission in the Gold Coast. The first continuing work was effected by the *Basel Evangelical Missionary Society,* whose pioneer missionaries arrived in Christiansborg in 1828. The Basel workers were from Germany and Switzerland. Death took a heavy toll and would have wiped out the mission had not reinforcements arrived in 1832. Of the three men who arrived in March of that year, only *Riis* was still alive three months later. Two additional missionaries joined Riis, only to die in a short time. But Riis refused to give up. After an extended furlough he returned in 1843, this time with a group of Moravian Christians from Jamaica. Because of their African background these people were better able to withstand the enervating climate of the Gold Coast. Fortunately they survived and lived to form the nucleus of the first Protestant church in the Gold Coast.

A characteristic feature of the mission in Ghana was the segregation into separate villages of Christians and pagans. This plan had its drawbacks, but it did result in a strong Christian church with high moral standards. After World War I the Basel Mission work in the Gold Coast was transferred to the *United Free Church of Scotland.* By that time church membership had risen to twelve thousand. Every village of any size had a bush school, and African church workers outnumbered the missionaries six to one. Today the *Presbyterian Church of Ghana* reports a communicant membership of fifty-five thousand and a Christian community of a quarter of a million.

The *Methodist Missionary Society* in 1831 became the second Protestant mission to take up work in the Gold Coast. The outstanding pioneer was *Thomas Birch Freeman,* a West Indian half-caste who received an education in England. With his arrival in 1838 the mission commenced work among the Ashanti. From the beginning great stress was laid on the training of African workers. Schools and Bible schools were opened. Today the *Ghana Methodist Church* has a huge investment in education— over one thousand schools with almost two hundred thousand pupils. Institutions include *Freeman College, Trinity College,* and *Kwadaso Women's Training Center.* Today the *Ghana Methodist Church* has eighty-five thousand members and a Christian community almost three times as large.

Recent Missions.   The Anglicans have been in Ghana for many years. Two missions have carried the burden of the work, the *Church Missionary Society* and the *United Society for the Propagation of the Gospel.* The Anglican community of sixty thousand is divided among nine centers in all parts of the country. The Diocese of Accra is part of the Anglican Province of West Africa.

The *Salvation Army* has been active in Ghana since 1922. Great Britain and the Netherlands are among the territories represented by the seventeen overseas officers serving in Ghana. An active evangelistic and social service program has resulted in almost one hundred congregations.

The *Assemblies of God,* whose work began in 1931, has eight centers in the far north as well as three on the coast and one in Kumasi. A strong indigenous church became independent in 1964. Two Bible schools have produced 104 national workers assisted by 40 missionaries. One hundred twenty churches have a combined membership of six thousand.

The early societies worked mostly in the coastal areas and slowly advanced north. The first mission to concentrate in the Northern Territories was the *Worldwide Evangelization Crusade* in 1940; its headquarters is in Kumasi. Medical work, evangelism, church planting, and theological and educational work are carried on in these tribal areas. Bible correspondence courses, literature distribution, and a radio ministry are the main outreaches from Kumasi.

Baptist Mid-Missions began work in 1946 in response to the call of some local Baptist Christians who had recently come from the Yoruba country and were without pastoral care. The BMM missionaries settled along the coast, where they established three main stations. Three years later they opened a second field in the Northern Territories. At the present time the mission has twenty-five missionaries in five centers, including Accra. Fifteen churches have a combined membership of two hundred.

The *Lutheran Church-Missouri Synod* work in Ghana was started by a Ghanian pastor in 1958. In 1960 the first resident missionary arrived. The following year the *Evangelical Lutheran Church of Ghana* was officially incorporated. Numerical growth has been slow in spite of the fact that seven congregations have been established in three major cities.

The first congregation of Baptists in Ghana, Yoruba-speaking traders from Nigeria, met in 1918. The Baptist churches started by these immigrants cooperated with the Nigerian Baptist Convention until the formation of the *Ghana Baptist Convention* in 1964. In the meantime, in 1947 the first *Southern Baptist* missionaries arrived. Their work is located in eight centers, extending from Accra on the coast to Nalerigu in the extreme north. Institutions include a hospital, seminary, bookstore, hostel, and school for pastors. The Ghana Baptist Convention has five thousand members.

Other groups in Ghana include the *Eastern Mennonite Board* (1957), *Church of God* (Cleveland), *Wycliffe Bible Translators* (1962), and the *Seventh Day Adventists.*

Bible Societies. The *British and Foreign Bible Society* has been in West Africa since 1807. For over one hundred fifty years Ghana was administered by the BFBS as part of the West African Agency, but it became an Independent Agency in 1964. Three years later the *Bible Society of Ghana* was established. The complete Bible is available in five languages, and Portions in five more. In 1965 the government ordered

500,000 Bibles from the BFBS for use in the schools. It was the largest single order ever received by the society in the 160 years of its existence. Scripture distribution in 1968 rose 38 percent over the previous year.

Church Union. Six denominations are carrying on talks looking forward to church union. They are the *Anglican Church, Methodist Church, Evangelical Presbyterian Church, Presbyterian Church of Ghana, African Methodist Episcopal Church,* and the *Mennonite Church.* These talks have been going on for over a decade.

Ecumenical Relations. Ghana has a strong Christian council. Three of Ghana's churches are members of the World Council of Churches. The *Church Hospital Association,* formed in 1967, coordinates the medical work of the various groups. *Trinity College,* a training school for ministers, is a joint operation of the Methodists and the Presbyterians. Recently the Anglicans have begun sending their young men to Trinity. In 1966 the Anglican Church gave limited sanction to intercommunion with those churches involved in church union negotiations. The *Ramseyer Memorial Retreat and Study Center* at Abetifi is related to the Division of World Mission and Evangelism of the World Council of Churches. The *Evangelical Fellowship of Ghana,* formed in 1969, has six members. Five churches and the Christian Council are members of the All Africa Conference of Churches.

The Church in Ghana. Church attendance was greatly reduced under the repressive measures of the Nkrumah regime, but increased significantly the year following the military coup of 1966. Seven of the eight members of the National Liberation Council are Christians. In October, 1969, however, the government ordered the expulsion of all aliens not holding valid passports and work permits. This resulted in near panic, with almost a million aliens returning to their neighboring homelands. Church membership was decimated. Particularly hard-hit were the Southern Baptist churches. Of the sixty-six congregations made up of Yorubas, only four remain. A large church in Kumasi with an average attendance of two thousand in October reported that attendance dwindled to approximately one hundred seventy in November.

Togo

Political History. Togo was ruled by Germany for thirty years and jointly by England and France for another forty-six. In 1957 British Togoland joined the Gold Coast to form the new nation of Ghana. French Togoland became an autonomous unit of the French Union in 1956 and received full independence in 1960.

The People. The population of Togo is two million. The Togolese are divided into eighteen ethnic groups. The two major tribes, the Ewes and the Kabres, make up more than half the population. French is the official language. Literacy is estimated at between 5 and 10 percent.

Religion. The majority of the Togolese are animists. Christians number almost four hundred thousand, mostly Roman Catholics. There are about one hundred fifty thousand Muslims.

Missions. It was only natural that a German colony should attract German missionaries. The *North German Mission* entered this part of Africa in 1847. Its missionaries labored there until they were expelled during World War I, at which time their work in British territory was transferred to the *United Free Church of Scotland;* and their work in French territory passed into the hands of the *Paris Evangelical Mission.* The church, now fully autonomous, is known as the *Evangelical Church of Togo.* With a Christian community of fifty thousand, it is the largest church in the country. Largely self-supporting, the church continues to welcome missionaries from the French and German societies and representatives from the United Church Board of World Ministries.

The *Methodist Church,* British in origin, is centered in the coastal area of Anecha. In 1968, eleven ministerial posts were vacant. "In Togo the Methodist Church is small and struggling. It is benefiting from being able to share in a sustained evangelistic effort by the larger Evangelical Church of Togo."[5]

The *Assemblies of God* opened its first station at Dapango, not far from the border of Upper Volta, in 1940. Today, with twelve missionaries at four stations, it is the only mission working in the northern part of Togo. A Bible school helps provide national leaders for twenty churches and fifty outstations. Church membership is two thousand.

When a *Southern Baptist* missionary in Ghana visited Togo in 1958 he found some six Baptist congregations recently formed by traders from Nigeria. In response to a request from one of these churches (Lome) for resident missionaries, the SBC sent its first members to Togo in 1964. The work is just getting under way; there are some three hundred members in two organized churches.

Dahomey

Political History. Dahomey achieved full independence in 1960 after being a protectorate of France since 1892. The government has been overthrown at least three times since independence, and political power has oscillated between military and civilian authority.

[5] *New Community,* Annual Report, 1969, p. 54.

The People. The population of 2.6 million is divided into forty-two ethnic groups. Four of them—the Fons, Adjas, Baribas, and Yorubas— account for more than half the population. The people of Dahomey are among the best educated in West Africa.

Religion. Most of the tribes are animists. Islam flourishes in the north. Christianity has registered its greatest gains in the south.

Missions. The *English Methodists* began work in Dahomey over one hundred years ago. Their main area of work is in the coastal region of the south. Several important institutions are located in Cotonou, including a girls' hostel and a Christian literature center. A lay training center is proposed. The Methodist Church today has about eight thousand members. "For years church life has been hampered by lack of personnel and money."[6]

The *Assemblies of God* is the only mission working exclusively in the northern part of the country. The work was begun in 1945 by a missionary couple transferred from Upper Volta. In the course of time five stations were opened. The Bible school, established in 1949, has had as many as thirty-five students enrolled. In 1970 the number had dropped to nineteen. Ten small churches and forty outstations are cared for by thirty-three national workers. The mission operates its own plane, called *Speed the Light.*

It was in 1946 that the *Sudan Interior Mission* opened its first station at Kandi among the Bariba tribe. Since then additional centers have been opened in neighboring areas. In 1961 the first and only mission hospital in Dahomey was opened at Bimbereke. A French-language Bible college at Kandi serves the needs of Dahomey, Upper Volta, and Niger.

The *Southern Baptists* have appointed to Dahomey a couple with long service in Nigeria. After a year in France to learn the French language, they were hoping to enter Dahomey sometime in 1970.

Ecumenical Relations. The *Protestant Methodist Church* is a member of the All Africa Conference of Churches.

Nigeria

Political History. The Republic of Nigeria received its independence from Great Britain on October 1, 1960. No colony in Africa was better prepared for independence, and it was hoped that Nigeria would become a showcase of British parliamentary democracy in Africa. Politics in the first decade were marred by coups and counter-coups, accompanied by assassi-

---

[6] *Ibid.*, p. 53.

nations which were prompted largely by tribal rivalries. A bloody massacre of some fifty thousand Ibos, mostly in the north, sent two million Ibos from all parts of Nigeria back to their own region in the east. The secession of the eastern region (Biafra) in 1967 set off a civil war which cost Nigeria one billion dollars and the Ibos one hundred thousand civilian lives, mostly from starvation. Peace was restored and the country reunified after thirty-two months of fratricidal war.

The People. With an estimated population of sixty-two million persons, Nigeria is by far the most populous country in Africa. It has 250 tribes dominated by three main groups: the Hausa-Fulani in the north, the Yorubas in the west, and the Ibos in the east. These three groups represent about 60 percent of the total population. The Ibos are the best educated, most aggressive, and most competent of the three groups. They are also the most Christian.

Religion. There are more Christians and more missionaries in Nigeria than in all the rest of West Africa combined. Christians represent about 10 percent of the population, Muslims 30 percent, and animists 60 percent. The constitution guarantees religious liberty, and the Supreme Court upheld this principle in 1964 when a Baptist pastor in a Muslim village was found guilty by a lower court of "insulting the Muslim faith" when he conducted a Christian service in a home. During the civil war American missionaries on the Nigerian side were often kept waiting for visas, doubtless because of the United States' refusal to sell arms to the federal government. After the civil war many of the missionaries on the Biafran side of the line were expelled for having "given aid and comfort to the enemy." Many Roman Catholic missionaries were involved in this exodus. Christianity is a required subject in government schools, and students must successfully pass the course in order to graduate.

Early Missions. First on the scene were the *Wesleyan Methodists,* who established a station in Yoruba country in 1842. After 130 years the autonomous Methodist Church, divided into four districts, has over thirteen hundred organized churches with an adult membership of fifty-five thousand persons. Educational work includes 522 primary schools with 125,000 students, 18 secondary schools with 3,500 students, and 15 teacher training colleges with an enrolment of 1,300. Medical work includes thirteen institutions. Still working with this church are sixty-five missionaries.

The *Church Missionary Society* has been in Nigeria for 125 years. *Henry Townsend* opened the first station in Yoruba country in 1845. Other centers were opened in rapid succession: Abeokuta in 1846, Lagos in 1852, and Ibadan in 1853. The first African bishop, Samuel Crowther, was consecrated in 1864; and from then until his death in 1893 he gave powerful leadership to the emerging church. The CMS work in Nigeria has long since been under the control of the autonomous church, known as the *Province of West Africa.* Today there are ten dioceses in Nigeria with a total of 175,000 communicant members and a Christian community many times that size. The Archbishop of the Province, Moses Scott, is the first African to hold that high office. The bishops of all ten dioceses are also Africans. The CMS still maintains a missionary staff of seventy-five in Nigeria. Those in the four dioceses of Biafra were evacuated, but they will be returning now that hostilities are over.

Nigeria is the oldest of the seventy-one mission fields in which the *Southern Baptist Convention* maintains work. It is second only to Brazil in the number of missionaries and the size of the church. It all began back in 1850 in the Yoruba country. The first half-century was not very productive. It ended with six missionaries, six churches, and six outstations. But the missionaries refused to give up. Gradually their perseverance paid off. It took an act of faith to create the Yoruba Baptist Association in 1914. Later the name was changed to the *Nigerian Baptist Convention.* From the beginning the churches were encouraged to assume responsibility for the evangelization of their own people. As early as 1919 they formed the Woman's Missionary Union of Nigeria. In 1960 the convention appointed its first foreign missionaries, two couples to Sierra Leone. The 455 churches in the convention are all fully self-supporting. They have more national pastors (539) than they have organized churches—a rare phenomenon on the mission field. The field is divided into three districts: Eastern, Northern, and Mid-Western. Institutions include two high schools, one teacher training college, three Bible schools, one seminary, and two hospitals, besides a school for missionaries' children. Two hundred career missionaries help man these institutions.

Another mission to get an early start in the first half of the nineteenth century was the *United Free Church of Scotland.* The first missionaries came not from Scotland but from Jamaica in 1846. They located in the coastal region of Calabar. Reinforcements from Scotland joined them, among them Mary Slessor, known as the "White Queen of Calabar," whose heroism is unmatched in the annals of missionary history. Her influence over the native chiefs, her administration of justice, and her success in abolishing intertribal warfare have made her a legend even to this day. In 1952 the *Presbyterian Church of Eastern Nigeria* became autonomous. In 1954 the *Canadian Presbyterian Church* was invited by the Church of Scotland to send its first two missionaries to Nigeria. Today both missions are working with the *Presbyterian Church of Nigeria,* whose 425 churches have an aggregate membership of 17,000 and a Christian community of 100,000.

Later Missions. The *Qua Iboe Mission* is an interdenominational faith mission whose origin can be traced to the influence of the great missionary statesman of the nineteenth century, H. Grattan Guinness. Samuel A. Bill, graduate of Guinness' Bible Institute in London, founded the mission in 1887 in the valley of the Qua Iboe River in eastern Nigeria. The 1930's saw advance into the Igala district of northern Nigeria. Later a third mission was started among the Bassa but few of them have turned to Christ. The civil war had an adverse effect on the work, with many of the missionaries unable to return to their stations. The *Qua Iboe Church,* now independent, has 850 congregations with a total membership of 40,000 and a Christian community of 100,000.

The *Sudan Interior Mission,* with a membership of almost twelve hundred, is the largest mission working exclusively in Africa. About one-half of its members are located in Nigeria, which makes it the largest mission in the country so far as personnel is concerned. *Rowland V. Bingham,* founder of the SIM, made two abortive attempts to reach Kano, losing his colleagues, Gowan and Kent, in the process. He began work in the Nupi tribe, 500 miles up the Niger River, in 1901. Another pioneer was *A. W. Banfield,* who translated the Bible into the difficult Nupi dialect and also compiled a dictionary. It was he who established the *Niger Press,* which for fifty-five years turned out a steady stream of Christian literature in nearly fifty languages. The *Reverend Thomas Titcombe,* another brave pioneer, was the first SIM missionary to a pagan tribe—the Tagba people, famous for their cannibalism. He served in Nigeria for fifty years and was still going strong at seventy-seven years of age.

In 1917 the mission began the evangelization of the Tangales. Eight years later it moved north to the city of Kano in the heart of Hausa country. Jos, entered in 1923, became the headquarters of the mission. The SIM churches, now known as the *Evangelical Churches of West Africa,* received their independence in 1956. Shortly thereafter they organized their own missionary society, which now supports more than one hundred missionaries in various parts of Africa. Its twelve hundred churches have 60,000 baptized members and a Christian community of 400,000, served by twelve hundred pastors and five hundred evangelists. There are 390 missionaries in Nigeria.

The SIM has pioneered in two important areas: gospel radio and a Christian news magazine, *African Challenge. Station ELWA* has already been described in the section on Liberia. *African Challenge* is a popular magazine designed to be sold on the newsstands of Africa. Now appearing in Yoruba and English, its circulation has climbed to 160,000 copies. The *Kano Hospital,* famous for its eye surgery, is known for hundreds of miles in all directions.

The SIM has chalked up a fantastically good record so far as casualties are concerned. From 1893 to 1963 the grand total of missionaries sent to Africa numbered 1,911. Of these, 76 died, 33 retired, 120 were on leave of absence, 401 resigned for all reasons, including health, personal and family problems, discipline, etc.; leaving 1,281 (67 percent) of all missionaries ever accepted still in active service. This represents a 33 percent loss over seventy years, compared with the Peace Corps' casualty rate of 17.2 per cent over a twenty-one-month period!

The *Sudan United Mission* was founded in London in 1904. Between 1906 and 1961 branches from other countries joined its ranks. The various branches are autonomous, appointing, supporting, and controlling their own missionaries, and to some extent occupying separate areas of operation on the field. Several well-known American boards are included in the SUM: *Christian Reformed Church,* with 110 missionaries in Nigeria; the *Church of the Brethren;* and the *Evangelical United Brethren,* now part of the Methodist Church. The largest field is in northern Nigeria, which now has sixty-four stations. The self-governing church TEKAS was constituted in 1955 and registered with the government in 1956. Known as the *Fellowship of Churches of Christ in the Sudan,* TEKAS now has thirty-eight hundred congregations with sixty-five thousand communicant members and a Christian community of half a million.

The *Synodical Conference of Lutheran Churches* began mission work in Calabar in 1936. Soon there was a Bible school, a teacher training school, and a seminary. Later a hospital and a clinic were opened. In 1963 the *Evangelical Lutheran Church of Nigeria* came into being. In 1964 the Lutheran Synodical Conference transferred its work in Africa to the *Lutheran Church-Missouri Synod.* When the civil war broke out all missionaries from the eastern region were evacuated; but by October, 1968, thirty of them had been able to return. The Christians, however, suffered greatly, and much relief and rehabilitation have been undertaken in the past year or two. The latest report indicates that the ELCN now has thirty-eight thousand baptized members in 220 churches. In 1965 there were eighty missionaries serving in various capacities.

The *Assemblies of God* initiated work in eastern Nigeria in response to a call from thirty-two indigenous churches needing assistance. Work was begun at Port Harcourt in 1939. Today the mission has work in seventeen centers in all parts of Nigeria. Five Bible schools have provided over five hundred national workers for 609 churches with twenty-five thousand members.

The *Salvation Army* with ten thousand members, and the *Seventh Day Adventist Church* with twenty thousand members, have both been in Nigeria for many years. Other missions include *Wycliffe Bible Translators, Christian Missions in Many Lands, Missionary Church Association,* and *Church of God* (Cleveland).

Relief Work. The civil war made necessary an enormous amount of relief work. All missions in the area did what they could, but their resources were hopelessly inadequate. Sizable assistance from outside was given by the *World Council of Churches, Church World Service, Lutheran*

World Federation, Mennonite Central Committee, and a host of smaller agencies from all over the Christian world.

The Bible Societies. In a country as large as Nigeria, which has 250 languages and dialects, Bible translation is of major importance. The complete Bible is available in seven languages, the entire New Testament in seven more languages, and Portions in an additional forty-five languages. The *Bible Society of Nigeria,* autonomous since 1966, has been distributing over a million copies of the Scriptures each year. With the end of the civil war the Bible Society made an urgent appeal for help to provide 250,000 Bibles, 55,000 New Testaments, 360,000 Gospel Portions, and 1,000,000 Scripture Selections. A program of Bible translation and revision is now under way. Plans include New Testaments in Hausa, Indoma, and Isoko. Bibles in Igala and Ogonu are in process of being printed.

Evangelism. The New Life For All campaign, patterned after Evangelism-in-Depth and widely supported by all evangelical groups, has resulted in a large ingathering of church members. Even in the Muslim north converts have been made in significant numbers. Some churches have more than doubled their membership in the last five years, largely as a result of the campaign.

Church Union. For many years church union talks involving the Anglicans, Presbyterians, and Methodists were carried forward. Substantial progress was made and it looked as if the plan would be consummated in 1966; but at the last minute the Methodists reversed their stand and the plan fell through. Since then the civil war has intervened and the talks have not been resumed.

Ecumenical Relations. There is a strong *Christian Council in Nigeria,* but it is not affiliated with any world body. There is one other organization, the *Nigerian Evangelical Fellowship.* It is a member of the Association of Evangelicals of Africa and Madagascar. The *Methodist Church* and the *Presbyterian Church* are members of the World Council of Churches. Six organizations are affiliated with the All Africa Conference of Churches.

The Ibo People. During the civil war the Ibo people suffered greatly; but in their hunger and poverty many of them turned to the Lord. The Assemblies of God reported sixty new churches during the time the missionaries were excluded. The Sudan Interior Mission churches doubled during the war, and have increased several times since then. Immediately at the close of the war thirty-nine tons of Bibles in four Nigerian languages were shipped to Lagos to replace the Bibles lost and destroyed during the war. The eastern region, once the stronghold of Roman Catholicism, is

now wide open to the evangelical groups and their churches are multiplying rapidly.

Niger

Political History. Although French pacification began before 1900,
Niger did not become a French colony until 1922. It became fully
independent in 1960 and is not a member of the French Community.
Under two-term President Diori, Niger has enjoyed a degree of political
stability rather rare in this part of Africa. Niger's only political party is the
Niger Progressive Party founded in 1946.

The People. The estimated population of Niger is 3.8 million, concentrated largely in a narrow band along the southern border. Half of the
people are Hausa. The Djerma-Songhai account for about one-fifth of the
population. Most of the other inhabitants are nomadic or semi-nomadic
tribes.

Religion. Niger is predominantly Muslim. Some tribes have resisted
the influence of Islam and cling tenaciously to their animistic practices.
Christianity has barely scratched the surface.

Missions. There are only two Protestant missions in Niger. The older
and larger is the *Sudan Interior Mission,* whose first station was opened in
1924 at Zinder, ancient hub of the slave trade and still a jumping-off place
for the camel caravans of the desert. Their second station was Tsibiri,
opened in 1928; it is now closed. In 1940 Newton Kapp opened Maradi,
which is SIM headquarters in Niger. After thirty years Mr. Kapp is still
going strong. President Diori, former student of Kapp's, awarded him the
Order du Chevalieax. Four other missionaries have been decorated by the
President for their part in the SIM hospital at Galmi—the only mission
hospital in Niger. The country's only leprosarium, outside Maradi, is
operated by the SIM. Because of chronic shortage of medical staff a single
nurse, Jo Rogers, handles over three hundred patients by herself. The
mission also has a Bible school and two girls' schools. The Niger Church
received government recognition in 1961. The SIM, with almost sixty
missionaries assigned to Niger, has a big stake in the future of the Christian
cause in this difficult Muslim country.

The only other mission in Niger is the *Evangelical Baptist Missions,* a
society dedicated to the spread of the gospel in French-speaking countries.
It entered in 1929 and established headquarters in the capital, Niamey.
Today it has some forty missionaries in seven main areas. Transportation
between these areas is by mission plane. The mission conducts elementary
schools and has plans to open a high school, always with the aim of

reaching the students with the gospel as well as giving them a good education. There is also a Bible school and a bookstore. The New Testament has been translated into the Djerma tongue. Work is proceeding on the Old Testament. The national church has formed its own missionary society.

XIV

Central Africa

Cameroon

Political History. Cameroon was controlled by Germany from 1884 to 1916. Following World War I it was divided between France and Britain, the larger, eastern part going to France. In 1960 the French trusteeship ended and Cameroon became an independent state. The British trusteeship of (West) Cameroon ended in 1961 with the northern half going to Nigeria and the southern part joining Cameroon. Cameroon has close ties with France and cordial relations with the United States.

The People. The estimated population is 5.7 million, which includes twenty thousand Europeans. Cameroon has some two hundred tribes speaking twenty-four major languages. French is the official language of East Cameroon and English the official language of West Cameroon. Eighty-five percent of the population is rural and illiteracy is about 80 percent.

Religion. Cameroonians living in the north are primarily Muslim, while those living in the south are Christians. About half the population remains animist. Both Muslims and Christians continue to be influenced by pagan practices. Although the constitution guarantees religious liberty, the rapid advance of Islam in the north is resulting in persecution of the Christians there. In August, 1966, two Swiss missionaries of the Paris Mission were murdered by a group of terrorists abetted by a Christian teacher on the staff of a church school. The four men responsible for the murders were later executed by the government. In March, 1967, Marjory Havlick, a Presbyterian missionary, suffered a fractured skull from a blow inflicted by a robber who entered her home.

Missions. The *Baptists* were the first on the scene in Cameroon. Their work breaks down into three rather well-defined periods which coincide roughly with the political fortunes of the territory. These periods are: the English (1842-1890); the German (1890-1936); the American and Canadian (1936-1970). At the end of the German period the mission was in danger of closing; but the infusion of new blood from the North America Baptist General Conference revived it and rapid progress has been made since that time. In 1953 the churches organized themselves into the *Cameroon Baptist Convention*. At present there are 480 organized congregations with a membership of thirty-two thousand. Some seventy-eight missionaries continue to serve in various capacities with the convention. Medical work includes a hospital, three maternity centers, and a leprosarium. In the educational field the convention maintains, with government grants, 112 primary schools, a teacher training school, and 2 colleges.

The second mission to take up work in Cameroon was the *Presbyterian Church in the USA*. The work began on the island of Corisco near the mouth of the Gabon River in 1850. Later the mission was extended to Gabon on the continent, and in 1871 the two fields, Corisco and Gabon, were united. It was not until the 1880's that the Presbyterians extended their work into Cameroon. Strong central mission stations were established, and these were used as bases from which the surrounding countryside was effectively evangelized. The plan worked well. Growth was steady and consistent. With only one field in Africa, the Presbyterian mission could afford to make a large investment in Cameroon. The *Presbyterian Church of Cameroon* was organized in 1957, at which time it had three synods and ten presbyteries. Since the church became independent, the number of fraternal workers has dropped 50 percent, but the number of national pastors has almost doubled and the number of Cameroon teachers with diplomas is almost three times as great. The church still depends on American doctors to operate its six hospitals. In addition it has twenty-five dispensaries, two leper colonies, one orphanage, and six dental centers. At *Dager Theological School* sixty students are training for the ministry. The *United School of Theology* at Yaounde opened its doors first in 1962. The *Presbyterian Church of Cameroon* reported a total of sixty-three thousand communicant members in 1967. It has 271 organized churches and 1,525 unorganized groups served by 124 ordained ministers and 1,240 evangelists.

A split developed in the Presbyterian Church of Cameroon at the tenth General Assembly in January, 1967. It stemmed from a long-standing difference of opinion over the church's participation in the ecumenical movement. Seven pastors and fourteen elders withdrew. The dissident group voted to form a new church which they called the *Reformed Presbyterian Church*. The new group had the support of 10 percent of the pastors in the Presbyterian Church. The stated clerk is reported to have taken a conciliatory attitude toward the dissidents and expressed the hope that they would return. In the meantime, they have made several abortive attempts to get government recognition of the new church. On the third attempt the president of the country received the group, but did not grant their request. Some of the dissidents were imprisoned for five months; by May of 1968 all but three of them had been released, but they were still prohibited, under penalty of heavy fine, from assembling for worship. During the past three years the *Independent Board for Presbyterian Foreign Missions* has tried to gain entrance to Cameroon to give assistance to this group, but to date it has been denied. Instead, it is sending Bible correspondence courses, New Testaments, and other forms of Christian literature from headquarters at Cape May, New Jersey.

When Germany seized control of Cameroon in 1887 the work begun by the English Baptists was turned over to the *Basel Evangelical Missionary Society.* Shortly after the transfer a mass movement occurred and several whole tribes asked for Christian instruction. Encouraged by this turn of events, the Basel Mission extended its work inland and by 1914 had established sixteen main stations and almost four hundred schools. Out of this effort came the *Presbyterian Church in West Cameroon,* with a total communicant membership of over fifty thousand.

When Britain and France occupied Cameroon during World War I, the German missionaries were expelled. The *Paris Evangelical Missionary Society* stepped into the breach, even though its own financial situation at the time was appalling. Being an interdenominational mission, the PEMS was able to supply Baptist missionaries for the Baptist churches and Presbyterian missionaries for the Presbyterian churches left without them. The church brought into existence by the PEMS, the *Evangelical Church of the Cameroon,* became autonomous in 1957. A decade later it reported a Christian community of a quarter of a million people divided among 1,035 churches.

The *American Lutheran Church* and the *Norwegian Missionary Society* continue to give assistance to the *Evangelical Lutheran Church of Cameroon.* The *Sudan United Mission,* with Swiss and Norwegian branches, has had missionaries in Cameroon since 1911. Their churches, 185 in all, have not yet been organized into an autonomous body. *Wycliffe Bible Translators* has six linguists working in cooperation with the University of the Cameroon.

Bible Societies. Work began in 1870. The area was included in the West Africa Agency prior to 1958. Then a new Joint Agency was established by the *British and Foreign Bible Society* and the *Netherlands Bible Society.* The *Bible Society of Cameroon* became independent in 1964. In a land with so many different tribes, Bible translation is a problem. Today the complete Bible is available in three languages, the New Testament in another seven, and Portions in three more. In less than six years the distribution of Bibles and New Testaments has increased 400 percent and

Portions and Selections even more. There are three contributing factors. (1) In 1964 the Evangelical Church of the Cameroon launched an evangelistic campaign designed to take the gospel to hitherto unreached areas. (2) The Roman Catholic Church is now encouraging the reading of the Bible. In some areas the Catholics are taking the lead in distribution. (3) In many tribes where literacy is on the increase the Scriptures are the only reading materials available.

Church Union. In 1964 three bodies initiated unity talks: *Presbyterian Church in West Cameroon, Evangelical Church of the Cameroon,* and the *Presbyterian Church of Cameroon.* In April, 1967, they were joined by the *Eglise Protestante Africaine,* a group which had separated from the Presbyterian Church in East Cameroon in the 1930's for language reasons. A constitution has been completed and submitted to the four denominations concerned. At one time the Evangelical Lutheran Church of North Cameroon showed an interest in the talks and in 1967 sent representatives to the sixth meeting; but it has not followed through. The Cameroon Baptist Convention in West Cameroon was invited to attend the meetings of the Church Union Committee, but declined.

Ecumenical Relations. Plans are being drawn up for an *Evangelical Council of Cameroon* to replace the Evangelical Federation of Protestant Churches and Missions of Cameroon and Equatorial Africa. The proposed council would coordinate the work, be the official voice of its member churches and missions, and maintain relations with the churches in Rio Muni, Gabon, and Congo-Brazzaville. The present federation is not affiliated with the World Council of Churches. Five denominations are members of the World Council of Churches. Four churches are affiliated with the All Africa Conference of Churches.

Chad

Political History. From 1900 to 1959 Chad was one of four territories that composed French Equatorial Africa. In 1960 it became an independent state and elected to remain in the French Community. All opposition parties were abolished in 1962 and prominent political leaders were arrested. A temporary state of emergency followed. A guerrilla type of civil war is developing and the government, with the help of French troops, is trying to contain it. At the root of the current strife is the traditional enmity between the Arab-speaking Muslims in the north and the pagan Negroid tribes in the south.

The People. The estimated population is 3.4 million, almost equally divided between the Caucasoid Muslim people in the north and the

Negroid Bantu tribes in the south. About five thousand Frenchmen remain in Chad, not including two thousand Legionnaires.

Religion. The dominant religion in the north is Islam. The people in the south are animists. The Christians, found mostly in the south, number about two hundred thousand, divided almost equally between Roman Catholics and Protestants.

Missions. The first Protestant mission to enter Chad was *Baptist Mid-Missions.* The year was 1925; the place was Fort Archambault. The Sara people were friendly enough; but opposition from the ruling chief was so strong that no progress was made until his death in 1937. Following his death the long-expected breakthrough occurred, after which the work grew rapidly. Churches and outstations sprang up in various places; and the first chapel, originally built to accommodate four hundred, had to be enlarged to take care of three times that number. As the number of Christians multiplied, the mission conducted short-term Bible schools to provide enough leaders for the expanding work. Soon the church in Fort Archambault was supporting twenty-one evangelists. The mission opened the first Christian high school in Chad in 1964. It also maintains a Bible school and a hospital at Koumra. The indigenous church, the *Association of Baptist Churches in Chad,* received its autonomy in 1964, at which time all mission property was transferred to the church. The church has a baptized membership of six thousand and a Christian community of twenty thousand. Thirty-seven BMM workers are assigned to Chad. They work out of four main centers, all in the extreme southern part of the country.

There are several other missions in Chad. *Christian Missions in Many Lands* entered the southwest section from its Kano base in Nigeria. *Dr. John R. Olley* began work in Fort Lamy in 1925 and was their outstanding leader for thirty years. He translated the New Testament first into Mbai and later into Kim, and established assemblies in various parts of the country. The present staff of nineteen missionaries from five different countries occupies five main centers in the south and two in the central part of the country, and there is one in Fort Lamy, the capital.

Canadian workers of the *Sudan United Mission* entered Chad in 1927. For the first decade opposition was strong and progress slow. The years 1940-1950 witnessed a great ingathering. From the beginning the mission employed the indigenous principle; as a result the churches today are self-supporting. In 1962 the church became independent; it is known as the *Evangelical Church of the Chad.* In 1955 the New Testament in Ngambai was completed. In 1969 the North American branch of the mission merged with *The Evangelical Alliance Mission.* There are now seventeen thousand baptized believers in 420 congregations, 260 of which are organized. The Evangelical Church of the Chad has organized its own

African Missionary Society and sent some of its best qualified men into the Lake Chad area to evangelize the Muslims. Five tribal Bible schools and the *French Theological School* provide a steady stream of pastors and evangelists. One hospital and three clinics constitute the medical work. About four thousand children and young people are enrolled in the *Flambeaux* and *Lumieres* programs, patterned after our Christian Service Brigade and Pioneer Girls.

The *Lutheran Brethren Mission* has been at work in Chad for many years and has 230 churches with almost four thousand members. The *Worldwide Evangelization Crusade* entered Chad in 1962 with a view to reaching the unevangelized Muslims in the north. Their initial request was for sixteen workers; but in 1970 they had only eight missionaries, all British, in three stations. The *Church of God* (Cleveland) reports a church of almost five hundred members. *Missionary Aviation Fellowship* provides air transportation for missionaries, pastors, evangelists, medical personnel, and others.

Bible Translation. There is no Bible agency in Chad. After fifty years of missionary work there is still no complete Bible in any language. The New Testament is available in seven languages and Portions have been produced in five more.

Central African Republic

Political History. The Central African Republic, formerly known as Ubangi-Shari, was for fifty years one of four territories of French Equatorial Africa. It achieved full independence in 1960. A swift coup d'etat on January 1, 1966, engineered by the military, was designed to eliminate waste and corruption, halt stagnation, and expel the Chinese communists whose presence threatened the security of the state. President Bokassa then abolished the constitution and dissolved the National Assembly. Since then he has ruled the country by decree. The Central African Republic remains a member of the French Community.

The People. The population is 2.6 million. Although there are about eighty different ethnic groups, two of them—the Baya-Mandjai and the Banda—account for more than two-thirds of the population. More than 80 percent of the people live in rural areas. The literacy rate is about 20 percent. French is the official language, but Sango is the lingua franca of the country.

Religion. In 1966 some 68 percent of the population professed to be Christians, 40 percent Protestant and 28 percent Catholic. Animism is still strongly entrenched and claims 27 percent of the people. Only 5 percent are Muslims.

Missions. The *Brethren Church* was the pioneer in this part of Africa. The first missionaries arrived in 1921 and began work among the Karre people. During the first twelve years three stations serving three different language areas were opened with fifteen missionaries engaged in itineration, translation, and medical work. During the second twelve-year period missionary personnel doubled and more stations were opened. A strong medical program revolves around the medical centers at Boguila in the north and Yaloke in the south. Dispensaries are maintained at other stations. Educational work includes a dozen elementary Bible schools for the training of local leaders. They also act as a feeder to the Bible institute at Bozoum. Attached to the latter is the School of Theology, taught entirely in French. The mission has to its credit the translation of the New Testament into Karre and Kabba. The entire Bible in Sango was produced by the cooperative efforts of the Brethren Church and Baptist Mid-Missions. The Brethren Church now has a baptized membership of fifty thousand and a Christian community of nearly seventy-five thousand. Some fifty missionaries are working happily with over two hundred full-time national workers.

Baptist Mid-Missions is responsible for the eastern part of the Central African Republic. Through the years its main emphasis has been on evangelism, church planting, Bible translation, and leadership training. Eighty-five missionaries are assigned to twelve main centers. Medical work includes a hospital, medical training school, six dispensaries, and dental work. Several elementary Bible schools and two advanced Bible schools prepare nationals for the work of the church. A seminary is available for those who are qualified for work at that level. The indigenous church has over three hundred congregations and a total of forty thousand baptized members. This figure would be higher had it not been for a split that occurred in 1956 when a sizable group left Baptist Mid-Missions and formed the Comite Baptiste, which in 1967 had an estimated membership of seven thousand.

The *Swedish Baptist Mission* established work in 1923 at Berberati in the southwest. It operates schools, clinics, and orphanages, and engages in evangelistic and church planting work. In 1968 the *Union of Baptist Churches* reported sixteen thousand members served by twenty-one ordained pastors and over two hundred other full-time workers.

In 1924 the *Africa Inland Mission* sent workers into the extreme eastern end of Central African Republic to the Zande tribe. The indigenous church, independent since 1965, is known as the *Evangelical Church of Central Africa.* At present it has about twelve hundred members with a Christian community of five thousand. Fifteen missionaries serve with the church.

The *Swiss Pentecostal Missionary Society* has been in Central African Republic since 1927 and has built up a church of sixty-five hundred members.

Bible Translation.   The whole Bible in Sango was completed in 1966. Two other languages have the New Testament and three additional languages have Portions of the Word of God.

Gabon

Political History.   After being for fifty years a part of French Equatorial Africa, Gabon became a sovereign state in 1960. Though not a member of the French Community, it maintains close ties with France. It has no diplomatic relations with any communist country. The Peace Corps program was terminated in 1967 at the request of the Gabonese government.

The People.   The population of Gabon is about half a million, which works out at four persons per square mile. There is no population explosion here. In fact, the population has decreased in the last eighty years because of disease. The people, almost all of Bantu stock, are divided into forty tribes, each with its own language. French is the official language. Illiteracy at 88 percent is high.

Religion.   Christians represent almost half the population, and most of these are Roman Catholics. Muslims are found in the north. The remainder are animists.

Missions.   In 1842 the *American Board of Commissioners* launched a mission on the lower reaches of the Gabon River. After much discouragement and little progress, the mission was transferred in 1870 to the *American Presbyterians*. In 1892 the Presbyterians pulled out in favor of the *Paris Evangelical Missionary Society*. It took several decades before significant results were seen. Church membership more than trebled between 1925 and 1950. It was under the Paris Mission that *Albert Schweitzer* served for half a century. His hospital at Lambarene was a veritable Mecca for all VIP's visiting that part of Africa. Since his death in 1965 the hospital has been modernized and the staff internationalized, which has added greatly to its efficiency as a medical institution. The church which has resulted from the work of the Paris Mission is independently organized. Known as the *Evangelical Church of Gabon,* it has a membership of almost twenty thousand and a Christian community more than three times that number.

The only other mission in Gabon is the *Christian and Missionary Alliance*. Its work in the southern part of the country dates back to 1934. Bongolo was the first, and is today the central, station. Medical work is confined to three dispensaries. Bible training is available in the *Central Bible School* at Bongolo and the *Regional Bible School* at Koula Moutou. During 1968 revival broke out in Bongolo and spread to other centers. Caught up in the revival were high school students, illiterate villagers, national workers, Bible school students, men, women, young, and old. Sinners were born again; backsliders were restored; the sick were healed; and alcoholics were delivered from the power of Satan. As a result church membership increased by 20 percent in one year to a new high of sixty-four hundred. The indigenous church, long since independent, is the *Evangelical Church of South Gabon*.

Bible Translation. The Fang people, the largest tribe in Gabon, are the only ones to have the entire Bible in their own tongue. The New Testament is completed in three languages; Portions are available in eight additional languages.

Ecumenical Relations. The *Evangelical Church of Gabon* is a member of both the World Council of Churches and the All Africa Conference of Churches.

Congo (Brazzaville)

Political History. Congo (B) was part of French Equatorial Africa from 1910 to 1960, when it became a sovereign state known as the Republic of the Congo. There are two Republics of Congo, one ex-French and the other ex-Belgian. The latter is by far the better known. To distinguish these two Congos it is customary to add the name of the capital, Brazzaville or Kinshasa as the case may be. Congo severed diplomatic relations with neighboring Congo (Kinshasa) in 1968. It has strong ties with communist countries, especially Communist China.

The People. The population of Congo is about one million and growing rapidly, largely because of immigration from the north. One-fifth of the population lives in two cities, Brazzaville on the Congo River and Pointe Noire, a seaport on the Atlantic Ocean. Some ten thousand Europeans, mostly Frenchmen, live in Congo. There are fifty ethnic groups, each with its own language. French is the official language.

Religion. Animism is the dominant religion. Most of the urban population is reported to be Christian, at least in name. Islam is not strong among the Congolese.

Missions. The *Swedish Evangelical Mission,* from its field in Belgian Congo, extended its work into French Congo in 1909 and eventually established twelve stations in the southern part of the country. The first mission school opened, in spite of serious difficulties, in 1911. Today the mission schools are subsidized by the state. Medical work presented even greater problems and it was not until 1961 that the mission had its own doctor. In the 1920's and again in 1947 and 1948 revival brought renewal to the churches. The *Evangelical Church of Congo/Brazzaville* became autonomous in 1961 and has since joined the World Council of Churches. Latest available statistics indicate a membership of sixty-six thousand and a Christian community twice as large. In 1970 it had fifty-three missionaries in Congo.

When in 1940 the *Norwegian Covenant Mission* in South Africa handed its work over to the national church, it transferred its missionary staff to French Congo, where over the years some thirty Norwegian missionaries have served. When the national church became independent in 1961 it merged with the Evangelical Church of Congo/Brazzaville.

The *United World Mission* sent its first missionary, a widow who had already given many years of service in Belgian Congo, to the region of Likouala in the northern part of the Congo, where three stations were developed. A four-year Bible school was founded in 1956, and a dispensary was opened in 1969. That same year the Christians organized themselves into a legal body—the *Evangelical Church of Likouala.* Nine missionaries are assigned to work with this church.

Another group in Congo is the *Baptist Church of the Sangha.* Cooperating with this church in the *Swedish Orebro Mission.*

The *Salvation Army* entered French Congo from Leopoldville in 1937. In 1953 it became a separate command. In 1968 it had in Congo sixteen officers from four European countries.

Ecumenical Relations. The *Evangelical Church of Congo* and the *Salvation Army* belong to the All Africa Conference of Churches. Only the former is a member of the World Council of Churches.

Congo (Kinshasa)

Political History. Formerly known to the world as the Belgian Congo, the Democratic Republic of Congo received its independence June 30, 1960. Unlike France and Great Britain, Belgium did almost nothing to prepare its colony for independence; and when it came there was not a single Congolese doctor, engineer, or lawyer in the whole country. Pandemonium broke out in July when the army rebelled against the Belgian officers and went on the rampage. The government changed hands several times. Left-leaning Lumumba died under mysterious circumstances; communist diplomats and technicians were expelled; and finally the United Nations intervened with 20,000 troops to keep the country from complete chaos. Katanga tried to break away from the central government. Leftist rebels, who called themselves "Simbas," captured Kisangani on August 5, 1964, and a month later proclaimed the People's Republic of Congo. For a time they controlled large areas in the northeast part of the country. It was during the fall of that year that the Simbas, looting, burning, and murdering as they went, left a swath of destruction in their wake. Some two thousand hostages, most of them foreigners, were rescued by Belgian paratroops on October 24, 1964. Many missionaries, both Roman Catholic and Protestant, were killed. Now, after almost ten years of turbulence, the country seems to be settling down to a peaceful existence.

The People. The population of Congo is close to seventeen million. There are two hundred tribes, each speaking a different dialect; but these can be classified into three main groups: Negroes, Hamites, and Pygmies. Four regional, or trade, languages are Lingala, Kingwana, Kikongo, and Tshiluba. The mass exodus of foreigners following independence has reduced their number from 115,000 to about 50,000 today.

Religion. Animism is the native religion of the Congolese. Roman Catholicism is strong, claiming some five million adherents. The Protestant community numbers at least two million; and the Kimbangu Church, reputed to be the largest separatist church on the continent, represents another half million. All told the Christian community might run as high as 45 percent of the total population. Islam has not yet penetrated deeply into this part of Africa, and there are probably not more than 125,000 Muslims in the country.

Protestant Beginnings. Following the death of David Livingstone, *Henry M. Stanley* decided to continue the exploration of Central Africa. In August, 1877, he became the first white man to descend the mighty Congo River to its mouth. His experiences, recorded in his *Challenge to Christendom,* made an enormous impact on the Christian church, especially in Great Britain. As a result two societies were prompted to begin work in Congo in 1878, the *Livingstone Inland Mission* and the *Baptist Missionary Society.* The pioneers encountered incredible difficulties —geographic, linguistic, and climatic. Only one out of four survived the first term of service. Twelve attempts were made before they finally opened a station in Kinshasa.

These two pioneer agencies are still in Congo. The Livingstone Inland Mission in 1900 changed its name to the *Regions Beyond Missionary Union.* Its *Evangelical Church of the Lulonga,* with a membership of thirty-five thousand, is practically on its own, with only four missionaries to help. The Baptist Missionary Society has branched out in many directions in the upper and middle areas of Congo. As a result three independent churches have come into being and today manage their own affairs. The combined membership of these churches is fifty thousand. Thirty-six missionaries, mostly medical personnel, are still cooperating with two of the churches. They maintain four overcrowded hospitals, but staffing them with qualified personnel is a continuing problem. Some of the missionaries are assigned to the *Evangelical Medical Institute* in Kimpese on the Lower Congo, where they are ministering to the refugees from Angola.

Between 1881 and 1884 the first two mission steamers were launched on the Upper Congo, after having been carried in sections by porters 225 miles from the coast. Three outstanding pioneers deserve honorable mention, *George Grenfell, Henry Richards,* and *W. Holman Bentley.* Grenfell, in his little steamer, *Peace,* preached the gospel and planted churches far up the Congo River. Richards concentrated on the Lower Congo, where, after seven years of unfruitful work, revival broke out and a mass movement swept thousands into the Kingdom. Bentley's great contribution was the translation of the New Testament into Kongo.

Early Missions. In 1881 Congo was the first field to be entered by the *Swedish Evangelical Mission.* After almost ninety years it still has sixty missionaries on the field. The national group, the *Evangelical Church of Congo,* received its independence in 1961. Its twenty-three organized churches have a membership of twenty-eight hundred. Educational institutions include sixty primary, seven middle, three high, and two normal schools. It operates a Bible school, seminary, and hospital.

In 1884 Congo became the first of twenty-six fields now served by the *Christian and Missionary Alliance.* Thirty years later, after thirty graves had been filled, there were only eight hundred believers. By 1924 the number had increased to four thousand. As early as 1931 the *Evangelical Church of the Alliance in Congo* received its independence and has been self-supporting ever since. Today its 224 congregations have a total of 23,500 members.

The *Plymouth Brethren,* under the leadership of *F. Stanley Arnot,* began their work in Katanga territory in the south in 1889. Later they opened a second region in the northeast. Congo, with eighty-two missionaries, is one of their largest fields.

The *Southern Presbyterians* started their work in Kasai in south central Congo in 1891. The first missionaries were *Samuel Lapsley* and *William Sheppard. William Morrison* reduced the Baluba-Lulua language to writing and translated the Bible. This is their only field in Africa, so the mission through the years has been able to make a large investment in Congo. Before the evacuation of 1960 they had 175 missionaries here. Today there are one hundred missionaries serving in eleven centers including Kinshasa, the capital. The *Presbyterian Church of the Congo,* with a membership of one hundred fifty thousand, was given full autonomy in 1969.

The *Disciples of Christ* entered Congo in 1899 and established work in the Equator Province. In recent years some of the missionaries have been seconded to ecumenical institutions in other parts of the country; but most of the sixty-five missionaries are assigned to four of twelve regions into which their field is divided. The *Church of Christ in Congo* (Disciples) became fully autonomous in 1963. The last few years have witnessed unprecedented growth, from 140,000 members in 1966 to 230,000 in 1969.

The *Congo Inland Mission* was founded in 1911 to engage interested Mennonite bodies in a united effort to evangelize the vast unreached areas of the Congo. Four groups of Mennonites responded and are today part of the Congo Inland Mission, which is working among six tribes in south central Congo. It has consistently maintained a large missionary staff which today numbers eighty. The church and mission merged in February, 1960, four months before the coming of independence. Known as the *Evangelical Mennonite Church in Congo,* it has a membership of forty thousand.

The *Africa Inland Mission* is by far the largest interdenominational mission in Congo. Its work goes back to 1912, when a party of eight led by *C. E. Hurlburt* crossed Lake Albert and entered northeast Congo from Uganda. The national church, known as the *Evangelical Church of Eastern Congo,* has been independent since 1960. In recent years its membership has soared from thirty thousand to seventy-five thousand and the Christian community to almost three hundred thousand. Some one hundred missionaries are working side by side with eighty-seven ordained pastors and over thirteen hundred evangelists. Educational work includes five high schools and a teacher training college. Almost two hundred young people are enrolled in three Bible schools and one seminary. Five hospitals and twenty-two dispensaries minister to the physical needs of the people.

Another American mission in Congo is the *United Methodist Board of Missions.* The first station was opened in 1914 in the extreme southern part near Lubumbashi, in what used to be the wealthy province of Katanga. Through the years it has branched out in other areas and today the nineteen districts of the *Methodist Church of Congo* are divided into two Annual Conferences: the Central Conference, which is largely rural; and the Southern Conference, which is chiefly urban. The General Conference of 1968 authorized the creation of the North Katanga Provisional Annual Conference, which comprises six districts. One of its outstanding institutions, the *Springer Institute,* has continued to function with few interruptions during the turmoil of this postindependence period. In 1968 the following report was filed: "All schools at Springer Institute are functioning which is rare in the Congo these days. Most schools are closed or holding one or two classes because many Europeans have not returned.

We have the largest group in seminary in our history, and primary and secondary classes are full."[1]

The *American Baptists* entered Congo in 1915, but managed to win only ten converts in the first ten years. After thirty years of perseverance a breakthrough occurred in 1946; since then the church has been growing at the rate of several thousand every year. The year 1969 marked the formation of the *Baptist Church of Western Congo,* which replaces both the ABFMS and the former national church organization; so in Congo the church and mission are now one. In 1968 church membership was reported to be 113,000, with a Christian community almost three times that number. Doubtless there has been significant growth in the past two years.

The *Evangelical Free Church of America* began work in the Ubangi area in northwest Congo in 1922 and has maintained a full program of work and a large staff of missionaries ever since. In 1937 the *Evangelical Covenant Church of America* entered this same area. The two missions linked up and through the years have worked together, producing a single church, the *Evangelical Church of Ubangi,* which became independent in 1960. It has a membership of thirty-one thousand. In the last year, however, the Congolese church decided to divide, at a time when most other churches are uniting. Dr. Paul Carlson, who was killed by the Simbas in November, 1964, was a member of the Covenant Mission.

Several missions entered the Congo in the 1930's. Among them were the *Unevangelized Fields Mission* (1931), the *Salvation Army* (1934), and the *Berean Mission* (1938). The Unevangelized Fields Mission, working in the northeastern section of the country, sustained the heaviest of all Protestant losses during the Simba rebellion of 1964. Thirteen missionaries and six children were killed under the most gruesome circumstances.

Two Baptist missions moved into Congo shortly after World War II, the *Conservative Baptists* in 1946 and *Baptist Mid-Missions* in 1953. The former is working in Kivu Province near the Uganda border. During the 1960's the missionaries had to evacuate on three separate occasions. In addition to evacuation, the missionaries in one district had to contend with an ugly situation that developed when a dissident group decided to take over the mission property. But in spite of all the difficulties and dangers, some fifty missionaries are now back in Kivu cooperating with the national leaders of a fourteen-thousand-member church. Institutions include three middle schools, one Bible school, a hospital, and two dispensaries.

Some missions had the courage to commence work in troubled Congo *after* independence in 1960. Included in this group are: *Missionary Aviation Fellowship* (1960), *United Church of Canada* (1961), *Mennonite Central Committee* (1962), and the *Free Methodists* (1963). MAF has four planes providing transportation for much-needed personnel and supplies,

---

[1] Board of Missions, The United Methodist Church, *1969 Annual Report,* p. 53.

in a country where there are very few all-weather roads and travel in wet weather is a nightmare. The MCC has over sixty missionaries in Congo, most of them engaged in relief and rehabilitation.

Missionary Evacuation. To evacuate or not to evacuate, that has been the bugbear of missionary work in countries torn by civil strife. Missionaries do not usually run at the first sight or sound of danger. On the other hand, they are too few and too valuable to be expendable. The situation in Congo became particularly dangerous when the civil war took on antiforeign overtones and Westerners, particularly Belgians, were singled out for special attention. Some missions evacuated their personnel in the summer of 1960. Others waited until later. In some cases evacuation was complete; in others only partial. Some missionaries were brought home to Europe and America; others were simply transferred temporarily to contiguous countries. Some missions went through three and four evacuations. Others, in areas not affected by the turmoil, did not find it necessary to evacuate at all. Never at any time was more than 50 percent of the missionary body affected. The author knows of no mission that pulled out and never returned. It goes without saying that there has been a good deal of attrition along the way. Many missionaries, for various reasons, did not get back to Congo; but other missionaries have entered Congo recently for the first time. Accurate statistics are difficult to secure, but the *World Christian Handbook,* 1968, lists only 1,057 missionaries in Congo as compared with 2,100 in 1960.

Missionary Martyrs. Some have questioned the use of the term "martyr" in connection with the killings in Congo. Were the missionaries killed because they were missionaries or because they were white and therefore identified with the old colonial regime? The latter is probably the case. The fact remains that had they not been missionaries they would not have been there in the first place, nor would they have stayed long enough to expose themselves to this kind of danger. Most of the casualties occurred during the Simba uprising in 1964. In all, 209 missionaries were killed between 1960 and 1965. The Roman Catholics, most of them Belgian, sustained 179 casualties and the Protestants 30. The Unevangelized Fields Mission took the brunt of the Protestant losses with nineteen persons, including children, involved.

Missionaries Return. Undaunted, the missionaries returned to their work. Without exception they received an enthusiastic welcome, not only from the Christians but also from the local populace and government officials. The first item of business was to rebuild the premises that had been destroyed and restock the hospitals and dispensaries. This took plenty of time and not a little money. The work of rehabilitation is still going on. MAF planes played a signal role in the transporting of supplies.

Beginning with 1968 the annual reports of the various missions began to speak with cautious optimism of future prospects in Congo. The political situation is greatly improved. Economic conditions are better, but still far from good. Many schools are still closed; others are operating with hopelessly inadequate staff and equipment; but progress is being made. The worst is doubtless over, and Congo will not only survive as a political unit but will probably become one of the strongest countries in Africa.

Bible Societies. It was not until 1954 that the *British and Foreign Bible Society* was able to establish an Agency in Congo. The *American Bible Society* joined the Agency in 1956. The *Bible Society of Congo* became independent in 1969. More Bible translation has been accomplished in Congo than in any other country of Africa. There are two reasons for this. First, there are two hundred tribes, each with its own dialect. Secondly, Congo has had the highest number of missionaries of all the countries in Africa. Today the complete Bible is available in twelve languages, the New Testament in twenty, and Portions in another thirty-four, making a total of sixty-six languages.

Kimbanguist Church. History was made in 1968 when the first Separatist church in Africa was accepted into the World Council of Churches. The full name of the church is the *Church of Jesus Christ on Earth through the Prophet Simon Kimbangu.* It was not officially recognized by the colonial government until 1959, but its origin goes back to 1921, when Simon Kimbangu began to preach the gospel and heal the sick. In no time at all he had a large following, in spite of the fact that he demanded the destruction of fetishes and prohibited licentious dances, polygamy, alcohol, and other vices. His popularity attracted first the attention and then the opposition of the Belgian officials and some of the missionaries. He was accused of subversive activities and after only five months of ministry he was arrested. Without witnesses or legal counsel, he was condemned to death by a military tribunal. Some missionaries interceded on his behalf and the death sentence was commuted to life imprisonment. He died in prison October 12, 1951.

In spite of persecution and the deportation of some thirty-seven thousand members, the church continued to grow in size and strength. It opened its first schools in 1953. Since 1963 they have been subsidized by the government. It also operates its own dispensaries, cooperatives, technical training centers, orphanages, etc. With several hundred thousand members, it is said to be the largest Separatist church in Africa.

Ecumenical Relations. The Congo Continuation Committee founded in 1911 became the *Congo Protestant Council* in 1925. All but two or three of the mission societies in Congo belonged to the council. For most of its history it was composed of conservative evangelicals, so much so that when the International Missionary Council at the Ghana Assembly in 1958 decided to join the World Council of Churches, the CPC withdrew from the IMC.

At the 48th General Assembly in March, 1970, the whole structure of the CPC was drastically altered. The crusade for organic unity was spearheaded by its secretary general, Jean Bokeleale, a strong-minded man, a dedicated ecumenist, and a member of the Executive Committee of the WCC. Patriotism, paternalism, politics, national unity, neo-colonialism—all were interjected into the eight days of heated debate. Finally, at 2:30 A.M. on Sunday morning, March 8, the sixty-year-old CPC was voted out of existence and in its place was born the *Church of Christ in the Congo*. Of the voting members, thirty-two voted in favor of the motion, fourteen voted against it, and two abstained. The new church adopted a "policy of neutrality with relation to all foreign religious movements, notably the World Evangelical Fellowship and the World Council of Churches." However, a representative of the All-Africa Conference of Churches was present at the meeting and made a "lengthy report." A few days later, Dr. Eugene Blake, General Secretary of the WCC, visited Congo and talked with Mr. Bokeleale.

The conservative evangelicals, still in the majority, were not happy with either the procedures of the Assembly or the outcome of the voting. But they are now faced with a *fait accompli* and it remains to be seen how the new organization will operate. The new church is in no sense a united church, such as has been produced, after twenty or thirty years of theological debate, in other parts of the world. Its constituent members are called "communities"; but each community has continuing authority over its own structures, organizations, functions, and doctrinal basis. The *Evangelical Alliance of the Congo,* formed in 1963, has fourteen members. It is linked with the *Association of Evangelicals of Africa and Madagascar.*

Three churches in Congo are members of the World Council of Churches. Six churches hold membership in the All Africa Conference of Churches.

Rwanda

Political History. Once part of German East Africa, and for many years administered as a mandated territory by Belgium, Rwanda achieved full independence in 1962.

The People. The population is about 3.3 million, divided into two main groups, the Hutus and the Tutsis. The former outnumber the latter nine to one. After four centuries of subjugation by the Tutsi elite, the

Hutus rose up in 1959 in bloody revolt and overthrew the Tutsi absolute monarchy. Thousands of Tutsis were murdered, and 120,000 fled to Burundi and other neighboring countries. In both Rwanda and Burundi the Hutus are now in power. Kigali, the capital, is one of the smallest and most backward of all the capital cities of the world.

Religion. More than 35 percent of the people are Christians, most of them Roman Catholics. The remainder are mostly animists. Islam is still weak. The missions once had a huge investment in education, but the primary schools have all been nationalized, leaving only a few high schools in the hands of the church.

Missions. Protestant missions were rather late in getting started in this Roman Catholic dominated part of Africa. The *Anglican Church* led the way in 1926. Its mission there is known as the *Ruanda Mission,* a theologically conservative subagency of the Church Missionary Society. The foundations of a strong indigenous church were laid in the 1930's and 1940's, and the succeeding years saw unprecedented development and growth in all directions. "And more than this, into the basic framework of our institutions the Lord poured the solid concrete of Revival which has withstood, and always will withstand, the test of time because it is compounded of the Broken Rock of Christ and numberless grains of sand which are the Christians, bonded to Him in the fellowship of His Redeeming Blood."[2] *Dr. Stanley Smith,* one of the first pioneers and now eighty years of age, is still working full time on a revision of the Bible which he translated many years ago for the people of Ankole-Kigezi. In 1968 the Anglican Church in Rwanda reported a Christian community of eighty-five thousand.

The *Seventh Day Adventists* have been in Rwanda for many years, long enough to build up the largest Protestant church in the country. It has a total membership of seventy-seven thousand. Strange as it may seem, they report no schools and only two dispensaries with twenty-three beds.

The *Protestant Mission of Belgium* began work in Rwanda in 1921. Three stations were opened—in 1921, 1922, and 1924. Eighteen missionaries from four European countries are now part of the mission. They are working in cooperation with the *Evangelical Presbyterian Church of Rwanda,* which became fully autonomous in 1959. The present membership of the church is close to five thousand.

The *Danish Baptist Mission* in 1928 assumed responsibility in Rwanda and Burundi for the work left vacant by the German Neukirchen Missionary Society after World War I. Pioneer missionaries were *Johanne and Niels Peter Andersen.* The first church was formed in 1931. The *Union*

---

2 Rwanda Notes Review Number, 1962-1963, *Building for Eternity,* p. 16.

of Baptist Churches has been independent since 1960. Only four missionaries are on the Rwanda staff at present.

The *Free Methodist Church of North America* sent its first missionaries to Rwanda in 1935. Their commitments there have not been large. At present they are operating a high school, a Bible school, and a hospital. Eleven missionaries are serving with the national church, which has almost five thousand full members and another one thousand in preparation.

Another mission with work in Rwanda is a Pentecostal group of the *Swedish Free Church.* The work in Rwanda began in the 1930's as an extension of the mission in Belgian Congo and for some years continued to be administered from there. Today some twenty missionaries are working with the *Pentecostal Churches,* with about two thousand members.

The first *Plymouth Brethren* missionaries, *Mr. and Mrs. John Lacey,* transferred from Burundi to Rwanda in 1961. In 1965 three Brethren missionaries, evacuees from Congo, joined the staff in Rwanda.

Ecumenical Relations. An interdenominational organization *Protestant Literature Audio-Visual and Radio Center* (CELTAR), has been established in Kigali. The founding of an interdenominational school of theology, eagerly anticipated by many, has encountered a number of problems. In 1969 the *Church Missionary Society,* the *Belgian Protestant Mission,* and the *Seventh Day Adventists* agreed to undertake jointly an entirely new translation of the only complete Bible (Kinyarwanda), which first appeared in 1954. Most of the churches belong to the *Protestant Council of Rwanda;* cooperation within the council has had its ups and downs. Two churches, *Baptist* and *Presbyterian,* are affiliated with the All Africa Conference of Churches.

Burundi

Political History. Burundi, which once formed the southern half of a UN Trust Territory administered by Belgium, was declared a sovereign nation in 1962. Four years later its absolute king (Mwami) was deposed and the monarchy was replaced with a republic. The Chinese communists, accused of subversive activities, were expelled in 1965.

The People. The population is 3.5 million. Here, as in Rwanda, we find the same two ethnic groups, the Hutus and Tutsis. The former are of Bantu stock and make up about 85 percent of the population. Ninety-eight percent rural, and with only one city of any size (the capital), Burundi is one of the most backward countries in Africa.

Religion. The Roman Catholics are strong in Burundi, as they are in Congo and Rwanda. Protestants got a much later start and today are considerably weaker. Together they represent about 60 percent of the population. The remaining 40 percent are largely animists.

Missions. The first Protestant mission to settle permanently in Burundi after World War I was the *Danish Baptist Mission.* Its first missionaries arrived in 1928 and took up the work left by the German missionaries who were compelled to leave during World War I. The Danish mission was able to assume responsibility for only three of the five former German stations, Rubura, Musema, and Ruhinga. Of the other two, Muyebe was given over to the Free Methodists in 1935 and Kibimba to the Society of Friends a few years later. In 1960 the Baptist churches of Burundi formed the *Union of Baptist Churches of Burundi.* Membership in 1968 was about twenty-five hundred.

Pentecostal missionaries of the *Swedish Free Church* have been working here since the 1930's. Through the years they have made a large investment in Burundi. With some seventy missionaries, it is one of their largest fields. The investment has paid off; today the Christian community is reported to be as high as 160,000.

The *Rwanda Mission, CMS,* opened its first station in Burundi in 1935. Medical facilities, always in great demand in Burundi, have been taxed to the utmost by the sudden influx of 120,000 refugees from Rwanda. Three hospitals in the mission's three main centers minister to the physical and spiritual needs of thousands of patients every year. The mission has its own teacher training college at Buhiga and cooperates with a united teacher training college at Kibimba. *Warner Theological College* at Buye provides priests and other full-time workers for some four hundred congregations, large and small. The *Anglican Church of Burundi* is self-governing and self-supporting.

The *Free Methodist Church of North America* was the first American society to take up work in Burundi. The year was 1935. Since then it has continuously maintained a staff of missionaries; there are twenty-two at present. Their medical work centers around the hospital at Kibuye and two dispensaries. From the beginning the mission encouraged the Africans to support their own churches. Today the *Burundi Free Methodist Church* is a full Conference with forty-five hundred members and another one thousand under instruction. During the troubles in 1965 and 1966 many of their pastors were imprisoned and some were executed. Nevertheless the work continued to grow. The Free Methodists send their young men to the Mweya Bible Institute operated by World Gospel Mission.

The *Kansas Yearly Meeting of Friends* has had an active missionary program dating back to 1935. Its missionaries cooperate closely with the World Gospel Mission and the Free Methodists. At present the Friends have twenty-seven missionaries in Burundi and a church membership of almost three thousand.

The *World Gospel Mission* work in Burundi began in 1938. Today their thirty missionaries are concentrated in two centers of work. In 1969 their Bible school at Mweya had its highest enrollment in history. Four missions besides their own are represented in the student body. There are plans to establish a union seminary. The mission is hard pressed to maintain its medical facilities. At the *Murore Hospital* there is neither doctor nor nurse in residence. One nurse is now responsible for two dispensaries some distance apart.

Evangelism. The missions in Burundi are all theologically conservative and completely dedicated to the work of evangelism. Hospitals and schools are expected to contribute to the growth of the church. In April, 1970, church and mission leaders met to lay plans for the New Life For All campaign. Prayer cells are being organized, and revival has already broken out in two schools. A spiritual awakening sparked by an all-night prayer meeting in a Bible institute resulted in confession, restitution, and deliverance from drink.

Christian Radio. Along with evangelism goes Christian broadcasting. CORDAC, an acronym for the French name *Corporation Radio Diffusion Afrique Centrale,* is one of three missionary radio stations on the continent. CORDAC is an independent organization with an executive board of three nationals and two missionaries. Founder and director is Robert Kellum, who spent ten years with the Far East Broadcasting Company in Manila. It is located in Bujumbara, the capital, and has a radius of twelve hundred miles. It first went on the air in January, 1964. Programs are aired in half a dozen languages and more are projected in the near future. Taped programs and music are supplied by a score of studios in various nearby countries. Seventy-five percent of the schedule consists of gospel programs, 25 percent of secular programs. Now in its sixth year, CORDAC's *Institute of Radio Arts and Sciences* is training African specialists in both programming and technique.

Refugee Relief. With 120,000 refugees in the country, the churches and missions found their resources taxed beyond capacity. It was necessary for outside agencies to come to their help. Four organizations cooperated in the relief program: *World Council of Churches, Church World Service, Mennonite Central Committee,* and the *National Association of Evangelicals.* The program terminated in December, 1968.

Ecumenical Relations. These come to focus in the *Protestant Alliance of Burundi,* in which all churches participate. In addition there are several joint enterprises. Three of the missions have joined together to establish the *Gitega Literature Center.* The same three missions plan to open a *Christian College of Burundi.*

XV

East Africa

Sudan

Political History. Sudan became a sovereign state in 1956 after being ruled jointly by Egypt and Britain since 1899. A bloodless coup d'etat in 1958 introduced a period of military rule which lasted until 1964. In May, 1969, a group of radical socialist army officers seized power. Among other reforms they promised regional autonomy to the three southern provinces, which were rebelling against the central government in Khartoum because it tried to impose Arab rule and Muslim culture on the Negro population in the south.

The People. The population is about fifteen million and is divided between the Arabs in the north and the Africans in the south. The country is divided, therefore, into two separate and distinct spheres, with Arab religion and culture in the north and the simple, more primitive tribespeople in the south. The Arabs outnumber the Africans two to one.

Religion. The Arabs are Muslims; the Africans are mostly animists. A small minority of Africans are Muslim, and there may be as many as half a million Christians, mostly Roman Catholics, among them. Sudan is an Arab state and Islam is the official religion; consequently it is unrealistic to expect genuine freedom of religion, regardless of what the constitution says.

Missions. Protestant missions in the Arab north have been represented for seventy years by two great missions: the *Church Missionary Society*, which opened its first station at Omdurman in 1899; and the *United*

371

Presbyterians, who entered Sudan from Egypt in 1900. It was not until 1935 that the CMS extended its work to include the pagans in the Nuba Mountains. The first station in the south was opened in 1906 and it was ten years before the first convert was baptized. After 1916 a period of growth set in and the number of Christians increased to tens of thousands. Strong and vigorous churches sprang up in six tribes, all under the guidance of their own pastors. In 1970 the CMS had two middle schools, a hospital, a girls' school, and a high school in Omdurman, and a clergy house school in Khartoum. In spite of all the difficulties of the past five years the *Episcopal Church in the Sudan* reported a membership in 1968 of 110,000.

The *United Presbyterians,* like the Anglicans, have work in both regions of Sudan. Two autonomous churches have resulted: the *Presbyterian Church in the Sudan* (Upper Nile), with a membership of twenty thousand in 1968; and the *Evangelical Church of the Sudan,* with a much smaller membership of fifteen hundred. There is close cooperation between the Presbyterians and the Anglicans. Most of the institutions are operated jointly. The Presbyterian property in Khartoum was destroyed in the riot of 1964. *Bishop Gwynne Divinity College,* originally an Anglican institution but now ecumenical, is temporarily closed because of partial destruction of its buildings and the absence of its faculty. The *Spearhead Press* was told it could do printing only on a noncommercial basis.

The *Sudan United Mission,* with members from Australia and New Zealand, has had work in Sudan ever since the first station was opened in 1913 at Melut.

The *Sudan Interior Mission* moved into Sudan after its missionaries were expelled from Ethiopia in the 1930's and opened four stations in the south. Other stations followed; but in 1961 the government closed three of the four stations in the Dinka tribe. At the same time the schools and dispensaries were also closed. In 1964 the SIM had thirty-six missionaries at nine stations. By 1970 only five missionaries remained.

John Boyce, veteran of almost fifty years of service in Kenya, spearheaded the advance of the *Africa Inland Mission* into south Sudan in 1949. By 1963 it had opened four stations and church membership had climbed to 250.

Expulsion of Missionaries.   Opposition to missionary work was nothing new in Sudan, but it came to a head in 1962 with the passing of the Missionary Societies Act. This Act formally and legally spelled out the many restrictions placed on the movements and activities of the missionary body. The final blow came on February 17, 1964, when the Minister of the Interior announced the "repatriation of foreign missionaries from the three southern provinces." Involved in this order were 270 Roman Catholic and 45 Protestant missionaries. They were given seven days to settle their affairs, including the closing of hospitals, schools, and dispensaries, and leave the country. The reason given by the government was that the missionaries were interfering in the internal affairs of the country, which was just a euphemistic way of accusing them of aiding and abetting the cause of the African insurgents who were fighting for their civil rights in the three southern provinces.

The real reason for the expulsion was that the government was about to commit genocide in its attempt to force Arab culture on the south, and it did not wish to have any foreigners on hand to witness the slaughter. So the missionaries had to leave. Those in the north were permitted to carry on for the time being. In the fall of 1970 the government ordered the expulsion of all American missionaries who were registered with the Ministry of Education and some who were registered with other Ministries. This leaves only a handful of non-American missionaries in the north, mostly in Khartoum and Omdurman.

Churches in the South. The freedom fighters in the south are no match for the well-equipped government troops, so they have had to resort to guerrilla warfare. In all such warfare it is the civilian population that suffers most, because it is caught in the cross-fire between the opposing forces. Despite denials from Khartoum, thousands of innocent persons have been killed, and as many as 250,000 refugees have fled to nearby countries. In 1966 the All African Conference of Churches was invited by the Sudanese government to send a deputation of four to investigate conditions in the south. They were given the red carpet treatment and flown by plane to see five garrison towns; they traveled by road only twelve miles, from Wau to Bussere, and reported that they saw no destruction anywhere. The leader of the group, Sir Francis Ibiam of Nigeria, later admitted that they had not been shown the real picture. The destruction, of course, has taken place in the smaller towns and villages in the bush country; and the Christians, because they are the educated elite, have been singled out for special attack. Pastors and other church leaders have been killed and churches and schools have been burned; but still the church not only survives but continues to grow. Revival has broken out in some places and thousands of new converts have registered their decision to follow Christ. One pastor wrote:

> God has been working *mighty* miracles among us. . . . Crowds and crowds of people filling the church, and all around it; saying they want to believe or that they want to study God's Word, or want to repent of sin and come back to the Lord! There were over 500 in a class for baptism. Hundreds accepted the Lord during these past ten months. . . . In six of the large villages of the district the dance places are empty, for there has been no pagan dancing since June, as so many have left all to follow the Lord Jesus.[1]

Ecumenical Relations. The cooperating agency is the *Sudan Council of Churches.* It and two churches, *Presbyterian* and *Episcopal,* are mem-

---

[1] *World Vision Magazine,* May, 1968, p. 32.

bers of the All Africa Conference of Churches. The *Presbyterian Church in the Sudan* is an associate member of the World Council of Churches.

Ethiopia

Political History. Ethiopia is a Christian kingdom with an unbroken dynasty going back hundreds of years before Christ. The ruling hou e is said to have descended from Menelik I, the son of King Solomon and the Queen of Sheba. Haile Selassie has been emperor since 1930. He lived in exile in London while the Italians occupied his country from 1935 to 1941. Eritrea, which united with Ethiopia in a federal union in 1952, became a province in 1962. Roughly one-third of the farm land in Ethiopia is owned by the government and the royal family. Another third belongs to the Coptic Church. The remainder is divided among members of the aristocracy, communal groups, and various small holders.

The People. Some twenty-five million people live in Ethiopia. The Amharas, which include the ruling family, the aristocracy, and high officials, are of Semitic origin, as are also the Tigreans. They account for about one-third of the population. The third group, the Gallas, are Hamitic in background. They include 40 percent of the people. The remainder is made up mostly of Negroid groups. A unique group are the Falashas, known as "Black Jews," who live in the northwest province of Amhara. Amharic is the official language. Illiteracy is high, about 95 percent.

Religion. On the basis of religion, the population breaks down into three groups of approximately equal size: Christians, Muslims, and pagans. The Christians inhabit the highlands; the others are found mostly in the coastal and lowland areas.

Ethiopian Orthodox Church. This church dates back to the fourth century, when Frumentius introduced Christianity from Egypt. Within ten years of his arrival, the king and two-thirds of his people embraced the new faith. Frumentius was consecrated bishop of the Ethiopian Church by the Patriarch of Alexandria, and through the centuries the church in Ethiopia was under the ecclesiastical jurisdiction of the Coptic Church in Egypt. It was not until 1956 that the affiliation ended; the Ethiopian Church now has its own patriarchate. It is the state church and the emperor is its titular head.

For many centuries the Ethiopian Church was decadent, reactionary, and feudalistic. Many of the priests were illiterate and immorality was not uncommon. But in recent years the church has undergone renewal and today there are signs of new life. For centuries the Bible was read in ancient Ge'ez, the liturgical language of the church; but Amharic has now replaced Ge'ez, and the Bible in the language of the common people is being widely used in church and study groups. The church's three seminaries have up-dated their programs in an effort to train modern and more effective leadership for the church. The church has also launched its own Gospel Missionary Association. On the home front the association is seeking to reach the pagan population. Overseas it has established missions in Trinidad, Guyana, and New York.

Like other Eastern Orthodox churches, the Ethiopian Church does not look with favor on the evangelical form of Christianity represented by missionaries from the West. In fact, if it were not for the influence of the emperor, missionary work in Ethiopia might long since have been terminated. To this day missionary activity is restricted to Muslim and pagan areas. Any attempt to "proselytize" the Coptic Christians is likely to incur the wrath of the hierarchy and result in expulsion from the country.

Missions. Ethiopia has attracted half a dozen Lutheran missions from Norway, Sweden, Denmark, Germany, Finland, and the United States. The first on the scene was the *Swedish Lutheran Mission,* whose first two missionaries landed at Massawa in 1866. Their ultimate destination was the Galla people in western Ethiopia; but unsettled conditions made their going impossible, so they settled among the Kunamas in Eritrea. In 1911 a second Lutheran mission, known as the *True Friends of the Bible,* entered the field. In 1938 the converts of these two missions joined to form one Lutheran church. The first missionary to penetrate inland was *Carl Cederquist,* who gained access to Addis Ababa in 1904. In 1927 the Swedish Mission began its fruitful work among the western Galla. That year the *German Hermannsburg Mission* also started work in the same general area.

Following the Italian occupation three additional Lutheran missions entered Ethiopia. In 1948 the *Norwegian Lutheran Mission* began work in the south among the pagan Sidamo and Galla tribes. The *Danish Lutheran Mission* followed in 1952. The *Icelandic Mission Society* opened a field in southern Ethiopia in 1954. It works in close cooperation with the Norwegian Mission. In 1957 the *American Lutheran Mission* joined the Continental Lutherans in the evangelization of Ethiopia. The *Finnish Missionary Society* joined the Lutherans in Ethiopia in 1968. Today there are 250 Lutheran missionaries in the country. The largest of the Lutheran churches is the *Ethiopian Evangelical Church—Mekane Jesus,* with a Christian community of 120,000.

The *United Presbyterians* were the first Americans to take up the challenge of Ethiopia. In 1920 their first missionaries settled among the Wallega Galla in western Ethiopia. Three years later *Dr. Thomas A. Lambie,* one of their outstanding pioneers, opened the *George Memorial Hospital* in Addis Ababa. The Presbyterian church in Ethiopia is known as the *Bethel Evangelical Church.* It came into existence during the Italian occupation when the missionaries were expelled from the country. When the war was over the Bethel Church declared itself an autonomous body. American missionaries working with the church number eighty-five, which makes Ethiopia the largest of some thirty fields in which the United Presbyterians are ministering at present. The Bethel Evangelical Church is not large as compared with Presbyterian churches in other parts of the mission field. At present it has a membership of sixty-five hundred and a Christian community three times that number. It works in close cooperation with the (Lutheran) Mekane Jesus Church. The *Reformed Church in America,* with a dozen workers in Ethiopia, works closely with the Presbyterian Mission. The *Orthodox Presbyterians* began work in 1943.

The *Sudan Interior Mission* is by far the largest mission and has produced the largest indigenous church in Ethiopia. Its work there began in 1927, when the *Abyssinian Frontiers Mission,* an independent work founded by Dr. Lambie, merged with the SIM. During the evacuation, 1935-1941, the believers in the Galla tribe increased from sixty to eighteen thousand! Today the SIM has 225 missionaries working with the national church, known as the *Word of Life Evangelical Church.* It is the largest in the country with 182,000 baptized members and a Christian community estimated at half a million. Ninety percent of these Christians, including some of the church leaders, are illiterate, and the mission is introducing a crash program in an effort to alleviate the situation. The Word of Life Evangelical Church has its own missionary society, which has sent hundreds of missionaries to neighboring tribes—a truly indigenous work. Some 1,438 pastors and 346 evangelists minister in 1,675 organized churches and 120 unorganized churches. The church operates 360 primary schools, most of them at the village level, and 64 Bible schools. The mission is responsible for thirty-seven primary schools, nine middle schools, and two high schools. In addition, the mission maintains fifteen high-grade Bible schools and one seminary. Its medical program includes four hospitals, twenty-five clinics, two dispensaries and two leprosaria—all under the supervision of seven doctors and forty nurses.

The Anglicans have been represented in Ethiopia by the *Bible Churchmen's Missionary Society* ever since 1934. They were just getting under way when the Italian invasion brought missionary work to a halt. The BCMS today is working within the Ethiopian Orthodox Church; its missionaries have opportunities undreamed of ten short years ago. They teach Bible and other subjects in the convents and seminaries, and even preach in Trinity Cathedral. In 1969 the bimonthly magazine, *Witness to the Light,* which formerly was the responsibility of the BCMS, became an ecumenical venture with five missions sharing the burden.

The *Seventh Day Adventists* have been in Ethiopia since the war and have the finest hospital in Addis Ababa. Their church of eighty-five hundred members is one of the larger ones in the country.

The *Eastern Mennonite Board of Missions and Charities,* which took up work in Ethiopia in 1948, continues in partnership with the Meserete Kristos Church. With forty-four Mennonite workers, Ethiopia is one of the mission's larger fields of operation. The church, still quite small, is trying to establish its own identity and administer its own affairs; but this has not been easy. Certain responsibilities rest with the mission, including relationship to the *All-Africa Leprosy and Rehabilitation Training Center.* The *American Leprosy Missions* and *The Leprosy Mission* (London) are also involved in the center.

The *Baptist General Conference of America* has been in Ethiopia since 1950. Its missionary force is now thirty-six. In the fall of 1968 the mission reported a breakthrough with two hundred persons turning to Christ in a series of special meetings in Gendeberet.

Two British missions moved into Eritrea in the 1950's and later extended their work westward to include Addis Ababa. One was the *Red Sea Mission Team,* dedicated to taking the gospel to the Muslims of the Red Sea area; the other was the *Middle East General Mission* (formerly the Egypt General Mission), which transferred some of its workers to this part of the world after the Suez crisis in 1956. It likewise has most of its work concentrated in Eritrea. Another mission working in Eritrea is the *Evangelistic Faith Missions.* It has been there since 1950.

Ethiopia is one of the most mountainous countries in Africa. *Missionary Aviation Fellowship,* with two planes, one operating in the east and the other in the west, is rendering invaluable service to all groups in Ethiopia.

Several missions have taken up work in Ethiopia during the 1960's. The first and largest of these is the *Baptist Bible Fellowship,* which now has thirty missionaries committed to that field. The *Southern Baptists* entered in 1967 and are already engaged in three centers.

Separatist Churches. Mention has been made of the revival in the Sudan Interior Mission district during the Italian occupation. When the mission returned, some of the churches refused to acknowledge its authority and in 1955 went off on their own. Two independent bodies were formed. The larger of the two is the *Kambatta Evangelical Church,* with twenty-five thousand adherents.

Radio Voice of the Gospel. RVOG is sponsored by the *Lutheran World Federation* and is affiliated with the Coordinating Committee for Christian Broadcasting, which represents the All Africa Conference of Churches, the East Asia Christian Conference, and the Near East Council of Churches. Its facilities include two 100,000-watt shortwave transmitters, one 1,000-watt mediumwave transmitter, and a system of antennas to beam the programs to twenty countries in sixteen languages. Recording studios are located in more than a dozen countries. It first went on the air in February, 1962.

Bible Societies. For many years the work was carried on through the Swedish Mission in Asmara under the Egyptian Agency. In 1915 a depot was set up in Addis Ababa. Ethiopia remained the responsibility of the *British and Foreign Bible Society* until it became a Joint Agency with the *American Bible Society* in 1960. Since 1967 the secretary of the Bible Society has been a national. The complete Bible is available in three languages, the New Testament also in three languages, and Portions in ten languages. The advisory council now includes members from Protestant, Orthodox, and Catholic churches. The Amharic Bible, first completed in 1840, was recently revised; as a result sales have increased greatly. Paperback editions of the Amharic New Testament and *Today's English Version* have been very popular.

Ecumenical Relations. From the beginning there has been an unusual degree of harmony and cooperation among the various missions and churches in Ethiopia. The only ecumenical organization is the *Inter-Mission Council,* to which all the groups belong. It is not affiliated with any world organization. Only one church is affiliated with any outside organization. The *Ethiopian Orthodox Church* holds membership in both the World Council of Churches and the All Africa Conference of Churches.

Somalia

Political History. At one time on the horn of Africa there were three Somalilands, British, French, and Italian. French Somaliland is still a French colony. The other two received their independence in 1960 and on July 1 merged to form one sovereign state, Somalia.

The People. No census has been taken for many years, hence the estimate of 2.7 million may be wide of the mark. The Somalis are a Hamitic people. There are four major tribal groups. The only other sizable ethnic group are the Arabs, who number thirty-five thousand. The foreign population includes some two thousand Italians and one thousand Indians and Pakistanis. There are three official languages, Arabic, English, and Italian. English is the medium of instruction in most schools after the fourth grade. Illiteracy is very high—estimated at 95 percent.

Religion. When the United Nations established its trusteeship in 1950 there was the guarantee of religious liberty. When in June, 1963, the government amended the constitution, it affirmed the right of every person to freely profess his own religion; at the same time it declared it to be illegal to spread or propagandize any religion other than the True Religion of Islam.

Missions. The *Eastern Mennonite Board of Missions and Charities* entered this Muslim land in 1953. Under existing conditions it is impossible to engage in direct evangelism; so the mission must be content with a nonverbal approach expressed through schools and hospitals. In 1968 the mission phased out its elementary schools in two locations and is now concentrating on intermediate schools (grades 5-7) instead. It also conducts adult eduction classes in night schools in three cities, including the capital. Medical work includes a clinic at Mahaddei and a hospital at Jamama. A bookstore in the capital is doing a thriving business. A Mennonite missionary, Merlin Grove, was stabbed to death by a Muslim fanatic in 1962. The assassin was later arrested and given life in prison. The government offered its apologies, and the popular sympathy seemed to be with the missionaries. In each of the half dozen centers where the mission maintains work there is a small nucleus of believers; but their lot is a hard one. It is not yet possible to organize these believers into a church.

The *Sudan Interior Mission* received permission to enter Somalia in 1954. For a time the mission operated several schools, but when the government in 1963 insisted that the Koran be taught in place of the Bible, the mission closed the schools. It found, however, that many of the best students continued to come to Bible classes in the homes of the missionaries; and there was greater freedom and higher interest than when the schools were in operation. A July, 1965, report says: "From Mogadishu comes word that each week finds new ones turning to Christ." That same year came another report: "The work, rather than folding up because of certain restrictions, is becoming more than we can handle." Night schools in English are very popular, especially among schoolteachers and government officials. In 1965 there were 350 people attending the night school and typing classes in the capital. Often fruitful contacts are established in this way. In 1966 the mission announced the translation of the complete New Testament into the Somali language. Work on the Old Testament will soon be completed. As yet no national church has been organized. There is, however, the *Somali Believers Fellowship,* made up of four groups with a membership that varies from sixty to seventy-five. Five young men have gone to Bible school in other countries to prepare for the evangelization of their own country. The mission operates two hospitals and three clinics under the supervision of two doctors and ten nurses. That the SIM means business in Somalia is seen in the fact that it has thirty missionaries there at present.

Another Christian organization, which wishes to remain anonymous, sent two workers to Somalia in 1969. In the country they are known as "Christians in Service Overseas."

To date practically all the converts in Somalia have been young men. Christian marriage for these men is a serious problem.

Kenya

Political History. Kenya became a British colony in 1905. The terrorist Mau Mau movement, which ravaged the country from 1952 to 1959, was a bloody prelude to independence, which came on December 12, 1963. Jomo Kenyatta, erstwhile leader of the Mau Mau, is now president of the republic. He has given strong and able leadership to one of the most stable governments in Africa. Tribal tensions run deep and were responsible for the assassination of Cabinet Minister, Tom Mboya, in July, 1969. It was feared at that time that Kenya might be plunged into a blood bath; but the situation seems to have been stabilized.

The People. The population of Kenya is about eleven million, of which 250,000 are non-Africans: Indians, Arabs, and Europeans. The principal ethnic groups are the Kikuyu, Luo, Baluhya, Kamba, Kisii, and Meru. The Kikuyu are a strong, aggressive, virile people; they dominate politics and control the government through the Kenya African National Union. Kenyatta is a Kikuyu; and in 1969, just prior to important elections, the only opposition party, Kenya People's Union, was banned.

Religion. About 25 percent of Kenya is Christian, divided among Catholics (1,230,000), Protestants (800,000), Separatists (600,000), and Orthodox (100,000). The Arabs and some of the Africans are Muslim. The Indians, the largest non-African group, are Hindu. The constitution guarantees religious liberty and the government has lived up to its commitment in this regard. Many missionaries feared that the coming of independence would mean the end of their work; but President Kenyatta has on more than one public occasion paid tribute to the work of missions and invited the missionaries to remain and help build a new Kenya. Relations between church and state are good, if not cordial. The decision of the government in 1965 to take over all church and mission schools caused a flurry of excitement in Christian circles; but the *Christian Churches Educational Association* worked hard to prepare the churches for this inevitable change.

Missions. The first Protestant mission to take up work in East Africa was the *Church Missionary Society.* Its pioneer was a German, *John Ludwig Krapf,* who arrived in Mombasa in 1844. Two months later his wife and only child died. Himself sick to death with fever, Krapf refused to give up. Instead, he called for more recruits from London. Two years later his request was granted in the arrival of *John Rebmann.* Together they explored the country and opened stations as they went. Ill health forced Krapf to return home in 1853, but Rebmann remained and reduced three tribal languages to writing. Stations were opened from Mombasa to

Nairobi, which was reached in 1906. Between 1900 and 1930 the CMS opened eight more stations in the Central Province. Today the Anglicans are by far the largest church in Kenya. The area is divided into five dioceses, in one of which the *Bible Churchmen's Missionary Society* is working. Over one hundred fifty missionaries are assigned to twenty-five major institutions, mostly educational. Included are two hospitals and several theological schools.

In 1900 the *Church of Scotland* took over a work which had been begun some ten years earlier by the East Africa Scottish Mission. Through the years the mission has maintained educational and medical work, along with evangelism and church planting. The African church, known as the *Presbyterian Church of East Africa,* is an interracial church including Africans, Europeans, and Asians. Communicant members number twenty-six thousand. Missionaries are still needed, not only in church work but also in three large hospitals, two teacher training colleges, two other schools, and *St. Paul's United Theological College* in Limuru.

The largest faith mission in east Africa is the *Africa Inland Mission* which now has six hundred missionaries in six African countries. The first field to be opened in 1895 was Kenya. *Peter Cameron Scott,* founder of the mission, led the way with a party of seven missionaries. The first center was Mombasa on the coast, where the combination of heat and humidity was too much for the newcomers. Peter Scott lived only fourteen months. One by one the other members of the little group sickened and died, until only one survivor was left. Eventually he had to return home. A second attempt, under the leadership of *Dr. Charles E. Hurlburt,* was made a few years later, this time with success. The first inland station was opened at Nzawi, in the Akamba country. In 1907 *Lee H. Downing,* with a party of twenty-three new workers, arrived in Mombasa. With such large reinforcements, the AIM was able to establish work among two additional tribes, the Masai and the Tugen.

The *Africa Inland Church,* independent since 1943, is organized along Congregational lines and bears some resemblance to Presbyterianism. At the insistence of the church leaders, missionaries have a place on the councils of the church. In 1970 the church requested complete integration of church and mission, but this was only partly granted. The AIC has a baptized membership of over one hundred fifty thousand. Some six hundred primary schools and about seventy high schools are under government control but sponsored by the church and mission. Medical work includes three hospitals and twelve dispensaries. Theological education includes six Bible schools and *Scott Theological College.* The *Rift Valley Academy* for missionaries' children is one of the largest and best in the whole of east Africa. Its choir has performed for President Kenyatta and over the government radio and television networks. Under the leadership of Timothy Kimau, radio pastor of the AIC, over one hundred programs are aired each month, free of charge, over the powerful government station, *The Voice of Kenya*. Recently television programs have been added to the schedule.

American Friends have been in Kenya since 1902. It is the largest of their five fields. The program centers around the main station of Kaimosi near Lake Victoria. The *East Africa Yearly Meeting* got its independence in 1964. Under African leadership the work continues to expand. Seventeen Monthly Meetings and three Quarterly Meetings were officially opened in 1968-69. Total membership is thirty-one thousand. A dozen or more missionaries continue to cooperate with the Yearly Meeting, most of them in various institutions. These include three high schools, a Bible institute, a farmers training center, and an international center in Nairobi. A hospital at Kaimosi and a health center at Lugulu, both with satellite dispensaries, are part of their medical program.

Of the thirty-six mission fields of the *Church of God* (Anderson, Indiana), only one is located in Africa, and that one is in Kenya. The first station, Kima, was opened in 1919 when that part of Kenya was covered with tropical jungles. Fifty years later this area is densely populated with Africans whose life-style has been completely changed, in large part by the gospel. A flourishing indigenous church, with 275 congregations and a membership of twenty thousand, is completely self-supporting. Institutional work includes four secondary schools and two hospitals.

The *World Gospel Mission* has been in Kenya for thirty-one years and has developed the *Africa Gospel Church* of three thousand baptized members. A staff of thirty-five missionaries is engaged in a variety of ways. Two bookshops are maintained at Nakuru and Kitale. The publications department produces Sunday school and vacation Bible school materials for churches and missions in all parts of east Africa. The only secondary school, with 180 students, now has an African headmaster. The seventy-two bed hospital at Tenwek continues to average twice as many patients as beds. Three clinics took care of twelve thousand outpatients last year. In 1969 the *Kenya Highland Bible College* added the third year of study in its four-year plan. Some sixty students are enrolled. The mission now has its own recording studio to produce radio programs which are aired over the Voice of Kenya, Radio Cordac in Burundi, and the Radio Voice of the Gospel in Addis Ababa.

The *Seventh Day Adventist* work in Kenya is divided into three fields with a total church membership of fifty-four thousand.

Kenya is by far the largest of the fifteen mission fields of the *Pentecostal Assemblies of Canada*. The work there dates back to 1921. Almost one-third of all its overseas missionaries are concentrated in this one country. Known as the *Pentecostal Assemblies of God,* the national church now has a membership of one hundred thousand, almost two-thirds of all the overseas church members of the mission. Two other Pentecostal missions are in Kenya: *Elim Missionary Assemblies* and *International Pentecostal Assemblies.* Both missions have a rather small work even though they have been there for forty years. Of some forty missions in Kenya only one is Baptist. The *Southern Baptists* have had work in West Africa for over a hundred years, but only recently have they moved into east Africa. Their work in Kenya began in 1956; today they have a missionary staff of seventy-seven in seven centers. They have not been as successful in Kenya as elsewhere. Their ninety-eight churches have 104 national pastors but only forty-two hundred members; and only nineteen of the churches are self-supporting.

Two Presbyterian missions from the USA are in Kenya: *Independent Board for Presbyterian Missions* (1942) and *World Presbyterian Missions* (1961).

International Missions entered Kenya in 1956 and has thirteen missionaries working among the Hindu population. *Missionary Aviation Fellowship,* in Kenya since 1959, has two planes working closely with the Africa Inland Mission and occasionally with other groups.

Two Mennonite groups have a heavy commitment in Kenya: *Mennonite Central Committee* (1962) and the *Eastern Mennonite Board of Missions and Charities* (1964). Three other newcomers are the *United Methodist Church* (1962), the *United Church of Canada* (1963), and the *Anglican Church of Canada* (1965). The latest arrival is the *World Mission Prayer League* (1968).

In recent years several supporting missions have taken up work in Kenya: *Navigators, Bible Club Movement, Child Evangelism Fellowship, Christian Service Corps,* and others. In the fall of 1970 a thirty-acre campsite outside Nairobi was purchased by *Word of Life.* It is part of a plan to develop Christian youth camps in one hundred countries in ten years.

Bible Societies. For its size Kenya is rather well-off when it comes to Bible translation. The complete Bible has been published in nine languages; the New Testament in six, and Portions in six more. Paperback editions of the New Testament in Swahili, Kikuyu, and Luo are selling well. *Today's English Version* and the RSV are also in great demand. The Joint Agency with Tanzania was dissolved in 1970 and now Kenya has its own independent Bible Society.

Church Union. Church union is not confined to Kenya but includes Tanzania as well. Five churches have representatives on the Negotiating Committee, which has held six meetings. The churches are: *Anglican Church of the Province of East Africa, Evangelical Lutheran Church of Tanzania, Methodist Church in Kenya, Moravian Province in Tanzania, Presbyterian Church of East Africa.*

Ecumenical Relations. There has always been a good deal of cooperation among churches and missions within Kenya and with groups in

Tanzania and Uganda. There are two ecumenical bodies in Kenya, the *National Christian Council* and the *Evangelical Fellowship of East Africa.* Neither of them belongs to any outside organization. Five of the churches in Kenya belong to the All Africa Conference of Churches. Three east Africa churches with headquarters in Kenya are members of the World Council of Churches: *Church of the Province of East Africa, Methodist Church in Kenya,* and *Presbyterian Church of East Africa.* The AACC *Broadcast Training Center* is located in Nairobi. Financial and other aid is given to the Training Center by RAVEMCCO, recently changed to Inter-media.

Separatist Movement. This movement has been very strong in Kenya, especially in recent years. The first major secession took place in 1957 and involved some seventy-five thousand members of the Church of Christ in Africa. An even larger break came when ninety-three thousand left the Roman Catholic Church in 1963. After independence in 1963 the movement began to snowball; three years later there were 160 dissident groups with a total of six hundred thousand adherents. In the last couple of years, however, relations between these independent groups and the historic denominations have begun to improve. By 1967 seven groups had joined the National Christian Council.

Uganda

Political History. Uganda is one place in the world where the cross preceded the flag. Protestant missionaries entered this part of Africa in 1877, whereas the Imperial British East Africa Company did not extend its influence to Uganda until 1890. From 1894 to 1962 Uganda was a protectorate of Great Britain. In 1967 it became a republic and all the traditional kingdoms, including Buganda, were abolished. Today the country is divided into eighteen administrative districts which are tightly controlled by the central government. A military coup took place in January, 1971.

The People. The population of Uganda is estimated to be 9.8 million. The Africans, who form 98 percent, are divided into four racial groups: Bantu, Nilotic, Nilo-Hamitic, and Sudanic. Of the four, the Bantu are the most numerous and include the powerful Baganda, with more than one million members. English is the lingua franca of Uganda; Luganda and Swahili are widely used in certain parts of the country. Illiteracy, at 75 percent, is not high for Africa.

Religion. Christianity has made great gains in Uganda and today claims over 50 percent of the population. The Roman Catholics are more numerous than the Protestants—60 percent as against 40 percent. Islam is on the increase and making inroads rapidly. The Africans who have not embraced either Christianity or Islam are animists; but their number is decreasing.

Missions. Both Roman Catholic and Protestant missions have done exceedingly well in Uganda, with the result that Christianity is now the dominant religion of the country. Men and women, chiefs and peasants, rich and poor are all found within the church. There is no phase of national life which has not been influenced by Christianity. On the Protestant side this has resulted mainly from the work of the *Church Missionary Society,* whose missionaries left a record of sacrifice and success seldom equaled and never surpassed.

In studying the situation in Uganda one is immediately struck by the lack of proliferation of mission boards. Until the 1960's, when eight American boards entered the country, the field was left pretty much to the oldest and largest society, the CMS, which accounts for 98 percent of the Protestants. The first party of CMS missionaries sailed for Uganda in 1876 under the leadership of *Alexander Mackay,* a highly-educated and gifted young Scottish engineer. Death took a heavy toll of that first party and after two years Mackay was the sole survivor. For twelve years he carried on alone in the face of overwhelming obstacles. More than once he was urged to return home, but each time he resolutely refused to abandon his post. Two other missionaries of outstanding stature in those days were *Pilkington* and *Hannington.*

The greatest gains were made under *Bishop Alfred R. Tucker* between 1890 and 1911. Of rugged physique, unflinching courage, sound judgment, and organizational ability, Tucker made an ideal bishop. When he arrived his flock numbered only two hundred; before he died church membership had climbed to sixty-five thousand. Since then there has been steady growth in all departments of the work. In 1929 the CMS was joined by the *Bible Churchmen's Missionary Society,* a conservative Anglican mission formed in 1922. Through the years it has maintained a small but important work among the Karamopong tribe north of the CMS area. At present there are four centers in the Diocese of Soroti. The response in these parts has not been great. The tribal spirit is still very strong, and pagan marriage customs militate against the baptismal vows taken by Christian young people.

The *Anglican Church of Uganda* became an independent Province in 1961. The highlight of the year 1966 was the election of the *Most Reverend Erica Sabiti,* the first African to become the Primate of the Anglican Church. One of the first projects of the African Primate was to inaugurate the Church of Uganda's Ten Year Plan, designed to enable the church to make a more effective contribution to both church and nation. Membership in the church is well over the 200,000 mark; the Christian community numbers 1,600,000. The CMS has 110 missionaries and the BCMS about a dozen missionaries serving in Uganda. Institutional work includes twenty-eight medical, educational, theological, and technical institutions.

The first station opened in Uganda by the *Africa Inland Mission* was Usambiro, where the famous Alexander Mackay began his missionary career many years before. After all five of its missionaries died, the CMS gave up the station and for sixty-three years it lay in ruins until the British branch of AIM took over in 1918. Through the years the AIM in Uganda has worked closely with the Anglicans, and their national church, with some four hundred congregations, forms the West Nile Diocese of the Church of Uganda, which has been independent for many years. Education at the lower levels is in the hands of the government. The church sponsors a teacher training school and a college. Other institutions include a Bible school, two hospitals, and two clinics.

The *Pentecostal Assemblies of Canada* entered Uganda in 1940 and has maintained a growing work to the present. The Uganda work began as a branch of the Kenya assemblies; but in 1966 those in Uganda were organized separately and ever since they have been autonomous. From the beginning they have been taught to be self-supporting. Some two hundred fifty pastors are responsible for the care of two hundred fifty churches with a membership of eight thousand. There is no medical or educational work. The one Bible school has one hundred students enrolled.

The *Seventh Day Adventists* operate four dispensaries in Uganda and report a church membership of about seven thousand.

The *Southern Baptists* entered in 1962 and their twenty-two missionaries are found in five centers, including Kampala, the capital. Their only educational work is a Bible school at Mbale. Their thirty-six churches are still small with a total membership of nineteen hundred. Twenty-eight of them are self-supporting.

The *Conservative Baptists* joined the missionary ranks in Uganda in 1963. Twelve missionaries are hard at work trying to develop an indigenous church. Already there are twenty organized churches and another twenty preaching points serving a Christian community of three thousand. As yet there is no medical or educational work.

Bible Societies. For many years Kenya, Uganda, and Tanzania were linked together under the *East African Bible Society*. More recently each area has been served by its own secretary. In 1968 the *National Bible Society of Uganda* was inaugurated. In June, 1969, two Scripture Distribution Training Conferences were held, and partly as a result, distribution increased by almost 200 percent in one year. The complete Bible is available in four languages, the New Testament in one, and Portions in five.

Ecumenical Relations. The Anglicans and the Catholics have maintained cordial relations for some time. In 1964 the two churches established the *Uganda Joint Christian Council.* The council enables both churches to take united action in several important spheres, especially in dealing with the government. The two churches have recently built a joint chapel in connection with the huge eight-hundred-bed *Mulago Hospital.* The Christian Council now includes representatives of all the Christian confessions. There are no church union talks in progress at this time. The *Evangelical Fellowship of Uganda,* formed in 1967, includes three church and mission groups. It has affiliations with the *Association of Evangelicals of Africa and Madagascar.* The *Church of Uganda, Rwanda and Burundi* is a member of both the World Council of Churches and the All Africa Conference of Churches.

Tanzania

Political History. Throughout the centuries the area known as Tanganyika was ruled by Arabs, Portuguese, Germans, and British. It achieved full independence in 1961. In April, 1964, Tanganyika united with Zanzibar to form the Republic of Tanzania. The Arusha Declaration of 1967 called for a form of socialism coupled with the concept of self-reliance. Tanzania has strong ties with Communist China, and a large number of Chinese technicians are helping the government to build a railroad.

The People. The population is twelve million. About 99 percent are Africans; they belong to 120 tribes, most of them of Bantu origin. Non-Africans include ninety thousand Indo-Pakistanis, twenty-six thousand Arabs, and twenty thousand Europeans. Race relations are not all that they might be, especially in Zanzibar. Swahili is the most widely spoken language; along with English, it is an official language.

Religion. The population is divided almost equally among animists, Muslims, and Christians. Islam was introduced by the Arab traders in the eighth century. Christianity arrived with the Portuguese in the sixteenth century, but their attempts at Christianization were not very successful. Protestant Christianity appeared much later.

Anglican Missions. There are no fewer than five Anglican societies working in various parts of Tanzania. The earliest of all societies entered in 1860. It was the *Universities' Mission to Central Africa,* one of four missionary organizations which owed their origin to the inspiration of David Livingstone. This mission was the outcome of Livingstone's visit to Oxford and Cambridge in 1857. His closing remarks at Cambridge were simple and direct:

I beg to direct your attention to Africa. I know that in a few years I shall be cut off in that country, which is now open; do not let it shut again. I go back to Africa to try and make an open path for commerce and Christianity; do you carry out the work which I have begun. I leave it with you.[2]

The UMCA is an independent organization of High Churchmen within the Church of England. It has established five dioceses in east Africa, three of them in Tanzania. In 1965 the UMCA merged with another High Church mission, the Society for the Propagation of the Gospel, to form the *United Society for the Propagation of the Gospel.*

After holding the fort alone for sixteen years the UMCA was joined by the *Church Missionary Society,* which established work on the south shore of Lake Victoria. For twenty years the CMS had only two stations in Tanganyika, but a period of expansion began in 1900 and nine additional stations were opened by 1930. About this time the *CMS of Australia* sent its first missionary to Central Tanzania, *Bishop George A. Chambers.* By 1967 one diocese had grown into four with hundreds of African clergy. In the meantime two other Anglican missions joined the work in Tanzania, the *Bible Churchmen's Missionary Society* and the *CMS of New Zealand.* The Anglican work in the Province of East Africa (Kenya and Tanzania) has grown so rapidly in the last few years that in 1970 the Province was divided in two. At that time the 222 Anglican missionaries were equally divided between Kenya and Tanzania. In 1968 in the eight dioceses of Tanzania there were over seventeen hundred churches with a Christian community of over three hundred thousand.

Lutheran Missions. The extension of German colonial power into this part of Africa paved the way for the advent of German missions. The first was the *Berlin Mission,* which started work in the coastal area in 1886 were Dar es Salaam now stands. Its plan was to minister to both Germans and Africans. Other societies from Leipzig and Bethel opened work in the north and northeastern parts in 1892 and 1893. Later on, when reinforcements arrived, the work was extended to the west and south. Following World War I, when German East Africa was broken up, the Lutheran churches in America were asked to come to the aid of the "orphaned" missions in Tanzania. The *Augustana Lutheran Church of America* was one of the missions that responded. It began work in the central province in 1924.

German missionaries were permitted to return to east Africa, but during World War II a second exodus took place; and again Lutheran churches in America and Scandinavia had to come to the rescue. The *Church of Sweden Mission* and the *Swedish Evangelical Mission* shared responsibility for the work in the west and south in 1942.

On the American side, the *Department of World Missions Cooperation of the National Lutheran Council, USA* assumed responsibility for

---

[2] *The Unfinished Task—Expanding Frontiers,* UMCA, p. 12.

three German missions in Tanzania. During the 1950's the *Finnish Mission-ary Society* and the *Danish Mission* worked in southern Tanzania in conjunction with the *Swedish Evangelical Mission.* During this period the *Norwegian Mission* took over the work of the *Swedish Evangelical Mission* begun in 1939 in the north-central part of the country. The seven Luther-an groups now in Tanzania are unified through the Federation of Lutheran Churches in Tanganyika, which dates back to 1937. The *Evangelical Lutheran Church in Tanzania* has been fully independent since 1961. Today it has a baptized membership of 470,000.

Other Societies. In 1860 the *London Missionary Society,* after ex-periencing much difficulty in establishing a work in Northern Rhodesia, launched an enterprise in the region of Lake Tanganyika. The LMS remained there for almost forty years before turning the work over to the *German Moravians.* When the Germans had to retire from the field during World War I, this mission was taken over temporarily by the *United Free Church of Scotland.* In 1926 it was returned to the Moravian Mission. During the 1930's the field was under the administration of the *Herrnhut Mission Board.* When World War II broke out, German missionaries were repatriated by government action, and the work was turned over to the *British Board of the Moravian Mission.* The Moravian work has been located in the southern and western parts of the country. The national church has been independent for more than twenty years, during which time it has made commendable progress in all departments. Since 1964 it has been known as the *Moravian Church in Southern Tanzania.* In 1968 it had four hundred congregations and a Christian community of seventy-two thousand. Some forty missionaries continue to serve with this church.

The *Africa Inland Mission,* with the largest number of missionaries in all of east Africa, expanded its Kenya work into Tanzania in 1910. At one time the mission operated three hundred schools with twelve thousand pupils, but these have passed into government hands and this part of the program has been phased out. The mission continues to operate one hospital and sixteen dispensaries. The church, independent since 1964, is the *Africa Inland Church.* It has twenty thousand members and is served by fifty-four pastors and 160 evangelists. The churches are all self-supporting. Two Bible schools furnish workers for the national church.

The *Pentecostal Assemblies of Canada,* after almost fifty years of work, report a church of five thousand members under the care of sixty-seven pastors and twelve evangelists. Eight missionaries serve with the church. The *Pentecostal Churches of Tanzania,* the work of the *Swedish Free Mission,* in 1968 reported a membership of almost nine thousand. The *Seventh Day Adventist Church* has a membership approaching the twenty-thousand mark.

The *Assemblies of God* sent workers into Tanganyika from Nyasaland in 1953 in response to a call from Pentecostal congregations which owed their existence to the ministry of an independent missionary, *Paul K. Derr,* in the 1930's. With a nucleus of fifteen national workers and about three hundred Pentecostal believers, *Wesley R. Hurst* began the task of organizing and consolidating the existing churches on an indigenous basis. Two Bible schools were established. Largely as a result of this the national workers today outnumber the missionaries almost five to one. Some fifty churches have been developed, but the membership is not large—an average of twenty members per church.

The *Eastern Mennonite Board of Missions and Charities* has been working in this part of the world since 1934. The *Tanzania Mennonite Church* has been independent for some time, but it still receives missionaries and money from the missions. Church growth in 1969 was reported as leveling off somewhat. The TMC schools, with an enrolment of seven thousand, provide one source of new members; but in some areas there is a large influx of adults. During the last decade the TMC has excelled in education, medicine, and scholarship. A half-million-dollar grant from the German Evangelical Central Agency enabled the TMC to completely rebuild and modernize the *Shirati Hospital.* The *Leprosy Control Center,* with assistance from the American Leprosy Missions, has been moved to the hospital.

The *Mennonite Central Committee* initiated work in Tanzania in 1962. Ten of its missionaries are serving in church-related schools. The other six are assigned to medical institutions, also church-related.

The only Baptist work in Tanzania is that of the *Southern Baptists,* who entered in 1956. Already they have fifty missionaries committed to this one field. They are serving in seven centers, engaged in medical, educational, and publication work. Institutions include a Bible school, seminary, hospital, bookstore, and community center. More than half the 144 churches are self-supporting. Unusual as it may seem, the church has more pastors than congregations.

Relief Work. There are over thirty thousand refugees in Tanzania from Mozambique, Rwanda, Congo, and Sudan. The local churches tried to provide sustenance for these destitute, displaced persons; but the job was too big for them. A good deal of help has come from outside groups such as the *Church World Service* and the *Lutheran World Federation.* In their deep despair, many of these unfortunate persons have been led to Christ through the kindness of His people.

Bible Societies. Tanzania is a branch of the *Bible Society of East Africa* located in Nairobi. With the use of Bible vans, Scripture distribution has increased significantly in recent years. Tanzania has done quite well in the matter of translation. The complete Bible is available in three languages, the New Testament in fifteen languages, and Portions in eleven more.

Ecumenical Relations. No church union talks are going on at present. There are two ecumenical groups: the *Christian Council of Tanzania,* which includes most of the missions and churches in the country; and the *Evangelical Fellowship of East Africa,* to which two Tanzanian missions belong. Three of the larger churches are members of the All Africa Conference of Churches. Two of them belong to the World Council of Churches.

XVI

South Africa

Angola

Political History. Except for a short period in the 1640's Angola has been under Portuguese rule for more than four hundred sixty years. The European rulers have no intention of ever giving home rule, much less independence, to Angola. By a constitutional amendment in 1951 the colony became an overseas province of Portugal and is represented in the 130-man National Assembly by seven delegates. All Angolans who accept Portuguese culture become citizens of Portugal. The others—and they are the vast majority—do not count.

The People. The population is estimated at 5.4 million, which includes 400,000 political exiles who have taken refuge in neighboring Congo. The Angolans are almost entirely of Bantu stock and are divided into four main tribal groups. Europeans, mostly Portuguese, number 275,000. After 460 years of colonial rule, the illiteracy rate among the Africans is about 88 percent.

Religion. Catholic priests accompanied the earliest Portuguese settlers, and ever since that time Catholic missions have been accorded preferential treatment. They have been subsidized and the priests have the status of state functionaries. All educational activities in Angola until 1908 were under the control of the church. Today there are an estimated two million Roman Catholics. Until the civil war erupted in 1961 the government looked with favor on Protestant missions. Indeed, there was more religious liberty in Angola than in Portugal. The vast majority of the tribespeople remain animists. Islam has not yet penetrated far enough south to be of any importance.

Missions. The *Baptist Missionary Society* was the first Protestant group in Angola, where they arrived in 1878. Their work was located in the extreme northern region of the country and through the years they established over 250 churches. This was one of the hardest hit areas of the civil war and the first to be evacuated. All the Baptist missionaries were out by 1966, and many of the Christians had fled across the border into Congo.

The *American Congregationalists* opened their mission in Angola in 1880. After twenty-five years they had only three hundred Christians. After 1914 growth became more rapid. One of their bigger centers is Dondi, where they have *Emmanuel Seminary,* the *Dondi Press,* and the *Publication Center.* Medical work includes five hospitals, all operating at present without resident doctors. The *Church Council of Central Angola* coordinates the work of eight churches which have grown up around mission stations of the United Church Board for World Ministries and the Board of Overseas Missions of the United Church of Canada. These churches have sixty thousand communicant members served by about eighty pastors. Only three UCBWM missionaries remain in the country.

The *American Methodists* entered Africa with a bang. In 1885 some forty-five missionaries (including women and children) under the leadership of the newly elected missionary bishop, William Taylor, set out to open six stations in Africa, five of them in Angola. Present day Methodist work is divided into two main regions: Luande and Malange. Since 1961 three districts have been closed; but the loss has been offset by new churches which have sprung up in other areas. Today the Methodist Church has thirty-eight thousand full and preparatory members served by sixty-one ordained men and sixty-eight supply pastors. Five American missionaries were arrested in 1961. During the following five years the number of Methodist missionaries dropped from forty-five to four.

In 1889 *Christian Missions in Many Lands* entered Angola. Their outstanding missionary was *Frederick Stanley Arnot,* who gave a lifetime of service to the cause of Christ in Africa. At one point the mission had a larger foreign staff than any other group in Angola. Their field is in the northeast section of the country where today there are hundreds of assemblies and preaching places. By 1969 their numbers were reduced to four American and seven British missionaries.

Two Canadian societies have had work in Angola. The older of these is the *United Church of Canada* which, since its inception in 1925, continued the work begun by the Canadian Presbyterians. In November, 1967, the Home Board made plans for the evacuation of the one missionary couple and twelve single ladies in Angola at that time.

The other Canadian mission, the *Canadian Baptists,* came much later, in 1957. It quickly augmented its staff until three years later it had twenty-four missionaries in Angola—all in the northwest corner. In the early years of the civil war the Canadian Baptists, along with their English brethren, had to evacuate. Many of them moved into Congo, where they are carrying on relief work among the refugees. They do not intend to establish permanent work there; they hope to return to the territory of the Angola Evangelical Mission, for which they assumed responsibility in 1954. In the meantime they and their refugee Christians are working in partnership with three groups in the lower Congo: The American Baptists, the English Baptists, and the Swedish Covenant Mission.

The *South Africa General Mission* (now known as the Africa Evangelical Fellowship) began work in Angola in Muie on the Kutsi River when *A. W. Bailey* arrived in 1914. The work is divided into two regions: southern and southwestern. As late as 1964 the mission reported continued growth, especially in evangelism. The number of evangelists doubled in one year to a total of fifty-six. The Bible institute at Catota had an enrolment of 180. But finally pressure was exerted. The missionaries had to leave Luonze in 1963 and Muie in 1967. By 1969 only two of their main stations in the south western region had resident missionaries. In the southern region there were missionaries only in Catota. The primary school and hospital were still open, but the Bible school was closed, awaiting the return of missionaries on furlough.

The Civil War. With a score of colonies getting their independence in 1960 it was only natural that the people of Angola should want it, too. Portugal refused even to discuss the matter. Civil war broke out in 1961 and has continued ever since. Stern repressive measures by the government and the military caused some 400,000 refugees to flee across the northern border into Congo; among them were many Christians and church leaders. Naturally the Protestant missionaries, most of them from North America, were in favor of self-determination for the people of Angola. This made them and the Christian church suspect in the eyes of the colonial administrators and there was a crackdown. The government got rid of them by the simple expediency of not granting visas to new or returning missionaries. Their number dropped from 260 in 1961 to below 70 by 1966. The missionaries who remained, some without furlough for ten years, found government restrictions so repressive that their work became virtually impossible. In the meantime, their very presence in Angola became a source of embarrassment, to say nothing of danger, to the church and its leaders. In November, 1967, the home boards of the two United Churches (Canada and the USA) decided to withdraw all remaining personnel at one time to dramatize their opposition to the reactionary colonial regime in Luanda.

The mass exodus of missionaries from Angola has not been an unmitigated tragedy. At least fifty of them are now in lower Congo ministering to the physical and spiritual needs of the refugees in that area. The Christian refugees are infusing new life into the churches in lower Congo, some of which stand in need of renewal. In Angola the church leaders have had new responsibilities thrust upon them, and they are rising to the occasion in a manner that can only strengthen the sinews of the indigenous churches. The work inside Angola goes on, albeit not without difficulty and danger.

The State of the Church.   The church in Angola is divided into three parts. The largest section is still functioning under the Portuguese authorities. The smallest group is witnessing courageously to those hiding in the bush and forests. The third group is in exile in Congo. Of this last group, some have kept their identity as a church in exile; but the majority have joined local churches. In the northern part of Angola no Protestant services of any kind are permitted. Medical work is extremely hard hit, with only three missionary doctors left in the country.

Strange as it may seem, as the other missionaries were leaving Angola the *Southern Baptist Convention,* in 1968, sent its first missionaries into the country. One couple, with former experience in Brazil, are located in the capital, Luanda. They are serving in cooperation with the Angola Baptist Convention and the Portuguese Baptist Convention, in which there are nine churches with 525 members.

The Bible Societies.   The *Bible Society of Angola* now has its own building on one of the main thoroughfares leading out of the capital. It continues to receive 98 percent of its budget from the United Bible Societies. Scripture distribution continues on the rise in spite of the adverse circumstances facing the Protestant church. The complete Bible is available in three languages besides Portuguese, the New Testament in two languages, and Portions in four others. As might be expected, Roman Catholic church leaders in Angola are dragging their feet in the matter of Bible reading and distribution. Nevertheless progress is being made. The archbishop has appointed a commission to study Vatican directives regarding relationships with the United Bible Societies and the use of the Bible.

Ecumenical Relations.   There is only one ecumenical organization. It is the *Evangelical Alliance of Angola,* which has no official affiliation with any outside group.

Mozambique

Political History.   Mozambique, on the east coast, has been a Portuguese possession since 1505. By a constitutional amendment in 1952 the colony became an overseas province of Portugal. As such it is an integral part of Portugal and, therefore, not eligible for independence.

The People.   The population is estimated at 7.7 million, of whom 130,000 are Europeans, mostly Portuguese. The African tribes are of

Bantu stock, each with its own dialect. The southern tribes, who have had more contact with European civilization, are more advanced culturally than those in the north. The literacy rate is low—about 5 percent.

Religion. The tribespeople are mostly animists. Roman Catholic missions have been active since the arrival of the Portuguese; consequently the Roman Catholic Church claims a million communicant members, of whom 130,000 are Europeans, and about 175,000 catechumens. Protestants of all denominations number approximately 175,000. There are almost 900,000 Muslims, most of them north of the Zambezi River. The Portuguese government favors Roman Catholic missions. Protestant missions are barely tolerated, and have to work under restrictions which vary from time to time and from place to place.

Education. In 1940 Portugal signed an agreement with the Vatican whereby all state-controlled schools were handed over to the Roman Catholic missions. No permits are given to Protestant-sponsored village schools other than religious education classes. Protestant churches are permitted to operate primary schools provided the schools are established on mission property. All instruction must be in Portuguese.

Missions. Several abortive attempts were made to start Protestant missions in Mozambique. The first abiding mission was established by the *American Methodists* under Bishop William Taylor in 1893. The first missionary of the Women's Foreign Missionary Society was appointed in 1903. The Methodist Church has grown and is still spreading into virgin territory under the inspiration of its own home missionary society. The first African bishop was elected in 1964. The Annual Conference in Mozambique is divided into six districts with over nine hundred places of worship. The more important institutions are the *Central Training School* (known as "Tuskegee in Africa"), *Hartzell School, Keys Memorial School,* two hospitals, a nurses training school, and a leprosarium. The Methodist Church in Mozambique is self-supporting as well as self-governing.

Free Methodist work in Mozambique was born in 1885 when an unknown chief sold land for "eighty yards of cloth and a flannel shirt, worth about five dollars" to pioneer missionaries Harry Agnew and Mr. and Mrs. W. W. Kelley. After a few years tribal uprisings caused the missionaries to withdraw; but Mr. Agnew later returned to establish permanent work. He erected the first Free Methodist chapel in Africa. He also laid the foundations for the future church by translating a handbook on Christian theology and portions of the Gospel of John. Today the church includes five thousand members, with half that number under instruction.

The Anglicans in Mozambique are represented by the *United Society for the Propagation of the Gospel.* Their work is situated in the north, near

Lake Nyasa. The Diocese of Lebombo, set up in 1893, is now part of the *Church of the Province of South Africa.* The church has some forty thousand members. In 1967 an Old Catholic priest, Dr. Pine Cabral, pastor of the Lusitanian Catholic Church in Oporto, Portugal, was appointed Suffragan Bishop of the Diocese of Lebombo. When Dr. Cabral becomes bishop, the Anglican Diocese of Lebombo is expected to become part of the Lusitanian Catholic Church of Portugal.

The *Africa Evangelical Fellowship,* after forty years of fruitless effort, finally succeeded in getting a foothold in northern Mozambique in 1936. In 1942 the AEF took over the work initiated in 1913 by the Church of Scotland and later transferred to the Nyasa Mission, which in turn retired from the field in favor of AEF. Government restrictions prevented the opening of new stations. Indeed, some established stations had to be given up for lack of reinforcements. No missionary of the AEF has resided in northern Mozambique since 1960. The number of Christians, now over ten thousand, has more than trebled in eight years.

The *Church of the Nazarene* is a newcomer to Mozambique, its first missionary couple having arrived in 1954. More than once its missionaries have been refused permits to enter the country; but in answer to prevailing prayer their number had climbed to twenty-four by 1969. They have met with good success, so that today they report 325 preaching points, almost one-third of them self-supporting, with a membership of eighty-six hundred. They have twice that number in their Sunday schools. They operate three Bible colleges with a total enrolment of 160.

The *Pentecostal Assemblies of Canada* entered Mozambique in the early 1950's. The pioneering couple, the Reverend and Mrs. C. Austin Chawner, spent fifteen years there and ended up in 1965 with three hundred assemblies and as many national workers, and some six thousand believers. The number has since grown to almost ten thousand. They have two large Portuguese-led, multi-racial assemblies, one in the capital, Lourenco Marques, and the other in Beira. The entire work in Mozambique is indigenous and self-supporting. Canadian missionaries stationed in South Africa give oversight as permits are available.

Another Pentecostal group, *Church of God* (Cleveland), reports 561 churches in Mozambique and a membership of over six thousand under the spiritual care of 525 national ministers.

The *Worldwide Evangelization Crusade* has been in Mozambique since 1966. Only two missionaries are there at present.

Other groups include the *Scandinavian Baptist Mission,* the *Presbyterian Church of Mozambique,* the *Congregational Church,* and the *Seventh Day Adventists.*

Bible Societies. All three Bible societies cooperate with the Bible Society in Mozambique. The whole Bible is published in five languages, the New Testament in three more, and Portions in another six. The demand for Bibles and New Testaments far exceeds the supply. For two weeks in October, 1967, the largest cinema in Lourenco Marques showed the film, "The Bible." Permission was given to distribute to the audience inside the cinema a four-page pamphlet on the Bible. The Scriptures are especially prized in the northern part of the country which is closed to missionaries, in an area where the number of Christians increased from ten thousand to twenty-five thousand in less than ten years.

Ecumenical Relations. The *Christian Council of Mozambique* is making efforts to coordinate all aspects of missionary work and is now publishing its own bulletin. Nearly all the Protestant churches and missions are members of the council, though at times there is tension between the conservative evangelicals and the ecumenical brethren. The very limited number of fully qualified Africans and the continuing lack of missionary personnel hamper the work of the council. At Ricatla, fifteen miles north of the capital, the Swiss Mission turned over one of its stations to the National Christian Council for the establishment of a *Union Theological Seminary* and *Ecumenical Center*. The seminary, opened in 1956, is supported largely by the Methodists and the Swiss Presbyterians. The Christian Council is not affiliated with the World Council of Churches.

Rhodesia

Political History. The ramifications of Rhodesian history during the past decade should have a chapter, not a paragraph. Southern Rhodesia has been a self-governing colony of Great Britain since 1923. In 1953 it merged with Northern Rhodesia and Nyasaland to form a federation, which fell apart ten years later. In 1965 Prime Minister Ian Smith took unilateral action and declared Rhodesia an independent state dominated by the white minority. The two African nationalist parties were outlawed and their leaders arrested. At Britain's insistence the United Nations called on all its members to apply economic sanctions against Rhodesia; but the Ian Smith regime seems to be firmly entrenched with moral and material support from South Africa. The situation is potentially explosive and guerrilla activity is on the increase. Rhodesia today is virtually a police state, at least so far as the Africans are concerned.

The People. The estimated population is 4.8 million, of whom 230,000 are Europeans, many of whose families have been there for several generations and who regard themselves as Rhodesians. The African population are of Bantu stock and are divided into two main tribal groups. The Mashona are the older and larger group. The Matabele, in the south-western part of the country, arrived within the last 150 years. English is the official language.

Religion. The Europeans belong to some branch of the Christian church and a fairly large number of Africans have embraced the Christian faith. The total Protestant community may be as high as nine hundred thousand. Islam, coming down the coast from the north, is making headway; but as yet it is not so great a threat as it is farther north.

Missions. The first Protestant missionary was the famous *Robert Moffat* of the *London Missionary Society*. In 1829 he made his first historic visit to this part of Africa. A second visit came in 1835; but it was not until 1859 that permanent work was established in the country north of the Limpopo River in Rhodesia. By that time Moffat was nearing the end of his missionary career. Broken in health, he returned to Scotland in 1870 and died in 1883.

Between 1870 and 1890 three missions attempted to establish work in Rhodesia, but none succeeded; so for thirty years the LMS was the only mission in this vast territory. In spite of many hardships and difficulties the LMS workers carried on; and today the work is part of the *United Congregational Church of Southern Africa.*

When in 1890 Great Britain extended its control to Rhodesia it began making grants of land to missionary societies. Immediately new societies took up work in Rhodesia. First on the scene was the *Church Missionary Society,* whose first efforts were directed to the spiritual needs of the white settlers. Later it began work among the Africans. Through the years the CMS missionaries have ministered to black and white alike with gratifying results. Today the *Anglican Church in Rhodesia* has two dioceses—Mashonaland and Matabeleland—with twenty-five thousand church members and a Christian community four times that number.

The second mission to enter that year was the *Methodist Missionary Society* of England. Taking advantage of the land grants, it soon established strong central stations surrounded by many outstations. Today the *Methodist Church* has thirty-one thousand full members and another ten thousand on trial, making it one of the largest in the country.

The *Salvation Army* pioneered in Rhodesia as early as 1891. In 1970 it was serving a Christian community of sixty thousand. The *American Board of Commissioners* inaugurated work at Mt. Silinda in 1893. It and Chikore are the two large stations on which most of today's thirty-five UCBWM missionaries are working. Medical work includes two hospitals, one of them with 140 beds staffed by only two doctors and three nurses plus African aides. The Rhodesia mission is responsible for sixty primary schools and two excellent secondary schools. *Epworth Theological School* is in Salisbury. Administrative authority has recently been transferred from the mission council to the United Church of Rhodesia. Membership is around forty-five hundred.

In 1895 the *Seventh Day Adventists* acquired a piece of land and developed a church which now has twenty-eight thousand members.

In 1897 *Methodist Bishop Joseph C. Hartzell* obtained from Cecil Rhodes a large tract of land with buildings. The first project in 1898 was a school for European children in Umtali. The Annual Conference was established in 1931. Today the Methodist Church, working in the eastern part of the country, is divided into four districts. The work includes two hospitals, several village clinics, and primary and secondary schools. In 1969 the Rhodesia Annual Conference had 15,000 enrolled as full members and 17,000 on probation, with another 6,250 enrolled as beginners.

The *South Africa General Mission* moved into Rhodesia in 1900. Its field is located in the eastern part of the country close to the western border of Mozambique. It is divided into three main districts, and the capital of Salisbury. Most of the missionaries are on two stations, Rusiti and Biriiri, where they are engaged in medical, educational, literature, and Bible school work. The *Africa Evangelical Church,* now independent, has seventeen hundred members.

The Evangelical Alliance Mission sent its first missionaries to Rhodesia in 1942. They settled on the Zambezi River, in bush country almost untouched by the gospel. As time went on ten centers were opened, including Salisbury. Today their work includes a hospital at Chironge established in 1959, a Bible school at Kapfundi opened in 1953, and a teacher training school begun in 1956. A high school department was added later. Some six thousand pupils are enrolled in primary schools.

European Baptists in Rhodesia established churches between 1917 and 1950, but did not conduct work among the Africans. *Southern Baptist* missionaries have worked almost exclusively among the Africans since 1950. A hospital was opened in 1953 and a seminary in 1955. The *Baptist Convention of Central Africa* was organized in 1963. Today forty-eight career missionaries are at work in ten strategic centers throughout Rhodesia. Twenty-seven national pastors serve forty-four churches, of which about half are self-supporting.

Three Pentecostal missions are working in Rhodesia: *Assemblies of God, Church of God* (Cleveland), and *Pentecostal Assemblies of Canada.* Besides the two large Methodist missions already mentioned there are two others, the *Free Methodists* and the *Wesleyan Church,* both from the USA. The *Plymouth Brethren* have both British and American missionaries here. The *Evangelical Lutheran Church in Rhodesia,* with fifteen thousand communicant members, is the result of the work of the *Church of Sweden Mission.*

Church and State. The Christian church in Rhodesia is on the horns of a dilemma. It finds itself at odds with a so-called Christian government that denies the Africans the right of self-determination, even though they outnumber the whites almost twenty to one. Church and mission leaders must walk a tightrope; one false step and down they go. To remain silent in the face of gross social injustice in order to curry favor with the

A GLOBAL VIEW OF CHRISTIAN MISSIONS

government is to sell one's Christian birthright for a mess of pottage. To oppose the Ian Smith regime is to invite a crackdown which might close the churches. It requires the wisdom of Solomon, the patience of Job, and the courage of Daniel to maintain a clear Christian witness in the political milieu of Rhodesia today. Be it said to the credit of the church, it is the only organized group that has taken a strong stand against the repressive measures adopted by the government. Protestant church leaders and Roman Catholic bishops alike called on their members to reject the constitutional proposals of 1969 that would lead to *apartheid*. The government, of course, has retaliated. Church leaders have been beaten, fined, jailed, and harassed in other ways. Missionaries, especially Americans, who have a penchant for sounding off, are in a most vulnerable position. They too have been fined and jailed, and some have been expelled from the country.

The churches have another problem, an internal one. The leaders do not always have the support of their constituencies. The church is under fire for its refusal to give exclusive support to either white supremacy or black nationalism. The white settlers accuse the church of being communist, or of paving the way for communism, and threaten to withdraw their support. On the other hand, the African church members are becoming impatient; they consider the church's protests to be too little and too late.

Bible Societies. The work begun in 1894 is administered by the *British and Foreign Bible Society*. Because of the unsettled conditions in the country, anyone distributing literature is suspect until he can prove that his business is legitimate. Thus colportage work has suffered. The first and only complete Bible is in the Chinau language; it did not appear until 1957. The New Testament is available in four languages, and Portions in one dialect.

Church Union. Five denominations are engaged in church union negotiations: *Anglican Diocese of Mashonaland and Matabeleland, Presbyterian Church, Methodist Church, Congregational Union,* and *United Church of Christ.*

Ecumenical Relations. The *Epworth Theological College* in Salisbury, begun by the English Methodists, is now supported by five denominations. The *United College of Education* at Bulawayo, opened in 1968, is jointly supported by seven bodies. The *Christian Council of Rhodesia* in 1967 reported seventeen full members and six associate members. It is affiliated with the World Council of Churches. The *Evangelical Fellowship of Rhodesia* is a member of the Association of Evangelicals in Africa and Madagascar. Seven organizations have membership in the All Africa Conference of Churches.

Zambia

Political History. Zambia is the new name for Northern Rhodesia. For ten years, from 1953 to 1963, it was part of a three-nation federation arranged by the British when they were about to pull out of this part of south Africa. The federation never had the support of the Africans and was dissolved in 1963. The following year Northern Rhodesia became the Republic of Zambia. President Kaunda is a sincere and dedicated Christian, the son of an African pastor, who is not afraid to express his Christian convictions. He is making an honest attempt to apply Christian principles to the problems of nation building.

The People. The population of Zambia is 4.2 million. Unlike its neighbor to the south (Rhodesia), it has a very small European community—about 2 percent of the people. The Africans, of Bantu stock, are divided into many tribal groups. The half dozen burgeoning cities that form the Copper Belt are attracting an ever-increasing number of tribespeople from the bush country. The literacy rate is about 20 percent. English is the official language.

Religion. The *International Review of Missions,* January, 1968, stated that 70 percent of the Zambians are Christians, which makes Zambia the most Christian country in Africa. This, of course, includes a large number of Roman Catholics. There is complete freedom of religion, and the government radio station gives free time to the various Christian groups. Primary education is rapidly passing into government hands. The churches and missions still play a major role in teacher training and secondary education, for which there is an enormous demand. African students in secondary schools of all kinds numbered only three thousand in 1961; by 1970 the number had increased to fifty thousand.

David Livingstone. Livingstone never settled in Zambia, but his travels took him back and forth across the country and indeed across Africa. He died in Zambia and his heart was buried there. It seems fitting then that mention should be made of this great man in the chapter on Zambia. The world remembers him as one of the great explorers of all time, but he always considered himself to be first of all a missionary. It is true that he won few converts and planted no churches; but he blazed the trail and prepared the way for all who followed. If all the explorers and administrators who went to Africa had been of Livingstone's caliber the subsequent history of that unhappy continent would have been quite different.

During his first term, which began in 1840, he was associated with the London Missionary Society. For a while he resided at Kuruman with

Robert Moffat and his family. Later he married their daughter, Mary. His first extended trip began in 1852 and lasted four years, during which he traced the Zambezi to its source, crossed the continent to the west coast, and then retraced his steps to the east coast. What he saw of the slave trade fired his soul with indignation against all those who engaged in this nefarious traffic.

Upon his return to England in 1856 he was given a hero's welcome and accorded all kinds of honors. He spoke at Oxford and Cambridge universities and out of this visit came the Universities' Mission to Central Africa. Everywhere he spoke against the iniquitous slave trade. In 1858 Livingstone returned to Africa, this time as an agent of the Royal Geographical Society. The remaining fifteen years, except for a brief visit home in 1864-65, were devoted to further exploration. For a long time nothing was heard of him and it was thought that he was lost. Henry M. Stanley of the *New York Herald* organized a relief party and found Livingstone at Ujiji on Lake Tanganyika. Stanley tried, without success, to persuade Livingstone to return home. But Livingstone was very adamant; he wanted to finish his work of exploration. Not long after, on May 1, 1873, he was found dead on his knees in an African hut in Ilala on Lake Banguelo.

United Church of Zambia. After twenty-five years of union negotiations, the *United Church of Zambia* was inaugurated in 1965. It is the result of the work of six famous missionary societies: *Paris Mission, London Missionary Society, Methodist Missionary Society, Church of Scotland, United Church of Canada,* and *United Church of Christ* (USA). All six missions continue to support the work of the UCZ. Their missionaries go where they are sent and do what they are told. Finances and manpower are two unsolved problems facing the UCZ. It is still dependent on foreign sources for 90 percent of its budget. Some one hundred foreign missionaries are serving with the UCZ, the United Church of Canada furnishing about forty-one of that number. Still there are never enough to meet the increasing demands. African personnel are also a problem, some of them leaving the church for government service. The government has taken over the two hospitals at Chitambo and Serenji and is now responsible for finances and administration; but the church (actually the missions) is expected to procure all expatriate personnel. This cumbersome form of cooperation poses serious problems and causes not a little frustration.

Educational work includes two secondary schools and two teacher training colleges. Most of the missionaries are in institutional work. Some who are assigned to rural areas feel they could make a better contribution working among students in the urban centers. The church has not always been wise in its use of manpower. The missionaries are needed; they are not sure they are wanted. "As an expatriate, you can't win! You are wanted, and yet not wanted. You are open to criticism for not attending political rallies, or, if you go, you may be told 'leave us to run our own country.' "[1]

Other Missions. The *Seventh Day Adventists* have been in Zambia since 1903 and today have a well-established church of nineteen thousand members. The Anglicans have been represented in Zambia ever since the *Universities' Mission to Central Africa* (now part of the United Society for the Propagation of the Gospel) entered in 1910. Today the Anglican Church, with almost twenty-five thousand communicant members and a Christian community twice that size, is one of the largest in the country. The *Church Missionary Society* has three missionaries in Zambia.

The *Africa Evangelical Fellowship* was another of the early comers to Zambia, its first missionaries arriving in 1910. They made themselves responsible for Kaondeland and part of Barotseland. More recently the work has extended to the Copper Belt in the north and to other towns along the railway, including Luskae, the capital. In the Copper Belt the church is making good progress. Primary schools have been taken over by the government. The new girls' school at Mukinge is growing rapidly. Medical work has developed and a second hospital has been opened. Its eighty-two missionaries are located in ten widely scattered centers. The mission maintains two Bible schools. The *Evangelical Church of Zambia* is quite independent of the mission. It has a membership of about five thousand and a Christian community three times as large.

The *Wesleyan Church* has been in Zambia since 1930. Presently there are 30 missionaries and 145 national workers engaged primarily in the southern province among the Batonge tribe.

A fairly recent arrival in Zambia was the *Southern Baptist Convention* in 1959. Its twenty-four career missionaries are divided among seven centers, and already twenty-six self-supporting churches have grown up in and around these places. Their seminary is in the capital.

The *Plymouth Brethren,* with 135 missionaries, have a big investment in Zambia. Their two hundred assemblies represent a Christian community of almost fifteen thousand. Other missions in the country include the *Church of Christ (Disciples)* and the *Pentecostal Assemblies of Canada.* The *African Reformed Church,* outgrowth of the Dutch Reformed Church of South Africa, has five hundred churches with twenty thousand members.

Bible Societies. The work began in 1894. The Rhodesias were administered under Equatorial Africa until the Rhodesia Agency was formed in 1939. The Rhodesias and Nyasaland became a Joint Agency with the National Bible Society of Scotland in 1957. In 1964 this area was reorga-

---

[1] USPG, *Kaleidoscope,* 1970, p. 87.

nized into three separate Agencies, with Zambia administered by the American Bible Society. A milestone was reached in 1968 with the formation of the Bible Society of Zambia. The complete Bible is published in two languages, the New Testament in five, and Portions in four more. Scripture distribution is carried on by thirty colporteurs. Distribution in 1968 went over the million mark, an increase of 34 percent over 1967.

Church Union. Three months after its inauguration in January, 1965, the United Church of Zambia invited the Synod of the Anglican Church to join in formal conversations with a view to closer links between the two churches. Later on two other churches were mentioned as possible candidates for the union, the African Reformed Church and the Presbyterian Church of Southern Africa. The 1968 and 1970 issues of the *Ecumenical Review* dealing with church union negotiations make no mention of these talks. Presumably they have been suspended.

Ecumenical Relations. Kitwe in the Copper Belt is the headquarters of the *All Africa Conference of Churches* and the home of the *Mindolo Ecumenical Foundation.* The latter was founded in 1958 by the Copper Belt Christian Service Council. It has three divisions: research, training, and consultation. It works closely with the AACC and the WCC. Half its $350,000 annual budget is raised by Africans. The remainder is furnished by Western churches, either directly or through the WCC. The AACC is an autonomous organization with a fraternal relationship to the WCC. There are two ecumenical organizations in Zambia: the *Christian Council of Zambia,* affiliated with the WCC; and the *Evangelical Fellowship of Zambia,* linked with the Association of Evangelicals of Africa and Madagascar. In Zambia there are six organizations which are members of the All Africa Conference of Christian Churches.

Malawi

Political History. Nyasaland was a protectorate of Great Britain from 1889 until 1953 when it, along with Northern and Southern Rhodesia, formed the Central African Federation; it was dissolved in 1963. On July 6, 1964, Malawi, as it is now known, became an independent member of the British Commonwealth. Two years later, after the adoption of a new constitution, it became a republic. Dr. Kamuzu Banda, its first and only president, is an elder in the Presbyterian Church.

The People. Malawi, with 4.5 million people, has the highest population density in Africa. Its annual growth rate is 3 percent, so the problem is likely to get worse rather than better. The people are of Bantu stock. Major tribes are the Nyanja, Yao, and Ngoni, who migrated respectively from Congo, Tanzania and Mozambique, and South Africa. English and Chi-Chewa are the official languages.

Religion. Almost 50 percent of the people are animists; 30 percent profess Christianity; and 20 percent are Muslims. There is complete freedom of religion.

Missions. The name of David Livingstone will ever be associated with Malawi, not only because he was the first European to visit the area, but also because three important missions there owe their existence to the inspiration of this great missionary-explorer: *Universities' Mission to Central Africa, Livingstonia Mission* of the Free Church of Scotland, and *Blantyre Mission* of the Church of Scotland.

In 1860 the first party of missionaries of the *Universities' Mission to Central Africa,* under the leadership of *Bishop Charles F. Mackenzie* and accompanied by Livingstone, established a station just south of Lake Nyasa. A series of misfortunes, including the death of Mackenzie, forced the mission to withdraw to Zanzibar. A second attempt was made in the 1870's and this time the enterprise prospered. The only Anglican mission in Malawi, the UMCA (now known as the *United Society for the Propagation of the Gospel*) has through the years maintained a well-rounded program of evangelistic, educational, medical, and industrial activities. The Anglican community of sixty thousand is served by forty-one African priests and twelve European priests.

The moving spirit back of the *Livingstonia Mission* was *James Stewart,* already a missionary of commanding stature and well known as the founder of the *Lovedale Institute* in South Africa. He had met Livingstone in Africa, and shortly after the latter's death he proposed to his church that work be undertaken in Malawi. To obtain funds Stewart sold his family plate and most of his patrimony. The first party arrived in 1875 and established headquarters on the west side of Lake Nyasa, but later transferred north to Livingstonia. The leader was *Robert Laws,* who was chiefly responsible for founding at Livingstonia an educational institution similar to Lovedale in South Africa. The slave trade, combined with tribal warfare, made the first few decades extremely difficult. After fifteen years there were only sixteen converts. Following the arrival of the British in 1891 the situation stabilized and the mission prospered.

The first missionaries of the *Blantyre Mission* arrived in 1876. They staked out an area on the Shire Highlands and called it Blantyre. Through the years the *Henry Henderson Institute* at Blantyre has trained hundreds of ministers, teachers, hospital attendants, clerks, printers, gardeners, carpenters, machinists, etc.

The *Dutch Reformed Church* (South Africa) initiated missionary work in 1888 with a cluster of stations in the central province.

The churches brought into existence by these three missions united to form the *Church of Central Africa Presbyterian.* Since 1956 the *Presbyterian Church in Ireland* has had a small group of missionaries cooperating with the Presbyterian Church. This church, already the largest in the country, is growing at a rapid pace, especially in the Blantyre Synod. The Church of Scotland 1968 Report said: "The growth of the church continues at an alarming rate." The 1969 Report added: "Church membership numbers continue to leap upwards, facing the Synod with special problems of Christian education." In 1968 the Christian community was 600,000. It is probably considerably larger today.

Both the *Seventh Day Adventists* and the *Seventh Day Baptists* have a mission in Malawi. The first is the older and larger, dating back to 1902. Today it has a church of twenty thousand members. The Seventh Day Baptist work in Malawi did not get under way until 1947. Malawi is its fastest growing field; some twenty churches have a combined membership of three thousand.

The *Africa Evangelical Fellowship* has four main centers of work, all in the deep south, dating back to 1902. Besides the regular forms of mission work—evangelism, church planting, Bible schools, medical work— the mission maintains a school for the blind in Lulwe where forty pupils go through the eighth standard and are thus prepared for a useful life. The AEF church is known as the *Evangelical Church of Malawi.* The Bible institute at Likubula is a cooperative effort of the AEF, the ECM, and the Zambesi Mission.

The *Assemblies of God* missionaries entered Malawi in 1944 to assist several existing Pentecostal groups. They eventually opened six stations in the northern, central, and southern parts of the country. The usual Bible school was established. The church received its independence in 1962. National workers outnumber missionaries six to one. The mission reports a "wonderful spirit of cooperation" between church and mission.

The most recent mission to enter Malawi was the *Southern Baptist Convention* in 1959. The work in five main cities centers around two bookstores, a Bible school, evangelism, and church planting. During the first decade ninety self-supporting churches were established.

Bible Societies. The Rhodesias and Malawi became a Joint Agency with the *National Bible Society of Scotland* in 1957. In 1964 Malawi was established as a separate Joint Agency under the administration of the NBSS. To date the complete Bible is available in only one language, Tumbuku. The New Testament is in five languages and Portions in one. Scripture distribution is keeping pace with the rapid growth in church membership; in one year, 1967, it increased 158 percent.

Church Union. Church union is not new in Malawi. Mention has already been made of the fact that three churches of Reformed background merged to form the *Church of Central Africa Presbyterian.* In more recent years union talks have been taking place among the Church of Central Africa Presbyterian, the Anglicans, and the Churches of Christ (Disciples). One of the three synods of the Presbyterian Church has withdrawn from the talks. The three participating churches have already agreed on Fourteen Steps Towards Unity.

Ecumenical Relations. In 1968 the *Christian Literature Association* was formed to coordinate the production and distribution of Christian literature throughout the country. Another organization is the *Private Hospital Association of Malawi,* which coordinates the medical programs of all Protestant and Catholic missions. The United Church of Christ (USA) has seconded a couple and the United Church of Canada has loaned a dentist to PHAM. In 1965, with the help of the World Council of Churches, the *United Lay Training Center* at Chilema was established. Student work in Malawi comes to focus in the *Student Christian Organization.* In May, 1968, the Presbyterians and the Anglicans joined forces to build the Chapel of the Holy Spirit at the Chilema Lay Training Center. There are two other ecumenical organizations: the *Christian Council of Malawi,* with no outside connections; and the *Evangelical Association of Malawi,* affiliated with the Association of Evangelicals of Africa and Madagascar. The *Christian Council of Malawi* and the *Diocese of Malawi* are members of the All Africa Conference of Churches.

South Africa

Political History. The Union of South Africa received Dominion status in 1910, when the four self-governing colonies of Cape of Good Hope, Natal, Transvaal, and Orange Free State were united to form one country. On June 1, 1961, it became a republic and withdrew from the British Commonwealth over the issue of *apartheid.*

The People. The population of 19.2 million is divided into four main groups: Africans (Bantus), 68 percent; Europeans, 19 percent; Coloreds (mixed European and African), 10 percent; and Asians (mostly Indians in Natal), 3 percent. Of the whites, approximately 60 percent are descended from Dutch, German, and French settlers. They are known as Afrikaners and speak Africaans. The other 40 percent are primarily English-speaking. The Afrikaners dominate the government and are responsible for the policy of *apartheid.*

Religion. South Africa is the most Christian country in Africa. The reason is the presence there of large numbers of white settlers of British and Dutch extraction. The Roman Catholic Church reports 1,175,000 members or 6.5 percent of the population. Of these, some two hundred thousand are white. Among the Protestant denominations, the Dutch Reformed Church, with three branches, is the largest. It accounts for almost half the white population. The Church of England claims about 15 percent. Methodists, Presbyterians, Baptists, Lutherans, and Congregationalists follow in that order. Among the Colored people, the Dutch Reformed Church is the largest. The Church Missionary Society is next. The Bantus are overwhelmingly Christian. There are 260,000 Hindus and 175,000 Muslims.

Church and State. Nowhere in the world outside the communist orbit is the controversy between church and state more severe than in the Republic of South Africa. It all stems from the government's avowed policy of *apartheid,* which is the law of the land. There are few countries in the world completely free of racism; but in South Africa the problem is rendered enormously difficult by reason of the fact that there it has constitutional validity as well as public support, especially among the Afrikaners. The Group Areas Act is the tool employed by the government to force the Whites, Coloreds, and Africans to live in strictly segregated areas. This policy of *apartheid* is the burning issue in South Africa today. It affects not only its internal affairs, but its foreign relations as well; and certainly it has serious repercussions for both church and mission in that unhappy land.

The church is about the only group which is offering any resistance; but the position of the church is weakened by two factors. First, it does not speak with a united voice. The Dutch Reformed Church, the largest in the country, supports the policy of *apartheid,* as do some others. Secondly, it is the leaders and not the members of the resistant churches who are doing battle with the government. Too many church members either agree with the policy of *apartheid,* or they feel a moral obligation to uphold the law so long as it remains on the books. Still others, not without qualms of conscience, do not want to rock the boat. So it is left pretty much to the church leaders and ecumenical councils to oppose the government. The Council of Churches has spearheaded the confrontation. In June, 1968, it published a courageous *Message to the South African People* expressing for its member churches its understanding of the gospel over against the perversions of *apartheid,* reminding the people that as Christians their first loyalty is to God and not to man. In recent years the *Christian Institute* in Johannesburg and the *University Christian Movement* have likewise spoken out against social injustice. But these groups can go only so far without encountering repressive measures which might invite disaster. Already church leaders have been jailed and missionaries have been expelled.

Ecumenical groups in various parts of the world have spoken out against the policy of *apartheid* in South Africa. Among these are the

British Council of Churches, the *National Council of Churches in the USA* and the *World Council of Churches.* The government has threatened to take action against churches in South Africa if they refuse to dissociate themselves from the WCC. In September, 1970, two churches voted to remain in the WCC. They were the United Congregational Church and the Presbyterian Church. The General Assembly of the latter reminded the Prime Minister "that its only Lord and Master is Jesus Christ, that it may not serve other masters, and that its task is not necessarily to support the government in power but to be faithful to the Gospel."[2] A very recent decision of the WCC to allocate $200,000 for the support of groups fighting racism in various parts of the world has provoked violent reaction on the part of the government of South Africa.

Missions. The earliest Protestant missionary work in Africa was that of the *Moravian Church* in South Africa. The pioneer was *George Schmidt,* who arrived in 1737. Ziegenbalg and Plutschau stopped off in South Africa on their way to India in 1705. They were so shocked by the treatment meted out to the Hottentots that they appealed to Herrnhut for missionaries to be sent to South Africa. When Schmidt arrived, he immediately set about to alleviate the oppression of the Hottentot slaves of the Dutch settlers. The Dutch looked with disdain on any attempt to convert the Hottentots, whom they regarded as little better than animals. The first converts were a long time in coming; but Schmidt persevered and eventually in 1743 he had the joy of baptising six Hottentots. This aroused the animosity of the Dutch authorities and Schmidt was expelled from the country.

The Moravians made a second attempt in 1792 and this time the mission succeeded. Under a pear tree that Schmidt had planted, three missionaries conducted a meeting which marked the beginning of a new era in missionary work in South Africa. To their surprise, they discovered an old woman who still possessed a New Testament given to her by Schmidt almost fifty years before. The first station was established among the Hottentots. In 1818 the work was extended to include the Kaffirs. The outstanding leader was *Bishop Hans Peter Hallbeck* (1784-1840). Under his direction the Moravians expanded their mission right up to the borders of the Orange Free State and Natal. After 170 years, the Moravians are still at work in South Africa.

The *London Missionary Society,* organized the year that the British occupied the Cape, sent its pioneer missionary, *John Theodore Vanderkemp,* to South Africa in 1799. His first concern was for the salvation of the Kaffirs. He succeeded in effecting a temporary entrance to one of their tribes, but withdrew when the situation became inflamed, owing to the oppression of the natives by the Dutch settlers. His second project was the

---

[2] *Ecumenical Press Service,* October 1, 1970, p. 2.

founding of a settlement for runaway slaves on Algoa Bay. This was not too successful owing to the presence in the settlement of those who refused to work. Vanderkemp carried the practice of identification a good deal further than most missionaries, so that he married a seventeen-year-old African girl whom he bought out of slavery. The fact that he was old enough to be the girl's father only aggravated the anomalous situation. The incompatibility of the union, according to his critics, saddened his later years and shortened his life. Some of his colleagues also married Hottentot women, not always with happy results.

One of the outstanding missionaries of the LMS in South Africa was *Robert Moffat,* who arrived in 1817. After spending some time in Capetown he received permission to enter the north country. One of his converts during those years was a native chief, Africaner, notorious for his terror tactics. In 1820 Moffat settled in Kuruman, the first station in Bechuanaland. Later he penetrated north of the Zambezi River into Matabeleland. The year 1829 witnessed the founding of the first Bechuana church in Kuruman. In 1857 Moffat completed the translation of the Bible into Bechuana. After fifty-three years of arduous labors, Moffat and his wife returned to England.

Mention should be made of *John Philip,* also of the *London Missionary Society,* who for thirty years championed the cause of the oppressed Africans. He was one of the first men to assert that, given the same advantages, the black man is in no wise inferior to the white man. Like missionaries in other parts of the world, he did his best to end the exploitation of the indigenous population. His efforts paid off, for in 1833 the slaves were emancipated. John Philip was not a lone crusader. He did his best to persuade others to join in the fight against evil. It was largely in response to his appeal that other societies initiated work in South Africa.

The *Methodist Church* is the largest group with work among the Bantu. Their mission dates back to 1816 when *Barnabas Shaw* arrived on the scene and began work among the Namaquas (Hottentots) south of the Orange River. In 1820 *William Shaw* established a Christian colony at Algoa Bay for the Hottentots. Three years later he started a mission for the Kaffirs. By 1831 the Methodist Missionary Society had established six centers among the Bantu. *John W. Appleyard* translated the Bible for one of the Kaffir tribes.

The first Presbyterian missionary arrived in South Africa in 1818. He was followed three years later by two missionaries of the *Glasgow Missionary Society.* The most famous of its many educational institutions was *Lovedale,* founded in 1841 after a visit by Alexander Duff of India. Its course of study ranged from primary grades to preparation for the ministry. It emphasized training in handicrafts and agriculture. It conducted medical and church work. It operated a press. Though it began as a Presbyterian institution, it later developed into a truly ecumenical center, drawing students from a number of denominations. Its second principal,

James Stewart, a former colleague of David Livingstone, was known worldwide for his ability as an educator and missionary statesman. *Lovedale* passed under government control when the Bantu Education Act was passed in 1953.

Another society with a long history in South Africa is the *Paris Evangelical Missionary Society.* Its first representatives arrived in 1829. One of them took up work among the Hottentots; two others proceeded to Bechuanaland and established a center at Kuruman. The most famous of its missionaries was *Francois Coillard,* who spent twenty years in Basutoland before heading up an indigenous work in Rhodesia. During the latter part of the century the mission was under the leadership of *Adolphe Mabille.*

The Anglicans were represented in South Africa by the *Church Missionary Society* and the *Society for the Propagation of the Gospel.* The work got under way in the 1830's. Work among the indigenous population began with the appointment of the first bishop, *Robert Gray,* in 1847. Almost at once he began training candidates for Holy Orders. In two years the number of clergy in the diocese increased from fourteen to forty-two, and more than twenty churches were built. By 1914 the Anglicans had missions in all four provinces of the Union. Today the *Church of the Province of South Africa* has fourteen dioceses and a Christian community of 1.5 million.

The *American Board of Commissioners* began work among the Zulus in 1835. The Zulu Bible was one of its contributions to the Zulu people. In 1967 the *United Church Board for World Ministries* joined with the *Congregational Union of South Africa,* the *London Missionary Society,* and the *Congregational Church in Africa* to form the *United Congregational Church of Southern Africa.* The church today has one hundred thousand members. Missionaries are engaged in education, Christian education, leadership training, evangelism, administration, and finance.

The Evangelical Alliance Mission established its first station in Swaziland in 1892. From there the work spread to Zululand, Tongoland, Natal, and Transvaal, and more recently to the Orange Free State. The *Union Bible Institute,* established in 1940 and now located in Sweetwaters, Natal, is a combined project of nine evangelical missions in South Africa. Through the years it has trained over seven hundred young men. A women's division was added in 1960. TEAM also has two other Bible schools, the *Evangelical Bible Institute* in Transvaal and the *Capetown Bible Institute.* The *Bantu Evangelical Church,* with more than one hundred self-supporting congregations, is the largest of three indigenous churches. TEAM is also developing churches among the Coloreds in Capetown and the Indians in Natal. Its largest medical institution is the *Mosvold Hospital.*

The *South Africa General Mission* (now the Africa Evangelical Fellowship) was formed in 1894 when two small missions already in South

Africa decided to join forces. Its first station was in the wild Zulu country. Podoland was entered in 1895. Work among the Indians of Natal was undertaken in 1896. The first American missionaries arrived in 1908. Today the AEF is the largest faith mission in southern Africa. Its international headquarters is in Johannesburg, where the Bible institute is also located. Durban is another large center of work. The mission has always had a deep concern for the Zulu people. The *African Evangelical Church*, already independent, has almost five thousand members. Special projects include the *Christian Radio Fellowship,* which produces programs for broadcasting over South Africa Broadcasting Company, Radio Swaziland, and Radio Lesotho. The *Africa Christian Literature Advance* acts as an agent for Gospel Light Publications, Back to the Bible Publications, Moody Press, and Scripture Audio-Visual Education. The mission also maintains its own press.

Mention should be made of the *Evangelical Lutheran Church in Southern Africa,* which has a total Christian community of half a million. This large church has grown out of the labors of several missions which have been in South Africa for over one hundred years: *American Lutheran Mission, Berlin Mission Society, Church of Sweden Mission, Norwegian Mission Society,* and *Hermannsburg Mission.*

The largest of all churches is the *Dutch Reformed Church,* which is divided into three ethnic groups: White, Colored, and Mixed, with a combined total Christian community of almost two million.

Another very large church is the *Methodist Church of South Africa,* with a Christian community of 1,250,000. Other large churches with their Christian communities are: *Full Gospel Church of God* (140,000); *Reformed Church in South Africa* (120,000); *Presbyterian Church of Southern Africa* (100,000); *Dutch Reformed Church of Africa* (150,000).

Smaller groups include the *Moravian Church* (62,000), *Pentecostal Assemblies of Canada* (60,000), *Salvation Army* (30,000), and *Seventh Day Adventists* (40,000).

Several American missions have work in South Africa: *Assemblies of God, Church of God* (Cleveland), *American Lutheran, United Methodist, Free Methodist, Wesleyan Church, Church of the Nazarene, Worldwide Evangelization Crusade,* and *Plymouth Brethren.*

Church Union.   As stated earlier, in 1967 a major union was consummated when four denominations merged to form the *United Congregational Church of Southern Africa.* In 1968 a Church Unity Commission was formed to initiate union talks between the United Congregational Church and five other denominations: *Bantu Presbyterian Church, Presbyterian Church of Southern Africa, Tsonga Presbyterian Church, Methodist Church of South Africa,* and *Church of the Province of South Africa* (Anglican). Five full meetings have been held in the past two years.

Ecumenical Relations. Eleven churches in South Africa belong to the *World Council of Churches*. Many more are members of the *South African Council of Churches*. Those churches which, for one reason or another, feel obliged to support the government's policy of *apartheid* are having second thoughts about their affiliation with such "liberal" councils. The *Baptist Union of South Africa* in November, 1969, withdrew from the South African Council of Churches. The statement read: "Over the past decade, differences with the Council's liberal stance have increased to the point of incompatibility. Full identification with this body has become so embarrassing that the Assembly decided by a large majority to dissociate itself from the Council."[3] Thirteen organizations are members of the All Africa Conference of Churches.

Separatist Churches. The largest number of *Bantu Separatist Churches* are found in South Africa. Two kinds are to be distinguished—the Ethiopian and the Zionist. These churches are found in all parts of the continent, but they are especially numerous in South Africa. One reason for this is the government policy of *apartheid,* which so blatantly discriminates against the indigenous population. The Ethiopian type of church is due in large measure to the color bar and emphasizes the African character of the church. The Zionist type is a much more significant and elaborate expression of the African mind. As might be expected, these Separatist Churches have developed an indigenous form of ritual which includes hand-clapping, dancing, native music, and faith healing. The movement began towards the end of the last century and has been expanding ever since. Almost every church has lost members to this movement. Today there are reputed to be over two thousand sects in South Africa. "The movement accelerated after 1927 and again after 1945, until by 1966 independents numbered over three million, or one-quarter of all Bantu Christians in the nation."[4]

At best they are only semi-Christian; in some instances they are anti-Christian. They are a strange mixture of animism, native customs, and magic, with certain Christian elements added and the whole embellished with the external symbols of Christianity. If the movement continues to grow at its present pace it will have serious repercussions on the church. There are signs that some sects are beginning to move back into the mainstream of Christianity. Their leaders are requesting and receiving theological training and other forms of assistance from the historic denominations. From time to time efforts have been made to bring these Separatist groups together; but only in recent years has any progress been made. Since 1965 two associations have been formed, the *African Independent Churches' Association* and the *Assembly of Zionist and Apostolic Churches.*

---

[3] *Ibid.*, November 13, 1969, p. 4.

[4] David B. Barrett, *Schism and Renewal in Africa* (Nairobi: Oxford Press, 1968), p. 23.

South West Africa

Political History. This part of Africa was annexed by Germany in 1884. Following World War I the League of Nations gave the mandate to South Africa. In October, 1966, the United Nations revoked the mandate and placed South West Africa under international control. The Republic of South Africa declared this action null and void and has continued its unilateral administration of the territory in defiance of the United Nations. The South African government is pursuing a policy of *apartheid* which will eventually divide the country into separate white and nonwhite areas. The new name chosen for South West Africa if and when it gets its independence is Namibia.

The People. The Bushmen were probably the earliest inhabitants, followed by the Hottentots (Namas). The Bantu-speaking Ovambos and Hereros came from the north later. The population is estimated at 675,000, of which about 100,000 are Europeans. There are a dozen different tribes, the largest (300,000) being the Ovambos. Afrikaans and English are the official languages, but German is more widely used than English. The Africans in South West Africa are much worse off than their brothers in the Republic of South Africa, and that is bad enough.

Religion. The European population is Christian. In addition there are about three hundred thousand non-whites who are Christians. The remaining 40 percent of the population is pagan. Religious liberty is by no means complete. The church must knuckle down to the dictates of the state, whose policy of *apartheid* is totally unacceptable. In 1968 Anglican Bishop Robert Mize was not permitted to return to the country after furlough.

Missions. From the early days of the missionary movement the Hottentots of South Africa have attracted the attention of missions working in that area. The first mission to do anything for the Hottentots was the *London Missionary Society* in 1805. For a time the *Methodist Missionary Society* also established a work among them. However, it was the *Rhenish Missionary Society* that inaugurated the largest continuing work among the Hottentots. It began in 1839. The outstanding pioneer was *Hugo Hahn*. His plan was to establish a self-supporting colony of Christians. However, the nomadic instincts of the Hottentots were too strong. Steady progress was made until 1946.

> In that year a massive schism occurred from the Rhenish Mission among the Nama, followed nine years later by an even larger split among the Herero resulting in the Oruuana (Community) church which claimed the entire tribe. At various times the Bergdama threatened mass secession, each time narrowly

averted by mission concessions. In 1959 a further large schism occurred among the Basters, or Coloureds of Rehoboth; eighty per cent of their membership left the Rhenish Mission to form the Independent Rhenish Mission of South Africa.[5]

The first mission field to be entered by the *Finnish Missionary Society* was South West Africa in 1870. The work is located among the Ovambo in the north. Through the years the mission has maintained a specially strong medical program with thirteen hospitals and twenty-four clinics. Two Bible schools and a seminary provide workers for the church, the *Evangelical Lutheran Ovambokavanga Church.* Independent since 1954, it is the largest in the country. Its one hundred ninety thousand members are served by 90 pastors and 200 evangelists, aided by 67 missionaries.

The Anglicans report a Christian community of forty-six thousand, of whom thirty-nine thousand are Africans. Through the years the Anglican mission has been the *United Society for the Propagation of the Gospel.* It maintains both schools and hospitals. The diocese of Damaraland, part of the Province of South Africa, covers the whole of South West Africa. Ovamboland is in the northern section of this area, where most of the church's work is done. In fact, in 1967 Ovamboland produced more converts than any other part of the entire Province.

The *United Evangelical Lutheran Church* (all white) reports a Christian community of about twelve thousand. The *Dutch Reformed Church* has a Christian community of thirty-three thousand. The *Methodist Church of South Africa* has a small work. The American missions in South West Africa are the *Seventh Day Adventists* and two newcomers, *Southern Baptist Convention* and *Church of God* (Cleveland).

Botswana

Political History. The first of Britain's High Commission Territories to achieve statehood, the Bechuanaland Protectorate joined the ranks of Africa's independent states as the Republic of Botswana in 1966. Botswana elected to remain in the British Commonwealth.

The People. The population of Botswana is 640,000 and is increasing at 3.5 percent each year. A large section of the west and southwest form part of the Kalahari Desert. Ninety percent of the people derive a livelihood of sorts from the raising of cattle, mostly for the South Africa market. The majority of the Botswana are Bantu, divided into eight main tribes. In addition there are about thirty thousand Bushmen and five

---

[5] *Ibid.,* pp. 24, 25.

thousand Europeans. The illiteracy rate is 80 percent. Only 10 percent of those who attend primary school ever stay to graduate.

Religion. The Protestant community is slightly over the one hundred thousand mark. Roman Catholics number ninety-eight hundred. The remainder of the people are animists.

Missions. *Robert Moffat,* one of Africa's most famous missionaries, made several journeys into what is now known as Botswana. However, inasmuch as his work centered in Kuruman, his story is told in the section on South Africa. The *London Missionary Society,* of which Moffat was a member, was the pioneering mission in former Bechuanaland. Its first missionary was *John MacKenzie* who arrived in 1864, just six years before Moffat retired from the field. In addition to being a missionary and an explorer, MacKenzie was something of a statesman and did not hesitate to make his views on politics known to the British authorities in South Africa. Like so many missionaries in all parts of the world, he conceived it his duty to champion the rights of the indigenous population against exploitation on the part of the white man. Consequently, he argued for the annexation of Bechuanaland to prevent it from falling into the hands of the Boers as they marched northward. He was convinced that this was the only way to safeguard the rights of the Africans.

The London Missionary Society (now part of the Congregational Council for World Mission) has for over one hundred years been the largest mission in south Africa. But in recent years it has suffered a severe decline in the number of missionaries, from 163 in 1967 to 120 in 1970. Of these, forty-seven are working with the *United Congregational Church of Southern Africa.* The church in Botswana is one of Six Regions of the United Church, which embraces 105,000 communicant members in over two hundred fifty organized churches.

The Anglican society in Botswana is the *United Society for the Propagation of the Gospel.* The small church of fifteen hundred communicant members belongs ecclesiastically to the Diocese of Matabeleland (Rhodesia), which is one of four dioceses which joined in 1955 to form the Province of Central Africa.

The *Assemblies of God* tried several times to gain entrance to Botswana but did not succeed until 1963; so their work is just getting under way. Even so, they have four missionaries and seven nationals working in seven strategic centers, including Gaberones, the capital.

Here in Botswana we meet again with the *Southern Baptists.* Their first couple began language study in Francistown in 1968. A missionary dentist and his wife joined them in 1970.

Several other groups have commitments of various kinds in Botswana. The *Church of God* (Cleveland) reports seven churches with five hundred members. The *Mennonite Central Committee* had seventeen workers there in 1969. The first *Plymouth Brethren* couple settled in Serowe in 1968. *Church World Service* makes contributions to many projects, including Mochudi Community Development Center and Swaneng Hill School.

Ecumenical Relations. The *Botswana Christian Council* formed in 1966 includes the Anglicans, Lutherans, London Missionary Society, Methodists, and the United Free Church of Scotland. Roman Catholics, Dutch Reformed Church, Seventh Day Adventists, Apostolic Faith Mission, and Assemblies of God are observers. The Council works closely with the All Africa Conference of Churches and the World Council of Churches. Most of the church relief sent to Botswana is channeled through the Christian Council. Four denominations, Presbyterians, Methodists, Quakers, and Congregationalists, have organized a union church at Gaberones, the capital. Funds for the building of the new church were donated by the participating groups, with help from the London Missionary Society, the Anglicans, and the World Council of Churches.

Lesotho & Swaziland

These were two High Commission Territories which for many decades formed enclaves within the Union of South Africa. They are now independent. Because they are so small, and because their economic, cultural, and religious ties with South Africa are so close, it does not seem wise to give them extended treatment here.

Lesotho. Formerly Basutoland, it received its independence in 1966. The earliest mission was the *Paris Mission,* which began work in 1833. Its outstanding missionary was *Francois Coillard,* who spent twenty of his notable forty years in Africa in Basutoland. The national church, independent since 1964, is known as the *Lesotho Evangelical Church;* it has a Christian community of two hundred thousand. The Anglican community, the work of the *United Society for the Propagation of the Gospel,* is organized into the Diocese of Lesotho. Now part of the Province of South Africa, it is the second largest church, with seventy-two thousand members.

Three Pentecostal groups have work in Lesotho: the *Assemblies of God* (1950), the *Pentecostal Churches of Canada* (1958), and the *Church of God* (Cleveland).

Christianity has made good headway in Lesotho. Out of a population of one million, 60 percent are Christians. Of these, 230,000 are Roman Catholics.

Ecumenical Relations. The *Lesotho Evangelical Church* is a member of the World Council of Churches and the All Africa Conference of Churches.

Swaziland. This territory got its independence in 1968. With a population of only four hundred thousand it is one of the smallest sovereign states in Africa. Approximately 25 percent of the population are Christians. Eighty percent of all the schools are run by the churches. The Swaziland Broadcasting Service provides time for religious broadcasts supplied by the various churches working through the *Swaziland Conference of Churches.*

Here again we meet the *United Society for the Propagation of the Gospel.* Since independence, the Anglicans have established a separate diocese for Swaziland. The *Africa Evangelical Fellowship* has been in this territory ever since 1891 and has established the *African Evangelical Church,* which has twenty-five congregations. The *Church of the Nazarene* has been there since 1910 and has over two hundred places of worship. The *Wesleyan Church,* after sixty years of work, still has only a small church of fewer than five hundred. The *Church of God* (Cleveland) reports seven churches with about one hundred members each. The *Methodist Church of South Africa* and the *Seventh Day Adventists* complete the picture in Swaziland.

Missionary Radio. *Trans World Radio* is now erecting a powerful shortwave radio station which will begin operations early in 1972. The new station will broadcast the gospel in a dozen languages to some eighty-five million people south of the equator.

Madagascar

Political History. "Madagascar" is the geographical name for the island. "Malagasy Republic" is its political name. But "Malagasy" is an adjective and cannot stand alone, so it seems proper to retain the old name, "Madagascar." In the eighteenth century it was a center of the infamous slave trade with the West Indies. For a time Britain and France fought for its control. The French won out and Madagascar became a protectorate in 1885 and a colony in 1895. The Merina monarchy was abolished and the last queen, Ranavalona III, went into exile. In 1958 the Malagasy Republic was created within the French Community. Two years later it achieved full sovereignty. The first decade has been marked by an unusual degree of political stability, with not a single coup.

The People. The population of Madagascar is 6.6 million. The people are of Malayan-Indonesian origin, with an intermingling of Arab and African strains. Of the island's eighteen ethnic groups, the largest is the Merina, or Hova, who occupy the central highlands. Foreign groups include the French (40,000), Indians (14,000), Chinese (8,000), and 35,000 immigrants from French Comoro Islands. The Malagasy language is understood universally throughout the island. Illiteracy is still high—around 65 percent.

Religion. About 40 percent of the people are Christian, divided almost equally between Roman Catholics and Protestants. The remainder of the population practice a form of animism combined with ancestor worship. Islam was introduced by the Arabs, but it is not a strong force.

Early Missions. The first attempt to reach Madagascar with the gospel came in 1818 when *David Jones* and *Thomas Bevan* of the *London Missionary Society* arrived in Tamatave. King Radama I was kindly disposed towards the new venture and appealed for more missionaries, including skilled craftsmen to train his people in the arts of civilization. The first institution was a Christian school established in Tananarive. In time other missionaries joined the task force in Madagascar, but some of them turned out to be a disappointment. The Bible was translated; schools and industries were begun. By 1833 there were thirty thousand persons who had learned to read. Some two thousand converts had joined the church.

Period of Persecution. During the reign of Queen Ranavalona I (1828-1861) a wave of terror swept the island and thousands every year perished at her bloody hands. Soon the queen turned upon the Christian church. Teaching, preaching, public worship, and the distribution of the Scriptures were banned. All missionaries, except those who were performing "useful" tasks, were expelled from the country. With the missionaries out of the way, the queen attacked the church and tried to destroy it. But the Christians, even on pain of death, refused to give up their faith. For some twenty-five years the reign of terror continued, but to no avail. When the wicked old queen died in 1861 the number of Christians had actually multiplied many fold.

Period of Prosperity. Shortly after her coronation in 1869 Queen Ranavalona II confessed Christianity and was baptized. Supported by royal patronage, Christianity became the religion of the realm and people flocked in droves to the Christian banner. The church was then in greater danger from its friends than it had been from its foes. For thirty years it enjoyed a period of peace and spiritual prosperity, during which new societies entered Madagascar and took up work in various parts of the country.

The *Church Missionary Society* sent out two men in 1864; but withdrew them ten years later. The *Society for the Propagation of the Gospel* likewise sent two missionaries in 1864. In 1866 the *Norwegian Missionary Society* sent out *John Engh* and *Nils Nilsen,* who settled in Betafo in the southern part of Central Province. The following year another mission entered Madagascar—the *British Friends*. During the 1890's two American groups took up work—the *Evangelical Lutheran Church* (1892) and the *Lutheran Free Church* (1895).

Second Period of Persecution.   In 1896 the French, after ten years of military conquest, finally annexed the island; and Madagascar was reduced to colonial status. A new wave of terror, incited by the Jesuits, swept over the church. Mission property was confiscated, schools were closed, seven hundred churches were destroyed, anti-Christian literature was circulated, and pagan customs were revived. For a time it looked as if all the missionaries would be expelled. The outlook brightened considerably when the *Paris Evangelical Missionary Society* decided in 1897 to enter Madagascar to assist the persecuted Protestants.

Later Developments.   By 1913 it had become apparent that something must be done to avoid overlapping and duplication of effort on the part of the various missions. As a concession to the newly established concept of comity, the London Missionary Society surrendered to other societies 1,290 schools and some five hundred of its seven hundred hard-won churches. The church which grew out of the LMS work is completely independent. Known as the *Church of Christ in Madagascar,* it had a Christian community of 350,000 in 1968. In recent years the LMS work has suffered from lack of men and money. The number of missionaries has fallen far too sharply and the church is unable to pick up the slack. The famous LMS Press in the capital was so heavily in debt that in 1965 it was sold to the Lutherans. In 1970 the LMS had fourteen missionaries in four centers working with the church.

The Triple-Jubilee Celebration of the arrival of the first LMS missionaries, Jones and Bevan, took place in 1968. The celebrations provided a great public and national occasion as well as a time of thanksgiving for the church. They culminated in a great assembly in the national stadium with some eighty thousand persons present. On hand for the occasion were the president of the republic, cabinet ministers, foreign ambassadors, and representatives of the churches and missions. In his speech the president paid tribute to the contribution which the church and the Bible have made to the life and culture of the Malagasy people.

Church growth in Madagascar has been most gratifying, and all churches have shared in it. In 1950 the three Lutheran groups united to form the *Malagasy Lutheran Church,* with six synods and ninety thousand members. In 1967 the MLC marked the one hundredth anniversary of the beginning of Lutheran mission work with special celebrations. At that time it reported 344 ordained national pastors assisted by 1,440 trained evangelists and a church membership of 267,000.

The Anglicans have been represented in Madagascar by the *United Society for the Propagation of the Gospel.* The *Episcopal Church of*

Madagascar, with three dioceses and its own bishops and clergy, has been independent for some time. Between 1965 and 1970 the number of Anglicans increased from thirty-eight thousand to sixty thousand.

The *Paris Mission* has likewise produced an indigenous church which is self-governing. Known as the *Evangelical Church of Madagascar,* it had a Christian community of 410,000 in 1968.

The *English Quakers,* with a much smaller commitment in Madagascar, have a church of seventy-five hundred members. The church brought into being by the *Seventh Day Adventists* has four thousand members.

The only new mission to enter Madagascar in recent decades is the *Conservative Baptist Foreign Mission Society.* Its first missionaries, *Mr. and Mrs. William Hunter,* went at the invitation of a group of Baptist churches which had been without outside help since the departure of missionary Brinley Evans twenty years before. The work in Madagascar will be generally centered in the cities and will be done in connection with established churches in leadership training and literature.

The State of the Church. The churches in Madagascar are numerically strong. It is estimated that the Protestant community numbers nearly 1.5 million and the Roman Catholic 1.2 million. Together they account for 40 percent of the total population. The churches are much stronger and wealthier in the cities than in the rural areas. All the churches are independent, and foreign funds and personnel are used at the discretion of the church councils and synods. Obviously evangelism through the years has played a major role; otherwise, churches would not be so large. Evidence of continuing concern for evangelism is seen in the decision of the Lutheran Church to publish *Revolution in Evangelism* by Dayton Roberts. The church plays a large role in education and there are many Christians in positions of influence. The program, however, is rather costly. In some regions the schools are maintained only in the face of much frustration and many difficulties, and at a standard that leaves much to be desired. There is complete separation of church and state, and both sides guard the principle with great care.

Bible Translation. This is no problem as the Malagasy language is universally known throughout the island. The Malagasy Bible, completed in 1835, is the only translation needed.

Church Union. Mention has already been made of the fact that three Lutheran churches united in 1950. A second union took place in 1968 after seventeen years of negotiations. The union involved three churches in the northern half of the island. They are the *Evangelical Church* (Paris Mission Society), the *Church of Christ* (London Missionary Society), and the *Friends' Church* (Quaker Mission). The new church is known as the

Church of Jesus Christ in Madagascar. With eight hundred thousand members it represents three-fourths of all Protestants in the island.

Ecumenical Relations. Most of the churches in the island belong to the *Christian Council of Madagascar,* which in turn is a member of the World Council of Churches. The *Malagasy Lutheran Church* and the *Church of Jesus Christ* are also members of the World Council. Two groups belong to the All Africa Conference of Churches.

Separatist Churches. Though isolated from the mainland, Madagascar has not completely escaped the inroads of the Separatist movement. The first dissident group dates back to 1894. The largest body, the *Eglise du Reveil,* with some fifty thousand followers, was organized in 1955. By 1967 the Separatists numbered approximately two hundred thousand.

XVII

South America

Brazil

Political History. Brazil is the only non-Spanish republic in South America. In 1500 Pedro Alvares Cabral landed on the Brazilian coast and claimed the land for Portugal. The first Portuguese governor-general was appointed in 1549. In 1822, after more than three centuries of colonization, Brazil was declared an independent monarchy by Dom Pedro. In 1889 the monarchy was overthrown in a bloodless revolution and Brazil became a republic. Although Brazil is recognized as a progressive state, military and civilian dictators come and go in rapid succession. At the moment the jails are filled with political prisoners.

The People. The population of Brazil is about ninety-one million and is growing at 3 percent annually. The basic ethnic stock is Portuguese, with African and Indian strains intermixed. Some 62 percent of the population is white, 27 percent mulatto, and 11 percent Indian. The Indians belong to two hundred tribes, more than half of which are completely monolingual. About one hundred sixty thousand Indians, living mostly in the Amazon valley, are untouched by modern civilization. During the twentieth century there has been an influx of Italians, Germans, and Japanese. Despite class distinctions, racial prejudice is almost nil. Brazil is the only Portuguese-speaking country in the Western Hemisphere. From every point of view Brazil is the largest, strongest, and potentially the richest country in Latin America. With a stable government, sound economic policies, and dynamic leadership, it could conceivably overtake the United States in another generation.

Religion. Brazil is a Roman Catholic country. Not so long ago the Roman Catholics accounted for 95 percent of the population. The recent phenomenal growth of the evangelicals, especially the Pentecostals, however, has reduced the percentage to slightly less than ninety. For more than four hundred years the Roman Catholic Church has been closely allied with the state; but its influence today is not as great as it was. Besides, the church itself is divided on many issues. Here, as elsewhere in South America, there is a paucity of clergy, making adequate oversight impossible. Church and state were separated in 1889, reunited in 1934, and separated again by the constitution of 1946. Religious liberty is a fact of life and evangelical Christianity is growing by leaps and bounds.

Early Missions. The first continuing Protestant work began with the arrival of *Dr. Robert Kalley* fron England in 1855. In 1911 his mission, *Help for Brazil,* amalgamated with two others to form the *Evangelical Union of South America,* with headquarters in London. Later an American branch was formed and it became responsible for five states in northeast Brazil. The British branch of the EUSA cooperates with the *Union of Evangelical Congregational Christian Churches* of Brazil, which now has thirteen thousand members.

Of the historic denominations, the *American Methodists* were the first to enter Brazil. Their first missionary was *Justin Spaulding,* who arrived in Rio de Janeiro in 1836. The mission was aborted in 1842 and reopened in 1885 by the *Methodist Episcopal Church.* During the 1880's *Bishop William Taylor* started self-supporting missions in northern Brazil, where the *Reverend Justus H. Nelson* spent forty-five years, earning his own support by teaching English, German, and Portuguese. In 1930 the *Methodist Church of Brazil* became autonomous. Today the church has six Conferences, each with its own bishop; five of them are Brazilians. All educational institutions are controlled, and the property held, by the church, not the mission. Some eighty-odd missionaries cooperate with the church through a central council consisting of twelve Brazilians and twelve missionaries. Most of these missionaries are engaged in the twenty-four major institutions maintained by the church. The Methodist Church of Brazil has 850 churches and almost twelve hundred preaching places, with a full membership of fifty-eight thousand.

The *American Presbyterians* have been in Brazil since 1859 and have built up a large and strong national church. The pioneer was the *Reverend Ashbel G. Simonton,* whose first audience consisted of two men who wanted to learn English. He was followed by the *Reverend George W. Chamberlain,* the great evangelist who spent forty years preaching and organizing churches in the state of Sao Paulo. In 1888 the churches established by the two Presbyterian missions (Northern and Southern) united to form the *Presbyterian Church of Brazil.* In 1903 a segment broke away from the Presbyterian Church and formed the *Independent Presby-*

terian Church, which has a present membership of about twenty-three thousand. The Presbyterian Church of Brazil has thirteen synods and seventy-one presbyteries. There are 520 ordained ministers and 140,000 communicant members. The Presbyterian work in Brazil is divided into four missions. The United Presbyterians have seventy missionaries working with the Central Brazil Mission. About 50 percent are engaged in evangelistic work; another 25 percent serve in specialized ministries. The remainder serve in theological and secondary education. The other three missions include 160 missionaries of the *Board of World Missions of the Presbyterian Church in the US.*

The *Southern Baptists* have a huge investment in Brazil. *William and Anne Bagby* were the first missionaries. They went to Rio de Janeiro in 1881. The Bagbys had nine children. Four of them died; the remaining five became missionaries. The following year they were joined by the Taylor family. The two families moved north that year to Salvador, Bahia, where the first Baptist church was founded in 1882. In 1884 the Bagbys returned to Rio de Janeiro, which became the center of Baptist work in the south. The dominant center in the north is Recife. In 1897 *Erik A. Nelson* and his wife opened a third field in Equatorial Brazil.

Almost from the beginning the mission was blessed with capable Brazilian leaders. The *Brazilian Baptist Convention* was organized in 1907 in Salvador, Bahia. Both home and foreign mission boards were organized. The former pioneered in four states and the latter sent missionaries to Argentina, Chile, Portugal, Bolivia, and Paraguay. In 1910 the American missionaries were organized into two missions, North and South Brazil. In 1950 the North Brazil Mission was divided into two missions, the new one called the Equatorial Brazil Mission. Today Southern Baptist work includes all twenty-two states and the four federal territories of Brazil.

The Southern Baptists have maintained a strong theological program with thirty Bible schools, and seminaries at Recife, Rio de Janeiro, Sao Paulo, and Belem. Medical work has not received the same degree of attention. The church has only one hospital, opened in 1968, and some three dozen clinics. The *Carroll Memorial Publishing House* in Rio de Janeiro has produced huge quantities of the Scriptures, theological texts, Sunday school materials, and Christian literature of all kinds. At the beginning of 1970 there were 290 Southern Baptist missionaries assigned to forty-seven centers in all parts of the country. The *Brazilian Baptist Convention* comprises 2,147 churches, with a total membership of almost 300,000 served by 1,500 pastors.

Although the Southern Baptists represent almost 95 percent of all the Baptist membership in Brazil, there are fourteen other Baptist missions, all but one, the *Baptist Missionary Society* (England), from the United States. Together they have about three hundred fifty missionaries in Brazil. The three largest are *Baptist Mid-Missions* (1936), *Association of Baptists for*

World Evangelism (1942), and the *Conservative Baptists* (1946). These account for almost two hundred of the three hundred fifty missionaries.

The worldwide Anglican Communion has only a small and feeble representation in South America. In the whole continent the *Church of England* has only twelve thousand communicant members. The *Protestant Episcopal Church* (USA) has one mission field in South America. That is in Brazil, where the three dioceses comprising the *Episcopal Church of Brazil,* with forty thousand communicant members, are still regarded as Missionary Districts of the American Church. So far as the Church of England is concerned, this stems directly from its insistence at the Edinburgh Conference in 1910 that Latin America not be considered a mission field because the Roman Catholic Church was already there in full force.

The American effort in Brazil began with the arrival in 1889 of two young seminarians, *James W. Morris* and *Lucien Kinsolving.* The first church was organized in Porto Alegre. From there it spread throughout the state of Rio Grande do Sul and into the states of Santa Catarina, Parana, Sao Paulo, Rio de Janeiro, and the Federal District. Its one seminary, in Porto Alegre, with only four hundred volumes in its library, was described by Canon Howard A. Johnson as "a fragile effort, enfeebled by pluralism and nepotism."[1] He adds, however, that both the pluralism and the nepotism have extenuating circumstances.

The Episcopal Church of Brazil, although eighty years old, is still largely dependent for support on funds from the United States. In 1962 only six of its 185 parishes were self-supporting. Canon Johnson blames this on the mission rather than the church. "It should be known that PECUSA has dollared the place almost to death. I mean, the American Church has habituated the Brazilians to an attitude of perpetual dependence."[2] There has been little or no effort to reach out into the community; consequently church growth has been slow. "Such growth as we can show is due, for the most part, to the fact that Brazilian Episcopalians have children."[3] Bishop Stephen Neill has urged that a fourth diocese be created so that a new, autonomous province of the Anglican Communion might be formed in Brazil; but to date this has not been achieved. Two of the three bishops are Brazilians.

Immigrant Churches. Two large Lutheran churches are found in the three southern states of Rio Grande do Sul, Santa Catarina, and Parana. These states account for 45 percent of Brazil's population, 75 percent of its agricultural goods, and 80 percent of its industrial production. These churches owe their origin more to European immigration than to missionary endeavor, though the latter has not been lacking. European immigra-

---

[1] Howard A. Johnson, *Global Odyssey* (New York: Harper & Row, 1963), p. 42.

[2] *Ibid.*

[3] *Ibid.*

tion, especially from Germany, began in the 1820's, and by the middle of the century Lutherans were there in sufficient numbers to warrant an organized effort to meet their spiritual needs. In 1861 the *Basel Missionary Society* sent its first missionaries to Brazil. A synod was organized in 1867. By 1881 ten Basel missionaries were in Brazil. Five years later there came into being the *Evangelical Synod of the Rio Grande do Sul.* This was followed by the formation of the *Lutheran Church in Brazil* in 1895. It experienced rapid growth during the first half of the twentieth century. In 1968 this church, now known as the *Evangelical Church of Lutheran Confession in Brazil,* reported over eleven hundred congregations with a Christian community of 650,000.

The first missionary pastor of the *Lutheran Church-Missouri Synod* arrived in Brazil in 1901 to become the pastor of the Sao Pedro church. In 1904 the Brazil District of the Missouri Synod was formed, with fourteen pastors and delegates of ten congregations in attendance. In 1921 the work spread northward into the states of Santa Catarina and Parana. In 1929 it extended into Espirito Santo, and in 1931 it reached Rio de Janeiro. A publishing house was established in 1923. Radio broadcasting began in 1937—before the Lutheran Hour was launched in the United States. Forty-three parishes have their own programs. Though its largest concentration is still in the three southern states, in recent years the Evangelical Lutheran Church of Brazil has branched out into ten additional states. Porto Alegre with eighteen churches is the headquarters of the work. The church maintains three seminaries but still is not able to furnish enough pastors for the 850 congregations. Parish pastors number only 130, which means that each pastor has to care for six or seven congregations. The baptized membership of the church is 125,000. The church in Brazil is still very dependent financially on the church here in America; but it is hoped that in the near future it will become autonomous. At present only five North American clergymen remain in Brazil, and they have been there for over twenty-five years.

Pentecostal Churches.   The historic denominations in Brazil are very large as compared with sister churches in other countries of South America; but they are completely dwarfed by the Pentecostal churches, whose extraordinary growth in recent years has attracted worldwide attention. *Pentecostal* missions in Brazil date back to 1910, when *Gunnar Vingren* and *Daniel Berg,* two Swedish ministers from Chicago, settled in Belem near the mouth of the Amazon. Supporting themselves as they preached, they soon won a group of zealous converts. With the coming of other Pentecostal missionaries (mostly Scandinavians in the early years) the work spread eastward and southward along the coast into all the major cities. A large number of Brazilians dedicated their lives to the ministry, and they extended the work into the interior. Almost all of the assemblies founded by the nationals were entirely indigenous.

The Pentecostal movement in Brazil breaks down into four groups: the *Assemblies of God,* the *Church of Christ in Brazil, independent churches,* and *churches related to mission boards.* By far the largest is the Assemblies of God, which has twenty-two hundred churches and sixty-six hundred outstations under the care of sixty-eight hundred national workers. Church membership is 1,550,000, with an additional 560,000 adherents. This rapidly-growing church is entirely self-governing and self-supporting. Several Pentecostal missions cooperate with the Brazilian Assemblies of God. These include the *Assemblies of God* in the USA, *Swedish Free Mission, Norwegian Pentecostal Mission,* and the *Independent Assemblies of God.*

A second large Pentecostal group is the *Congregacio Cristo do Brazil* (Church of Christ), which began in 1910 when two lay preachers of Italian descent, residents of Chicago, arrived in Brazil. One of these men was *Louis Francescon,* who became the founder and leader of the Congregacio Cristo. The church is made up almost entirely of Italian immigrants, and for many years all preaching was in that language. The church is located in the two states of Sao Paulo and Parana, where 90 percent of the annual baptisms take place. The movement has grown rapidly. The ministers receive no remuneration at all; the tithes and offerings go towards the construction of church buildings, which in 1967 numbered over one thousand. Communicant membership is more than half a million.

One other Pentecostal church is worthy of mention, *Brazil for Christ,* founded by the best-known, most dynamic evangelical leader in Brazil, *Manoel de Melo.* For a time during the 1950's he was associated with the Foursquare Gospel Church and participated in their huge tent campaigns, which drew one hundred thousand persons to a single meeting. Manoel de Melo soon became the most popular and most controversial Pentecostal leader in Brazil. He left the Foursquare Gospel Church and started a new movement, which he called "Brazil for Christ," in a downtown office in Sao Paulo. Through his nationwide radio broadcast he became known all over Brazil, and wherever he went people flocked to his meetings by the tens of thousands. The power of God rested on his ministry to an unusual degree. Thousands were healed; speaking in tongues was another feature of his movement. His warm personality, his dynamic leadership, the spontaneous informality of his services, and his charismatic gifts greatly endeared him to the Brazilian people. At the same time his unorthodox practices excited the suspicion of some and the open opposition of others. The fact that he drew converts from the historic denominations did nothing to enhance his reputation in those circles. Under construction at present is a mammoth church building in Sao Paulo which will accommodate twenty-five thousand persons. When completed it will be the largest church in the world. Brazil for Christ is growing so rapidly that any statistics are out of date in six months. William Read estimated half a million adherents in

1963 and suggested an annual increase of eighty thousand.[4] The *World Christian Handbook* (1968) sets the figure at seven hundred thousand. Who knows? By now it may be approaching one million.

Manoel de Melo attended the Uppsala Assembly of the World Council of Churches in 1968 and said that he "felt like Ezekiel in the valley of dry bones."[5] Nevertheless in April, 1969, he announced his intention of applying for membership in that body. He says that Brazil for Christ needs the "social orientation" of the WCC and the WCC needs the "evangelical emphasis" of Brazil for Christ. It will be an interesting marriage.

Faith Missions. In recent years there has been a vast proliferation of missionary bodies working in Brazil, doubtless drawn there by reports of church growth among the Pentecostals. At least fifty interdenominational faith missions have entered Brazil in this postwar period, bringing the total number of missionaries to three thousand. It is quite impossible to make individual mention of these missions, especially as some of them are very recent newcomers and have only one or two missionaries in the country. Church growth among these missions, even the older ones, has not been great. Three missions, however, have been there for some years and have a large investment in the evangelical cause in Brazil.

The *Unevangelized Fields Mission* has been in Brazil ever since 1931. Working out from headquarters at Belem, where it was founded, it has evangelized more than twelve Indian tribes, some of them very hostile. Three mission launches enable the missionaries to evangelize the villages along the Amazon River. The mission now has 130 missionaries in the country. In recent years it has been recruiting Brazilian missionaries from the Sao Paulo area; three have already joined the mission. A church of ten thousand members, known as the *Evangelical Christian Church*, has been autonomous since 1948. Two Bible schools and a seminary train workers for the church.

The *New Tribes Mission* has work in five countries of South America. Brazil was the last to be entered, in 1949; but today, with 156 missionaries, it is the largest of all twelve fields in which NTM is working. The work is confined to primitive Indian tribes. Evangelism, linguistic work, Bible translation, and other forms of pioneer work are still going forward. As yet no indigenous church has emerged.

Another faith mission, *Wycliffe Bible Translators,* has been in Brazil since 1956. Its 170 linguists are working out from four main centers and have entered some forty tribes, where Bible translation is now taking place. Bible translation is needed for at least forty more tribal languages. Field offices of the Summer Institute of Linguistics are maintained in Brasilia and Rio de Janeiro.

---

[4] William R. Read, *New Patterns of Church Growth in Brazil* (Grand Rapids: Eerdmans, 1965), p. 154.

[5] *Ecumenical Press Service,* April 24, 1969, p. 6.

Missionary Aviation. Brazil has more territory than all the rest of South America combined, and much of its hinterland is dense jungle never yet penetrated by the white man. Under such conditions the airplane is hardly a luxury. Four missions operate their own planes: *Southern Baptists, Southern Presbyterians, United Presbyterians,* and *Wycliffe Bible Translators. Missionary Aviation Fellowship* has four planes located in four strategic centers and provides transportation for more than a dozen missions operating in the hinterland of Brazil. In addition its mechanics service the planes of the four missions mentioned above.

Theological Education. The historic denominations have done a good job in training an educated ministry. Three of them have three seminaries and the Southern Baptists have four. Most of the other missions, especially the older and larger ones, operate their own Bible schools. But among the independent and Pentecostal churches the situation is well-nigh desperate. It is estimated that of the sixteen thousand Brazilian pastors, only forty-five hundred have received any form of Bible school or seminary training. Forty thousand additional workers are not included in this figure. The Assemblies of God alone have three thousand pastors who have never had any theological training. Little wonder when they have only three Bible schools for a church of a million and a half members. To help solve this enormous problem the conservative evangelicals have formed the *Evangelical Theological Association for Extension Training.* Membership in AETTE is open to the more than eighty seminaries and Bible schools in Brazil. Nearly one-third of these institutions were represented at AETTE's Constituent Assembly in Sao Paulo on October 12, 1968. To preserve the conservative evangelical nature of the association a doctrinal statement was unanimously adopted. The creation of this association represents a breakthrough in theological education. Instead of having the pastors, many of them older men with farms, shops, and families to care for, come to a central seminary or Bible school, the Bible school will be taken to them. Programmed texts are being prepared which will greatly aid in self-education. Periodically the student-pastors will gather in some nearby center for a short period of instruction, counsel, supervision, and examination by qualified teachers, both missionary and national. In this way it is hoped that the thousands of untrained pastors will in time receive the equivalent of at least a Bible school training.

An older association of theological schools is the *Association of Evangelical Theological Seminaries.*

Ecumenical Relations. Three churches in Brazil are members of the World Council of Churches, and a fourth, *Brazil for Christ,* has applied for membership. The *Evangelical Confederation of Brazil* is the ecumenical organization within the country which attempts to coordinate the activities of its many members. It is affiliated with the Division of World

Mission and Evangelism of the WCC. An important development in May, 1965, was the formation of the *Evangelical Institute of Research.* Created jointly by the Evangelical Confederation and the Association of Evangelical Theological Seminaries, this institute will be at the service of the churches.

Bible Societies. The *British and Foreign Bible Society* first sent Scriptures to Brazil in 1822. An agent was appointed in 1862. In 1903 the two societies, British and American, divided Brazil between them. In June, 1948, the *Bible Society of Brazil* was created. The British and American secretaries withdrew in 1961. In 1969 a record of seven million Scriptures were distributed. The major publication of the year was the New Testament in popular Portuguese, which gained the recommendation of the Roman Catholic authorities and sold out its first edition of fifty thousand in a few months. The government has offered the Bible Society a site in the new capital, Brasilia, for the erection of a new Bible House. The 1968 Report of the United Bible Societies reports that Portions of the Scriptures were available in nine Indian dialects; but Wycliffe Bible Translators on their own have added Mark in seven additional dialects and Luke in two more.

Argentina

Political History. Argentina was discovered by Don Juan Diaz de Solis in 1516. The first Spanish governor arrived in 1534 and Spanish rule lasted until 1816, when independence was declared. A constitutional government was established in 1853 after almost forty years of anarchy. Conservative political forces dominated Argentina until 1916. Since then conservative and radical governments have followed one another, interspersed now and again with military coups.

The People. More than one-third of the twenty-four million people of Argentina live in and around the capital city of Buenos Aires, the largest city in Latin America. Argentina has been called the melting pot of South America. Ninety-seven percent of the population is Caucasian, primarily of European descent with Italian and Spanish strains predominating. The population growth rate is only 1.37 percent, one of the lowest in Latin America. The Indian and mestizo population, estimated at six hundred fifty thousand, is concentrated in the peripheral provinces of the north, northwest, and south. The Indians live in widespread poverty. As might be expected, the literacy rate—about 86 percent—is the highest in Latin America. Spanish is the language of all of Latin America except Brazil.

Religion. Roman Catholicism is the religion of Argentina and claims more than 90 percent of the people. It is no longer taught in the schools, however, as it was under the Perón dictatorship. Here, as elsewhere in Latin America, the Roman Catholics do not take their religion too seriously. In Argentina many of the people are antichurch, anticlergy, and quite materialistic. Protestants account for about 5 percent of the population. The Jewish community numbers almost half a million.

Missions. The first Protestant missionary was *James Thompson,* who represented both the British and Foreign Bible Society and the Lancastrian Educational Society. Arriving in Buenos Aires in 1820, he received a cordial welcome, was made an honorary citizen of the country, and for a brief period achieved considerable success in the distribution of the Scriptures and the founding of schools, one hundred of which were located in Buenos Aires.

The *American Methodist* mission in Argentina was launched with the arrival of *Justin Spaulding* and *John Dempster* in 1836. For several decades the work was confined to European immigrants, who were arriving in large numbers. Spanish work began with *John F. Thompson* in 1867. Two single ladies, representing the *Women's Foreign Missionary Society,* arrived in Rosario in 1874. The *South American Annual Conference* was organized in 1893. In 1946 Argentina and Uruguay became one conference of the Latin American Central Conference. In 1954 the two countries were separated and Argentina set up its own Annual Conference. It was divided into two in 1963, the second being the Patagonia Provisional Annual Conference in the south. The Patagonia field includes pastors from Argentina, Germany, Wales, and the USA. Pastors are trained at *Union Theological Seminary* in Buenos Aires. The *Methodist Publishing House,* founded in 1883, is one of the chief centers for the production of Protestant literature throughout Latin America. Educational institutions include three academies. There are 114 churches with an average membership of forty.

The *South American Missionary Society,* an independent conservative mission of the Church of England, has just recently celebrated its 124th anniversary. Its early years were marked by one tragedy after another. The first party, including the founder, *Captain Allen Gardiner,* died of starvation. Six years later a second party was massacred by the aborigines. But the intrepid missionaries refused to give up, and at last a mission was founded. In 1888 *Barbrooke Grubb* penetrated the Chaco region and began work among the Indians. Today SAMS has forty-seven missionaries in six centers of northern Argentina. The first Indian was ordained in 1966; now there are twenty-three Indian pastors. The mission is responsible for seventeen schools for Indians. Evangelism, Bible translation, and medical and agricultural work also form part of the program.

The *Christian and Missionary Alliance* began work in 1897. Two of its early churches were turned over to the Baptist Society, and later certain sections were ceded to the Mennonites. The CMA headquarters is in

Buenos Aires, where the Bible school and the bookstore are located. Missionary activity reached a peak in 1925, after which a new policy of self-support for the churches and the Depression of the early 1930's depleted the staff. Today the *Argentine Christian and Missionary Alliance* has twenty-six churches, twenty preaching places, and a total membership of fourteen hundred.

A Swiss pastor began Baptist work in Argentina in 1881, and three churches had been established when the *Southern Baptists* entered in 1903. Five years later the *Argentine Baptist Convention* was organized. Their international seminary was opened in Buenos Aires in 1950. Today all but one of the seventeen main centers are found in the middle of the country. With eighty-six missionaries on its staff the SBC is the largest mission in the country. Of its 250 churches, 210 are self-supporting. Total membership is almost twenty thousand. The Argentine Baptists are in the midst of their "Decade of Advance." In ten years they hope to double the number of churches.

Other Baptist missions have work in Argentina. Oldest and largest is the *Conservative Baptist Foreign Mission Society,* which began work in 1948. Forty missionaries and a national staff of sixty-two are engaged in evangelism, church planting, radio broadcasting, and Bible school ministries. Already they have thirty-eight organized churches and another thirty-four preaching places, with a baptized membership of fifteen hundred. The *Baptist General Conference* has been at work since 1958 and the *Baptist Bible Fellowship* since 1960.

The *Plymouth Brethren* have been working in Argentina since the beginning of the century. In 1970 they had seventy-seven national leaders and 300 assemblies. Fifty-five missionaries from six countries constitute the foreign staff. Lay leadership on the part of the Argentines is a big factor in their growth. In 1969 a split occurred in the Brethren ranks due to several factors. One was a difference of opinion regarding youth work. Another was the appearance of a charismatic movement in the dissident group. The new group still regards itself as Plymouth Brethren. Estimates of the size of the schism range from one thousand to five thousand.

Lutheran Churches. The *Lutheran Church-Missouri Synod* entered Argentina from Brazil in 1906. Though the work was begun in the German language, Spanish is rapidly taking over as the language of worship. Through the years the work has extended into sixteen states, and today there are forty-six parishes with a baptized membership of twenty-three thousand. In spite of the existence of *Concordia Seminary* in Buenos Aires, there is a severe shortage of pastors. Only one church (Buenos Aires) has its own pastor.

There are three other Lutheran groups in Argentina. The largest of these is the *Evangelical Church of the River Plate.* German in background, it numbers about fifty thousand. The *Danish Lutherans* have their own church with a communicant membership of twenty thousand. There is also the *United Evangelical Lutheran Church in Argentina,* to which the Lutheran Church in America is directly related. It is quite small, with a membership of five thousand. The Lutherans form the largest confessional group in Argentina after the Pentecostals.

Pentecostal Churches. The Pentecostals in Argentina got off to a slow start; it was not until the mid-1950's that their growth rate suddenly and dramatically accelerated. The Pentecostals are fragmented here as they are in Brazil. The *Assemblies of God* (Swedish Free Mission) have at least twenty thousand communicants. The *Pentecostal Assemblies of Canada* report 160 churches, with five thousand members. The *American Assemblies of God* have seventy churches and a membership of five thousand. In all three churches the national workers outnumber the missionaries about ten to one. This doubtless is one source of strength. There are two other churches—the *Christian Assemblies* (Italian in background) with twenty-five thousand members, and the *Church of God* (Cleveland) with ten thousand members. In addition, a large number of Pentecostals from Chile have emigrated to Argentina in search of work. Naturally they have located in the larger cities, where they have multiplied rather rapidly. Their membership may be as high as fifteen thousand. There is also a host of smaller independent Pentecostal churches for which figures are not available. A conservative estimate of total Pentecostal membership in Argentina is around one hundred thousand, which makes it the largest of all the groups.

Other Groups. Though the membership is not large, mention should be made of the *Waldensian Church* made up of immigrants from the mother church in Italy, which is the oldest Protestant church in the world. Its members number about sixty-five hundred. Other missions include the *Brethren Church, Christian Churches* (Disciples), *Church of the Nazarene, Mennonite Board of Missions and Charities, Salvation Army, Seventh Day Adventists,* and the *Christian Reformed Church.*

Comparatively few faith missions have been attracted to Argentina, and most of them have begun work in the last decade. A dozen groups have a total of about fifty missionaries, half of whom belong to the *Evangelical Union of South America.* It has been there since 1956. The EUSA is working in Patagonia, the bleak, wind-swept, arid region forming the southern part of Argentina. Their work includes evangelism, literature, youth work, and a Bible school.

Ecumenical Relations. One church, the *Evangelical German Synod of Rio de la Plata,* is a member of the World Council of Churches. Most of the churches in Argentina are members of the *Federation of Evangelical*

Churches. * The *United Evangelical Lutheran Church* is an associate member of the WCC.

Uruguay

Political History. After fighting first Portugal and Spain and later Argentina and Brazil, Uruguay finally gained full independence in 1828. The new nation continued to be plagued by civil war, foreign intervention, and invasion until the end of the nineteenth century. With the exception of a coup in 1933, the twentieth century has been marked by stable democratic government. It is the most progressive of all the South American countries and is known as a citadel of freedom and a center of culture and education.

The People. The three million people of Uruguay are almost wholly of European descent. The prevailing culture is Spanish, though much of the population is of Italian origin. Some 45 percent of the people live in and around the capital city of Montevideo. Uruguay is noted for its high literacy rate (about 91 percent), its high standard of living, and a large urban middle class. Mestizos account for 10 percent of the population.

Religion. Although Roman Catholicism is the dominant religion, there is complete separation of church and state. Uruguay is the least Catholic of all the South American countries. There is freedom of religion, but not many people take advantage of it. Uruguay is virtually a secular state. The people are largely unchurched, without any religious convictions.

Missions. The *American Methodists* were the first to enter Uruguay, arriving in 1839; but their permanent mission was not established until the arrival of *John T. Thompson* in 1870. The first member of the *Women's Foreign Missionary Society* arrived in 1878 and opened a school for young women. The Methodists have never had a large number of missionaries in Uruguay; consequently the growth has been slow. It was not until 1954 that the work was separated from that in Argentina and Uruguay got its own *Provisional Annual Conference.* There are twenty circuits in the conference with one hundred members to a circuit. Its outstanding institution is *Crandon Institute* in Montevideo, founded in 1879. The institute includes a kindergarten, primary and secondary grades, and junior college. Enrolment is eleven hundred.

The *Southern Baptist* missionaries moved into Montevideo from Argentina in 1911. The staff there has always been too small. At times

---

* It should be understood that all Protestants in Latin America, regardless of their theological stance, are known as Evangelicals.

during the first four decades there were only two couples in Uruguay. The number did not increase to six until 1954. The *Uruguay Baptist Convention* was organized in 1948. With twenty-two missionaries in five centers, the SBC is now the second largest mission in the country. Only seven of the twenty-four organized churches are self-supporting, which is strange for a country where the standard of living is so high.

Assemblies of God missionaries entered Uruguay about 1946. The first church was established in Montevideo. For fifteen years not much progress was made; but beginning in 1960 a number of American evangelists held campaigns in Uruguay with gratifying results. In 1961 there were only five organized churches and seven preaching places. Today there are twenty-nine churches and one hundred outstations. A Bible school was opened in 1960. A weekly radio broadcast, *The Voice of Truth,* dates back to 1946 and is the oldest continuing radio program of the Assemblies in any foreign field. The broadcast is heard not only in Uruguay but also in Argentina, Paraguay, and southern Brazil. The missionaries in Uruguay report that the people, long considered pleasure-loving and indifferent to religion, are more responsive to the gospel than ever before. Another Pentecostal mission is the *Church of God* (Cleveland), whose first contacts with Uruguay were in 1945. By 1949 two churches had been established. During the past two decades progress has been slow but steady. Today there are sixteen churches and thirteen missions with a total membership of five hundred.

Two Lutheran missions have a small work in Uruguay. The *Lutheran Church-Missouri Synod* has had a church in the capital city since 1936. The Augustana Lutheran Church, now the *Lutheran Church in America,* sent its first missionary to Montevideo in 1952. He was *Paul Benson.* In 1954 a new work was begun in Rivera, a town of forty thousand on the border of Brazil. The Lutherans report meager results after almost two decades of work. Although services are held in five different places, no congregation has yet been organized.

The *Worldwide Evangelization Crusade,* the first faith mission to enter Uruguay, launched its work in 1950. The five missionaries there at present belong to the British branch of the mission and are working in the northeast section of the country. Three other faith missions are found in Uruguay, *New Testament Missionary Union, Worldwide European Fellowship,* and *Evangelical Mission to Uruguay.*

The *Mennonite Board of Missions and Charities* began work in Uruguay in 1954. The two oldest churches, in La Paz and Sauce, have a combined baptized membership of about seventy-five. The *Evangelical Biblical Seminary* in Montevideo, founded in 1956, is now a cooperative effort of the Mennonite Board of Missions and the General Conference Mennonite Church, whose first missionaries reached Uruguay in 1960. Teaching is done in both German and Spanish and is designed to prepare

Christian workers for Mennonite churches of various backgrounds in Paraguay, Uruguay, Brazil, and Argentina.

The *Waldensian Church* in Uruguay owes its origin to *Pastor Armand-Hugon,* who arrived in 1877 and for forty-two years gave himself indefatigably to the work of the Lord. During that time he built schools, organized a lay ministry, and divided the settlements into parishes, each with its own church. By 1905 they were sufficiently organized to become the sixth district of the Mother Church. A later development united the churches in Uruguay and Argentina, making them the seventh district of the Waldensian Church. One of the outstanding features of the church in Uruguay is the ministry of laymen. In the northern part of the country most of the churches are in charge of laymen. The Waldensian population today is about thirteen thousand, divided among seventeen churches under the supervision of eleven pastors.

The *Church of the Nazarene* after twenty years of work in Uruguay reports thirteen churches and preaching points, none of them self-supporting. Missionaries number eight. The only institution is a Bible school with eight students.

The *Seventh Day Adventists* have no schools or medical work in Uruguay, but they do have twenty-one churches with a membership of 3,170. The *Salvation Army* work in Uruguay dates back to 1890. It was not until January, 1917, that the SA was recognized by the Ministry of the Interior as a Juridical Person. In 1968 it reported twelve hundred members.

During the last two decades some half dozen Baptist missions have begun work in Uruguay: *Independent Bible Baptist Missions* (1950), *Baptist Bible Fellowship* (1959), *Free Will Baptists* (1962), *Baptist World Missions* (1964), *National Baptist Convention* (1965), and *Baptist Missionary Association of America* (1965).

Several supporting groups have moved into Uruguay: *Christian Literature Crusade* (1950), *Campus Crusade* (1966), and *Child Evangelism Fellowship.*

The *Plymouth Brethren* from New Zealand have had a small band of missionaries in Uruguay since the 1930's. The *Pocket Testament League* held a six-month campaign in 1965-66, during which time two teams had nearly four hundred meetings and distributed a quarter of a million Gospels of John. Some six thousand persons enrolled in a free correspondence course in John's Gospel. These people were all referred to evangelical churches near their homes.

Ecumenical Relations. The *Evangelical Institute of Montevideo,* sponsored by the Lutheran Church in America in cooperation with other churches and interdenominational organizations, was established in 1966. Catholics as well as evangelical theologians are attached to this institute. Another ecumenical organization is the *Center for Christian*

Studies in Montevideo. The most inclusive of all groups is the *Federation of Evangelical Churches in Uruguay.* The headquarters of the *Provisional Committee for Latin American Evangelical Unity,* sponsored by the World Council of Churches, is located in Montevideo. Known as UNELAM, the committee has seven councils or national federations in various countries. Its executive secretary is Emilio Castro.

Paraguay

Political History. Paraguay threw off the Spanish yoke in 1811. During much of the nineteenth century the country was ruled by three strong dictators who provided political stability and economic prosperity. The country lost half its population in a fratricidal war in the 1860's with its three neighbors. A war with Bolivia in the 1930's won the bulk of a vast disputed territory but left Paraguay exhausted.

The People. The population of 2.3 million is the most homogeneous in South America. About 95 percent of the people are mestizo. The large majority live in the east, most of them within a hundred-mile radius of the capital. The official language is Spanish; but Guarani has been described as "the strongest and most freely held national tie, the passport and seal of Paraguayan authenticity, the voice of the Paraguayan soul." Literacy is about 30 percent.

Religion. Roman Catholicism has been strong in Paraguay ever since the Jesuits established the reductions (Christian villages for the Indians) in the seventeenth and eighteenth centuries. On August 2, 1967, over the vigorous protest of the Protestant churches, Roman Catholicism was declared the state religion. Other religions are tolerated. The Protestant denominations, which represent only 1 percent of the population, are located in Asunción and a few country towns.

Missions. Here again, for the third time in South America, we find the Anglican mission, the *South American Missionary Society.* Its pioneer, *Adolpho Henricksen,* reached the Chaco in 1888 but lived only one year. His successor, *Wilfred B. Grubb,* was the first white man to live among the Lengua Indians of Paraguay. His term of service extended over twenty years, during which he reduced languages to writing, translated the Scriptures, and prepared grammars. Today there is a small, poverty-stricken Chaco church among the Lengua Indians. Three Indians with hardly any education have been ordained and are the leaders of the church. This Indian church is still without the complete New Testament; but it is growing. The 1968 Annual Report mentioned sixty new congregations. The Paraguayan ministry is centered in Asunción and Concepción. The twenty-one missionaries are located in four zones: Chaco, Concepción, River, and Central.

The second mission to enter Paraguay was the *New Testament Missionary Union* founded by John Hay in 1902. At that time it was known as the Paraguayan Evangelistic and Medical Mission. The name was changed in 1931. Its missionaries have not engaged in educational and institutional work. Instead, they have concentrated on church planting; and when a church can stand on its own feet, the missionaries move on. The plan seems to have paid off, for today the *New Testament Church,* with fifteen hundred members, is the largest Protestant church in the country.

The *United Christian Missionary Society* (Disciples) initiated work in Paraguay in 1917. The educational work centers around *International Academy,* which maintains a position of prominence in Paraguay. *Friendship Mission* ministers to the physical and social needs of the people. There are some fourteen or fifteen congregations, including an English-speaking group in Asunción. A dispensary and three rural service centers form part of the work. With a better educated national ministry the church in Paraguay is about to enter a new era. The nineteen missionary pastors will still be needed to promote church growth.

There is a good deal of Mennonite work in Paraguay, most of it dating back to 1935. The work among the Indians in the Chaco was begun by the *Evangelical Mennonite Brethren, General Conference Mennonite,* and the *Mennonite Brethren Churches* in Filadelfia. These three groups formed a mission called *Light to the Indians;* but they soon learned that they lacked the necessary financial resources. The Mennonite Brethren Church, being the largest of the three, was asked to communicate with the Mennonite Brethren Board of Missions of North America to apply for help. The response was favorable and now these two churches support the *Light to the Indians.*

The *Mennonite Central Committee's* six missionaries sponsor a variety of programs in Paraguay, including the immigration of Mennonites, the establishment of Mennonite colonies, Indian and Paraguayan settlements, home industries, leprosy work, and others. Since the MCC director left Paraguay in July, 1969, these projects are directly related to the Mennonite organizations which are responsible for administering the cooperative projects. The total number of baptized Indians in Paraguay in 1968 was 1,150.

Assemblies of God missionaries first arrived in Paraguay in 1945 and worked among Pentecostal Christians who had fled from the Slavic countries of Europe. Churches were established in Encarnación, Asunción, and other cities. The *Paraguay Assemblies of God* was formed in 1958. The following year a Bible institute was opened in Asunción. The first *Women's Missionary Council* was organized in 1960. Literature, Bible correspondence courses, and radio ministry round out the program. The national church, with 480 members, is served by thirty-one national workers. Eleven missionaries continue to work with the church.

A second Pentecostal mission, the *Church of God* (Cleveland), has been at work since 1954, when *Dr. Hargrave* and *Jose Minay* met in Paraguay and laid plans for the evangelization of the new field. By the end of the year a church had been planted in Asunción, and a Bible school was opened in 1957. In 1970 the work had grown to include thirty churches and sixty missions, with a total membership of 1,050.

The *Southern Baptist Convention* entered Paraguay in 1945; but Baptist work in that country dates back to 1919, when the *Argentine Baptist Convention* sent *Mr. and Mrs. Fernandez* to Asunción as its first missionaries. The *Paraguay Baptist Theological Institute* opened in 1956. Medical work was begun by Miss Miriam Willis. Later, in 1953, a fifty-bed hospital was opened—the first Baptist hospital in South America. A school of nursing has been connected with the hospital since 1961. The *Paraguay Baptist Convention,* organized in 1956, has recently adopted a plan whereby it hopes to double Baptist work, including stewardship, in the next five years. The PBC has fourteen churches and 1,475 members. Twenty-six missionaries cooperate with the church; but Paraguay "sorely needs additional field missionaries" for work in the interior.

In 1946 the *New Tribes Mission,* then a fairly new organization, took up work among the Indian tribes in the northeastern section of the country. The mission works closely with the Indian Affairs Department. The government offered NTM the responsibility of a large Indian reservation of over thirty thousand acres. The Maka Indian work near Asunción was turned over to the mission in 1962. In 1967 the government gave about six thousand acres of land for a reservation in the far northern part of the Chaco where the Moro Indians roam. The mission has work also on the Chamacoco Indian reservation. Today there are fifty NTM missionaries in Paraguay; they are working among six tribes and in five other centers, including Asunción and Concepción.

The year 1946 witnessed the beginning of the *Free Methodist* mission in Paraguay. The *Reverend and Mrs. Harold Ryckman* led the way. The mission began by purchasing the *Samaritan Orphanage* in Asunción; it had been operated for many years by an independent missionary. Later this was converted into a Bible school. The work has not been easy. After almost a quarter of a century there are only eight churches and eight preaching points, with a total baptized membership of 151. There is no medical or educational work. Four Free Methodist missionaries are in Paraguay.

Two other missions with a fairly long record in Paraguay are the *Seventh Day Adventists* and the *Plymouth Brethren. Campus Crusade* is a newcomer, having arrived only in 1966. The *Pocket Testament League* visited Paraguay in the summer of 1965 and distributed twenty-five thousand copies of the Gospel of John. A Bible correspondence course offered by the PTL drew more than one thousand registrations.

Evangelism. Representatives of fourteen evangelical bodies met during April, 1970, and took formal action toward planning a nationwide program of Evangelism-in-Depth to begin in July, 1971. The campaign is expected to have the support of seventeen of the country's twenty denominations and the participation of more than twenty-five thousand Christians.

Chile

Political History. Once part of the Spanish empire, Chile proclaimed its independence in 1810. In a war with Bolivia and Peru (1879-1884) it expanded its territory by one-third. Its present constitution was adopted in 1925. Since 1932 all presidents have been duly elected by the people, including a communist, Salvador Allende, in October, 1970. If Allende is a genuine Marxist and remains in power for any length of time, civil liberties, including freedom of speech, press, assembly, and religion, will gradually but surely disappear.

The People. The population of Chile is 9.5 million, half of whom are under twenty-one years of age. About 68 percent of the population is mestizo, 30 percent European, and 2 percent Indian. Education is free and compulsory; but it is estimated that only 30 percent of those who start first grade complete the six years of primary school. Chile has a high degree of urbanization—about 70 percent—one-third of which is found in the province which includes the capital.

Religion. The Roman Catholic Church claims 80 percent of the population, including the Indians; but only 10 percent of them attend mass. The evangelicals have been growing at a fast rate, mostly among the Pentecostal groups. The old-line denominations remain stagnant. In 1966 the Frei government promulgated a decree which authorized the teaching of Roman Catholicism in public schools. Mass meetings by evangelicals in major cities throughout Chile, including a thirty-thousand-person demonstration in the center of Santiago, prompted the government to rescind the decree a year later. Up to the present, evangelicals have enjoyed a large measure of religious freedom. It remains to be seen what the future holds under a communist regime.

Missions. The earliest continuing work in Chile was started by the *United Presbyterians* in 1873, when they took over an independent work started in Valparaiso in 1847. Chile has been the least productive of all the nine countries in South America in which the American Presbyterians have worked. After 123 years the church is still a small body of some twenty-five hundred members. In 1950 a Ten-Year Plan was adopted whereby the mission would progressively transfer its responsibilities to the church. The plan was somewhat changed in 1957 when it was agreed that a phased withdrawal of missionary personnel would be effected until all missionaries had left the country. In 1963 the *Presbyterian Church in Chile* became independent, and for the last two years there have been no fraternal workers in Chile. The only continuing support is that given to the Evangelical Theological Community, an ecumenical project shared by Anglicans, Methodists, and Pentecostals.

In 1944 a schism occurred in the Presbyterian Church in Chile. A group of young people known as Group Evangelical Action launched a movement designed to foster more prayer, more Bible study, more evangelism, and tithing within the church. George Gilchrist, Presbyterian missionary, and Alivero Maufras, Chilean pastor, gave encouragement and leadership to the movement, which soon gained wide support in the denomination. The presbytery, in an attempt to suppress the movement, ordered the two men to terminate their activities in connection with the Group Evangelical Action. When they refused, they were suspended from the ministry, whereupon one-fifth of the denomination withdrew in protest.

The leaders of the new group, called the *National Presbyterian Church,* asked for help from the United States. Two conservative missions, *World Presbyterian Missions* and the *Independent Board for Presbyterian Foreign Missions,* went to their rescue immediately. Unfortunately, the new church split in 1956 over issues that had their origin in the USA and not Chile. As a result the Independent Board organized a new church and called it the *Fundamentalist National Presbyterian Church of Chile.* The World Presbyterian Missions has six couples working with the National Presbyterian Church, which now has eleven organized churches under the supervision of nine ordained pastors. Four young men are now studying at John Calvin Seminary in Quillota. The Independent Board has five missionaries working with the Fundamentalist Church. The seminary at Quinta, closed for several years, has been reopened with seven students. The church has five pastors. The mission operates a Christian day school in Chillan.

American Methodist work in Chile began when the *Reverend William Taylor* in 1877-78 toured the west coast of South America seeking to establish self-supporting schools in English-speaking communities. These schools were expected to produce leaders for the evangelical churches which hopefully would emerge. The work in Chile became a part of the South American Annual Conference in 1893. In 1905 Chile established its own Annual Conference. In May, 1969, the *Chilean Methodist Church* held its own national assembly, constituted itself an autonomous church, and elected the Reverend Raimundo Valenzuela as its first bishop. The

Annual Conference is divided into five districts. Institutions include two high schools, a Christian training institute, a student center, and a rural life center. Theological training is provided in the ecumenical Theological Community. The Methodist Church has fifty-two hundred full members and half as many preparatory members served by forty-four pastors, thirty-four national and ten missionary.

In 1898 the *Christian and Missionary Alliance* assumed the support of two independent missionaries already in Chile. Several additional missionaries went to Chile at the turn of the century. The first chapel was dedicated in Valdivia in 1900. A Bible institute was started in 1921. Between 1920 and 1927 some fifteen missionaries joined the work in Chile. Besides having work in half a dozen cities in Chile, the C&MA has work on the island of Chiloe. Today the mission has fifty-two organized churches and 136 unorganized churches, all of them self-supporting.

The *Soldiers' and Gospel Mission,* now known as the *Gospel Mission of South America,* was founded by *William M. Strong* in 1923. Before leaving for Chile at forty-five years of age, Mr. Strong had been in the insurance business in New York. After spending two months in Bolivia, Mr. Strong landed in Chile where he immediately went to work, preaching the gospel to the soldiers in Tacna. In 1925 the work was extended to Valparaiso and Concepción. In 1933 *William M. Strong, Jr.* joined the work in Chile and initiated work among the Indian population in and around Galvarino. Reinforcements from the United States and Great Britain arrived in the 1930's and new stations were opened in various parts of the country. As the mission expanded its work more time and thought were given to the civilian population. When the soldiers' part of the work was phased out several years ago, the mission changed its name. In 1970 the mission had sixty-five missionaries on its roll, all of them in Chile.

Baptist Missions. German immigrants established the first Baptist church in Chile in 1892. The *Chilean Baptist Convention* was organized in 1908. The *Southern Baptist Convention* sent its first missionaries to Chile in 1917. Today the work centers in seven cities from Antofagasta in the north to Punta Arenas in the extreme south. The *Chilean Baptist Convention* now comprises 118 churches, most of them self-supporting. It has a membership of almost eleven thousand, which represents an increase of 55 percent in the last decade. The seminary, established in Santiago in 1939, provides a steady flow of pastors for the churches. There are two primary schools and a high school. The only medical work is a clinic in Antofagasta. The publication work is located in the capital.

The second largest Baptist group is the *Association of Baptists for World Evangelism,* which entered Chile in 1953 and now has twenty-two missionaries on its staff. Its work is located in two large cities, Santiago and Valparaiso, where it is engaged in evangelism and church planting. By

1965 five congregations were meeting and three of them were organized churches.

Three other Baptist organizations have entered Chile recently: *Baptist Bible Fellowship* (1955), *Maranatha Baptist Mission* (1963), and *World Baptist Fellowship Mission Agency* (1969).

Anglican Mission. The only Anglican mission in Chile is the *South American Missionary Society* of England. It began medical work about the turn of the century among the Mapuche Indians in the south. The mission is also engaged in direct evangelism, education, agriculture, literature, student work, and theological training. The adoption of a "Forward Move" plan in 1961 almost doubled the number of missionaries and permitted the mission to open new churches in Santiago, Valparaiso, Concepción, and Temuco. Very few of the Anglican congregations are self-supporting. The half-hour radio program in Valparaiso was taken off the air in 1968 because of lack of funds to meet the rising costs. The *Dorothy Royce Hospital,* ministering to the Indians, was closed in 1969 for lack of personnel. Since then it has been operating as a clinic with a Chilean nurse in charge. The SAMS has fifty missionaries in Chile.

Lutheran Missions. The *Lutheran Church-Missouri Synod* began work in Chile in 1954, but the investment was never large. For several years now there have been no missionaries in Chile. In 1967 a small church of 141 baptized members was served by two national pastors. The *Lutheran Church in America* entered Chile in 1963 and has been working with the *Lutheran Church in Chile,* almost entirely a German-speaking church. In 1969 two Spanish-speaking congregations were organized in Santiago as the direct result of the work of the Board of World Missions of the LCA.

Pentecostal Missions. There are at least half a dozen Pentecostal missions working in Chile. The *Church of God* (Cleveland) work got under way in fits and starts by short visits from various missionaries in 1917, 1940, and 1951. It was not until 1954 that missionaries took up residence and organized the first church. Today there are forty-five organized churches. The *Assemblies of God* work in Chile began with the arrival in Santiago of *Mr. and Mrs. H. C. Ball* in 1941. Other missionaries settled in Valparaiso in 1947. The *Assemblies of God in Chile* was organized in 1950. Today thirty-three organized churches have a membership of 1,350.

Other Pentecostal missions are in Chile but they have experienced very little growth. At first these missions all wanted to help the Chilean Pentecostal churches; but because of serious disagreements regarding baptism and the nature of supernatural manifestations, they were obliged to go their own way and establish their own churches, none of which is large even after many years.

Pentecostal Churches. The real growth in Chile has taken place in the indigenous Pentecostal churches. So great has been their growth that today they represent 80 percent of all evangelicals in Chile. Sad to relate, these churches are fragmented so badly that today there are 125 different denominations of Pentecostals.

The Pentecostal movement in Chile goes back to 1910, when *Dr. W. C. Hoover,* a Methodist minister, received the "Baptism of the Holy Spirit" and led the members of his congregation into the same experience. Other congregations followed and in no time at all the movement began to snowball. The Methodist hierarchy repudiated Hoover and declared his doctrines to be "anti-Methodist, contrary to the Scriptures and irrational"; whereupon the majority in the three churches in Santiago and Valparaiso withdrew and founded the *Methodist Pentecostal Church.* Dr. Hoover became its leader. From 1910 to 1930 the MPC grew by accepting dissenters from the old-line denominations founded by expatriate Protestants. From 1930 on, the church drew its members from the Chilean masses, mostly nominal Catholics, who joined its ranks in search of spiritual reality. Since 1950 it has grown by leaps and bounds, until today it has a communicant membership of about one hundred fifty thousand.

There are other large Pentecostal churches in Chile, all of them completely indigenous. The *Evangelical Pentecostal Church* has approximately one hundred twenty thousand communicant members. Other churches, though much smaller, are far larger than those founded by expatriate missions. The Pentecostal community in Chile today is estimated at over half a million.

Ecumenical Relations. At one time three churches held membership in the World Council of Churches: *Evangelical-Lutheran Church in Chile, Pentecostal Church of Chile,* and *Pentecostal Mission Church.* These two Pentecostal churches made history when, at the New Delhi Assembly in 1961, they became the first Pentecostal groups to join the WCC. The Pentecostal Mission Church is no longer a member of the world body. The *Evangelical Council of Chile* is related to the Division of World Mission and Evangelism of the WCC. In recent years the council has been torn by internal strife. The *Methodist Pentecostal Church,* largest in Chile, withdrew from the council in 1968. The *Evangelical Theological Community,* inaugurated in 1965, is an ecumenical training center for Methodists, Anglicans, and some Pentecostal groups. For a time the Presbyterian Church of Chile participated, but it withdrew in 1968. In 1965 there were four denominations in the Chilean Confederation of Evangelical Fundamentalist Churches.

Bolivia

Political History. Bolivia was once part of the famous Inca Empire which was destroyed by the Spanish. Independence from Spain was declared in 1825 and the new country was named after the great Latin-American liberator, Simon Bolivar. At one time or another Bolivia has gone to war with its five neighbors, and in the process has lost over half its original territory. As a result it is today a landlocked country. Politically Bolivia has been notoriously unstable. Since independence it has undergone well over two hundred revolutions. This has affected the economy. It has received more U.S. aid per capita than any other Latin American country; but it is still the poorest country after Haiti.

The People. The estimated population of Bolivia is 4.7 million. It is one of several Latin American countries where the Indians outnumber the rest of the population. They represent about 55 percent, European stock 15 percent, and mestizos 32 percent. The ruling class is of Spanish descent. Spanish is the official language. The Indians speak their own dialects, the two principal ones being Quechua and Aymara. Through the years the Indians have been exploited and oppressed.

Religion. Roman Catholicism has been the dominant religion ever since it was first introduced by the Spanish conquerors. It has not, however, made much impression on the Indians. The colorful Indian festivals are a strange mixture of Christian and pagan rites. Approximately two-thirds of the priests in Bolivia are foreigners. Protestant missions have been in Bolivia for over seventy years and enjoy a good measure of religious liberty. The government has looked with favor on evangelical missions, and not a few missionaries have been decorated for their humanitarian work. There are thirty-three Protestant groups working in the country.

Missions. The distinction of being the first mission in Bolivia belongs to the *Canadian Baptists,* who began their work in 1898. In those early days missionary work was both difficult and dangerous, for the penal code of the state declared that anyone conspiring to establish a religion other than the Catholic religion "is a traitor, and shall suffer the penalty of death." The lives of the missionaries and their converts were often in danger. The Canadian Baptists pioneered in evangelism, education, agrarian reform, theological education, radio work, and interdenominational cooperation. The *Southern Cross Radio Station* blankets Bolivia with the gospel and also beams it into other parts of South America. It accepts commercial advertising, which helps to balance the budget. The *Bolivian Baptist Union* received its independence in 1966; since then the thirty-four missionaries have been under its jurisdiction. The mission maintains a clinic and a theological seminary. The latest addition, in 1969, was the *Carlos Merrick Collegiate Institute.*

The *Plymouth Brethren* took up work in Bolivia shortly after the Canadian Baptists. Through the years they have supported a large staff of missionaries from five home countries. Today thirty missionaries are at work in ten centers.

The *American Methodist* work grew out of the attempts of *Bishop William Taylor* to establish self-supporting schools and churches among the English-speaking communities as a springboard for work among the Spanish-speaking peoples and the Indian tribes. The *American Institute* in Cochabamba, founded in 1912, is one of the outstanding institutions in Bolivia. *Pfeiffer Memorial Hospital* in La Paz is a modern and well-equipped private hospital. Connected with it is a school of nursing, the first in the country. In the last ten years the Methodist Church has grown rapidly, extending its work from two into eight of the nine departments into which the country is divided. Much of this is due to the influence of Keith Hamilton, who got a vision for church planting while attending the Institute of Church Growth. Today the Methodist work in Bolivia is divided into six districts. *Wesley Institute* in Montero, which offers a four-year course, has facilities to train forty church workers. Some sixty-two missionaries are serving with the Methodist Church in Bolivia.

The largest church in Bolivia is the *Seventh Day Adventist Church,* whose twelve thousand members are found in all parts of the country. The largest concentration, however, is found in the areas of La Paz and Lake Titicaca, where a mass movement among Aymara Indians took place between 1915 and 1934. Much of their growth can be attributed to their fine system of schools. In 1970 they reported 326 primary schools, nine secondary schools, and one college in their Inca Union Mission. At Chulumani they have a hospital and a sanitarium.

Shortly after the beginning of the century *George Allan* and five other New Zealanders arrived in Bolivia with a burden for the Quechua and Aymara Indians. For a time they cooperated with the Canadian Baptists; but in 1907 Mr. Allan established the *Bolivian Indian Mission,* which concentrated most of its efforts in the departments of Potosi and Cochabamba. Mr. Allan translated the New Testament into Quechua. In 1950 the churches formed their own organization, *Evangelical Christian Union,* which became fully autonomous in 1966 and the following year joined the Bolivian Association of Evangelicals. The mission changed its name to the *Andes Evangelical Mission* in 1965 to conform more closely to its new goals of reaching non-Indians in Bolivia and branching out into Peru and other countries of South America. Under the dynamic leadership of *Joseph S. McCullough* and *C. Peter Wagner,* the AEM has acted as a catalyst in evangelical circles in Bolivia and beyond. It was largely instrumental in bringing into existence the *Bolivian Association of Evangelicals* and the *Bolivian Evangelical Social Action Committee.* It is a member of six or seven interdenominational organizations in Latin America. In Bolivia it has sponsored special campaigns by the Gideons (1959), Youth for Christ (1961), Pocket Testament League (1963), Evangelical Literature Overseas Workshops (1960, 1964), and Evangelism-in-Depth (1965).

With Indians predominating in Bolivia, it is only natural that several "Indian" missions should be located in that country. The *South America Indian Mission,* founded by *Joseph A. Davis,* began in the eastern part of the country in 1922. For many years it worked only among the Ayoreo and Chiquitano Indians, but more recently it has undertaken work among the Bolivians as well. On September 1, 1970, the name of the mission was changed and the word "Indian" was deleted. Today its eighteen missionaries are located in six centers engaged exclusively in evangelism and church planting. In 1969 the mission moved its headquarters to Santa Cruz, which is the main supply center for the entire eastern part of Bolivia, where its work is located.

Bolivia is one of four countries in which the *Evangelical Union of South America* has work. The program in Bolivia got under way in 1937 in the highlands in the southwest part of the country. Three main stations and many outstations have been opened there. In 1944 the mission moved into the eastern lowlands. The following year the *Eastern Bolivian Fellowship,* laboring among the Chane and Chirguano Indians, merged with the EUSA. At present there are eight main stations in the lowlands. Twenty-seven missionaries are engaged in evangelism, youth work, radio, literature, and church planting. The *Hebron Bible Institute* in Camiri offers courses in Spanish and Guarani. The EUSA also has a British branch working in Bolivia which is quite distinct from the North American branch.

The *World Mission Prayer League,* a Lutheran faith mission, has had missionaries in Bolivia since 1938. Their thirty missionaries are located in four main centers. In the capital, La Paz, they have their headquarters, bookstore, Spanish-speaking church, and Indian work. In Coaba there is a farm and a Bible school. The latest center is Caranavi, opened in 1967. It is here that they are erecting the Parish Radio Station. Two other centers are Apolo and Mocmoco. The *Bolivian Evangelical Lutheran Church* voted in 1967 to dissolve the church synod. Since then the pastors and congregations have continued to function as before.

In 1942 Bolivia became the first country to be occupied by the *New Tribes Mission.* Today, with eighty-eight missionaries, it is the second largest of NTM's twelve fields. Only Brazil, where they have 156 missionaries, is larger. The missionaries are located in fifteen centers and are working among seven different tribes. The mission operates a primary school, a middle school, and a high school. Its medical work is confined to a dental clinic.

The *World Gospel Mission* has a large investment in Bolivia dating back to 1943. Mission-sponsored institutions include the *Berea Bible School, Berea High School,* and *Nueva Esperanza* (evangelistic center). By means of *Radio Centenario* in Santa Cruz the mission is able to reach all four of its districts with long and shortwave broadcasts. A mission plane carries commercial passengers during the week to pay for evangelistic flights on the weekends. The national church received its independence in 1969. Cooperation between church and mission is through a Joint Planning Committee of twelve members. Extension theological education is carried on from seven centers.

The *United World Mission* entered Bolivia in 1944. Santa Cruz is the headquarters of the mission and the home of two of its three missionary couples. Some six national workers cooperate with the program in Santa Cruz, which includes radio, literature, evangelism, and church planting.

The *Church of the Nazarene* has been in Bolivia for twenty-five years. The missionary staff at present numbers twelve. Serving with them are sixty-five national workers in a church of two thousand members. The Bible college, closed for some time, was due to reopen in 1970.

Several Pentecostal missions are in Bolivia. The first to arrive was the *Assemblies of God,* in 1946. The basic strategy was to establish centers in the cities and branch out into the surrounding areas. In the early years three important cities were occupied: La Paz, Cochabamba, and Santa Cruz. Today the mission and church are working among the Spanish-speaking people and the Aymara Indians. Three Bible schools have provided strong leadership for a growing church. In 1967 the church and the mission cooperated in a program of Total Evangelism. As a result church membership increased from 1,700 to 2,850 in two years. Ten missionaries assist ninety national workers in an on-going program of evangelism and church planting.

Two other Pentecostal missions are in Bolivia. The *International Church of the Foursquare Gospel* has maintained a work among the savage Siriono tribe since 1929. Their main work centers in a large compound in the Green Hell jungle, where some three hundred Indians are living under Christian instruction. The *Church of God* (Cleveland), a newcomer in the 1960's, reports eight churches with sixty-four members.

Wycliffe Bible Translators began work in Bolivia in 1955. Their eighty linguists are working in sixteen tribes. They have analyzed many dialects and reduced several languages to writing. The Gospel of Mark has been produced in eight languages and Luke and nine other books of the New Testament in various others.

The *Mennonite Central Committee,* which coordinates the social and relief work of the many Mennonite groups in North America, has some forty missionaries in Bolivia engaged in agriculture and rural development projects. They have recently rounded out a decade of service. The *Oregon Yearly Meeting, Friends Church,* has been in Bolivia since 1930. Their

National Evangelical Church, with three thousand members, has been autonomous since 1963. They have no medical work. Educational work includes thirty primary schools, one normal school, and a Bible school.

Theological Education. In recent years the *Andes Evangelical Mission* has pioneered in new forms of theological training. In April, 1969, it established the *George Allan Theological Seminary* by merging two Bible schools. The seminary, a joint effort of church and mission, has three programs, urban, rural, and extension, which operate on six levels to meet the requirements of a multicultural society with vastly differing needs. One unique feature of the seminary is the extension department which provides on-the-job theological training for older pastors who cannot leave their farms, families, and churches long enough to take advantage of the more conventional type of centralized theological training. Known as Extension Theological Education, this program is being rapidly expanded into all parts of South and Central America; and programmed textbooks are being prepared in Spanish and Indian languages for use throughout Latin America. Through the good offices of the *Committee to Assist Missionary Education Overseas* (a joint IFMA-EFMA project), this new concept of theological training has spread to Africa and Asia, where the first workshops were conducted in the summer of 1970. Africa has requested five more workshops for 1971, three in French and two in English. Five countries in Asia have made similar requests.

Bible Societies. The work here began in 1827. In 1905 Bolivia was added to the Republic of the Andes Agency. In 1940 it became a Joint Sub-Agency with Chile of the British and American Societies. The Bolivian Sub-Agency was separated from that of Chile in 1956. The year 1968 saw the first Advisory Committee of the Bible Societies in Bolivia. Members of the committee represent all the major denominations in the country. That same year the Bible Society dedicated its own building in the heart of Cochabamba. Not a single Indian language has the complete Bible. Two tribes, Quechua and Aymara, have the New Testament. A popular version of these New Testaments is under way. Nine additional Indian languages have at least a Portion. The translations done by the *Wycliffe Bible Translators,* mentioned earlier, are not included in these figures. Scripture distribution is on the increase, sparked by special campaigns by the Baptists and the Adventists. The Roman Catholic community is showing a real interest in the study of the Bible.

Church Union. In 1959 the churches planted by the *Evangelical Union of South America* merged with the *Evangelical Christian Union,* a church body which in 1950 grew out of the work of the *Andes Evangelical Mission.* At its biennial convention on November 2, 1968, the Evangelical Christian Union of Bolivia voted to establish a confederation with the

Evangelical Church of Peru. The ECP took similar action at its annual assembly in Peru on September 1, 1968. This is the first known instance of two churches founded by faith missions crossing international boundaries. The new confederation will include almost seven hundred fifty churches and a membership of over twenty thousand.

In August, 1970, three missions, the Andes Evangelical Mission and the British and American branches of the Evangelical Union of South America, held a joint business meeting in Cochabamba in which they discussed the possibility of a merger. Two of the missions agreed to the idea in principle. The EUSA (UK) proposed a waiting period of two years.

Ecumenical Relations. Various members of the thirty-three Protestant agencies work together in local councils of churches and in the *Aymara Literature and Literacy Committee.* The American Methodists and other groups have cooperated with the Canadian Baptists' *Southern Cross Radio Station* in La Paz. The *Bolivian Evangelical Social Action Committee* (COMBASE) was organized in 1963. The widest fellowship is the *National Association of Evangelicals in Bolivia* (ANDEB), which was established in 1967. Its constitution calls for affiliation with the *World Evangelical Fellowship.* Its original purpose was to combat the growing influence of the ecumenical movement, especially the overtures made to the national churches by such ecumenical organizations as the *Provisional Committee for Evangelical Unity in Latin America* (UNELAM) which, though independent, has indirect ties with the World Council of Churches. Since its founding three years ago ANDEB has been the battleground between the conservative evangelicals on the one hand and the ecumenists on the other. The Methodist Church has never joined ANDEB and the Canadian Baptists have withdrawn.

Peru

Political History. Peru was the center of the ancient Inca Empire which was destroyed by the Spanish conqueror, Francisco Pizarro. In colonial times Peru was the principal source of Spanish wealth and power in South America. It was liberated in 1824 by Sam Martin and Simon Bolivar. Since then it has been dominated by strong-man rule, both military and civilian. It is presently ruled by a military junta which came to power by a bloodless coup d'etat in October, 1968. The seizure of American industries has worsened American-Peruvian relations.

The People. Peru's population is estimated at 13.5 million and is divided three ways. Approximately 46 percent is Indian, 43 percent mestizo, and 11 percent white. A certain degree of racial tension exists among the three groups. The official language is Spanish, but many of the

Andean Indians speak only Quechua or Aymara. The forest Indians of the eastern jungles (about one hundred thousand and diminishing rapidly) speak a wide variety of unrelated languages and dialects. The population is increasing annually at 3 percent. Literacy is estimated at 55 percent.

Religion. The Roman Catholic Church claims 99 percent of the people of Peru. The 1915 Constitution provided for religious freedom, but Roman Catholicism has been given preferential treatment, and since 1929 has been the only religion allowed to be taught in any school, public or private. Catholic-Protestant relations have improved greatly since 1960. Protestant parades were permitted in the interior for the first time in 1967. A census in the mid-sixties indicated 153,000 Protestants in the country, a net increase of 100,000 in twenty years. According to figures released by the National Evangelical Council, church membership is now increasing at an annual rate of 20 percent.

Missions. *American Methodists* were the first to undertake missionary work in Peru. Permanent work was begun by *Thomas B. Wood* in 1891. From the beginning the Methodists have regarded their schools as basic to their evangelistic outreach. The school started by Mr. Wood in Callao grew into one of the outstanding private schools in the country. Its graduates occupy positions in the professional and business life of the country. Besides *Callao High School,* there are two other high schools, several primary schools, a normal school, and an *Institute for Christian Workers.* Three social centers are also maintained. In January, 1968, the Methodist Church had a sufficient number of full members to become an Annual Conference. It is now seeking autonomy before 1972. The church is divided into three districts and has a membership of about fifteen hundred, two-thirds of whom come from city slum areas.

The *Church of the Nazarene* sent its first missionaries to Peru in 1917. Through the years it has maintained a steady staff of workers, mostly in the northern part of the country where the mission operates a primary school, a Bible school, and a dispensary. Nineteen missionaries are there at present. The national church comprises some one hundred eighty congregations, large and small, with a total membership of thirty-eight hundred, which includes those on probation. These churches are all self-supporting.

The *Seventh Day Adventists* have the largest church in Peru. Their work dates back to 1907 and began with a mass movement among the Aymara Indians around Lake Titicaca. A major factor in their growth has been their fine system of schools, whose teachers come from the Adventist normal school in Lima. The work in Peru is divided into four districts: Central, East, North, and South. In spite of several schisms, church membership at the close of 1969 was forty thousand.

The *Assemblies of God* is one of the larger missions in Peru. It has been at work there since 1919 and its church-planting program seems to have brought results, for today they report 220 churches with a membership of twelve thousand and an additional eight thousand adherents. Other Pentecostal missions include the *Church of God* (Cleveland), *Elim Missionary Association, United Pentecostal Church,* and *Swedish Free Mission.*

Peru, with fifty missionaries, is the largest of the four fields of the *South America* (Indian) *Mission.* The work began in 1921 and for almost half a century the mission has been working in Peru's vast jungle lowland among the Spanish-speaking and mixed-blood peoples as well as the scattered Indian tribes. The Spanish work includes itinerant river and road evangelism, literature, Bible training, camp, and children's work. The SAM has labored over thirty years among the Shipibo, Conibo, and Campa Indians, many of whom have come to Christ. More recently work has been established in two more tribes.

The *Regions Beyond Missionary Union* has two branches working in Peru, one from North America and the other from the United Kingdom. It entered Peru at the request of the *Peru Inland Mission* in 1922 and for many years worked in cooperation with that mission in the eastern section of the country. The main center of work is Lamas, where the hospital and the Bible school are located. In recent years more attention has been given to work among the Quechua Indians. Several years ago the PIM became integrated with the RBMU.

The *Christian and Missionary Alliance* opened its first station at Huanuco in 1926. In 1933 the mission founded the *Peruvian Bible Institute* and invited the Evangelical Union of South America and the Free Church of Scotland to cooperate in the training of nationals. In 1946 the school was reorganized and the C&MA established its own Bible school in Huanuco. The Alliance now has work in three main areas, the coast, the Sierra, and the eastern jungle. Its three centers on the coast are Lima, Trujillo, and Chimbote. The *Alliance Church in Peru* has been independent since 1955. The membership of almost fourteen hundred is divided among forty-four organized churches and seventy-five unorganized congregations.

The *Association of Baptists for World Evangelism* entered Peru in 1939 and has seven centers of work on the Ucayali and Amazon rivers. The hub of their work is in Iquitos, the largest river town in Peru. Today there are five churches associated in a fellowship through ABWE effort. A national missionary agency has been established. The Bible school, radio ministry, youth camp, and literature work are all located at Iquitos, a town of one hundred thousand with a very rapidly growing population. The missionary staff in Peru numbers thirty-three.

Baptist Mid-Missions has been in Peru since 1937. Its twenty-one missionaries assigned to Peru are located in Lima, Trujillo, Callao, and Cuzco. The *Southern Baptists* entered in 1950. Their thirty missionaries are working in five coastal cities from Arequipa in the south to Piura in the north. They maintain three bookstores and a theological seminary, the latter opened in 1959. The *Peruvian Baptist Convention* was organized in 1966. It has a membership of almost one thousand. Six of its fifteen churches are self-supporting. When the government completes the highway into the interior, the mission plans to acquire properties for future expansion. Five other Baptist missions have entered Peru within the last decade and their work there is just getting under way. None of them is large.

Wycliffe Bible Translators sent its first team of linguists into Peru in 1946. Since then it has greatly enlarged its program until today Peru, with 240 missionaries, is one of the larger fields of the mission. It has work in thirty-four tribes and plans to enter five more. The *Jungle Aviation and Radio Service* began in Peru.

The *Oregon Yearly Meeting, Friends Church* entered Peru in 1960. From the beginning the work has been on a purely indigenous basis, with the local congregations supporting themselves and in a great measure governing themselves. They have only church work in Peru. There are four organized churches and nineteen outstations, with a total membership of three hundred. These are served by four ordained pastors, two evangelists, and twenty-four lay pastors.

The British branch of the *Evangelical Union of South America,* under the leadership of *John Ritchie,* was instrumental in bringing into existence the *Evangelical Peruvian Church,* which in 1967 had an estimated membership of fourteen thousand. The great weakness of the church is the paucity of trained leaders, due in part to Ritchie's policy of encouraging lay rather than professional leadership. The church has no Bible school of its own and must depend for trained workers on the Lima Bible Institute, which trains leaders for the mestizo churches rather than for the more primitive Indian churches. In 1969 the *Andes Evangelical Mission* (Bolivia) sent its first missionary couple to Peru. In October, 1970, AEM entered into an alliance with EPC.

Naturally most of the missions operating in Peru are from North America; but there are half a dozen other missions, most of them rather small, from Switzerland, Sweden, Scotland, Ireland, Chile, and Australia. In addition there are several supporting missions, such as *Christian Service Corps, Missionary Dentist, Inc., Scripture Union, World Home Bible League.* Most of these are newcomers to Peru and are cooperating with the evangelical bodies in that country.

World Presbyterian Missions entered Peru in 1947. Like others, they have not found Peru an easy field. The mission has work in two of the three regions of the country. The hub of their work is in Huanta in the Sierra, where the mission began. A *National Presbyterian Church* has been formed. It has fourteen churches and more than forty unorganized congregations. To serve this field the presbytery has only two national pastors, a small number of partially trained lay workers, and thirteen missionaries.

The *Plymouth Brethren* have long been at work in Peru and today have over thirty missionaries there from Canada, the United Kingdom, and the USA. Their greatest concentration is in the city of Lima, where some four hundred thousand slum dwellers live. In the interior they have eight other centers of work.

The *Mennonite Brethren Church* has had a mission in Peru since 1946. At present they have seven missionaries there. The Indian work is confined to the Campa tribe, which numbers from twenty thousand to thirty thousand. There is also work among the Spanish-speaking Peruvians. From time to time missionaries have been loaned to other groups: Peruvian Seminary in Lima, Wycliffe Bible Translators, Evangelism-in-Depth, and others.

Christian Radio.   Although there is little cooperative programming in Peru, some local pastors have programs in Lima. Most denominations place weekly programs on commercial stations. *The Evangelical Alliance Mission* owns and operates the only missionary broadcasting station in Peru—*Radio del Pacifico,* which has a 10,000-watt mediumwave transmitter with simultaneous FM programs and a shortwave transmitter. The *Southern Baptists* have a recording studio in Lima. In 1970 gospel television came to Peru. A daily TV program, *Message to the Conscience,* is being broadcast over HCJB-TV in Lima. This program is being produced by *Latin American Radio Evangelism* and is the result of a citywide campaign by Paul Finkenbinder.

Evangelism.   Churches and missions are always engaging in evangelism. That is their chief business; but now and again special concerted efforts are put forth on a grand scale. One such was Evangelism-in-Depth, which was conducted in Peru in 1967. Churches were revived as they accepted the challenge to mobilize all their members for continuous, effective witnessing. The year was one of unprecedented sowing and harvesting as Christians united for a nationwide campaign. In twenty-five cities united regional crusades won thousands to Christ. No fewer than sixteen public parades were held in as many cities. The crusade concluded on Sunday, November 26, in the proud city of Lima with an overwhelming public demonstration of evangelical fervor. In a campaign in Peru the *Pocket Testament League* distributed thirty-five thousand gospels. In February, 1965, *World Vision* sponsored a training institute for pastors and Christian workers in Lima. Six hundred leaders from twenty-five groups attended, including eight teachers and pastors from the jungle tribes. The institute helped to prepare the way for Evangelism-in-Depth two years later.

Bible Societies.   *James Thompson* and *Francisco Penzotti,* of the British and American societies respectively, were the pioneers in Peru. In

1946 the *American Bible Society* and the *British and Foreign Bible Society* in Peru and Ecuador united as a Joint Agency, under BFBS administration. Peru and Ecuador became separate agencies in 1964. No Indian tribe, not even the Quechuas, as yet has the complete Bible in its native tongue. Three tribes have the New Testament, and twenty-seven have one or more Portions. The large number of translations of New Testament Portions in recent years has been mostly the work of Wycliffe Bible Translators. They alone have produced 110 translations and various New Testament books in 24 languages. In addition, they have translated the entire New Testament into the Piro language. The Bible societies are doing all they can to promote the distribution and reading of the Scriptures. To this end they conduct a score of distribution training courses each year. Distribution in recent years has been helped greatly by *Evangelism-in-Depth,* the Baptist *Crusade of the Americas,* and the Seventh Day Adventist program, *The Bible Speaks.* In 1968 more than thirty-eight thousand Scriptures were distributed through Roman Catholic churches.

Theological Education. Most of the missions have their own Bible schools and some of them have their own theological seminaries. There is only one interdenominational seminary, the *Evangelical Seminary of Lima* supported by the *Peruvian Fellowship,* which has headquarters in Toronto, Canada. The seminary trains leaders for all groups in Peru. It also has a Bible institute department. An *Association for Theological Education* was formed in 1965 and included, at that time, ten theological schools.

Ecumenical Relations. Several years ago Protestant missions and national churches in Peru formed the *Peruvian Evangelical Council.* The Methodists played a leading role in the council until 1966, when they withdrew as a protest against what they described as "a mission dominated organization." There may be more to the problem than appears on the surface. In 1968 the Peruvian Evangelical Council made the following statement:

> We alert the brethren that UNELAM and the affiliated groups are a threat to the evangelical movement because of their ecumenism. In the light of this the Board of Directors of the Peruvian National Evangelical Council after deep study has decided to abstain completely from all affiliation with UNELAM and for this reason has written a letter to them on this point.[6]

In a surprise move in August, 1969, the *Peruvian Evangelical Church,* largest in the country, decided to sever relations with the Bible Societies because of their alleged ecumenical position and their publication of a "Common Bible" with the Catholic Church.

---

[6] *Pulse,* Vol. III, No. 5, September, 1968, p. 6.

Ecuador

Political History. Ecuador became a separate, independent state in 1830 after being part of Greater Colombia for eight years. During the nineteenth century Ecuador witnessed a veritable parade of presidents, dictators, and juntas—forty in all. From 1925 to 1948 the country changed presidents twenty-two times. Since then a measure of political stability has been achieved. The last military coup was in 1963.

The People. The population of 5.8 million is divided four ways: approximately 40 percent Indian; another 40 percent mestizo; 10 percent Caucasian (mostly of Spanish descent); and 10 percent Negro. Spanish is the official language. Most of the Indians speak Quechua. Primary education is free and compulsory. Not all Indian children are in school, however.

Religion. Although Ecuador is a Roman Catholic country there is genuine freedom of religion. Protestant missions have been in Ecuador since the turn of the century but have made little impact on the religious life of the people. In fact, Ecuador has the smallest percentage of Protestants of all the Latin American countries—approximately twenty thousand out of a population of almost six million, about one-third of 1 percent of the total population. Of the forty Protestant groups only five have a Christian community of more than a thousand. There are, however, contributing factors to this situation.

Ecuador was one of the last countries of South America to open its doors to evangelical missionaries. Only four of the forty missions were there prior to 1940. The others are of more recent vintage, and only nine have more than ten missionaries in the country. Most of the missionaries worked among the Spanish-speaking mestizo population, where Roman Catholic influence was very strong. Consequently results were meager. As for the large Indian population, it was for many years "off limits" to the Protestant missionaries; and in more recent years when the limitations were lifted, few missionaries have learned the Indian's language.

Missions. The first Protestant mission to begin work in Ecuador was the *Gospel Missionary Union*. Mr. George Fisher and two companions arrived in 1896, shortly after a revolution opened Ecuador to non-Catholic missions. The mission has three distinct fields of labor: the mestizos in the lowlands, the Quechua Indians in the highlands, and the Jivaro Indian head-hunters on the upper reaches of the Amazon. Medicine plays an important role, especially among the Jivaros. Elementary schools are conducted for the Indians, in Spanish as well as the tribal languages. Most of the teaching is now done by Ecuadorians. A literature distribution center is maintained in Guayaquil. GMU operates three radio stations in

Ecuador. *Station HCGM-7* at Macuma broadcasts the gospel several hours daily to the Jivaro Indians; *HCUE*-6 and *HCUE*-5 are located in the Andes Mountains and broadcast in Quechua and Spanish. In spite of the fact that GMU has eighty-three missionaries in Ecuador, most of them in evangelism and church-planting ministries, in 1968 they reported only fifteen churches with a total membership of 535 after seventy-five years of work.

Pioneer missionaries of the *Christian and Missionary Alliance* arrived in Ecuador in 1897. During the early years in Quito persecution was so severe that only the timely intervention of the police prevented bloodshed, and it was impossible to hold public meetings. Tract distribution and personal work were all that could be attempted. Through the years the C&MA has been working in three areas: the coast, the Sierra, and the Oriente. Four coastal cities now have churches. Six main centers have been opened in the Sierra and four in the Oriente. Headquarters is in Quito, where the *Alliance Academy,* with an enrolment of 250, serves eighteen missionary societies in Ecuador. The largest church is in Guayaquil, where the city church has opened ten satellite churches in various parts of the city and suburbs. The mission conducts many short-term Bible schools and two long-term schools, one at Guayaquil, which operates on two levels, and one for Indians at Dos Rios. The mission, with subsidies from the government, also maintains elementary schools in the jungle areas. Two important ministries, the Bible schools and the Alliance Academy, draw heavily on the fifty missionaries in Ecuador. The national church, known as the *Ecuadorian Evangelical Church,* has fourteen organized churches, forty-nine unorganized churches, and forty-one outstations. Twelve of the forty-seven national workers are ordained pastors. Baptized church members number twenty-three hundred.

The third mission to open work in Ecuador was the *Seventh Day Adventists* in 1906. The ready response of the Aymara Indians in Bolivia and Peru which enabled the SDA to build up a large church in those two countries was not repeated in Ecuador. Consequently the SDA have been no more successful than any other group. Their entire foreign staff consists of only eight missionaries. Nineteen churches with a membership of thirty-three hundred represent the extent of their evangelistic work. Even so, it is the largest church in Ecuador.

In 1945 four of the old-line denominations joined forces to form the *United Andean Indian Mission.* The mission established its first station, Picalqui Farm, sixty miles north of Quito, in 1946. Later two other centers were opened. Its program included evangelism, education, agriculture, and medicine. The Heifer Project has cooperated with the agricultural part of the work. The UAIM merged its evangelistic work with that of the *Church of the Brethren.* This resulted, in 1965, in the formation of the *United Evangelical Church of Ecuador,* with twelve congregations and four hundred members. The church embraces both rural and urban groups. Developing Indian leadership has been difficult; but work among the more responsive mestizos and whites has grown. Through the years the number of missionaries in this cooperative effort has varied from ten to sixteen.

The *Missionary Church Association* has twelve missionaries working in the northwest province of Esmeraldas. The Ecuadorian mission got under way in 1945, and by 1952 the *National Evangelical Church of Ecuador* had been organized. Today the church comprises seven organized congregations and thirty-five unorganized groups with a total of 216 members. Seven national pastors and seven teachers are working with the national church.

The *Evangelical Covenant Church of America* opened its work in Ecuador in 1947. From the beginning the main emphasis has been on evangelism. At present Covenant churches are found in Quito, Guayaquil, Ibarra, Tulcan, and other cities located mostly in the north central province. A national Covenant Church was organized in 1961. At one time their missionaries in Ecuador numbered twenty-two. At present they are down to ten. Institutional work includes three elementary schools and a medical clinic.

The year 1950 marked the beginning of *Southern Baptist* work in Ecuador. The first center was Quito, where they have a bookstore and a primary school. The first Baptist churches, officially recognized as such in 1954, were two small congregations which for many years had been independent but had held Baptist doctrines and used Baptist literature. At present the mission has twenty-six missionaries in six centers, three along the coast and three in the interior. A theological institute was opened in Guayaquil in 1961. The mission is now developing an agricultural project. Twenty-seven churches report a total of 1,150 baptized members under the care of thirty-seven pastors.

The *World Mission Prayer League* (Lutheran) has a small work in the inland city of Cuenca dating back to 1951. Most of the dozen missionaries there are new recruits. They are engaged in church and school work.

The *Inter-American Missionary Society* (South America branch of the Oriental Missionary Society) entered Ecuador in 1952, intending at first that it should be part of the Colombia field, which at that time was in danger of folding up. Mission headquarters is established in Guayaquil. The IAMS churches in Ecuador are organized under the name of the *Inter-American Church*. In 1958 the Night Cultural Bible Institute work began. That same year the mission began work among the Araguro Indian tribe, where the mission's one clinic is now located. The national church comprises ten organized congregations and eight preaching points, with a total baptized membership of 366. Nine pastors cooperate with eighteen missionaries in church and school work. A small Bible school with thirteen students is training men for the ministry.

In Ecuador we meet again with the *Wycliffe Bible Translators*. Their first team arrived in 1953, and since that time translators have begun work in seven tribes, including the Auca Indians. Seventy-five missionaries are now located in Ecuador. The Gospel of Mark has been translated into four Indian languages.

There are five Pentecostal missions in Ecuador and several splinter groups which call themselves Pentecostals. The largest mission is the *International Church of the Foursquare Gospel,* whose first missionaries, *Mr. and Mrs. Arthur Gadberry,* arrived in Guayaquil in 1956. Opening a Bible school, they reached some adults. Later a vacant lot was rented and for ten weeks services were held with an average attendance of fourteen. By 1962 two churches were organized in Guayaquil and El Milagro with a total of seventy members. A breakthrough occurred in 1962 as a result of a citywide evangelistic and healing campaign conducted in Guayaquil by Roberto Espinoza. Attendance reached forty thousand, largely because of the miraculous healings which took place and which attracted the attention of the entire city. By 1964 the mission reported fifteen churches, nineteen meeting places, and almost twenty-three hundred converts. The *United Pentecostal Church* has shown similar growth. The *Assemblies of God* has been in Ecuador since 1962 and has only eight missionaries there; but already they report eight churches with a combined membership of almost nine hundred.

The *Berean Mission* is a more recent arrival, having sent its first missionaries in 1959. It is concentrating its efforts in the mountain province of Bolivar, where its six missionaries are working among twenty thousand Quechua Indians. As soon as possible the mission hopes to have short-term Bible schools for Spanish- and Quechua-speaking peoples. Field headquarters is located in the provincial capital, Guaranda, where there is a weekly broadcast on the local radio station.

Some half dozen supporting missions are in Ecuador, one having arrived as recently as 1970. Chief among these is *Missonary Aviation Fellowship,* which began operations in 1948. Its two planes are stationed at Shell Mera, where they provide transportation for five evangelical missions.

A dozen *Plymouth Brethren* missionaries from the United States, Canada, and the United Kingdom are located in five centers in the northern part of the country.

Missionary Radio. There are five Christian radio stations in Ecuador. Mention has already been made of the three operated by the *Gospel Missionary Union.* The *National Evangelical Church* operates *Station HCET* in Ambato. The largest and best known is *HCJB* in Quito, owned by *World Radio Missionary Fellowship.* It is the oldest of all the missionary radio stations in the world. Its first broadcast took place on Christmas Day, 1931, over a 250-watt transmitter when there were only seven receiving sets in Quito. Today it is interdenominational and international in character and worldwide in scope. Its staff comprises some 350 persons divided almost equally between Ecuadorians and expatriates. Through almost forty years of broadcasting HCJB has made an outstanding contribution to the evangelization not only of Ecuador and Latin America, but of the world as well. Today, with almost half a million watts of power, it is presenting fifty programs daily in fifteen languages. By means of short-wave it beams the gospel into all parts of the world. Several evangelical missions cooperate with HCJB in various capacities. Ever since 1941 the *Slavic Gospel Association* has been responsible for the broadcasts in the Russian language beamed into the USSR. In 1959 it inaugurated its television programs, which have been very popular in Quito. In fact, for several years it was the only TV station in the country. In 1947 it organized the *Bible Institute of the Air* in which tens of thousands of persons in all parts of the world have enrolled. WRMF also has a medical program, the *Rimmer Memorial Hospital* and the *Palmer School of Nursing* opened in 1955, and the *Epp Memorial Hospital* at Shell Mera opened in 1958.

World Radio Missionary Fellowship in 1962 inaugurated the *All-Ecuador Gospel Network* designed to saturate Ecuador with gospel programs presented over commercial radio stations throughout the republic. In 1966 Ecuador had about one hundred commercial stations, more than sixty of which were involved in the AEGN program. The project is rather unique. AEGN agrees to supply each station with cultural programs if the station will agree to present an equal number of sustaining gospel programs. In this way there is no charge for air time.

Evangelism. Evangelism-in-Depth conducted a countrywide crusade in Ecuador in 1970. It began with two huge rallies, one in Quito and one in Guayaquil. In Quito there were fifteen hundred professions of faith and in Guayaquil, three thousand. In the last week of June the very conservative Roman Catholic city of Cuenca was the scene of an evangelistic campaign without precedent. Although it is a large city, there are only two small Lutheran churches with a total membership of sixty. For several years "Hermano Pablo," Latin American-born Paul Finkenbinder, radio and TV evangelist of the Assemblies of God, has aired his daily continent-wide five-minute radio program over a local station in Cuenca. It was not the most promising place for a citywide campaign, but "Hermano Pablo" decided to go there. Throughout the six nights of the crusade some fifteen hundred people crowded into the auditorium. Every night a TV program called "Hermano Pablo Answers" made a great impact on the city. At the end of the week there had been recorded a total of three thousand professions of faith—in a city where previously there had been but sixty believers.

Bible Societies. In March, 1964, Ecuador became a separate Joint Agency, under the administration of the *British and Foreign Bible Society*.

Before that it had been united with Peru. The Indian tribes in Ecuador, as elsewhere, are still waiting for the complete Bible. Only one language, Quechua, has the New Testament. Six other Indian tribes now have at least one Portion of the Scriptures in their own language; four of these translations were executed by *Wycliffe Bible Translators*. Scripture distribution is on the increase, due largely to the *Evangelism-in-Depth Crusade* and the *Crusade of the Americas*. But each year the Bible societies themselves conduct an average of fifteen to twenty Penzotti Scripture Distribution Workshops in which church leaders are taught the techniques of successful Scripture distribution. In addition, the Bible societies are urging every Christian to sell one Bible every two months and a New Testament every month as a mark of his faith.

Ecumenical Relations. The all-missionary Inter-Mission Fellowship was dissolved in 1965 after fifteen years of existence. Taking its place is the *Ecuadorian Evangelical Fellowship,* which includes churches as well as missions, with the churches assuming more of the leadership role. In 1967 it sponsored study sessions on family planning, missionary-national cooperation, and Evangelical-Roman Catholic relations. Tension exists in the EEF between the conservatives and the ecumenists. Also in 1967 the small Episcopal Church established an Ecumenical Library in Quito in cooperation with Lutheran and Roman Catholic leaders.

Postscript. In January, 1956, the world was shocked to learn of the killing of five missionaries by the Auca Indians. Shortly after the tragedy friendly contacts were established with the Aucas, and *Rachel Saint* and *Betty Elliot,* sister and wife respectively of two of the five martyrs, lived and worked among them. Miss Saint translated the Gospel of Mark into Auca, and it was presented to them on Easter Sunday, 1965. Some thirty members of the tribe have been baptized, including the five men who killed the missionaries. One of the Auca women, *Dayuma,* has been to the United States where she was baptized by Dr. V. Raymond Edman, then president of Wheaton College. Two of the Auca Christians attended the Berlin Congress on Evangelism. The world has seldom seen a finer example of Christian love or a greater demonstration of the power of the gospel.

Colombia

Political History. In 1819 the Republic of Colombia was established after 300 years of Spanish rule. At that time Greater Colombia included what is now Panama, Venezuela, and Ecuador. Venezuela and Ecuador withdrew in 1830. Panama, with a "little help" from the United States, broke away in 1903. The past century has been marked by a long and bloody struggle between the Liberal and Conservative parties. One civil war which ended in 1902 took one hundred thousand lives. Twice as many persons were killed in *La Violencia* from 1948 to 1952.

The People.   With 21.5 million people, Colombia is the fourth largest country in Latin America. Only Brazil, Mexico, and Argentina are larger. The mestizos account for almost 60 percent of the population. An estimated 20 percent are European. Other groups include mulatto, 14 percent; and Negro, 4 percent. Not more than 2 percent are pure Indian. The population is increasing at an annual rate of 3 percent. The literacy rate is about 60 percent.

Religion.   Colombia is the most Roman Catholic dominated country in Latin America. The 1887 Concordat with the Vatican declared Roman Catholicism to be the official religion of Colombia. An Agreement on Missions, signed in 1953 between the government and the Vatican, gave the Roman Catholic Church a monopoly on Christian work among the fifty or sixty Indian tribes in the country. In October, 1970, the Roman Catholic Church initiated steps to revise the Concordat, giving the people the right to educate their children as they please. It is also prepared to revoke the Agreement on Missions, which is due to expire in 1978. The constitution guarantees freedom of religion, but this has not been observed. In recent years, however, the evangelicals have enjoyed an unprecedented degree of liberty, engaging in open-air meetings, street parades, city-wide campaigns, and radio broadcasting.

Missions.   The *United Presbyterian Church, USA,* has been in Colombia fifty-six years longer than any other Protestant group. The pioneer was *Henry B. Pratt,* who arrived in 1856 and whose translation of the Bible into modern Spanish was published in 1893. Through the years the Presbyterians have maintained a fine system of schools, including twenty-one elementary and eight secondary schools. Church and mission were integrated in 1959. Since then all institutions and all thirty-five fraternal workers have been under the direction of the church. The *Presbyterian Church of Colombia* has three presbyteries and twenty-five organized churches, with twenty-four hundred members. Membership, though small for 114 years of work, has almost doubled in the past decade.

The *Gospel Missionary Union,* which in 1896 had been the first Protestant mission to enter neighboring Ecuador, extended its work to Colombia in 1912. A printing plant was set up and a monthly paper, *El Mensaje Evangelico,* was started. In fifty-two years it has not missed a single issue. It now has a circulation of forty-two hundred. The GMU is working in four provinces along the Pacific coast. Palmira is the headquarters of the national convention of the GMU. In addition to three churches, it has the following institutions: Bible institute, Maranatha Hospital, Aurora Bookstore, and Christian Education Center. The influence of these institutions is felt by the entire population. The GMU was particularly hard hit during *La Violencia,* when it lost three-quarters of its thirty-two churches.

The Evangelical Alliance Mission has a small work in eastern Colombia which is really an extension of its much larger mission in western Venezuela. Resident work began in Cucuta in 1922. The first missionaries were *Mr. and Mrs. John Christiansen,* who had helped pioneer the work in Venezuela. The national church, the *Association of Evangelical Churches of Eastern Colombia,* has been independent since 1949. Today it has thirty-one churches and thirty-eight other meeting places, with a total of 850 members and a Christian community of twenty-six hundred. Educational work centers in nine primary schools. Some thirty missionaries assist thirteen pastors and fourteen evangelists in the work of the church. The one Bible school has an enrolment of seventy-five.

The *Christian and Missionary Alliance* began work in Colombia in 1923, when Roman Catholic persecution made missionary work almost impossible. But the missionaries persevered and today the C&MA has work in seven departments in the southern part of the country. Bogota, the capital, was entered in 1961. The Aurora Bookstore in Cali supplies 80 percent of all gospel literature sold by evangelical bookstores throughout Colombia. The *Alianza en Marcha* daily broadcast over Trans World Radio from Bonaire is undoubtedly one of the best-known programs in the Western Hemisphere. During 1969 almost thirteen thousand letters from thirty-one countries were received. Besides thirty-six broadcasts a week over TWR, the program can now be heard forty-six times a week over five stations in Colombia. The Alliance conducts two main Bible schools, Central and Indian. Theological extension courses are available in five other centers. Colombia youth are turning to Christ in increasing numbers and are actively participating in the ministry of the local churches. Forty-eight organized churches and ninety-three outstations have a baptized membership of almost thirty-two hundred.

The *Seventh Day Adventist* work in Colombia goes back to 1930. For the first two decades the work was hard and growth was slow; but since 1940 the growth rate has picked up considerably, so that by the close of 1969 they reported a church membership of eighteen thousand.

There are some nine or ten Pentecostal groups in Colombia. The *Assemblies of God* mission is the outcome of the pioneer efforts of *Mr. and Mrs. Edward Wegner,* independent missionaries who began work in Sogamoso in 1932. Eleven years later this work became affiliated with the Assemblies of God. *Templo Betel* was started in Bogota by *Harry Bartel* in 1956. Today there are eighteen organized churches in the city. In 1960 a Bible school was opened in Bogota. Churches have been started in seven new state capitals in the past three years. Paul Finkenbinder's daily radio program, *Message to the Conscience,* is transmitted over nineteen local radio stations covering the entire country. When the *Colombia Assemblies of God* was organized in 1958 there were only three churches represented. Today there are 50 churches and 150 outstations.

The *Worldwide Evangelization Crusade* has been in Colombia since 1932. WEC ministry today is found in seven centers including the capital, Bogota. More than forty autonomous churches have been established. There are a Bible school with forty students, fourteen primary schools, a hospital, and a printing press. Thirty-four missionaries from seven home countries serve in Colombia.

The *South America Mission* entered Colombia in 1934 and has been working in the Guajira Peninsula in the northeast tip of the country. Churches for Latin Americans have been established in the four centers where most of the twenty-four missionaries are stationed. Two couples are working among the Guajira Indians, and another couple are giving their time to three small Indian tribes that inhabit the Sierra Nevada de Santa Marta.

The *Latin America Mission* is best known for its sponsorship of Evangelism-in-Depth in ten countries of Latin America. Through this means it acts as a catalyst to encourage other missions and churches to assume responsibility for the complete and systematic evangelization of their own countries. In more recent years it has reached out and given aid and counsel to churches and missions in Africa and Asia. Less known is the fact that LAM has its own permanent work in two Latin American countries, Colombia and Costa Rica. Two single ladies pioneered the work in Colombia in 1937. In the face of great odds they laid the foundations for an evangelistic and church-building ministry which now covers three provinces along the northern coast. Churches are established in the major cities: Sinceleja, Cartagena, Magangue, and Monteria. A Bible school was opened in 1942. Three years later the *Association of Caribbean Evangelical Churches* was formed. The association became autonomous in 1962. Today it includes twenty-eight organized churches and forty unorganized groups, with a total membership of twenty-two hundred. Twenty-eight missionaries serve alongside fifty-five national pastors. Ten primary schools and one high school represent the extent of the educational work.

The *Southern Baptists* took up work in Colombia in 1941, and since that time they have experienced steady growth. After six short years they were able to organize the *Colombia Baptist Convention.* The SBC has a larger missionary staff (61) than any other mission in Colombia except Wycliffe Bible Translators, which has 175. These missionaries are located in seven major cities. The hospital, opened in 1953, is in Barranquilla. The international seminary, also opened in 1953, is in Cali. Only three of the fifty-six organized churches are self-supporting. Total membership is 5,350, making the church one of the largest in Colombia.

The *Wesleyan Church* entered Colombia in 1941 and settled in the city of Medellin, where they established a publishing house as well as a church. More recently a church has been organized in Bogota. Seven missionaries and eighteen national workers are occupied in ten organized churches and twenty-eight unorganized congregations.

The American branch of the *Evangelical Union of South America* entered Colombia in 1942 and began work in practically virgin territory in the department of Magdalena in the northeast corner of the country. Today mission work is carried on in three distinct geographical areas. The program includes evangelism, schools, Bible conferences, literature, and, more recently, radio. A farm training center, known as Carmel Colony, was started in 1955. It also serves as a Bible school. A school for missionaries' children is also part of the colony. Radio broadcasts, something new in Colombia, are now aired over local stations in El Banco and Santa Marta.

The *Inter-American Missionary Society,* a subsidiary of the Oriental Missionary Society, chose Colombia as the first of three fields in South America. *Dr. and Mrs. B. H. Pearson* arrived in Medellin in August, 1943, followed a week later by the Gillams. In six months they had established a seminary on the property of the Wesleyan Church in that city. The following year they acquired their own property in Medellin. In 1950 the *Mission to the Andes,* which had been in Colombia for some years, merged with the IAMS. In 1951 the local churches established by the mission were organized into the *Association of Inter-American Churches of Colombia.* Sixteen Christian day schools were started for Protestant children excluded from the public schools dominated by the Roman Catholics. A vocational Bible training institute, opened in Cristalina in 1955, combines training in technical skills with a knowledge of the Bible. The national church, which received full autonomy in 1968, comprises thirty-five organized congregations and eighty-one preaching places, with a total of fourteen hundred baptized members. It is experiencing some difficulties in achieving self-support. The seminary in Medellin, with a limited enrolment of fourteen, is to become the *United Evangelical Seminary* serving the entire evangelical community in Colombia.

Colombia in 1944 became the second of five South American countries to be entered by the *New Tribes Mission.* The work stretches from the rain forest of the Choco in the north to the vast plains in the east and the jungle regions in the south. There are some sixty or seventy tribes in Colombia, and NTM with its thirty-seven missionaries is working out from four bases and the capital, Bogota. The immense *Comisaria of Guainia* in the eastern plains region is now 40 percent Protestant, largely the result of the work of the New Tribes Mission. Between 1960 and 1966 their communicants increased from three hundred to almost three thousand. The NTM brings local churches into existence and immediately puts them on their own. Most of them remain without any affiliation. The mission makes no attempt to form fellowships or associations of any kind.

The *American Lutheran Church,* in Colombia since 1944, works through the Evangelical Lutheran Church-Colombia Synod. In 1958 it was organized under its own constitution with six member congregations. Two others joined in 1961 and still another in 1965. The baptized membership is small—only 750. The national ministerium numbers only three Colombians. During the early years the Lutherans concentrated on rural areas; but in more recent times they have begun work in Bogota and Cali, where they hope to establish a base among the urban middle class.

The *Mennonite Brethren* have been in Colombia since 1945. For the first fifteen years they worked on the plains of the Cauca and San Juan rivers. Since then they have concentrated on the city of Cali, where at present they have some forty missionaries, about half of them engaged in teaching. More recently they have opened work in Medellin, where they have three couples. Church membership is slightly over the five hundred mark.

Wycliffe Bible Translators, a comparative newcomer, having entered in 1962, already has 175 missonaries working among thirty tribes. The base at Lomalinda in the eastern plains is within two hours flying time of an estimated forty tribes.

Colombia is one of the overseas missionary districts of the *Episcopal Church in USA.* Aid is mostly in the form of money rather than men. Two missionaries are there at present. The Episcopal Church is extending its work in Colombia and there were in 1965 several congregations in Bogota and Barranquilla.

The *Plymouth Brethren* have thirteen missionaries from three countries in four major cities of Colombia.

La Violencia. For a ten-year period, from 1948 to 1958, the Protestants of Colombia suffered persecution at the hands of the Roman Catholic Church. During that time no new missionaries were permitted to enter the country; and missionaries going on furlough were not permitted to return. According to reliable statistics, forty-seven churches and chapels were completely destroyed and scores of others were closed. Over two hundred primary schools were closed, most of them by government order, thus depriving Protestant children of an education. Altogether seventy-eight Protestants were killed on account of their faith. But in spite of the persecution, the worst in the history of Protestant work in Latin America, Protestant church membership increased some 400 percent from 1948 to 1960. In 1968 the total number of baptized communicants numbered 84,500. This was an increase of almost fourteen thousand over the previous year. The total Protestant community is probably three times the communicant membership and in 1970 was probably close to the three hundred thousand mark. Even so, it represents only 1.3 percent of the population.

Pentecostal Churches. Pentecostal churches constitute the most rapidly growing sector of Colombian Protestantism. They accounted for

16 percent of the total Protestant membership in 1960 and 39 percent in 1969. Numerically there were six and a half times as many Pentecostals in 1969 as in 1960. Four Pentecostal churches have a membership of over one thousand. They include *United Pentecostal Church* (2,500), *International Church of the Foursquare Gospel* (4,365), *Assemblies of God* (1,442), and *Panamerican Mission* (1, 100).

Evangelism. *Overseas Crusades,* which majors in mass evangelism, entered Colombia in 1963. In 1966, in cooperation with the Office of Evangelism of the Evangelical Confederation of Colombia, it sponsored large-scale evangelistic campaigns in ten cities with remarkable results. In Medellin 750 persons made public confession of faith in Christ. The mayor lent the Olympic Stadium to the crusade committee. City officials granted permission for advertising, public meetings, and even a parade. The most powerful radio station in the city gave some free time. When it was all over one veteran missionary with twenty-seven years in Colombia remarked: "This wouldn't have been possible even a year ago. The last time we tried to make an impact on this city with the gospel we were stoned and they threw dirt all over our clothes."[7] In Bogota Luis Palau preached to twenty thousand persons from the steps of the National Capitol. The *Times of Colombia* gave excellent coverage and the crusade was on television seven times. Hundreds made decisions for Christ.

Under the leadership of the *Latin America Mission* the evangelical churches of Colombia conducted an Evangelism-in-Depth campaign in 1968. Christians of all denominations united to sponsor nineteen regional crusades and three even larger meetings in Barranquilla, Cali, and Medellin. Over seven thousand prayer cells were formed, and more than twenty thousand decisions for Christ were registered. On the first official visitation day an estimated 17,500 members of the 600 participating churches visited 100,000 homes, finding interest in 25 percent of them. The campaign came to a climax on Sunday, December 15, when thirty thousand Protestants paraded through downtown Bogota to the plaza in the center of the city. The parade, held with government permission and full cooperation from the police, dramatized the increasing religious freedom and the growing strength of the evangelical church in Colombia.

The *First Latin American Congress on Evangelism* met in Bogota in November, 1969. The motto was "Action in Christ for a Continent in Crisis." Some 920 delegates from twenty-five countries attended the congress, held on the International Fair Ground in Bogota. In all, twenty-eight major addresses were delivered, all but two of them by Latin Americans. The final document, entitled "The Evangelical Declaration of Bogota," set forth ten points relating to evangelism and other aspects of

---

[7] Overseas Crusades, *Cable* March-April, 1967.

the church's ministry. "Evangelism is not something optional," it stated; "it lies at the very essence of the church. It is her supreme task."

Not directly related to evangelism but certainly contributing to it was the third *World Vision Pastors Conference* in Medellin in April, 1967. Some six hundred pastors and Christian leaders from all parts of Colombia participated in the five-day conference. Representatives of the various denominations remained for another five days to plan for the 1968 Evangelism-in-Depth campaign.

Bible Societies. Work began in Colombia in 1825, but it was not until 1901 that the first agent for Peru, Ecuador, and Colombia was appointed. In 1946 the agency was reorganized and Colombia and Venezuela were brought together under the supervision of the *American Bible Society*. Since 1961 Colombia has had its own Agency. Bible translation in the Indian languages has lagged. In 1968 only one tribe had the complete New Testament and only four tribes had at least one Portion. In the last two years several languages have been added to the list. A record distribution of the Scriptures was achieved in 1968 with an increase of 147 percent over the previous year. Evangelism-in-Depth campaign accounted for much of the increase. Eighteen bookstores located throughout the country help the Bible society in the work of distribution.

Ecumenical Relations. The *Evangelical Confederation of Colombia,* formed in 1951, includes most of the nearly fifty groups working in the country. In November, 1966, twenty Protestant groups formed the *Asociacion Evangelica Pro-Indigenas de Colombia* to train Colombians for Indian work and to publish literacy and Bible study materials for the aborigines.

Venezuela

Political History. Venezuela was one of the first colonies in Latin America to break away from Spain in 1810; but it was not until 1821 that full independence was achieved under Simon Bolivar, Venezuela's national hero and native son. It was part of Greater Colombia until 1830. Like other countries in Latin America, Venezuela has had its share of political instability. Only in recent years has it been able to develop effective representative government. Romulo Betancourt (1959-1964) became the first popularly elected president to complete his term of office. The discovery of huge oil reserves has greatly enriched the country and resulted in an economic boom.

The People. With an estimated population of 10.2 million, Venezuela is one of the least densely populated countries in South America. About 95 percent of the population lives in the Andes and along the coast, leaving only 5 percent in the region south and east of the Orinoco River, which represents half the territory of Venezuela. Some 65 percent of the people are mestizo, 21 percent of European origin, 7 percent Negro, and 7 percent pure Indian. Literacy is 34 percent. Spanish is the official language.

Religion. Roman Catholicism is the dominant religion of Venezuela. An agreement between Venezuela and the Vatican in 1964 caused evangelicals some concern; but their fears proved groundless. Following the Vatican Council a *rapprochement* has been taking place between the Roman Catholics and the Protestants. In Caracas every month Catholic priests attend ministerial meetings of various denominations—Lutheran, Presbyterian, Anglican, Pentecostal, and Orthodox—and attend official functions in Protestant churches. Presbyterian and Lutheran pastors have given lectures in Roman Catholic seminaries, and Catholic priests have spoken in Presbyterian churches. The conservative evangelicals have grave doubts about the wisdom of this kind of dialogue.

Missions. The *United Presbyterian Church in the USA* was the first to initiate permanent work in Venezuela. The year was 1897 and the city was Caracas, which remains the hub of the Venezuelan mission. Besides two churches, Caracas has *Colegio Americano,* opened in 1896. Present enrolment is 750. In 1969 it was reorganized under the authority of a semi-autonomous association in which the Presbytery and the Commission, and probably several educational groups, will participate. The Presbyterians now have ten centers of work, six of which were opened in the 1960's. The *Evangelical Presbyterian Church of Venezuela* includes twelve churches and 950 members. Some of the newer churches are manned by consecrated laymen. Fifteen fraternal workers are in Venezuela, mostly in institutional work.

The *Plymouth Brethren* (Christian Missions in Many Lands) is the largest and fastest growing evangelical group in Venezuela. Their settled work began in Caracas in 1910. Through the years they have maintained a constant staff of missionaries. Today they have sixteen missionaries in seven centers working with the national assemblies. Their membership grew from two thousand in 1955 to seven thousand in 1967. Their emphasis on lay workers and the autonomy of the local assembly has paid off.

Venezuela was the first country in South America to be entered by *The Evangelical Alliance Mission.* The first station, Maracaibo, was opened in 1906 by *Mr. and Mrs. T. J. Bach* and *Mr. and Mrs. John Christiansen.* One of their first projects (1907) was the publication of *La Estrella de la Manana* (The Morning Star), an evangelical magazine with a circulation of six thousand which reaches into every country in Latin America. *Ebenezer Bible Institute,* located in San Cristobal since 1944, has six modern buildings and is one of the finest in Latin America. TEAM has two Bible camps, one in San Cristobal and the other on the shores of Lake Maracaibo. A radio studio connected with the Bible institute prepares tapes which are aired over commercial stations and TEAM's own 10,000-watt station, *Radio Victoria,* in Aruba. TEAM's churches, known as the *Evangelical Churches of Venezuela,* have been autonomous since 1927. Fifty-six organized churches and fifty-six unorganized churches, with a membership of twenty-one hundred, are manned by twenty-one pastors and eighteen evangelists. TEAM has ninety missionaries in Venezuela.

The *Assemblies of God* work stems from the pioneer efforts of independent Pentecostal workers who went to the field in 1920. Undaunted by hardships, they saw many people turn to the Lord; and local churches were established which later affiliated with the Assemblies of God. Among the early workers were *Mr. and Mrs. Gottfried Bender,* who located in Barquisimeto in 1919 and began the first evangelical church in that city and state. In 1927 a church was set up in Coro. Revival broke out in that area in 1966 and spread throughout the whole district. The Bible institute in Barquisimeto is a major factor in the growth of the church. Six evening Bible institutes have recently been started. In 1962 the Assemblies launched their work among the Guajiro Indians. Already there are more than four hundred believers. In 1970 the AOG reported seventy-six self-supporting churches and 134 outstations with thirty-one hundred baptized members. Eighty-eight national workers and sixteen missionaries are working with these churches.

Several other Pentecostal groups are found in Venezuela: *Church of God* (Cleveland), *International Church of the Foursquare Gospel, United Pentecostal Church, Ebenezer Church,* and *Venezuelan Pentecostal Union.*

An interdenominational mission working only in Venezuela is the *Orinoco River Mission.* It was founded in 1920 by *Van Eddings* after he and his wife had spent one term on the island of Margarita. On their return to Venezuela they made their headquarters in Carupano on the mainland. The first years brought much persecution. They were stoned, mobbed, and intimidated; and on one occasion their chapel was destroyed. *Donald and Faith Turner* joined the Eddings in 1921. During the next four years primary schools were opened in four cities. In 1939 a Bible institute began in Las Delicias. The school for the children of missionaries is located in the same city. A gospel launch acquired in 1952 enables the missionaries to reach many remote villages on the Orinoco River. The mission maintains a bookstore in Puerto La Cruz. The fiftieth anniversary project is the erection of a $50,000 gospel center there. In 1969 the ORM had sixty-six churches with twenty-four hundred members. Another fourteen hundred Christians in eastern Venezuela, once affiliated with the ORM, have now formed their own association. The mission has some fifty missionaries in Venezuela.

The *Evangelical Free Church of America* in 1920 took over three churches which had been established by *David E. Finstrom* of the South American Evangelical Mission. This work was in La Victoria in the state of Aragua. A second field was opened in 1925 in the state of Guarico. This latter was known as the Venezuela Interior Mission. As additional recruits arrived new stations were opened throughout north central Venezuela. A Bible institute was begun in 1954. During the first decade more than one hundred young people were trained for evangelistic and pastoral work in the emerging churches. The *Evangelical Free Church Association* received its independence in 1953. At present it comprises thirty-one organized and eleven unorganized churches, with a baptized membership of over one thousand. Nine pastors and fourteen evangelists have the oversight of the work. The EFC has always worked in close cooperation with *The Evangelical Alliance Mission* in Venezuela. Jointly they operate a printing press, publishing house, two bookstores, a magazine, and correspondence courses. The latest cooperative effort is the *United Evangelical Seminary* established in 1969 in El Limon.

The *New Tribes Mission* began the Venezuelan mission in 1946. Its sixty missionaries are located in seven centers in the extreme southern section of the country known as the Amazon Territory and sandwiched between Colombia and Brazil. Educational work includes two schools, one primary and one middle. The NTM keeps no records of its churches; consequently it is difficult to say how much progress has been made.

The *United World Mission* is rounding out twenty-five years of work in Venezuela. Its work is divided into three major areas; Caracas, Barquisimeto, and El Tocuyo. Three missionary couples and a single lady make up the missionary staff. There is a Bible school at El Tocuyo, and headquarters is located in Barquisimeto. The work in Caracas is just getting under way and no church has yet been established. At the end of 1969 a total of six churches reported a combined membership of 275.

As in other parts of Latin America, *Southern Baptist* work in Venezuela was begun by local Christians who had studied the Spanish-language Baptist literature published in El Paso. A self-supporting Baptist church was already in existence when SBC missionaries arrived. The first church was organized in Caracas in 1945 and the second in Maracaibo the following year. American missionaries transferred from Colombia arrived in 1949. The *Venezuelan Baptist Convention* was organized in 1951. It maintains boards of evangelism, education, benevolences, finances, legal affairs, publications, and home missions. For a period of six years (1958-1964) tension between the mission and the convention became so great that the two were obliged to go their separate ways. Fortunately reconciliation was effected, and progress has been renewed. Here, as in other parts of the world, the Southern Baptists have had a burden for Americans living abroad. Under their leadership English-speaking churches have been established in Caracas and Maracaibo. As 1970 began, a total of twenty-three missionaries were assigned to seven cities along the northern coast of Venezuela. The Venezuelan Baptist Convention now has twenty-nine churches with almost seventeen hundred members.

The first Evangelical Lutheran church was organized in Caracas in 1893. From that time to the present the Lutheran faith has been confessed by Lutherans in Venezuela. Over the decades Lutheran churches from Europe and the United States, working through the Lutheran World Federation, have faithfully supported the ministries of various national groups. In 1951 the *Lutheran Church-Missouri Synod* moved into Venezuela and opened two missions, one in San Antonio in the east and another in Caracas. For some time all services were conducted in German, but today practically all the worship services and instruction are in Spanish. The Lutheran congregations in Venezuela have not experienced great numerical growth; but the Word of God is being proclaimed and greater attempts are being made to reach the Venezuelans for Christ. At the close of 1969 there were still no national pastors. Eight missionaries have the spiritual oversight of 750 baptized members.

The *Worldwide Evangelization Crusade,* in Venezuela since 1953, has eight missionaries located in Barquisimeto and Acarigua in the eastern part of the country. Outreach includes extensive literature work, house-to-house visitation, church planting, evangelistic campaigns, and conference ministries. Young people's retreats and children's classes are also held. A bookstore, a bookmobile, and correspondence courses complete the program.

Other missions in Venezuela include *Baptist Mid-Missions, Churches of Christ* (Disciples), *Baptist Bible Fellowship, Baptist International Missions.* Several missions have entered Venezuela during the past decade: *Anglican Church of Canada, Christian Union General Mission Board, United Christian Missionary Society. Missionary Aviation Fellowship* has one plane in Venezuela cooperating with New Tribes Mission, Orinoco River Mission, and the Evangelical Free Church.

Bethel Evangelical Church, a purely indigenous work started by a layman, *Aristides Dias,* had an estimated membership of six thousand in 1966. Its 150 churches are located in the state of Apure in the southern part of the country.

Evangelism. An Evangelism-in-Depth campaign was held in 1964-1965. More than five hundred evangelical churches united in the fifteen-month effort. Some eighteen thousand Christians participated in the training course. More than seventeen thousand professions of faith were recorded. The campaign in Venezuela did not appear to be so successful as similar campaigns in other Latin American countries. During 1967 the Billy Graham Evangelistic Association held crusades in three cities.

Ecumenical Relations. For many years Venezuela was the only country in Latin America without a national council of any kind. This was changed in 1967 when the *Venezuelan Evangelical Council* was organized. It unites the majority of churches and missions in the country. Its two major goals are to represent evangelical work before the government and to promote freedom of religion. The Presbyterian Church of Venezuela has made a firm decision to conduct open dialogue with the Roman Catholics, and this has alienated it from the more conservative element in the Evangelical Council.

Bible Societies. Work began in Venezuela when *James Thompson* of the *British and Foreign Bible Society* visited the country in 1832. At various times through the years the Agency has been connected with the Colombia, Puerto Rico, Caribbean, and West Indies Agencies. In 1961 Venezuela became a separate Joint Agency (British and American), administered by the *American Bible Society*. Bible translation has not been of major concern, perhaps because there are comparatively few Indians in the country. To date only six tribes have any part of the Scriptures in their own tongue. The first New Testament, in Marquiritare, is on the press at the present time. It will probably be many years before the complete Bible is available. Scripture distribution continues to increase, largely as the direct result of some twenty to thirty Penzotti Scripture Distribution Workshops conducted each year in all parts of the country. The Bible society enjoys excellent relations with newspapers, radio, and television. Four colporteurs are working full time for the Bible society, and a Bible van is of particular help in reaching the central and western regions of the country.

XVIII

Central America & Caribbean

Mexico

Political History. The Spanish conquest of Mexico began in 1520 and lasted three hundred years. Full independence was achieved when the republic was established in 1822. The bloody revolution of 1910 was social as well as political and resulted in one of the most stable and progressive governments in the underdeveloped world. During the past sixty years Mexico has confronted its many problems in an orderly fashion with a peculiar institutional framework somewhere between dictatorship and democracy. In foreign affairs Mexico has remained neutral and today enjoys friendly relations with both Cuba and the United States.

The People. With 47.5 million people Mexico is the second largest country in Latin America in terms of population. The growth rate, currently at 3.5 percent, is one of the highest in the world. About 60 percent of the Mexicans are mestizos. Indians account for 25 percent, Negroes 10 percent; the remaining 5 percent includes Americans, Canadians, and other expatriates, mostly Latin Americans. Spanish is the official language and about 70 percent of the people are literate. Over one hundred Indian tribes speak their own languages, some of which have not yet been reduced to writing.

Religion. During the Spanish period Mexico was under the domination of the Roman Catholic Church. The revolution of 1910 was directed largely against the church; as a result it was stripped of all its property and much of its power. Since then relations have gradually improved to the point where church and state have made their peace, though the former is still subject to certain restrictions. Mexico, however, remains, for all practical purposes, an overwhelmingly Catholic country. Evangelicals have had to live with government restrictions and at the same time contend with Roman Catholic opposition. The latter is on the decrease. A prominent daily newspaper in Mexico City is now featuring a regular weekly column of Protestant news. In 1965, for the first time, the American Bible Society was permitted to have a display at the annual Home Fair which attracted thousands of persons, including the Archbishop of Mexico.

Proliferation. According to the ninth edition of the *North American Protestant Ministries Overseas Directory,* there are now 1,391 missionaries serving under 119 missions in Mexico. Of these 119 boards, 17 have no resident missionaries at the present time. Another fifty-six boards have one to five missionaries; and twenty-one boards have from six to ten missionaries. Thirty-seven of the missions have entered Mexico in the last decade; forty-eight furnish no information concerning their date of entrance. Most of them are new and small and presumably have begun work in Mexico in the last decade.

Identification. Obviously it is impossible to include 119 missions in this survey. It will be necessary to restrict our consideration to a dozen or more of the older, larger, and more representative missions. It might be wise, however, to give some indication of the various kinds of missions that are operating in Mexico and some idea of their number and size. Besides the American Baptist Convention, which has been in Mexico since 1870, there are ten other Baptist missions with a total of 130 missionaries. There are fourteen Pentecostal missions with seventy missionaries. Lutheran missions number four, and they have some three dozen missionaries. The Mennonites have seven different missions with a total of 126 missionaries. Nondenominational missions form the largest single bloc. They number almost twenty and report a total of 140 missionaries. There is another category, smaller than the others but nevertheless significant. These are groups that fill a supporting role, whose workers are likely to come and go. There are eight such missions. In addition there are four Holiness groups and two Friends missions.

Early Missions. The first evangelical church in Mexico was the First Baptist Church in Monterey founded in 1864 by *James Hickey,* a former Irish Roman Catholic. Six years later the first missionary of the *American Baptist Home Mission Society* arrived in Monterey. After a hundred years there are four Baptist churches with over two thousand members in that city. The latest report indicates that the American Baptists in Mexico now have thirty-nine churches and eighty mission stations, with a baptized membership of 3,550. Six of the eight missionaries are teaching in the Baptist Seminary in Mexico City.

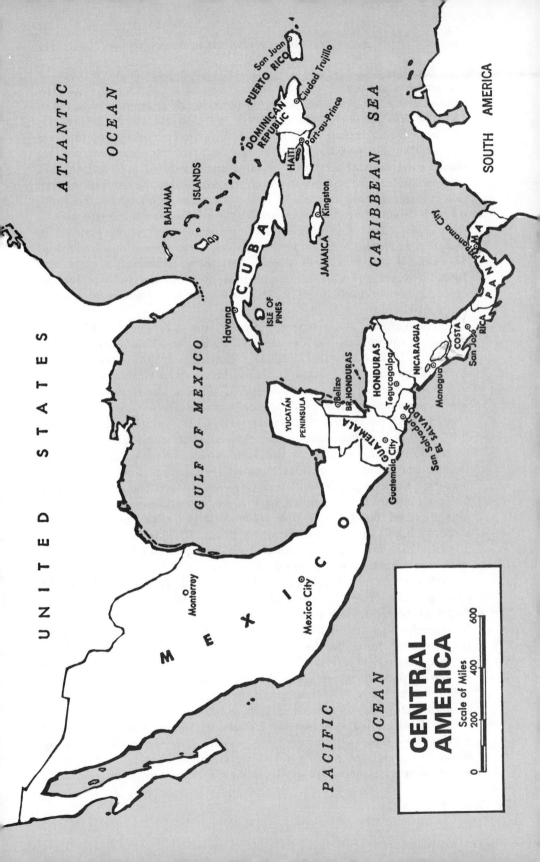

CENTRAL
AMERICA

Scale of Miles

0   200   400   600

ATLANTIC

OCEAN

UNITED STATES

GULF OF MEXICO

BAHAMA

ISLANDS

CUBA

Havana

ISLE OF
PINES

San Juan

PUERTO RICO

DOMINICAN
REPUBLIC

Ciudad Trujillo

HAITI

Port-au-Prince

JAMAICA

Kingston

CARIBBEAN SEA

PANAMA

Panama City

SOUTH AMERICA

NICARAGUA

Managua

COSTA
RICA

San José

HONDURAS

Tegucigalpa

Belize

BR. HONDURAS

EL SALVADOR

San Salvador

GUATEMALA

Guatemala City

YUCATÁN
PENINSULA

MEXICO

Monterrey

Mexico City

PACIFIC

OCEAN

The *American Board of Commissioners for Foreign Missions* (now the United Church Board for World Ministries) entered Mexico in 1872. The following year it took over an independent work in Monterey started in 1855 by *Miss Melinda Rankin*. One of the pioneers was *J. L. Stephens,* who organized a church in Guadalajara. Mob violence incited by the local Roman Catholic priest resulted in the death of Mr. Stephens and his Mexican evangelist. Here again the missionaries refused to be intimidated; the work continued and eventually prospered. Today the work of thirteen Congregational churches on the west coast is coordinated by the Junta (Church Council), whose superintendent is a layman of the first church in Guadalajara. Two fine educational institutions, *Colegio El Pacifico* in Mazatlan and *Institute Colon* in Guadalajara, are under national leadership. The same is true of a medical clinic and three community centers. The Junta is working toward self-support of the churches in time for the centenary celebrations in 1972. The Board for World Ministries has two couples in Mexico.

The *Northern Presbyterians* (now the United Presbyterian Church of the USA, Commission on Ecumenical Mission and Relations) sent four couples to Mexico City in 1872. The following year the *Southern Presbyterians* launched their mission in the southern part of Mexico. In 1901 the two groups merged to form the Synod of Mexico. The General Assembly was inaugurated in 1947. Today the *National Presbyterian Church of Mexico,* with seventeen presbyteries and 632 organized churches, has thirty-one thousand communicant members. The administrative work is centered in Mexico City, as are the *Presbyterian Theological Seminary* and the *Central Bible School for Women.* Three other Bible schools are preparing lay evangelists and other Christian workers for the rural areas. *Colegio Americano,* established in 1917, is a coeducational school with nine hundred pupils from first grade through junior college. It helps prepare Christian leaders for the whole Yucatan Peninsula. At the close of 1969 COEMAR had twenty-four and the Presbyterian Church in US had thirty-seven fraternal workers in the country.

Missionary work was begun in Mexico in 1873 by both the *Methodist Episcopal Church* and the *Methodist Episcopal Church, South.* Dr. *William Butler* pioneered for the former and *Bishop John C. Keener* for the latter. In general, the work of the two churches was focused in different areas, the northern church in the Federal District and nearby states and the southern church in the northern region of the country. The *Methodist Church of Mexico,* which resulted from the merger of the two groups in 1930, is completely autonomous. All the ministers and officers are Mexicans. Church members number 26,600, a net gain of only 800 in the past decade. Institutional work includes ten schools, four hostels, three cultural centers, two Bible schools, and one hospital. The *Methodist Publishing House* is located in Mexico City, as is *Union Theological Seminary.* Thirty-three missionaries are serving in these various institutions.

Mexico was the first of all the Latin American countries to be entered by the *Foreign Mission Board of the Southern Baptist Convention.* The year was 1880 and the pioneer missionary was *John Westrup,* an Englishman already in the country. Within a few weeks Westrup and his helper were killed, either by religious fanatics or by Indian bandits. *William D. Powell* went from Texas to fill the vacancy. *The National Baptist Convention of Mexico* was organized in 1903. The *Baptist Seminary* was opened in Torreon in 1901. There are plans to move it to Mexico City, where there are a student center and a bookstore. Today seventy Baptist missionaries are assigned to fifteen centers in all parts of Mexico, from Oaxaca in the south to Hermosillo in the north. The National Baptist Convention comprises 195 churches and almost sixteen thousand members under the care of 215 national pastors. Not all churches and pastors are Southern Baptist.

The *Protestant Episcopal Church* has had mission work in Mexico ever since the House of Bishops in 1904 made the country a Missionary District and sent *Bishop Aves* to minister to the American Episcopalians there. The bishop was instructed to give ecclesiastical oversight to the *Church of Jesus,* founded some years before by a converted Dominican friar, *Manuel Aguas.* Three Mexican bishops-elect were waiting and ready for consecration; but consecration was not conferred, and the Church of Jesus, which might have become a strong indigenous church, surrendered its autonomy and became part of the Missionary District of the American Episcopal Church. In the meantime, after "wandering in the wilderness" for thirty-five years, it had lost most of its members to other groups and was only a fraction of its former size. The *Mexican Episcopal Church,* with its own bishop and staffed almost entirely by Mexican clergy, in 1968 reported a communicant membership of 5,350.

Pentecostal Missions. As already intimated, there are some fourteen Pentecostal missions working in Mexico; in addition there are many indigenous groups large and small. Together they account for an aggregate communicant membership of three hundred thousand. The first Pentecostal assembly was established in Ciudad Muzquiz in 1919. In 1921, through the ministry of an American missionary, *Mrs. Anna Sanders,* a Pentecostal assembly was formed in Mexico City. Later she labored in the Yucatan Peninsula. In 1931 a national organization was formed and registered with the government as the *Assemblies of God in Mexico.* From the beginning this organization has been completely autonomous. The general conference is divided into three districts, each with a full-time superintendent. More than a score of American missionaries continue to assist in the work. Growth has been steady and rapid. In 1970 there were 875 national workers serving 430 churches and 300 outstations, with a total membership of almost sixteen thousand. Much of the growth is due to the strong leadership training program carried on in six Bible schools.

Space permits the mention of only one indigenous Pentecostal group, the *Apostolic Church,* which dates back to 1914. This church follows the Methodist Episcopal form of polity. It has churches in all but one of Mexico's twenty-nine states. In 1967 it had over 1,000 officers, including 13 bishops, and 1,050 preachers. Each of its 425 organized churches is expected to be responsible for the evangelization of its own territory.

Indian Missions. Some missions are working exclusively among the many Indian tribes in Mexico. The largest of these is *Wycliffe Bible Translators,* whose first field, in 1935, was Mexico. Since then Wycliffe translators have begun work in ninety-six languages, Scriptures have been published in seventy-nine languages, and there are believers in seventy-six tribes. Today WBT has 335 translators, including 18 short-term assistants, in Mexico. It is also the site of the Jungle Training Camp at which all their Latin America new workers get their basic training. WBT is the fastest growing mission in the world. In thirty-five years it has grown from nothing to almost twenty-five hundred missionaries in 450 tribes in nineteen countries of the world. WBT is determined to complete the task of Bible translation within this century. Its organizational structure and methods of operation are geared towards realizing this goal of giving every tribe a translation of the New Testament by the year 2000. There are still two thousand tongues to go. Five thousand additional translators will be needed in the next fifteen years.

The *Mexican Indian Mission* is an undenominational faith mission founded by *Dr. James G. Dale* in 1931, when he was sixty years of age and had already given a generation of service to the cause of Christ in Mexico. Dr. Dale opened the first station in the village of Tamazunchale in the heart of Indian territory. Today Tamazunchale, with its dozen or more buildings, is the nerve center of an ever-expanding work which has reached into seven states. The number of missionaries has dropped in the last decade from twenty-seven to eighteen, but more and more the work is being taken over by the Mexicans trained at the Bible school in Tamazunchale.

Other Missions. The *Seventh Day Adventists* have been in Mexico long enough to build up a large and flourishing work which is divided into six missions, or regions. Some two hundred fifty churches have been established. Total communicant members number forty-four thousand. They have no medical work; but their educational work includes thirty-four grade schools, five secondary schools, and one college.

The *Wesleyan Church* sent its first missionaries, *Mr. and Mrs. F. H. Soltero,* to Mexico in 1920 to "found and conduct a Pilgrim mission, Bible school, and printing plant." Started in San Luis Potosi, the church grew and multiplied in spite of persecution and discouragement. Today four missionaries are teaching in the Bible school at Valles. Eighty national workers are serving a church with a membership approaching six thousand.

The *Lutheran Church-Missouri Synod* began work in Mexico in 1940. The mission there has never been a large operation and at present only two missionaries are serving in Mexico. Progress has been slow and the Mexican churches have tended to depend too much on American support. In 1968 nine congregations formed the *Lutheran Synod of Mexico.* In order to allow close relations with other Lutheran congregations in Mexico the new synod eliminated from its constitution an article on doctrinal standards.

Mexico was the first country to attract *Missionary Aviation Fellowship* when it first went into operation in 1946. It began with one small plane and a Christian pilot. Two more planes and the necessary personnel were added later on as the Fellowship expanded its program. It now has four planes serving six evangelical missions in Mexico. But Mexico is not the only country in which MAF is operating. Altogether it has sixty-four planes serving scores of missions and churches in nineteen countries around the world. For many years it was an American operation. More recently it has acquired two new home bases, Great Britain and Australia.

For sixty-five years the *Central American Mission* lived up to its name and confined its ministry to the republics of Central America. In 1955 it moved into Mexico and established headquarters in the fast-growing city of Pueblo southwest of the capital. The main work there is the Bible school, which began day classes in the Baptist church and evening classes in the Methodist church in the spring of 1959. Since then it has acquired its own new property and buildings, and some thirty students are enrolled in the three-year course. In 1963 the mission transferred its entire publication project to Mexico. At present the operation consists mainly of translating and adapting Scripture Press Sunday school materials to meet the needs of Sunday schools all over Latin America. Medical work includes two dispensaries and a dental clinic. Church work is only now getting under way, with two organized and eleven unorganized churches. Thirty-three CAM missionaries are in Mexico.

Evangelism by Radio. Until recently Christian radio in Mexico was impossible due to legal restrictions. During the administration of President Lopez Mateos (1958-1964) the law was revised. Religion is now permitted on the air provided it keeps out of politics and does not attack other religions. It took some time before station managers would accept evangelical programs; but perseverance paid off, and today there are hundreds of programs throughout the country every week. There are plans to establish Christian radio stations in various locations. By 1967 *Radio Maranatha* in Mexico City was broadcasting twelve hours a day on an FM station. The Presbyterians in the jungles of Chiapas have been given the opportunity of starting a 10,000-watt station with full cooperation from the local authorities. The Seventh Day Adventists were the first group to buy time on commercial stations. In 1968 they were broadcasting over forty-four stations. The Mennonites and the Southern Baptists have also sponsored Christian programs on local stations. In March, 1967, the first interdenominational program, *Prisma,* began its ministry over XEX network of ten stations. This is a fifteen-minute Sunday morning program directed by *Juan M. Isais* of the Latin America Mission. During the 1968 Olympics, Campus Crusade sponsored seventy brief programs on some of which Christian athletes gave their testimonies. During the 1969 Christmas season Luis Palau, Overseas Crusades Latin American evangelist, preached to an estimated TV audience of seven hundred thousand. In March, 1970, Overseas Crusades inaugurated TV crusades in eight countries in Central and South America. The Mexico City Rally in March was nationally televised in three countries. Plans are already under way for a nationwide Evangelism-in-Depth campaign in Mexico in 1971.

Bible Societies. Several attempts were made before the Bible Society was able to open a depot in Mexico City in 1863. In 1878 it was agreed that the *American Bible Society* should take over the work of the Agency. In 1962 Mexico became a Joint Agency of the two Bible societies, under ABS administration. A good deal of Bible translation work has been accomplished, most of it by Wycliffe Bible Translators. Ninety tribes in Mexico now have the Scriptures. Of these, eight have the complete New Testament; the others have one or more Portions. No tribe has the complete Bible. Scripture distribution is running around three million copies per year.

Theological Education. With over one hundred missions in Mexico it is not surprising to find about forty Bible schools and theological seminaries. *Union Theological Seminary,* established in Mexico City in 1919, has been a cooperative effort of the Methodists, Disciples, and Congregationalists. In 1969 Union Seminary moved to a joint campus with three others, Episcopal, Lutheran, and Baptist, located adjacent to the University of Mexico. Each seminary maintains its own identity but shares certain common facilities, such as library, chapel, and instruction hall. A corporate institution of graduate study is in process of organization with the help of the Theological Education Fund. In January, 1969, thirty-five representatives of nine denominations and eighteen Bible institutes convened the first meeting of the *Mexican Association of Institutions of Theological Education.*

Ecumenical Relations. The *Evangelical Council of Mexico* is the most inclusive Protestant fellowship in the country. It is affiliated with the Division of World Mission and Evangelism of the World Council of Churches. Another organization, the *Center for Ecumenical Studies,* was recently established in Mexico City. A third ecumenical organization is

CAVE (Centro Audio-Visual Evangelico de Mexico). The *National Evangelical Convention,* supported by the conservative evangelicals, meets once a year.

Guatemala

Political History. Prior to the Spanish conquest Guatemala was the center of the Mayan civilization, which flourished for a thousand years. The colonial period lasted from 1524 to 1821. During the nineteenth century Guatemala experienced a series of dictatorships, broken only by short periods of representative government. The modernization of Guatemala began with the revolution of 1944. Since then political life has been marked by crisis and confusion. The Communist Party, given legal recognition in 1952, was outlawed in 1954. The 1960's witnessed guerrilla activity, at least one military coup, and the assassination of three American officials, including the ambassador.

The People. The population of Guatemala is 5.1 million and growing at an annual rate of 3.1 percent. Pure-blooded descendants of the Mayan Indians make up slightly more than half the population. The ladinos (mestizos) account for 43 percent, and the remaining 2 percent are white. The Indians are divided into some twenty tribes, each speaking its own dialect. About 70 percent of the people are illiterate. Spanish is the official language.

Religion. Guatemala is a predominantly Roman Catholic country. The 1965 constitution guarantees religious liberty and the right of religious bodies to own property free of taxes. Religion is taught in both Roman Catholic and Protestant schools. According to some estimates, Protestants represent 10 percent of the population, which is high for Latin America. Roman Catholic-Protestant relations, though not particularly good, are gradually improving. The first Protestant university in Latin America, *Universidad Mariano Galvez,* was established in 1966. It is sponsored by a group of evangelical professionals. Two Presbyterian missionaries are on the faculty.

Missions. The oldest mission in Guatemala is the *American Presbyterian* whose work dates back to 1882. The pioneer missionary was the *Reverend J. C. Hill,* who received a personal invitation from the president of Guatemala, Don Justo Rufino Barrios, who was interested in updating his country and thought that Protestantism could be used to that end. His original call was to China, but when this invitation came from Guatemala, Mr. Hill decided to accept it. So eager was the president to get on with the modernization of his country that he made Mr. Hill a member of his official party. In this rather strange way Protestant missions began in Guatemala. Except for one or two short periods, the Presbyterian mission has maintained a staff in Guatemala for almost ninety years and is now one of the leading Protestant groups in the country. The *National Evangelical Presbyterian Church of Guatemala,* fully autonomous since 1961, has eighty-four organized churches and many unorganized congregations in its six presbyteries, fifty-five ordained pastors, and twenty-five fraternal workers. The *Quiche Bible Institute,* a joint venture with the Primitive Methodists, tries to meet the basic needs of the Quiche Indians. The *Evangelical Presbyterian Seminary* in San Felipe has developed a new pattern of theological education which is rapidly spreading to other groups throughout Latin America, and, indeed, to Africa and Asia. Ten regional centers have replaced the traditional campus situation. About two hundred men and women, who live at home, are enrolled in these centers, which receive weekly visits from the seminary professors. The studies are carried on at three different academic levels to tailor the curriculum to the background and capacity of the students.

The *Central American Mission,* founded by the well-known C. I. Scofield, entered Guatemala in 1899. Today the CAM has work in all six of the republics of Central America and Mexico. Pioneer missionary *A. E. Bishop* gave forty-five years of service to Guatemala, during which he laid the foundations of the work. From every point of view Guatemala is the largest and most important of all seven fields of the mission. The indigenous church, the *Central American Evangelical Church,* has been fully autonomous since 1927. Today it has 170 organized churches and 200 unorganized congregations, with thirteen thousand members and a Christian community of thirty thousand. The seventy-one missionaries in Guatemala are divided among several important institutions. The *Robinson Bible Institute,* now in Chimultenango, has been training leaders for the Indian work since 1923. The Bible institute in Guatemala City, dating back to 1929, added a seminary department in 1966. This institution trains leaders for all the Central American countries. Three other Bible schools are maintained, and a school for missionaries' children. *Radio Station TGNA,* which first went on the air in 1950, is now preparing to introduce television. Medical work includes two dental clinics.

The *California Yearly Meeting of Friends* entered Guatemala in 1902. They have experienced solid though not spectacular growth. The 1969 report indicated seventy-three hundred professed believers. During the year close to one thousand accepted Christ as Savior. The hub of their work is in Chiquimula, where they have a daily broadcast over a local station. The *Berea Bible Institute* has greatly expanded its extension program, with 158 students in twenty-five centers enrolled at the beginning of 1970. The residence program, suspended in 1967 for lack of students, was reactivated in 1969. Almost two hundred students are enrolled in the Amigos schools in Chiquimula.

The *Church of the Nazarene* has been in Guatemala since 1904. Today the church reports a membership of twenty-seven hundred in eighty-six congregations under the supervision of sixty-three national workers. Thirteen missionaries help to staff two Bible colleges.

The *Church of God* (Cleveland) work in Guatemala was initiated by *Charles T. Furman* and *Thomas A. Pullin* in 1916. They settled for a time in the Department of Totonicapan. In 1920 they moved to Santa Cruz del Quiche and began pioneer work among the Quiche Indians. In 1932 the missions in both places experienced a great outpouring of the Holy Spirit. The work was divided into three districts in 1955. Today in Guatemala there are 287 churches and 296 missions with a membership of 10,250.

The *Primitive Methodist Church* has only one mission field and that is Guatemala. The first missionary was *Charles Furman,* a Pentecostal who arrived in 1916 but who did not become a member of the Primitive Methodist Missionary Society until 1921. Furman was dropped by the Methodists after a charismatic movement swept the field in 1932. The Primitive Methodists are working almost exclusively among the Indian tribes. Reported membership is above one thousand. The *Quiche Bible Institute* trains leaders for the churches.

The first *Assembly of God* missionaries, *Mr. and Mrs. John L. Franklin,* arrived in Jutiapa in 1937 and linked up with several indigenous Pentecostal groups. Four years later they moved to Guatemala City, where there are twenty-three churches today. A Bible school was opened in the capital in 1950. Later on a Bible school for Indians was opened at Panajachel. Assembly pastors are responsible for twelve daily radio programs in various parts of the country. Some 315 churches are all self-supporting and self-governing. In addition there are 460 outstations. Together they account for almost eleven thousand baptized members. Only ten missionaries are in Guatemala.

The *Lutheran Church-Missouri Synod* began work in Zacapa in 1947 in answer to three distinct calls from English, German, and Spanish groups. After almost twenty-five years of work Guatemala has a very heavy emphasis on Americans and Europeans in key positions. Only two vicars are nationals. The church in the capital conducts services in Spanish, English, and German. Spanish work extends to five other centers in different parts of the country. In 1969 there were five parishes in Guatemala with almost seven hundred communicant members.

The first *Southern Baptist* missionaries arrived in Guatemala in 1948, but Baptist churches were in existence before that. In fact the *Guatemalan Baptist Convention* was formed in 1946, with the assistance of a member of the SBC Home Mission Board. The Foreign Board now has eighteen missionaries located in six centers. The theological institute and the bookstore are in the capital. The Guatemalan Baptist Convention now has thirty-four organized churches with slightly fewer than one hundred members per church. The Baptists in Guatemala have pioneered in live tele-vision broadcasting.

Wycliffe Bible Translators has almost sixty translators working in seventeen tribes of Guatemala. The work began in 1952. Today there are believers in all the tribes.

The *Seventh Day Adventists* have a long-established work in Guate-mala. In 1969 they reported forty churches with a membership of sev-enty-four hundred.

During the 1960's thirteen new missions entered Guatemala. For the most part these are small missions, just getting under way. Total mission-aries in this group number thirty.

Evangelism. The *Latin America Mission* sponsored an Evangelism-in-Depth campaign in 1962. It took a full-time team of thirteen LAM coordinators plus an uncounted multitude of volunteers a whole year to do the job. The organizational problem was massive. A national executive committee supervised the work of thirty-two regional committees. Over six thousand prayer cells were organized. Between forty thousand and fifty thousand believers took a two-month training course in personal evangelism. It is impossible to know how many Christians made personal calls on friends and relatives during the year; but in two days of organized house-to-house visitation, more than five thousand evangelicals made two hundred forty thousand calls and distributed half a million Gospels and a million tracts. The campaign ended with a month-long united national campaign in Guatemala City. On the last day some fifteen thousand Christians marched in a parade to the Olympic Stadium, where an enthusi-astic crowd of over thirty thousand braved the drizzle and the threat of revolution to attend the final meeting.

Bible Societies. Originally the Central American Agency included five countries, with headquarters in Guatemala City. By mutual agreement in 1913 the *American Bible Society* withdrew from Iran and the *British and Foreign Bible Society* from Central America (with the exception of British Honduras). In 1946 when the Colombia-Venezuela Joint Agency was established, the Caribbean Agency again became the Central American Agency. In 1960 the headquarters returned to Guatemala. On January 1, 1970, the first Guatemalan executive secretary of the Bible Society took office. The Reina Bible (Spanish) has been in existence for four hundred years. Only six Indian tribes have the complete New Testament. The latest one, for the Mam-speaking people, appeared in 1969. Eleven other tribes have at least one Portion. Distribution among the Indians is not large, owing to the low rate of literacy. Scripture distribution for the entire country in 1969 registered an increase of 54 percent over the previous year. In 1968 the Bible Society provided one hundred thousand Selections to be used in various campaigns sponsored by the Billy Graham Evangelistic Association.

Ecumenical Relations. There is no national council or its equivalent in Guatemala. The *Evangelical Committee for Social and Cultural Service,* founded in 1963 at the initiative of the Church World Service, coordinates the social work of the churches in addition to carrying out its own projects, which include leadership training, campaigns against illiteracy, public health programs, and others. The National Presbyterian Church of Guatemala is a member of the *Latin American Commission of Christian Education* (CELADEC).

Honduras

Political History. Honduras became an independent state in 1838 after three centuries of Spanish rule. Since then its history has been marked by frequent revolutions. Only since 1930 has relative stability been achieved, and then not without frequent setbacks. The latest military coup took place in 1963. A long-standing border dispute with El Salvador led to open warfare in 1969.

The People. The population of Honduras is 2.5 million and growing at an annual rate of 3.5 percent, slightly higher than the average for Latin America. About 90 percent of the people are mestizo. Minority groups include Indians, Negroes, and Europeans, in that order. Spanish is the official language, though English is spoken along the north coast and on the Bay Islands. The literacy rate is almost 50 percent.

Religion. The dominant religion is Roman Catholicism. In 1959 the president and the archbishop dedicated the nation to the Sacred Heart of Jesus and the Immaculate Heart of Mary. The Constitution, however, guarantees religious liberty, and Protestant missions have operated with a good deal of freedom.

Missions. Protestant missionary work began with the arrival in 1896 of a party of five missionaries of the *Central American Mission.* Through the years the CAM has maintained a strong staff in eight or nine centers in the western part of the country. Almost half of its thirty-four missionaries are concentrated in two institutions, the *Evangelical Hospital* and the *American Academy.* The mission has one doctor and three nurses. Church growth has been rather slow. After almost seventy-five years there are only two thousand church members. The *Association of Central American Churches in Honduras,* which became fully autonomous in 1948, comprises fifty organized churches and thirty unorganized congregations. Forty pastors serve these churches.

In 1909 the *California Yearly Meeting of Friends* entered Honduras. Its mission there has never been large; its staff at present numbers seven. It has no work other than church work. Church membership, slightly over one thousand, is divided among some two dozen congregations.

One British mission, the *Methodist Missionary Society,* has been working among the English-speaking people in the Bay Islands and in the inland city of San Pedro Sula for more than half a century. During the Depression in the 1930's all of their work on the islands was swept away, and the church and secondary school in San Pedro Sula had to close. Again in 1967 they were confronted with retrenchment at a time when the opportunities called for expansion. This was due in part to the devaluation of the pound. In 1968 they reported thirty-five churches and over twenty-three hundred members.

The *Evangelical and Reformed Church* (now the United Church Board for World Ministries) has been working in the three northern departments since 1921. Today the *Evangelical and Reformed Synod of Honduras* comprises twenty organized churches with one thousand members. Four of its eighteen pastors have given a total of one hundred years of service to Christ and the church. All thirteen missionaries now in Honduras have been appointed in the past decade. The medical and social work is carried on in cooperation with the Association of Evangelical Institutions of Honduras.

The *Seventh Day Adventists* have been in Honduras for many decades and through all this period their work has shown steady growth. Today, with twenty-six churches and thirty-seven hundred members, they are the largest church in the country.

The *American Moravian Church* established its first station at Kaurkira in 1930. Since then half a dozen centers have been opened in the eastern region of the country among the ten thousand Miskito Indians. Medical, educational, and agricultural work all form part of the program. The *Honduran Synod of the Moravian Church* has twenty-four pastors serving twenty-six congregations with sixteen hundred members.

The *Assemblies of God* launched its missionary work in Honduras from its base in El Salvador in 1940, in response to an appeal for help from three already existing Pentecostal churches. Today there are four main centers of work in the northwest and two centers in the south. The *Honduran Bible School,* opened in 1946, has moved twice and is now located in San Pedro Sula, where new buildings were dedicated in 1965. From the beginning the work has been indigenous and self-supporting. Nearly every year new assemblies are established and new churches built. Today there are forty-one churches and seventeen outstations in charge of sixty-four national workers; but the growth here has not been comparable to that in El Salvador. Total membership is about eleven hundred.

The *World Gospel Mission* has been at work in Honduras since 1943. With headquarters in the capital city of Tegucigalpa, WGM is responsible for the evangelization of over three hundred thousand people in the central part of the republic. A strong national church, the *Honduran Holiness Church,* lost many members during the war in 1969, when the Salvadorans in Honduras were either sent home or detained. The mission maintains a Bible school and a high school in the capital. The latter has about one hundred students.

The *Church of God* (Cleveland) began work on the Bay Islands in 1944. Through the years there has been a large turnover of missionaries, due to the mission's policy of transferring its members from one country to another. Later on work was started along the northern coast of the mainland. In 1950 *Josue Rubio,* a Mexican, became the first Church of God missionary to the interior, where through the years he has had a remarkable ministry. During the 1950's revival broke out along the border near Guatemala. Today the Church of God is one of the larger churches, with a membership of over twenty-one hundred divided among fifty-nine churches and twenty-nine missions. Sixty-two ministers and four missionaries minister to these groups.

In 1949 *Mr. and Mrs. Wilbur Ackerman* of the *United Brethren Mission* went to Honduras to take over a work abandoned by the Zion Methodist Mission in 1930. For a time they worked with English-speaking people in La Ceiba, Tela, and Cortez, where a church and elementary school were established. In 1952 the mission began work among the Spanish-speaking people. Today the *Church of the United Brethren in Christ* has three hundred members meeting in thirteen congregations. Five missionaries are in Honduras.

The *Eastern Mennonite Board of Missions and Charities* has forty-one missionaries in Honduras, including six associates and fifteen overseas volunteers. The work started in 1950 and today includes a Bible institute, *Pine Grove Academy,* and medical and church work. Total church membership is about three hundred, divided among some twenty-five small congregations numbering anywhere from two to thirty-two members.

The first Baptist group to enter was the *Conservative Baptist Home Mission Society* in 1951. Their first missionaries were *Mr. and Mrs. Lee Irons,* who had been in Honduras as independent workers before joining CBHMS. La Ceiba, one of the largest coastal cities, is the center of the English-speaking work. Work was begun later among the Spanish-speaking people of the Aguan River Valley. In 1960 *Radio Station HRVC,* located in the capital, began broadcasting the gospel on shortwave; mediumwave was added in 1965. Today the programs can be heard in all parts of the country. In 1969 a dozen new churches were started through the extension Bible institute program conducted by the missionaries in the San Juan Valley. Ten pastors have the spiritual care of some seven hundred church members. Ten missionaries carry the burden of the radio and Bible institute work.

Southern Baptist work began in the late 1940's, though the first resident missionaries did not arrive until 1954. Four years later the *Association of Honduran Baptist Churches* was organized. It now has eleven churches and almost seven hundred members. A theological institute is located in the capital, along with a bookstore. Thirteen missionaries are stationed in five centers. A mobile medical unit operates out of El Porvenir. Student work was begun in 1970. *Baptist Mid-Missions* has been in Honduras for fifteen years, during which time it has established four small churches. Six missionaries serve there now.

The *Wesleyan Church* has two missionaries in Honduras. The work began in 1957 and today is located in four centers, Puerto Cortes, Tela, La Ceiba, and Puerto Castilla. Six churches report a combined membership of around one hundred.

Missionary Aviation Fellowship entered Honduras in 1968 and has four planes cooperating with more than a dozen evangelical groups.

Eight missions initiated work in Honduras during the 1960's. To date their investment in terms of personnel has not been large—a total of only fourteen missionaries in all.

Evangelism. Evangelism-in-Depth held its campaign in 1963-64. An estimated fifteen thousand Christians met in 2,650 prayer cells and some six thousand took the training courses. At least 110 new congregations were formed and the churches in San Pedro Sula had their membership more than doubled as a result of the united crusade in that city.

Ecumenical Relations. The *Evangelical Alliance,* a conference of Protestant groups, meets each year; but its effectiveness has declined in recent years due to the withdrawal of several member groups and the lack of an effective united program.

British Honduras

Political History. Although Britain sent an official representative to the area in the eighteenth century, Belize was not formally termed "the colony of British Honduras" until 1840. It became a crown colony in 1860. Guatemala and Britain have quarreled over this territory for a long time. In 1968 the United States, after more than two years of mediation, offered a solution which was rejected by both parties. Under the 1964 Constitution Honduras enjoys almost full internal self-government.

The People. With only 125,000 people, British Honduras is the smallest nation in Central America. One-third of the population lives in the capital city, Belize. Forty percent is of African descent, 40 percent of Latin-Indian descent. Indians represent 16.5 percent, and Europeans 3.5 percent. English is the official language. The literacy rate is about 75 percent.

Religion. More than 50 percent of this traditionally Protestant country is now claimed by the Roman Catholics, who have made great headway in the last few years, especially with their fine system of schools, into which they have poured a good deal of money. Very little Protestant work has been done among the Indians.

British Missions. Four British missions were pioneers in this part of the world. The first was the *Society for the Propagation of the Gospel,* whose chief concern was the Negro laborers from Jamaica. In 1914 a bishop and about fifteen clergy cared for the spiritual needs of the people. Today there are about twenty thousand Anglicans living in a dozen centers, from Punta Gorda in the south to Coroxal in the north.

The *Methodist Missionary Society* began work in 1825 and in spite of many vicissitudes has continued to the present. Mission work centers in four cities, Belize, Toledo, Stann Creek, and Coroxal. *Wesley College* in Belize has served the district for eighty-six years. High schools are located in the other centers. The Methodist church reports a membership of about two thousand but a Christian community of fifteen thousand.

The *Salvation Army* sent its first workers to British Honduras in 1915. The *Plymouth Brethren* for many years have had a small work there.

American Missions. The *Church of the Nazarene* entered British Honduras in 1934. After thirty-five years of work there were twenty-four churches and preaching points, only one of which is self-supporting. Fifteen missionaries are working there.

The *Assemblies of God* began permanent work with the arrival in 1951 of *Mr. and Mrs. Walter Clifford,* former missionaries to India and Ceylon. As early as 1956 plans were laid for the establishment of indigenous churches. Today the work centers in four cities, including the capital. British Honduras is one of the very few fields in which the Assemblies do not have a Bible school. Perhaps this accounts for the lack of growth—only five small churches, with a total of eighty members after almost twenty years.

The *Gospel Missionary Union* sent its first missionaries, *Mr. and Mrs. Gordon Lees,* to British Honduras in 1955. They settled in Belize, where they established the Yarborough Bible Church. In 1956 the mission acquired twenty-acre Carol Farm, thirty miles out of Belize, where they have opened a girls' camp, a conference grounds, and a Bible school. In 1960 work was begun among the Indians at Orange Walk. The mission operates several schools subsidized by the government. Fifteen missionaries, including six short-termers, are in British Honduras.

The *Eastern Mennonite Board of Missions and Charities* has been in British Honduras since 1960. There is a strong emphasis on service programs, which center around three Mennonite colonies and one Amish settlement. The workers are on a completely self-supporting basis. Two radio programs over *Radio Belize* are sponsored by the mission.

The *Conservative Baptists* have been in the country for ten years. Five organized churches have been established. Four missionaries, four pastors, and seven teachers constitute the permanent staff. The mission operates three primary schools.

The most recent arrival is the *Elim Missionary Association,* which entered the country in 1967. Its six missionaries are just now getting down to work.

Ecumenical Relations. The *Protestant Council* includes the Methodists, Presbyterians, Salvation Army, and the Church of the Nazarene. An attempt to form a Christian council embracing all Christian groups has met with little success. There is a *Christian Social Council,* originally set up by Church World Service and now supported by the Division of Inter-Church Aid, Refugee and World Service of the World Council of Churches. There is a growing ecumenical consciousness. Roman Catholics have joined with Protestants in national services; and in 1965, for the first time in history, a Methodist minister was invited to preach in the Anglican Cathedral. Also for the first time, an Anglican bishop has spoken in a Pentecostal church.

El Salvador

Political History. El Salvador revolted against Spain in 1821 and became an independent republic in 1829. As elsewhere in Central America, frequent revolutions have marked El Salvador's history. Relative stability did not come until 1900 and lasted only thirty years. From 1930 to 1960 the country again reverted to coups and countercoups. The new constitution of 1962 restored constitutional government, and free elections in 1964, 1966, and 1968 were carried out without major incidents.

The People. The population of 3.3 million is about 90 percent ladino (mestizo) and 6 percent Indian. The remainder is made up mostly of white people. Approximately half the population is illiterate. Spanish is the official language. Education is free and compulsory.

Religion. Roman Catholicism is the dominant religion. The total Protestant community is approximately one hundred thousand, or about 3 percent of the population; and this in spite of the fact that El Salvador is the most densely populated country in Central America. Fifteen missions are listed as having work in El Salvador; but together they have only sixty-five missionaries, almost half of whom belong to one mission, the Central American Mission. In 1968 Protestant missionaries were notified that as foreign residents they and their children must pay $800.00 for residence permits. Roman Catholics were not included in this new ruling.

Missions. After six years of work in Costa Rica, in 1894 the *Central American Mission* made plans to enter other nearby fields. The venture ended in disaster when two missionaries en route to El Salvador contracted yellow fever and died within a few days of each other. Two years later a second attempt succeeded and the first missionary landed in El Salvador. In April of the following year *Robert H. Bender* began his impressive ministry in this republic. The mission's work today is centered in San Salvador, where eighteen of its thirty missionaries are located. The mission maintains three primary schools and a short-term Bible school. The national church, called the *Evangelical Church of El Salvador,* received its autonomy in 1935. Between 1935 and 1940 it lost several hundred members. Today there are sixty churches and thirty-six unorganized congregations with a baptized membership of thirty-three hundred.

The *American Baptist Home Mission Society* has been working in El Salvador since 1911. A good deal of dedication has gone into the work; but growth was slow, especially until 1950. Since that time the pattern has improved somewhat. The two outstanding institutions are the Baptist academies in Santa Ana and San Salvador, both of which have a capacity enrolment. The *Baptist Association of El Salvador* voted in 1967 to participate in the *Crusade of the Americas,* 1968-1970, which the Convention here in the USA failed to support. There are only four American missionaries in El Salvador, but a good deal of American money is still used for expansion purposes. The Association's 1967 report spoke of the need of pastors with a higher level of preparation. The bottleneck is not lack of institutions or candidates, but of money to support the students in training. In 1970 the Baptist Association of El Salvador reported thirty-one churches, forty-four missions and stations, and a church membership of 2,450.

The *Seventh Day Adventists* have two missionaries in El Salvador at present. In the El Salvador mission, however, there are thirty-five churches and almost sixty-three hundred members.

The *Assemblies of God* entered El Salvador in response to a call for help from twelve Pentecostal churches founded by an independent Pentecostal missionary some years before. *Mr. and Mrs. Ralph Williams* arrived in 1929 and immediately formed a national church organization in which national leaders shared responsibility with the missionaries. In 1931 Williams established the *Bethel Bible Institute* in San Salvador; today it has eighty-six students enrolled. San Salvador is the hub of their work. The

Evangelistic Center in the heart of the city is open for evangelistic services every night in the year. National workers sponsor a dozen daily radio broadcasts and four weekly programs in various parts of the country. With the cooperation of three other evangelical missions, *Radio Station YSHQ* was erected on the Bible school property. This 10,000-watt station reaches into adjoining republics sixteen hours a day. Since its inception the station has been financed largely by the four leading evangelical church organizations in El Salvador. A phenomenal Sunday school program reaches over twenty-nine thousand pupils every week. Two Christian day schools are in operation. The one in the capital includes kindergarten through junior college and has an enrolment of about one thousand. Often referred to as the showcase of Assemblies of God missions in Latin America, El Salvador has demonstrated the wisdom of using indigenous methods of missionary work. The Assemblies of God Church is the largest denomination in the country. More than one thousand national workers are serving 325 churches and 760 outstations with a total membership of ninety-six hundred. The Christian community is estimated at sixty-three thousand. This entire work is self-supporting and self-propagating; only eight missionaries are connected with it.

The pioneer missionary of the *Church of God* (Cleveland) in El Salvador was *H. S. Syverson,* who arrived in 1940. He undertook to build on a sagging foundation laid by an independent Pentecostal missionary, *Frederick W. Mebius,* who had worked in El Salvador since 1904. At one time Mebius headed a large and thriving work, but in later years it had gradually been reduced to five mission stations. In 1944, shortly after the death of Mebius, Syverson opened a Bible school which through the years has provided a steady stream of workers for the churches of El Salvador. Most of the 117 ministers are graduates of this school. Today the Church of God in El Salvador reports 117 organized churches, 78 missions, and a membership of forty-three hundred.

In addition to the two above-mentioned Pentecostal missions, there are indigenous Pentecostal groups in El Salvador which have never been identified with any foreign mission. Their total membership is estimated at ten thousand. Taken together, the Pentecostals represent at least 75 percent of all the evangelicals in the country today.

Other groups with missionaries in El Salvador include the *Plymouth Brethren, Church of the Nazarene, Churches of Christ,* and *Baptist International Missions.*

Ecumenical Relations.   There is no national council of churches or its equivalent in El Salvador. The only group with ecumenical connections is the *Association of Baptists,* which is a member of the *Latin American Commission of Christian Education* (CELADEC). A rather surprising degree of *rapprochement* has been achieved between the Roman Catholics and the Protestants. In 1967, for the first time in the country's history,

Roman Catholic priests and nuns, attending a service in the First Baptist Church of San Salvador, were singing with a Protestant congregation Luther's famous hymn, "A Mighty Fortress Is Our God." The previous year a similar united service had been held in El Rosario Church. Most of the Protestant denominations were reported as being present. Here, as elsewhere in Latin America, this kind of fraternization has tended to polarize the Protestant community, the ecumenists hailing the new conciliar spirit and the conservative evangelicals deploring it.

Nicaragua

Political History. Nicaragua became a sovereign, independent state in 1838 after some three hundred years of Spanish rule. In the early part of the twentieth century U. S. Marines intervened several times in Nicaragua to restore peace and guarantee political stability. Since 1936 Nicaragua has been ruled by the members of the Somozo family.

The People. Seventy percent of the 1.9 million people are mestizos, 17 percent European, 9 percent Negro, and 4 percent Indian. About 40 percent of the population is urban. Fifty percent of the people over ten years of age are literate.

Religion. Roman Catholicism is the dominant religion, with 96 percent of the people belonging to that faith. In 1966 the National Congress approved an amendment to the constitution permitting the teaching of religion in public schools. This has caused some concern in evangelical circles, where it is regarded as a violation of the principle of the separation of church and state.

Missions. Nicaragua is the oldest of all the mission fields of Central America. The first missionaries were *German Moravians* who arrived in 1849. During World War I the work was transferred to the *American Moravians,* who have been there ever since. The *Moravian Church,* with ten thousand members and a Christian community of twenty-five thousand, is the largest in Nicaragua. Its Christians are mostly English-speaking West Indians who work on the banana plantations. Work is carried on in nineteen centers, nine on the east coast, four along the Mexican border, and six inland, one of which is Managua, the capital. Medical work includes four clinics and two hospitals, both of which have a nurses training program. The Moravians have twenty-five hundred students enrolled in their schools, and twelve thousand in their Sunday schools. *Moravo Academy,* which began in the early 1920's, has 580 in the elementary school and 320 in the secondary school. The Bible institute trains workers for the church. Today there are nineteen ordained nationals, seven Creoles and twelve Miskito Indians. Self-support is a continuing problem, but the synod has devised a plan whereby a local church will pay part of its pastor's salary direct to the pastor rather than through a central fund. Mission subsidies are being progressively lowered.

The *Central American Mission* started work in Nicaragua in 1900. By 1925 it had some seven hundred church members; but since that time growth has been painfully slow. The national church received its autonomy in 1948. Notwithstanding this, the CAM has had trouble with its churches. In 1955 half of the twenty-two churches declared themselves independent. In 1965 several remaining congregations broke away and formed their own association. This in great measure explains the lack of growth in the CAM churches, whose total membership in 1970 was only eight hundred. Eight of the sixteen missionaries are in the Bible school located in Managua. The others are engaged in various forms of evangelism.

In 1917 *Miss Blackmore* became the first Baptist missionary to Nicaragua. That same year the First Baptist Church of Managua was organized. Within a year Miss Blackmore had opened four schools. In 1922 the *American Baptist Home Mission Society* helped to establish the *Baptist Academy,* also in Managua. In 1927 the Women's Society opened the *Evelyn Briggs Cranska Memorial Hospital,* which through the years has done much for the evangelical cause. The *Nicaragua Baptist Convention* was organized in 1937. Between 1940 and 1960 the membership doubled from 1,422, to 2,821, but during the past decade it has remained about the same. In 1968 the convention, with the help of the mission, established the *Polytechnic Institute* in Managua. The *Baptist Hospital* is now included as one of its schools. Three hundred students were enrolled the first year. The institute is situated on the spacious grounds of the Baptist Academy.

The *Assemblies of God* entered Nicaragua in 1936 and built on a foundation laid by independent Pentecostal missionaries, first in Matagalpa and later in Leon, dating back to 1912. In 1936 a national church organization was formed, and the following year the *Nicaragua Bible Institute* was opened in Matagalpa. The consolidation of the work into a church organization and the founding of the Bible school made greater progress possible, and the coming of new missionaries advanced it still further. The past thirty-four years have seen slow but steady growth. In 1970 there were 37 churches and 147 outstations, with twenty-two hundred members.

The *Church of the Nazarene* began work in Nicaragua in 1943. Today there are forty-two churches and preaching points, six of which are self-supporting. Institutions include two dispensaries and a Bible college. Seventeen missionaries are teamed up with eighty national workers.

The *Church of God* (Cleveland) mission in Nicaragua began in January, 1951, when *Miguel Flores,* a native of El Salvador, crossed the border and began preaching to the Indians. In three months he had won enough converts to organize a church in Managua. By the end of the year he had established four congregations. He remained in Nicaragua until funds were exhausted and then returned to El Salvador. He was followed by *Pedro Abreu,* who had been a carpenter before becoming a missionary. He preached the gospel, won converts, and built several churches with his own hands. Today the Church of God, with 1,750 members, is one of the larger denominations in Nicaragua. Forty ministers have the oversight of thirty-five churches and twenty-two missions.

During the 1960's nine other missions entered Nicaragua. Together they represent a missionary force of only twenty-one persons.

Evangelism. In 1960 Nicaragua became the first country in which Evangelism-in-Depth held a nationwide campaign. It lasted only five months and was in the nature of an experiment; but it was sufficiently successful to encourage the Latin America Mission to repeat the performance in other countries. To date EID campaigns have been held in ten countries of Latin America.

Christian Radio. Most gospel radio stations are owned and operated by missionary bodies; but *Radio Station YNOL* in Managua is sponsored by Christian laymen from the various churches, with the technical advice and help of several evangelical missions. It began broadcasting in March, 1959. Since that time it has developed its program and increased its power to the place where it is now a powerful instrument for the preaching of the gospel in Nicaragua.

Ecumenical Relations. Compelled by the need for concerted action in matters pertaining to church and state, nine of the larger denominations decided in 1966 to constitute a *National Evangelical Council of Churches.* Roman Catholic-Protestant relations are gradually improving. In one city, Tashapaunie, the Anglicans, Roman Catholics, and Moravians decided in 1969 to join forces and conduct one good day school rather than three second-rate schools.

Bible Societies. The work in Nicaragua comes under the Agency in Honduras, whose new executive secretary, the *Reverend Saul Gomez,* was appointed in 1969. With only 4 percent of the people pure Indian, it is not surprising to learn that the complete New Testament, translated in 1905, is available only to the Miskito Indians. Roman Catholics are reading the Scriptures with the blessing of the church. In 1967 in the town of Bluefields the Roman Catholic churches joined with the Protestant churches in a joint Bible Day Celebration.

Costa Rica

Political History. Costa Rica was discovered by Columbus on his fourth and last voyage to the New World. After more than three hundred years of Spanish rule, it became a sovereign, independent state in 1838. It is the most progressive and democratic of all the Central American states. Since 1889 there have been only two short interruptions in constitutional government. Since the revolution in 1948 there have been four presidential elections, all of them peaceful.

The People. The estimated population of Costa Rica is 1.8 million, the overwhelming majority of Spanish descent. Negroes, whose ancestors came from Jamaica, number about twenty-five thousand and live in the province of Limon on the Caribbean coast. The Indian population has dwindled from twenty-five thousand in 1520 to three thousand today. The annual population growth of almost 4 percent is one of the highest in the world. The literacy rate is 85 percent—one of the highest in Latin America.

Religion. Costa Rica is a Roman Catholic country, but ever since the anti-clerical laws were passed in 1884 the power of the church has been weakened. Consequently there has been complete freedom of religion during the twentieth century. Evangelicals number about fifty thousand. There are few cities in Costa Rica without a Protestant church of some denomination.

British Missions. Evangelical Christianity was first introduced into Costa Rica by Baptists and Methodists from Jamaica, who emigrated to Costa Rica in large numbers in the nineteenth century. The *Jamaica Baptist Missionary Society* felt concern for these compatriots and in 1887 it sent the *Reverend Joshua Sobey* to Costa Rica to establish a mission there. The following year the First Baptist Church in Limon was organized. Not until 1894 did *Methodist* mission work get under way, and it was two years before a permanent pastor was available to shepherd the Methodist flock. The pioneer missionary was a layman, *Sydney Stewart,* a native of Jamaica. The *Methodist Missionary Society* (England) works with the Methodist churches of Costa Rica. The *Society for the Propagation of the Gospel* began missionary work in Central America in the eighteenth century. In 1896 *Bishop Ormsby* visited Costa Rica and instituted the Anglican form of worship in San Jose and Limon, where he found Anglican Christians. By 1906 the Anglicans had twelve well-organized missions between Limon on the coast and the capital city of San Jose. Today the *Episcopal Church in Costa Rica* has over one thousand members.

American Missions. The first mission from North America was the *Central American Mission,* whose pioneer missionaries, *Mr. and Mrs. William W. McConnell,* arrived in San Jose in 1891. At first he preached only in English; but after a visit from Francisco Penzotti of the Bible Society he began work among the Spanish-speaking people, who, of course, were Roman Catholics. Three new missionaries arrived in 1893 and five more in 1895. The emphasis was on widespread evangelism rather than on church planting; consequently church growth was tardy. By 1937 there were only three hundred church members. Between 1950 and 1960 there was a period of sustained growth, but during the decade of the sixties the number of churches and congregations remained about the same. The indigenous church, the *Association of Evangelical Churches,* has been autonomous since 1948 and today has a membership of 1,225 and a Christian community four times that number.

The first continuing work of the *United Methodists* was begun in 1918 by *Sidney W. Edwards.* During the Depression the work was carried on by means of special funds and the use of national workers. Today the *Costa Rica Provisional Annual Conference* is divided into three districts. Total membership is almost twelve hundred. The Methodists have their own seminary in Alajuela which serves the churches of Panama as well as Costa Rica. The *Methodist Academy* in San Jose is one of two Protestant schools with government recognition. Graduates may enter the university with full credits.

The largest mission in Costa Rica is the *Latin America Mission,* well known throughout the world for its promotion of Evangelism-in-Depth. The LAM was founded in 1921 by *Harry Strachan.* Its purpose was "to reach for Christ, by any and all means, in cooperation always with the local missionary organizations, the vast unevangelized masses of Spanish-speaking America." Harry Strachan and his Latin American colleagues threw caution to the winds and launched out on a program of mass evangelism which involved large campaigns in the major cities of Latin America. The results were beyond all expectations. Wherever they went, thousands packed the theaters and public halls. It was LAM, under the inspiration of the then general director, *R. Kenneth Strachan,* which in 1960 launched the first Evangelism-in-Depth campaign in Nicaragua. Since then ten campaigns have been held in Latin America; and similar campaigns, under different names, have been held in Nigeria, Congo, and other countries. Today Evangelism-in-Depth is organized on an international scale, with *Ruben Lores* as the executive director. LAM operates several important institutions in Costa Rica. One is *Radio Station TIFC,* which was erected in 1948. Another is the *Latin American Biblical Seminary,* whose fifty-four students represent twenty-six denominations and missions in seventeen countries. In 1968 the seminary got its first Latin American president, the *Reverend Plutarco Bonilla.* Its new international administrative board met for the first time in March, 1970, electing as president

Adalberto Santizo, rector of the evangelical Universidad Mariano Galvez in Guatemala. The publishing arm of LAM, *Editorial Caribe,* in 1965 began publishing Gospel Light Sunday school materials in Spanish. Editorial Caribe is now operating under a new banner, LAMP (Latin America Mission Publications). The *Bible Hospital,* which LAM operated in San Jose for thirty-nine years, was turned over to an enterprising group of local Christians in 1968. LAM is one of the more progressive missions and has pioneered in a number of areas. Latin Americans have for some time been full members of the mission. Ruben Lores, a native Cuban but now a United States citizen, is assistant general director. The mission is not content to talk about indigenization. It is doing something about it. One-third of all the missionaries in Costa Rica are members of LAM.

The first *Church of God* (Cleveland) church to be organized in Costa Rica was in Limon in 1935. The congregation was made up of English-speaking Negro immigrants from Jamaica. For fifteen years this church was the only Church of God in Costa Rica. In 1950 the first Spanish-speaking work was begun with the arrival of a young Panamanian missionary. He established work in San Jose, and was arrested some forty times because of his preaching. Beginning in 1950, the Church of God has experienced almost continuous revival. Thirty churches and nineteen missions are now served by twenty-eight national pastors. Total membership is 780. The Church of God would be larger today had it not experienced several schisms along the way.

In 1943 *Mr. and Mrs. Lawrence Perrault* were the first *Assemblies of God* missionaries appointed to Costa Rica. In 1950 a national was elected pastor of the assembly in San Jose. Other assemblies followed this pattern, and now all the churches are pastored by nationals who are fully supported by their own congregations. Most of the assemblies are in the south. Plans are being made to plant churches in the central plateau, the northwest region, and along the Caribbean coast. In 1965 the *Costa Rica Conference* organized its own missions department to promote worldwide missions. The Bible school has thirty-five students. The conference in 1970 had thirteen hundred members divided among thirty-five churches and forty-two outstations.

The first *Southern Baptist* missionaries were sent to Costa Rica by the Home Mission Board; the work was transferred to the Foreign Mission Board in 1949. In the meantime the *Baptist Convention of Costa Rica* had been organized in 1947. A theological seminary was established in San Jose in 1950. Today eight of the twenty-one churches in the convention are self-supporting. Twenty pastors and ten missonaries are involved in the work.

The *Seventh Day Adventists* have been in Costa Rica since the 1930's. In the intervening years they have slowly but steadily built up the largest church in the country, with 2,750 members in thirty-five congregations.

During the 1960's ten additional missions entered Costa Rica. Among them they have some two dozen missionaries. The largest of these is the *World Baptist Fellowship* with ten.

Mention should be made of the *Spanish Language Institute,* originally planned for Presbyterian personnel in Colombia. Later on it opened its doors to other missions and in 1950 was transferred to San Jose, where it now has an annual enrolment of over three hundred. During its twenty-eight-year history the institute has helped to train almost four thousand young missionaries representing 134 mission agencies.

Evangelism. Costa Rica was the second country in which Evangelism-in-Depth held a nationwide campaign in 1961. In 1963 and again in 1966 Costa Rica, headquarters of the Latin America Mission, was host to international workshops on EID.

Ecumenical Relations. There is a good spirit of cooperation among the various evangelical groups in Costa Rica. Doubtless some of this is fostered, at least indirectly, by the Spanish Language Institute. The Latin America Mission, interdenominational in membership and irenic in spirit and representing more than a third of all the missionaries in Costa Rica, has done much to promote interdenominational cooperation. The *Evangelical Alliance* embraces most of the Protestant groups. It is a very active organization and continues to flourish, largely because of its policy of nonalignment with international organizations. Its Committee on Rural and Social Work sends Goodwill Caravans into the rural areas to minister to the physical and spiritual needs of the people.

Panama

Political History. Panama achieved independence from Spain in 1821 and until 1903 was part of Colombia. The break with Colombia was the direct result of American intrigue, and the Canal Zone is one of the few remaining pockets of imperialism in the world today. Time and again Panama has tried to rectify the situation but without success.

The People. The estimated population of Panama is 1.4 million. Some 65 percent is mestizo or mulatto; 13 percent, Negro; 11 percent, white; 10 percent, Indian; and 1 percent, Chinese. Nearly one-third of the people live in Panama City and Colon. The culture, customs, and language are basically Spanish, though English is widely understood. The few Indian tribes live along the Caribbean coast.

Religion. Roman Catholicism is the dominant religion of Panama. Freedom of religion is practiced and there is complete separation of church and state.

Missions. The *Southern Baptists* were among the first to evangelize the Panamanians in 1905. They are represented there by the Home Mission Board, which took over the work of the *Jamaica Baptist Missionary Society*. The Southern Baptists still have a flourishing work in the Canal Zone, the nearby San Blas Islands, and in Panama itself. The *Baptist Convention* is the third largest denomination, with a membership of fifty-five hundred.

The *Seventh Day Adventists* began work in Panama about the same time as the Baptists and today their conference reports a membership of forty-seven hundred. The *American Episcopalians* entered in 1906 and took over the work begun years before by the Society for the Propagation of the Gospel. Communicant membership is about the same as that of the Seventh Day Adventists. *American Methodists* entered the Canal Zone in 1905; but with the formation of union churches under the National Council of Churches, the Methodists retired from the Canal Zone. For eleven years the work was administered as part of the *North Andes Mission Conference*. In 1916 it became a separate mission. In Panama today there are twelve congregations with almost five hundred members. There is close cooperation between the American and British Methodists.

The *Church of God* (Cleveland) moved into Panama in 1935 and incorporated two existing Pentecostal groups, one in Colon and the other in Panama City, into the Church of God. In 1939 the mission extended its work into the interior. *Bolivar DeSouza* was for many years the outstanding evangelist. A period of rapid growth from 1955 to 1966 resulted from a revival. Today the Church of God reports twenty-nine churches and thirty missions with over one thousand members.

The *International Church of the Foursquare Gospel,* with almost fourteen thousand members, is the largest church in the country. The first missionaries entered Panama in 1928. Much of the success is due to the use of laymen in the work of evangelism, and also to the fact that the mission maintains two Bible schools. The *Lutheran Church-Missouri Synod* began work in the Canal Zone in 1942; today its *Redeemer Church* of 225 communicant members is composed mostly of American military personnel. A branch church was formed in Panama in 1967 as the Panamanians felt uncomfortable in Redeemer Church.

Since 1944 missionaries of the *Central American Mission* have been sowing the good seed of the Word in the soil of Panama from one end of the country to the other. The indigenous church that is emerging, known as the *Association of Evangelical Churches,* received its autonomy in 1961. Today the association comprises seven churches and ten outstations with a total membership of 235. Sixteen missionaries and nine pastors are cooperating in the work of the gospel.

The *Gospel Missionary Union* moved into Panama in 1953 and set up headquarters at Sunrise Farm, eighteen miles from Panama City. Today it is the site of *Bethel Bible Institute* and the campgrounds. On the Atlantic side *Bethesda Clinic* treats six thousand patients a year. The goal of the mission is to establish self-supporting, self-propagating churches. The latest report indicates that nine churches have been brought into being. The *New Tribes Mission* entered Panama in 1953. Today one missionary couple is in the Canal Zone; three other couples are located in Chepo; and the remainder of the twenty-six missionaries are divided almost equally between the Guaymi and Choco tribes.

Other missions in Panama include *Free Will Baptists, Conservative Baptists, Church of the Nazarene, Assemblies of God, Church of God* (Anderson, Indiana), and *Mennonite Brethren.*

Missionary Radio. *Radio Station HOXO, The Voice of the Isthmus,* has been broadcasting the gospel to the people of Panama since 1950. From a small beginning with homemade equipment and only a few hours of programming each day, HOXO has grown to a 5,000-watt AM voice which broadcasts eighteen hours daily in both Spanish and English. It also carries special programs in the language of the San Blas Indians. For nine years HOXO was operated jointly by the *Latin America Mission* and the *World Radio Missionary Fellowship.* On March 1, 1963, LAM withdrew from the union; since that time the station has been the sole responsibility of WRMF. The twentieth anniversary project is a $20,000 fund to install FM broadcasting equipment.

Haiti

Political History. Haiti revolted against France in 1804. Two separate regimes emerged after independence; but the country was unified in 1820 when Haiti conquered the eastern part of the island. In 1844 Santo Domingo (now the Dominican Republic) broke away and became a separate republic. By 1910 rebellions had ousted thirteen of Haiti's first eighteen presidents. Woodrow Wilson ordered U. S. Marines to occupy Haiti in 1915 and they remained there until 1934, giving Haiti the only true peace it has ever known. Dr. François Duvalier ("Papa Doc"), who took office in 1957 and proclaimed himself president for life, ruled the country through voodoo mysticism and the strong-arm terror of his five-thousand-man secret police force. His son succeeded him after his death in April, 1971.

The People. Some 95 percent of Haiti's population of 4.8 million people are of African descent. The remainder are mostly of mixed African and Caucasian ancestry. The population density is one of the highest in the world, and the standard of living is the lowest in the Western Hemisphere. Added to the perils of dictatorship are racial strife, land erosion, and illiteracy. French is the official language, but it is spoken only by the literate 10 percent of the people. The others speak only Creole.

Religion. The 1860 concordat with the Vatican made Roman Catholicism the state religion. The Catholic clergy is supported by public funds. The Jesuits returned in 1956 after an exile of two hundred years. Evangelicals enjoy complete freedom to preach the gospel, conduct schools, and establish churches. The response has been very good. Churches are filled to capacity; Protestants now constitute more than 10 percent of the population.

One of the peculiar features of religion in Haiti is voodooism, a mixture of African fetishism and Roman Catholicism. Here, as in many other places, the Catholic Church incorporated into its worship certain features of the indigenous pagan religion. Today voodooism in Haiti is related to the whole sweep of Catholic life and teaching. The *lao* are saints. The "island below the sea" is purgatory. *Paquets* resemble Catholic amulets. The *hougan's* temple ceremonies are similar to the mass. His services for the deceased have much in common with Catholic prayers for the dead. The sign of the cross and voodoo signs are used interchangeably. In Haiti there is little to choose between voodooism and Roman Catholicism.

Missions. In 1861 the *Episcopal Church* went to Haiti. The *Reverend James T. Holly,* a black priest of the church in the USA, emigrated to Haiti with about 110 black Americans in the hope of establishing a colony in that country. The colony failed, but the church survived. In 1874 the *Eglise Orthodoxe Apostolique Haitienne* was recognized and Mr. Holly was consecrated its first bishop. After his death the church asked that it be made a missionary district of the Protestant Episcopal Church of the USA. In 1923 the first missionary bishop, the *Right Reverend Harry R. Carsons,* was consecrated. During the twenty years of his leadership the church grew and local clergy were trained. The church in Haiti remains a missionary district of the church in the USA. The number of Haitian clergy has increased 50 percent in the past decade, but communicant membership remains about the same, 13,500.

The *American Baptist Home Mission Society* entered Haiti in 1923 and took over a small work which originated with the English Baptists. A theological seminary, opened in 1947, has provided over sixty pastors for the churches in Haiti and others for service overseas. The *Haitian Baptist Convention,* organized in 1963, did not really get off the ground until 1968. Educational work includes 108 elementary schools and 1 secondary school, with a total enrolment of almost twelve thousand. The *Good Samaritan Hospital* serves thirty-six thousand outpatients and fifteen hundred inpatients each year. One doctor and four nurses carry the entire load. At the close of 1969 the convention reported eighty-six churches and almost six hundred mission stations. Baptized membership increased from twenty-five thousand to thirty-six thousand in the past decade. The Christian community is estimated at 120,000.

Haiti is one of five fields of the *Lott Carey Baptist Foreign Mission Convention* organized in 1897. Its first missionaries went to Haiti in 1927. The missionary staff now numbers forty. Its principal institution is a girls' school at St. Marc.

The *West Indies Mission* has a thriving work in the Tiburon Peninsula of Haiti dating back to 1936, when it established a Bible school in Aux Cayes. The churches, known as the *Evangelical Baptist Mission of South Haiti,* have been self-governing from the beginning. The WIM has made a large investment in Haiti (over fifty missionaries at present) and it has paid off. In 1970 there were 211 organized churches and 350 unorganized churches with a total membership of ten thousand. Ordained pastors number 29 and evangelists 302. Educational work includes 150 primary schools and 1 secondary school. The Bible school, the secret of their success, has an enrolment of fifty. The WIM is promoting a new concept in theological training whereby the seminary is taken to the students, rather than having the students come to the seminary. Sixty-four students are enroled in the extension program as compared with ten in the seminary itself.

The *Unevangelized Fields Mission* sent its first missionaries to Haiti in 1943. They settled in the northwest part of the country, where a strong indigenous church has grown up. Besides evangelism and church planting, the program includes correspondence courses, camps, radio broadcasts, a printing press, and orphanages. Educational work includes forty-five primary schools, four middle schools, and two high schools. The Bible school has an enrolment of ninety. Medical work has not been neglected. One doctor and four missionary nurses are responsible for a hospital, a dispensary, and two clinics. The *Mission Evangelique Baptiste d'Haiti,* autonomous since 1949, comprises 56 organized churches and 142 other congregations, with a total membership of 7,350. Forty-two missionaries are working alongside 19 ordained pastors and 125 evangelists.

The *Church of God* (Cleveland) entered Haiti in 1934 at the invitation of a Pentecostal pastor, *Vital Herne,* who had a thriving church in Port-au-Prince. A small Bible school was established and churches sprang up in various parts. Two tragedies overtook the work. Pastor Herne had to be dismissed for unseemly conduct, and the government closed all their churches for two years. When the churches reopened in 1943 the membership had dropped by two-thirds. Since that time the losses have been recouped, and today there are 193 organized churches and 170 missions, with a total membership of 17,500.

The *Seventh Day Adventists* report a membership of thirty-seven thousand in 135 churches, which makes them the second largest Protestant group in Haiti.

The *Methodist Missionary Society* (England) has been in Haiti for several decades. It has thirty rural schools in every circuit. It also operates two colleges, one in Port-au-Prince and the other in Cap-Haitien; and it sponsors several clinics. The church suffers from an acute shortage of workers. In 1968 the Jeremie circuit, with forty-three country chapels, had only one minister.

The *Wesleyan Church* has had missionaries in Haiti since 1946. Their main work is in Port-au-Prince, where eleven of their sixteen missionaries are located.

Baptist Mid-Missions work in Haiti began in 1949. It grew out of a work started by a pastor from Switzerland. *Mr. and Mrs. B. F. Sherwood* were the first couple to be appointed to Haiti, where they had been working under another mission. Prejudice and dissension plagued the work in the early years. The missionary staff has never been large; consequently growth has not been rapid. In 1968 there were only 560 church members.

In January, 1952, the first *Missionary Church Association* personnel began arriving on the field. Within a few months five missionaries were located in the town of Pignon. The MCA inherited five indigenous churches started years before by a young Frenchman, *Elie Marc,* and shepherded during the 1940's by an independent missionary, *Reuben Clark.* In 1957 a division split the national church, cutting deeply into the total work. Primary schools were started at the beginning, but it was not until 1960 that the people began to see the need of sending their children to school. Medical work was established in 1956. The *Association of Evangelical Churches of Haiti* became autonomous in 1967. Eleven organized churches have a combined membership of 1,650.

The *Assemblies of God* established permanent work in Haiti in 1957 with headquarters in Petionville. A Bible school was opened in 1964. In 1967 a church building seating fifteen hundred was acquired in Port-au-Prince. During a two-week campaign attendance reached twenty-five thousand, with more than five hundred making decisions for Christ. As a result membership in the Assemblies of God in Haiti has almost doubled in the last two years.

The *Inter-American Mission* has a staff of thirty-nine in Haiti. The work dates back to 1958, when *Radio Station 4VEH* went on the air. A small evangelical church of 250 members has emerged. The *Evangelical Church of Haiti* has experienced rapid growth in the last few years, from 250 to 660 members. The mission sponsors nine primary schools and a clinic.

Relief Work. The people of Haiti are pitifully poor, and malnutrition is endemic. The *Mennonite Central Committee* with twenty-five missionaries has been seeking for eleven years to meet the physical and spiritual needs of the people. *Church World Service,* whose efforts go back to 1954, has done much to alleviate human suffering. These and other missions have engaged in large-scale relief and rehabilitation after the various hurricanes that have devastated Haiti.

Christian Radio. Haiti is fortunate in having two Christian radio stations. The first of these is *Station 4VEH,* owned and operated by the *Inter-American Mission* at Cap-Haitien. It has been broadcasting the gospel to the people of Haiti for twenty years. Today its 10,000-watt station broadcasts in French, Creole, Spanish, and English. *Radio Lumiere,* sponsored by the *West Indies Mission,* began broadcasting in 1958. Pretuned transistor radios have been placed in churches all over the island. The station is expanding to a seventeen-hour day, and plans are afoot to erect three more transmitters in different parts of the country.

Dominican Republic

Political History. The Dominican Republic occupies the eastern two-thirds of the island of Hispaniola, which was discovered by Columbus in 1492 and used as a springboard for the Spanish conquest of the Western World. Since becoming a sovereign state in 1865 it has had more than its share of trouble, economic as well as political. It was occupied by the U. S. Marines from 1916 to 1924. From 1930 to 1961 it was under the tyrannical control of Rafael L. Trujillo. In 1965 U. S. troops intervened when civil war threatened to bring a communist regime to power.

The People. The estimated population of 4.1 million is divided three ways. About 70 percent is mestizo; 15 percent is Caucasian; and 15 percent is Negro. Approximately 70 percent of the population is rural, and only 50 percent is literate.

Religion. A 1954 concordat with the Vatican made Roman Catholicism the state religion. Protestants enjoy a fair degree of toleration, however, especially since the Vatican Council.

Missions. The Dominican Republic was one of the last countries of Latin America to be entered by Protestant missions. The *Seventh Day Adventists* got an early start and today, with twelve thousand members, they are the largest church in the country. The *Free Methodists* entered the republic in 1907 at the invitation of an independent missionary who had labored there since 1889. Headquarters was established in Santiago, where they opened a Bible institute, a coeducational boarding school (the first in the country), and the largest Protestant church on the island. The Bible institute has become a theological seminary operating at three academic levels. The *Dominican Free Methodist Church* became autonomous in 1948. In 1970 it was one of the larger churches with forty-five hundred members in thirty-two organized churches and three hundred preaching places.

The *Protestant Episcopal Church* began work in Santo Domingo in 1918. For thirty years the mission was confined to the English-speaking population. In 1948 it branched out to include Spanish work as well. The Dominican Republic is a Missionary District of the Protestant Episcopal Church in the USA. It received its first American bishop in 1960. Assisting him at that time were five American and three Dominican priests. Communicant members now number 1,250, an increase of only one hundred in the past decade.

In 1938 *Cecil Samuels,* a Jamaican by birth and a graduate of the Cuba Bible Institute, was sent by the *West Indies Mission* to do pioneer work in the town of La Vega. The following year missionaries arrived. La Vega became the headquarters of the work in the Dominican Republic. A Bible school was opened in 1942. The churches, known as the *Association of Evangelical Temples,* have been self-governing from the start. Today the association includes twenty-nine organized churches and fifteen outstations, with a total membership of 550. Nineteen missionaries, three pastors, and seventeen evangelists are all engaged in church planting. There is no institutional work.

The *Assemblies of God* entered the republic in 1941 but had the advantage of starting off with several churches which had been established over a period of eight years by a Puerto Rican evangelist. A Bible school was opened in 1945 on a thirty-acre farm fifteen minutes from downtown Santo Domingo. The AOG work has been built on citywide evangelistic campaigns conducted by visiting American and Puerto Rican evangelists, as well as by missionaries and local pastors. The missionary staff has never been large. Today it numbers only 6; but there are 160 national workers, who serve 98 organized churches and 415 outstations with a total membership of sixty-one hundred.

The Dominican Republic is the only country in Latin America in which the *Evangelical Mennonite Church* has work. The first missionary, *Lucille Rupp,* arrived in 1945 and settled in El Cercado. The church organized in 1952 is now known as the *Evangelical Mennonite Church.* The work includes several bookstores, a day school, and a Bible school. Much of it is now centered in San Juan. Church growth has been slow. In 1958 total membership in eleven churches was 214; in 1968 it was 236.

The *Missionary Church Association* sent its first group of missionaries, four couples and a single lady, to the northwestern part of Dominican Republic in 1945. Roman Catholic opposition was very stiff, but the government adhered to its policy of religious freedom guaranteed in the constitution. The *Simon Bolivar Christian School* was opened in 1956 to relieve the children of Christian families from the pressures and persecutions of the public schools. A strong church and a fine bookstore are located in Santo Domingo. The indigenous church, known as the *Mission-*

ary Church, received its independence in 1969. It is not large; total membership is only 235. Eight missionaries and twelve pastors make up the full-time staff.

Baptist Mid-Missions began work in 1950 and today has seven missionaries in Santo Domingo. The *Plymouth Brethren* have increased the number of their assemblies from thirty to sixty in the past decade. Twenty missionaries and eleven evangelists are ministering in these assemblies. The *Unevangelized Fields Mission* has been in Dominican Republic since 1949. The national church, *Alianza Biblica Cristiana,* became autonomous in 1952. It now includes eight churches and five outstations. Institutional work is confined to two primary schools and a small Bible school. The *Seventh Day Adventists* are by far the largest Protestant group in the country. They report seventy-six churches with twelve thousand members. The *Dominican Evangelical Church* was founded in 1920 as a union of the Methodist, Presbyterian, and Evangelical United Brethren Churches. The *Moravians,* whose work in the Dominican Republic dates back to 1907, merged with the Dominican Evangelical Church in 1960. With twenty-seven hundred members it is one of the larger churches in the country. *Southern Baptist* work began in 1962 when a missionary couple was transferred from Ecuador. The *Dominican National Baptist Convention* was organized in 1968. A training program for ministers and lay leaders has been launched, and an indigenous medical ministry is helping relieve human suffering in the nation.

Evangelism. The Evangelism-in-Depth campaign in 1965-66, which coincided with an armed revolution, was conducted in spite of adverse conditions. More than three hundred thousand homes were visited after the first training classes. Some 175,000 Scripture Portions and 200,000 tracts were distributed. Goodwill Caravans were a feature of the campaign in the rural areas. The campaign closed with a three-week crusade in the capital city, Santo Domingo. During the campaign some twelve thousand persons registered their decision for Christ.

Cuba

Political History. Cuba was discovered by Columbus on October 28, 1492. It remained under Spanish rule until the close of the Spanish-American War in 1898. Dictator Batista ruled Cuba from 1934 until he was ousted from power by Fidel Castro on January 1, 1959, after almost six years of guerrilla warfare. Two years after taking office Castro came out in his true colors and announced to the world that he was a communist. The United States broke off diplomatic relations with Cuba in January, 1961. Economic sanctions against Cuba have damaged but not destroyed Castro's regime. Beginning in late 1965 Castro allowed those who wished to leave the country to do so. An estimated half million Cubans have gone into exile, most of them in the USA.

The People. The estimated population of 8.3 million is divided into three major ethnic groups: 72 percent is of Spanish ancestry; 15 percent, mulatto; 12 percent, Negro. Orientals represent a tiny minority of 1 percent.

Religion. The dominant religion is Roman Catholicism; but here, as elsewhere in the West Indies, it is mixed with pagan practices introduced by the slaves brought over from Africa. Under Castro's communist regime both Roman Catholics and Protestants have suffered a diminution of religious liberty, though the situation has been much better than in other communist countries.

Missions. The first Anglican services were held in 1762. More than one hundred years later *American Episcopalians* established contact with the island. In 1885 a bishop from Florida paid a visit to Cuba, but permanent work was not undertaken until 1898. In 1906 the first bishop, the *Right Reverend Albion W. Knight,* reported ten clergy and 450 communicants. By the early 1960's the Episcopal Church had a Cuban bishop. All twenty-three clergy were also Cuban. Communicants numbered 8,650, but the Anglican community was estimated at seventy-four thousand. From the beginning Cuba was a missionary district of the Protestant Episcopal Church in the USA. In 1967 it became an autonomous diocese outside the usual Anglican provincial organization, but linked to the rest of the Anglican communion through the Metropolitan Council comprising the Primate of Canada, the Archbishop of the West Indies and the President of the Ninth Province of the Caribbean.

Methodist work in Cuba had its beginnings among Cubans in Florida. Methodist preachers visited Cuba in 1881 and 1883. The first missionary was *George N. MacDonell,* who reached Havana in 1899. In 1907 the Cuban mission was organized. It developed into a Mission Conference in 1919 and an Annual Conference in 1923. Methodism has become firmly established in the six provincial capitals and in other important towns and cities as well as in the rural areas. In 1966 the Methodist Church reported a membership of eight thousand, a decrease of about twenty-five hundred from 1960. The Christian community is estimated at fifty thousand.

The *Southern Baptist* work in Cuba is under the *Home Mission Board.* It too began among Cubans in Florida and from there it was extended to Cuba. Membership in the *Cuban Baptist Convention* has been as high as nine thousand, but the exodus of Cubans in recent years has doubtless lowered that figure somewhat. Two other Baptist missions have been at work in Cuba: the *American Baptist Home Mission Society* and the

National Association of Free Will Baptists. The latest report from the American Baptists indicates a slight increase in membership from the 6,550 reported in 1967. The executive secretary wrote: "Tell the brethren we are well and happy to have the privilege of doing something for our Lord here." The Free Will Baptists got a much later start than the other two missions. Their work in Cuba got under way in 1936, and in 1962 the church became autonomous. A 1969 report indicated that the work continues under national leadership in the eight fields of the FWB. There were forty-seven organized churches, twenty-six national pastors, twenty-eight hundred baptized believers, and five thousand attending church.

The *United Presbyterians* began their Cuban mission about the turn of the century. The *First Presbyterian Church* in Havana was founded in 1901. The work is divided into the central and western regions of the island. In 1966 the *Presbyterian Reformed Church in Cuba* became autonomous. Up to that time it had been a presbytery of the Synod of New Jersey. The denomination hoped to become fully self-supporting by 1969.

The *American Friends* have been represented in Cuba since 1900. In 1960 they had work in ten centers and a Christian community of about one thousand. In 1969 *Miss Betty Nute,* a British Friend living in the USA, visited Cuba and reported four Monthly Meetings still functioning with perhaps two hundred members.

Pentecostal missionary work in Cuba was begun by *Assemblies of God* personnel in 1920. During the first decade the work was conducted at various intervals by several women evangelists. In May, 1936, it was placed directly under the Foreign Missions Department. In 1949 the *Assemblies of God in Cuba* received their independence. Missionaries continued to work with the church but the nationals were in charge. Following the revolution the missionaries had to withdraw. During the past decade the number of churches has increased from thirty-three to forty-two. The Bible school in Manacas is closed.

The *Church of God* (Cleveland) sent its first missionary couple to Cuba in 1943. They settled in Santiago de Cuba in Oriente Province. From Oriente the work spread and churches were established in various places. In 1970 two dozen pastors were in charge of nineteen churches and two missions with a total membership of 530.

Cuba became the first field of the *West Indies Mission* when it was founded in 1928 by *Elmer V. Thompson* and Cuban-born *B. G. Lavastida.* Through the years the main emphasis has been on the training of nationals and through them the evangelization of the island. The *Cuba Bible Institute* opened its doors to fifteen eager students on September 25, 1928. Hundreds of graduates of CBI are serving churches in Cuba and other islands of the West Indies. At one time the WIM had over thirty missionaries in Cuba, but they were evacuated shortly after Castro came to power. For a time the Bible school was closed; but it was reopened when the Canadian missionary, *Wolfe Hansen,* returned to Cuba in 1962. In January, 1969, the Canadian secretary of WIM visited Cuba and reported seventy-five churches still open and "filled to the doors for services."

The *Berean Mission* began work in Cuba in 1945. In 1952 it acquired a twelve-acre tract of land in Oriente Province, which became the headquarters of the work. The plan was to develop a self-supporting Bible school. At one time five families were located there. The work included radio broadcasting, correspondence courses, a bookstore, and a school for missionaries' children. The missionaries evacuated Cuba in September, 1960. Since then the mission has been working among the Cuban refugees in Miami.

Evacuation. Fidel Castro was hailed as a national hero when he toppled Batista and seized power on January 1, 1959; but when he brought communists into his government and announced that he was going to establish a socialist state in Cuba, the whole picture changed. Some missions, seeing the handwriting on the wall, pulled out in 1960. When the United States severed diplomatic relations in 1961 a second wave of evacuees left Cuba; but a small number of American missionaries and most Canadian and British missionaries remained at their posts. American missionaries, of course, were *persona non grata,* and for the Cubans to fraternize with them was to excite suspicion. No matter how much its validity is denied, there *is* such a thing as guilt by association. Several missionaries have been able to return to Cuba for short visits. They have always been welcomed by the Christians. Some of them were able to hold meetings.

The Church In Cuba. There does not appear to have been any open, organized persecution of the church by the government. The policy has been one of opposition, harassment, and suppression. Pastors and missionaries have been sent to prison, but always on charges other than religious. There was a period in 1963 when the evangelicals were singled out by Castro as "undesirable reactionaries" and a crackdown was ordered. One report stated that only 10 percent of the two hundred thousand copies of the Scriptures sent to the Cuban Bible Society ever arrived. The remainder were ground into pulp. Several missionaries were jailed and others were expelled from the country for no known reason. In 1965 more than fifty Baptist pastors were arrested simultaneously. Thirty-four of them were brought to trial and sentenced for a variety of reasons.

As in other communist countries, the church is required to confine its program to purely religious activities. Education is the prerogative of the state, so parochial schools are no more. The only religious instruction is that given in the churches and this hardly offsets the mass indoctrination conducted by the schools. Orphanages and other social agencies have been either abandoned or turned over to the state. Compulsory military training has removed some pastors from their charges and has decimated the enrolment in theological training institutions. Most pastors are continuing to preach the gospel as they understand it. A few have become firm *Fidelistas,* trusted and used by the regime; their messages, cluttered with political propaganda, parrot the party line. During the first years of the Castro regime there was a severe falling away; but as confidence was restored, many returned to the church. The mass exodus of more than half a million Cubans in the mid-sixties included many Christians and not a few pastors. Their departure was a great blow to the church. In recent years, in spite of continued harassment by the government, the churches have not only held their own but have actually shown signs of virility and growth.

As might be expected, the Cuban churches are particularly eager to be free of American domination. The *Episcopal Church* consecrated its first Cuban bishop in 1967 and declared itself autonomous. The *Presbyterian Church* became independent; so did the *Methodist Church*. Self-support, however, is another thing. Some denominations still require outside assistance. Funds can be sent to Cuba through mission boards in Canada, the Evangelical Alliance in London, and the World Council of Churches in Geneva.

Ecumenical Relations. In the last couple of years two churches in Cuba have become associate members of the World Council of Churches. They are the *Methodist Church in Cuba* and the *Presbyterian-Reformed Church in Cuba.*

XIX

Oceania

Geography. Few persons have an accurate understanding of the vastness of the Pacific Ocean, which covers one-quarter of the earth's surface. In the southwestern part of the Pacific, north and east of Australia, are fifteen hundred islands divided into some thirty clusters and many lesser groups. These islands are usually divided into three major groups. The first of these is known as Polynesia (Many Islands) and includes the Society, Austral, Cook, Tonga, Samoa, and Phoenix islands. The second, Micronesia (Little Islands), includes the Gilbert, Marshall, Mariana, and Caroline islands. The third, Melanesia (Black Islands), includes Fiji, New Caledonia, New Hebrides, Solomon, and New Guinea islands.

Political History. The Pacific Ocean was named in 1520 by Magellan, who was the first European to explore that part of the world. Other navigators followed Magellan; but it was left to Captain Cook in the latter half of the eighteenth century to bring the Pacific islands to the attention of England and Europe. It was his *Voyages Around the World* that fired the imagination of William Carey and set him thinking of missionary work. After that it was only a matter of time until Spain, Britain, France, and Germany each took possession of various islands. In Micronesia the Marianas, the Marshalls, and the Carolines were ruled successively by Spain, Germany, and Japan. The Marshalls and the Carolines are now administered by the United States under a United Nations trusteeship. The Gilbert Islands still belong to Britain. In Polynesia France is still in control of the Society, Austral, Marquesa, and Tuamoto islands. The Tonga Islands, though an independent kingdom, are under the protection of Britain. Eastern Samoa belongs to the United States. Western Samoa, after half a century of New Zealand control, became independent on January 1, 1962. Fiji, once a British colony, became independent in 1970. New Caledonia is a French Overseas Territory. New Hebrides is an Anglo-French Condominium. New Guinea in the far west is divided into two parts. The western area, West Irian, is now part of Indonesia. The eastern section, which includes Papua and New Guinea, is Australian External Territory.

The People. Approximately 2.5 million people live in this region of the Pacific. It is thought that they came in prehistoric times from the mainland of Asia via Indonesia and the Philippines. More recently they have been joined by several hundred thousand Indians, who in some areas, such as Fiji, account for half the population. Before the coming of the missionaries interisland warfare was a way of life and cannibalism was raised to the status of a cult. Whalers, traders, and other white men invaded these parts and exploited the islanders in a shameful fashion. Here, as elsewhere, it was the missionaries who befriended the islanders; and in so doing they incurred the wrath of their fellow white men whose avarice and cruelty knew no bounds.

Religion. Before the coming of Christianity animism was the dominant religion. Ancestor worship was practised. The outstanding characteristic of their form of animism was *tabu*, by which certain articles of food, certain localities, and certain occupations were forbidden on pain of death. This was applied with particular strictness to the womenfolk. The large Indian population is partly Hindu and partly Muslim. Christianity has made spectacular gains in this part of the world. Today some of these islands are more Christian than the so-called Christian countries of the West.

Society Islands

Space forbids the inclusion of all the major islands; it will be necessary to confine ourselves to half a dozen of the more important ones. We begin with the Society Islands because in point of time they were the first to receive the gospel; also they became the seedbed from which Christianity was transplanted to other islands.

The first missionaries to reach Tahiti in 1797 were members of the *London Missionary Society,* which had been organized only two years before. The party consisted of thirty persons, only four of whom were ordained; the others were artisans. It was expected that with their tools and skills they would be self-supporting in a country with a warm climate and fertile soil. Eighteen of the members of the party disembarked at Tahiti; eleven went on to the Tonga Islands and one to the Marquesas. The

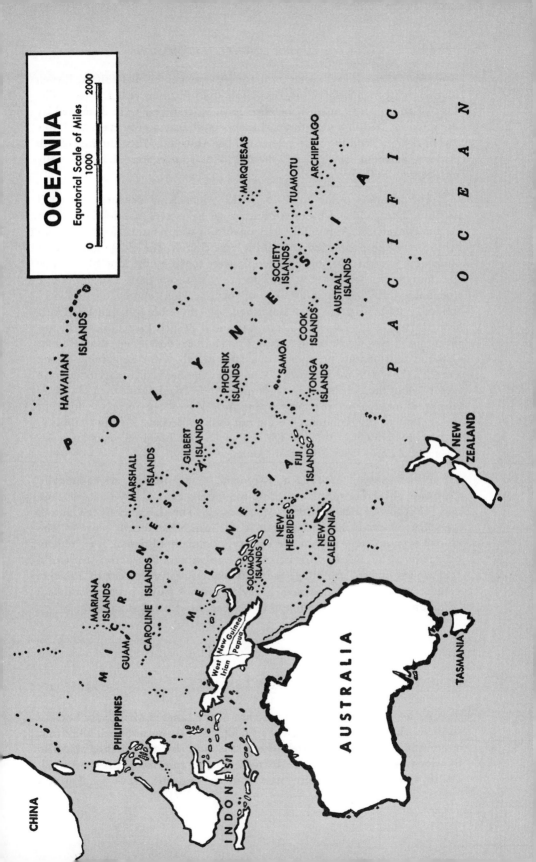

enterprise encountered severe and totally unexpected difficulties. Eleven of the eighteen members on Tahiti left the following year for Australia. Two of those who remained married local women and were dismissed by the mission. Within a year three of the men on Tonga were massacred, one "went native," and the others departed for Australia. When the nineteenth century dawned, only five men and two women were left, the only missionaries in Oceania.

The turning point came in 1812 when King Pomare requested baptism. This followed by one month a special prayer meeting in London for his conversion. Apparently his conversion was genuine, for he gave up his idolatry and proceeded to build a large church. The old gods and their cults were overthrown, and the people were urged by the king to embrace the new faith, which they did. In a very short time Tahiti became nominally Christian. Schools were opened, teachers and evangelists were trained, a printing press was established, and the Bible was translated into Tahitian by 1838. In 1842 Tahiti became a French Protectorate. In the meantime, five years before, the French had demanded that Roman Catholic missionaries be admitted to the island. With the coming of the French, the LMS missionaries found it increasingly difficult to operate under what they called "the bishop and the gunboat." In 1886 they withdrew in favor of the *Paris Evangelical Missionary Society,* which, at the request of the islanders who did not wish to become Roman Catholics, had begun work in Tahiti in 1863. Exactly one hundred years later the *Evangelical Church* became autonomous.

Now known as French Polynesia, these islands are nominally Christian, the Protestant community numbering about forty-two thousand and the Roman Catholic, thirty-one thousand. The character of the church has changed drastically from what it was in the nineteenth century. The church is completely French and society, nominally Christian, is extremely permissive. The Tahitian Christians have to witness in a permissive world that smiles on sex, gambling, and drunkenness. Fifty percent of Tahitian couples are not legally married. Every so often a parish priest conducts a communal ceremonial "clean-up" to legalize the existing situation.

Tonga Islands

As we have seen, the first attempt of the London Missionary Society to establish a mission on Tonga proved abortive. It was not until 1822 that a continuing work was established, this time by the Methodists. The pioneer was *Walter Lawry* of Australia, but his career was cut short by ill health and he had to retire after fourteen months. However, Lawry's reports made the British *Methodist Missionary Society* and the *Australian Methodist* group all the more keen to continue the work in the Tonga Islands, and in 1826 *John Thomas* and *John Hutchison* reached Tongatapu. Such was the opposition that a year later John Thomas asked permission for the two men to withdraw. The committee in Sydney did not agree, but sent two more missionaries to help them. In time opposition weakened and results came. Thomas remained in the islands for twenty-eight years, during which the entire population became Christian. In 1834 a mass movement occurred on Vavau and spread rapidly to other islands in the group. In 1854 the Tongan mission was transferred from the Methodist Missionary Society (England) to the newly constituted Australian Conference. *Tobou College* on Tongatapu, which opened its doors in 1866, became a training center for young chiefs preparing for government service.

The Methodist work in the Tonga Islands soon became self-supporting and self-propagating; and having evangelized their own islands, the churches sent their own missionaries first to Samoa and then to Fiji. The work in Tonga progressed for many years and the missionaries were able to guide the Tongans in the establishment of a monarchial form of government which, side by side with the church, provided a happy and contented life for the people and enabled them to remain free at a time when other Pacific Island groups were coming under colonial rule.

About ninety years ago division crept in by way of personality clashes between certain missionaries. The resulting split affected both church and state. It took years of patient endeavor to heal the breach; and there still remain in Tonga two small denominations which resulted from the split and are outside the main stream of Methodism. They are the *Church of Tonga* and the *Free Church of Tonga*. Together they represent a Christian community of fifteen thousand. The *Methodist Church of Tonga* became fully autonomous in 1926. Today it has a membership of seventy-nine hundred and a Christian community of thirty thousand. It reports 153 church schools with an enrolment of 10,245. It conducts a seminary with fifteen students in residence.

Early in the twentieth century the *Anglican Church* entered Tonga, but its strength has never been great. In 1968 it had a communicant membership of only five hundred and a Christian community seven times that figure. Another group in the Tonga Islands is the *Seventh Day Adventist Church* with about one thousand members. The *Assemblies of God* held a Good News Crusade in Tonga in 1966 and out of this effort has come the beginnings of a Pentecostal church. There are twenty-five national workers, but no missionaries, in the islands. Four small churches and fifty-one outstations were reported in 1970. Today 70,000 of the 85,000 inhabitants are Christians, of whom 15,000 are Roman Catholics and 55,000 are Protestants.

Western Samoa

The first missionaries to Samoa were not Europeans but Polynesian teachers from Tahiti and Tonga. As early as 1828 a Samoan on a visit to Tonga learned of Christianity and became a Christian. On his return to Samoa he shared the gospel with his own people. Friends and neighbors believed and churches sprang up everywhere. In 1830 *John Williams,* of the *London Missionary Society,* paid a visit to Samoa to strengthen the churches there. On his departure he left behind eight Tahitian teachers. Five years later there was a Christian church with a membership of over two thousand. In less than two years the number had increased to thirteen thousand. In a matter of a few years the entire population embraced Christianity.

The *London Missionary Society* and the *Methodist Missionary Society,* in order to avoid competition and duplication of effort, decided to divide this part of the Southwest Pacific between them. Tonga was to go to the Methodists and Samoa was to belong to the Congregationalists. The decision was made without consulting the Christians. When they were apprised of the plan they refused to accept it. The Christians in Samoa had received the gospel from the Methodists; and with the Methodists they would remain.

In 1855 the *Australian Methodist Church* became autonomous and took over the work of the British conference. It immediately took steps to send missionaries to Samoa to shepherd the Samoan Methodists who remained orphans after they refused to join the Congregationalists. Gradually the Methodist Church gained in strength without affecting the growth of the LMS work. In 1875 when *George Brown* was appointed to pioneer the work in New Guinea, several Samoans joined with the Fijians to form the pioneer team; and through the years Samoans have continued to share in the missionary work of the new fields. Since 1915 the Samoan Methodists have assumed increasing responsibility, especially in financial affairs. In 1964 the Samoan District became a Conference within the Methodist Church of Australia. The first president was an Australian; he was followed by two Samoans. Today the Methodist Church has a communicant membership of 7,350 and a Christian community of 21,000.

The really large church in Samoa is the *Congregational Christian Church,* with a membership of twenty-two thousand and a Christian community of eighty thousand. Only two missionaries remain with this church. The CCC in Samoa continues its substantial missionary contribution to the United Church in Papua.

Two other groups have work in Samoa. The *Anglican Church of the Province of New Zealand* (Diocese of Polynesia) has a membership of twelve hundred. The *Seventh Day Adventist Church* is about the same size.

The population of Samoa (140,000) is almost wholly Christian. Of these, 100,000 are Protestants and 30,000 are Roman Catholics.

Fiji Islands

The history of Christianity in Fiji is both tragic and exciting. Notorious for intertribal warfare and cannibal feasts, Fiji for many years proved to be barren soil for the good seed of the gospel, and only after great sacrifice and courage did the missionaries succeed in disarming prejudice and overcoming opposition.

The first missionaries were not Europeans but two Tahitian teachers placed on the island of Oneata by the London Missionary Society in 1830. When it was decided that Fiji should be the responsibility of the *Methodist Missionary Society* they continued their work under the Methodists. It was following the great spiritual awakening in the Tonga Islands in 1834 that the decision to take the gospel to Fiji was put into effect. *William Cross* and *David Cargill*, with some of the best Tongan teachers, formed the first team that landed on the eastern island of Lakemba on August 12, 1835. Only the restraining hand of God kept the chief and his warriors from killing and eating the little band of missionaries and teachers. The party was allowed to stay and given a rubbish heap as the site for their houses. They worked hard but saw little fruit. Most of their early converts were Tongans living in Lau, but the few Fijians who accepted Christ began to witness under strong persecution. The work of grace through the power of the Holy Spirit had begun.

Cross moved on to other parts of Fiji but encountered even stronger opposition; and when he died in 1842 at Somo Somo on the island of Taveuni, it was as much from a broken heart as a broken body. During his eight years in Tonga he had witnessed a Pentecostal visitation resulting in thousands of converts, but found very little response in Fiji and none at Taveuni. Additional missionaries were sent to Fiji, but the response was the same—opposition and persecution. In spite of all the difficulties and dangers, however, only one European missionary was martyred in Fiji. *Thomas Baker* and nine Fijian helpers were killed and eaten in 1867.

The turning point came with the conversion of the paramount chief, Thakombau, who called himself "The Root of War." Immediately upon his conversion in 1854 he gave orders to destroy all heathen temples and to use the foundation stones to build the great church in Lau which stands to this day. The old killing-stone was dedicated as the baptismal font.

In 1875 when *George Brown*, former missionary to Samoa, passed through Fiji on his way to open a new field in the wilds of New Guinea, he visited the training school seeking for recruits. When the challenge was given, all eighty-three students stood to their feet indicating that they were ready and willing to go. When the British Administrator warned them of the dangers and tried to dissuade them from engaging in such a hazardous undertaking, they replied, "If we die, we die; if we live, we live." Only one of them lived; but they formed the spearhead of a Fijian missionary movement northward and westward across the Pacific in which 270 men (wives not included) took the message of the Cross to the Solomon, New Hebrides, Gilbert, and New Guinea islands.

In 1964 the Fiji District became a Conference of the *Methodist Church of Australia.* In 1970 the Methodist Church in Fiji reported 38,000 communicant members and a Christian community of 165,000. Three other Protestant churches are found in Fiji: the *Anglican Church,* with a Christian community of 6,000; the *Seventh Day Adventists,* with 7,000; and the *Assemblies of God,* with 10,000. The total Protestant community is in the neighborhood of 190,000. The Roman Catholic community is 42,000. Together the two communions account for 230,000 of the 490,000 inhabitants, which means that practically all the indigenous Fijians are now Christians by profession. It should be noted that almost half the population of Fiji today is composed of Indians, who are either Hindus or Muslims. Efforts to win them to Christ have not been very successful. Only 3 percent of them have become Christians.

New Hebrides

New Hebrides has the distinction of being a condominium, ruled jointly by Great Britain and France. Each power retains sovereignty over its own nationals resident in New Hebrides, but neither may exercise authority separately over the group of islands. There are only two towns in New Hebrides, Vila, the capital, on Efate and Luganville on Santo.

As we have already seen, in each of the major islands one mission or denomination has been dominant. In the Society and Samoan islands it was the Congregationalists. In Tonga and Fiji it was the Methodists. In New Hebrides we meet a third group, the Presbyterians.

The first attempt to introduce Christianity into New Hebrides occurred in 1839 on the southern islands of Tanna and Erromanga. The intrepid pioneer was *John Williams* of the *London Missionary Society,* who had already given two decades of service to the cause of Christ in the Society Islands. His plan was to use native teachers rather than foreign missionaries in pioneer work. Taking with him Samoan teachers, he set forth to occupy new territory for Christ. He left three teachers on Tanna and proceeded to Erromanga, where he and *James Harris* were killed immediately upon landing. News of his murder stirred both the London Missionary Society and the Samoan Christians to greater efforts on behalf of New Hebrides. In 1840 a second attempt was made. When missionaries arrived on Tanna they found the Samoan teachers safe. The missionaries remained on Tanna for a while, but then were obliged to leave when they were blamed for an epidemic of dysentery. In 1841 Samoan teachers were placed on a third island, Aneityum. Things went well and four years later additional Samoan missionaries were sent to help them. In 1845 a second attempt was made to place Samoan workers on Tanna. When disease broke out the following year the missionaries were blamed and two of them were killed.

In 1848 the *Presbyterians* entered the picture in the person of *John Geddie* of Nova Scotia. He took up work on the southernmost island of Aneityum. Later he was joined by reinforcements from the Reformed Presbyterian Church of Scotland. In six short years half the population embraced the Christian faith. By 1860 the New Testament had been translated and almost half the population had become literate. A plaque in one of the churches in memory of John Geddie reads: "When he landed in 1848 there were no Christians here; when he left in 1872 there were no heathen."

Perhaps the most famous of all South Sea missionaries was *John G. Paton,* sent out in 1858 by the *Reformed Presbyterian Church of Scotland.* He and two couples who accompanied him spent four years on Tanna until the islanders, infuriated by another epidemic, drove them off. With support from the Presbyterian Church of Victoria, Paton decided to make a new beginning on the nearby island of Aniwa. Here the people were more friendly. Christianity spread rapidly among the inhabitants and before long the entire island was nominally Christian. In his later years he founded the *John G. Paton Mission Fund,* which continues to the present time.

In 1869 the *Presbyterian Church of New Zealand* sent its first missionary to New Hebrides. He was *William Watt. Peter Milne* followed him in 1870. Milne was assigned to Nguna. In twenty-five years the entire island became Christian. Eventually Presbyterians from Canada, Australia, and other countries joined in supporting the mission in New Hebrides. In 1948 the *Presbyterian Church of New Hebrides* became fully autonomous. It continues to receive missionaries and support from the Presbyterian Churches of Australia and New Zealand. Communicant members number eighty-six hundred. The Christian community is about thirty thousand. The church is divided into thirty-nine parishes under the care of thirty-five pastors. Thirty-nine missionaries assist the church in various capacities. Institutions include 148 schools and two hospitals. The British government is beginning to assume more responsibility for the schools. Theological education has been carried on at *Tangoa Training Institute,* which closed in 1970. In 1971 it will be replaced by a Bible college for lay workers.

Bible translation begun by John Williams was continued by the Gordon brothers, and by 1870 the four islands of Erromanga, Nguna, Tanna, and Futuma had the Scriptures in their own languages. By 1901 the Scriptures had been published in twenty-two languages.

The *Anglicans,* under the leadership of *George A. Selwyn,* the first Bishop of New Zealand, initiated mission work in the northern islands about 1850. The Australian Board of Missions, on which the Anglicans of Australia and New Zealand were represented, organized the Melanesian Mission. To avoid competition with the Presbyterians, the Anglicans kept to the northern islands. By the turn of the century they had about one thousand baptized members on three small islands. Today the *Anglican Church in New Hebrides* is part of the Province of New Zealand.

The *Seventh Day Adventists* have had a mission in New Hebrides for many years. They report some two dozen churches with a membership of twenty-three hundred. The *Australian Churches of Christ* have about two thousand members.

Solomon Islands

The *Anglicans* represent the oldest and largest Protestant group in the Solomon Islands. Their work goes back to the 1850's when *George A. Selwyn,* the first Anglican Bishop of New Zealand, founded the *Melanesian Mission,* in which the Anglicans of Australia and New Zealand cooperated. Bishop Selwyn made several extensive visits throughout the islands; but the foundations of the work were laid by *John C. Patteson,* who in 1861 was consecrated the first missionary bishop of Melanesia. For ten years he superintended the Anglican work in the Solomon Islands, until his untimely death at the hands of the natives in the Santa Cruz Islands in 1871. His plan was to bring promising young men to a central place for training and then send them back as missionaries to their own people. For a time they were sent to New Zealand, but later they used Norfolk Island. *John Selwyn,* son of Bishop George Selwyn, succeeded Patteson as missionary bishop of Melanesia, in which capacity he visited the many islands of Melanesia. Here also the Anglican church is part of the Province of New Zealand. In 1968 the Anglican community was estimated at thirty-five thousand.

The *South Sea Evangelical Mission,* which began work in the Solomon Islands in 1904, grew out of another undenominational mission, the *Queensland Kanaka Mission* founded by *Florence S. H. Young* in 1886. She was the first of many missionaries to serve under the newly organized board. It was with this mission that the famous *Dr. Northcote Deck* and twelve members of the Deck family served for many years. Centers were opened on three islands, Malaita, Makira, and Guadalcanal. The *South Sea Evangelical Church* became independent in 1963. In 1970 it comprised 285 churches with approximately three hundred pastors and evangelists. Over one hundred teachers, some of them without formal teacher training, are teaching in sixty schools. The enrolment in six Bible schools is one hundred. Twenty-seven missionaries are serving with the church.

Australian Methodists began missionary work in the Solomon Islands in 1902. The first group of workers included teachers from Fiji and Samoa as well as missionaries from Australia. There was a good deal of opposition, but the presence of the South Sea Islanders did much to overcome the initial suspicion and fear. In the first decade some thirty churches were organized, with seven thousand in attendance. In 1922 the New Zealand Methodists asked to be allowed to take full responsibility for the Solomon Islands District. The Japanese occupation destroyed everything, and when the war was over the missionaries were faced with the problem of rehabilitation. The national church has been autonomous since 1968, when it merged with other churches to become part of the *United Church in Papua, New Guinea and the Solomon Islands.*

The *Seventh Day Adventists* got off to a slow start in 1914; but in more recent years the rate of growth has accelerated considerably. In 1969 they reported 163 churches with a total membership of fourteen thousand.

Micronesia

Micronesia represents a land area half the size of Rhode Island but spread over an expanse of the Pacific as large as mainland USA. It has been a United States Trust Territory since 1947. Three groups of islands, the Carolines, the Marshalls, and the Gilberts, have been the scene of Protestant missionary endeavor. Four missionary societies have carried the burden of the evangelization of these islands: the *American Board of Commissioners for Foreign Missions,* the *Hawaiian Evangelical Association,* the *Liebenzell Mission,* and the *London Missionary Society.*

The *American Board* began work in the Carolines in 1852. The first party contained both American and Hawaiian missionaries. Two islands were occupied, Kusaie and Ponape. The first *Liebenzell* missionaries arrived in 1906 and were stationed on Truk, Palau, and Yap islands. Through the years there has been close cooperation between the German and American missionaries.

The *American Board* extended its work to the Marshall Islands in 1857. Today there are thirteen American missionaries working there under the *United Church Board for World Ministries.* Eight of them are teaching in *Mizpah High School* on Truk.

In 1857 the *American Board* began work on the Gilbert Islands. The *Hawaiian Evangelical Association* also sent missionaries. The *London, Missionary Society* entered the islands in 1870 and occupied the southern part. After World War I the American Board withdrew in favor of the London Missionary Society. The *Gilbert Islands Protestant Church* is now independent. A small number of missionaries continue to give assistance. Two important institutions are the *Hiram Bingham High School* and the *Tangintebu Theological College.*

Papua-New Guinea

The island of New Guinea is divided into two parts. The western region, known as West Irian, now belongs to Indonesia. The eastern region is divided into two parts, Papua in the south and New Guinea in the north. Papua and New Guinea are administered by Australia as a Trust Territory under the United Nations.

Four historic denominations entered this part of the world in the closing decades of the nineteenth century: the *Congregationalists* of England, the *Anglicans* and *Methodists* of Australia, and the *Lutherans* of Germany.

Congregationalists. Here, as in other parts of the world, the *London Missionary Society* led the way. *Samuel McFarlane* in 1871 and *W. G. Lawes* in 1874 were the pioneers. Both men had seen service in islands to the east and brought with them national teachers and evangelists. McFarlane established a base on Murray Island near the mouth of the Fly River, and Lawes took up residence in Port Moresby on the mainland of Papua. They were followed in 1877 by *James Chalmers.* All three of these outstanding missionaries gave several decades of service to the evangelization of Papua. Chalmers met a martyr's death in 1901. The memory of Chalmers and Lawes has been perpetuated in two theological colleges which bear their names. In 1962 the *Papua Ekalesia* was finally inaugurated. It included the work of the LMS, the Presbyterian Church of New Zealand, and the District Work of the Kwato Mission. In 1968 the church reported a communicant membership of twenty-three thousand and a total Christian community of sixty-two thousand.

Methodists. New Guinea was the first mission field of the *Australian Methodist Church.* The pioneer was *George Brown,* who was accompanied by a team of Fijian and Samoan volunteers. They landed at Molot in the Duke of York Islands in 1875. Outstations were opened on the islands of New Britain and New Ireland. In 1878 a Fijian minister and three young Fijian teachers were killed and eaten. When the news reached Fiji others offered to take their place. The work was hard, the conditions difficult, the dangers frequent; but in spite of everything the Holy Spirit was at work, and in 1886 the mission was able to report almost five hundred members and another two hundred in training. World War II brought tragedy to the Methodists in New Guinea. Under the Japanese the people were subjected to privation, torture, and death; but they remained loyal to

Christ. The wives of the missionaries and all but four of the women missionaries were evacuated. The four women and eleven of the men were captured. The men perished in a prison ship on their way to Japan.

Methodist work in Papua was launched in 1890. *William Bromilow,* who had spent ten years in Fiji, was chosen as the leader of a team of four ministers and a carpenter from Australia and twenty-two teachers from Tonga, Samoa, and Fiji. Papua was not greatly affected by either of the two World Wars. Being British territory, it was not involved in World War I; and the Japanese did not reach this area during World War II. Since the war there has been considerable development in every branch of the work. More schools have been established; technical education has been extended; and timber milling and plantation work have been organized, with the dual purpose of training Papuans and assisting the institutional work of the church financially. The first Papuan bishop was consecrated in 1968.

A third field was opened in Mendi in 1950 among the Stone Age people in the Highlands of Papua-New Guinea. The first party consisted of *Mr. and Mrs. Gordon Young,* a missionary nurse, a teacher, and several New Britain pastors. They lived in tents for some time and then in simple native-type houses. In 1953 a second station was opened at Tari. For almost a decade the missionaries labored without any fruit. The break came in 1960 in Tari and then spread to Mendi. By 1961 there had been two hundred conversions. In 1967 some three thousand persons were added to the church. There is a desperate need for educated ministry in the Highlands. About 90 percent of the men employed in the circuits as pastors and evangelists are illiterate.

Lutherans. The *Lutherans,* with 400,000 baptized members, constitute the largest Protestant group in New Guinea, and one of the largest mission churches in the world. The pioneer agency was the *Neuendettelsau Mission Society* of Germany. The leader was *Johann Flierl,* who established the first mission station at Finschhafen in 1886 and for forty-four years guided the destiny of the rapidly growing mission. During the first thirteen years progress was slow; but after that a people's movement began and has continued to this day. From the beginning the *Lutheran Church of Australia* has been deeply involved and has provided the lion's share of resources, both men and money. Following the devastation of World War II the *American Lutheran Church* went to the aid of the Lutheran mission in New Guinea. In 1956 the *Evangelical Lutheran Church of New Guinea* became fully autonomous. Present baptized membership is 350,000. The sponsoring mission is the Lutheran Mission New Guinea, whose constituent members are the *Lutheran Church of Australia,* the *American Lutheran Church, Neuendettelsau Mission,* and *Leipzig Mission.* Together the cooperating missions have six hundred missionaries in New Guinea. The Evangelical Lutheran Church of New

Guinea plays a vital and leading role in the evangelization of New Guinea. Today there are at least three thousand full-time workers in the church, serving in its evangelistic, medical, and educational programs. Of these, at least three hundred are ordained pastors. The church operates four theological seminaries and six Bible schools. Educational institutions include 140 primary schools, 4 technical schools, and 4 high schools. The medical program includes fourteen full-fledged hospitals and ten small congregational hospitals run by New Guineans.

The *Lutheran Church-Missouri Synod* entered New Guinea in 1948 and established a station at Yaramanda among the Enga people in the Central Highlands. Its missionaries have worked in close cooperation with other Lutherans. A national church, known as the *Wabag Lutheran Church,* was organized in 1961. Today it has a baptized membership of thirty-six thousand and over four hundred evangelists. Serving with the church are almost one hundred fifty missionaries engaged in evangelistic, educational, and medical work.

Anglicans. The first group of *Anglican* missionaries, under the leadership of *Albert Maclaren,* landed at Dogura on the northeast coast of New Guinea in 1891. They were greeted by a band of warriors, each with a spear in his hand. Fortunately the warriors were more interested in barter than battle and accepted tobacco, knives, beads, and pipes in exchange for a sizeable tract of land. Forty years later a cathedral seating two thousand persons was built on the site where the work began. During World War II when the island was occupied by the Japanese, the white residents were ordered to evacuate to Australia; but the missionaries heeded the admonition of their bishop:

> We must endeavor to carry on our work in all circumstances, no matter what the cost may ultimately be to any of us individually. God expects this of us. The church at home, which sent us out, will surely expect it of us. . . . The people whom we serve expect it of us. We could never hold up our faces again, if for our own safety we forsook Him and fled when the shadows of the passion began to gather around Him in His spiritual and mystical body, the church in Papua.[1]

During the Japanese occupation both church and mission suffered staggering losses. Some missionaries succeeded in hiding; others were herded into concentration camps. Still others were killed, among them the Anglican bishop and eight of his staff. In 1951 the volcanic eruption of Mount Lamington buried four thousand persons and all but extinguished the church. It snuffed out the lives of fourteen missionaries and a much larger number of the indigenous clergy. Slowly but surely the work of rehabilitation went forward and today the schools and churches are

---

[1] Henry P. Van Dusen, *They Found the Church There* (New York: Charles Scribner's Sons, 1945), p. 94.

functioning normally. The first Papuan to be consecrated bishop was *George Ambo,* whose father had been a headhunter and a cannibal.

Faith Missions. Oldest of the faith missions is the Australian branch of the *Unevangelized Fields Mission,* which began work among the great Gongodala tribe on the lower Fly River in 1932. In 1945 the mission pushed north into the upper Fly River area; and in 1950 the first advance into the Highlands to the north and east was made. Today the UFM has about one hundred thirty missionaries in Papua working alongside an equal number of national workers. The entire New Testament has been translated into one language and Portions into eight other tongues. Thousands have been baptized in sixteen well established centers. The national churches are carrying more and more responsibility for their own government, support, and expansion.

The *South Seas Evangelical Mission* (Australia) entered New Guinea in 1948 and established a work on the Sepik River. Today thirty-eight missionaries and eleven national workers are engaged in church and school work. Two Bible schools report an enrolment of seventy; but as yet no national church has been organized.

The *New Tribes Mission* has been in New Guinea since 1949. Today the mission has eighty-five missionaries in four main areas working in ten different tribes. *Wycliffe Bible Translators* entered New Guinea in 1956 and reports 521 known languages in the Papua-New Guinea area. Today the mission has 318 missionaries and eighteen short-term assistants working in eighty-three tribes. This makes New Guinea the largest of all eighteen fields in which WBT has work. Hundreds of missionaries belonging to some thirty-five different organizations have the *Missionary Aviation Fellowship* to thank for the transportation services it is providing in a land where roads simply do not exist and air travel is the only way to get from one valley to the next. MAF has thirteen planes operating in Papua-New Guinea, which makes it the largest of the nineteen fields in which MAF is now serving.

Other Missions. The *Plymouth Brethren* have been in New Guinea for many years and in 1970 reported 153 missionaries working in seventy-five assemblies. The *Church of the Nazarene* entered in 1955 and today has twenty-eight missionaries in New Guinea. In the past decade several other missions have initiated work in this part of the world. Included in this group are the *Baptist Bible Fellowship* (1962), *Wesleyan Church* (1962), *Church of Christ in Christian Union* (1963), and *Association of Baptists for World Evangelism* (1967).

Church Union. Mention has already been made of the organization in 1962 of the *Papua Ekalesia,* which included the churches brought into existence by the London Missionary Society, the Presbyterian Church of

New Zealand, and the Kwato Mission. The life of the Papua Ekalesia was, however, a short one. Almost from its inauguration it began to participate in conversations leading to a wider union. In 1968 the *United Church of Papua, New Guinea and the Solomon Islands* was formed by a union of the *Papua Ekalesia,* the *United Synod of the Methodist Church of Melanesia,* and the *Union Church in Port Moresby.* This church brings together 1,305 organized churches and 820 unorganized groups with a total membership of 80,000 and a Christian community three times that number. Some 240 missionaries continue to assist this large and rapidly growing church, whose own full-time workers include 83 ministers, 1,808 evangelists, 681 teachers, and 440 others. Connected with the church are 211 primary schools, 4 secondary schools, and 3 vocational schools. Five Bible schools report an aggregate enrolment of eighty. One union seminary is preparing the more promising young men for the ministry. Medical work includes 28 hospitals, 283 clinics, and 43 dispensaries. For all this medical work there are only five doctors. Most of the work is carried on by 213 nurses, many of them nationals.

Ecumenical Relations.   Four churches in Oceania are full members of the World Council of Churches: *Evangelical Church in New Caledonia, Presbyterian Church of the New Hebrides, Congregational Christian Church in Samoa,* and *Evangelical Church of French Polynesia.* The inauguration of the *Pacific Conference of Churches* took place in 1966 on the island of Lifou in the Loyalty Islands. Most of the autonomous churches in the area are now members of the conference. At the same time *National Christian Councils* came into being in Fiji, New Hebrides, and Melanesia. Other councils are planned in the Solomon Islands and the Samoan group. With substantial assistance from the Theological Education Fund two associations were formed in 1969: the *Melanesian Association of Theological Schools* and the *South Pacific Association of Theological Schools.* The *Pacific Theological College,* Suva, Fiji, is an ecumenical training center for the Christian ministry.

XX

Europe

Ever since the beginning of the Holy Roman Empire, about A.D. 800, Christianity has been the dominant religion of Europe. At the height of its power the Roman Catholic Church was the wealthiest, most powerful organization on the continent. Europe was the home of the Protestant Reformation. It was the scene of the Pietist Movement and the Great Revival under the Wesleys and Whitefield. It was also the birthplace of the modern missionary movement. For hundreds of years Christianity provided both the matrix and the motif of Western civilization, including art, music, sculpture, literature, philosophy, and, of course, theology. Medieval history is largely church history.

Today Europe is fast becoming de-Christianized. It can no longer be regarded as a Christian continent. Hans Lilje, bishop of the German Evangelical Church and one of the presidents of the World Council of Churches, stated: "The era when Europe was a Christian continent lies behind us." Speaking of the situation in Europe, Kenneth Scott Latourette stated: "Christians are tending to become minorities, . . . the trend is toward de-Christianization of a predominantly nominal Christian population."

Several factors have contributed to this sad state of affairs. Secularism and humanism were spawned by the Renaissance. German rationalism and higher criticism undermined the veracity and authority of the Holy Scriptures. Two world wars among the so-called Christian countries of the West and the failure of the Christian church in Germany to offer more than token resistance to Nazism hardly enhanced the image of Christianity in Europe. The rise of the USSR and the emergence of communist governments in Eastern Europe have imposed severe restrictions on the activities of the church in those countries. The new theology and the new morality espoused by some Protestant leaders in Western Europe have removed the ancient landmarks and left nominal church members in a spiritual vacuum. Vatican II and the rapid changes taking place in the Roman Catholic Church have thrown the faithful into confusion. Non-Christian religions from the East, particularly Buddhism and Hinduism with their mysticism and esoteric rites, are attracting a good deal of attention. Muslims from Pakistan and North Africa are emigrating in large numbers to Europe in search of employment, higher wages, and a better way of life. As a result, mosques are being erected in the larger cities.

An estimated 160 million people in Europe make no profession of religion. Among those who still claim allegiance to Christianity there are few who take their religion seriously. France, though nominally Roman Catholic, is the most pagan country in Europe. Fear and superstition abound, especially in the rural areas, and more and more people are turning to spiritism; so much so, that the Roman Catholic Church now regards France as a mission field. In England 66 percent of the population are baptized by the Church of England; 26 percent go on to Confirmation; but only 9 percent remain as regular churchgoers. In the state churches of Europe the situation is even worse. Only 5 percent of the German Lutherans and 3 percent of the Swedish Lutherans attend church on a regular basis. By no stretch of the imagination can Europe be called a Christian continent. Oddly enough, the most virile form of Christianity is found in the communist countries of Eastern Europe and the USSR.

It is difficult for Americans to understand and appreciate the difference between the religious situation in Europe and that in the United States. In the whole of Europe there is only one Christian radio station, and that was erected and is maintained by an American mission, *Trans World Radio*. It is possible to buy time on *Radio Luxembourg* and *Radio Monte Carlo;* but prime time is almost impossible to secure, and when available is extremely expensive. Even in England the local churches cannot buy time on the British Broadcasting Corporation network. The Bible, available in so many editions and versions in the USA, is a rare book in many countries of Europe. The Bible school movement of the USA and Canada, which has done so much for the cause of evangelical Christianity at home and overseas, is practically unknown in Europe. The few Bible schools that do exist are largely the result of American initiative in this postwar period. During the last two centuries Europe has produced no great evangelists such as Charles G. Finney, Dwight L. Moody, or Billy Graham. In fact, mass evangelism as we understand it is an American phenomenon and not particularly appreciated by most European church leaders. The two largest confessional groups in Europe are the Anglicans and the Lutherans, both of which believe in baptismal regeneration. The emphasis is on religious education rather than individual conversion. The Methodists and the Baptists, who have traditionally preached repentance

MODERN EUROPE

Scale of Miles

0   100   200   300   400

and faith as an integral part of the conversion experience, form a very small minority in Europe.

American Missions. It was not until recent years that Europe came to be regarded as a mission field; and even today the historic denominations in the USA are reluctant to accept this point of view. The only large historical denomination with missionary work in Europe is the *Southern Baptist Convention.* It reports ninety-one missionaries in eight countries. More than half of them are in Italy and Spain. Most of the American groups now working in Europe are evangelical and evangelistic and understand the missionary mandate to include all unregenerate persons regardless of their ecclesiastical connections. Nominal Christians have as much need for the gospel as the so-called pagans of the non-Christian world.

At present there are over eighty American societies in Europe. Together they account for 1,535 missionaries. In addition there are several hundred missionaries from Great Britain and the Commonwealth countries. The idea of Europe as a mission field did not really catch on until after World War II, when there was a sudden influx of missions from North America. Prior to that, however, there were several well-established America-based missionary societies in Europe: *Belgian Gospel Mission* (1919), *Bible Christian Union* (1922), *Eastern European Mission* (1927), *European Evangelistic Society* (1927), and *Slavic Gospel Association* (1934). Several missions concentrating wholly on Europe came into being shortly after World War II: *Greater Europe Mission, European Evangelistic Crusade, Worldwide European Fellowship,* and *Society for Europe's Evangelization.*

Several specialized agencies have extended their work to Europe in this postwar period. These include the *Pocket Testament League, Campus Crusade for Christ International, Child Evangelism Fellowship, Bible Club Movement, Navigators, Youth For Christ International, Young Life Campaign, International Fellowship of Evangelical Students,* and the *Billy Graham Evangelistic Association.*

Special mention should be made of the radio ministry of *Trans World Radio,* which began broadcasting from Monaco in 1960. Today it is beaming the gospel in thirty-one languages into all parts of Europe, Russia, North Africa, and the Middle East. TWR broadcasts seven days a week over medium, short, and longwave transmitters with a total of more than half a million watts. Studios in various parts of Europe and the Middle East furnish tapes which are mailed to Monte Carlo. A German branch, *Evangeliums-Rundfunk,* is now part of TWR and, with a staff of fifty full-time workers, produces five daily programs in German. The German branch is a work of faith and is entirely self-supporting. In some countries behind the Iron Curtain the German programs are the only spiritual nourishment available to German Christians.

Mass evangelism is something new to Europe and it is just now beginning to catch on. The *Janz Brothers Gospel Association* of Canada, majoring in evangelistic campaigns, has been operating in Germany since 1956. Billy Graham has conducted many crusades in Great Britain and on the continent. The latest was the EURO 70 Crusade held April 5-12 in Dortmund, Germany. Described as the largest evangelistic effort ever held in Europe, it used modern technology to transmit the messages simultaneously in eight languages to thirty-six cities by means of closed-circuit television. Combined nightly audiences ranged from 83,000 to 127,000. Over fifteen thousand inquirers were counseled. The *World Congress on Evangelism,* sponsored by *Christianity Today* under the leadership of Dr. Carl F. H. Henry and Billy Graham in 1966 in Berlin, fired the imagination of evangelicals in all parts of the world. Growing directly out of that congress came regional congresses on evangelism in Africa, South America, Singapore, and other places. A European Congress on Evangelism is planned for September, 1971, in Amsterdam. It should be noted that mass evangelism, with "decisions for Christ," is not popular in some circles, especially in the state churches. But there are signs that this is changing at the grassroots where people in search of spiritual reality are responding in ever increasing numbers.

In the state churches theological education is at the university level and seminary graduates usually know more about Barth, Brunner, and Bultmann than they do about the Bible. Among the free churches there are several indigenous Bible schools in the United Kingdom and ten on the continent, of which six belong to the Pentecostal churches. Additional Bible schools have been established in this postwar period by American missions. A leader in this field is *Greater Europe Mission* which now operates Bible schools in France, Germany, Italy, Sweden, and England, and is in the process of acquiring one in Belgium. If the people of Europe are ever to be reached with the gospel, it will have to be by Europeans themselves. An unsolved problem is the reluctance of the state churches to accept the humble Bible school graduates as "men of the cloth." This too is changing as an acute shortage of pastors is forcing some state churches to accept Bible school graduates as assistant pastors.

There is a pressing need for evangelical seminaries on the graduate level. Efforts have been made by various missions to meet this need. In recent years two theological seminaries have been established, one in France and the other in Switzerland. In addition, the *Southern Baptists* have established a seminary near Zurich which is making an impact in Baptist circles.

What is the best way to evangelize Europe? To work through the existing churches, many of which are state or quasi-state churches, or to start new churches? Most people would agree that the former is the more desirable; but is it feasible? When Protestant missionaries first went to the Middle East in the early part of the nineteenth century it was with the idea of reviving the Eastern churches and through them evangelizing the Muslim population. The attempt was not very successful because the Orthodox churches did not wish to be revived and resented any attempt on the part of the Western missionaries to infiltrate their ranks. Something of the same situation exists in the state churches of Europe. It has not proved easy to cooperate with them for reasons which are both theological and cultural.

For the most part, missionaries involved in church planting are working outside the state churches. Among the free churches and some independent groups they have been more successful. In some parts, where the free churches do not exist, the missionaries have had to start from scratch and build churches of their own. Most of the interdenominational missions in Europe are devoting considerable time and energy to church planting; among them are *Greater Europe Mission, The Evangelical Alliance Mission, Conservative Baptists, Worldwide European Fellowship, Bible Christian Union,* and others.

Theological literature of an evangelical stripe is in short supply. There are in Europe only two million French-speaking Protestants. For every book in French, there are 150 in English. In the evangelical field about one thousand titles are available. Only recently has a Bible dictionary been published. They are still waiting for a one-volume Bible commentary. There are very few biblical or theological textbooks. In the German language the works of Barth, Brunner, and Bultmann can be found everywhere. Evangelical literature is much more difficult to procure. In fact, very little is available. In Italy there are only two hundred thousand Protestants among fifty-three million people. As might be expected, the list of evangelical books is very small. About thirty titles have been published by Abele Biginelli, Scripture Gift Mission in Rome. The Waldensian Church has done some noteworthy publishing, and so have the Conservative Baptists. Only recently has the ban on evangelical literature in Spain been lifted. It will be a long time before the supply catches up with the demand. In the meantime the evangelicals can use Spanish books published in Latin America.

Several missions have been engaged in widespread distribution of evangelistic literature. *Operation Mobilization,* conducted by Send the Light Mission, sends several hundred young people to Europe every summer, where they engage in mass distribution of gospel literature. The *Pocket Testament League* has conducted campaigns in various countries of Europe during which millions of copies of the Gospel of John have been given out. *World Literature Crusade, Scripture Gift Mission,* and *Missionary Prayer and Literature Fellowship* have also been working in Europe.

Missionary work in Europe differs in many respects from that in other parts of the world. Illiteracy is no problem. Mission schools, which played an important role in the evangelization of Africa, are nonexistent. The same is true of medical work. Bible translation is no problem, since the Bible has been available in most of the languages of Europe for many years. Indeed, many of the European countries for decades have had their own Bible societies. In some countries schools for missionaries' children are not needed; the children attend local public schools. This sets the missionaries free for evangelism, church planting, radio broadcasting, and theological education.

Protestant Europe

There are approximately 110 million Protestants in Europe. The two largest groups are the Lutherans (sixty million) and the Anglicans (thirty million). The Lutherans are found in Germany and the four Scandinavian countries, Denmark, Norway, Sweden, and Finland. About 80 percent of the people of East Germany are Lutherans and some 50 percent of the West Germans are Lutherans. In Scandinavia the percentage is anywhere from 90 to 97. Of the thirty million Anglicans, almost twenty-eight million are found in England; the other two million are divided among Scotland, Wales, and Northern Ireland. There are no Anglican churches on the continent and no Lutheran churches in the United Kingdom, except for expatriates.

The remaining Protestants, made up of Baptists, Methodists, Pentecostals, Presbyterians, and Reformed, are found in relatively small groups in various parts of Europe. The Waldensian Church, the oldest Protestant Church in the world, is located in Italy. It has a constituency of thirty-five thousand.

Many of the Protestant churches are state churches, supported by state funds and subservient to government control. Under such a system all citizens, Christian and non-Christian, are required to support the church. Such an arrangement is a source of irritation to the non-Christians and a serious detriment to the initiative of the church members, who feel no obligation to give to the support of the church. The pastors on their part have no great urge to seek the lost, to preach the gospel, or even to fill the pews. Their position is secure and their income is guaranteed regardless of performance. In England both church membership and seminary enrolment are decreasing rapidly. Religion is at its lowest ebb since the days of John Wesley. The situation is much better in Scotland and Northern Ireland, where the Presbyterians are numerically strong and church attendance is high. Even so, England is much better off than the Lutheran countries. In the Anglican Church there is a strong evangelical wing. In addition there are some six million non-Conformist church members in Great Britain, and church attendance among them is much higher than is the case with the Anglicans. Among the non-Conformists there are evangelical denominations; and in all denominations there are evangelical churches and preachers.

Of the 1,535 North American missionaries in Europe, only 600 are in the predominantly Protestant countries. West Germany heads the list with 313, and the United Kingdom has 104. Switzerland and the Netherlands have eighty-two and fifty-four respectively. Sweden has twenty-seven. The remaining twenty are divided among Norway, Denmark, and Sweden. *Campus Crusade* and *Navigators* account for more than half of all the missionaries in the United Kingdom. Ever since the Reformation the Netherlands has been a predominantly Protestant country. This is true no longer. In recent years the Roman Catholics have overtaken the Protestants and now outnumber them by approximately three hundred thousand.

Greece is the only country in Free Europe which is predominantly Eastern Orthodox. Over 95 percent of the population belongs to the Greek Orthodox Church. Although the constitution guarantees religious freedom, it recognizes the Orthodox Church as the state church and all but forbids the preaching of the gospel to any but evangelicals. There are two evangelical denominations of approximately equal size, the *Greek Evangelical Church* and the *Free Evangelical Church*. The former is Presbyterian in polity and the latter is similar to the Plymouth Brethren. Both denominations are permitted to minister only to their own constituency; any attempt to share the gospel with the Greek Orthodox is regarded as proselytizing. Evangelical pastors have been jailed from time to time. Some of the forty missionaries in Greece are natives of the country who came to the United States, some for theological training, and became American citizens. All missionaries must use great discretion in their presentation of the gospel lest they be deported as undesirable aliens. The *American Mission to Greeks* supports one hundred national workers. It is the leading publisher and distributor of evangelical literature in Greece. It has its own printshop in Athens and bookstores and colporteurs covering the entire country. For ten years now it has been placing gospel messages in the form of ads in newspapers and magazines. It also supports children in seventeen orphanages, and sends 150-200 tons of food, clothing, and drugs to Greece each year.

Catholic Europe

Europe with 252 million Roman Catholics is still a predominantly Roman Catholic continent. Fifty million of these 252 million, however, are behind the Iron Curtain, leaving roughly 200 million Roman Catholics in Free Europe. The three largest concentrations are in France, Italy, and Spain, which account for 127 million of the 200 million Catholics in Free Europe. These are the three countries which have attracted the most missionaries from North America—France (328), Italy (174), and Spain (118).

The Roman Catholic Church is passing through a time of crisis. It began with Pope John XXIII and has continued with ever increasing tension under Pope Paul VI. There are many facets to this highly complex situation; but it really boils down to a crisis of authority. Many of the younger clergy and theologians are openly rebelling against what they consider the outmoded rites and dogmas of the church. Others are trying to bring the church into line with biblical revelation; but progress is too slow for some of the more radical elements, particularly those in the Netherlands and Germany. Its best efforts are always too little and too late to suit the radicals. On the other hand, Pope Paul has spoken out more than once against the heat and haste of those who are in danger of destroying the church from within. So far as the Vatican is concerned, they are moving too fast and too far.

While strife within the church is increasing, tension between Catholics and Protestants is decreasing. Ever since John XXIII substituted the term "separated brethren" for "heretics," a general *rapprochement* has been taking place between Roman Catholics and Protestants in all parts of the world. Two archbishops of Canterbury have visited the Vatican, but the pope has not yet returned the compliment. There is a growing spirit of cooperation between the Roman Catholic Church and the World Council of Churches. The General Secretary of the WCC has more than once visited the Vatican, and Pope Paul paid a historic visit to Geneva in June, 1969. A Joint Working Committee is only one of many cooperative ventures of the two world bodies. While it is still too early to talk about the RCC joining the WCC, the RCC is now definitely part of the ecumenical movement.

The winds of change blowing through the Vatican have been felt to the ends of the earth, and Protestant missionaries in Roman Catholic countries are grateful for an increasing measure of religious liberty. This is particularly true in Italy and Spain, and to a lesser degree in Portugal.

Ever since the Inquisition, Spain has been notorious for its treatment of non-Catholics. In 1939 Generalissimo Franco outlawed all Protestant churches. For more than two decades Protestants were second class citizens who suffered all kinds of discrimination, social and economic as well as religious. Commencing in the early 1960's the climate began to change. In his encyclical *Pacem in Terris* John XXIII said: "Among human rights we must recognize the right a man has to honor God according to the dictates of his own conscience and to profess religion in private and in public." In 1965 the Vatican Council issued its pronouncement on religious liberty. Its language left no room for doubt. Now that Rome had spoken, Catholic Spain could not fail to respond.

In 1962 the Spanish Minister of Foreign Affairs initiated a move toward government recognition of Protestant churches. The following year the *British and Foreign Bible Society* resumed operations in Spain after the interruption of its activities in 1956. The first evangelical bookstore was opened in Barcelona in 1965 by the *Worldwide European Fellowship*.

That same year a simultaneous nationwide evangelistic campaign was conducted in spite of prohibitions against the use of mass methods of evangelism. Ads placed in four Barcelona newspapers brought new people to the meetings. In 1966 the New Press Law modified censorship of the press and made possible the publication of some Protestant literature.

For some years the *Evangelical Defense Commission,* representing nearly all Protestant denominations in Spain, fought a running battle with the authorities, demanding and finally achieving an unprecedented measure of freedom. In June, 1968, the Religious Liberty Act, a comprehensive document of forty-five articles, was passed by the Cortes and became law. It granted legal status to all Protestant churches willing to register with the government, but the act of registration included disclosure of church membership and financial records. This was unacceptable to three of the Protestant denominations (*Spanish Evangelical Church, Spanish Reformed Episcopal Church,* and *Evangelical Baptist Union*) and to date they have refused to register. The government has not pressed the matter one way or the other; and the churches continue to function with slowly increasing freedom. Until the 1953 concordat with the Vatican is revised or revoked, it will be difficult for the government to grant full religious liberty to the Protestants. In the meantime the evangelicals rejoice in the degree of liberty they have. They can now educate their own children, train their own clergy, own their own cemeteries, and hold public office. They have come a long way in the past decade.

The Protestant movement in Spain dates back to 1868. Through the decades there has been much discrimination and not a little persecution, with the result that growth has been slow. Today there are about forty-five thousand evangelicals out of a population of thirty-three million. The three largest groups are the *Evangelical Baptist Union,* the *Federation of Evangelical Independent Churches,* and the *Plymouth Brethren.* Together they account for two-thirds of the Protestant community.

Missionary work was begun by the *American Baptists* in the 1870's but was later given up. The *Swedish Baptists* commenced work in 1881 and continued until 1921, when they turned it over to the *Southern Baptists,* who are now the oldest and largest mission in Spain. The *Spanish Christian Mission* entered in 1943. Most of the twenty-four missions now in Spain have entered during the last two decades.

The Roman Catholic Church claims 98.4 percent of the people of Portugal; but most of the people are unchurched. The constitution guarantees religious liberty; but this has not prevented the Catholic hierarchy from curtailing the rights and privileges of the Protestant minority. Even so, there has been more religious freedom in Portugal than in Spain. In the early 1960's an evangelistic campaign in Lisbon attracted three thousand persons a night for a total of seventy thousand during the entire campaign. There were at least fourteen hundred decisions, including priests, atheists, and persons from all walks of life. After three weeks the meetings were banned by the police. A protest to the governor of Lisbon was unavailing. In 1970, however, evangelist John Haggai conducted a twelve-day crusade in Lisbon without interference of any kind. The closing service witnessed nearly eight thousand people jammed into the pavilion, the largest indoor arena in the city.

While there is little open persecution of Protestants, there is underground opposition. Protestants are severely restricted in their public activities and are not permitted to own property. Baptist churches in Lisbon have been trying for some time to secure incorporation and thus qualify for property-owning rights; but there has been no response from the government. In the summer of 1970 the government agreed to consider a religious liberty law which it was hoped would grant legal status to religious minorities; but later the premier postponed action and returned the bill to parliament for further study. Evangelicals in Portugal number about thirty thousand. There are eleven missions in the country. The *Southern Baptists* and the *Plymouth Brethren,* each with six missionaries, have the largest contingent of workers. A nationwide program of Evangelism-in-Depth was launched in 1969 under the sponsorship of evangelical churches, initiated by the *Conservative Baptist* missionary, *Samuel Faircloth.*

Italy is reputed to be 98.8 percent Roman Catholic, yet it has the largest communist party in the free world. It is generally assumed that a communist cannot be a Christian and a Christian cannot be a communist; but in Italy it is possible to be both at the same time. The enigma is not as puzzling as it appears. Many devotees of Rome are only nominal Christians, and many party members are communists simply because they are fed up with the atrocious economic and social conditions prevailing in the country.

The 1948 constitution guarantees religious liberty; but until the 1960's this was honored mostly in the breach. In recent years several court cases have been won by evangelical pastors and missionaries who were arrested for holding public meetings without a permit. Since then the atmosphere has cleared, and evangelicals enjoy an unprecedented degree of religious liberty. Indeed, their chief foe now is not the Catholic Church but the communist party. Several open-air meetings have been broken up by party members. It remains to be seen whether Italy can long remain free.

The evangelical community in Italy numbers approximately two hundred thousand. The Pentecostals are the largest group; they account for 65 percent of the Protestants. The second largest group are the Waldensians, who number approximately thirty-five thousand. Nearly half of them live in what is known as the Waldensian Valleys, north of Turin. Some five thousand live in Turin, Milan, and Rome, and ten thousand are scattered all over Italy and Sicily. In addition there are some twenty thousand Waldensians in Uruguay and Argentina. There are also Waldensian congregations in Switzerland, France, United States, and Canada.

The Waldensians of Italy are descendants of Valdo, "the poor man of Lyons." The Archbishop of Lyons, alarmed by the rapid growth of the movement, forbade Valdo to preach; and in 1184 the Council of Verona excommunicated him and his followers. From the beginning the movement was characterized by a strong attachment to the Word of God. In 1532 the Waldensians decided to accept the Reformation and took their place in the family of Reformed Churches. In 1555 they began to conduct their worship in public and for this purpose they built churches. The period from 1555 to 1690 was one of severe persecution. It was not until 1848 that official persecution ended and the Waldensians obtained their civil rights.

For over a century the Waldensian Church has had its own theological seminary, first in Florence and since 1922 in Rome. At present the church has about one hundred ministers. Several new congregations have been established since the war. The Waldensian Church maintains a college, a Latin school, several primary schools, three hospitals, four orphanages, and half a dozen eventide homes. It is a member of the *Federal Council of Protestant Churches in Italy* and works closely with the Methodist Church. It is a member of the *World Alliance of Reformed Churches* and the *World Council of Churches*. Its motto is "The light shines in darkness." The Waldensian Church is the only truly indigenous church; the other churches have been started by missionaries from abroad.

At the present time there are twenty-three North American missions working in Italy. Together they represent a total of 175 missionaries. The two largest missions are the *Southern Baptists,* who have been there since 1870, and the *Conservative Baptists,* who entered in 1950. Each has twenty-five missionaries in Italy. The Southern Baptists report ninety-two churches with a combined membership of five thousand. Only twenty of the churches are self-supporting.

Most of the missions entered Italy since 1950 and are just now getting established. The majority of the missionaries are located in the large cities of the west and central parts. The north, east, and most of the south are desperately in need of an evangelical witness. There are half a dozen Bible schools in Italy with a total enrolment of fifty-three.

Special mention should be made of the Pentecostals, who represent 65 percent of all the Protestants in the country. Pentecostal work commenced in 1908, led by *Giacomo Lombardo,* an Italian immigrant who lived for a time in Chicago. Scores of churches were established as nationals and Italian-Americans joined him in preaching the gospel. Steady growth continued until 1934, when Fascist persecution closed the churches and the work went underground until the Allied armies arrived in 1944. In 1947 about 95 percent of the Pentecostal churches organized under the name of the *Assemblies of God in Italy.* For a time there was severe persecution; but in May, 1954, the decision of the Supreme Court opened the way for official recognition of the Assemblies of God in Italy. Since then the work has grown by leaps and bounds. Italian-American ministers and lay workers returning to their native towns and villages are winning converts. New churches are springing up everywhere. The number of congregations has tripled in the last ten years. Today five hundred churches are under the care of 258 national workers, assisted by 14 missionaries. The greatest weakness seems to be in the area of theological training. There is only one Bible school with an enrolment of twenty-three. At this rate it will be a long time before all the churches have trained leadership.

France must be included in Catholic Europe. Indeed, the Roman Catholic Church claims 87 percent of its fifty million people. It is doubtful, however, if more than 10 percent of the population attend mass regularly. For all practical purposes, France is a pagan country.

Protestants number slightly less than one million, or about 2 percent of the population. Two Reformed and two Lutheran denominations account for 85 percent of the Protestant community. These four denominations presently are engaged in talks looking forward to federal union.

Since World War II a large number of North American missions, most of them evangelical and independent, have taken up work in France. At present there are forty mission boards reporting a total of 330 missionaries. The larger missions include: *Baptist Mid-Missions* (twenty), *Bible Christian Union* (thirty-two), *Conservative Baptists* (sixteen), *The Evangelical Alliance Mission* (twenty-four), *Greater Europe Mission* (thirty-two), *North Africa Mission* (twenty-nine), *Unevangelized Fields Mission* (twenty-one). The largest mission in terms of workers is *Christian Missions in Many Lands* (Plymouth Brethren), with forty-four workers in France. Not all of them, however, are from North America. Some are from the Commonwealth countries.

The *North Africa Mission* moved to Marseilles in 1963 when the government of Tunisia closed its bookstore in Tunis. The Bible correspondence course work continues unabated. More recently the NAM has been concerned for the spiritual welfare of the many North Africans living in southern France. The *Greater Europe Mission's* oldest and largest Bible school is located in Lamorlaye, outside Paris. Today its graduates are serving Christ in all parts of Europe and some have gone farther afield to other continents.

Most evangelical missions are engaged in various forms of evangelism, church planting, student work, summer and winter camps, literature distribution, etc. Mass evangelism has met with considerable success in France. Billy Graham crusades in Paris have greatly strengthened the cause of evangelism, especially among evangelicals. A committee is now trying to secure the endorsement of the major Protestant denominations for a nationwide evangelistic effort along the lines of Evangelism-in-Depth.

A new magazine entitled *Ichthus* has recently been launched by French evangelicals. Another new development is a conservative Faculty of Evangelical Theology at Vaux-sur-Seine, with a growing number of students drawn from Baptist, Brethren, Methodist, Reformed, and Independent churches.

The *Assemblies of God* are by far the fastest growing group in France. In recent years the Christian community has tripled from thirty thousand to ninety thousand. Six American missionaries are assisting the French assemblies. The *Seventh Day Adventists* report a total constituency of ten thousand.

Communist Europe

Besides the USSR there are eight communist countries in Eastern Europe. They are East Germany, Poland, Rumania, Czechoslovakia, Hungary, Bulgaria, Yugoslavia, and Albania. Three of these countries are predominantly Roman Catholic in religion: Poland, Hungary, and Czechoslovakia. Three are predominantly Eastern Orthodox: Bulgaria, Rumania, and Yugoslavia. Albania is 70 percent Muslim. In the USSR there are probably forty million members of the *Russian Orthodox Church* and perhaps as many as five million evangelicals. So when we think of communist Europe we must not assume that all, or even a majority, of the people are communists. Only a small fraction of the population are card-carrying communists, even in the USSR. In all nine countries there are probably not more than twenty-five million communists out of a total population of 375 million.

According to orthodox Marxism, religion is the opiate of the people; the church is an anachronistic, reactionary institution; and full-time religious workers are parasites on the body of society. This being so, one would not expect the church to fare very well under a communist government. On the other hand, communists the world over pose as the authors and guardians of genuine democracy and are careful to include in their constitution an article guaranteeing religious freedom. However, there is always a gap between the promise and the performance. Liberty, as we in the West understand the term, simply does not exist in a communist country. Sooner or later every organization and institution is required to toe the party line. This is the price of survival. The church has usually been the last and the most difficult institution to bring under control.

In none of the countries except Albania has the church been outlawed; nor has it been obliged to go underground. It has legal status, and within certain well-defined limits it is free to minister to the spiritual needs of its own constituency. With the passing of time conditions have tended to improve, though there have been setbacks and reverses along the way. In the early years of the Russian occupation the churches had a rough time. In 1948 all evangelical pastors in Bulgaria were arrested. Four were given life terms; four received fifteen-year terms; and others got shorter terms. In September, 1950, some 150 Polish pastors were arrested and given sentences of two to four years. Following Khrushchev's denunciation of Stalin in 1956 the situation gradually improved. In all of Eastern Europe today it is hard to find a single evangelical pastor who has not spent some time in prison.

The picture in Eastern Europe is spotty. The degree of religious freedom varies from country to country. Indeed, it may well vary from place to place within a given country; or it may change overnight without any apparent reason. The most predictable thing about the communists is their unpredictability. One thing, however, seems certain. The communists have not changed their view of religion. It is a bourgeois invention and will completely disappear when scientific socialism becomes universal. In the meantime the church will be permitted to exist but not grow. It can worship but not witness. Religious services must be confined to church buildings. To hold a meeting in a private home is to invite trouble. Open-air meetings are out of the question. However, there will be no persecution. The state will not make martyrs. If certain influential leaders must be removed, it will be on trumped-up charges with a moral or political complexion. Under these conditions, so they think, the church will gradually wither and die.

To ensure the success of their antireligious program, the communists insist on having the children and young people under their care. Students in the schools are subjected to a relentless barrage of communist propaganda; but Christian children under eighteen years of age are not permitted to receive religious instruction either in the churches or in their own homes. In the place of baptism and confirmation, Christian youth are expected to take the communist oath. In East Germany the ceremony is known as "Allegiance to the Dedication of Youth." It is difficult for school children to avoid joining the Young Communist League.

Theological education is greatly restricted. In the Soviet Union only three seminaries are still open and they belong to the Russian Orthodox Church. There are no training schools for the evangelicals. So their pastors must get their training abroad—a very difficult thing to do—or go without.

Bibles are in short supply. For many decades no Bibles were printed in the Soviet Union. During 1969 some 750,000 copies of the Scriptures were distributed in seven countries, including Russia. In the past eighteen months 94,000 copies were printed in Czechoslovakia, and 100,000 in Rumania in 1968-1969. Some 200,000 copies are shipped annually to Poland under a standing license. Thirteen translation projects are under way.

The *United Bible Societies* has budgeted $420,000 for Eastern Europe in 1971.

The church, like all other organizations, must be completely subservient to the state. It must agree to support the establishment of socialism leading to communism; and this must be done under the leadership of the communist party. The Russian Orthodox Church suffered greatly under Stalin; but when the church supported the government in its war against Hitler the situation improved. Now the Orthodox Church enjoys a measure of freedom. For a long time it was completely isolated from the rest of Christendom, but in 1961 it was permitted to join the World Council of Churches; and since that time its leaders have been active in the ecumenical movement. These leaders, of course, have never been known to disagree with government policy, not even when Czechoslovakia was invaded in 1968. Even the churches in Czechoslovakia failed to speak out against the invasion of their country. An exception was Dr. Joseph L. Hromadka, winner of the Lenin Peace Prize, who courageously wrote a letter to the Soviet ambassador in which he described the invasion as a "tragic error" and called for the speedy withdrawal of the occupying forces. But we must bear in mind that this is the price of survival. When the issues are political and not religious, Christian leaders take the path of least resistance and support the party line. Only those who have lived under a communist regime can possibly appreciate the enormous pressures that a totalitarian government can exert on its hapless citizens.

On the whole, church membership and attendance have declined. In Rumania in 1954 there were fifteen hundred Baptist churches; today there are only eight hundred, with 130 pastors. Their seminary in Bucharest is permitted to enroll only six new students each year. Other groups have suffered a similar fate. Brethren Assemblies are down from eight hundred to five hundred; Pentecostal churches from one thousand to six hundred; and Seventh Day Adventist churches from eleven hundred to six hundred.

After more than fifty years of repression religion is by no means dead in the Soviet Union. The largest church is the *Orthodox Church* with some forty million members. The *All Union Council of Evangelical Christians-Baptists,* which includes Mennonites, Plymouth Brethren, and Pentecostals, represents a community of about five million. In recent years a rift has appeared among the Evangelicals, with a militant group known as the Initiators, demanding full religious freedom and accusing their leaders of collaboration with the government. Some members of this "dissident" group have been arrested and others have been sent to labor camps in Siberia. In some instances their children have been placed in state institutions where they are indoctrinated with communist ideology. Lutherans, found mostly in Latvia and Estonia, number approximately one million. The Roman Catholic Church reports 3,200,000 members. There are also small groups of Methodists and Adventists.

There is ample evidence that in the last few years the government of the Soviet Union has stepped up its persecution of both Jews and Christians. In November, 1969, sixty-two members of the Evangelical Christian and Baptist Church addressed an open letter "to all Christians of the world," in which they clearly documented the many instances of persecution and imprisonment, giving names, dates, and places. Towards the end the letter states:

> We accept the ever-increasing persecutions and sufferings as from the hand of our heavenly Father. They cannot separate us from the love of God in Christ Jesus. . . . We are condemned as in the days of Esther; all, one after another to be sent to prison, harsh camps and exile. We have carefully studied the findings of investigations, the interrogation of witnesses at trials, sentences; and we declare before all the world that our relatives have been sentenced and are suffering for professing faith in God. Proof of this is provided by the universal offers of freedom in the camps and prisons in return for apostasy; by the denying of Bibles to prisoners; by the constant and universal confiscation of spiritual and religious literature.

The letter closes with an earnest plea:

> Dear children of God! The intention of our appeal to you is a heartfelt request to take warm part in prayer to our omnipotent Father, that He might look upon the threats of our persecutors and give His servants strength to speak the Word of God with all boldness. (Acts 4:29).[1]

The letter is a most moving document. Evangelicals around the world gave it prominence and called for prayer on behalf of our persecuted brethren in the USSR. The letter must have reached the ecumenical leaders in Geneva, New York, London, and other places; but there is no evidence that the World Council of Churches took any action on behalf of these Baptists in the Soviet Union, whose only offense was their insistence on worshiping God according to the dictates of their consciences. The WCC has long championed the cause of freedom fighters in all parts of the world and recently allocated $200,000 to eighteen civil rights groups in twelve countries. So far as one can tell, the WCC has remained silent on this particular issue. No public statement of any kind has been made; nor was the letter, in whole or in part, reproduced in the *Ecumenical Press Service*. We are certainly living in strange times. Civil rights are held to be most sacred. Religious liberty is a matter of indifference. Political prisoners are heroes. Religious prisoners are allowed to languish in jail with no one to plead their cause.

Of all the countries in this part of the world Albania is the only one where religion has been destroyed. Previously Albania was 70 percent Muslim, 20 percent Orthodox, and 7.5 percent Catholic; but in November, 1967, more than 2,150 churches, mosques, monasteries, and convents were closed and converted to other uses. Albania declared itself to be "the

---

[1] World Evangelical Fellowship, *Monograph Series,* No. 2, p. 7.

first atheistic state in the world." Of the other seven countries (not counting the Soviet Union) Bulgaria enjoys the least religious liberty and Poland the most.

East Germany is the only predominantly Protestant country in the communist bloc. At one time 83 percent of the people belonged to the Lutheran Church; but in the last two decades the number has dropped. Among the millions of refugees from East Germany in the 1950's were many Lutherans. Twenty-five years of communist indoctrination of youth has further reduced the number of professing Lutherans.

Poland, the largest of all the satellite countries, is 93 percent Roman Catholic; consequently the evangelicals are a small minority. The Baptists were permitted to open a Bible school in 1967—the first since World War II. The year 1966 commemorated two important events, the coming of Christianity to Poland one thousand years ago and the 150th anniversary of the work of the Bible society. A highlight of the celebration was the publication of the New Testament in modern Polish. There are no restrictions on worship services, Sunday schools, young people's meetings, national conventions, and even open-air meetings. *Trans World Radio* in Monte Carlo broadcasts the gospel to Poland once a week. The program, known as "The Voice of the Gospel from Warsaw," is prepared in government studios in Warsaw. Listeners are encouraged to write to a Warsaw address for spiritual counsel, Scripture portions, and Christian literature.

The *Eastern European Mission* helps to support pastors in Poland who are too poor to support themselves. *Paul Peterson* of EEM, *Peter Dyneka* of the Slavic Gospel Association, *Paul Freed* of Trans World Radio, and other mission executives have paid many visits to Eastern Europe and Russia. To a man they report a great famine for the Word of God, crowded churches, long meetings, and a warm and enthusiastic reception on the part of church members and leaders. It is no exaggeration to say that the beleaguered churches in the communist countries of Eastern Europe are among the most dynamic churches in the world today. They are living and thriving under conditions which closely approximate those of the first century. Their Christian faith is their most precious possession and they are prepared to die for it.

Doubtless the most effective outside aid now being given to the evangelical Christians behind the Iron Curtain is the radio ministry. The gospel is beamed into Russia, including Siberia, from powerful shortwave transmitters in Quito, Addis Ababa, Manila, and Seoul. So effective are these broadcasts that they have attracted the attention of the Soviet authorities and have been denounced in *Pravda*. In many isolated communities these Christian programs are the only spiritual nourishment available to the evangelicals.

Christian leaders from the West are now permitted to pay short visits to most of these communist countries. In some cases they have been invited to preach in the churches. Billy Graham held a short rally in Yugoslavia. In all cases they reported a warm reception from the church leaders and a deep hunger for the Word of God on the part of the Christians. Doubtless it will be some time before missionaries from the West are permitted to resume normal operations in that part of the world.

Change of Nomenclature

In recent years almost fifty missions have changed their names for various reasons. Some changes were politically expedient. Others were occasioned by a change of location which rendered the old name obsolete. Still others reflected a change in the internal structure of the mission. In ten cases the new name was the result of a union of two or more missions.

OLD NAME	NEW NAME
Air Mail from God Mission	Trans World Mission
American Board of Commissioners for Foreign Missions	United Church Board for World Ministries
American Mission to Lepers	American Leprosy Missions, Inc.
Bolivian Indian Mission	Andes Evangelical Mission
British Syrian Mission	Lebanon Evangelical Mission
Ceylon & India General Mission	International Christian Fellowship
China Inland Mission	Overseas Missionary Fellowship
Church Mission to Jews	Church's Ministry among the Jews
Disciples of Christ	United Christian Missionary Society
Egypt General Mission	Middle East General Mission
Evangelical United Brethren / The Methodist Church	United Methodist Church Board of Missions
India Mission	International Missions, Inc.
Indo-Burma Pioneer Mission	Partnership Missions, Inc.
London Missionary Society / Commonwealth Missionary Society	Congregational Council for World Ministries
London Missions to Jews	Church's Ministry among the Jews
Mission to Lepers	The Leprosy Mission
National Holiness Missionary Society	World Gospel Mission
Nile Mission Press	Arabic Literature Mission
Oriental Crusades	Overseas Crusades
Oriental Missionary Society	Inter-American Missionary Society (South America only)
Pioneer Bible Mission / United Faith Mission	United Missionary Fellowship
Plymouth Brethren	Christian Missions in Many Lands
Poona Village Mission / International Christian Fellowship	International Christian Fellowship

OLD NAME	NEW NAME
Presbyterian Church in USA United Presbyterian Church of NA }	United Presbyterian Church in USA Commission on Ecumencial Mission and Relations
Radio, Visual Education and Mass Communication Committee Committee on World Literacy and Christian Literature }	Intermedia
Religious Tract Society Christian Literature Society for India and Africa Christian Literature Society for China } . . .	United Society for Christian Literature
Society for the Propagation of the Gospel United Literature Society Universities' Mission to Central Africa } . . .	United Society for the Propagation of the Gospel
Soldier's and Gospel Mission of South America	Gospel Mission of South America
South Africa General Mission	Africa Evangelical Fellowship
South America Indian Mission	South America Mission
South China Boat Mission International Missions, Inc. }	International Missions, Inc.
Sudan United Mission (Chad)	The Evangelical Alliance Mission
United Missionary Society Missionary Church Association }	Missionary Church, Overseas Missions Department
Wesleyan Methodist Church Pilgrim Holiness Church }	Wesleyan Church, Department of World Missions
Woman's Union Missionary Society	United Fellowship for Christian Service
Zenana and Medical Missionary Fellowship	Bible and Medical Missionary Fellowship

Bibliography

Early Period

Beda, *Venerabilis. Ecclesiastical History of the English People.* Oxford: Clarendon Press, 1969.

Burkitt, F. C. *Early Christianity Outside the Roman Empire.* Cambridge, England: Cambridge University Press, 1899.

Conference on Christianity in Roman and Sub-Roman Britain. *Christianity in Britain, 300-700.* Leicester: Leicester University Press, 1968.

Cook, Harold R. *Historic Patterns of Church Growth.* Chicago: Moody, 1971.

Dvornik, Francis. *Byzantine Missions Among the Slavs.* New Brunswick, N.J.: Rutgers University Press, 1970.

Edman, V. Raymond. *The Light in Dark Ages.* Wheaton, Ill.: Van Kampen, 1949.

Eusebius. *Ecclesiastical History.* Washington, D.C.: Catholic University of America Press, 1965

Foster, John. *After the Apostles.* London: SCM Press, 1951.

———. *Beginning from Jerusalem.* London: Lutterworth, 1956.

———. *They Converted Our Ancestors: A Study of the Early Church in Britain.* London: SCM Press, 1965.

Gibbon, Edward. *The Triumph of Christendom in the Roman Empire.* New York: Harper & Row, 1958.

Green, Michael. *Evangelism in the Early Church.* Grand Rapids: Eerdmans, 1970.

Harnack, Adolf. *The Mission and Expansion of Christianity in the First Three Centuries.* 2 vols. New York: Putnam, 1908.

Henderson, A. *A Historical Survey of Christian Missions from the First Century to the End of the Seventeenth.* London: Faith Press, 1927.

Hoare, Robert J. *Christianity Comes to Britain.* London: Chapman, 1968.

Lebreton, Jules, and Zeiller, Jacques. *The Triumph of Christianity.* New York: Collier, 1962.

Maclear, G. F. *History of Christian Missions During the Middle Ages.* Cambridge: Macmillan, 1863.

Merivale, Charles. *The Conversion of the Roman Empire.* New York: Appleton, 1865.

Ramsey, William M. *The Church in the Roman Empire Before A.D. 170.* Grand Rapids: Baker Book House, 1954.

Stewart, John. *Nestorian Missionary Enterprise: The Story of a Church on Fire.* Edinburgh: Clark, 1928.

Talbot, C. H. *The Anglo-Saxon Missionaries in Germany.* New York: Sheed & Ward, 1954.

Walroud, F. F. *Christian Missions Before the Reformation.* London: S.P.C.K., n.d.

Modern Period

Bates, M. Searle and Pauck, W. *Prospects of Christianity Throughout the World.* New York: Scribners, 1964.

Boer, Harry R. *The World Missionary Situation Today.* Grand Rapids: Eerdmans, 1958.

Cook, Harold R. *Highlights of Christian Missions.* Chicago: Moody, 1967.

Dennis, James S. *Centennial Survey of Foreign Missions.* New York: Revell, 1902.

Forman, Charles W., ed. *Christianity in the Non-Western World.* Englewood Cliffs, N.J.: Prentice-Hall, 1967.

——. *The Nation and the Kingdom: Christian Mission in the New Nations.* New York: Friendship Press, 1964.

Foster, John. *To All Nations: Christian Expansion From 1700 to Today.* London: Lutterworth, 1961.

Harr, Wilber C., ed. *Frontiers of the Christian World Mission Since 1938: Essays in Honor of Kenneth Scott Latourette.* New York: Harper & Row, 1962.

Howard, David M. *Student Power in World Evangelism.* Downers Grove, Ill.: Inter-Varsity, 1970.

Latourette, Kenneth Scott. *The Christian World Mission in Our Day.* New York: Harper & Brothers, 1954.

——. *Christianity in a Revolutionary Age.* 5 vols. New York: Harper & Row, 1958-1962.

——. *Emergence of a World Christian Community.* New Haven: Yale University Press, 1949.

Leonard, Delavan L. *A Hundred Years of Missions: Progress Since William Carey.* New York: Funk & Wagnalls, 1913.

Lyall, Leslie T. *Mission Fields Today: A Brief World Survey.* London: Inter-Varsity Fellowship. 1963.

Merk, Frede and Lois. *Manifest Destiny and Mission in American History: A Reinterpretation.* New York: Knopf, 1963.

Neill, Stephen. *Colonialism and Christian Missions.* New York: McGraw-Hill, 1966.

Orr, J. Edwin. *The Light of the Nations.* Grand Rapids: Eerdmans, 1965.

Payne, Ernest A. *The Growth of the World Church.* London: Edinburgh House, 1955.

Pierson, Arthur T. *The Modern Missionary Century.* New York: Baker & Taylor, 1901.

Speer, Robert E. *Missions and Modern History.* 2 vols. New York: Revell, 1904.

Sundkler, Bengt. *The World of Mission.* Grand Rapids: Eerdmans, 1965.

Thiessen, John C. *A Survey of World Missions.* Chicago: Moody, 1961.

Thompson, R. W. *British Foreign Missions 1837-1897.* London: Blackie, 1899.

Van Dusen, Henry P. *One Great Ground of Hope: Christian Missions and Christian Unity.* Philadelphia: Westminster Press, 1961.

——. *World Christianity Yesterday, Today and Tomorrow.* New York: Abingdon-Cokesbury, 1947.

Warneck, Gustaf. *History of Protestant Missions.* New York: Revell, 1904.

Warren, Max. *The Missionary Movement from Britain in Modern History.* London: SCM Press, 1965.

——. *Social History and Christian Mission.* London: SCM Press, 1967.

Winters, Ralph D. *The Twenty-five Unbelievable Years 1945-1969.* South Pasadena, Calif.: William Carey Library, 1970.

General History

Aberly, John. *An Outline of Missions.* Philadelphia: Muhlenberg Press, 1945.

Barnes, L. C. *Two Thousand Years of Missions Before Carey.* Chicago: Christian Culture Press, 1900.

Carver, William O. *The Course of Christian Missions.* New York: Revell, 1932.

Hardy, E. R., Jr. *Militant in Earth: Twenty Centuries of the Spread of Christianity.* New York: Oxford University Press, 1940.

Glover, Robert H., and Kane, J. Herbert. *The Progress of Worldwide Missions.* New York: Harper & Row, 1960.

Hutchison, Paul. *The Spread of Christianity.* New York: Abingdon, 1922.

Latourette, Kenneth Scott. *Christianity Through the Ages.* New York: Harper & Row, 1965.

——. *A History of the Expansion of Christianity.* 7 vols. New York: Harper & Brothers, 1937-1945.

Mason, Alfred D. *Outlines of Missionary History.* London: Hodder & Stoughton, 1912.

Mathews, Basil J. *Forward Through the Ages.* New York: Friendship Press, 1951.

Neill, Stephen. *A History of Christian Missions.* New York: McGraw-Hill, 1964.

Robinson, Charles H. *History of Christian Missions.* New York: Scribner, 1915.

Directories and Handbooks

Allen, Yorke, Jr. *A Seminary Survey.* New York: Harper & Brothers, 1960.

Barkman, Paul F., Dayton, Edward R., and Gruman, Edward L., eds. *Christian Collegians and Foreign Missions.* Monrovia, Calif.: Missions Advanced Research & Communication Center, 1969.

Coxwell, H. Wakelin, and Grubb, Kenneth, eds. *World Christian Handbook, 1968.* Nashville: Abingdon Press, 1968.

Goddard, Burton L., ed. *The Encyclopedia of Modern Christian Missions: The Agencies.* Camden, N.J.: Nelson, 1967.

Interpretative Statistical Survey of the World Mission of the Christian Church. New York: International Missionary Council, 1938.

Kane, J. Herbert. *Faith Mighty Faith: Handbook of Interdenominational Foreign Mission Association.* New York: IFMA, 1956.

Missions Advanced Research And Communication Center. *North American Protestant Ministries Overseas Directory.* 9th Edition, 1970. Waco, Tex.: Word Books, 1970.

Neill, Stephen, Anderson, Gerald H., and Goodwin, John, eds. *Concise Dictionary of the Christian World Mission.* London: Lutterworth, 1970.

Missions and Ecumenics

Beaver, R. Pierce. *Ecumenical Beginnings in Protestant World Mission.* New York: Nelson, 1962.

Fey, Harold E., ed. *A History of the Ecumenical Movement: 1948-1968.* Philadelphia: Westminster Press, 1970.

Hogg, William R. *Ecumenical Foundations: A History of the International Missionary Council and Its Nineteenth Century Background.* New York: Harper, 1952.

Rouse, Ruth, and Neill, Stephen, eds. *A History of the Ecumenical Movement, 1517-1948.* Philadelphia: Westminster, 1948.

Weber, Hans-Reudi. *Asia and the Ecumenical Movement, 1895-1961.* London: SCM Press, 1966.

Denominational Missions

Band, Edward. *Working His Purpose Out: The History of the English Presbyterian Mission 1847-1947.* London: Presbyterian Publishing Office, 1948.

Barclay, Wade C. *History of Methodist Missions.* 3 vols. New York: Board of Missions of the Methodist Church, 1949-1957.

Berry, L. L. *A Century of Missions of the African Methodist Episcopal Church 1840-1940.* New York: Gutenberg, 1942.

Bingham, Rowland V. *Seven Sevens of Years: The Story of the Sudan Interior Mission.* Toronto: Evangelical Publishers, 1943.

Brown, Arthur J. *One Hundred Years: The Story of Presbyterian Missions.* New York: Revell, 1937.

Burgess, Andrew S. *Lutheran Churches in the Third World.* Minneapolis: Augsburg, 1970.

Canton, W. *A History of the British and Foreign Bible Society.* 5 vols. London: John Murray, 1904-1910.

Cauthen, Baker J. *Advance: A History of Southern Baptist Foreign Missions.* Nashville: Broadman Press, 1970.

Clarke, W. K. Lowther. *A History of the S.P.C.K.* London: S.P.C.K., 1959.

Conn, Charles W. *Where the Saints Have Trod: A History of Church of God Missions.* Cleveland, Tenn.: Pathway Press, 1959.

Cook, Frank S. *Seeds in the Wind: The Story of Radio Station HCJB, Quito, Ecuador.* Miami: World Radio Missionary Fellowship, n.d.

Danker, William J. *Two Worlds or None.* St. Louis: Concordia, 1964.

Delong, R. V., and Taylor, M. *Fifty Years of Nazarene Missions.* 3 vols. Kansas City, Mo.: Beacon Hill Press, 1952-58.

Disciples of Christ. *This is Missions.* St. Louis: Bethany Press, 1953.

Dwight, Henry Otis. *Centennial History of the American Bible Society.* New York: Macmillan, 1916.

Emery, Julia C. *A Century of Endeavor, 1821-1921.* New York: Department of Missions, Protestant Episcopal Church, 1921.

Engle, Anna R., Climenhaga, John A., and Buckwalter, Leoda A. *There Is No Difference* (Brethren in Christ). Nappanee, Ind.: Evangelical Visitor House, 1950.

Eubanks, Annie. *I Sent You to Reap.* Indianapolis: Pilgrim Holiness Mission, 1962.

Field Literature Committee. *From His Hand to Ours: Being an Account of the Work of the Nepal Evangelistic Band until 1959.* Printed in Great Britain, n.d.

Findlay, G. G., and Holdsworth, W. W. *The History of the Wesleyan Methodist Missionary Society.* London: Epworth, 1921.

Forbes, Jean Gordon. *Wide Windows.* Toronto: United Church of Canada, 1951.

Freed, Paul E. *Towers to Eternity: Trans World Radio.* Waco, Tex.: Word Books, 1968.

Goodall, Norman. *A History of the London Missionary Society 1895-1945.* London and New York: Oxford University Press, 1954.

Goodsell, Fred F. *You Shall Be My Witnesses.* Boston: American Board of Commissioners for Foreign Missions, 1959.

Harris, L. F. *Our Days Are in His Hands: A Short History of the Unevangelized Fields Mission.* London: UFM, n.d.

Harvey, G. Winfred. *The Story of Baptist Missions in Foreign Lands.* St. Louis: Chancy R. Barns, 1885.

Hewat, Elizabeth G. K. *Vision and Achievement, 1796-1959: a History of the Foreign Missions of the Churches United in the Church of Scotland.* London: Nelson, 1960.

Hewitt, Gordon. *Let the People Read.* London: United Society for Christian Literature, 1949.

Holmes, Kenneth. *The Cloud Moves.* London: Regions Beyond Missionary Union, n.d.

Hooton, W. S., and Wright, J. Stafford. *The Bible Churchmen's Missionary Society.* London: BCMS, 1947.

Hudspith, Margarita A. *Ripening Fruit* (Bolivian Indian Mission). Harrington, N.J.: Harrington Press, 1958.

Hutton, J. E. *A History of Moravian Missions.* London: Moravian Publication Office, 1923.

Johnson, Howard A. *Global Odyssey: The Anglican Communion in Eighty Countries.* New York: Harper & Row, 1963.

Jones, Christine H. *American Friends in World Missions.* Elgin, Ill.: Brethren Publishing House, 1946.

Jordan, Artishia W. *The African Methodist Episcopal Church in Africa.* New York: Patane Press, 1961.

Jordan, Bernice C. *How Many Loaves: History of Bible Club Movement.* Upper Darby, Pa.: Bible Club Movement, 1962.

Kent, Homer A., Sr. *250 Years . . . Conquering Frontiers: A History of the Brethren Church.* Winona Lake, Ind.: Brethren Missionary Herald Company, 1958.

King, Louis L., ed. *Missionary Atlas: A Manual of the Foreign Work of The Christian and Missionary Alliance.* Harrisburg, Pa.: Christian Publications, 1964.

Kraybill, Paul N. *Called to be Sent.* Scottdale, Pa.: Herald Press, 1964.

Kulbeck, Gloria. *What Hath God Wrought.* Toronto: Pentecostal Assemblies of Canada, 1958.

Lamson, Byron S. *Venture: The Frontiers of Free Methodism.* Winona Lake, Ind.: Light and Life Press, 1960.

Ledyard, Gleason. *Sky Waves: The Incredible Far Eastern Broadcasting Company Story.* Chicago: Moody, 1964.

Lovett, Richard. *History of the London Missionary Society, 1795-1895.* 2 vols. London: Henry Frowde, 1899.

Lueking, F. Dean. *Missions in the Making: 1846-1963.* St. Louis: Concordia, 1964.

Lyall, Leslie T. *A Passion for the Impossible: The China Inland Mission 1865-1965.* Chicago: Moody, 1965.

Mann, Wendy. *The Unquenched Flame.* London: South American Missionary Society, 1967.

Maxwell, J. Lowry. *Half a Century of Grace: A Jubilee History of the Sudan United Mission.* London: SUM, 1954.

Medford, Hampton T. *Zion Methodism Abroad.* Washington D.C., 1937.

Miller, A. Donald. *An Inn Called Welcome: The Story of the Mission to Lepers 1874-1917.* London: The Mission to Lepers, 1965.

Mitchell, David. *Seventh Day Adventists Faith in Action.* New York: Vantage Press, 1958.

Moomaw, I. W. *To Hunger No More* (Agricultural Missions). New York: Friendship Press, 1963.

Moyer, Elgin S. *Missions in the Church of the Brethren.* Elgin, Ill.: Brethren Publishing House, 1931.

New Tribes Mission. *The Early History of New Tribes Mission.* Woodworth, Wis.: Brown Gold Publications, 1962.

Norton, H. Wilbert. *History of Free Church Missions.* Moline, Ill.: Christian Service Foundation, 1964.

Overholtzer, J. Irvin. *A Modern Weeping Prophet: A History of International Child Evangelism Fellowship.* Pacific Palisades, Calif.: International Child Evangelism Fellowship, Inc., 1953.

Pannabecker, S. F. *The Christian Mission of the General Conference Mennonite Church.* Newton, Kans.: Faith and Life Press, 1961.

Perkin, Noel and Garlock, John. *Our World Witness: A Survey of Assemblies of God Foreign Missions.* Springfield, Mo.: Gospel Publishing House, 1963.

Peters, Gerhard Wilhelm. *The Growth of Foreign Missions in the Mennonite Brethren Church.* Hillsboro, Kans.: Board of Foreign Missions, 1948.

Pollock, J. C. *Shadows Fall Apart: The Story of the Zenana Bible and Medical Mission.* London: Hodder & Stoughton, 1968.

Richardson, Kenneth. *Garden of Miracles: A History of the Africa Inland Mission.* London: Victory Press, 1968.

Roe, James M. *The History of the British and Foreign Bible Society, 1905-1954.* London: British and Foreign Bible Society, 1965.

Ross, Emory. *New Hearts—New Faces* (American Leprosy Missions). New York: Friendship Press, 1954.

Rycroft, W. Stanley. *The Ecumenical Witness of the United Presbyterian Church in the USA.* New York: COEMAR, 1968.

Salter, Doris. *The Story of Bible Christian Union.* Brooklyn: Bible Christian Union, 1968.

Sandall, Robert. *History of the Salvation Army.* 2 vols. New York: Nelson, 1950.

Scott, Frances E. *Dare and Persevere: The Story of One Hundred Years of Evangelism in Syria and Lebanon, From 1860 to 1960.* London: Lebanon Evangelical Mission, 1960.

Scripture Gift Mission. *Publishing Salvation.* London: Radstock House, 1961.

Spain, Mildred W. *And In Samaria.* Dallas: Central American Mission, 1940.

Stevens, George H. *Go, Tell My Brethren: Church Mission to the Jews 1809-1959.* London: Olive Press, 1960.

Stock, Eugene. *The History of the Church Missionary Society.* 4 vols. London: CMS, 1899-1916.

Storms, Everek R. *History of the United Missionary Society.* Elkhart, Ind.: Bethel Publishing Company, 1958.

Strong, William Ellsworth. *The Story of the American Board.* Boston: Pilgrim Press, 1910.

Sudan Interior Mission. *Root From Dry Ground: The Story of the Sudan Interior Mission.* London: SIM, 1966.

Swanson, J. F., ed. *Three Score Years . . . And Then.* Chicago: The Evangelical Alliance Mission, 1950.

Taylor, Mendall L. *Fifty Years of Nazarene Missions.* 3 vols. Kansas City, Mo.: Nazarene Publishing House, 1952-1958.

Thompson, H. P. *Into All Lands: The History of the SPG.* London: S.P.C.K., 1951.

Torbet, Robert G. *Venture of Faith: The Story of the American Baptist Foreign Mission Society 1814-1954.* Philadelphia: Judson, 1955.

Townley-Lord, F. *Achievement* (Baptist Missionary Society). London: Carey Press. 1941.

Turner, Faith. *Out of Weakness Strength.* Orinoco River Mission, 1969.

United Christian Missionary Society. *The Growing World Mission of Disciples of Christ.* Indianapolis: United Christian Missionary Society, 1959.

Unruh, John D. *In the Name of Christ: A History of the Mennonite Central Committee and Its Service 1920-1951.* Scottdale, Pa.: Herald Press, 1952.

Webb, Pauline M. *Women of our Company: Methodist Missions.* London: Cargate Press, 1958.

Wobig, John. *A Look at Baptists.* Forest Park, Ill.: North American Baptist General Conference, 1958.

World Presbyterian Missions. *The Principles, History, Work, Organization of World Presbyterian Missions.* Wilmington, Del.: World Presbyterian Missions, Inc., 1964.

Roman Catholic Missions

De Vaulx, Bernard. *History of the Missions.* New York: Hawthorn, 1961.

Millott, Rene P. *Missions in the World Today.* New York: Hawthorn, 1961.

Morner, Magnus. *The Expulsion of the Jesuits from Latin America.* New York: Knopf, 1965.

Schmidlin, Joseph. *Catholic Mission History.* Techny, Ill.: Divine Word Press, 1933.

Missions in America

Berkhofer, Robert F. *Salvation and the Savage: An Analysis of Protestant Mission and American Indian Response.* Lexington: University Press of Kentucky, 1965.

Grubb, Kenneth G. *Religion in Colonial America.* London: World Dominion Press, 1937.

Gunther, Peter F., ed. *The Fields at Home: Studies in Home Missions.* Chicago: Moody, 1963.

Humphreys, Davis. *An Historical Account of the Incorporated Society for the Propagation of the Gospel in Foreign Parts.* New York: Arno Press & The New York Times, 1969.

Keiser, Albert. *Lutheran Mission Work Among the American Indians.* Minneapolis: Augsburg, 1922.

Posey, Walter B. *Frontier Mission: A History of Religion West of the Southern Appalachians to 1861.* Lexington: University Press of Kentucky, 1961.

Rutledge, Arthur B. *Mission to America: A Century and a Quarter of Southern Baptist Home Missions.* Nashville: Broadman, 1969.

India and Pakistan

Asirvatham, Eddy. *Christianity in the Indian Crucible.* Calcutta: Association Press, 1955.

Banker, Floyd and Hazel. *From Famine to Fruitage: An Account of Fifty Years of Wesleyan Methodism in Western India.* Marion, Ind.: Wesley Press, 1960.

Fishman, Alvin T. *For This Purpose.* Guntur, India: American Baptist Mission, 1958.

French, W. E. *The Gospel in India.* London: Carey, 1947.

Hagen, Kristofer. *Bells Still Are Calling: Church and Mission in India.* Minneapolis: Augsburg Publishing House, 1965.

Hayward, Victor E. W., ed. *The Church as Christian Community: Three Studies of North Indian Churches.* London: SCM Press, 1968.

Hollister, John W. *The Centenary of the Methodist Church in Southern Asia.* Lucknow, India: Lucknow Publishing House, 1956.

Hooper, John S. *Bible Translation in India, Pakistan and Ceylon.* New York: Oxford University Press, 1963.

Lehman, E. Arno. *It Began at Tranquebar.* Madras: Christian Literature Society, 1956.

Liddick, Ruth S. *Fifty Years in India.* Marion, Ind.: Department of World Missions, Wesleyan Methodist Church, 1960.

Mathews, James K. *South of the Himalayas: One Hundred Years of Methodism in India and Pakistan.* New York: Board of Missions of the Methodist Church, 1955.

Menzel, Emil W. *I Will Build My Church.* Philadelphia: Board of International Missions, Evangelical and Reformed Church, 1943.

Moraes, George Mark. *A History of Christianity in India: From Early Times to St. Francis Xavier, A.D. 52-1542.* Bombay: Manaktalas, 1964.

National Christian Council of India. *Christian Handbook, 1970.* Nagpur: NCCI, 1970.

Neill, Stephen. *The Story of the Christian Church in India and Pakistan.* Grand Rapids: Eerdmans, 1970.

Paul, Rajaiah D. *The First Decade: An Account of the Church of South India.* Madras: Christian Literature Society, 1958.

Pickett, J. Waskom. *Christian Mass Movements in India.* New York: Abingdon Press, 1933.

Potts, E. Daniel. *British Baptist Missionaries in India 1793-1837* Cambridge, England: University Printing House, 1967.

——. *The History of Serampore and Its Missions.* Cambridge, England: Cambridge University Press, 1967.

Ratzlaff, Mrs. Harold. *Fellowship in the Gospel, India 1900-1950.* Newton, Kans. Mennonite Publication Office, 1950.

Reformed Church in America. *One Hundred Years with Christ in the Arcot Area: 1853-1953.* Madras: Ahura Press, 1955.

Richter, J. *History of Protestant Missions in India.* New York: Revell, 1908.

Robbins, J. C. *Following the Pioneers: A Story of American Baptist Mission Work in India and Burma.* Philadelphia: Judson, 1922.

Sundkler, Bengt G. M. *The Church of South India: The Movement Toward Union, 1900-1947.* London: Lutterworth, 1954.

Swavely, C. H. *The Lutheran Enterprise in India.* Madras: Federation of Evangelical Lutheran Churches of India, 1952.

Taylor, J. T. *Our Share in India: The Story of the Central India Mission of the United Church of Canada.* Toronto: United Church of Canada Board of Foreign Missions, 1931.

Thomas, P. *Christians and Christianity in India and Pakistan.* London: Allen & Unwin, 1954.

Wilder, Harriet. *A Century in the Madura Mission.* New York: Vantage Press, 1962.

Southeast Asia

Anderson, Gerald H., ed. *Christ and Crisis in South East Asia.* New York: Friendship Press, 1968.

——. *Christianity in Southeast Asia: A Bibliographical Guide.* New York: Missionary Research Library, 1966.

Baker, Gilbert. *The Church on Asian Frontiers.* London: Church Information Office, 1963.

Brown, Russell E. *Doing the Gospel in Southeast Asia.* Valley Forge: Judson Press, 1968.

Browne, Lawrence E. *The Eclipse of Christianity in Asia.* New York: Howard Fertig, 1967.

Bull, Geoffrey T. *Coral in the Sand.* Chicago: Moody, 1965.

Devanandan, P. D. *Christian Issues in Southern Asia.* New York: Friendship Press, 1963.

Dowdy, Homer E. *The Bamboo Cross: Christian Witness in the Jungles of Vietnam.* New York: Harper & Row, 1965.

Eastman, Addison J., ed. *Branches of the Banyan: Observations on the Church in Southern Asia.* New York: Friendship Press, 1963.

Fletcher, Grace N. *The Fabulous Flemings of Kathmandu.* New York: Dutton, 1964.

Fridell, Elmer A. *Baptists in Thailand and the Philippines.* Philadelphia: Judson, 1956.

Howard, Randolph L. *Baptists in Burma.* Philadelphia: Judson, 1931.

Irwin, E. F. *With Christ in Indo-China.* Harrisburg, Pa.: Christian Publications, 1937.

Kuhn, Isobel. *Ascent to the Tribes: Pioneering in North Thailand.* Chicago: Moody, 1956.

Lyall, Leslie T. *Urgent Harvest.* London: China Inland Mission, 1961.

Manikam, Rajah B. *Christianity and the Asian Revolution.* New York: Friendship Press, 1954.

Manikam, Rajah B. and Thomas, Winburn T. *The Church in Southeast Asia.* New York: Friendship Press, 1956.

Mathews, Basil J. *Unfolding Drama in Southeast Asia.* New York: Friendship Press, 1944.

McFarland, G. B., ed. *Historical Sketch of Protestant Missions in Siam, 1828-1928.* Bangkok: Bangkok Times Press, 1928.

Pollock, J. C. *Earth's Remotest End.* New York: Macmillan, 1961.

Rattenbury, H. B. *Let My People Know* (Methodists in Burma). London: Cargate Press, 1947.

Roy, Andrew T. *On Asia's Rim.* New York: Friendship Press, 1962.

Shwe Wa and Sowards, G. and E. *Burma Baptist Chronicle: 1813-1963.* Rangoon: Burma Baptist Publications, 1963.

Smith, Mrs. Gordon H. *Victory in Viet Nam.* Grand Rapids: Zondervan, 1965.

Tegenfeldt, Herman. *Through Deep Waters* (Burma). Valley Forge, Pa.: American Baptist Foreign Mission Society, 1968.

Trachsel, Laura. *Kindled Fires in Asia.* Marion, Ind.: World Gospel Mission, 1960.

Wells, Kenneth E. *History of Protestant Work in Thailand 1828-1958.* Bangkok: Church of Christ in Thailand, 1958.

Indonesia

Bentley-Taylor, David. *The Weathercock's Reward: Christian Progress in Muslim Java.* London: Lutterworth Press, 1967.

Cooley, Frank L. *Indonesia: Church and Society.* New York: Friendship Press, 1968.

Hitt, Russel T. *Cannibal Valley* (West Irian). New York: Harper & Row, 1962.

Koch, Kurt. *The Revival in Indonesia.* Grand Rapids: Kregel, 1970.

Kraemer, Hendrik. *From Missionfield to Independent Church: Report on a Decisive Decade in the Growth of Indigenous Churches in Indonesia.* London: SCM Press, 1958.

Pedersen, Paul B. *Batak Blood and Protestant Soul.* Grand Rapids: Eerdmans, 1970.
Smith, Ebbie C. *God's Miracles: Indonesian Church Growth.* South Pasadena, Calif.: William Carey Library, 1970.
Sunda, James. *Church Growth in West Guinea.* Lucknow, India: Lucknow Publishing House, 1963.

Philippines

Anderson, Gerald H., ed. *Studies in Philippine Church History.* Ithaca, N.Y.: Cornell University Press, 1969.
Deats, Richard L. *Nationalism & Christianity in the Philippines.* Dallas: Southern Methodist University, 1967.
———. *The Story of Methodism in the Philippines.* Manila: National Council of Churches, 1964.
Gowing, Peter G. *Islands Under the Cross: The Story of the Church in the Philippines.* Manila: National Council of Churches in the Philippines, 1967.
A Half Century in the Philippines. New York: National Council Protestant Episcopal Church, 1952.
Kretzmann, Herbert. *Lutheranism in the Philippines: 1952-1966.* St. Louis: Concordia Seminary, 1966.
McGavran, Donald A. *Multiplying Churches in the Philippines.* Manila: United Church of Christ in the Philippines, 1958.
Osias, Camilo and Lorenzana, Avelina. *Evangelical Christianity in the Philippines.* Dayton: United Brethren Publishing House, 1931.
Pitts, Joseph S. *Mission to the Philippines.* Kansas City, Mo.: Beacon Hill Press, 1956.
Rodgers, James B. *Forty Years in the Philippines.* New York: Board of Foreign Missions of the Presbyterian Church in the U.S.A., 1940.
Taglucop, Angel B. *Philippine Directory, 1961.* Manila: Philippine Bible House, 1961.
The United Church of Christ in the Philippines. Manila: Federation Press, 1954.
Whittemore, Lewis Bliss. *Struggle for Freedom: Philippine Independent Church.* Greenwich, Conn.: Seabury, 1961.

China

Bush, Richard C., Jr. *Religion in Communist China.* New York: Abingdon, 1970.
Cary-Elwes, Columbia. *China and the Cross: A Survey of Missionary History.* New York: P. J. Kenedy, 1957.
Clark, Willie H. *The Church in China: Its Vitality; Its Future.* New York: Council Press, 1970.
Cohen, Paul A. *China and Christianity: The Missionary Movement and the Growth of Chinese Anti-Foreignism, 1860-1870.* Cambridge: Harvard University Press, 1963.
Dawson, Christopher. *The Mongol Mission: Narratives and Letters of the Franciscan Missionaries in Mongolia and China in the 13th and 14th Centuries.* London and New York: Sheed and Ward, 1955.
Dunn, George H. *Generation of Giants: The Story of the Jesuits in China in the Last Decades of the Ming Dynasty.* London: Burns & Oates, 1962.
Foster, John. *The Church of the T'ang Dynasty.* London: S.P.C.K., 1939.
Hoy, William Edward. *History of the China Mission.* Philadelphia: Board of Foreign Missions of the Reformed Church in the United States, 1914.

Jones, Francis P. *The Church in Communist China: A Protestant Appraisal.* New York: Friendship Press, 1962.

——, ed. *Documents of the Three-Self Movement: Source Materials for the Study of the Protestant Church in Communist China.* New York: Far Eastern Office, Division of Foreign Missions, National Council of Churches of Christ in the U.S.A., 1963.

Kilen, Juline R. *Forty Years in China: The Lutheran Brethren Mission in China 1902-1942.* Fergus Falls, Minn.: Broderbaandet Publishing Company, 1943.

Latourette, Kenneth Scott. *A History of Christian Missions in China.* New York: Macmillan, 1929.

Liu, Kuang-ching. *American Missionaries in China.* Cambridge: Harvard University Press, 1966.

Lutz, Jessie G. *Christian Missions in China: Evangelists of What?* Boston: Heath, 1965.

Lyall, Leslie T. *Come Wind, Come Weather.* Chicago: Moody, 1960.

——. *Red Sky at Night: Communism Confronts Christianity in China.* London: Hodder and Stoughton, 1969.

MacGillivray, D., ed. *A Century of Protestant Missions in China 1807-1907.* New York: American Tract Society, 1907.

Matthews, H. S. *American Board of Commissioners for Foreign Missions: Seventy-Five Years of the North China Mission.* Peking: Yenching University, 1942.

Outerbridge, Leonard M. *The Lost Churches of China.* Philadelphia: Westminster, 1952.

Paton, David M. *Christian Missions and the Judgment of God.* London: SCM Press, 1953.

Patterson, George N. *Christianity in Communist China.* Waco, Tex.: Word Books, 1969.

Rose, John. *A Church Born to Suffer: An Account of the First Hundred Years of the Methodist Church in South China 1851-1951.* London: Cargate Press, 1951.

Stauffer, M. T., ed. *The Christian Occupation of China.* Shanghai: China Continuation Committee, 1922.

Swanson, Allen. *The Missing Fourth of the China Protestant Church.* Pasadena: Institute of Church Growth, 1968.

Varg, Paul A. *Missionaries, Chinese and Diplomats: The American Protestant Missionary Movement in China 1890-1952.* Princeton, N.J.: Princeton University Press, 1958.

Wehrle, Edmund S. *Britain, China and the Anti-missionary Riots, 1891-1900.* Minneapolis: University of Minnesota Press, 1966.

Williamson, Henry R. *British Baptists in China 1845-1952.* London: Carey Kingsgate Press, 1957.

Taiwan

Band, Edward, ed. *He Brought Them Out* (Movement among the tribes). London: British & Foreign Bible Society, 1960.

Mackay, George L. *From Far Formosa.* New York: Revell, 1895.

MacMillan, Hugh A. *First Century in Formosa.* Taipei: China Sunday School Association, 1963.

——. *Then Till Now in Formosa.* Taipei: English and Canadian Presbyterian Missions in Formosa, 1953.

Swanson, Allen J. *Taiwan: Mainline versus Independent Church Growth: A Study in Contrasts.* South Pasadena, Calif.: William Carey Library, 1970.
Tong, Hollington K. *Christianity in Taiwan: A History.* Taipei: China Post, 1961.

Japan

Boxer, Charles R. *The Christian Century in Japan.* Berkeley: University of California Press, 1951.
Cary, Otis. *History of Christianity in Japan.* 2 vols. New York: Revell, 1909.
Drummond, Richard H. *A History of Christianity in Japan.* Grand Rapids: Eerdmans, 1970.
Germany, Charles H., ed. *The Response of the Church in Changing Japan.* New York: Friendship Press, 1967.
Iglehart, Charles W. *A Century of Protestant Christianity in Japan.* Tokyo: Tuttle, 1959.
———. *Cross and Crisis in Japan.* New York: Friendship Press, 1957.
Lee, Robert. *Stranger in the Land: A Study of the Church in Japan.* London: Lutterworth, 1967.
Mann, J. C. *The Last Fifty Years in Japan.* London: Church Missionary Society, 1948.
National Christian Council. *Japan Christian Yearbook, 1970.* Tokyo: Christian Literature Society, 1970.
Natori, Junichi. *Historical Stories of Christianity in Japan.* Tokyo: Hokuseido Press, 1957.
Rigmark, William. *Covenant Missions in Japan.* Chicago: Covenant Press, 1959.
Society of Friends. *Fifty Years of Quakerism in Japan.* Tokyo: Yearly Meeting of Friends, 1937.
Spae, Joseph J. *Christian Corridors to Japan.* Tokyo: Oriens Institute for Religious Research, 1967.
———. *Christianity Encounters Japan.* Tokyo: Oriens Institute for Religious Research, 1969.
Syrdal, Rolf A. *Mission in Japan: Studies in the Beginning and Development of the Indigenous Lutheran Church in Japan.* Minneapolis: Augsburg, 1958.
Thomas, Winburn T. *Protestant Beginnings in Japan: 1859-1889.* Rutland, Vt.: Tuttle, n.d.
Tomonobu, Yanagita. *Christianity in Japan.* Sendai: Bible Library Publishers, 1957.
Tucker, Henry St. George. *A History of the Episcopal Church in Japan.* New York: Scribner, 1938.
Verbeck, Guido H. F. *History of Protestant Missions in Japan.* Yokohama: Meiklejohn, 1883.
Young, John M. L. *The Two Empires in Japan.* Tokyo: Bible Times Press, 1958.

Korea

Brown, George T. *Mission to Korea.* Nashville: Board of Missions, Presbyterian Church in U.S., 1962.
Clark, Allen D. *History of the Korean Church.* Seoul: Christian Literature Society, 1961.
Paik, L. George. *The History of Protestant Missions in Korea 1832-1910.* Pyeng Yang: Union Christian College Press, 1929.

Rhodes, Harry A. *History of the Korea Mission, Presbyterian Church U.S.A., 1884-1934.* Seoul: Chosen Mission Presbyterian Church U.S.A., 1934.
—— and Campbell, Archibald. *History of the Korea Mission, Presbyterian Church U.S.A., 1935-1959.* New York: COEMAR, 1960.
Shearer, Roy E. *Wildfire—Church Growth in Korea.* Grand Rapids: Eerdmans, 1966.

Middle East

Arpee, Leon. *A Century of Armenian Protestantism 1846-1946.* New York: Armenian Missionary Association, 1946.
Baly, Denis. *Multitudes in the Valley: Church and Crisis in the Middle East.* Greenwich, Conn.: Seabury, 1959.
Batal, James. *Assignment: Near East.* New York: Friendship Press, 1950.
Bridgeman, Charles T. *The Episcopal Church and the Middle East.* New York: Morehouse-Gorham, 1958.
Finnie, David H. *Pioneers East: The Early American Experience in the Middle East.* Cambridge: Harvard University Press, 1967.
Grabill, Joseph L. *Protestant Diplomacy and the Near East: Missionary Influence on American Policy, 1810-1927.* Minneapolis: University of Minneapolis Press, 1970.
Jessup, Henry Harris. *Fifty-Three Years in Syria.* 2 vols. New York: Revell, 1910.
Noshy, Ibrahim. *The Coptic Church: Christianity in Egypt.* Washington, D.C.: Ruth Sloan Associates, 1955.
Penrose, S. *That They May Have Life: The Story of the American University 1866-1941.* New York: Trustees of the American University of Beirut, 1942.
Richter, Julius. *A History of Protestant Missions in the Near East.* New York: Revell, 1910.
Thompson, A. E. *A Century of Jewish Missions.* New York: Revell, 1902.
Van Ess, Dorothy F. *History of the Arabian Mission 1926-1957.* New York: Board for the Christian World Mission of the Reformed Church in America, 1958.

Africa: Genral

Baeta, C. G., ed. *Christianity in Tropical Africa.* London: Oxford University Press, 1968.
Barrett, David B. *Schism and Renewal in Africa.* Nairobi: Oxford Press, 1968.
Beetham, T. A. *Christianity and the New Africa.* London: Pall Mall Press, 1967.
Blyden, Edward. *Christianity, Islam and the Negro.* Edinburgh: Edinburgh University Press, 1967.
Carpenter, George W. *The Way in Africa.* New York: Friendship Press, 1959.
Du Plessis, J. *The Evangelization of Pagan Africa.* Capetown: Juta, 1930.
Groves, C. P. *The Planting of Christianity in Africa 1840-1954.* 4 vols. London: Lutterworth, 1948-1958.
Hasting, Adrian. *Church and Mission in Modern Africa.* Bronx, N.Y.: Fordham University Press, 1970.
Hayward, Victor E. W., ed. *African Independent Church Movements.* London: Edinburgh House Press, 1963.
International Missionary Council. *The Church in Changing Africa.* New York: IMC, 1958.

Naylor, W. S. *Daybreak in the Dark Continent.* New York: Young People's Missionary Movement, 1912.

Northcott, Cecil. *Christianity in Africa.* Philadelphia: Westminster, 1963.

Society of African Missions. *One Hundred Years of Missionary Achievement 1856-1956.* Cork, Ireland: African Missions, 1956.

Sundkler, Bengt. *The Christian Ministry in Africa.* London: SCM Press, 1962.

Taylor, John V. *The Primal Vision: Christian Presence Amid African Religion.* London: SCM Press, 1963.

Trachsel, Laura. *Kindled Fires in Africa.* Marion, Ind.: World Gospel Mission, 1960.

Westermann, Diedrich. *Africa and Christianity.* London: Oxford University Press, 1937.

North Africa

Cooley, John K. *Baal, Christ, and Mohammed: Religion and Revolution in North Africa.* New York: Holt, Rinehart and Winston, 1965.

Kerr, Robert. *Morocco After Twenty-five Years.* London: Murray and Evenden, 1912.

———. *Pioneering in Morocco.* London: Allenson, 1894.

Warren, T. J. P. *North Africa Today.* Tunis: North Africa Mission, 1947.

West Africa

Ajayi, J. F. Ade. *Christian Missions in Nigeria, 1841-1891: The Making of a New Elite.* London: Longmans, Green and Co., 1965.

Ayandele, E. A. *The Missionary Impact on Modern Nigeria 1842-1914: A Political and Social Analysis.* London: Longmans, Green and Co., 1966.

Bartels, F. L. *The Roots of Ghana Methodism.* New York: Cambridge University Press, 1964.

Carter, Charles W. *A Half Century of American Wesleyan Missions in West Africa.* Marion, Ind.: Wesley Press, 1940.

Clarke, George and Lane, Mary. *American Wesleyan Mission of Sierra Leone.* Marion, Indiana: Wesley Press, 1912.

Debrunner, Hans W. *A Church Between Colonial Powers: A Study of the Church in Togo.* New York: Friendship Press, 1965.

———. *A History of Christianity in Ghana.* Accra: Waterville Publishing House, 1967.

DeKorne, John C. *To Whom I Now Send Thee: Mission Work of the Christian Reformed Church in Nigeria.* Grand Rapids: Eerdmans, 1945.

Dike, K. O. *Origins of the Niger Mission (CMS) 1841-1891.* Ibadan: Ibadan University Press, 1957.

Foster, Raymond S. *The Sierra Leone Church: An Independent Anglican Church.* London: S.P.C.K., 1961.

Fuller, Harold W. *Aftermath: The Dramatic Rebirth of Eastern Nigeria.* New York: Sudan Interior Mission, 1970.

Garrett, T. S. and Jeffrey, R. M. C. *Unity in Nigeria.* London: Edinburgh House Press, 1965.

Grimley, John B. and Robinson, Gordon E. *Church Growth in Central and Southern Nigeria.* Grand Rapids: Eerdmans, 1966.

Johnson, T. S. *The Story of a Mission: The Sierra Leone Church: First Daughter of CMS.* London: S.P.C.K., 1953.

Lageer, Eileen. *New Life for All* (Nigeria). Chicago: Moody, 1970.

McFarlan, Donald M. *Calabar: The Church of Scotland Missions 1846-1946.* New York: Nelson, 1946.

Nan, Henry. *We Move Into Africa: The Story of the Planting of the Lutheran Church in Southwestern Nigeria.* St. Louis: Concordia, 1945.

Olson, Gilbert W. *Church Growth in Sierra Leone.* Grand Rapids: Eerdmans, 1968.

Sadler, George W. *A Century in Nigeria.* Nashville: Broadman, 1950.

Smith, Noel. *The Presbyterian Church of Ghana, 1835-1960.* Accra: Ghana Universities Press, 1966.

Trimingham, J. Spencer. *The Christian Church and Islam in West Africa.* London: SCM Press, 1955.

Walker, Frank D. *A Hundred Years in Nigeria: The Story of the Methodist Mission in West Nigeria 1842-1942.* London: Cargate Press, 1942.

———. *The Romance of the Black River: The Story of the CMS Nigeria Mission.* London: Church Missionary Society, 1930.

Ward. W. J. *In and Around the Oron Country: The Story of Primitive Methodism in Southern Nigeria.* London: Hammond, n.d.

Webster, James Bertin. *The African Churches Among the Yoruba 1888-1922.* Oxford: Clarendon Press, 1964.

Whetstone, Harold V. *Lutheran Mission in Liberia.* New York: Board of Foreign Missions of the United Lutheran Church in America, 1955.

Wold, Joseph Conrad. *God's Impatience in Liberia.* Grand Rapids: Eerdmans, 1967.

Central Africa

Almquist, L. Arden. *Covenant Missions in Congo.* Chicago: Covenant Press, 1958.

Andersson, Efraim. *Churches at the Grass Roots: A Study in Congo-Brazzaville.* London: Lutterworth, 1968.

Carpenter, George W. *Highways for God in Congo.* Leopoldville: La Librairie au Congo, 1952.

Faupel, J. E. *African Holocaust: The Story of the Uganda Martyrs.* London: Geoffrey Chapman, 1965.

Fullerton, W. Y. *The Christ of the Congo River.* London: Carey Press, 1928.

Jobson, Orville D. *Conquering Oubangi-Chari for Christ.* Winona Lake, Ind.: Brethren Missionary Herald, 1957.

Reid, Alexander J. *Congo Drumbeat: History of the First Half Century in the Establishment of the Methodist Church Among the Atetela of Central Congo.* New York: World Outlook Press, 1964.

Schneider, G. *A Graphic Portrayal of a Christian Mission at Work in the Cameroons, West Africa.* Forest Park, Ill.: North American Baptist General Conference, 1957.

Smith, A. C. S. *Road to Revival: The Story of the Ruanda Mission.* London: Church Missionary Society, 1946.

Weaver, W. B. *Thirty-Five Years in Congo.* Chicago: Congo Inland Mission, 1945.

Wilson, George Herbert. *The History of the Universities' Mission to Central Africa.* Westminster: UMCA, 1936.

East Africa

Allison, Oliver. *A Pilgrim Church's Progress* (Anglican Church in Sudan). London: Highway Press, 1965.

Anderson, William B. *Ambassadors by the Nile: The Church in North-East Africa.* London: Lutterworth Press, 1963.

Bernander, Gustaf. *The Rising Tide: Christianity Challenged in East Africa.* Rock Island, Ill.: Augustana Press, 1957.

Church of Scotland Foreign Missions Committee. *Kenya 1898-1948: The Jubilee Book of the Church of Scotland Mission, Kenya Colony.* Glasgow: CSFMC, 1948.

Davis, Raymond J. *Fire on the Mountains: The Study of a Miracle — The Church in Ethiopia.* Grand Rapids: Zondervan, 1966.

Eby, Omar. *Whisper in a Dry Land* (Somalia). Winona Lake, Ind.: Herald, 1968.

Forsberg, Malcolm I. *Dry Season: Today's Church Crisis in the Sudan.* New York: Sudan Interior Mission, 1964.

———. *Last Days on the Nile.* Philadelphia: J. B. Lippincott, 1966.

Hellberg, Carl J. *Missions on a Colonial Frontier West of Lake Victoria: Evangelical Missions in NW Tanganyika to 1932.* Lund, Sweden: Gleerups, 1965.

Kitching, A. L. *From Darkness to Light: A Study of Pioneer Work in the Diocese of the Upper Nile.* London: S.P.C.K., 1935.

Oliver, Roland A. *The Missionary Factor in East Africa.* New York: Humanities, 1968.

Taylor, John V. *The Growth of the Church in Buganda.* London: Student Christian Movement Press, 1958.

Trimingham, J. Spencer. *The Christian Approach to Islam in the Sudan.* New York: Oxford University Press, 1948.

———. *The Christian Church and Mission in Ethiopia.* London: World Dominion Press, 1950.

Ullendorff, Edward. *Ethiopia and the Bible.* London: Oxford University Press, 1968.

Willmott, Helen M. *The Doors Were Opened: The Remarkable Advance of the Gospel in Ethiopia.* London: Sudan Interior Mission, n.d.

South Africa

Davies, Horton and Shepherd, R. H. W. *South Africa Missions 1800-1950.* London: Nelson, 1954.

Du Plessis, J. *A History of Christian Missions in South Africa.* New York: Longmans, Green and Co., 1911.

Evans, H. St. J. T. *The Church in Southern Rhodesia.* London: Society for the Propagation of the Gospel, 1945.

Eveleigh, William, ed. *The Story of a Century 1823-1923.* Capetown: Methodist Publishing House, 1923.

Gerdener, G. B. A. *The Story of Christian Missions in South Africa.* Johannesburg: Linden Christian Church, 1950.

Griffith, Robert. *Madagascar, a Century of Adventure.* London: London Missionary Society, 1919.

Hinchcliff, Peter. *The Anglican Church in South Africa.* London: Darton, Longman & Todd, 1963.

Lennox, John. *The Story of our Missions: South Africa.* Edinburgh: Offices of the United Free Church of Scotland, 1911.

Matthews, F. T. *Thirty Years in Madagascar.* London: Religious Tract Society, 1904.

McMahon, E. O. *Christian Missions in Madagascar.* Westminster: Society for the Propagation of the Gospel, 1914.

Randall, Max Ward. *Profile for Victory: New Proposals for Missions in Zambia.* South Pasadena, Calif.: William Carey Library, 1970.

Richards, Elizabeth. *Fifty Years in Nyanza 1906-1956.* Maseno, Kenya: Nyanza Jubilee Committee, 1956.
Rotberg, Robert I. *Christian Missionaries and the Creation of Northern Rhodesia.* Princeton, N.J.: Princeton University Press, 1965.
Sales, Jane M. *The Planting of Churches in South Africa.* Grand Rapids: Eerdmans, 1971.
Sales, Richard, ed. *Adventuring with God: The Story of the American Board Mission in South Africa.* Durban: Lutheran Publishing House, 1967.
Sibree, J. *Fifty Years in Madagascar.* New York: Houghton Mifflin, 1924.
Sundkler, Bengt. *Bantu Prophets in South Africa.* New York: Oxford University Press, 1961.
Syrdal, Rolf A. *Mission in Madagascar.* Minneapolis: Augsburg, 1957.
Taylor, James Dexter. *The American Board Missions in South Africa.* Durban: John Singleton, 1911.
White, Winifred M. *Friends in Madagascar: 1867-1967.* Oxford: Church Army Press, 1967.
Whiteside, J. *History of the Wesleyan Methodist Church of South Africa.* London: Stock, 1906.
Wilson, T. E. *Angola Beloved.* New York: Loizeaux, 1967.
Wishlade, R. L. *Sectarianism in Southern Nyasaland.* London and New York: Oxford University Press, 1965.

South America

Beach, Harlan P., et. al. *Protestant Missions in South America.* New York: SVM, 1907.
Crabtree, Asa R. *Baptists in Brazil.* Rio de Janeiro: Baptist Publishing House of Brazil, 1953.
Davis, J. Merle. *The Evangelical Church in the River Plate Republics.* New York: International Missionary Council, 1943.
Drown, Frank and Marie. *Mission to the Headhunters* (Ecuador). New York: Harper and Row, 1961.
Duey, Charles J. *Covenant Missions in Ecuador.* Chicago: Covenant Press, 1965.
Edwards, Fred E. *The Role of the Faith Mission: A Brazilian Case Study.* South Pasadena, Calif.: William Carey Library, 1971.
Hamilton, Keith. *Church Growth in the High Andes.* Eugene, Oreg.: Institute of Church Growth, 1962.
Hawthorne, Sally R. *Cloud Country Sojourn.* Cochabamba: Bolivian Indian Mission, 1957.
Howard, David M. *Hammered as Gold* (LAM in Colombia). New York: Harper and Row, 1969.
Mackay, John A. *Christianity on the Frontier.* New York: Macmillan, 1950.
Montgomery, J. Dexter. *Disciples of Christ in Argentina 1906-1956.* St. Louis: Bethany, 1956.
Nickel, Ben J. *Along the Quichua Trail.* Smithville, Mo.: Gospel Missionary Union, 1965.
Porterfield, Bruce E. *Commandos for Christ* (Bolivia). New York: Harper and Row, 1963.
Read, William R., Monterroso, Victor M., and Johnson, Harmon A. *Church Growth in Latin America.* Grand Rapids: Eerdmans, 1969.
Read, William R. *New Patterns of Church Growth in Brazil.* Grand Rapids: Eerdmans, 1965.
Rycroft, W. Stanley. *Religion and Faith in Latin America.* Philadelphia: Westminster, 1958.

Sinclair, John H., ed. *Protestantism in Latin America: A Bibliographical Guide.* Austin, Tex.: Hispanic American Institute, 1967.

Taylor, Clyde W. and Coggins, Wade T., eds. *Protestant Missions in Latin America: A Statistical Survey.* Washington, D.C.: Evangelical Foreign Missions Association, 1961.

Trachsel, Laura. *Kindled Fires in Latin America.* Marion, Ind.: World Gospel Mission, 1960.

Turner, Faith. *Out of Weakness Strength* (Orinoco River Mission). Miami: World Radio Missionary Fellowship, 1968.

Wagner, C. Peter. *The Protestant Movement in Bolivia.* South Pasadena, Calif.: William Carey Library, 1970.

Wallis, Ethel Emily. *The Dayuma Story.* New York: Harper and Row, 1960.

Yoder, Howard W. *Present Limitations on Religious Liberty in Latin America and their Effects on the Evangelical Communities.* New York: National Council of Churches of Christ in the U.S.A., 1955.

Young, Robert. *From Cape Horn to Panama.* London: South American Missionary Society, 1905.

Central America and the Caribbean

Bennett, Charles. *Tinder in Tabasco: A Study of Church Growth in Tropical Mexico.* Grand Rapids: Eerdmans, 1968.

Borhek, Mary Virginia. *Watchman on the Walls* (Nicaragua). Bethlehem, Pa.: Board of Christian Education, Moravian Church, 1949.

Gonzales, Justo L. *The Development of Christianity in the Latin Caribbean.* Grand Rapids: Eerdmans, 1969.

Johnson, Harmon A. *The Growing Church in Haiti.* Coral Gables, Fla.: West Indies Mission, 1970.

McGavran, Donald. *Church Growth in Mexico.* Grand Rapids: Eerdmans, 1963.

Mitchell, James E. *The Emergence of a Mexican Church: The Associate Reformed Presbyterian Church of Mexico.* South Pasadena, Calif.: William Carey Library, 1970.

Nelson, Wilton M. *A History of Protestantism in Costa Rica.* Lucknow, India: Lucknow Publishing House, 1963.

Oceania

Burton, J. W. and Deane, Wallace. *A Hundred Years in Fiji.* London: Epworth, 1936.

Colwell, James. *A Century in the Pacific.* New York: Kelly, 1915.

Crawford, David and Leona. *Missionary Adventures in the South Pacific.* Rutland, Vt.: Tuttle, 1967.

Davies, John. *The History of the Tahitian Mission: 1799-1830.* Cambridge, England: Cambridge University Press, 1961.

Frerichs, A. C. *Anutu Conquers in New Guinea.* Minneapolis: Augsburg, 1957.

Koskinen, Aarne A. *Missionary Influence as a Political Factor in the Pacific Islands.* Helsinki: Academia Scientiarum Fennicae, 1953.

Murray, A. W. *Forty Years' Mission Work in Polynesia and New Guinea from 1835 to 1875.* London: Nisbet, 1876.

——. *Missions in Western Polynesia: Historical Sketches 1839-1863.* London: John Snow, 1863.

——. *The Kingdom in the Pacific.* London: London Missionary Society, 1913.

——. *The Triumph of the Gospel in the New Hebrides.* New York: Doran, 1908.

Shevill, Ian. *Pacific Conquest: The History of 150 Years of Missionary Progress in the South Pacific*. Sydney: Pacific Christian Literature Society, 1949.
Taylor, Richard S. *Our Pacific Outposts: Nazarene Missions*. Kansas City, Mo.: Beacon Hill Press, 1956.
Tippett, Alan R. *Solomon Islands Christianity*. New York: Friendship Press, 1967.
Van Dusen, Henry P. *They Found the Church There*. New York: Scribner, 1945.
Vicedom, C. F. *Church and People in New Guinea*. New York: Association Press, 1961.

Europe

Bourdeaux, Michael. *The Christian Religion in the USSR*. Indianapolis: Bobbs-Merrill, 1965.
De Grunwald, Constantin. *The Churches and the Soviet Union*. New York: Macmillan, 1962.
Evans, Robert B. *Let Europe Hear*. Chicago: Moody, 1964.
Harris, W. Stuart, ed. *Eyes on Europe*. Chicago: Moody, 1970.
Hedlund, Roger E. *The Protestant Movement in Italy*. South Pasadena, Calif.: William Carey Library, 1970.
Hutten, Kurt. *Iron Curtain Christians*. Minneapolis: Augsburg, 1967.
Mäläskä, Hilkka. *The Challenge for Evangelical Missions to Europe: A Scandinavian Case Study*. South Pasadena, Calif.: William Carey Library, 1970.
Pollock, J. C. *The Faith of the Russian Evangelicals*. New York: McGraw-Hill, 1965.
Shuster, George N. *Religion Behind the Iron Curtain*. New York: Macmillan, 1954.
Solberg, Richard W. *God and Caesar in East Germany*. New York: Macmillan, 1961.

Conference Reports

INTERNATIONAL MISSIONARY COUNCIL MEETINGS:

World Missionary Conference, Edinburgh, 1910. 9 vols. New York: Revell, 1910.
Jerusalem Meeting of the International Missionary Council, 1928. 8 vols. New York: IMC, 1928.
International Missionary Council Meeting at Tambaram, Madras, 1938. 7 vols. New York: Oxford University Press, 1939.
Ransom, Charles W., ed. *Renewal and Advance: Christian Witness in a Revolutionary World* (Whitby, 1947). London: Edinburgh House Press, 1948.
Goodall, Norman, ed. *Missions Under the Cross* (Willingen, 1952). New York: Friendship Press, 1953.
Orchard, R. K., ed. *The Ghana Assembly of the International Missionary Council*. New York: Friendship Press, 1958.
Report to the Final Assembly of the International Missionary Council and the Third Assembly of the World Council of Churches. New Delhi, 1961.
Latham, Robert O. *God For All Men* (Mexico City, 1963). Geneva: World Council of Churches, 1963.

INTER-VARSITY URBANA CONVENTIONS:

1946 Convention: *Completing Christ's Commission*. Chicago: IVP, 1947.
1948 Convention: *From Every Campus to Every Country*. Chicago: IVP, 1949.

1951 Convention: *By All Means—Proclaim Christ.* Chicago: IVP, 1952.
1954 Convention: *Changing World—Unchanging Christ.* Chicago: IVP, 1955.
1957 Convention: *One Lord, One Church, One World.* Chicago: IVP, 1958.
1961 Convention: *Commission, Conflict, Commitment.* Chicago: IVP, 1962.
1964 Convention: *Change, Witness, Triumph.* Chicago: IVP, 1965.
1967 Convention: *God's Men: From All Nations to All Nations.* Downers Grove, Ill.: IVP, 1968.
1970 Convention: *Christ the Liberator.* Downers Grove, Ill.: IVP, 1971.

WHEATON CONGRESS, 1966: Lindsell, Harold, ed. *The Church's Worldwide Mission.* Waco, Tex.: Word Books, 1966.

ANNUAL REPORTS:

Division of Overseas Ministries. *Annual Report.* 475 Riverside Drive, New York, N.Y. 10027.
Evangelical Foreign Missions Association. *Annual Report.* 1405 G. Street, N.W., Washington, D.C. 20005.
Interdenominational Foreign Mission Association. *Annual Report.* 54 Bergen Avenue, Ridgefield Park, N.J. 07660.

Index

It should be noted that this index is selective rather than inclusive. If *every* item had been included the index would have reached unmanageable proportions. Moreover, not every reference to the *listed* items has been included. The author has included only those references which have some significance or afford some information. In this way the reader will be spared the frustration of referring to many passages only to discover that they offer no additional information.